MW01221727

ASPA CLASSICS

Conceived of and sponsored by the American Society for Public Administration (ASPA), the ASPA Classic Series publishes volumes on topics that have been, and continue to be, central to the contemporary development of the field. The ASPA Classics are intended for classroom use, library adoptions, and general reference. Drawing from the *Public Administration Review (PAR)* and other ASPA-related journals, each volume in the series is edited by a scholar who is charged with presenting a thorough and balanced perspective on an enduring issue.

Each volume is devoted to a topic of continuing and crosscutting concern to the administration of virtually all public sector programs. Public servants carry out their responsibilities in a complex, multidimensional environment, and each collection will address a necessary dimension of their performance. ASPA Classics volumes bring together the dialogue on a particular topic over several decades and in a range of journals.

The volume editors are to be commended for volunteering to take on such substantial projects and for bringing together unique collections of articles that might not otherwise be readily available to scholars and students.

ASPA CLASSICS

The Age of Direct Citizen Participation
Nancy C. Roberts, ed.

Administrative Leadership in the Public Sector
Montgomery Van Wart and Lisa Dicke, eds.

Public Personnel Administration and Labor Relations
Norma M. Riccucci, ed.

Public Administration and Law
Julia Beckett and Heidi O. Koenig, eds.

**Local Government Management:
Current Issues and Best Practices**
Douglas J. Watson and Wendy L. Hassett, eds.

The Age of Direct Citizen Participation

An ASPA Classics Volume

Advancing excellence in public service . . .

Edited by
Nancy C. Roberts

ME.Sharpe
Armonk, New York
London, England

Library of Congress Cataloging-in-Publication Data

The age of direct citizen participation / edited by Nancy C. Roberts.
    p. cm. — (ASPA series)
 Includes bibliographical references and index.
 ISBN 978-0-7656-1512-1 (cloth : alk. paper)—ISBN 978-0-7656-1513-8 (pbk. : alk. paper)
 1. Political participation—United States. 2. Direct democracy. 3. Representative government and representation.
I. Roberts, Nancy Charlotte.

JK1764.A35 2008
323′.0420973--dc22   2007022268

Printed in the United States of America

The paper used in this publication meets the minimum requirements of
American National Standard for Information Sciences
Permanence of Paper for Printed Library Materials,
ANSI Z 39.48-1984.

♾

BM (c)   10   9   8   7   6   5   4   3   2   1
BM (p)   10   9   8   7   6   5   4   3   2   1

CONTENTS

Part 1. Direct Citizen Participation: Challenges and Dilemmas   **3**

Part 2. Administrative Theory and Direct Citizen Participation   **19**

2.1. Citizens as Social Learners   26

1. The Recovery of Civism in Public Administration
   H. George Frederickson   26

2. Toward a Public Philosophy of Public Administration: A Civic Perspective
   of the Public
   Curtis Ventriss   38

3. Facilitating Community, Enabling Democracy: New Roles for Local
   Government Managers
   John Nalbandian   49

4. The New Public Service: Serving Rather than Steering
   Robert B. Denhardt and Janet Vinzant Denhardt   63

2.2. Citizens as Coproducers, Owners, and Co-Investors   78

5. Citizenship and Service Delivery: The Promise of Coproduction
   Charles H. Levine   78

6. Reinventing Government or Reinventing Ourselves: Two Models for
   Improving Government Performance
   Hindy Lauer Schachter   93

7. Reframing the Metaphor of the Citizen-Government Relationship:
   A Value-Centered Perspective
   Gerald E. Smith and Carole A. Huntsman   104

Part 3. Arenas of Direct Citizen Participation   **119**

3.1. Policy Implementation: Programs and Sectors   124

8. Citizen Participation in Community Action and Model Cities Programs
   John H. Strange   124

9. Decentralization and Citizen Participation in Education
   Marilyn Gittell   143

10. Decentralization and Citizen Participation in Criminal Justice Systems
    Richard A. Myren   164

11. Community Participation and Modernization: A Reexamination of Political Choices
    Curtis Ventriss and Robert Pecorella   193

3.2. Policy Analysis, Initiation, and Budgeting   205

12. The Democratization of the Policy Sciences
    Peter deLeon   205

13. Public Deliberation: An Alternative Approach to Crafting Policy and
    Setting Direction
    Nancy Roberts   212

14. The Relationship Between Citizen Involvement in the Budget Process and City
    Structure and Culture
    Carol Ebdon   226

Part 4. Mechanisms of Direct Citizen Participation   **237**

4.1. Individual Participation   243

15. Institutionalized Use of Citizen Surveys in the Budgetary and Policy-Making
    Processes: A Small City Case Study
    Douglas J. Watson, Robert J. Juster, and Gerald W. Johnson   243

4.2. Small Group Participation   254

16. Emergent Citizen Groups and Emergency Management
    Robert A. Stallings and E.L. Quarantelli   254

17. Citizens Panels: A New Approach to Citizen Participation
    Ned Crosby, Janet M. Kelly, and Paul Schaefer   266

4.3. Large Group Participation   279

18. Consensus-Building for Integrated Resources Planning
    Lance deHaven-Smith and John R. Wodraska   279

19. State Strategic Planning: Suggestions from the Oregon Experience
    *Gerald R. Kissler, Karmen N. Fore, Willow S. Jacobson, William P. Kittredge,
    and Scott L. Stewart*   286

20. The Practice of Deliberative Democracy: Results from Four Large-Scale Trials
    Edward C. Weeks   296

4.4. Electronic Participation   314

21. Reinventing the Democratic Governance Project Through Information Technology?
    A Growing Agenda for Debate
    Andrew Kakabadse, Nada K. Kakabadse, and Alexander Kouzmin   314

Part 5. Assessments of Direct Citizen Participation   **337**

22. Resident Participation: Political Mobilization or Organizational Co-optation?
    David M. Austin   341

23. Citizen Participation in the Philadelphia Model Cities Program:
    Retrospect and Prospect
    Erasmus Kloman   356

24. Citizen Participation: Can We Measure Its Effectiveness?
    Judy B. Rosener   365

25. Making Bureaucrats Responsive: A Study of the Impact of Citizen Participation
    and Staff Recommendations on Regulatory Decision Making
    Judy B. Rosener   374

26. The Question of Participation: Toward Authentic Public Participation
    in Public Administration
    Cheryl Simrell King, Kathryn M. Feltey, and Bridget O'Neill Susel   383

27. Assessing Public Participation in U.S. Cities
    XiaoHu Wang   401

28. Administrative Agents of Democracy? A Structural Equation Modeling
    of the Relationship between Public-Sector Performance and Citizenship Involvement
    Eran Vigoda   416

Part 6. Building Theories of Direct Citizen Participation   **441**

29. Public Involvement in Public Management: Adapting and Testing a Borrowed Theory
    John Clayton Thomas   443

30. Putting More Public in Policy Analysis
    Lawrence C. Walters, James Aydelotte, and Jessica Miller   458

31. From Responsiveness to Collaboration: Governance, Citizens, and the Next
    Generation of Public Administration
    Eran Vigoda   473

Part 7. Direct Citizen Participation: Coming of Age   **491**

Index   501
About the Editor   512

The Age of
Direct Citizen
Participation

PART 1

DIRECT CITIZEN PARTICIPATION
Challenges and Dilemmas

> As soon as public service ceases to be the main business of the citizens, and they prefer to serve with their pocketbooks rather than with their persons, the State is already close to its ruin. Is it necessary to march to battle? They pay troops and stay home. Is it necessary to attend the council? They name deputies and stay home. By dint of laziness and money, they finally have soldiers to enslave the country and representatives to sell it.
> —*Jean-Jacques Rousseau*

INTRODUCTION

Citizenship participation is the cornerstone of democracy, but there is a deep ambivalence about citizens participating *directly* in their government. On the one hand, the active role of citizens in governance is an important ideal in American life (Box 1998; Skocpol and Fiorina 1999). Direct democracy keeps community life vital and public institutions accountable. It resolves conflict through "a participatory process of ongoing, proximate self-legislation and the creation of a political community capable of transforming dependent private individuals into free citizens and partial and private interests into public goods" (Barber 1984, p. 151). Proponents of direct democracy argue that the United States has reached a point where an increase in direct involvement is not only desirable, but feasible. Citizens have the knowledge and the ability to participate more fully in the political, technical, and administrative decisions that affect them. They have demonstrated this capability when given the chance. Most important, citizens have the right to be engaged in the decisions that touch their lives (Barber 1984; Box 1998).

On the other hand, direct citizen participation in government is viewed with skepticism, even wariness. Representative democracy, or indirect citizen participation, has its advantages. It protects citizens from the dangers of direct involvement: It buffers them from uninformed public opinion; it prevents the tyranny of the majority; and it serves as a check on corruption. Representative democracy also meets the needs of a complex, postindustrial society that requires political, technical, and administrative expertise to function. Unlike public officials, citizens typically do not have the time or the interest to deliberate for the purpose of developing informed public judgment. Therefore, given the size and complexity of the modern nation-state, direct citizen participation is not a realistic or feasible expectation (Dahl 1989).

3

The ongoing debate about direct versus indirect citizen participation has a bearing on administrative theory and practice (Cooper 1984; Rohr 1984; Stivers 1990; Wamsley et al. 1987; Frederickson 1997; King and Stivers 1998; Warner 2001). In the course of their work, public officials and administrators make decisions and take actions that land them on either side of the great divide. They can invite direct citizen participation and include citizens in developing bureau policy, or they can discourage it, even prevent it, in the execution of their duties (Thomas 1995). Administration thus becomes an important focal point, and some would say battleground, in discussions over public involvement in government. As Camilla Stivers (1990) notes, "A key question in the history of the U.S. administrative state has been the extent to which the administration of a representative government can accommodate citizens actively involved in public decision making" (p. 88).

What makes this question even more intriguing for administrative theory and practice is the "social experiment" that has been under way over the course of the last century, especially since 1950. Citizen participation has been mandated in many public policies and programs. Citizens have been included more directly (either by law or administrative discretion) into administrative practice (Advisory Commission on Intergovernmental Relations 1979). Direct citizen participation is no longer hypothetical; it is very real, and public administrators are central to its evolution.

The first goal of this book, then, is to document and describe where we are in this "social experiment" and to identify some of the more notable efforts of direct citizen participation as reported in the literature. The articles selected for this volume provide a good overview of the scope and depth of citizen involvement in public administration. The second goal of this book is to help readers interpret the results of these social experiments. We need to understand what has succeeded, what has not, and why. This task is much more difficult than the first. There are the standard challenges of doing assessments and evaluations given value and goal conflicts, especially on such a complicated and "contested concept" as citizen participation (Day 1997). This is not a trivial undertaking in and of itself; but there is more at stake. Assessments quickly land us deep into normative territory. Knowledge of results always begs the next question: Given what we know, should citizens be directly involved in government and administrative practice? Here things get very complicated. Let us use some hypothetical examples to illustrate the point.

Suppose we find "failure" in some of these social experiments, either in terms of outcomes or in terms of the process. What exactly would that mean? There could be at least two interpretations. On the one hand, failure could "prove" that critics were right in their cautions about direct citizenship participation. Citizens should not be directly participating in administration any more than they should be directly involved in setting legislative or executive policy. Citizen involvement cannot work and does not work as predicted, and the consequences for participation are not good for the long-term health of the democracy. On the other hand, failure could document the "success" of those who have structured a system in such a way as to limit direct citizen participation. Since the system discourages, or as some would say, to a large extent prevents, substantive citizen involvement, it would be reasonable to conclude that when asked to participate, citizens either do not know how to, do not want to, or do not even care to try. Thus failures in direct participation could be attributed to learned helplessness and the "success" of a system that prevents their substantive participation in the first place.

Alternatively, suppose we find some "successes" in direct citizen participation. People actually did participate and the consequences were positive, assuming we could achieve a consensus on what positive means. How do we interpret these results? First, we would need to establish whether the study results could be generalized to all settings. Does direct citizen participation function at all levels of government, in all sectors, for all issues, during all phases in the policy process, with all mechanisms of involvement? Or does direct citizen participation only function with certain kinds of people (both leaders and participants), in small face-to-face groups, on simple, nontechnical issues? Finding answers to these questions is an enormous undertaking, given the numbers of variables, levels, and units of analysis in a federated system with three branches of government reliant on a growing involvement of businesses and nonprofits to operate. And the complications do not stop there. If we identify certain constraints and limitations on direct involvement, how do we interpret them? Are they the result of an institutional system that conditions behavior so that its removal or redesign would enable citizens to behave differently, or are people likely to behave the same way no matter what the system's design? Sorting myths from reality becomes a major challenge under these circumstances (Reidel 1972; Buck and Stone 1981).

Thus, our examination of citizen participation in public administration research and practice has the potential of pushing us further into the normative debates about democratic and administrative theory. We might just end up where we started—enmeshed in the ambivalence about direct citizen participation and its expression. We will take our chances. The hope is that in more than fifty years of research there will be something substantive to say about the status of direct citizen participation in American administrative practice. If nothing more, we can hope for better guidance on what directions we should pursue in the future.

Before we turn to this literature, we need to lay some groundwork. This is the function of this introductory chapter. We begin by defining direct citizenship participation. Since it is a contested concept, the literature built up around it is complex and difficult. We start by acknowledging the differences between the legal and the substantive definitions. We then chose a substantive definition that includes the important elements of power and decision making. *Direct citizen participation* is defined herein as the process by which members of a society (those not holding office or administrative positions in government) share power with public officials in making substantive decisions related to the community. Although participation inside organizations is considered to be an important component of the overall participatory process (Vigoda and Golembiewski 2001), especially as it has a direct bearing on how citizens treat one another and interact with public officials, space considerations preclude its coverage in this volume.

Next, we provide a brief history of direct citizen participation as it pertains to administrative practice. Administrators and researchers have amassed an enormous amount of knowledge about direct citizen participation. An overview of its foundations, especially the governmental interventions that have prompted its resurgence, provides a good backdrop for the volume's articles.

Direct citizen participation also provokes debates among democratic and administrative theorists. To help flesh out different perspectives, we include a brief summary of the reasons to be supportive and the reasons to be cautious about direct citizen participation. There are substantive arguments on both sides. The reader will find it easier to see linkages and make comparisons across the articles with this general overview in mind.

Finally, we summarize the tensions over direct citizen participation provoked by the debates. The tensions are natural outgrowths of our competing perspectives on democratic and administrative theory and some of the contradictions inherent in modern life. Coping with them is a requirement for both researchers and practitioners. Researchers need to address the questions they prompt in order to develop better theory, which at this point is not well formulated. Administrators, at the front line of daily contact with citizens, need to use the questions as a catalyst to improve administrative practice. For our purposes, we return to the tensions over direct citizen participation in the book's conclusion. They become our guideposts in determining what progress, if any, has been made and the extent to which direct citizen participation is a viable alternative in modern democratic societies to indirect representation.

DEFINITIONS OF CITIZEN PARTICIPATION

Research on citizen participation produces a complex and untidy literature (Kweit and Kweit 1981). As a contested concept (Day 1997), it is not surprising that it is plagued with definitional problems.[1] Citizen participation can refer to a range of different actions by different people (Pateman 1970).

For some, citizenship is a legal concept. It is a political status or role conferred upon people (Cooper 1984). Legal definitions emphasize the procedural aspects of involvement—the extent to which citizenship is defined in constitutions and statutes that prescribe the qualifications, rights, and obligations within a particular government's jurisdiction (Cooper 1984). Although the U.S. Constitution is virtually silent on the role of citizens in a democratic society, it is understood that citizens owe allegiance to the republic, must abide the laws, and risk their lives for the national defense (Walzer 1980). In turn, citizens are guaranteed the rights of voting, universal suffrage, and formal equality. For proponents of legal definitions such as Schumpeter (1943), democracy becomes procedural, nothing more than an institutional arrangement used to arrive at legislative and administrative decisions with no particular goal or end in mind. Citizenship serves its purpose to the extent there are enough citizens to choose among leaders for the purpose of policy making.

For others, citizenship is more than a legal concept. It is a substantive ethical and sociological statement. "It is like John Dewey's idea of community, Ernest Baker's concept of duty, and Walter Lippmann's emphasis on civility all rolled into one" (Dimock 1990, p. 21). For example, the Greek philosophers viewed "citizenship as the main goal of life" (Dimock 1990, p. 23). Central to this ideal is the belief that government must be guided by a moral purpose—the realization of values in the lives of its citizens (Hart 1984). The citizen's primary responsibility is "to know what those values are, why they should believe in them, and what the implications for action might be" (Hart 1984, p. 114). Furthermore, "each individual should act as an independent and responsible moral agent" (p. 115). If any situation should compromise regime values, the citizen has to act with civility in defense of those values (Hart 1984).

This perspective on citizenship requires both collective and individual virtue and moral purpose. Its scope is broader than the legal definition; it extends not only to formal governmental arrangements, but also includes voluntary organizations and community involvement. Its focus is on building and sustaining community—political, economic, and social—and the development of the community's values, norms, and traditions (Cooper 1984). Its requirements are a sense of responsibility and civic devotion to one's commonwealth and a dedication to human and environmental betterment throughout the world (Dimock 1990). A natural expression has been in various social movements throughout U.S. history—abolitionist, populist, labor union, feminist, civil rights, environmental, and neighborhood movements (Cooper 1984). Indeed, the ethical tradition of substantive citizenship has prompted changes in legal definitions. It has been credited with the democratization of the elitist form of government in the Constitution through the extension of the franchise to nonwhites and women, the abolition of slavery, the expansion of civil rights, the establishment of equal employment opportunities, and the mandates for citizen participation in public policy making (Cooper 1984).

If we adopt *Webster's* definition of participation as the means to have a share in common with others, to partake with others, then direct citizen participation would alternatively mean fulfillment of one's legal rights and duties as specified in the Constitution, or alternatively, active involvement in substantive issues of government and community. Sherry Arnstein's (1969) definition is illustrative of the latter when she incorporates substantive interests of the polity, such as race, class, and gender, to define citizen participation as a categorical term for citizen power. It is the redistribution of power that enables the have-not citizens, presently excluded from the politics and economic processes, to be deliberately included in the future. It is the strategy by which the have-nots join in determining how information is shared, goals and policies are set, tax resources are allocated, programs are operated, and benefits like contracts and patronage are parceled out. In short, it is the means by which they can induce significant social reform which enables them to share in the benefits of the affluent society (p. 216).

The preference here is to adopt a substantive definition that is more inclusive and extends to both "haves" and "have-nots." Citizens come in many different stripes and colors; focusing on one type of citizen to the exclusion of others subverts the concept. Although redistribution of power may be an intention or an outcome of citizen participation, it should not be a limiting factor in its definition. The most logical differentiation among participants is between those who hold elected and administrative government positions and those who do not. In this sense, citizen participation would refer to those members of society who serve without pay and do not have formal governmental decision-making authority in the formulation or implementation of public policy.

On the other hand, Arnstein's emphasis on power and decision making are central to the concept of direct citizen participation. In her work on the "ladder of participation," she clearly distinguishes citizen participation from manipulation and tokenism (Arnstein, 1969) as others have distinguished it from cooptation (Selznick 1949, Dryzek 1990). What is implied in her definition is a reconceptualization of power. Direct participation requires power sharing among the citizens and public officials. It is not a form of control that enables those in authority to get citizens to do what they want them to do. Shared power is power *with* citizens as opposed to power *over* citizens (Follett 1940; Roberts 1991). Citizens are viewed as an integral part of the governance process, and their active involvement is considered essential in the substantive decisions facing a community. Substantive decisions, in this instance, are defined as those that are important and critical in community life as defined by the members of the community.

Combining the expanded view of citizen, and the concepts of shared power and decision making, citizen participation is defined as the process by which members of a society (those not holding office or administrative positions in government) share power with public officials in making substantive decisions and in taking actions related to the community. The focus is on direct participation (when citizens are personally involved and actively engaged) as opposed to indirect participation (when citizens elect others to represent them) in the decision process.

BRIEF HISTORY OF DIRECT CITIZEN PARTICIPATION

The concept of citizen participation has a long lineage. The first written record of direct citizen participation came from the Greek city-states, and one of its earliest expressions was in the *Ecclesia* of Athens. The *Ecclesia* was an assembly open to all free, male citizens, 18 and older, for the purpose of debate, consensus seeking, and democratic decision making. Its policymaking power was checked by the council of 500 (elected members who screened the agenda), and by a court (members chosen by lot who ruled on the constitutionality of the measures that were passed) (Cunningham 1972; Fishkin 1991). During the Middle Ages, after the decay and fragmentation of the Roman Empire, urban artisans formed associations to control public matters central to their work. They formed guilds, which were an oligarchy with some voting rituals and limited citizen involvement. Voluntary associations that provided charity, education, and other services also had limited participation (Cunningham, 1972). Eventually, direct citizen participation began to reassert itself in the popular assemblies of the ninth-century English township, in some Swiss cantons and communes in the thirteenth century, and the city-states of Renaissance Italy.

In 1215, Virginia and New England colonial settlements launched their own variants of citizen participation built on the Magna Carta, which guaranteed due process for all citizens and the self-rule of church congregations. Virginians assembled in 1619 to pass laws, and the Pilgrims established their own government when 41 adult males met aboard the *Mayflower*. The New England colonists also held town meetings, a latter-day successor to the *Ecclesia,* that enabled free, white, property-owning, adult male citizens to jointly hold certain decision-making powers. Although dominated by elite citizens, town government was democratic in form and neighborhood-oriented in practice. Other influences came from the Native Americans, who made important decisions during full councils of warriors; from the Spanish settlers, who used a *cabildo abierto* (open council); and from black Americans, who were accustomed to village assemblies (Cunningham 1972).

Beginning with the presidency of Andrew Jackson, the nineteenth century saw a broadening of democratic practice both at state and national levels. Property qualifications were dropped, and self-educated citizens, rather than elites, became part of the civil service. However, as large urban areas developed, political elites—party and caucus leaders—became powerful and pushed direct participation in local government into the background (Cunningham 1972). To deal with the increasing number of unattended city problems, people turned to voluntary associations such as churches, charity organizations, settlement houses, and trade unions. Rural areas also developed their own voluntary organizations such as the National Grange. Later, the Morrill Acts of 1862 and 1890 underwrote land-grant colleges to support agriculture and launch field demonstrations. The Cooperative Extension Service was set up in 1914 to enable county agents to educate farmers and their families. Working with county agents, local people were required to mutually agree upon plans and implement them (Cunningham 1972).

The first three decades of the twentieth century witnessed the growth of other expressions of direct participation. They included voluntary city and regional planning, attempts to improve the environmental through the City Beautiful Movement, and slum eradication (Day 1997). At the same time, tribal organizations dealt with the Bureau of Indian Affairs and the Indian Division of the Public Health Service, citizens served on the Selective Service Boards, and tenants' associations formed in low-rent public housing projects (Stenberg 1972). Later, farmers' committees would set production quotas and make decisions for agricultural programs associated with the New Deal (Cunningham 1972).

After World War II, when the federal government reassumed the preeminent role in social and economic life it had established in the 1930s, direct citizen participation received a growing number of endorsements, at least on paper. The Housing Act of 1949 required participation in urban renewal through public hearings. The Housing Act of 1954 (the Workable Program for Community Improvement) and the Juvenile Delinquency Demonstration Projects involved citizen participation through citywide advisory committees composed of leading citizens (Hallman 1972). The Urban Renewal Act of 1954 mandated citizen participation and called for the formation of advisory boards to be comprised of citizen leaders, such as contractors, bankers, and developers, who could make development "work" (Day 1997). However, these participation efforts involved "non-indigenous, blue-ribbon citizens" in an advisory capacity with little or no direct participation by residents of affected areas (Stenberg 1972).

The War on Poverty in the 1960s changed the requirements of citizen participation. The Economic Opportunity Act of 1964 established the Community Action Program (CAP) that contained the very controversial "maximum feasible participation" clause. Although the actual origin of this clause has not been identified, the support for direct citizen participation emerged from a number of sources: the civil rights movement and its push for participatory democracy; the strategy of those working on a National Service Corps who believed the poor should have a voice in planning and administering local programs; and the political force of Robert Kennedy and the young people in the Kennedy administration who championed maximum involvement of the poor (Boone 1972). The clause sought to include "residents of the areas and members of the groups served" in decision making. The vehicle of their participation became the nonprofit Community Action Agency (Stenberg 1972). The national demonstration projects of Head Start and Legal Aid also attracted citizen participation in that local poor people were recruited to develop and manage the programs. In all of these programs, the type of participating citizen changed from affluent white to poor minority member. In the case of the Community Action Program, administrative guidelines decreed that a third of the CAP's boards of directors should be representatives of the poor.

The face of participation began to shift yet again with the Model Cities Program, established by the Demonstrations Cities and Metropolitan Development Act of 1966 that combined urban renewal with the war on poverty. In an effort to avoid the political conflicts engendered by the 1964 act, it provided only for "widespread citizen participation" (Day 1997). The ultimate authority was to rest with local governments that were given control so as to tailor the program to their needs (Hallman 1972). Later, mandatory participation was replaced with "adequate opportunity for citizen participation" in the Housing and Community Development Act of 1974 and the "encouragement of the public" in the Costal Zone Management Act of 1972 (Day 1997). The National Environmental Policy Act of 1969 instructed members of the President's Council on Environmental Quality to consult with the Citizens' Advisory Committee on Environmental Quality and other groups "as it deems advisable" (Day 1997).

Despite this apparent shift in emphasis from mandatory to advisable involvement, the 1970s was marked by an "explosive growth" in federally mandated citizen participation. The Federal Advisory Committee Act of 1972 required citizen advisory boards throughout the federal bureaucracy and encouraged the participation of organized interests. A symposium on *Citizen Participation in Public Policy* cited impressive statistics: 137 (61 percent) of the 226 public participation programs operating in federal agencies had been created during the decade (Rich and Rosenbaum 1981, p. 439). The Advisory Commission on Intergovernmental Relations (1979) presented similar data: 124 (80 percent) of the 155 federal grant-in-aid programs requiring public participation were adopted in the 1970s. A smaller surge appeared at state and local levels. Gormley (1981) estimated that 75 percent of state utility regulatory commissions had a high level of citizen participation. And Cole's (1974) surveys of state and county governments indicated growing opportunities for citizen involvement.

Although the federal government did not pursue one policy toward participation (Stenberg 1972), through its interventions, direct citizen participation became more of a feature in urban renewal, juvenile delinquency, poverty, manpower training, model cities, neighborhood health centers, and community mental health programs. There appeared to be a two-level process: the national level provided funds and guidelines and the local level executed plans and programs. The locus of implementation was in the neighborhood with ordinary citizens exercising varying degrees of control depending on the community and its citizens. This trend was compatible with the ever-broadening power of the citizen in the electoral process through political parties and their conventions, the direct primary, initiatives, referenda and recalls, boards and commissions, and public opinion polls that are considered to be "unofficial" referenda in the minds of elected officials.

Demands for direct citizen participation in issues of basic welfare and quality of life expanded in the last two decades of the twentieth century. A confluence of voices from students, union members, working and middle-class whites, government workers, environmentalists, feminists, and consumers amplified the movement. Becoming more suspicious of the growing size of government, the power of experts, and the impact of technology, activists of all persuasions wanted more direct control and power in the decisions that affected them. To date, these voices and their demands have not shown any signs of abating.

CITIZEN PARTICIPATION AND DEMOCRATIC THEORY: SOURCES OF AMBIVALENCE

There are two central questions for any democratic system: Who should rule, and how should that rule be configured in practice? For a good part of U.S. history, the answer has been that an elite group of citizens should rule through a representative system of government. In the *Federalist Papers,* for example, one finds an aversion to direct citizen participation. Hamilton argued that direct citizen participation would not be necessary, that a sound administrative system would keep people's allegiance (Stivers 1990). In Federalist 63, Madison explicitly rejected a direct role for citizens and called for exclusion of the people who needed protection against their errors and delusions (Rohr 1984). Thus, the Constitution was drawn up to minimize direct citizen participation by relying on an educated and propertied elite to govern. Although there is now a universal franchise, the idea of representative government is very much alive, as witnessed in the 2000 election when the electoral college and the Supreme Court, rather than the popular vote, determined who would be president of the United States.

The question of how well elites have ruled through a representative system has been widely debated. Some, like Schumpeter (1943), believe representation works well enough as long as the masses elect their leaders and otherwise stay out of politics and do not attempt to influence or control their representatives. Others see representation as a malfunctioning system that endangers democracy, especially a representative system based on pluralism.[2] Critics of pluralism believe that vested interests often override public interests (Fishkin 1991, 1997; Burnheim 1985) due to the "mobilization of bias" (Bachrach and Baratz 1962) and the "spillover effect" (Fishkin 1991). Groups with money often are advantaged over other groups who lack the knowledge, skills, and resources to be heard in the political process.

Other advocates of reform push for greater citizen involvement to curb the abuses of a representative system (Pateman 1970; Barber 1984; Box 1998). They propose direct rather than indirect citizen involvement. The following statements summarize some of the basic arguments in support of direct citizen participation.

Reasons to Support Direct Citizen Participation

Direct citizen participation is developmental. As first postulated by Aristotle and later elaborated by Jean-Jacques Rousseau (Pateman 1970) and John Stuart Mill (Krouse 1982; Warner 2001), citizen participation is intrinsically valuable because it develops the highest human capacities and fosters an active, public-spirited moral character. The state exists to establish the conditions for the exercise of citizenship so members can live well—the ultimate aim of which is to achieve virtue (Stivers 1990, p. 87). Thus, through direct participation, people are able to realize their potential (Hart 1972). Simply put, "good processes produce good people" (Hart 1972, p. 613). Any obstacle to direct participation inhibits this self-development (Cunningham 1972).

Direct citizen participation is educative. Rousseau and Mill believed that democracy has to be learned and it can only be learned through practice (Pateman 1970). The more one participates, the more one develops the attitudes and skills of citizenship, and the more others will be drawn into the process, making the system more democratic. To sustain this virtuous cycle (Oldfield 1990), all institutions in a society should be supportive of democratic ideals. Authoritarian conditions at work will have a detrimental effect, especially since people spend a great deal of time in their jobs. Thus, a participatory government requires a participatory society that reinforces and sustains it, especially at the local level (Pateman 1970). Also, according to Rousseau (Pateman 1970) and Mill (Krouse 1982; Warner 2001), citizens need to deliberate to make good collective decisions. Instead of relying on one another's raw public opinion, citizens need to come to public judgment (Yankelovich 1991). Public judgment evolves from taking into account others' interests, hearing competing arguments, objections, and counterarguments before any collective decision is made. It emerges from face-to-face dialogue and deliberation (Dryzek 1990; Bohman and Rehg 1997, Bohman 1998; Elster 1998) during which time citizens come to identify and share a common conception of what Rousseau calls the general will and Mill calls the common good (Pateman 1970). Anyone outside the deliberative process is prevented from learning the norms by which this consensus is achieved, resulting in a divide between those who participate and those who do not. This divide ultimately can engender rifts and conflicts between participants and nonparticipants. By involving everyone who wants to participate, direct citizen participation has the potential to be a "solvent of social conflicts" (Salisbury 1975).

Direct citizen participation is therapeutic and integrative. Most citizens suffer from alienation and "only through participation will or can they be made well." Direct citizen participation is "justified as therapy—a process as the healing of the sick" (Hart 1972, p. 614). Participants achieve psychic rewards, a sense of freedom and control over their lives and strong feelings of political efficacy with higher levels of participation. They also gain, according to Rousseau and Mills (Pateman 1970), a sense of belonging in their community.

Direct citizen participation is legitimating. As citizens participate in governmental affairs and give their consent to decisions, they legitimate those decisions and the regime that makes them (Pateman 1970; Salisbury 1975). This legitimacy produces stability within the system and the regime that makes the rules.

Direct citizen participation is protective of freedom. According to Rousseau, participation enables people to be and remain their own masters and ensures that no man or group is master of another (Pateman 1970). Freedom comes from participation in decision making because people gain a very real degree of control over their lives and their environment (Pateman 1970). The people themselves are the best guarantors of their rights, and it is the rule of law, not men, that will protect their freedoms. Direct citizen involvement also fosters more responsive policy and administrative systems that are more in concert with what citizens desire, especially in the early stages of the policy process when the agenda is set.

Direct citizen participation is instrumental. It is necessary to obtain power and power is required to recoup losses, enhance gains, and enlarge the benefits for self or for one's group (Salisbury 1975). Direct citizen participation is a mechanism for those without power to challenge those who have it. It is a lever for making changes, whether it is to ensure material or psychic rewards. Its intent is to give those without power a platform and voice for change (Arnstein, 1969) and to reduce the tyranny of the haves over the have-nots.

Direct citizen participation is realistic. It is impossible to govern without the consent of the governed. Modern society is complex. People have to be included as a source of information and collective wisdom in order for society to use its resources wisely. Their direct participation can minimize delays and can be a source of innovative ideas and approaches (Barber 1984). Centralized systems, even representative ones, do not have the capability to adapt quickly and flexibly, especially given the technological and social transformations taking place in postindustrial societies.

Reasons to Oppose Direct Citizen Participation

Many regard direct citizen participation with distrust (Dahl 1989). They doubt the ability of the masses to make a positive contribution to governance; in fact, they are viewed as a potential threat to the system. The masses, says Schumpeter (1943), are "incapable of action other than a stampede" (p. 283). Such views are consistent with "a long-standing consensus in Western political thought: that substantive involvement by citizens in governance is unworkable, however desirable it may be" (Stivers 1990, p. 87). Reasons against direct citizen participation rest on the following assumptions.

Direct citizen participation is based on a false notion. "Human nature is flawed." People are either "too passionate and selfish or too passive and apathetic" (Stivers 1990, p. 87) to be directly involved. Studies have "demonstrated that the common man is not the rational, self-motivating, and thoughtful democrat of the Jefferson ideal. Rather the picture that emerges is of a lethargic, irrational, and prejudiced individual who neither understands nor is particularly committed to democratic principles" (Hart 1972, p. 610). Since individual citizens cannot realistically be trusted, they need "benevolent, but firm, guidance from an informed and politically active minority" (Hart, 1972, p. 611).

Direct citizen participation is inefficient. We live in a large, complex, bureaucratic society. Government is too big to support face-to-face relationships on which participatory democracy depends (Stivers 1990; Fishkin 1991). Mass involvement is undesirable because it would be too expensive, too slow, and too cumbersome to try "to get everybody in the act and still get some action" (Cleveland 1975). Moreover, the average citizen does not have the ability to comprehend the management of complex public affairs and institutions (Hart 1972, DeSario and Langton 1987, Fishkin 1991). As society has become more culturally and technologically sophisticated, it needs to rely on more refined, expert decision making. Extensive participation implies a "negation of the expertise built up by the specialist" (Kaufman 1969, p. 9). Elected officials and administrators have ultimate responsibility to formulate and execute public policy. We should rely on their professional expertise to do what they are "hired" to do. Otherwise, decision making will be more difficult (protracted and contentious), if not altogether uninformed, when "amateurs" are involved.

Direct citizen participation is politically naive. Governance should rest on an informed, knowledgeable elite. Only a small minority needs to be actively and directly involved in politics. When given the chance, citizens will choose a system that provides security and well-being, even though it begets hierarchy and control. "Oligarchy is the outcome of organic necessity" (Michels 1949, p. 402) and is indispensable in complex societies. It is not possible to have both complex organization and democracy. Besides, interest-group politics are too entrenched for the individual citizen to compete. Direct citizen participation cannot prevent powerful cliques from dominating the policy process nor can it eliminate differences in power that it is supposed to equalize (Kweit and Kweit 1981). Not everyone is equally qualified to decide thoughtfully on all issues. Individuals differ and there are limits to eliminating the differences among them (Fagence 1977).

Direct citizen participation is unrealistic. Direct citizen involvement is a luxury that modern societies cannot afford. It requires skills, resources, money, and time that most citizens do not have (Grant 1994; King et al. 1998). Citizens are too busy making a living and supporting their families to be more actively involved in politics. The assumption that people will participate if given the opportunity does not fit with reality. For the most part, relatively few people take advantage of opportunities that do exist (Almond and Verba 1989). Furthermore, not all people want to participate and should not be coerced into participating, which then would raise questions of the inequality of participation that would favor some and exclude others.

Direct citizen participation is disruptive. Too much citizen involvement heightens political conflict and is dysfunctional. High levels of mobilization lead to disequilibria that destroy social stability (Barber 1984). Public sympathies are almost without exception incoherent, incompatible with one another, of variable consistency, and imprecise (Fishkin 1991). The increased "noise" in the system (Kweit and Kweit 1981) makes it hard for decision makers to respond. Furthermore, heightened expectations for direct participation cannot be filled, and as a result they are likely to breed low self-esteem, alienation, and distrust—everything that citizen involvement is supposed to prevent (Kweit and Kweit 1990). In contrast, limited citizen participation has a positive function. It cushions "the shock of disagreement, adjustment and change" (Pateman, 1970, p. 7). Citizen apathy, in fact, helps maintain the stability of the system. In addition, citizens' preferences or interests have a strong tendency to be expressed in terms of vested interests. There is no guarantee that common interests and the welfare of the whole will be addressed or protected. What is more likely is an emotional fragmentation that ends up polarizing people without any mechanism that brings them back together. Reliance on the bureaucracy to direct and execute strategies and programs of citizen participation does not reduce the concern. When some members of society participate and others do not, for whatever reason, then their lack of involvement creates a vacuum that can be filled too easily by bureaucracy's preferred clientele (Fagence 1977). This opening has the potential for corruption and the exploitation of public policy for private interest (Etzioni-Halevy 1983).

Direct citizen participation is dangerous. It can lead to extremism as the totalitarian systems with their high rates of citizen participation have demonstrated during the twentieth century (Pateman 1970). Data from large-scale empirical investigations also reveal that lower socioeconomic groups have nondemocratic and authoritarian attitudes (Pateman 1970). Their preference is to adopt antidemocratic or antisocial policies that value stability over uncertainty. Known injustices have been preferable under the conditions of unpredictability and change (Fishkin 1991).

DILEMMAS OF DIRECT CITIZEN PARTICIPATION

The critiques of direct citizen participation summarized above raise a number of dilemmas that have to be addressed if direct citizen participation is to be treated more seriously in a complex, technologically advanced society. We briefly summarize them here for two purposes. They are important themes that are raised throughout the articles that follow. The reader will find it easier to sort through the myriad of perspectives and views if they are kept in mind. We also return to the dilemmas in the book's conclusion, where they serve as guideposts in our assessment of how well direct citizen participation has fared to date and what its prospects may be in the future.

The dilemma of size. The modern administrative state is very large and complex. Direct citizen involvement will have to accommodate numerous groups and individuals. Direct democracy was formulated for small groups meeting face-to-face and operating in relatively constrained public spaces. How can direct citizen participation overcome the limitations of scale (Dahl 1989; Fishkin 1991)?

The dilemma of excluded or oppressed groups. There are disadvantaged citizens who have been systematically excluded from representative democracy (Dahl 1989; Sanders 1997). Will there be room in the participatory process for ethnic and religious minorities, indigenous peoples, women, the old, gays and lesbians, youth, the unemployed, the underclass, and recent immigrants? And who will speak for future generations?

The dilemma of risk. Many complex technologies pose substantial hazards and risks to individuals, communities, regions, or even to the entire planet. Imposition of risks on people without even their tacit consent is an act of tyranny (Ellul 1964). Those exposed to risks (chemical, radioactive, and biotechnological hazards) "are so numerous, and so capable of political mobilization, that they threaten the stability of the political-economic order, and thus place legitimation at issue" (Dryzek 1996, p. 480). How do we deal with these risks?

The dilemma of technology and expertise. Citizens find it difficult to compete with professionals in terms of their knowledge, information, and expertise (Dryzek and Torgerson 1993). Administrative and technical elites crowd out both citizens and their representatives in the participatory process. How can ordinary citizens participate in the decisions made about complex technologies, especially when there can be wide disagreements among the experts, and the costs of gaining the knowledge, information, and expertise to stay current in these debates can be prohibitive?

The dilemma of time and crises. We are in an era of accelerating crises (Hart 1972; Toffler 1971). Decisions often have to be made quickly, without involving large numbers of people. There may not be time for large-group deliberations. Besides the decision costs involved in reaching agreements (Fishkin 1997), citizens may not have a great deal of time to give to participatory processes (Grant 1994). How will we deal with time constraints and crises?

The dilemma of the common good. Direct participation may not truly reflect the common good. The common good depends on deliberation, not just assurance of political equality or the capture of public opinion through the latest polls, faxes, 800 numbers, computers, and other technological marvels. Power to the people does not necessarily produce thoughtful deliberative power. Incentives have moved us toward direct democracy at the cost of deliberative democracy (Fishkin 1991). How can direct democracy be more deliberative to enable people to think more seriously and fully about public issues?

BOOK ORGANIZATION

The articles in this anthology on direct citizen participation have been chosen from among the journals sponsored by the American Society for Public Administration (ASPA). Those selected are excellent representatives of the book's major themes. Many articles could not be included due to size constraints and journal limitations. Readers should consult the introductions to each section, where additional articles have been referenced.

The articles are organized in five sections (Part 2 through Part 6). Each section represents a different way to approach the study of direct citizen participation—its position in administrative theory and practice, its manifestation throughout the policy process (implementation, initiation, budgeting), its practice through a range of mechanisms at various levels of analysis, its results based on assessments, and its theories developed and tested by scholars and practitioners.

Part 2, "Administrative Theory and Direct Citizen Participation," positions the topic of direct citizen participation within public administration theory. Competing public administration models exist, each with its own assumptions and expectations concerning the roles of administrators and citizens. Since direct citizen participation most often rests on the shoulders of public administrators for successful execution, it is important to know how the citizen and his or her direct involvement are viewed within a particular framework. If direct citizen participation is not seen as compatible or appropriate, and administrators discourage citizen involvement, then one would not expect to find many successful examples of it in practice.

Part 3, "Arenas of Direct Citizen Participation," provides a broad-brush view of the major arenas where direct citizen participation has been attempted. The articles chosen for this section illustrate the scope of citizen participation across various policy sectors and the depth of citizen participation throughout all phases of the policy process.

Part 4, "Mechanisms of Direct Citizen Participation," illustrates the many ways to include citizens directly in their governance. They range from public hearings and surveys to large collaborative planning meetings and citizen panels. The goal in this section is not to be comprehensive, but to illustrate mechanisms that appear to show the most promise in overcoming some of the major hurdles of direct citizen involvement. New mechanisms are evolving daily, and as is evident in the most recent articles, there is a growing interest in the use of new information and computer technology to support direct citizen participation.

Part 5, "Assessments of Direct Citizen Participation," summarizes key studies that have evaluated the processes and outcomes of direct citizen involvement. Although there is little consistency in terms of research design, variables selected, methodologies employed, or levels and units of analysis chosen, taken as a whole, these studies give us an important status report on the effectiveness of direct citizen participation as it has been practiced thus far.

Part 6, "Building Theories of Direct Citizen Participation," presents three articles that illustrate the state of theory development. Although theory about direct citizen involvement is least developed compared to the other themes in this collection, the articles demonstrate the progress that has been made to date and suggest potential avenues that could be explored in the future.

Part 7, "Direct Citizen Participation: Coming of Age," returns to the six major dilemmas introduced in this chapter and briefly summarizes the progress that has been made in overcoming these challenges to direct citizen involvement. The chapter concludes with an overview of the next steps. It highlights the innovative social technology that can be used to accommodate larger numbers of citizens, and it recommends research that will be required at the individual, group, and institutional levels to establish substantive theories of direct citizen participation.

NOTES

1. For an expanded analysis of the many different strands in the definition and conceptualization of citizenship, see Kalu (2003).

2. Pluralist theory (Dahl 1971) assumes that citizens assemble into interests groups and pressure the political elite in government to formulate policy to support their interests. Since everyone is assumed to have a chance to be part of an interest group and get their ideas considered by the political elite, then those whose ideas are adopted and "win" out over other ideas are considered to be, by definition, in the public's interest.

REFERENCES

Advisory Commission on Intergovernmental Relations. 1979. *Citizen Participation in the American Federal System.* Washington, DC: U.S. Government Printing Office.

Almond, G.A., and S. Verba. 1989. *The Civic Culture.* 3d. ed. Newbury Park, CA: Sage.

Arnstein, S.R. 1969. "A Ladder of Citizen Participation." *Journal of the American Institute of Planners,* 35(4): 216–24.

Bachrach, P., and M.S. Baratz. 1962. "Two Faces of Power." *American Political Science Review,* 56: 947–52.

Barber, B. 1984. *Strong Democracy: Participatory Politics for a New Age.* Berkeley and Los Angeles: University of California Press.

Bohman, J. 1998. "Survey Article: The Coming of Age of Deliberative Democracy." *The Journal of Political Philosophy,* 6(4): 400–25.

Bohman, J., and W. Rehg. 1997. *Deliberative Democracy: Essays on Reason and Politics.* Cambridge, MA: MIT Press.

Boone, R.W. 1972. "Reflections on the Citizen Participation and the Economic Opportunity Act." *Public Administration Review* (September): 444–56.

Box, R.C. 1998. *Citizen Governance: Leading American Communities in the 21st Century.* Thousand Oaks, CA: Sage.

Buck, J.V., and B.S. Stone. 1981. "Citizen Involvement in Planning: Myth and Reality." *The Journal of Applied Behavioral Science,* 17(4): 550–65.

Burnheim, J. 1985. *Is Democracy Possible?* Berkeley: University of California Press.

Cleveland, H. 1975. "How Do You Get Everybody in on the Act and Still Get Some Action?" *Public Management,* 57 (June): 3–6.

Cole, R.L. 1974. *Citizen Participation and the Urban Policy Process.* Lexington, MA: Lexington Books.

Cooper, T.L. 1984. "Citizenship and Professionalism in Public Administration." *Public Administration Review* (March): 143–49.

Cunningham, J.V. 1972. "Citizen Participation in Public Affairs." *Public Administration Review* (October): 589–602.

Dahl, R.A. 1971. *Polyarchy: Participation and Opposition.* New Haven: Yale University Press.

———. 1989. *Democracy and Its Critics.* New Haven: Yale University Press.

Day, D. 1997. "Citizen Participation in the Planning Process: An Essentially Contested Concept?" *Journal of Planning Literature,* 11(3): 412–34.

DeSario, J., and S. Langton, eds. 1987. *Citizen Participation Public Decision Making.* Westport, CT: Greenwood.

Dimock, M. 1990. "The Restorative Qualities of Citizenship." *Public Administration Review,* 50(1): 21–25.

Dryzek, J.S. 1990. *Discursive Democracy: Politics, Policy, and Political Science.* Cambridge: Cambridge University Press.

———. 1996. "Political Inclusion and the Dynamics of Democratization." *American Political Science Review,* 90(3): 475–87.

Dryzek, J.S., and D. Torgerson. 1993. "Democracy and the Policy Sciences: A Progress Report." *Policy Sciences,* 26(3): 127–37.

Ellul, J. 1964. *The Technological Society.* New York: Random House.

Elster, J., ed. 1998. *Deliberative Democracy.* Cambridge: Cambridge University Press.

Etzioni-Halevy, E. 1983. *Bureaucracy and Democracy: A Political Dilemma.* London: Routledge and Kegan Paul.

Fagence, M. 1977. *Citizen Participation in Planning.* Oxford, U.K.: Pergamon.

Fishkin, J.S. 1991. *Democracy and Deliberation: New Directions for Democratic Reform.* New Haven: Yale University Press.

———. 1997. *Voice of the People: Public Opinion and Democracy.* New Haven: Yale University Press.

Follett, M.P. 1940. "Power." In *Dynamic Administration: The Collected Papers of Mary Parker Follett,* ed. Henry Metcalf and L. Urwick, 95–116. New York: Harper.

Frederickson, H.G. 1997. *The Spirit of Public Administration.* San Francisco: Jossey-Bass.

Gormley, W.T. 1981. "Public Advocacy in Public Utility Commission Proceedings." *The Journal of Applied Behavioral Science,* 17(4): 446–62.

Grant, J. 1994. *The Drama of Democracy: Contention and Dispute in Community Planning.* Toronto: University of Toronto Press.

Hallman, H.W. 1972. "Federally Financed Citizen Participation." *Public Administration Review* (September): 421–27.

Hart, D.K. 1972. "Theories of Government Related to Citizen Participation." *Public Administration Review* (September): 603–21.

———. 1984. "The Virtuous Citizen, the Honorable Bureaucrat, and 'Public' Administration." *Public Administration Review* (March): 111–20.

Kalu, K.N. 2003. "Of Citizenship, Virtue, and the Administrative Imperative: Deconstructing Aristotelian Civic Republicanism." *Public Administration Review,* 63(4): 418–27.

Kaufman, H. 1969. "Administrative Decentralization and Political Power." *Public Administration Review,* 29(1): 3–14.

King, C.S., K.M. Feltey, and B.O. Susel. 1998. "The Question of Participation: Toward Authentic Participation in Public Administration." *Public Administration Review,* 58(4): 317–26.

King, C.S., and C. Stivers. 1998. *The Government Is Us: Public Administration in an Anti-Government Era.* Thousand Oaks, CA: Sage.

Krouse, R.W. 1982. "Two Concepts of Democratic Representation: James and John Stuart Mill." *The Journal of Politics,* 44(2): 509–37.

Kweit, M.G., and R.W. Kweit. 1981. *Implementing Citizen Participation in a Bureaucratic Society: A Contingency Approach.* New York: Praeger.

———. 1990. *People and Politics in Urban America.* Belmont, CA: Wadsworth.

Michels, R. 1949. *Political Parties.* New York: Free Press.

Oldfield, A. 1990. *Citizenship and Community: Civic Republicanism and the Modern World.* London: Routledge.

Pateman, C. 1970. *Participation and Democratic Theory.* Cambridge: Cambridge University Press.

Reidel, J.A. 1972. "Citizen Participation: Myths and Realities." *Public Administration Review,* 32(3): 211–20.

Rich, R.C., and W.A. Rosenbaum. 1981. "Introduction to Symposium on Citizen Participation in Public Policy." *The Journal of Applied Behavioral Science,* 17(4): 439–45.

Roberts, N.C. 1991. "Towards a Synergistic Model of Power." In *Shared Power,* ed. J.M. Bryson and R.C. Einsweiler, 103–21. Lanham, MD: University Press of America.

Rohr, J.A. 1984. "Civil Servants and Second-Class Citizens." *Public Administration Review* (March): 135–40.

Salisbury, R.H. 1975. "Research on Political Participation." *American Journal of Political Science,* 29(2): 323–41.

Sanders, L.M. 1997. "Against Deliberation." *Political Theory,* 25(3): 347–76.

Schumpeter, J. 1943. *Capitalism, Socialism and Democracy.* London: Allen and Unwin.

Selznick, P. 1949. *TVA and the Grass Roots.* Berkeley: University of California Press.

Skocpol, T., and M.P. Fiorina, eds. 1999. *Civic Engagement in American Democracy.* Washington DC: Brookings Institution Press.

Stenberg, C.W. 1972. "Citizens and the Administrative State: From Participation to Power." *Public Administration Review,* 32(3): 190–98.

Stivers, C. 1990. "The Public Agency as Polis: Active Citizenship in the Administrative State." *Administration & Society,* 22(1): 86–105.

Thomas, J.C. 1995. *Public Participation in Public Decisions.* San Francisco: Jossey-Bass.

Toffler, A. 1971. *Future Shock.* New York: Bantam House.

Vigoda, E., and R.T. Golembiewski. 2001. "Citizenship Behavior and the Spirit of New Managerialism: A Theoretical Framework and Challenge for Governance." *American Review of Public Administration,* 31(3): 273–95.

Walzer, M. 1980. *Obligations: Essays on Disobedience, War and Citizenship.* Cambridge, MA: Harvard University Press.

Wamsley, G.L., C.T. Goodsell, J.A. Rohr, C.M. Stivers, O.F. White, and J.F. Wolf. 1987. "The Public Administration and the Governance Process: Refocusing the American Dialogue." In *A Centennial History of the American Administrative State,* ed. R.C. Chandler, 291–20. New York: Free Press.

Warner, B.E. 2001. "John Stuart Mill's Theory of Bureaucracy Within Representative Government: Balancing Competence and Participation." *Public Administration Review,* 61(4): 403–13.

Yankelovich, D. 1991. *Coming to Public Judgment.* Syracuse, NY: Syracuse University Press.

Table P2.1

Citizen and Administrator Roles in Public A

System	Citizen role
Authority system	Subject
Representative system	Voter
Administrative state	Client
Pluralist system	Interest-group advo
Political/market economy	Consumer/custome
Civil society	Volunteer, coproduc
Social learning system	Co-learner

Citizen as Voter in a Representative System citizen. It is centered on the electoral process t will represent him or her in the legislature. It and political contributions, as well as other forn the military and on juries. Administrators are d Their role is to be the implementer of legislativ

Citizen as Client in an Administrative State assumptions: The prime value in decision mak the least cost. Administrators who staff public competitively on the basis of competence and m free decisions. Politics and bureau administrati be separated. To ensure accountability to politi basis of merit and expertise, specialization of of responsibilities and duties. Good public dec management. The elected chief executive, who and coordinates all parts of the political and bur They are to respect and defer to the expertise ar who are responsible to politicians for implemen interest, and ensuring equal and equitable proc specialized skills, knowledge, or ability to be d their role is to provide the required input and su can be properly designed, implemented, and ev

Citizen as Interest-Group Advocate in a Plu that democracy is best achieved through collec interests more effectively in groups rather tha autonomous advocacy groups exist to represe a whole, since each group tends to focus on sp the groups are believed to serve as the best wa interest-group conflicts, the full diversity of aff approximation of responsive policy can be deve interest groups multiple access points and mean centers of power are arranged both vertically and the opportunity to be heard at critical stages c compromise, and power sharing among power

racts ambition and absolute power is checked. heir interests, support the creation and mainte- ect public officials who represent their interests, g competing interests. The administrator's role re that all interest groups have equal access and

Market Economy.[5] In this model, individualism ssumed that the best way to reflect individual much the same way consumers/customers rely erences. If bureaus do not meet citizen needs, in government or in the private and nonprofit en have incentives to change and adapt in order these arrangements, the "steering" and produc- ing encourages entrepreneurial leadership and eeds. Production of public services then can be asi-private). In fact, competition among service service at the least cost. Relationships among rative arrangements, informal agreements, and e a set of associations often described as net- ging these relationships adds to the complexity system, administrators act as liaisons, brokers ley are expected to understand and apply busi- both public and private organizations as well mance and other private-sector techniques. In zed, deregulated and flexible government units erences.

ciety.[6] This model focuses on civil society—those sector. As Dryzek (1996) notes, civil society is ocratization. . . . It can be a place where people nt problems" (p. 482). Civic engagement cre- of volunteer in nonpaying activities to support nd civic life in general. For example, volunteers ugh neighborhood watches and citizen patrols school facilities, participation in cleanup cam- The second is the role of coproducer. Citizens ough neighborhood associations, community and deliver government services. Their mutual vice outputs. Citizen-agency collaborations in ernment, but the most prevalent are at the local ption during budget cutbacks, mounting service lies in the creation of network ties that are es- aining a healthy democratic system.

cess.[7] Solutions to public dilemmas and prob- . They are not "givens." Social learning occurs ials, and employees who are required to make problem definitions and solutions in order to —enabling participants to respect and listen to one another's opinions, and through deliberation—enabling competing perspectives to be aired and considered before decisions are made. In their roles as stewards of the public trust, public executives and administrators serve as facilitators of the learning process. They also promote the restructuring of political institutions so that supportive political cultures can be built and sustained. They advocate learning in smaller, decentralized and flatter government units to encourage citizen and employee involvement, and they develop new techniques to accommodate collaborative problem solving and decision making in large groups. Ultimately, the goals of social learning are to develop citizen identity, increase civic virtue, build learning communities, and harness the energy and talents of all members of a democratic society.

Citizen empowerment, a fundamental tenet of direct citizen participation, is an important element in six of the seven models summarized above. Citizens can be empowered in their roles as voters, advocates, consumers, customers, volunteers, coproducers, and co-learners. However, only the social learning model puts citizens on an equal footing with public officials. As co-learners and full partners, it requires them to be fully engaged in the democratic enterprise by being directly involved in problem solving and decision making about the public's business. The articles that follow all concur that democracy rests on the direct involvement of the citizens, although they disagree on how that involvement should be expressed. The first set of four articles is compatible with the social learning model. The second set illustrates variations on the theme in their descriptions of citizens as coproducers, owners, and co-investors.

CITIZENS AS SOCIAL LEARNERS

H. George Frederickson opens this section with the article "The Recovery of Civism in Public Administration." His fundamental premise is that "effective public administration of the future should be intimately tied to citizenship, the citizenry generally, and to the effectiveness of public managers who work *directly* with the citizenry" (p. 27). He traces the origins and traditions of civism in public administration and concludes that public administration has lost its focus on civism. Its restoration requires "an emphasis on the *public* aspects of the field and to the basic issues of democratic theory" (p. 29). Three issues are particularly important to restore the sense of community to American life: the directness of the democratic process; the principles of justice; and the principles of individual freedom. Public administrators have critical roles to play in this transition. They need to discover new methods of building consensus, including those that would employ modern technology, and keep people fully and directly involved in the policy process. They need to help public organizations become more responsive and adaptive to the tremendous changes that are occurring worldwide. Educational institutions also have a part to play by increasing civic learning in the schools at all levels and making civic education a lifelong process. The recovery of civism, he believes, will provide "the anchor that both the practice and study of public administration need, not only to find its identity but to be effective once again" (p. 29).

Building on this same theme, Curtis Ventriss's article, "Toward a Public Philosophy of Public Administration: A Civic Perspective of the Public," advocates developing a new philosophy of public administration based on civic purpose. He asks, "Is public administration's public purpose always restricted to responding to state direction, or does it entail broader social responsibilities?" (p. 41). It entails broader social responsibilities, he answers, because the polity is more than government institutions. To meet its social responsibilities, public administration must expand its conceptualization of the public and incorporate a new public purpose based on citizenship. Citizenship should be shaped by acceptance of societal interdependencies, a renewed emphasis on public learning, and a revitalized public language. Interdependencies acknowledge multiple levels of social, political, and economic realities in which everything depends on everything else, prompting administrators to serve as stewards of a multiplicity of public actors and interests. Public learning enables public dialogue and an open exchange of information in the shared definition of social problems and their solutions. A new public language "examines the value assumptions of policy decisions and openly explores the relationship of political means to political ends" (p. 45). This new civic purpose ultimately requires a shift from the "scientization of social science" to the creation of a new public social science.

In "Facilitating Community, Enabling Democracy: New Roles for Local Government Managers," John Nalbandian illustrates how the roles, responsibilities, and values of city management professionals have been transformed to accommodate the new civic purpose. Based on data from survey questions, correspondence, and in-depth panel discussions, he finds that city managers now aspire to be community builders and enablers of democracy. They expect to take on a facilitative leadership role to encourage citizen participation, develop community partnerships, and build consensus among diverse community interests. As part of their new responsibilities, they work to empower the governing body and the citizens and help both to develop and use the tools of engagement to address community problems. Their work is informed by new values based on individual rights, fairness, representation, and the belief that collectively a community can accomplish some tasks more efficiently and effectively than its individual members could do on their own. Local government managers have become much more process oriented, with less adherence to the "one best form" of government.

In "The New Public Service: Serving Rather than Steering," Robert B. Denhardt and Janet Vinzant Denhardt juxtapose what they call the New Public Service model with two other normative models—"Old Public Administration" and "New Public Management." To make the comparisons, they lay out three ideas that provide the conceptual foundation for New Public Service: (1) An active and involved citizenry concerned with the public interest and collaboratively engaged with public officials in governance; (2) a rebirth of civil society, where people work out their personal interests in the context of community concerns, and government plays a role in creating, facilitating, and supporting connections between citizens and their communities; and (3) new approaches to knowledge acquisition that are based on sincere and open discourse (e.g., dialogue and deliberation) among all parties, including citizens and administrators.

The New Public Service model has seven basic tenets as its foundation:

1. The role of the public servant is to help citizens articulate and meet their shared interests, rather than to attempt to control or steer society in new directions.
2. Building a collective shared notion of the public interest is the aim of public service, not finding quick solutions driven by individual choices.
3. Public policies and programs can most effectively and responsibly be achieved through collective efforts and collaboration.
4. The public interest and decisions result from dialogue about shared values rather than an aggregation of individual self-interests.
5. Accountability is complex, stemming from markets as well as statutory and constitutional law, community values, political norms, professional standards, and citizen interests.
6. Public organizations and the networks in which they operate are more likely to succeed if they are based on collaboration, shared leadership, and a respect for all people.
7. The public interest is best advanced by public servants and citizens rather than by entrepreneurial managers.

CITIZENS AS COPRODUCERS, OWNERS, AND CO-INVESTORS

In "Citizenship and Service Delivery: The Promise of Coproduction," Charles Levine asks how one designs a system that builds citizen trust in government, citizen efficacy, and a shared conception of the common good, especially when the current conceptualization of the citizen is predicated on narrow self-interest? He reviews six service delivery models, the dominant strategy for each one, and the roles the citizens are expected to play. He eliminates five alternatives and believes the answer lies in coproduction: "the joint provision of public services by public agencies and service consumers" (p. 83). Coproduction devolves service responsibility to neighborhood organizations, individual service, and public-private partnerships. Besides its potential for saving tax dollars, it has many beneficial results that include shared responsibility, mutual respect between citizens and public officials, and joint problem solving. Using community-based crime prevention groups as an example, he outlines their benefits as well as their problems and what must be done to overcome them. He also believes that coproduction can be generalized to other services, providing an important bridge between government and citizens.

Hindy Lauer Schachter offers an alternative role for citizens in her article "Reinventing Government or Reinventing Ourselves: Two Models for Improving Government Performance." In contrast to customer-centered models, she introduces an owner-based model of citizenship. This model derives from the New York Bureau of Municipal Research, a progressive organization incorporated in 1907 to help solve urban political problems. The bureau posited that urban citizens owned their government, and their ownership required them to mind their business—the public's business. As owner-shareholders in city corporations, citizens needed to work for administrative improvements by gathering information on how public services were performing, analyzing the data, presenting the results to politicians and public administrators, and demanding that changes be made if corporations were not functioning well. Although both the customer-centered and owner-centered models of citizenship are metaphors, and each has its own inconsistencies, Schachter believes that only the owner-citizen model keeps the focus on the citizen as a primary actor in a democratic society. To ensure the model's implementation, however, requires public empowerment through citizen education, consistent information exchange between government and citizens, and service learning that reinforces the citizen's responsibility for assuming a role in his or her community.

Gerald E. Smith and Carole A. Huntsman challenge both the citizen-owner model and the citizen-customer model. In "Reframing the Metaphor of the Citizen-Government Relationship: A Value-Centered Perspective," they offer a third model—the citizen as co-investor. This model draws from economic theory and the marginalist theory of value. Central to it is the belief that as citizens are motivated to increase incremental value for themselves and their communities, so should public organizations be motivated to create incremental value for their constituents. In this value-based model, government becomes the trustee—a steward and manager of assets, resources, and the public trust—whose purpose it is to deliver incremental value for citizens. In turn, citizens are equal shareholders of the common wealth of the community. They are expected to invest with other citizens and government in wealth creation by influencing the community's collective goals and direction. Both administrators and citizens need to be proactive and focus on creating value through the use of partnerships, cooperative ventures, volunteering, and sharing with each other. Field research demonstrated the application of economic value analysis to a local government context. Although citizens were unaccustomed to thinking in value terms, the researchers found that they expressed opinions, engaged in activities, and co-invested personal resources consistent with a value perspective.

NOTES

1. See Vigoda (2002) for a fuller description of this model.
2. See Dahl (1998) for an elaboration of this model.
3. See Wilson (1941), Gulick and Urwick (1937), and Yates (1982) for an overview of this model.
4. See Dahl (1956) and Yates (1982) for a summary of this model.
5. For a general overview of this perspective, see Osborne and Gaebler (1992). For a description of vouchers that enable citizens to purchase services of their choice from authorized suppliers, see Crompton (1983).
6. See Brudney and England (1983), Ferris (1984), Skopol and Fiorina (1999), and Putnam (2000) for an overview of this perspective.
7. See Dewey (1966), Gawthrop (1984), and Korton (1980, 1981) for a more complete description of the learning process.

REFERENCES

Box, R.C. 1998. *Citizen Governance.* Thousand Oaks, CA: Sage.
Brudney, J.L., and R.E. England. 1983. "Toward a Definition of the Coproduction Concept." *Public Administration Review,* 43(1): 59–65.
Crompton, J.L. 1983. "Recreation Vouchers: A Case Study in Administrative Innovation and Citizen Participation." *Public Administration Review,* 43 (September): 537–46.
Dahl, R.A. 1998. *On Democracy.* New Haven: Yale University Press.
———. 1956. *Preface to Democratic Theory.* Chicago: University of Chicago Press.
Dewey, J. 1966. *Democracy and Education.* New York: Macmillan.
Dryzek, J.S. 1996. "Political Inclusion and the Dynamics of Democratization." *American Political Science Review,* 90(3): 475–87.
Ferris, J.M. 1984. "Coprovision: Citizen Time and Money Donations in Public Service Provision." *Public Administration Review,* 44(4): 324–33.
Gawthrop, L.C. 1984. "Civis, Civitas and Civilitas: A New Focus for the Year 2000." *Public Administration Review,* 44 (March): 101–107.
Gulick, L., and L. Urwick. 1937. *Papers on the Science of Administration.* New York: Institute of Public Administration, Columbia University.
Held, D. 1996. *Models of Democracy.* 2d. ed. Stanford: Stanford University Press.
Herbert, A.W. 1972. "Management Under Conditions of Decentralization and Citizen Participation." *Public Administration Review,* 32 (October): 622–37.
Korten, D.C. 1980. "Community Organization and Rural Development: A Learning Process Approach." *Public Administration Review,* 40(5): 480–511.
———. 1981. "The Management of Social Transformation." *Public Administration Review,* 41(6): 609–18.
Osborne, D., and R. Gaebler. 1992. *Reinventing Government: How the Entrepreneurial Spirit Is Transforming the Public Sector.* Reading, MA: Addison-Wesley.
Putnam, R.D. 2000. *Bowling Alone: The Collapse and Revival of American Community.* New York: Simon and Schuster.
Skopol, T., and M.P. Fiorina, eds. 1999. *Civic Engagement in American Democracy.* Washington, DC: Brookings Institution Press.
Van Meter, E.C. 1975. "Citizen Participation in the Policy Management Process." *Public Administration Review,* 35 (December): 804–12.
Vigoda, E. 2002. "From Responsiveness to Collaboration: Governance, Citizens, and the Next Generation of Public Administration." *Public Administration Review,* 62(5): 527–40.
Wilson, W. 1941. "The Study of Administration." *Political Science Quarterly,* 56(2): 197–222. (Originally published in 1887.)
Yates, D. 1982. *Bureaucratic Democracy: The Search for Democracy and Efficiency in American Government.* Cambridge, MA: Harvard University Press.

CHAPTER 1

THE RECOVERY OF CIVISM
IN PUBLIC ADMINISTRATION

H. GEORGE FREDERICKSON

Something is wrong. Virtually all of our institutions seem to be in trouble. The family is deteriorating, schools seem to be ineffective, there is deep suspicion of most large-scale organizations, including industry, business, and government. There is dwindling support for churches. Crime is alarmingly common. We are balkanized into racial, economic, ethnic, demographic, and sexual division. Privatism, greed, self-interest, and self-indulgence challenge the notion of community.[1] Old assumptions of trust and integrity have slipped into a quagmire of litigiousness which jams the courts. The economy sputters, managing to violate Keynesian notions of the relationship between inflation, unemployment, and interest rates.

Government is at the center of virtually all of these problems. The people, the citizens, are very perceptive and know that something is wrong. Survey research indicates a sharp decline in confidence in government as well as most of our institutions.[2] While we continue to enjoy great political freedom, the lack of support for and confidence in our institutions results in despair and, in some cases, fear. Despair and fear are crippling emotions and can result in one of the oldest of political axioms: given the choice, people will be tempted to trade some freedom for greater security.[3] That special American genius for maintaining widespread personal freedom while building public and private institutions that work is being seriously tested, because our institutions are not working as well as they once did. Translating the genius for *building* institutions to genius in *changing* institutions to meet new and different circumstances, while preserving individual freedom, is the challenge of our time.

The media ordinarily present announcements of declining public support for public institutions in an alarming tone which the people receive with a combination of alarm and despair. Something would be wrong if the people were not responding with expressions of declining respect or support for government institutions. The fact is that our public institutions are not coping. We should be seriously concerned if the people, the citizens, thought that everything was fine. Everything is not fine; the people see that and are responding.

From *Public Administration Review*, 42, 6 (November/December 1982): 501–507. Copyright © 1982 by American Society for Public Administration. Reprinted with permission.

That response takes many forms; some are negative and some are positive. The negative responses include seeking to blame government employees, the bureaucracy, for problems in governmental effectiveness. Both Jimmy Carter and Ronald Reagan ran for the presidency on platforms which blamed the bureaucracy for government ineffectiveness. They tapped the vein of fear and distrust, they found in the bureaucracy a convenient scapegoat; and they went to Washington to cut out the fat, eliminate the waste, and uncover the fraud. Many mayors and governors have also been elected by standing on the same plank. When these people take office they soon discover that what *they* thought was fat and waste are very likely major priorities in the legislative branch.

On the positive side, expressions of disquietude over our ineffective institutions signify searches for better ways to organize, to manage, and to govern. Harlan Cleveland captures this perception well by indicating that the crucial question of the 1980s is "how do we get more governance with less government?"

"It is clear that many people want less government," he says, "but in the 1970s people also decided that they wanted more decisions made in the public interest, decisions concerning civil rights, children's rights, women, the purposes to which science and technology should be put. People have come to expect a lot more decisions from government but that doesn't necessarily mean that government has to deliver more services. It is possible to think of ways we could have more governance with less government."[4]

The citizens are groping for changes that they believe will improve the effectiveness of government agencies. There is no question that the citizens are deeply concerned about the education of their children, but those same citizens have very serious questions about the effectiveness of the public schools. Citizens are deeply concerned about lawlessness, crime, and law enforcement but they have serious reservations about the effectiveness of the police. What the citizens are saying in their expressions of declining support for the schools, the police, and other government organizations is that they want those institutions to *change.*

The first response on the part of public officials to the citizens' desire for change is far too defensive. To be sure, much of the blame directed at civil servants, particularly by elected officials, is baseless. The second most obvious response to this desire for change has been to develop systems for humanely cutting back on government activities. If there has been a theme in the *Public Administration Review* and in public administration circles generally in the last five years, it has been "cutback administration."

What the citizens want is *change,* and they want fundamental change. What the public service tends to want is either more or less of what they presently do. In response to demands for change, we cut back. We have fewer school teachers as enrollments decline, but we have great difficulty in addressing what is at the base of citizen's concerns about schools. Cutback is a short-range strategy. What is needed is long-range change. Public administration needs to sharpen its creative abilities and its capacity to develop alternatives. Where innovation, change, and responsiveness is occurring, it tends, in my judgment, to be associated with what is called here "a new civism." The effective public administration of the future should be intimately tied to citizenship, the citizenry generally, and to the effectiveness of public managers who work *directly* with the citizenry.

THE ORIGINS AND TRADITIONS OF CIVISM IN
PUBLIC ADMINISTRATION

In its origins, public administration was closely connected to the great over-arching issues of government. Almost 100 years ago, when the founding fathers began to formulate the field, it was presumed that public administration was directly associated with definitions of what constitutes a community, and the role and place of the citizens in the community. The early formulations of public administration dealt with concepts of majority rule and minority rights, questions of direct citizen participation in government, questions regarding the representational or republican style of democracy, questions of justice, freedom, equality, privacy, and due process. Woodrow Wilson, in his seminal essay, "The Study of Administration" in 1887 noted that in a democracy it is not the monarch that is sovereign, but the people.[5]

To Wilson, public administration should have a direct linkage to the sovereign, the people. Public administration was to be influenced by the opinions of the people and to be generally responsive to them. In another context, Wilson described the fiduciary responsibilities of administrators in the broadest possible fashion. Although administration is technical, essentially managerial, and is removed from electoral politics, "it is, at the same time, raised very far above the . . . level of mere technical detail by the fact that through its greater principles, it is directly connected with the lasting maxims of political wisdom, the permanent truth of political progress."[6]

That Wilson was concerned about the greater principles, the lasting maxims and the permanent truth of government, is clear later when he states: "Liberty depends incomparably more upon administration than upon constitution."[7]

It should not be assumed that Wilson was naive about the relationship between public opinion and the functioning of government administration. He certainly understood how administration was to be responsive to public opinion.

> The problem is to make public opinion efficient without suffering it to be meddlesome. Directly exercised in the oversight of the daily details and in the choice of the daily means of government, public criticism is, of course, a clumsy nuisance, a rustic handling delicate machinery. But, as superintending the greater forces of formative policy like in politics and in administration, public criticism is altogether safe and beneficent, altogether indispensable. Let administrative study find the best means for giving public criticism this control and for shutting it out from all other interference.[8]

Wilson was likewise concerned with the great questions of the maintenance of a democratic polity. "Our own politics must be the touchstone for all theories. The principles on which to base a science of administration for America must be principles which have democratic policy very much at heart."[9]

The early practices of public administration, both in the academy and in the bureau, clearly reflected the Wilsonian perspective on public administration. It was simply *assumed* that public administration was a full partner in the search for good government. It was assumed that the great civic issues were issues of significance not only to the courts, to the legislative branch, and to the executive office (mayors, governors and the president) but also to those who conduct the daily affairs of government. The early traditions of public administration were closely associated with the municipal reform movement, the good government movement, civil service reform, and other government changes associated with the latter years of the 19th century and the early years of this century [20th century]. Public administration, at the time, was closely connected with the fields of political science and public law. The issues that concerned those fields were assumed to be the issues that also concerned public administration. The early schools of public administration, particularly the Maxwell Graduate School of Citizenship and Public Affairs at Syracuse University, the School of Public Administration at the University of Southern California (originally called the School of *Citizenship* and Public Administration), and others all reflected this civic perspective on public administration. Using the Maxwell School at Syracuse University as an example, not only was there an MPA degree designed to prepare young people for public service, there was a general pattern of courses for all students majoring in the liberal arts on issues of democracy, the constitution, and public policy.

Dwight Waldo points out in *The Administrative State,* that early public administration constituted a marriage of the science of politics and the science of organization and management.[10] In the early years, the study and practice of the art of government and politics was dominant. The *public* part of public administration received the emphasis. Gradually that emphasis shifted to the sciences of management and administration, the "principles of public administration," and notions such as POSDCORB [Planning, Organizing, Staffing, Directing, Coordinating, Reporting, and Budgeting]. By the 1930s, both in the practice and in the study of public administration, there began a drift away from an explicit linkage between citizenship and notions of general responsibility for good government and the field of public administration. The major theoretical argument of the time centered on the question of a politics-administration dichotomy.

During this time, the Depression and World War II caused governments at all levels to grow dramatically. Just after World War II, Herbert Simon attacked the "principles" of public administration and moved the concept of efficiency and rational decision making to center stage.[11] Waldo argued that Simon had subtly reintroduced the politics-administration dichotomy. He further suggested that Simon had assumed levels of rational analytic abilities and means-ends assumptions that were simply not present in a complex world. The argument was joined by Charles Lindblom in "The Science of Muddling Through" in which he suggested that the "rational-comprehensive method" attributed to Simon is neither empirically verifiable nor practical. In application, he suggested a model called "successive-limited comparisons" which has come to be known as the "incremental model."[12]

While these issues were central to the thinking of people both in the practice and study of public administration, there was little interest in matters of citizenship and the role of citizens in democratic government. Questions of democratic theory and questions of ethics in government were less often asked. By the late 1960s and early 1970s, government was huge. Public administration was experiencing an identity crisis as were most institutions and the citizens were in the early stages of declining support for most of the institutions in our society. Civism was lost from public administration. The recovery of civism will help provide the anchor that both the practice and study of public administration need, not only to find its identity but to be effective once again.

THE RECOVERY OF CIVISM IN PUBLIC ADMINISTRATION:
DEMOCRATIC THEORY

The process of restoring support and legitimacy to government will require responding to citizens' concerns and needs. For public administration, both in practice and in education, this will mean a return to an emphasis on the *public* aspects of the field and to the basic issues of democratic theory. If public administration is to be effective, persons who practice it must be increasingly familiar with issues of both representational and direct democracy, with citizen participation, with principles of justice, and principles of individual freedom. Likewise if there is to be a restoration of government effectiveness and legitimacy, the citizenry will need to be significantly more conversant with these issues.

The directness of the democratic process is a basic issue for public administration. Stephen K. Bailey saw narrow limits around the directness with which citizens can participate in effective government:

Because of the ultimate capacity of American citizens to make wise fundamental value choices, attempts to induce them into making superficial technical choices are ill-advised. Representatives, legislators and officials are supported by an educated bureaucracy, informed by myriad interest groups and experts, checked by an independent judiciary and a free press, and held accountable to the larger public through periodic elections, intermittent correspondence, and occasional face-to-face meetings. All this constitutes not only a reasonable apparatus for conducting modern public business in an economically and technically complex-free society like the United States, but also the only reasonable apparatus.[13]

Bailey was fairly accused of supporting what has come to be known as the "pluralist elite model" of citizen participation.

Richard Flathman recently reviewed the concept citizenship in a democratic polity.[14] Political theory may be divided into those who support concepts of "high citizenship" and those who follow concepts of "low citizenship." In high citizenship (Pericles, Aristotle, and Rousseau in the classical tradition, and Arendt, Barber, Pateman, Thompson, and Walzer in contemporary literature) "citizens are free, equal, and engaging with one another in pursuing matters of high and distinctively human import. Citizenship is the distinct of human activity and the distinctively important feature of a political society."[15] In low citizenship (Schumpeter, Downs, Berelson, Lipset, Dahl, Sartori) empiricists can demonstrate that high citizenship cannot work in the modern world. "Whatever the merits of this ideal from a normative perspective, the ideal is unachievable in, and, hence, irrelevant to, political life and practice in the modern nation state. The continuous, intense, moral uplifting interactions that the ideal presumes can obtain, if at all, only among sub-groups within the large, complex, and impersonal societies of the modern world. Attempts to achieve and sustain such interactions at the level of the political society are distracting and destabilizing."[16] Flathman argues that the proponents of low citizenship are wrong. Whatever weaknesses the high participation model may have, it is still necessary if democracy is to succeed. High citizenship gives legitimacy to the exercise of authority in a democratic polity and provides for the power necessary to have effective yet open government. He calls for "self awareness as persons . . . including the role of citizen. Flathman's analysis is fully compatible with the recovery of citizenship in public administration.

Would not direct involvement in the democratic process between the public servants and citizens undermine the processes of electoral democracy? The answer to this is yes, if the public administrator is not sensitive to the point at which his or her prerogatives and responsibilities end and the elected official's prerogatives and responsibilities begin, and yes, if the public administrator is bent on self-recognition or power. The answer is decidedly no, if public administrators are part of a decision process which includes elected officials, citizens, and public servants and which is not dominated by the concerns, needs, and interests of the public servants.

Are not forms of direct democracy slow, cumbersome, time-consuming and non-risk taking? Yes, if public administrators are not skilled in working effectively with citizens and elected officials. Yes, if there is too great an emphasis on process and not sufficient emphasis on closure. On the other hand, even if direct patterns of involvement on the part of citizens have a slowing effect, that may be a worthy trade-off for the development of policies and programs more suited to the general interests of the citizenry.

For the public administrator to be effective, there must be an understanding of the workings of democratic government. Understanding the subtleties of politics in the machinery of government is important. An understanding of the constant process of mediation and adjustment in the policymaking process is important. These "arts" must be a part of the education of public servants.

A second concept in democratic theory is justice. Justice is a long-standing element in most social contacts. Justice has generally come to mean "that which is fair." The courts are ultimately responsible for the administration of justice in matters of civil and criminal law. Governments, and particularly democratic governments, through their decision-making processes deal routinely with questions of what is and what is not just. Much of the present low regard for government organizations has to do with the wide-spread view that there are great breaches in the fair treatment of citizens or in justice. It may be assumed that any enduring sense of community or any lasting common agreement as to the purposes of government will require justice and fairness. This is critical to public administration because it is the public servant who must administer the programs that carry out government policies.

John Rawls' *A Theory of Justice* should be required reading for everyone practicing public administration. It helps one to understand why there is so much dissatisfaction with contemporary institutions. When speaking of governmental institutions, Rawls states: "For us the primary subject of justice is the basic structure of society, or more exactly, the way in which the major social institutions distribute fundamental rights and duties and determine the division of advantages from social cooperation. By major institutions I understand the political constitution and the principal economic and social arrangements."[17]

Rawls is concerned with self-sufficiency and order in a society or a community. A common agreement on the same principles of justice makes people secure in their relationships with one another. Even though individuals are inclined to self-interest and different aims and purposes, if they share a common sense of fairness or justice it will assist in ordering their association. When that common sense of fairness or justice is lacking, then human associations are fragile, the legitimacy of institutions is in doubt, and the structure and endurance of government is in question. The point is that it is not just political philosophers or jurists who must concern themselves with justice. Those who are responsible for administering government agencies must be acquainted with these concepts and have a commitment to the notion of fairness.

Freedom is a third concept in democratic theory that is important to public administration. Constitutionally, of course, there are many freedoms: expression, religion, press, and so forth. For public officials, the issue of freedom goes two ways. First, the government is responsible for ensuring each individual's freedoms in the society. Probably more important, the government is responsible to see to it that government does not infringe these freedoms. In much of the history of the world, the biggest single threat to individual freedom has been government. In our time, too often the large scale public organization and the persons who work in those organizations are perceived to be a threat to individual freedom. It is widely believed that organizations are dehumanizing and threaten the freedom not only [of] the individuals who work in them, but [of] the persons they serve. In fact, it is our large scale organizations that free us. The American population is better educated than ever before because of large scale and complex educational institutions. We are healthier than ever before because of large and intricately-related health service organizations. We may long for the corner grocery store, but in fact, the advantages of the supermarket are compelling. Indeed, the world of large scale organization enhances freedom. The trick is to make those organizations changeable and responsive and not to allow them to exist primarily for the persons who work in them or profit from them but for those who are to be served by them.

The more extreme capitalists believe that the economy will only function adequately if there is complete freedom for business. The fact is that the corporate system is undergirded and underwritten by government policy and programs. A small and weak government would not only weaken the corporate system, but would leave the citizens without an ability to check corporate tendencies toward taking advantage of consumers. Effective and responsive government (local, state and federal) are vital to the maintenance of the free enterprise system.

The shared commitment to notions of citizenship, justice and freedom are manifest through the community. There has been a decided loss of sense of community in contemporary America. The single greatest conceptual and theoretical problem we face is the reconstruction of this sense of community. We must discover new methods of building consensus, methods that employ modern technology yet keep the people fully and directly involved in the policy process. Without a strong sense of community, public administration will continue to constitute a threat for the citizens and a scapegoat for elected officials.

THE RECOVERY OF CIVISM IN PUBLIC ADMINISTRATION: ORGANIZATION THEORY

Few concepts are more fundamental to the functioning of large-scale organizations than hierarchy. The scaler principle, workers ordered in a pyramid from greater to lesser positions, is found in most government agencies. Although the concept of hierarchy has been under attack in the literature of organization theory for many years, the actual practice indicates that hierarchy is a remarkably resilient concept. Still, there have been changes. Matrix organizations, for example, are increasingly common. Rensis Likert's concept of linking pins and overlapping tasks are rather good descriptions of what often happens in well-managed adaptive organizations.[18]

The modern world is so complex and fluid that strict notions of hierarchy simply are not workable. Harlan Cleveland predicts that: "The organizations that get things done will no longer be hierarchical pyramids with most of the real control at the top. They will be systems—interlaced webs of tension in which control is loose, power diffused, and centers of decision plural. 'Decision making' will become an increasingly intricate process of multi-lateral brokerage both inside and outside the organization which thinks it has the responsibility for making, or at least announcing, the decision."[19]

Cleveland's description is fully compatible with concepts of direct citizen involvement in the policy-making process. Citizen input can be accommodated at the "line" level of the organization, the point at which the organization serves its clients. Formal advisory or feedback systems at that level are ordinarily useful anyway. This concept of hierarchy also accommodates the horizontal entry of citizen views at the middle level of the organization, and of course, accommodates citizen preferences along with the dominant views of elected officials at the upper reaches of the hierarchy. The point is that modern public officials will need to have a conception of hierarchy that can tolerate the ambiguity involved in multiple levels of citizen involvement in the policy process. Moreover, they will need to be comfortable with organizational structures and administrative practices that accommodate rather than attempt to curtail citizen involvement.

Uncertainty is the fundamental problem for complex organizations, and coping with uncertainty is the essence of the administrative process.[20] The environment in which organizations function is constantly changing, therefore reducing certainty in the purposes and practices of those organizations. The "technology" with which organizations deal also changes rapidly, therefore adding to uncertainty. Depending on their size and type, complex organizations respond to uncertainty in different ways. Public organizations are subject to the same uncertainties as are private organizations, but government organizations are somewhat unique because they have difficulty articulating, measuring, and defining goals and purposes. For example, if the size of a police force [were] quadrupled, would that have any particular effect on the level of crime? Conversely, if a police department [were] cut in half, would it have any particular effect on the level of crime?

Where cause/effect relationships are difficult to verify, then symbols such as uniforms, pieces of machinery, elaborate jargon and fads become especially important and become strategies for dealing with uncertainty.

When an organization's purpose is relatively clear and generally understood, and where the cause/effect relationship is quite clear, the basic threat to that organization may have to do with its dependence on an environment which may not cooperate. An example might be the transportation department that provides busses, but few wish to ride the bus. Under those circumstances, the organization tries to deal with uncertainty and to make its functions more predictable through "transactions at the boundaries" or attempting to adjust its activities to match fluctuations in the environment. This requires the organization to hold certain positions or staff members in reserve for discretionary purposes, these positions to be assigned to whatever interests seem to be expressed at a particular time. Large-scale complex organizations cannot have monolithic authority because of rapid shifts in environment and because of the need to decentralize so that some units of the organization can be responsive. Full rationality, that is the entire organization working consistently on one clear goal or a hierarchy of goals, cannot work because at a particular time and in a particular setting, some part of the organization may need to work on different and perhaps even occasionally contrasting goals. These conditions are very common in our present environment and call for structural decentralization, the creation of semi-autonomous sub-units and modified or buffered concepts of rationality.

How does the modern day administrator cope with uncertainty? James Thompson says that effective managers of modern complex organizations are aggressive in keeping several groups involved in the policy process and in making the organization responsive to the widest possible range of needs and concerns. Thompson expresses concern that administrators perceive uncertainties in different ways and too often misread uncertainties and respond inappropriately with an overemphasis on hierarchy, on technology, or on rationality.[21]

Students of organization theory have long argued the merits of centralization versus decentralization. We are presently in an era of decentralization, and that bodes well for the prospect of greater citizen association with government functioning. In our federal system of government, we appear to be in the early stages of a fundamental decentralization. Virtually every change that has occurred in the dynamics of federalism since the origin of the country has been in the direction of a greater involvement of the national government in most functional areas of government and in most policy fields. When decentralization is discussed in the national government it has ordinarily meant setting up field offices or providing somewhat greater autonomy to the bureaus and services within the departments. A *real* decentralization in the federal structure means returning to the states and cities exclusive or nearly exclusive responsibility for particular government functions. The process of decentralization of this sort will be wrenching because of its fiscal implications. However, if it is even partially successful, it too will be hospitable to the prospects for greater citizen involvement in the policy process. Besides that, it makes good sense theoretically. As Stephen K. Bailey put it: "The American commonwealth is far too complex for rational control at the center—at least without the use of punitive government sanctions quite out of keeping with our peacetime national heritage."[22]

If there is a dominant theme in contemporary organization theory it is the rational model. It has a superficial orderliness to it, an orderliness based on assumptions about setting agreed upon organizational goals, and discovering the best means to achieve those goals. The elaborate logic behind this simple idea is seductive and receives unwarranted attention in the academy. The field of public administration has gradually evolved in the direction of schools of policy sciences or programs in policy analysis. The curriculum of these schools tends to be rational, technical, mathematical, and analytical. The assumption is that with the right data and a proper analysis, the answer will be clear and that answer will make government better. While data and analysis are necessary, they are not sufficient. An understanding of the policy process, a clearer perception of democratic values and of modern theories of organization, and effectiveness with elected officials and citizens are the keys to making government better. Public administration programs in higher education must balance their rational tendencies with the practical concerns of making government responsive.

While there continues to be an interesting debate between the rationalists and the incrementalists, in fact both the rational model and the incremental model are rational. As Camille Cates points out, the incremental model "is not irrational, it is just not perfectly rational."[23] Cates argues that what is needed is not more rationality or less rationality, *but something other than rationality.* Instead of rational or incremental decision making, Cates recommends what she calls creative decision making. Creative decision making is an artistic process of discovery of new alternatives by knowledgeable and perceptive policy makers. A high tolerance for ambiguity is called for. Rational premises may not always enhance the creative process. One does not abandon rationality or rational techniques but seeks a balance between rational and non-rational approaches, neither being sufficient to stand alone. The creative public official knows his or her own mind, is willing to change perspectives, take the opposite view, and support the creative process by asking different questions.[24]

CONCLUSIONS

One should not assume that what is described here is speculation about a preferred, or even a likely, future. In fact, much of what is described here is presently underway. The civism movement is gaining momentum across the land. In many cities, so-called public-private partnerships are developing whereby business, civic, and political leaders are working together on civic problems. New networks of concerned citizens dealing with safety, education, health care, housing, and other public policy matters are forming. Changes in government functioning involving fewer public employees and only necessary services are being invented. We are gradually learning how to have less government and more governance. Moreover, these innovations will go through a process of diffusion not unlike the diffusion that carried civil service reform across the land in the first half of this century. Public administrators are often at the forefront of these innovations, yet in the modern theory of public administration we read little of this movement.

In the social sciences, theory tends to come after, rather than before, discovery. As Peter Drucker so aptly puts it: "A new theory to fit a new reality will be a long time coming. For a new theory to be more than idle speculation and vague dreaming, it must come after the event. It codifies what we have already learned, have already achieved, have already done; but we cannot wait until we have the theory we need. We have to act. We have to use the little we know."[25]

If we must act, based on what we know at this hour, what role does the public administrator play? In the opinions of Scott and Hart, public administrators play not only an important part in making government more adaptive and responsive, they play the critical role.[26] There is no doubt that the general citizenry want the changes described earlier. The managers have two advantages. First, they can synthesize, summarize, and articulate the inchoate "preferences" or "feelings" or "mood" of the citizenry. The people know how they feel, but it takes skill and perception to capture those feelings and translate them into coherent and plausible positions. Scott and Hart are of the opinion that perceptive administrators who are in touch with their clientele are best able to do that. Second, public managers have the advantage of knowing best how the government works and how it can be changed. The trick, of course, is freeing the imagination and creative abilities of public managers, and freeing them from their preoccupation with organizational maintenance.

An understanding of the great issues of citizenship was once a vital part of education. If we are to be effective in the future, there must be a return to these understandings in the educational process.

The Carnegie Foundation for the Advancement of Teaching in their recent report, *Higher Learning in the Nation's Service,* calls for increased levels of civic learning in schools and colleges. Their opinions are similar to the civism perspective presented here. They point out that many Americans now seek:

> simple solutions to complex problems, they turn to repressive censorship, align themselves with narrowly focused special-interest groups, retreat into nostalgia for a world that never was, succumb to the blandishments of glib, electronic soothsayers, or—worst of all—simply withdraw completely, convinced that nothing can be done. . . .

> As a nation, we are becoming civically illiterate. Unless we find better ways to educate ourselves as citizens, we run the risk of drifting unwittingly into a new kind of Dark Age—a time when small cadres of specialists will control knowledge and thus control the decision-making process. . . .

> The replacement of democratic government by a technocracy or the control of policy by special-interest groups is not tolerable. . . .

> We are convinced that both formal and informal education must rise to meet the challenge. Specifically, we believe that that tired old academic work horse "civics" must be updated and restored in the curriculum to what was once an honored place.[27]

They call for civic education to be a life-long process, not just a part of the baccalaureate curriculum. While we deal here with civism for public administrators, the Carnegie Foundation, as major spokesmen for American higher education, call for civic education both for college age and adult citizens. David Mathews of the Kettering Foundation suggests the development of undergraduate curriculum changes that result in "the liberal arts as the civic arts and the civic arts as the liberal arts." Many campuses are experimenting with this return to traditional approaches to the liberal arts. In the long run, a more effective government will depend on both a civically enlightened and literate population and a sensitive public service committed to effective and responsive government.

In many ways, our universities are part of the problem. Over the last 50 years universities have developed a form of semi-autonomy for each discipline or department. Consequently, the requirements for majors are increasingly narrow and specialized. Until recently, the general education courses required of all who graduate were far too relaxed and permissive. As a result, graduates tend to have a limited set of interests, not to mention a general lack of concern for their responsibilities as citizens. As is often said on the campus, "The world has problems, the university has departments."

American management education has recently been soundly condemned for failing to develop breadth and vision in tomorrow's leaders. Too often the emphasis in management education is on analytical techniques, balance sheets and internal management strategies or techniques. William G. Scott points out that management education "discourages risk taking, innovation and long-range perspectives; it encourages gamesmanship, overcautiousness, and unimaginativeness."[28] Perhaps the single most important step necessary to correct this problem would be for university programs in public administration and its allied fields such as social services administration and education administration to return civism to the curriculum.

The first dean of the Maxwell School, William E. Mosher, edited an early book titled *Responsible Citizenship*. In it he wrote this about public administration:

> Our task is to preserve the democratic ideal. This involves a type of moral and political self-discipline, and above all behaviors, acts and deeds that spring from a dynamic faith in the democratic *way of living*. As a people we freely, even profusely, profess democracy, but are there enough "doers of the deed" to give us assurance that democracy will ultimately and inevitable prevail?[29]

The recovery of civism in our era is one of the keys to a more effective public administration, indeed, a more effective government.

ACKNOWLEDGMENTS

I wish to acknowledge the excellent work of Professor Beverly Henry of the University of Alabama at Birmingham, who provided a thorough and perceptive critique of an earlier draft of this essay.

NOTES

1. Stephen K. Bailey, "Political and Social Purposes of Education," *Education for Responsible Citizenship,* New York: McGraw-Hill (1977), p. 29.

2. Harlan Cleveland, "Renewing the Boundless Resource," Washington, D.C.: The American Association of State Colleges and Universities, 1979, p. 11.

3. Stephen K. Bailey, *op. cit.*

4. Harlan Cleveland, "The Chronicle of Higher Education," October 28, 1981, p. 11.

5. Woodrow Wilson, "The Study of Administration," *Political Science Quarterly,* Vol. II, No. 1 (June 1887), as reprinted in Jay M. Shafritz and Albert C. Hyde (editors), *Classics of Public Administration,* Oak Park, Ill.: Moore Publishing Company (1978), pp. 8–9.

6. *Ibid.,* p. 10.

7. *Ibid.,* p. 11.

8. *Ibid.,* p. 13.

9. *Ibid.,* p. 16.

10. Dwight Waldo, *The Administrative State,* New York: Ronald Press (1948).

11. Herbert A. Simon, *Administrative Behavior,* New York: Macmillan (1951).

12. Charles Lindblom, "The Science of Muddling Through," *Public Administration Review* 19, 1959, pp. 79–88.

13. Stephen K. Bailey, "Political and Social Purposes of Education," *Education for Responsible Citizenship: The Report of the National Task Force on Education,* New York: McGraw-Hill (1977), p. 33.

14. Richard Flathman, "Citizenship and Authority: A Chastened View of Citizenship," *News for Teachers of Political Science,* Summer, 1981, No. 30, pp. 9–19.

15. *Ibid.,* p. 9.

16. *Idem.*

17. John Rawls, *A Theory of Justice,* Cambridge, Mass.: The Belknap Press of Harvard University Press (1971), p. 7.

18. Rensis Likert, *New Patterns of Management,* New York: McGraw-Hill (1961), p. 105.

19. Harlan Cleveland, *The Future Executive,* New York: Harper and Row (1972), p. 13.

20. James D. Thompson, *Organizations in Action,* New York: McGraw-Hill (1967).

21. *Ibid.,* p. 162.

22. Stephen K. Bailey, *op. cit.,* p. 27.

23. Camille Cates, "Beyond Muddling, Creativity," *Public Administration Review,* Vol. 36 (November/December, 1979), No. 6, pp. 528–529.

24. *Ibid.,* pp. 530–532.

25. Peter Drucker, *Management: Tasks, Responsibilities, Practices,* New York: Harper and Row (1973), p. 5.

26. William G. Scott and David K. Hart, *Organizational America,* Boston: Houghton-Mifflin (1979).

27. Ernest L. Boyer and Fred M. Hechinger, *Higher Learning in the Nation's Service,* Washington, D.C.: The Carnegie Foundation for the Advancement of Teaching (1981), pp. 46–47.

28. William Ouchi, *Theory Z: How American Business Can Meet the Japanese Challenge,* Reading, Mass.: Addison-Wesley (1981). See also William G. Scott, "Barnard on the Future of Elitist Responsibility," *Public Administration Review,* Vol. 42 (May/June, 1982), pp. 197–201.

29. William E. Mosher, (editor), *Responsible Citizenship,* New York: Henry Holt and Company (1941), p. 853.

CHAPTER 2

TOWARD A PUBLIC PHILOSOPHY OF PUBLIC ADMINISTRATION
A Civic Perspective of the Public

CURTIS VENTRISS

What role should public administration play in the development of a public philosophy? At first glance, it seems presumptuous for public administration even to think about developing such a grandiose idea as a public philosophy. However, in an era of fiscal limits and declining confidence in public institutions, the abdication of responsibility for development of a public philosophy adequate to the issues the field faces might result in a political wilderness where there is, to use Richard Pells's apocalyptical phrase, "action without theory, realism without imagination, movement without vision."[1] Even if one dismisses Pells's phrasing as too overdrawn, the field could surely fall prey to what S.M. Miller aptly referred to as the "blind forces of the factual."[2] To be walled in by the blind forces of the factual runs the serious risk of keeping administrators cloistered in the administrative world of what they think they do best: implementing managerial and procedural reforms. As sufficient as this may appear to some, it ultimately leads to a pedantic public purpose. It becomes pedantic, as Louis Gawthrop points out, because such a cloistered existence divorces public administration from the public it serves and, more critically, it fails "to revive the character of citizenship and the notion of the citizen."[3]

In short, the intellectual malaise which confronts the field has less to do with managerial or analytical competency or even intellectual commitment to democratic principles (as important as these factors are) than it has to do with *an inability to articulate a public philosophy central to public administration's civic purpose and duty and to the reexamination of the field's role in shaping public affairs.* Thus, a reexamination of a *theory of governance* and a *new substantive relationship with the public* is needed in an era when public administration, according to the ASPA Centennial Agendas Project, is "alienated from society, bedeviled by complexity, and guided by limited knowledge and understanding."[4] A new public philosophy is now called for which reinvigorates the best in public administration's tradition while envisioning new and creative roles that the field can and should play in the future.

If this contention is accepted, a nagging question needs posing: how would one define a public

From *Public Administration Review,* 49, 2 (March/April 1989): 173–179. Copyright © 1989 by American Society for Public Administration. Reprinted with permission.

philosophy as it relates to public administration? As applied to public administration, a public philosophy is less a vehicle to develop some overarching framework to define or interpret political events than it is a prerequisite to formulate a new substantive outlook on public affairs—one that redefines the field by redefining the meaning of "the public" and the field's relationship to it. As important as it is for public administration to adhere to American regime values, these values may be substantively diminished if those in the field do not maintain a vigilant view of the public consonant with those values. Thus it is argued here that a public philosophy of public administration must be formulated, not upon the romantic and technocratic characteristics of past efforts, but instead upon a revitalized concept of the public that emphasizes public interdependency, public learning, a new public language, and a critical evaluation of the relationship between the role of the state and public administration. Such a public philosophy has important implications for the respective responsibilities of both academic and professional public administration.

CONTEMPORARY PUBLIC ADMINISTRATION

In 1981, on a cold brisk January day in Washington, Ronald Reagan, the newly inaugurated president of the United States, stepped up to the podium to outline a "new beginning" that he believed represented a definitive break with the past. His campaign rhetoric attacked alleged deleterious effects of social programs that Reagan said had produced a government too big, too intrusive, and too expensive, and which gave too much power to faceless bureaucrats. His message, in many respects, represented a pre-New Deal public philosophy that found new relevance in a time when many questioned whether America had lost its self-confidence. According to one astute political analyst, Reagan's public philosophy is tied to four basic premises, all of which shun abstract consistency: antigovernment nationalism, communitarian individualism, free-market radicalism, and a nostalgic assurance of America's role in the future.[5] Although empirical data on public perceptions still indicate that the majority of the public strongly support governmental social programs like Social Security and Medicare,[6] Reagan successfully shifted the public debate from expanding or initiating new social programs to curtailing the growth of domestic spending in areas other than defense. Moreover, while Reagan's public philosophy hardly replaced interest-group liberalism, his administration cleverly controlled the focus and tenor of discussion. Critics of Reagan's public philosophy have been content, for the most part, to engage in a statistical pillow fight about how the impacts of Reagan's policies adversely affected the poor and the middle class. Those who question the efficacy of his approach, however, have abdicated a broader responsibility when it comes to how such statistics add up to a new public philosophy.

Needless to say, Reagan's public philosophy made many in public administration increasingly nervous and defensive, and with good reason. What made some even more nervous was that the intellectual roots that were instrumental in legitimizing Reagan's general approach came, in part, from the neoconservative movement. Not all people associated with this school of thought agreed with Reagan's policy proposals, but collectively most tried to repudiate much of the Great Society's version of the welfare state by claiming that it permitted the growth of a paternalistic state which has overloaded government, thus rendering it less manageable. These critics asserted that the redistributive state had promised too many entitlements, too much democracy, and too much equality.[7]

In the eyes of its critics, public administration—caught awkwardly in the middle of this onslaught—was seen as part of the problem. In particular, the new public administration sadly found itself in an intellectual swamp with only a modicum of theoretical legitimacy. More importantly, the new public administration and other theoretical cohorts became relatively immobilized when dealing with the historically ingrained issue of the "conflict between mass democracy and elite professionalism in the American political structure [which] is what really shapes the American meaning of bureaucracy and American attitudes toward it."[8]

Not surprisingly, by the 1980s, one proclivity was to further depoliticize the field's public language under the rubric of fostering managerial efficiency and economy. Although this inclination is certainly understandable, it only exacerbated the constant wavering of the field between theoretical despair and managerial technocracy. This wavering, moreover, intensified the general uneasiness which has been present in public administration since its early beginnings: the field lacks a coherent theoretical foundation, thus borrowing theories and analytical approaches that more or less sustain public administration's pragmatic appeal.[9] While some have argued that this amalgamation of theories and analytical approaches is more of a virtue than a vice, it has done little, if anything, to temper the incessant tendency by public administration to emulate the presumed efficiencies of business administration. Perhaps this tendency will always be prevalent in public administration, but it carries the risk of incorporating business values that are inconsistent with the field's public purpose. Business values are not American regime values—only their tragic parody.

In its own messy way, public administration appears to be acknowledging that any theoretical concern outside a managerial and economic mindset only leads, in the end, to utopian hopes and emotional pleas. In other words, the respectability and legitimacy of the field seems now to rest uncomfortably on how well public administration actually succeeds in marrying scientific rationality with the calculus of efficiency, along with appropriate courteous hymns to the public interest and professional responsibility. Whatever the merits of this approach, it unfortunately serves notice to those who advocate exclusively normative goals for the field that what cannot be demonstrated as empirically valid or pragmatically useful comes dangerously close to being folly. Simply put, normative theorizing, even if clothed in the substantive garments of public relevancy, is becoming viewed as ill-suited to deal with the stark administrative realities which are associated with the rough-and-ready world of the political marketplace. Theorizing in economics is tolerated because it can lead to analysis and can be utilized by decision makers. On the other hand, normative-theory building, as seen by a growing constituency of scholars, leads to one unmistakable thing: theoretical (and practical) ambiguity. When all is said and done, utilitarianism is still a widely accepted academic and professional philosophy which guides America's approach to social problems.

This characterization of conceptual approaches is probably overdrawn given that the political geometry of the field is shaped by many intersecting lines of human inquiry. Nonetheless, this begs the important question as to whether any of these approaches can forge new linkages to "the public" while defining the field's future role and public purpose in shaping social and political affairs. Public administration's weakness in answering this question offers the opportunity for others to take advantage of this vulnerability. One of the key elements in developing a new link with the public is to examine public administration's relationship with the state and the implication of that relationship. This issue is pivotal because it deals to a large degree with the very raison d'être of American public administration.

STATE AND THE PUBLIC

Max Weber noted that no modern state can exist without an administrative system. Similarly, Carl Frederich argued that "administration is the core of the modern [state]."[10] While the relationship between an administrative system and the modern state seems self-evident today, the definition of the state is more elusive. Although the meaning of the state is fraught with difficulties (as political scientists openly admit), Morton Fried has provided a good working definition: "A state is not simply a legislature, an executive body, a judiciary system, an administrative bureaucracy, or even a government. . . . A state is better viewed as the complex of institutions by means of which the power of society is organized."[11] Arguing from a related perspective, Edward Laumann and David Knoke declare that the state is not a unitary actor, "but a complex entity spanning multiple policy domains, comprised of both governmental organizations and those private-sector participants whose interest must be taken into account."[12]

If these definitions are correct, they raise some interesting questions for public administration. Because public administration is largely regarded as a state function, does this mean, as some on the political left maintain, that public administration plays a crucial role in legitimizing the present arrangement of social power? Or more cynically, "is public administration, when stripped of its normative overtones, nothing more than an instrument of the state that acts as the authoritative structure promoting an artificial and ultimately unsatisfying social harmony?"[13] And finally, has public administration fallen into a Hegelian trap that the "real is the rational," that to question the "real" is to undermine the primordial goals of American public administration?

Such questions make many in public administration understandably nervous. And although one reaction is to be defensive about asking these polemical questions in the first place, they do focus on a central point: is public administration's public purpose always restricted to responding to state direction, or does it entail broader social responsibilities? Does the field's responsibility to the public stop at the institutional gates of the state? The difficulty in answering these questions stems, in part, from the widely held assumption that, because public administration serves the needs of the state, it also serves the needs of the public, as if the public and the state are one in the same.[14] Terry Cooper exposes the fallacy of this notion quite effectively:

> . . . the etymology of the term public indicates a breadth and depth of meaning that transcends government. Its most fundamental denotations are the shared, communal, universally accessible dimensions of collective life, as well as those things which have general impact upon the interest of all; the realm of interdependence. The normal connotations of the word, as found in res public have to do with the common good or well being. The state is clearly included in the meaning of the public, but in a secondary apparently derivative state.[15]

Even given the confusion that the public and the state are synonymous, Nicholas Henry maintains that the field continues to think of the meaning of the public in institutional terms, i.e., the public's relationship to the state.[16] But this view of the public is too pedantic. It does not confront the issue of citizenship and how it can be cultivated. This is not to imply that public administration does not play a pivotal role, if not the pivotal role, in addressing public needs within the confines of the state. But does public administration have a concern outside the managerial ethos demanded by the state? As George Will explains, a substantive meaning of the public—

> . . . is about the polity, which is much more than government institutions. It includes all the institutions, dispositions, habits and mores on which government depends and on which therefore, government should strive to have a shaping influence. . . . Democratic government must be a tutor as well as a servant to its citizens, because citizenship is a state of mind.[17]

What is hinted at here should now be more directly stated: *Public administration's conceptualization of the public must be expanded to include a new public purpose and obligation that enhances the development of citizenship—a citizenship that will be increasingly shaped by soci-*

*etal interdependencies and thus will require a civic perspective of a renewed emphasis on public
learning and a revitalized public language.*

What is at stake is a public philosophy of public administration that is not bound to (or victimized by) a pro-state liberalism but to a reconstituted meaning of the public. That is, a public philosophy that can address "the current imbalance between the political order's meticulous concern for material well-being and its fastidious withdrawal from concern for the inner lives and moral character of citizens."[18] Public administration's role in this admittedly ambitious endeavor can be achieved if the field proceeds on the theoretical and pragmatic basis of recognizing the importance of public interdependency, public learning, and a new public language. The following section briefly discusses each of these elements.

THE RELEVANCE OF INTERDEPENDENCY, LEARNING, AND LANGUAGE

Rexford Tugwell, one of the early intellectual recruits to the New Deal, lucidly argued in 1950 that Franklin Roosevelt's policies failed to achieve their key purpose because Roosevelt never offered a public philosophy for an interdependent society.[19] What Tugwell inchoately observed is a little clearer today: the growing interdependency of modern life necessitates a new kind of thinking that acknowledges the ecological axiom that everything is now related to everything else. Unfortunately, the field's present propensity is to think in term of dualities, not interdependencies. This perspective should come as no surprise since, as Michael Walzer notes, modern liberalism itself preaches and practices the art of separation.[20] Or put more candidly, as Gerald Frug argues in the *Harvard Law Review,* liberalism forces one to view the world as a series of complex dualities, thus preventing policymakers from formulating policies for an increasingly interdependent society.[21] From a somewhat different perspective, Gary Brewer put it this way:

> A system becomes more complex as the number of interconnected elements increases; most social systems are both large and highly interconnected. . . . These characteristics largely account for the astonishing diversity of social systems and behavior. Our limited intellectual apparatus, however, prompts us to seek ordered regularity. Our images are poor proxies for reality. Analyses frequently reflect these defective images, and so too do our policies.[22]

The point is real even if the language has become difficult. The call for interdependency means that public administration's thinking must readjust to multiple levels of social, political, and economic realities without losing its conceptual footing. In short, the field must not become the conceptual prisoner of a modern liberal philosophy that tries to reduce the richness of interdependency to a series of fragmented political realities. To avoid this fate, public administration must take note of four conditions of interdependency that require rethinking of the field's approach to public affairs:

- Public action occurs in expanding and crowded policy environments in which everything depends on everything else, and power is disbursed and shared by a multiplicity of publics and public actors;
- Capacity for any one government jurisdiction or policy actor to effectively act unilaterally is significantly reduced;
- An enlarged ring of often unforeseen, unintended, or indirect consequences increases vulnerability and openness to outside influences, with public managers increasingly dependent on other individuals and organizations outside of one's view;

- The consequences of policy choices and public actions are often far-ranging, delayed, and have indirect or hidden costs beyond the normal externalities; desirable and undesirable consequences are difficult to separate, and important and often critical second and third-order effects of policy choices may go unnoticed.[23]

What does this mean for a public philosophy dealing with the character of citizenship? First, as William Sullivan posits, "it is the general discussion of [societal] interdependency that brings a *public* into being."[24] He goes on to state that "public discussion [of interdependency] aims to bring before the whole civic community an understanding of the *externalities of policy choices* . . . precisely in terms of what pursuing these options will mean for the situation of various groups."[25] If public administration takes seriously the interdependent environment in which it operates, the practice of public administration can no longer be comfortably confined to institutional skyscrapers, but it must be somehow diffused into the communal bungalows where the interdependencies are directly felt. In short, the practice of public administration must be expanded to civic and voluntary associations that mediate between individuals and the state. These associations may thus be transformed into lively democratic laboratories for civic engagement and responsibility. These civic associations, as potential educative vehicles for nurturing citizenship, can serve as vital public forums (with the assistance of public managers) to facilitate critical discussion of the interrelated character of public issues and the implications of public interdependency on the body politic. This approach, of course, does not confront the vexing problem of how to manage the effects of interdependency. Instead, it suggests that the administrator's public stewardship in the future involves increasing the public's understanding of policy under conditions of interdependency and complexity. A step in this direction requires a focus on the need for public learning.

Defined briefly, public learning involves increasing the capacity and knowledge of the public by facilitating politically educative interactions between the public and adminstrators.[26] This learning process is critical, because at the heart of any new conceptualization of the public is the importance of democratic political education which implies, as Tocqueville so well understood, "the transformation of commitments, the cultivation of public virtue."[27] Saying this, public learning has the following characteristics:

- It assumes that public organizations are more than mere instruments to produce public goods and services; they provide a larger mechanism for political decision making in a democratic polity.
- It focuses on social values, and it seeks critical and reflective awareness by both administrators and the public in order to identify unintended and indirect outcomes or other normative consequences of public action.[28]
- It is facilitated by an emphasis on a social knowledge transfer and a disaggregated approach to public affairs.

While space does not permit an extended discussion on each of these characteristics, for purposes of brevity the following discussion focuses on disaggregated policymaking and social knowledge transfer. What is meant by these two approaches? First, disaggregated policymaking refers to a client-oriented approach to policy—an approach that recognizes the unique needs of different publics and the importance of defining those needs in the policy process. In brief, this approach recognizes that public interests and needs cannot be treated as one homogeneous unit by administrators. The public in this regard (as simple as it may sound) is composed of *individuals* who cannot be merged under the analytical category of some aggregate grouping. Robert Biller has correctly emphasized that this forces administrators to confront the fact that they deal with "person[s] [who] bring questions that are uniquely contextuated in a lifetime's increasingly particular experiences. . . . Persons are different with respect to their unique social histories."[29] Biller's central idea is that administrators need to begin experimenting with policies that are designed in a nonaggregate manner, although he is vague about how this can be achieved.

If the importance of Biller's point is accepted, social-knowledge transfer becomes imperative. Social-knowledge transfer refers to the direct exposure of the administrator to the unique knowledge of clients and the provision of a forum for public dialogue and open exchange of information of direct importance to the community. As idealistic as this may sound, M. Brian Murphy, arguing from a similar perspective, makes the point that administrators must "think beyond their own interests, and . . . understand the relationship between their own interests and that of the community, and see themselves as needing the knowledge of public things in order to make better decisions."[30]

Certainly, not all public goods and services can be delivered in a nonaggregated manner. And, more importantly, how can social-knowledge transfer work given the serious issue of the size and complexity of governmental operations? Benjamin Barber[31] and Ithiel de Sola Poole[32] have provided a hint on how public administration might deal with issues of size and complexity. Barber argues that size is an elastic term because of the growing influence of communication technology. According to Ithiel de Sola Poole, citizens can obtain critical policy information through a nationwide computerized system, if such a system is properly instituted. Furthermore, citizen surveys could be more widely utilized to ascertain public needs. Two scholars, for example, have recently developed what they refer to as a "value stretch methodology."[33] This model attempts to define the specific needs of clients in a large community on a cross-cultural basis. While no one approach can be expected to be entirely effective, public learning must be seen for what it is: a public service that enhances public involvement. That is, it is a process which recognizes that because social problems are shared, they require shared solutions. In this sense, administrators cannot simply view the public as some abstraction, but as part of a public learning process which concretely links the administrator to the unique experiences and knowledge of the community. If nothing else, this is a noble calling. If the need for public learning is taken seriously, leaving aside some of the logistical difficulties, a new public language designed for public dialogue and debate is desperately needed.

The noted historian Eric Foner, in explaining the relationship between political language and social change, believed that Thomas Paine's philosophical writings helped to spark revolutionary action not only because his ideas struck a political nerve in the American psyche, but also because "Paine helped to transform the meaning of the words of political discourse."[34] In public administration, interestingly, scant attention has been given to how political language has shaped views of social reality. It has been left to scholars, like J.G.A. Pocock, to argue that the lexicon of political language is part and parcel of a political phenomena which serves to support the legitimation of an authoritative structure.[35] Political language, in other words, molds political images of reality and thus confines, often unconsciously, approaches congruent to those images.

What is the political language of the United States today? Generally speaking, until World War I, America's political language had a tendency to frame political issues in legal and moral terminology.[36] The political language started to change with the growing importance of science, technology, and the modern state. Americans required a new political language more congruent with the spirit of the state, a discourse that would be supportive of a modern economy bent on rationalizing the tempo of economic change. America thus acquired a new public language and a new public philosophy built on the dubious validity of economics. In public policy terms, economics alone seemed able (and willing) to fulfill the dictates of a new public philosophy based on the requisite values of a technocratic and market-centered society.

One of the important virtues of economics is its ability to cloak its terminology under a veil of scientific objectivity. One need not look far to see how this has crept into the political arena: the emphasis of the Reagan Administration on cost-benefit analysis and the sacrosanct worship of the economist's empirical tool kit among professional schools of public affairs are but two examples. The intellectual baggage, so to speak, that accompanied this approach is not without its price tag. First, the public philosophy described by this language moves public discourse away from such issues as political authority and moral considerations. It remolds them into questions of economic choice. This degradation of political language attempts to "economize" the polity, denying the citizenry a public language with which to discuss, debate, and understand critical political issues. In its crudest form, this economic language transforms political language into expressions that must ultimately conform to economic reasoning with all its adamantly posited assumptions. Sheldon Wolin appropriately describes this public philosophy predicated on economics as anti-political power "because it contains no principle for transcending conflict to find common ground. There is no reconciliation, only winners and losers; there is no basis for common action . . . [and] when the economy becomes the polity, *citizen and community* become subversive words in the vocabulary of the new public philosophy."[37]

This is not to dismiss the importance of economic analysis. It is, rather, to maintain that public administration accepts this troubling public philosophy at its own peril. It anesthetizes the public by lulling citizens into a false sense of security and into accepting simplistic answers to complex political questions. With a self-interested ethos which is ingrained in the premises of modern economic thought, it is no wonder that a utilitarian calculus based upon one's private interest dominates discussion of policy issues when the reconciliation of the private interest and interdependency must be addressed. Given this situation, should one really be surprised, as one astute observer declared, that "public virtue [becomes] a kind of ghost town into which anyone can move and declare himself sheriff."[38]

A new public language is needed to confront this reductionistic public philosophy. *It must be a public language that examines the value assumptions of policy decisions and openly explores the relationship of political means to political ends.* It must nurture more sophisticated political judgment that can clarify differing policy choices and constructively address political conflicts. A poignant example of what is referred to here is the issue of economic development. Economic development has been traditionally sold as an attempt to increase jobs; but recently an attempt has been made by citizen groups like the United Neighborhood Organization in Los Angeles to view economic development as interrelated with the broader issues of cultural, social, and educational issues.[39] Simply put, economic issues cannot be divorced from the common good of the citizenry. As one research analyst in Los Angeles county put it:

> . . . if economic development implies some sort of need for economic self-sufficiency and control over one's destiny, it cannot be effective without the transformation of the citizen. Economic development has been unfortunately too narrowly defined and that's why we sometimes have meager results regardless of the money spent. . . . I think we are beginning to understand that economic development is also an integral part of citizen development.[40]

In brief, economic development is not just about "economic issues." It involves "noneconomic concerns" that economic analysis and reasoning are not designed to address. To explore these noneconomic concerns implies a *public language that gives a primacy to substantive political ends and societal interdependencies over the utility-language of economics.* A public language, in other words, does not use a reified vocabulary that constrains political dialogue or masks its assumptions under the thick fog of sophisticated methodologies. If public administration abdicates the task of developing such a public language, it risks further detachment from reality and continuing decline in public confidence.

CONCLUSION

But what does this public philosophy mean for the field in general? Having previously touched upon some of the implications of this public philosophy for professional managers, attention should also focus on academic public administration. For purposes of discussion, three important implications for the study of the field are these:

- A shift is needed away from the scientization of social science to an emphasis on developing a *public social science* that refuses to reduce public issues of *public relevancy* into a methodistic framework devoid of normative considerations. A public social science is distinguished by its recognition of the validity of methodological pluralism; that is, the utilization of a variety of analytical approaches that can encourage a critical, interpretative, and empirical inquiry into public affairs.[41] Methodological flexibility is needed to avoid political reductionism which ignores the public's multidimensional substantive needs.
- The field needs to move away from academic discourse that is restricted exclusively to academic circles. Academic scholars need to become *public scholars* who engage citizens in taking interests in knowledge that has public relevance.
- A shift is needed away from the present fixation on a Cartesian educational perspective that is manifested in economics and some management approaches. A more balanced pedagogical view is needed that critically exposes students to the myopic assumptions of these perspectives and their view of the public, especially in regard to interdependency, learning, and public language.

This is hardly a definitive list. Nevertheless, these suggestions force one to reconsider the view that the field can sustain needed credibility and legitimatization by primary dependence on, and devotion to, economy and efficiency. Nor can the field afford to assume a defensive posture by pleading that public administrators are often unduly scapegoated and that candidates for public office should show respect for the public bureaucracy and its cadre of competent and dedicated careerists. Obviously, these concerns need to be conveyed to the public at large. But to be content with these strategies as the answer to public administration's difficulties merely blinds those in the field to the real challenges that confront it.

Yet, like so many other social sciences, a manichean conflict pervades the field: many sense the shortcomings of a public philosophy built on scientific rationality that debases the public realm. Yet, the old positivist framework appears to provide protection from political subjectivism and supports services to the state. This conflict leaves public administration with the discomforting prospect that efficiency is its own legitimacy and that "what works" is the theoretical adhesive for the field's actions. These are not bad things in themselves, but they are hardly enough for public administration or for the public to live by. In the end, the real issues which confront the field remain the old ones: authority and purpose. And the old answers of Western political thought remain strong answers: democratic citizenship in search for human dignity. The challenge of public administration continues to be to facilitate that sort of constitutional self-governance.

NOTES

Thanks to individuals who provided feedback on earlier drafts of this essay: Professors Phil Cooper, SUNY (Albany), Marshall Dimock, and anonymous editorial referees. Thanks also to Donna Ventriss, Suzanne Bacon, and to Dawn Wales for assistance. This is a shortened version of the article that appears in *Democracy and Bureaucracy: A Minnowbrook Perspective.*

1. Richard H. Pells, *Radical Visions and American Dreams* (New York: Harper, 1973), p. 84.

2. Cited in Lewis A. Coser and Irving Howe, *The New Conservatives* (New York: Quadrangle, 1973), p. 8.

3. Louis C. Gawthrop, "Civis, Civitas, and Civilitas: A New Focus for the Year 2000," *Public Administration Review,* vol. 44 (March 1984), p. 103.

4. Chester A. Newland, *Public Administration and Community: Realism in the Practice of Ideals* (McLean, VA: Public Administration Service, 1984), p. 6.

5. Hugo Heclo, "Reaganism and the Search for a Public Philosophy," in John Palmer, ed., *Perspectives on the Reagan Years* (Washington: Urban Institute, 1986), pp. 37–49.

6. Consult the following evidence that demonstrates that Reagan's policies do not reflect a conservative public philosophy held by the general public: Vincente Navarro, "The 1984 Election and the New Deal: An Alternative Perspective," *Social Policy* (Spring 1983), pp. 3–10; John E. Chubb and Paul E. Peterson, *New Directions in American Politics* (Washington: Brookings Institution, 1986).

7. Consult Michel Crozier, Samuel P. Huntington, and Joji Watanuki, *The Crisis of Democracy: Report on the Governability of Democracies to the Trilateral Commission* (New York: New York University Press, 1975).

8. Barry D. Karl, "The American Bureaucrat: A History of a Sheep in Wolves' Clothing," *Public Administration Review,* vol. 47 (January/February 1987), p. 31.

9. See Emmanuel Wald, "Toward a Paradigm of Future Public Administration," *Public Administration Review,* vol. 32 (May/June 1973), pp. 366–372.

10. Cited in Ralph C. Chandler, *A Centennial History of the American Administrative State* (New York: Macmillan, 1987), p. 300.

11. Morton H. Fried, *The Evolution of Political Society* (New York: Random House, 1967), p. 229. Some of the ideas in this section are drawn from Curtis Ventriss, "Two Critical Issues of American Public Administration," *Administration and Society,* vol. 19 (May 1987), pp. 31–34.

12. Edward O. Laumann and David Knoke, "The Increasingly Organizational State," *Society,* vol. 25 (January/February 1988), p. 23.

13. Curtis Ventriss, "Two Critical Issues of American Public Administration," p. 32. Although never mentioning public administration by name, Robert Nisbet makes this claim in his book *The Quest for Community* (New York: Oxford University Press, 1953).

14. See David Mathews, "The Public in Practice and Theory," *Public Administration Review,* vol. 44 (March 1984), pp. 120–125.

15. Terry L. Cooper, "The Public and Private Dimensions: From Dichotomy to Interdependence" (unpublished manuscript, 1984), p. 3. For space reasons, the difference between *public* and *private* cannot be discussed here.

16. Nicholas Henry, "Considering the Cornerstone Questions: Resurrecting the Public Private Distinction," *Eleventh Conference on Teaching Public Administration* (Atlanta, GA: March 24, 1988), p. 7.

17. George F. Will, *Statecraft as Soulcraft* (New York: Touchstone, 1983), p. 24.

18. *Ibid.,* p. 65.

19. Rexford Tugwell, "The New Deal: The Progressive Tradition," *Western Political Quarterly,* vol. III (September 1950), pp. 390–427.

20. Michael Walzer, "Liberalism and the Art of Separation," *Political Theory,* vol. 12 (October 1984), pp. 309–320.

21. Gerald Frug, "The City as a Legal Concept," *Harvard Law Review,* vol. 93 (Fall 1980), pp. 1060–1078.

22. Gary Brewer, "Decisionmaking and Limits of Technique," in P. Schorr, ed., *Critical Cornerstones of Public Administration* (Boston: Oelgeschlagen, Gunn, and Hain, 1985), p 110

23. See Curtis Ventriss and Jeff Luke, "Organizational Learning and Public Policy" (unpublished manuscript, 1988), pp. 23–25. Also see Jeff Luke, "Managing Interconnectedness: The Need for Catalytic Leadership," *Futures Research Quarterly,* vol. 17 (Winter 1986), pp. 73–82.

24. William Sullivan, *Reconstructing Public Philosophy* (Berkeley: University of California Press, 1986), p. 166.

25. *Ibid.,* p. 166.

26. See Curtis Ventriss and Jeff Luke, "Organizational Learning and Public Policy," p. 2.

27. Alexis de Tocqueville, *Democracy in America* (New York: Mentor, 1956), pp. 207–220.

28. See Clarence N. Stone, "Efficiency versus Social Learning: A Reconsideration of the Implementation Process," *Policy Studies Review,* vol. 4 (February 1985). The following discussion parallels my discussion in "Two Issues of American Public Administration," pp. 41–42.

29. Robert P. Biller, "Toward Public Administration Rather than an Administration of Publics," in Ross Clayton and William Storm, eds., *Agenda for Public Administration* (Los Angeles: University of Southern California, 1979).

30. M. Brian Murphy, "Towards a Theory of Democratic Planning" (unpublished manuscript, 1983), p. 17.

31. Benjamin Barber, *Strong Democracy* (Berkeley: University of California Press, 1984).

32. Ithiel de Sola Poole, *Talking Back: Citizen Feedback and Cable Technology* (Cambridge, MA: MIT Press, 1973).

33. Baruch Kipnis and Curtis Ventriss, "Operationalizing Quality of Life Issues: From General Goals to Workable Objectives" (unpublished manuscript, 1985).

34. Eric Foner, *Tom Paine and Revolutionary America* (Oxford: Oxford University Press, 1976).

35. J.G.A. Pocock, *Politics, Language, and Time* (New York: Atheneum, 1973).

36. This discussion is drawn from Sheldon Wolin, "The New Public Philosophy," *Democracy,* vol. 1 (October 1981), pp. 23–36.

37. *Ibid.,* p. 36.

38. Allan Bloom, *The Closing of the American Mind* (New York: Simon and Schuster, 1987), p. 58.

39. See Curtis Ventriss and Robert Pecorella, "Community Participation and Modernization: A Reexamination of Political Choices," *Public Administration Review,* vol. 44 (May/June 1984).

40. *Ibid.,* p. 230.

41. Richard Bernstein, *The Restructuring of Social and Political Theory* (Philadelphia: University of Pennsylvania Press, 1976), p. 235.

CHAPTER 3

FACILITATING COMMUNITY, ENABLING DEMOCRACY
New Roles for Local Government Managers

JOHN NALBANDIAN

Dennis Hays, administrator of the Unified Government of Wyandotte County/Kansas City, Kansas, found himself in an unfamiliar role. In the presence of the governor, the mayor, and other dignitaries, Hays was asked to take the lead in a press conference announcing that the International Speedway Corporation had begun negotiating with the Unified Government as a partner in the construction of a NASCAR racetrack. His highly visible role in the project was being recognized and future expectations were being cast.

Kansas City, Kansas, once a manufacturing stronghold in northeast Kansas, is a city searching for lost pride. Hays, analytical and compassionate, and educated to believe that the role of the manager is to work backstage, found himself leading a project that would have significant effect on the sense of community in this city and on his own definition of professionalism.

This research, based on data gathered from open-ended survey questions, correspondence, and in-depth panel discussions, also utilizes earlier findings for a "then and now" examination of the contemporary roles, responsibilities, and values of city managers. City managers are seen as community builders and enablers of democracy. With those goals, they have become skilled at facilitative leadership and at building partnerships and consensus.

Also, they have become more aware that legitimacy of the city manager role demands more than a legal foundation in council-manager government, the manager's adherence to the value of efficiency, and making recommendations based on "the greatest good for the greatest number over the long run." In today's political environment of diverse and conflicting interests, managers must anticipate and attend to claims for equity, representation, and individual rights if they are to succeed as partner to the elected officials and citizens they serve and as leader of the professional staff they supervise.

THE PAST

In my earlier review of professionalism in local government I concluded that city management had transformed itself over several decades in three fundamental ways. It had "moved from an

From *Public Administration Review,* 59, 3 (May/June 1999): 187–197. Copyright © 1999 by American Society for Public Administration. Reprinted with permission.

orthodox view of a dichotomy between politics and administration to the sharing of functions between elected and appointed officials; from political neutrality and formal accountability to political sensitivity and responsiveness to community values themselves; and from efficiency as the core value to efficiency, representation, individual rights, and social equity as a complex array of values anchoring professionalism" (Nalbandian, 1991, 103). The first change represented an evolution of roles, the second a broader statement of professional responsibility, and the third set out to capture the contemporary value base of city management.

Those familiar with professionalism in local government will see that to a large extent many recent changes have reinforced these transformations. During the ten years, the following changes stand out:

- Community building has become part of the city management professional's responsibility.
- Managers are expected to facilitate participation and representation and to develop partnerships.
- There is less adherence to council manager government as the "one best form."
- The manager's internal administrative role has become more process oriented.

WHAT'S NEW

Community Building

Historical reviews of city management reveal a continuing search for the meaning of professionalism (Stillman, 1974). As social, economic, political, and technological trends create new contexts, the roles, responsibilities, and values of practicing professionals change. In my earlier project, I tried to define professionalism in local government as grounded in a broader array of community values than had been posited traditionally. But what I failed to articulate was the search for a *sense of community* as a way to conceptualize a context for contemporary professional work [see Figure 3.1].

Since the original research in the late 1980s, many voices have spoken to the themes of building community, civil society, and civic infrastructure as partial solutions to the growing distance between citizens and governing institutions. In his study of Italian regional governments, Putnam (1993) found that the presence of social capital, identified with the concepts of a rich network of local associations, active engagement in community affairs, egalitarian patterns of politics, and trust and lawfulness, positively affected economic development and the performance of governing institutions. Rice and Sumberg's (1997) research, focusing on the United States, reinforces Putnam's conclusions. In another academic vein, many have argued that reconnecting citizens to government requires government oriented toward citizen involvement rather than control by professional elites (Box, 1998; Lappé and Du Bois, 1994; Mathews, 1994). Frederickson poses a complementary challenge, asserting that local government professionals are in a unique position to enhance civil society and help build social capital if "the community paradigm were to become part of the bureaucrat's understanding of how the city ought to be" (1997, 31).

None of the city managers in this study actually used the term *community building* to describe his or her work. But the term seems apropos to how they describe what they do, especially when considered in the following theoretical way. From a public official's perspective, community building essentially involves building political capacity—the capacity to make collective decisions amidst diverse and conflicting interests. A crucial component of this capacity is developing a sense of responsibility among citizens to participate in and obligate themselves to collective decisions. The obligation stems: (1) from an understanding that certain tasks require collective

Figure 3.1

Methodology

Ten years ago Raymond G. Davis and I set out to explore the meaning of professionalism in local government through a series of interviews with city and county managers. Around the same time, George Frederickson invited a group of city management professionals to Lawrence to discuss "ideal and practice" in council-manager government. Each project resulted in publications commenting on the meaning of professionalism in local government (Frederickson, 1989; Nalbandian 1989; 1990; 1991).

In order to make a ten-year comparison, I contacted the professionals who had participated in the original projects and who were still connected with local government, asking them to review their ten-year-old interview or essay. To that number I added city managers who had written "state of the profession" articles in *Public Management* over the past five years. In addition, I contacted ICMA winners of the Mark E. Keane Award for Excellence in Local Government and I invited participation of a few more local government professionals who, over the years, I have found particularly draw to this topic.

I asked these 26 professionals to answer the following three questions in writing:

- What are the most significant changes that have occurred in local government in the last ten years?
- What changes have occurred in relationships between the governing body and chief administrative officer and in the politics of local government?
- What parts of the manager's job have remained the most stable over the last ten years? Which parts have changed the most?

I collected the responses and convened two panel discussions at the 1997 annual ICMA meeting in Vancouver with six of the participants. I added their transcribed remarks to the original comments, then reviewed everything I had received along with the few articles that appeared in *Public Management* magazine. I selected passages exemplifying what appeared to me as emergent themes and conveyed those remarks to all of the participating managers, asking for additional comments. With those in hand, I settled on the themes that best describe the meaning of professionalism in local government as it have evolved over the past ten years. Seeking additional feedback, I sent a draft of the resulting manuscript to the managers who had provided comments I quoted. Where possible, I have used the words of local government professionals extensively to illustrate the changes that have occurred, as experienced by these public servants.

and public action rather than private, individual decisions, and (2) from an expectation that the agents of governing institutions will respect the values of representation, individual rights, and social equity so that individual citizens do not suffer from capricious or arbitrary collective decisions (Tussman, 1960). In short, getting problems solved collectively while respecting the values of representation, individual rights, and social equity builds a sense of obligation to the collective good and constitutes one way of looking at community building.

With renewed interest nationwide in the paradigm of community, one can argue that in the future the legitimacy of professional administrators in local government will be grounded in the tasks of community building and enabling democracy—in getting things done collectively, while building a sense of inclusion. Contemporary comments by Karma Ruder, director of the Neighborhood Planning Office in Seattle, and Eric Anderson, city manager in Des Moines, illustrate this point.

Describing the professional's role in local government, Ruder (August 12, 1997) writes, "Who is doing the work that makes people respect their government and become committed to making life in their communities better? The crucial issue is how local governments stay legitimate in the eyes of those they serve."

Anderson (August 26, 1997) writes:

> I am increasingly convinced that we are accountable for more than the quality of our management. We are also accountable for how well we have performed in the governance of our communities. Our jobs are to assure a fundamentally productive combination of the two [politics and administration] in the daily life of local governments. We need to be more specific about the responsibility we carry for governance as well as service delivery.

He (Anderson, September 17, 1997) develops this notion further with these thoughts:

> We have a strong responsibility to make sure that we provide not only information to our governing bodies, but to support the processes of governance that support the representative nature of the city council. I'm not talking about getting involved in electoral politics, but in things like public hearings, discussion, and deliberation; training people in the organization to anticipate and foster participation; and building structures of participation that will be seen as legitimate. I don't think we have done a very good job on the governance side of our responsibilities.

In a panel discussion at the ICMA conference in Vancouver, British Columbia, Norm King (September 16, 1997), executive director of San Bernardino Associated Governments in southern California and former ICMA president, said, "There is a remarkable degree of value consistency in what we all represent. And I heard it today, especially in terms of the focus on the engagement of citizens in creating a more just society."

He went on to talk about how he would advance that goal. "The primary goal of government, and especially local government, is to create conditions that insure, foster, or encourage responsibility. This means creating responsibility in the people who work for us; in our customers; and in our citizens."

Community building is a theme that expresses our understanding of how the city management profession is evolving, but this work does not come without a challenge. On the one hand, community building as a context for grounding professional practice seems a clarion call from many voices (Etzioni, 1995; Glendon, 1991; Mathews, 1994; Selznick, 1992). In Howard Gardner's (1995) terms, *it is a good story;* it conveys a noble message Americans today want to hear even as they strive to enhance the quality of their private lives. The concept of community building is attractive as a base for the practice of city management, because with it comes an understanding that both politics and administration are crucial, often inseparable, and must work in the kind of partnership that most local government professionals value rather than the adversarial relationship with their governing body in which they occasionally find themselves.

The challenges to the call for community building are the long-term social, political, and economic trends that have fragmented society and insufficient transferable knowledge of how exactly to build and maintain a sense of community. In addition, for city managers, as issues become broadly regional or narrowly oriented around neighborhoods, municipal boundaries become less relevant demarcations of community (Church, November 27, 1997; O'Neill, Jr., October 29, 1997). But perhaps the most formidable challenge to the community paradigm is a compelling counterstory. This is the respected and enduring tale of self-reliance and self-interest, adherence to market-based values, and skepticism regarding the value of government (Fowler, 1991). As local government professionals come to realize that their work connects them to the processes of governing through community building, they also come to acknowledge that those advocating market values pose a vigorous challenge.

Local government professionals regard this challenge in contrasting ways. For some, it appears simply as another political change to be accommodated. Examples include comments from William Buchanan (October 17, 1997), manager in urban Sedgwick County, Kansas, which includes Wichita. "Today, I believe elected officials are clearly more diverse and have a higher sense of public service than witnessed recently. They certainly come to the task from a much more 'Reaganesque' approach than ten years ago. Government is to be used only as a last resort, power is to be shared, and partners are to be used to solve problems. This kind of reluctant use of power requires a different style of leadership [for the manager]."

David Watkins (July 21, 1997), city administrator in Lenexa, Kansas, a conservative suburb of Kansas City, writes, "I think the movement toward customer service as a value has helped our image. In Lenexa, we work hard trying to create an image that we are tough but fair problem solvers who value the benefits of business and residents in the community and who want to work with you, not against you."

Jan Perkins (July 13, 1997), city manager in Fremont, California, adds, "The city manager needs to lead the organization in changing and adapting to community expectations—becoming entrepreneurial, customer focused, citizen involved—in order for the city council to have faith and confidence in the direction the city manager is taking the organization."

Buchanan, Watkins, and Perkins help us understand that local government professionals must ground their practices in the political context of their work. In contemporary America, they are working in various partnerships to build a sense of community in places where "community" and "individual" compete vigorously in determining public purposes and the role of government.

Facilitative Role of the Manager

Participation and Representation. Local government professionals from California to Virginia comment that the greatest change they have seen over the past ten years is the amount and character of participation expected in public policymaking and problem solving. The theme is not new; it has been emphasized in city management literature since the 1960s, and it is completely consistent with the community building/enabling democracy theme (Rutter, 1980). What seems different now is its pervasiveness and its transforming quality. Bill Buchanan (October 17, 1997) writes, "We are required to share power. How we manage special needs and the fragmentation of centralized power seem to me to be the parts that have changed the most. How we define and then use and manage democracy to provide service will control the styles and types of skills municipal managers will need to be successful." And Charles Church (November 27, 1997), city manager in Lynchburg, Virginia, writes, "Reform should allow citizens to be fully engaged in the processes of local governance. I anticipate that neighborhood councils will increasingly take over many of the responsibilities of city councils and administrators for setting priorities and evaluating service delivery." The participation and representation theme is seen in working with diverse council members; through community problem-solving processes; and in a variety of partnerships.

Diversity. The diversity on councils is seen with more representation of race and gender, with more special interest candidates, and with more antigovernment council members. Potentially, each represents a difference way of viewing the role of government, the council's work, and relationships with citizens and professional staff (Bledsoe, 1993). The differences would seem to be greater than those seen in the past, at least from a local government professional's perspective.

These differences produce contrasting consequences. On the one hand, when effectively blended they increase the problem-solving capacity of the governing body. On the other hand, the differences can easily consume a council and render it ineffective (Mahtesian, 1997). The diversity on councils can be more extensive than the differences confronted in familiar daily work groups. In the absence of hierarchy, task specialization, systematic and credible feedback, and specific task definition, it is no wonder that councils flounder and the local government professionals seeking leadership and policy guidance from them become frustrated.

When effectively managed, this diversity seems to make a positive difference in communities. David Mora (December 5, 1997), city manager in Salinas, California, writes:

> The local government manager is responsible for advocating comprehensive participation and representation in governance issues. Part of the frustration today is the diversity and overwhelming nature of service demands from parts of the community that in the past either were not represented or were taken for granted by both elected and appointed local government officials. The new generation of local elected officials, representing a significantly diverse variety of interests, is demanding legitimate and comprehensive responses from management.

He continues by suggesting that the way to deal with diversity on the council is by reflecting that diversity among staff. He says that he himself had to learn to be more inclusive, to accept the diversity of the community. He and Eric Anderson argue that as city managers trying to relate to councils more representative of the community, it is easier to work with a staff that reflects an array of values and anticipates the council's expectations because then staff can tacitly understand them.

The connection between diversity and problem solving marks a significant departure from diversity as affirmative action. What was seen in the past, sometimes cynically as diversity for the sake of political correctness or, more positively, as moral virtue, is now seen as diversity for the sake of problem solving. What was once seen as the "right thing to do" is now seen as a prudent way to staff an organization for problem solving, especially in environments in which problem solving among diverse interests and political legitimacy go hand in hand.

Problem Solving. The relationship between politics, participation, problem solving, and legitimacy marks a departure from previous conceptions of the connection between citizens and local government officials. John Thomas (1986) notes that local governments began a few decades ago to invite a relationship based on the negotiation of interests. He contrasted this to the historic relationship based on "petition" or "redress." Current comments from local government professionals suggest that this association may be moving again, this time from "adversarial negotiations" toward "interest-based policy-making."

Karma Ruder (December 15, 1997) states, "Citizens more and more want to be part of establishing the framework for standards and for balancing the trade-offs between technical standards and perception of services or different values regarding what services are more important." The director of the Neighborhood Planning Office in Seattle characterizes her task as "figuring out how we make people shift from being fighters against city hall to having lots of different perspectives getting together to solve problems" (September 16, 1997).

Partnerships. Another expression of participation and community engagement is the number of partnerships that local governments are involved in both externally and internally. The external partnerships are evident in joint undertakings with school districts, counties, non-profits, community-based organizations, neighborhood associations, and private sector organizations. The importance of the partnerships appears to have affected the manager's role significantly. Perkins (July 13, 1997) writes, "[the prevalence of partnerships] requires the city manager to lead by example and foster relationships within the community to help pave the way for those organizational partnerships to be formed."

In Mora's (September 16, 1997) experience, the trend has had a similar impact on staff, especially regarding the partnerships with neighborhood groups. He notes that when hiring department heads, he specifically considers the ability to develop "partnerships, and work with community goals, and elected officials. The partnership element and involvement of neighborhoods and elected officials as well as the connections within and between departments is crucial."

Having been a city manager and now serving as executive director of a civic group of business leaders in Kansas City, Missouri, Jewel Scott (July 25, 1997) observes that there has been a significant shift toward community involvement and ownership of programs and service delivery.

> If I were a manager today, I would focus on finding ways to work creatively with the not-for-profit community to provide services and to evaluate and design service delivery systems. Also, I would be more open to building community ownership of issues and projects and to seeking the assistance of others in the community to do so. Finally, I would think very differently about what is important to a community's well-being. I would work harder to move decisions out into the community.

This discussion of community building and facilitative leadership points the profession of city management in a particular direction—away from professional elitism and toward a community paradigm. It appears that local government administrators must be able to move in this direction if they are to maintain their effectiveness and influence. There is a tacit understanding here that council-manager government itself no longer provides a comfortable, protective cover for the city manager's legitimacy.

Form of Government and the Added Value of City Managers

Frederickson (1996) has shown how adaptations to both council-manager and strong mayor forms of government have moderated the distinctions between the two. It is hard to imagine that to the average citizen the remaining differences really do make a difference. Whether they are important remains a point of contention among city management professionals. Tom Downs (November 24, 1997), former chairman of AMTRAK and a former city manager, argues that they do.

He observes, "The institutions we create are more important [than he formerly thought], endur-ing, and effective over the long term." He suggests that the collapse of local government in the nation's capital should teach us something about unfulfilled faith in charismatic leadership. Also, it should reinforce our belief that there is long-term value in governmental institutions that sustain and protect continuity, stability, expertise, and the value of public service—like those fostered by council-manager government.

In contrast, Mora (December 5, 1997) observes that council-manager government in its tra-ditional definition is not always the best or most appropriate for a community. He writes, "Our emphasis as professionals must be on providing expert local government management, regardless of the form of government. This 'ideal' of service can and should be a core value of the profession without dependence on the form of government." Ruder (August 12, 1997)—who formerly worked in Phoenix and Billings, both council-manager cities, and now works in Seattle, a strong mayor city—adds: "Distinctions about form of government seem much less critical to me than whether people are engaged as problem solvers in their own neighborhoods."

Anderson (August 26, 1997) suggests that the success of council-manager government in eliminating corruption has actually diminished its contemporary attractiveness. Its success has eliminated its original raison d'être. While the reform story is diminishing in attractiveness, strong mayor cities have come to rely more on professionally trained staff and accepted business practices, thus increasing their administrative effectiveness step by step.

As a corollary, Anderson observes, "Mayors have somehow emerged in this decade as the politi-cal 'reformers,' with mayors in Indianapolis, Philadelphia, New York, Chicago, and Los Angeles getting excellent press and praise as the standard bearers for progressive municipal government." Jan Perkins (July 13, 1997) concurs by suggesting that the perceived responsiveness of high-pro-file mayors easily leads to the notion that "we" [professional managers and advocates of council manager government] may be seen as the institution that needs reforming.

The popularity of the charismatic mayor elicited many comments from participants in this research. In many ways the discussion about form of government and concern over the present emergence of the strong mayor as a "reformer" is crucial to the meaning of local government professionalism. It calls into question the value city managers add to municipal government, and thus aims at the heart of professional legitimacy.

For years, the value of city mangers has been embedded in the form of government itself. Council manager government without a city manager is inconceivable, by definition. And as long as the form of government retained its prominence as "good government," the value and credibility of the city manager was, in large measure, unquestioned. Robert O'Neill, Jr. (October 29, 1997), county executive in Fairfax County, Virginia, observes that among the greatest changes in the rela-tionship between elected and appointed officials is the increasing skepticism that elected officials have regarding the value of senior management. As the contemporary reform story unfolds with the "mayor taking on the bureaucracy," council-manager government becomes an old story, and the value of the city manager is exposed. This calls for a new definition of the local government professional's roles, responsibilities, and values. Norm King (December 10, 1997) says it best: "The primary issue is not the council-manager plan. The issue is better articulating the added value of professional management. And in doing so, we must distinguish a well run city from a poorly run city *in a way which is understood by the citizenry* [emphasis added]."

In sum, as prominent mayors become seen as the new reformers, council-manager government becomes an old story. The search for legitimacy is really a search for identifying what value the city manager adds to a community. This is where the community-building, facilitative leadership paradigm holds promise.

Process-Oriented Management

Some of the changes identified by the local government administrators in this research focused on managing their internal, organizational role. Technological, demographic, and market-based pressures on governing institutions bring about these changes (Klingner and Nalbandian, 1998, chps. 1 and 8). Technological advances are noteworthy for two reasons—the amount of knowledge that is generated and the rapidity of change. Increasing knowledge often requires occupational specialization. More specialization means that teamwork is even more necessary to link diverse specialists. Interdepartmental differences in perspective are greater than in the past and are articulated more clearly and forcefully by better-educated, technically trained staff. The rapidity of technological change suggests that the occupational specializations themselves can become obsolete more quickly than in previous generations. This means that many teams have to exist as temporary organizational fixtures, and employees must become accustomed to working in more than one setting.

Demographic changes are reflected both in the diversity of people who constitute the workforce and in the tremendous demands for flexible work arrangements to accommodate family needs of today's single parents and dual income families. The challenge of workforce diversity manifests itself in different expectations that employees have of one another. In addition, men and women often approach problem solving and managing people differently. Accommodations to family needs include newer benefits such as child care, long-term care, and elder care; and work arrangements include flex-time, flex-place, job sharing, and a greater desire for part-time, yet permanent work.

George Caravalho (October 20, 1997), city manager in Santa Clarita, California, says, "The most significant change that has occurred in our profession is the impact that women have had in the workplace. Women seem less concerned with hierarchy and structure, tending to be more facilitative in their style. They look for areas of commonality; and they often have a calming approach to problem solving and conflict." Sandra Tripp-Jones (December 30, 1997), city administrator in Santa Barbara, California, adds, "Women have provided more behaviors not stereotypically male, so that both men and women have more freedom to use styles and skills that suit them individually. Among firefighters, for example, women have added and made it acceptable for men also to demonstrate compassion, empathy and sensitivity to people in traumatic situations. In addition, the offices of women managers often seem safe places for others to talk/vent/try out ideas in a less competitive setting."

And last, competitiveness in the marketplace puts a premium on responsiveness, quality, and speed. As David Watkins (December 10, 1997) says, "I understand that the role of government does not lend itself entirely to the service model of the private sector, but certain values such as fairness, timeliness, and unified decision making are transferable. Lenexa is moving toward a system where applicants will be viewed in a positive manner and staff will serve as problem solvers."

Gene Denton (June 25, 1997), county manager in suburban Johnson County, Kansas, indicates the kinds of internal changes that have come about in response to these types of external pressures:

> The structure of government has flattened. We have retrained most of our workers to be more self-reliant and departments to be interdependent. Creativity and innovation have replaced the more sterile values of efficiency and economy. Leadership has leaped ahead of management. Coaches have replaced supervisors. Connectedness, communication, and cooperation have outclassed competition. Quality is more valued than speed. The respected leader is one who is more concerned about how workers are progressing and what they *should be,* rather than what they *should do.*

The flattening of hierarchy is prudent when seeking rapid response by technically trained staff. City managers today cannot mandate changes because, more than before, they do not command the technical knowledge to fully understand what they are asking for. A city manager cannot tell a public works director that the council favors a proposed development that requires hooking up to a particular sewer line because it is more economical for the applicant, when the public works director says the downstream capacity won't handle the added load of wastewater. In addition, as city staff begins to incorporate facilitative management practices into their own work, city managers who exercise hierarchical control over them put at risk the often fragile agreements staff has negotiated among contending parties. For example, on a controversial development project involving landowners, regulatory bodies, financial institutions, and neighbors, planning staff may have negotiated an agreement that incorporates provisions regarding annexation, payment for infrastructure, and land use. City managers who would exercise hierarchical control over planning staff could jeopardize this agreement. Professional norms and the confidence that comes with the mastery of technical knowledge *and process skills* permit and sometimes encourage technical workers to question hierarchy. Because managers cannot dictate to staff, Denton's statement about being concerned with what workers *should be* rather than what they *should do* seems on target.

Denton observes that as managers are forced to reduce reliance on hierarchy, the personal attributes of workers become more crucial to performance. In fact, in the personnel field, it is not uncommon in the private sector to incorporate "personal attributes" into discussions about merit and competence (Borman and Motowidlo, 1993). This flies in the face of traditional personnel practices in which personal attributes are excluded from considerations of knowledge, skills, and abilities.

King's (September 16, 1997) comments capture the overarching thrust of the city manager's administrative role when he says, "I think the most important responsibility of any manager is to manage the values of the organization and to instill a sense of responsibility in employees for them." This is exactly what David Mora was referring to when he commented that the values of staff were crucial to him in his dealings with a diverse council, thus the hiring process must attend to more than just technical competence.

Furthermore, King says that while the vast majority of a city's work can be handled through traditional departments, the most important problems fall outside traditional departmental boundaries. In Denton's words, hierarchy is of little use in handling those problems that require "independence, creativity and innovation, connectedness, communication, and cooperation." This is precisely what Donald Schon predicted in 1974 when he wrote *Beyond the Stable State* and suggested that amidst continual change, values provide stability.

Complicating internal, administrative transitions, according to several managers, is the increasing tendency of councils to become involved in the "how to" rather than the "what" part of governance. Svara's (1985; 1998) work shows how the politics/administration dichotomy is more fruitfully viewed in terms of relative involvement of the city manager and city council members in the city's mission, policy, administration, and management functions. Using his terminology, elected officials have become more involved in administration and management, according to the participants in this research.

Buchanan (October 17, 1997) sums up the involvement of elected officials in this way:

> In an evaluation not too long ago, one of the Commissioners suggested that she would be more comfortable if I brought to her the projects as I was working on them rather than when they were completed. She used the analogy of a baby. She said she was part of the family and she wanted to see the baby. She wanted not only to see the clean baby with a shiny ribbon in her hair, but she wanted to see the baby, messy diaper and all.

Commenting on Buchanan's metaphor, Sandra Tripp-Jones (December 30, 1997) writes:

> They [the governing body] like being able to "dress the baby," to plan how to promote the idea. I need to be comfortable brainstorming with them as opposed to "providing the best and only answer." This is a change from even five years ago. Like the facilitation skills needed to foster more public participation without controlling it, the professional manager needs the self-confidence to brainstorm with council and be wrong, and to not need to have all the answers. This also means developing staff who can do the same.

The increasing interest elected officials show in "how to" is understandable if one recognizes that how decisions are reached conveys as much about representation, individual rights, and equity—*essential values in community building*—as the substance of the decision itself. If professional staff fails to acknowledge this council interest, it distances itself from the council and plants the seeds of council skepticism and distrust.

DISCUSSION AND CONCLUSIONS

Several years ago I described the changes that had occurred in the meaning of professionalism in local government as three transformations in roles, responsibilities, and values of city managers. I conclude by returning to those three transformations, relating them to the primary conclusions in this present research.

As long as the council-manager plan symbolized reform government, the city manager's roles, responsibilities, and values were protected—even if they were not easily articulated or understood. The legitimacy of the city manager rested in the form of government and the story it promised—nonpolitical, efficient, and responsive government. But as the memory of patronage and widespread corruption has faded, the most persuasive rationale for council-manager government is lost not only for citizens, but for governing body members themselves. In this environment, city managers are vulnerable to elected officials and citizens skeptical of the expertise of any government employee, even questioning the value of government itself.

Burdened with maintaining their legitimacy, some managers seek from their peers and ICMA a renewed and vigorous defense of council-manager government. My impression is that the value of professionalism in local government must be established independent of government form, and I think the comments of several managers in this study point in that direction. In searching for the connection between political leadership and administrative capacity, the concepts of community building and facilitative leadership are recurring themes. These themes provide clues to the present and future roles, responsibilities, and values of city managers as models for local government professionals in general.

Roles

Many aspects of the manager's job remain the same; keeping the council informed, providing continuity and stability, telling the council what it does not necessarily want to hear, and balancing short-run interests against a long-run, "greater good" perspective. The difference between now and ten years ago is in the emphasis on the facilitative role of the manager. Some 20 years ago, the International City Management Association's Future Horizons Committee (Rutter, 1980, 2) characterized its dialogue with the sentence: "Welcome, I am Jennifer Stene, the city coordinator." After examining the comments I received for this study, it appears that the future is now! Frederickson's (1997, chp. 3) review of literature on governance includes numerous references to academic studies emphasizing partnerships, networking, coordinating, and connecting as the essence of the "new public management."

Throughout the discussion of building community, the internal and external facilitative roles of the manager have been emphasized. These roles grow from the emphasis on partnerships, responsiveness and customer service, quality management, and coordinating divergent departmental perspectives. In short, "how" a city government conducts its business, whether with its own employees or with the governing body or citizens, has become as important as "what" is done.

In this environment, supporting the council's work—a long-standing role expectation of the chief administrative officer and staff—requires a facilitative orientation as part of the definition of professionalism in local government. There is a growing understanding that facilitative work is not designed to "make people feel better." It is designed to help promote a problem-solving orientation and to develop consensus among diverse interests. Eric Anderson (September 17, 1997) says, "This is not warm and fuzzy stuff; it is hard work. I have found it to be the toughest work we do. You've got to be incredibly patient and thick-skinned, and you have to have some sense that there truly is value in these processes because they are tremendously time consuming and occasionally abusive."

The connection he makes between facilitative staff work, support for the governing body, and building governance capacity and credibility places the facilitative role into a more important theoretical perspective than local government professionals commonly understand. Developing facilitative staff work requires more than just skill building. It takes us back to the values argument that King and Mora made earlier. Managing the value of the organization means connecting the overarching organizational sense of what is good/right with the work of the governing body *and* the community.

Responsibilities

The second tenet discussed in 1991 asserted that managers were responsive to their governing body but responsible to values expressed in the community more broadly. That responsibility is given more form when linked to community building.

The partnership between staff and governing body achieved through facilitative leadership is targeted toward community building. The concept of community building, as elusive as it might be to define, nevertheless provides more guidance than the vague, simplistic counsel that staff and the governing body are partners in governance, with the governing body establishing priorities and staff carrying out policy. The community-building concept provides a legitimate anchor because it establishes a concrete purpose of government that citizens can readily understand and endorse. It is not the only one, but it can provide a fruitful point of departure for real governing bodies and real managers seeking an effective relationship and a way to engage citizens. It provides a way to make democracy work.

The responsibility of the city manager is to empower the governing body *and* citizens by helping to develop and use the tools of engagement. This is where the facilitative leadership roles enter—framing issues and processes (1) to deal with diverse interests, (2) to focus on interests rather than positions when problem solving, and (3) to develop collaborative partnerships in policymaking and service delivery.

Values

As a third tenet, in 1991, I argued that representation, individual rights, and social equity combined with efficiency to form a value base for professionalism in city management. The concept of community building organizes those values. It suggests that building a sense of community requires a foundation of rights, fairness, and representation along with evidence that collectively a community can accomplish some tasks more efficiently and effectively than its members could do on their own—streets and sewer maintenance, storm water management, land-use planning, and so on. Giving up some freedom on behalf of the collective good is made more palatable when rights, equity, and representation of interest are guaranteed (Tussman, 1960).

In addition to providing a connection among these values, the community-building concept can help us see the future of facilitative leadership within an internal organizational community as well as within external political communities. Increasing levels of diversity within organizations place a premium on facilitative leadership aimed at building commitment to collective organizational purposes. The same can be said when hierarchy is replaced by collegiality and teamwork.

In asserting that the contemporary meaning of professionalism incorporates facilitative leadership and community building, I have chosen to downplay "the enduring commitment to public service" (Frederickson, 1997) as a central feature. I do not doubt this sense of obligation to the public good as a defining element for those who choose to become city managers. I have serious reservations, however, whether those outside of academic and professional circles find that commitment believable enough to grant city managers legitimacy. Those who come to our governing institutions seeking satisfaction of their private interests always find ways to mask those interests as the public good. We have become so facile at manipulating data to suit these hollow portrayals that claims of advancing, nurturing, or living by the public interest have become suspect by dispassionate citizens and governing body members alike. Brint (1994) has shown that professional status is more likely to be conferred upon those who can demonstrate skills employed in ways average citizens value rather than in the virtue of self-proclaimed motives. That is why skill in community building rather than a calling to public service is more persuasive to me as an anchor for contemporary professionalism.

Finally, the success at postulating facilitative leadership and community building as the anchors for contemporary professionalism in local government will depend upon two factors. The first is whether city managers are willing to acknowledge that the value they add to governing processes can be found in facilitative leadership and community building rather than associated principally in the issue of form of government. A second, and more challenging, task is whether the profession can formulate these two concepts into a "new story" that will connect and build on the reform heritage in a way that appeals to citizens.

ACKNOWLEDGMENTS

I would like to thank George Frederickson, Barbara Romzek, and Joe Freeman for helpful comments on a draft of this article.

REFERENCES

Anderson, Eric (1997). Correspondence with John Nalbandian, 26 August.
——— (1997). Panel discussion at ICMA conference in Vancouver, British Columbia, 17 September.
Bledsoe, Timothy (1993). *Careers in City Politics: The Case for Urban Democracy.* Pittsburgh: University of Pittsburgh Press.
Borman, W.C., and S.J. Motowidlo (1993). "Expanding the Criterion Domain to Include Elements of Contextual Performance." In F.L. Schmitt, W.C. Borman, and Associates, eds. *Personnel Selection in Organizations.* San Francisco: Jossey Bass.
Box, Richard C. (1998). *Citizen Governance: Leading American Communities into the 21st Century.* Thousand Oaks, CA: Sage.
Brint, Steven (1994). *In an Age of Experts.* Princeton, NJ: Princeton University Press.
Buchanan, William (1997). Correspondence with John Nalbandian, 17 October.
Caravalho, George (1997). Correspondence with John Nalbandian, 20 October.

Church, Charles (1997). Correspondence with John Nalbandian, 27 November.
Denton, Eugene (1997). Correspondence with John Nalbandian, 25 June.
Downs, Thomas (1997). Correspondence with John Nalbandian, 24 November.
Etzioni, Amitai, ed. (1995). *New Communitarian Thinking.* Charlottesville: University Press of Virginia.
Fowler, Robert Booth (1991). *A Dance with Community: The Contemporary Debate in American Political Thought.* Lawrence, KS: University Press of Kansas.
Frederickson, H. George (1997). "Facing the Community." *Kettering Review* (December): 28–37.
———, ed. (1989). *Ideal and Practice in Council-Manager Government.* Washington, DC: International City Management Association.
——— (1997). *The Spirit of Public Administration.* San Francisco: Jossey Bass.
——— (1996). "Type III Cities." Unpublished manuscript. Department of Public Administration, University of Kansas.
Gardner, Howard (1995). *Leading Minds.* New York: Basic Books.
Glendon, M.A. (1991). *Rights Talk: The Impoverishment of Political Discourse.* New York: Free Press.
King, Norm (1997). Correspondence with John Nalbandian, 10 December.
——— (1997). Panel discussion at ICMA conference in Vancouver, British Columbia, 16 September.
Klingner, Donald E., and John Nalbandian (1998). *Public Personnel Management: Contexts and Strategies,* 4th ed. Upper Saddle River, NJ: Prentice Hall.
Lappé, Frances Moore, and Paul Martin Du Bois (1994). *The Quickening of America: Rebuilding Our Nation, Remaking Our Lives.* San Francisco: Jossey Bass.
Mahtesian, Charles (1997). "The Politics of Ugliness." *Governing Magazine* 10: 18–22.
Mathews, David (1994). *Politics for People: Finding a Responsible Public Voice.* Urbana, IL: University of Illinois Press.
Mora, David (1997). Correspondence with John Nalbandian, 5 December.
——— (1997). Panel discussion at ICMA conference in Vancouver, British Columbia, 16 September.
Nalbandian, John (1989). "The Contemporary Role of City Managers." *American Review of Public Administration* 19: 261–278.
——— (1991). *Professionalism in Local Government: Roles, Responsibilities, and Values of City Managers.* San Francisco: Jossey Bass.
——— (1990). "Tenets of Contemporary Professionalism in Local Government." *Public Administration Review* 50: 654–663.
O'Neill, Robert, Jr. (1997). Correspondence with John Nalbandian, 29 October.
Perkins, Jan (1997). Correspondence with John Nalbandian, 13 July.
——— (1997). Correspondence with John Nalbandian, 21 July.
Putnam, Robert D. (1993). *Making Democracy Work: Civic Traditions in Modern Italy.* Princeton, NJ: Princeton University Press.
Rice, Tom W., and Alexander F. Sumberg (1997). "Civic Culture and Government Performance in the American State." *Publius* 27: 99–114.
Ruder, Karma (1997). Correspondence with John Nalbandian, 12 August.
——— (1997). Correspondence with John Nalbandian, 15 December.
——— (1997). Panel discussion at ICMA conference in Vancouver, British Columbia, 16 September.
Rutter, Lawrence (1980). *The Essential Community.* Washington, DC: International City Management Association.
Schon, Donald (1974). *Beyond the Stable State.* New York: Norton.
Scott, Jewel (1997). Correspondence with John Nalbandian, 25 July.
Selznick, Philip (1992). *The Moral Commonwealth: Social Theory and the Promise of Community.* Berkeley, CA: University of California Press.
Stillman, R.J., III (1974). *The Rise of the City Manager.* Albuquerque: University of New Mexico Press.
Svara, James H. (1985). "Dichotomy and Duality: Reconceptualizing the Relationship Between Politics and Administration in Council-Manager Cities." *Public Administration Review* 45: 221–232.
——— (1998). "The Politics-Administration Dichotomy Model as Aberration." *Public Administration Review* 58(1): 51–58.
Thomas, John C. (1986). *Between Citizen and City.* Lawrence, KS: University Press of Kansas.
Tripp-Jones, Sandra (1997). Correspondence with John Nalbandian, 30 December.
Tussman, Joseph (1960). *Obligation and the Body Politic.* New York: Oxford University Press.
Watkins, David (1997). Correspondence with John Nalbandian, 21 July.
——— (1997). Correspondence with John Nalbandian, 10 December.

CHAPTER 4

THE NEW PUBLIC SERVICE
Serving Rather than Steering

ROBERT B. DENHARDT AND JANET VINZANT DENHARDT

Public management has undergone a revolution. Rather than focusing on controlling bureaucracies and delivering services, public administrators are responding to admonishments to "steer rather than row," and to be the entrepreneurs of a new, leaner, and increasingly privatized government. As a result, a number of highly positive changes have been implemented in the public sector (Osborne and Gaebler 1992; Osborne and Plastrik 1997; Kettl 1993; Kettl and DiIulio 1995; Kettl and Milward 1996; Lynn 1996). But as the field of public administration has increasingly abandoned the idea of rowing and has accepted responsibility for steering, has it simply traded one "adminicentric" view for another? Osborne and Gaebler write, "Those who steer the boat have far more power over its destination than those who row it" (1992, 32). If that is the case, the shift from rowing to steering not only may have left administrators in charge of the boat—choosing its goals and directions and charting a path to achieve them—it may have given them more power to do so.

In our rush to steer, are we forgetting who owns the boat? In their recent book, *Government Is Us* (1998), King and Stivers remind us of the obvious answer: The government belongs to its citizens (see also Box 1998; Cooper 1991; King, Feltey, and O'Neill 1998; Stivers 1994a,b; Thomas 1995). Accordingly, public administrators should focus on their responsibility to *serve and empower citizens* as they manage public organizations and implement public policy. In other words, with citizens at the forefront, the emphasis should not be placed on either steering or rowing the governmental boat, but rather on building public institutions marked by integrity and responsiveness.

BACKGROUND

As it is used here, the "New Public Management" refers to a cluster of ideas and practices (including reinvention and neomanagerialism) that seek, at their core, to use private-sector and business approaches in the public sector. While there have long been calls to "run government like a business," the contemporary version of this debate in this country was sparked in the 1990s by President Clinton's and Vice President Gore's initiative to "make government work better and cost less." Modeled after concepts and ideas promoted in Osborne and Gaebler's 1992 book *Reinventing Government* (as well as managerialist efforts in a variety of other countries, especially Great Britain and New Zealand), the Clinton administration championed a variety of reforms and projects under the mantle of the National Performance Review. In part, what has distinguished these reforms and similar efforts at the state and local level from older versions of the run-government-like-a-business movement is that they involve more than just using the techniques of business. Rather, the New Public Management has become a normative model, one signaling a profound shift in how we think about the role of public administrators, the nature of the profession, and how and why we do what we do.

Yet many scholars and practitioners have continued to express concerns about the New Public Management and the role for public managers this model suggests. For example, in a recent *Public Administration Review* symposium on leadership, democracy, and public management, a number of authors thoughtfully considered the opportunities and challenges presented by the New Public Management. Those challenging the New Public Management in the symposium and elsewhere ask questions about the inherent contradictions in the movement (Fox 1996); the values promoted by it (deLeon and Denhardt 2000; Frederickson 1996; Schachter 1997); the tensions between the emphasis on decentralization promoted in the market model and the need for coordination in the public sector (Peters and Savoie 1996); the implied roles and relationships of the executive and legislative branches (Carroll and Lynn 1996); and the implications of the privatization movement for democratic values and the public interest (McCabe and Vinzant 1999). Others have suggested that public entrepreneurship and what Terry (1993, 1998) has called "neomanagerialism" threaten to undermine democratic and constitutional values such as fairness, justice, representation, and participation.

We would like to suggest that, beyond these separate critiques, what is missing is a set of organizing principles for an alternative to the New Public Management. We reject the notion that the reinvented, market-oriented New Public Management should only be compared to the old public administration, which, despite its many important contributions, has come to be seen as synonymous with bureaucracy, hierarchy, and control. If that is the comparison, the New Public Management will always win. We would like to suggest instead that the New Public Management should be contrasted with what we term the "New Public Service," a set of ideas about the role of public administration in the governance system that places citizens at the center.

While there have been many challenges to the New Public Management and many alternative ideas prominently advanced by scholars and practitioners, there have been no attempts to organize these efforts and underscore their common themes. This article is an effort to do so. First, it briefly summarizes the foundations and major arguments of the new public management as it contrasts with the old public administration. It then describes an alternative normative model we call the "New Public Service." This new model further clarifies the debate by suggesting new ways of thinking about the strengths and weaknesses of all three approaches. We conclude by considering the implications of placing citizens, citizenship, and the public interest at the forefront of a New Public Service.

THE NEW PUBLIC MANAGEMENT AND THE OLD
PUBLIC ADMINISTRATION

Over the past decade and a half, the New Public Management (again, including the reinvention movement and the new managerialism) has literally swept the nation and the world. The common theme in the myriad applications of these ideas has been the use of market mechanisms and terminology, in which the relationship between public agencies and their customers is understood as based on self-interest, involving transactions similar to those occurring in the marketplace. Public managers are urged to "steer, not row" their organizations, and they are challenged to find new and innovative ways to achieve results or to privatize functions previously provided by government.

In the past two decades, many public jurisdictions and agencies have initiated efforts to increase productivity and to find alternative service-delivery mechanisms based on public-choice assumptions and perspectives. Public managers have concentrated on accountability and high performance and have sought to restructure bureaucratic agencies, redefine organizational missions, streamline -agency processes, and decentralize decision making. In many cases, governments and government agencies have succeeded in privatizing previously public functions, holding top executives accountable for performance goals, establishing new processes for measuring productivity and effectiveness, and reengineering departmental systems to reflect a strengthened commitment to accountability (Aristigueta 1999; Barzelay 1992; Boston et al. 1996; Kearns 1996). The effectiveness of this reform agenda in the United States, as well as in a number of other countries, has put governments around the world on notice that new standards are being sought and new roles established.

These ideas were crystallized and popularized by Osborne and Gaebler's book, *Reinventing Government* (1992; see also Osborne and Plastrik 1997). Osborne and Gaebler provided a number of now-familiar principles through which "public entrepreneurs" might bring about massive governmental reform—ideas that remain at the core of the New Public Management. Osborne and Gaebler intended these principles to serve as a new conceptual or normative framework for public administration, an analytical checklist to transform the actions of government: "What we are describing is nothing less than a shift in the basic model of governance used in America. This shift is under way all around us, but because we are not looking for it, because we assume that all governments have to be big, centralized, and bureaucratic, we seldom see it. We are blind to the new realities, because they do not fit our preconceptions" (1992, 321).

Other intellectual justifications for the New Public Management evolved as well. These justifications, as Lynn (1996) notes, largely came from the "public policy" schools that developed in the 1970s and from the "managerialist" movement around the world (Pollitt 1990). Kaboolian notes that the New Public Management relies on "market-like arrangements such as competition within units of government and across government boundaries to the non-profit and for-profit sectors, performance bonuses, and penalties [to] loosen the inefficient monopoly franchise of public agencies and public employees" (1998, 190). Elaborating this point, Hood writes that the New Public Management moves away from traditional modes of legitimizing the public bureaucracy, such as procedural safeguards on administrative discretion, in favor of "trust in the market and private business methods . . . ideas . . . couched in the language of economic rationalism" (1995, 94).

As such, the New Public Management is clearly linked to the public choice perspective in public administration. In its simplest form, public choice views the government from the standpoint of markets and customers. Public choice not only affords an elegant and, to some, compelling model of government, it also serves as a kind of intellectual road map for practical efforts to reduce government and make it less costly. And it does so unabashedly. John Kamensky, one of the architects of the National Performance Review, comments that the New Public Management is clearly related to the public choice movement, the central tenet of which is that "all human behavior is dominated by self-interest" (1996, 251).

The New Public Management is not just the implementation of new *techniques,* it carries with it a new set of *values,* specifically a set of values largely drawn from the private sector. As we have already noted, there is a long-standing tradition in public administration supporting the idea that "government should be run like a business." For the most part, this recommendation has meant that government agencies should adopt practices, ranging from "scientific management" to "total quality management," that have been found useful in the private sector. The New Public Management takes this idea one step further, arguing that government should not only adopt the *techniques* of business administration, but should adopt certain business *values* as well. The New Public Management thus becomes a normative model for public administration and public management.

In making their case, proponents of New Public Management have often used the old public administration as a foil, against which the principles of entrepreneurship can be seen as clearly superior. For example, Osborne and Gaebler contrast their principles with an alternative of formal bureaucracies plagued with excessive rules, bound by rigid budgeting and personnel systems, and pre-occupied with control. These traditional bureaucracies are described as ignoring citizens, shunning innovation, and serving their own needs. According to Osborne and Gaebler, "The kind of governments that developed during the industrial era, with their sluggish, centralized bureaucracies, their preoccupation with rules and regulations, and their hierarchical chains of command, no longer work very well" (1992, 11–12). In fact, while they served their earlier purposes, "bureaucratic institutions . . . increasingly fail us" (15).

What are the tenets of this bureaucratic old public administration, and is it reasonable to characterize any contemporary thinking which falls outside New Public Management as evidence of the old public administration? Certainly there is not a single set of ideas agreed to by all those who contributed over the decades to the old public administration (just as there is not a single set of ideas that all associated with the New Public Management would agree to). But there are elements of public administration theory and practice that seem to constitute a guiding set of ideas or a normative model that we now generally associate with the old public administration. We suggest this model includes the following tenets:

- Public administration is politically neutral, valuing the idea of neutral competence.
- The focus of government is the direct delivery of services. The best organizational structure is a centralized bureaucracy.
- Programs are implemented through top-down control mechanisms, limiting discretion as much as possible.
- Bureaucracies seek to be closed systems to the extent possible, thus limiting citizen involvement.
- Efficiency and rationality are the most important values in public organizations.
- Public administrators do not play a central role in policymaking and governance; rather, they are charged with the efficient implementation of public objectives.
- The job of public administrators is described by Gulick's POSDCORB (Planning, Organizing, Staffing, Directing, Coordinating, Reporting, and Budgeting; 1937, 13).

If we compare the principles of New Public Management with these principles, the New Public Management clearly looks like a preferred alternative. But even a cursory examination of the literature of public administration demonstrates that these traditional ideas do not fully embrace contemporary government theory or practice (Box 1998; Bryson and Crosby 1992; Carnavale 1995; Cook 1996; Cooper 1991; deLeon 1997; Denhardt 1993; Farmer 1995; Fox and Miller 1995; Frederickson 1997; Gawthrop 1998; Goodsell 1994; Harmon 1995; Hummel 1994; Ingraham et al. 1994; Light 1997; Luke 1998; McSwite 1997; Miller and Fox 1997; Perry 1996; Rabin, Hildreth and Miller 1998; Rohr 1998; Stivers 1993; Terry 1995, 1998; Thomas 1995; Vinzant and Crothers 1998; Wamsley et al. 1990; Wamsley and Wolf 1996). The field of public administration, of course, has not been stuck in progressive reform rhetoric for the last 100 years. Instead, there has been a rich and vibrant evolution in thought and practice, with important and substantial developments that cannot be subsumed under the title "the New Public Management." So there are more than two choices. We will now explore a third alternative based on recent intellectual and practical developments in public administration, one that we call the New Public Service.

ROOTS OF THE NEW PUBLIC SERVICE

Like the New Public Management and the old public administration, the New Public Service consists of many diverse elements, and many different scholars and practitioners have contributed, often in disagreement with one another. Yet certain general ideas seem to characterize this approach as a normative model and to distinguish it from others. While the New Public Service has emerged both in theory and in the innovative and advanced practices of many exemplary public managers (Denhardt 1993; Denhardt and Denhardt 1999), in this section we will examine the conceptual foundations of the New Public Service. Certainly the New Public Service can lay claim to an impressive intellectual heritage, including, in public administration, the work of Dwight Waldo (1948), and in political theory, the work of Sheldon Wolin (1960). However, here we will focus on more contemporary precursors of the New Public Service, including (1) theories of democratic citizenship; (2) models of community and civil society; and (3) organizational humanism and discourse theory. We will then outline what we see as the main tenets of the New Public Service.

Theories of Democratic Citizenship

Concerns about citizenship and democracy are particularly important and visible in recent political and social theory, both of which call for a reinvigorated and more active and involved citizenship (Barber 1984; Mansbridge 1990; Mansbridge 1992; Pateman 1970; Sandel 1996). Of particular relevance to our discussion is Sandel's suggestion that the prevailing model of the relationship between state and citizens is based on the idea that government exists to ensure citizens can make choices consistent with their self-interest by guaranteeing certain procedures (such as voting) and individual rights. Obviously, this perspective is consistent with public choice economics and the New Public Management (see Kamensky 1996). But Sandel offers an alternative view of democratic citizenship, one in which individuals are much more actively engaged in governance. In this view, citizens look beyond self-interest to the larger public interest, adopting a broader and longer-term perspective that requires a knowledge of public affairs and also a sense of belonging, a concern for the whole, and a moral bond with the community whose fate is at stake (Sandel 1996, 5–6; see also Schubert 1957).

Consistent with this perspective, King and Stivers (1998) assert that administrators should see citizens *as* citizens (rather than merely as voters, clients, or customers); they should share authority and reduce control, and they should trust in the efficacy of collaboration. Moreover, in contrast to managerialist calls for greater efficiency, King and Stivers suggest that public managers seek greater responsiveness and a corresponding increase in citizen trust. This perspective directly undergirds the New Public Service.

Models of Community and Civil Society

Recently, there has been a rebirth of interest in the idea of community and civility in America. Political leaders of both major political parties, scholars of different camps, best-selling writers and popular commentators not only agree that community in America has deteriorated, but acknowledge that we desperately need a renewed sense of community. Despite increasing diversity in America, or perhaps because of it, community is seen as a way of bringing about unity and synthesis (Bellah et al. 1985, 1991; Etzioni 1988, 1995; Gardner 1991; Selznick 1992). In public administration, the quest for community has been reflected in the view that the role of government, especially local government, is indeed to help create and support "community."

In part, this effort depends on building a healthy and active set of "mediating institutions" that simultaneously give focus to the desires and interests of citizens and provide experiences that will better prepare those citizens for action in the larger political system. As Putnam (1995) argues, America's democratic tradition depends on the existence of engaged citizens, active in all sorts of groups, associations, and governmental units. Collectively, these small groups constitute a "civil society" in which people need to work out their personal interests in the context of community concerns. Only here can citizens engage one another in the kind of personal dialogue and deliberation that is the essence of community building and of democracy itself. Again, as King and Stivers (1998) point out, government can play an important and critical role in creating, facilitating, and supporting these connections between citizens and their communities.

Organizational Humanism and Discourse Theory

Over the past 25 years, public administration theorists, including those associated with the radical public administrationists of the late 1960s and early 1970s (Marini 1971), have joined colleagues in other disciplines in suggesting that traditional hierarchical approaches to social organization and positivist approaches to social science are mutually reinforcing. Consequently, they have joined in a critique of bureaucracy and positivism, leading, in turn, to a search for alternative approaches to management and organization and an exploration of new approaches to knowledge acquisition—including interpretive theory (for example, Harmon 1981), critical theory (Denhardt 1981), and postmodernism (Farmer 1995; Fox and Miller 1995; McSwite 1997; Miller and Fox 1997). Collectively, these approaches have sought to fashion public organizations less dominated by issues of authority and control and more attentive to the needs and concerns of employees inside public organizations as well as those outside, especially clients and citizens.

These trends have been central to interpretive and critical analyses of bureaucracy and society, but they have been even further extended in recent efforts to employ the perspectives of postmodern thinking, especially discourse theory, in understanding public organizations. While there are significant differences among the various postmodern theorists, they seem to arrive at a similar conclusion—because we depend on one another in the postmodern world, governance must be based on sincere and open discourse among all parties, including citizens and administrators. And while postmodern public administration theorists are skeptical of traditional approaches to public participation, there seems to be considerable agreement that enhanced public dialogue is required to reinvigorate the public bureaucracy and restore a sense of legitimacy to the field of public administration. In other words, there is a need to reconceptualize the field, both practically and intellectually, so as to build a New Public Service.

THE NEW PUBLIC SERVICE

Theorists of citizenship, community and civil society, organizational humanists, and postmodernist public administrationists have helped to establish a climate in which it makes sense today to talk about a New Public Service. Though we acknowledge that differences exist in these viewpoints, we suggest there are also similarities that distinguish the cluster of ideas we call the New Public Service from those associated with the New Public Management and the old public administration. Moreover, there are a number of practical lessons that the New Public Service suggests for those in public administration. These lessons are not mutually exclusive, rather they are mutually reinforcing. Among these, we find the following most compelling [see Table 4.1].

1. *Serve, rather than steer.* An increasingly important role of the public servant is to help citizens articulate and meet their shared interests, rather than to attempt to control or steer society in new directions.

While in the past, government played a central role in what has been called the "steering of society" (Nelissen et al. 1999), the complexity of modern life sometimes makes such a role not only inappropriate, but impossible. Those policies and programs that give structure and direction to social and political life today are the result of the interaction of many different groups and organizations, the mixture of many different opinions and interests. In many areas, it no longer makes sense to think of public policies as the result of governmental decision-making processes. Government is indeed a player—and in most cases a very substantial player. But public policies today, the policies that guide society, are the outcome of a complex set of interactions involving multiple groups and multiple interests ultimately combining in fascinating and unpredictable ways. Government is no longer in charge.

In this new world, the primarily role of government is not merely to direct the actions of the public through regulation and decree (though that may sometimes be appropriate), nor is it to simply establish a set of rules and incentives (sticks or carrots) through which people will be guided in the "proper" direction. Rather, government becomes another player, albeit an important player in the process of moving society in one direction or another. Government acts, in concert with private and nonprofit groups and organizations, to seek solutions to the problems that communities face. In this process, the role of government is transformed from one of controlling to one of agenda setting, bringing the proper players to the table and facilitating, negotiating, or brokering solutions to public problems (often through coalitions of public, private, and non-profit agencies). Where traditionally government has responded to needs by saying "yes, we can provide that service," or "no, we can't," the New Public Service suggests that elected officials and public managers should respond to the requests of citizens not just by saying yes or no, but by saying: "Let's work together to figure out what we're going to do, then make it happen." In a world of active citizenship, public officials will increasingly play more than a service delivery role—they will play a conciliating, a mediating, or even an adjudicating role. (Incidentally, these new roles will require new skills—not the old skills of management control, but new skills of brokering, negotiating, and conflict resolution.)

2. *The public interest is the aim, not the by-product.* Public administrators must contribute to building a collective, shared notion of the public interest. The goal is not to find quick solutions driven by individual choices. Rather, it is the creation of shared interests and shared responsibility.

The New Public Service demands that the process of establishing a vision for society is not something merely left to elected political leaders or appointed public administrators. Instead, the activity of establishing a vision or direction is something in which widespread public dialogue and deliberation are central (Bryson and Crosby 1992; Luke 1998; Stone 1988) The role of government will increasingly be to bring people together in settings that allow for unconstrained and authentic discourse concerning the direction society should take. Based on these deliberations, a broad-based vision for the community, the state, or the nation can be established and provide a guiding set of ideas (or ideals) for the future. It is less important for this process to result in a

Table 4.1

Comparing Perspectives: Old Public Administration, New Public Management, and New Public Service

	Old public administration	New public management	New public service
Primary theoretical and epistemological foundations	Political theory, social and political commentary augmented by naïve social science	Economic theory, more sophisticated dialogue based on positivist social science	Democratic theory, varied approaches to knowledge including positive, interpretive, critical, and postmodern
Prevailing rationality and associated models of human behavior	Synoptic rationality, "administrative man"	Technical and economic rationality, "economic man," or the self-interested decision maker	Strategic rationality, multiple tests of rationality (political, economic, organizational)
Conception of the public interest	Politically defined and expressed in law	Represents the aggregation of individual interests	Result of a dialogue about shared values
To whom are public servants responsive?	Clients and constituents	Customers	Citizens
Role of government	Rowing (designing and implementing policies focusing on a single, politically defined objective)	Steering (acting as a catalyst to unleash market forces)	Serving (negotiating and brokering interests among citizens and community groups, creating shared values)
Mechanisms for achieving policy objectives	Administering programs through existing government agencies	Creating mechanisms and incentive structures to achieve policy objectives through private and nonprofit agencies	Building coalitions of public, nonprofit, and private agencies to meet mutually agreed upon needs
Approach to accountability	Hierarchical—administrators are responsible to democratically elected political leaders	Market-driven—the accumulation of self-interests will result in outcomes desired by broad groups of citizens (or customers)	Multifaceted—public servants must attend to law, community values, political norms, professional standards, and citizen interests
Administrative discretion	Limited discretion allowed administrative officials	Wide latitude to meet entrepreneurial goals	Discretion needed but constrained and accountable
Assumed organizational structure	Bureaucratic organizations marked by top-down authority within agencies and control or regulation of clients	Decentralized public organizations with primary control remaining within the agency	Collaborative structures with leadership shared internally and externally
Assumed motivational basis of public servants and administrators	Pay and benefits, civil-service protections	Entrepreneurial spirit, ideological desire to reduce size of government	Public service, desire to contribute to society

single set of goals than it is for it to engage administrators, politicians, and citizens in a process of thinking about a desired future for their community and their nation.

In addition to its facilitating role, government also has a moral obligation to assure that the solutions generated through such processes are fully consistent with norms of justice and fairness. Government will act to facilitate the solutions to public problems, but it will also be responsible for assuring those solutions are consistent with the public interest—both in substance and in process. In other words, the role of government will become one of assuring that the public interest predominates, that both the solutions themselves and the process by which solutions to public problems are developed are consistent with democratic norms of justice, fairness, and equity (Ingraham and Ban 1988; Ingraham and Rosenbloom 1989).

In short, the public servant will take an active role in creating arenas in which citizens, through discourse, can articulate shared values and develop a collective sense of the public interest. Rather than simply responding to disparate voices by forming a compromise, public administrators will engage citizens with one another so that they come to understand each other's interests and adopt a longer range and broader sense of community and societal interests.

3. *Think strategically, act democratically.* Policies and programs meeting public needs can be most effectively and responsibly achieved through collective efforts and collaborative processes.

To realize a collective vision, the next step is establishing roles and responsibilities and developing specific action steps to move toward the desired goals. Again, the idea is not merely to establish a vision and then leave the implementation to those in government; rather, it is to join all parties together in the process of carrying out programs that will move in the desired direction. Through involvement in programs of civic education and by developing a broad range of civic leaders, government can stimulate a renewed sense of civic pride and civic responsibility. We expect such a sense of pride and responsibility to evolve into a greater willingness to be involved at many levels, as all parties work together to create opportunities for participation, collaboration, and community.

How might this be done? To begin with, there is an obvious and important role for political leadership—to articulate and encourage a strengthening of citizen responsibility and, in turn, to support groups and individuals involved in building the bonds of community. Government can't create community. But government and, more specifically, political leadership, can lay the groundwork for effective and responsible citizen action. People must come to recognize that government is open and accessible—and that won't happen unless government *is* open and accessible. People must come to recognize that government is responsive—and that won't happen unless government *is* responsive. People must come to recognize that government exists to meet their needs—and that won't happen unless it does. The aim, then, is to make sure that government is open and accessible, that it is responsive, and that it operates to serve citizens and create opportunities for citizenship.

4. *Serve citizens, not customers.* The public interest results from a dialogue about shared values, rather than the aggregation of individual self-interests. Therefore, public servants do not merely respond to the demands of "customers," but focus on building relationships of trust and collaboration with and among citizens.

The New Public Service recognizes that the relationship between government and its citizens is not the same as that between a business and its customers. In the public sector, it is problematic to even determine who the customer is, because government serves more than just the immediate client. Government also serves those who may be waiting for service, those who may need the service even though they are not actively seeking it, future generations of service recipients, relatives and friends of the immediate recipient, and on and on. There may even be customers who don't want to be customers—such as those receiving a speeding ticket.

Moreover, some customers of government have greater resources and greater skill in bringing their demands forward than others. Does this justify, as it would in the private sector, that they be treated better? Of course not. In government, considerations of fairness and equity play an important role in service delivery; indeed, in many cases, these are much more important considerations than the desires of the immediate customer.

Despite the obvious importance of constantly improving the quality of public-sector service delivery, the New Public Service suggests that government should not first or exclusively respond to the selfish, short-term interests of "customers." Instead, it suggests that people acting as citizens must demonstrate their concern for the larger community, their commitment to matters that go beyond short-term interests, and their willingness to assume personal responsibility for what happens in their neighborhoods and the community. After all, these are among the defining elements of effective and responsible citizenship. In turn, government must respond to the needs and interests of citizens. Moreover, government must respond to citizens defined broadly rather than simply in a legalistic sense. Individuals who are not legal citizens not only are often served by government programs, they can also be encouraged to participate and engage with their communities. In any case, the New Public Service seeks to encourage more and more people to fulfill their responsibilities as citizens and for government to be especially sensitive to the voices of citizens.

5. *Accountability isn't simple.* **Public servants should be attentive to more than the market; they should also attend to statutory and constitutional law, community values, political norms, professional standards, and citizen interests.**

The matter of accountability is extremely complex. Yet both the old public administration and the New Public Management tend to oversimplify the issue. For instance in the classic version of the old public administration, public administrators were simply and directly responsible to political officials. As Wilson wrote, "[P]olicy will have no taint of officialism about it. It will not be the creation of permanent officials, but of statesmen whose responsibility to public opinion will be direct and inevitable" (1887, 22). Beyond this, accountability was not really an issue; politicians were expected to make decisions while bureaucrats carried them out. Obviously, over time, public administrators assumed great capacities for influencing the policy process. So, at the other end of the spectrum, in the vernacular of the New Public Management, the focus is on giving administrators great latitude to act as entrepreneurs. In their entrepreneurial role, the new public managers are called to account primarily in terms of efficiency, cost effectiveness, and responsiveness to market forces.

In our view, such models do not reflect the demands and realities of public service today. Rather, public administrators are and should be influenced by and held accountable to complex constellations of institutions and standards, including the public interest, statutory and constitutional law, other agencies, other levels of government, the media, professional standards, community values and standards, situational factors, democratic norms, and of course, citizens. Further, the institutions and standards which influence public servants and to which they are held accountable interact in complex ways. For example, citizen needs and expectations influence public servants, but the actions of public servants also influence citizen expectations. Laws create the parameters for public administrators' actions, but the manner in which public servants apply the law influences not only its actual implementation, but also may influence lawmakers to modify the law. In other words, public administrators influence and are influenced by all of the competing norms, values, and preferences of our complex governance system. These variables not only influence and are influenced by public administrators, they also represent points of accountability.

The New Public Service recognizes the reality and complexity of these responsibilities. It recognizes that public administrators are involved in complex value conflicts in situations of conflicting and overlapping norms. It accepts these realities and speaks to how public administrators can and should serve citizens and the public interest in this context. First and foremost, the New Public Service demands that public administrators not make these decisions alone. It is through the process of dialogue, brokerage, citizen empowerment, and broad-based citizen engagement that these issues must be resolved. While public servants remain responsible for assuring that solutions to public problems are consistent with laws, democratic norms, and other constraints, it is not a matter of their simply judging the appropriateness of community-generated ideas and proposals after the fact. Rather, it is the role of public administrators to make these conflicts and parameters known to citizens, so that these realities become a part of the process of discourse. Doing so not only makes for realistic solutions, it builds citizenship and accountability.

6. *Value people, not just productivity.* Public organizations and the networks in which they participate are more likely to succeed in the long run if they are operated through processes of collaboration and shared leadership based on respect for all people.

In its approach to management and organization, the New Public Service emphasizes the importance of "managing through people." Systems of productivity improvement, process reengineering, and performance measurement are seen as important tools in designing management systems. But the New Public Service suggests that such rational attempts to control human behavior are likely to fail in the long term if, at the same time, insufficient attention is paid to the values and interests of individual members of an organization. Moreover, while these approaches may get results, they do not build responsible, engaged, and civic-minded employees or citizens.

If public servants are expected to treat citizens with respect, they must be treated with respect by those who manage public agencies. In the New Public Service, the enormous challenges and complexities of the work of public administrators are recognized. They are viewed not just as employees who crave the security and structure of a bureaucratic job (old public administration), nor as participants in a market (New Public Management); rather, public servants are people whose motivations and rewards are more than simply a matter of pay or security. They want to make a difference in the lives of others (Denhardt 1993; Perry and Wise 1990; Vinzant 1998).

The notion of shared leadership is critical in providing opportunities for employees and citizens to affirm and act on their public service motives and values. In the New Public Service, shared leadership, collaboration, and empowerment become the norm both inside and outside the organization. Shared leadership focuses on the goals, values, and ideals that the organization and community want to advance; it must be characterized by mutual respect, accommodation, and support. As Burns (1978) would say, leadership exercised by working through and with people transforms the participants and shifts their focus to higher level values. In the process, the public service motives of citizens and employees alike can be recognized, supported, and rewarded.

7. *Value citizenship and public service above entrepreneurship.* The public interest is better advanced by public servants and citizens committed to making meaningful contributions to society rather than by entrepreneurial managers acting as if public money were their own.

The New Public Management encourages public administrators to act and think as entrepreneurs of a business enterprise. This creates a rather narrow view of the objectives to be sought—to maximize productivity and satisfy customers, and to accept risks and to take advantage of opportunities as they arise. In the New Public Service, there is an explicit recognition that public administrators are not the business owners of their agencies and programs. Again, as King and Stivers (1998) remind us, government is owned by the citizens.

Accordingly, in the New Public Service, the mindset of public administrators is that public programs and resources do not belong to them. Rather, public administrators have accepted the responsibility to serve citizens by acting as stewards of public resources (Kass 1990), conservators of public organizations (Terry 1995), facilitators of citizenship and democratic dialogue (Chapin and Denhardt 1995; King and Stivers 1998; Box 1998), catalysts for community engagement (Denhardt and Gray 1998; Lappé and Du Bois 1994), and street-level leaders (Vinzant and Crothers 1998). This is a very different perspective than that of a business owner focused on profit and efficiency. Accordingly, the New Public Service suggests that public administrators must not only share power, work through people, and broker solutions, they must reconceptualize their role in the governance process as responsible participant, not entrepreneur.

This change in the public administrator's role has profound implications for the types of challenges and responsibilities faced by public servants. First, public administrators must know and manage more than the requirements and resources of their programs. This sort of narrow view is not very helpful to a citizen whose world is not conveniently divided up by programmatic departments and offices. The problems that citizens face are often, if not usually, multifaceted, fluid, and dynamic—they do not easily fall within the confines of a particular office or a narrow job description of an individual. To serve citizens, public administrators not only must know and manage their own agency's resources, they must also be aware of and connected to other sources of support and assistance, engaging citizens and the community in the process.

Second, when public administrators take risks, they are not entrepreneurs of their own businesses who can make such decisions knowing the consequences of failure will fall largely on their own shoulders. Risk in the public sector is different. In the New Public Service, risks and opportunities reside within the larger framework of democratic citizenship and shared responsibility. Because the consequences of success and failure are not limited to a single private business, public administrators do not singlehandedly decide what is best for a community. This need not mean that all short-term opportunities are lost. If dialogue and citizen engagement is ongoing, opportunities and potential risks can be explored in a timely manner. The important factor to consider is whether the benefits of a public administrator taking immediate and risky action in response to an opportunity outweighs the costs to trust, collaboration, and the sense of shared responsibility.

IMPLICATIONS AND CONCLUSIONS

From a theoretical perspective, the New Public Service offers an important and viable alternative to both the traditional and the now-dominant managerialist models. It is an alternative that has been built on the basis of theoretical explorations and practical innovations. The result is a normative model, comparable to other such models. While debates among theorists will continue, and administrative practitioners will test and explore new possibilities, the commitments that emerge will have significant implications for practice. The actions that public administrators take will differ markedly depending on the types of assumptions and principles upon which those actions are based. If we assume the responsibility of government is to facilitate individual self-interest, we will take one set of actions. If, on the other hand, we assume the responsibility of government is to promote citizenship, public discourse, and the public interest, we will take an entirely different set of actions.

Decades ago, Herbert Kaufman (1956) suggested that while administrative institutions are organized and operated in pursuit of different values at different times, during the period in which one idea is dominant, others are never totally neglected. Building on this idea, it makes sense to think of one normative model as prevailing at any point in time, with the other (or others) playing a somewhat lesser role *within* the context of the prevailing view. Currently, the New Public Management and its surrogates have been established as the dominant paradigm in the field of governance and public administration. Certainly a concern for democratic citizenship and the public interest has not been fully lost, but rather has been subordinated.

We argue, however, that in a democratic society, a concern for democratic values should be paramount in the way we think about systems of governance. Values such as efficiency and productivity should not be lost, but should be placed in the larger context of democracy, community, and the public interest. In terms of the normative models we examine here, the New Public Service clearly seems most consistent with the basic foundations of democracy in this country and, therefore, provides a framework *within which* other valuable techniques and values, such as the best ideas of the old public administration or the New Public Management, might be played out. While this debate will surely continue for many years, for the time being, the New Public Service provides a rallying point around which we might envision a public service based on and fully integrated with citizen discourse and the public interest.

REFERENCES

Aristigueta, Maria P. 1999. *Managing for Results in State Government.* Westport, CT: Quorum.
Barber, Benjamin. 1984. *Strong Democracy: Participatory Politics for a New Age.* Berkeley, CA: University of California Press.
Barzelay, Michael. 1992. *Breaking through Bureaucracy.* Berkeley, CA: University of California Press.
Bellah, Robert, et al. 1985. *Habits of the Heart.* Berkeley, CA: University of California Press.
———. 1991. *The Good Society.* New York: Knopf.
Boston, Jonathan et al. 1996. *Public Management: The New Zealand Model.* New York: Oxford University Press.
Box, Richard. 1998. *Citizen Governance.* Thousand Oaks, CA: Sage Publications.
Bryson, John, and Barbara Crosby. 1992. *Leadership for the Common Good.* San Francisco, CA: Jossey-Bass.
Burns, James MacGregor. 1978. *Leadership.* New York: Harper and Row.
Carnavale, David. 1995. *Trustworthy Government.* San Francisco, CA: Jossey-Bass.
Carroll, James, and Dahlia Bradshaw Lynn. 1996. The Future of Federal Reinvention: Congressional Perspectives. *Public Administration Review* 56(3): 299–304.
Chapin, Linda W., and Robert B. Denhardt. 1995. Putting "Citizens First!" in Orange County, Florida. *National Civic Review* 84(3): 210–215.
Cook, Brian J. 1996. *Bureaucracy and Self-Government.* Baltimore, MD: Johns Hopkins University Press.
Cooper, Terry. 1991. *An Ethic of Citizenship for Public Administration.* Englewood Cliffs, NJ: Prentice-Hall.
deLeon, Linda, and Robert B. Denhardt. 2000. The Political Theory of Reinvention. *Public Administration Review* 60(2): 89–97.
deLeon, Peter. 1997. *Democracy and the Policy Sciences.* Albany, NY: State University of New York Press.
Denhardt, Robert B. 1981. *In the Shadow of Organization.* Lawrence, KS: Regents Press of Kansas.
———. 1993. *The Pursuit of Significance.* Pacific Grove, CA: Wadsworth.
Denhardt, Robert B., and Joseph E. Gray. 1998. Targeting Community Development in Orange County, Florida. *National Civic Review* 87(3): 227–35.
Denhardt, Robert B., and Janet Vinzant Denhardt. 1999. *Leadership for Change: Case Studies in American Local Government.* Arlington, VA: Price Waterhouse Coopers Endowment for the Business of Government.
Etzioni, Amitai. 1988. *The Moral Dimension.* New York: The Free Press.
———. 1995. *The New Communitarian Thinking.* Charlottesville, VA: University of Virginia Press.
Farmer, John David. 1995. *The Language of Public Administration.* Tuscaloosa, AL: University of Alabama Press.
Fox, Charles. 1996. Reinventing Government as Postmodern Symbolic Politics. *Public Administration Review* 56(3): 256–61.

Fox, Charles, and Hugh Miller. 1995. *Postmodern Public Administration.* Thousand Oaks, CA: Sage Publications.

Frederickson, H. George. 1996. Comparing the Reinventing Government Movement with the New Public Administration. *Public Administration Review* 56(3): 263–9.

———. 1997. *The Spirit of Public Administration.* San Francisco, CA: Jossey-Bass.

Gardner, John. 1991. *Building Community.* Washington, DC: Independent Sector.

Gawthrop, Louis C. 1998. *Public Service and Democracy.* New York: Chandler.

Goodsell, Charles T. 1994. *The Case for Bureaucracy.* Chatham, NJ: Chatham House Publishers.

Gulick, Luther. 1937. Notes on the Theory of Organization. In *Papers on the Science of Administration,* edited by L. Gulick and L. Urwick, 1–46. New York: Institute of Government.

Harmon, Michael. 1981. *Action Theory for Public Administration.* New York: Longman.

———. 1995. *Responsibility as Paradox.* Thousand Oaks, CA: Sage Publications.

Hood, Christopher. 1995. The "New Public Management" in the Eighties. *Accounting, Organization and Society* 20(2/3): 93–109.

Hummel, Ralph. 1994. *The Bureaucratic Experience.* 4th ed. New York: St. Martin's Press.

Ingraham, Patricia W., and Carolyn Ban. 1988. Politics and Merit: Can They Meet in a Public Service Model? *Review of Public Personnel Administration* 8(2): 1–19.

Ingraham, Patricia W., Barbara S. Romzek, and associates. 1994. *New Paradigms for Government.* San Francisco, CA: Jossey-Bass.

Ingraham, Patricia W., and David H. Rosenbloom. 1989. The New Public Personnel and the New Public Service. *Public Administration Review* 49(2): 116–25.

Kaboolian, Linda. 1998. The New Public Management. *Public Administration Review* 58(3): 189–93.

Kamensky, John. 1996. Role of Reinventing Government Movement in Federal Management Reform. *Public Administration Review* 56(3): 247–56.

Kass, Henry. 1990. Stewardship as Fundamental Element in Images of Public Administration. In *Images and Identities in Public Administration,* edited by H. Kass and B. Catron, 113–30. Newbury Park, CA: Sage Publications.

Kaufman, Herbert. 1956. Emerging Conflicts in the Doctrines of Public Administration. *American Political Science Review* 50(4): 1057–73.

Kearns, Kevin, 1996. *Managing for Accountability.* San Francisco, CA: Jossey-Bass.

Kettl, Donald F. 1993. *Sharing Power.* Washington, DC: The Brookings Institution.

Kettl, Donald F., and Jon J. DiIulio, eds. 1995. *Inside the Reinvention Machine.* Washington, DC: The Brookings Institution.

Kettl, Donald F., and H. Brinton Milward, eds. 1996. *The State of Public Management.* Baltimore, MD: Johns Hopkins University Press.

King, Cheryl Simrell, Kathryn M. Feltey, and Bridget O'Neill. 1998. The Question of Participation: Toward Authentic Public Participation in Public Administration. *Public Administration Review.* 58(4): 317–26.

King, Cheryl, and Camilla Stivers. 1998. *Government Is Us: Public Administration in an Anti-government Era.* Thousand Oaks, CA: Sage Publications.

Lappé, Frances Moore, and Paul Martin Du Bois. 1994. *The Quickening of America: Rebuilding Our Nation, Remaking Our Lives.* San Francisco, CA: Jossey-Bass.

Light, Paul. 1997. *The Tides of Reform.* New Haven, CT: Yale University Press.

Luke, Jeffrey. 1998. *Catalytic Leadership.* San Francisco, CA: Jossey-Bass.

Lynn, Lawrence E. 1996. *Public Management as Art, Science, and Profession.* Chatham, NJ: Chatham House.

Mansbridge, Jane, ed. 1990. *Beyond Self-Interest.* Chicago: University of Chicago Press.

———. 1992. Public Spirit in Political Systems. In *Values and Public Policy,* edited by Henry J. Aaron, Thomas Mann, and Timothy Taylor. Washington, DC: The Brookings Institution.

Marini, Frank. 1971. *Toward a New Public Administration.* San Francisco: Chandler.

McCabe, Barbara, and Janet Vinzant. 1999. Governance Lessons: The Case of Charter Schools. *Administration and Society* 31(3): 361–77.

McSwite, O.C. 1997. *Legitimacy in Public Administration.* Thousand Oaks, CA: Sage Publications.

Miller, Hugh, and Charles Fox. 1997. *Postmodern "Reality" and Public Administration.* Burke, VA: Chatelaine Press.

Nelissen, Nico, Marie-Louise Bemelmans-Videc, Arnold Godfroij, and Peter deGoede. 1999. *Renewing Government.* Utrecht, Netherlands: International Books.

Osborne, David, and Ted Gaebler. 1992. *Reinventing Government.* Reading, MA: Addison-Wesley.
Osborne, David, with Peter Plastrik. 1997. *Banishing Bureaucracy.* Reading, MA: Addison-Wesley.
Pateman, Carole. 1970. *Participation and Democratic Theory.* Cambridge, UK: Cambridge University Press.
Perry, James L., ed. 1996. *Handbook of Public Administration.* 2nd ed. San Francisco, CA: Jossey-Bass.
Perry, James L., and Lois Wise. 1990. The Motivational Bases of Public Service. *Public Administration Review* 50(3): 367–73.
Peters, B. Guy, and Donald Savoie. 1996. Managing Incoherence: The Coordination and Empowerment Conundrum. *Public Administration Review* 56(3): 281–9.
Pollitt, Christopher. 1990. *Managerialism and the Public Service.* Cambridge, UK: Basil Blackwell.
Putnam, Robert. 1995. Bowling Alone. *Journal of Democracy* 6(1): 65–78.
Rabin, Jack W., Bartley Hildreth, and Gerald J. Miller, eds. 1998. *Handbook of Public Administration.* 2nd ed. New York: Marcel Dekker.
Rohr, John A. 1998. *Public Service, Ethics and Constitutional Practice.* Lawrence, KS: University Press of Kansas.
Sandel, Michael. 1996. *Democracy's Discontent.* Cambridge, MA: Belknap Press.
Schachter, Hindy Lauer. 1997. *Reinventing Government or Reinventing Ourselves.* Albany, NY: State University of New York Press.
Schubert, Glendon. 1957. "The Public Interest" in Administrative Decision-Making: Theorem, Theosophy, or Theory. *The American Political Science Review* 51(2): 346–68.
Schwartz, N.L. 1988. *The Blue Guitar: Political Representation and Community.* Chicago: University of Chicago Press.
Selznick, Phillip. 1992. *The Moral Commonwealth.* Berkeley, CA: University of California Press.
Stivers, Camilla. 1993. *Gender Images in Public Administration.* Thousand Oaks, CA: Sage Publications.
———. 1994a. Citizenship Ethics in Public Administration. In *Handbook of Administrative Ethics,* edited by Terry Cooper. New York: Marcel Dekker.
———. 1994b. The Listening Bureaucrat. *Public Administration Review* 54(4): 364–9.
Stone, Deborah. 1988. *Policy Paradox and Political Reason.* New York: HarperCollins.
Terry, Larry D. 1993. Why We Should Abandon the Misconceived Quest to Reconcile Public Entrepreneurship with Democracy. *Public Administration Review* 53(4): 393–5.
———. 1995. *Leadership of Public Bureaucracies.* Thousand Oaks, CA: Sage Publications.
———. 1998. Administrative Leadership, Neo-Managerialism, and the Public Management Movement. *Public Administration Review* 58(3): 194–200.
Thomas, John Clayton. 1995. *Public Participation in Public Decisions.* San Francisco, CA: Jossey-Bass.
Vinzant, Janet. 1998. Where Values Collide: Motivation and Role Conflict in Child and Adult Protective Services. *American Review of Public Administration* 28(4): 347–66.
Vinzant, Janet, and Lane Crothers. 1998. *Street-Level Leadership: Discretion and Legitimacy in Front-Line Public Service.* Washington, DC: Georgetown University Press.
Waldo, Dwight. 1948. *The Administrative State.* New York: Ronald Press.
Wamsley, Gary, et al. 1990. *Refounding Public Administration.* Thousand Oaks, CA: Sage Publications.
Wamsley, Gary, and James Wolf. 1996. *Refounding Democratic Public Administration.* Thousand Oaks, CA: Sage Publications.
Wilson, Woodrow. 1887. The Study of Administration. *Political Science Quarterly* 2 (June).
Wolin, Sheldon. 1960. *Politics and Vision.* Boston: Little-Brown.

CHAPTER 5

CITIZENSHIP AND SERVICE DELIVERY
The Promise of Coproduction

CHARLES H. LEVINE

One of the latent functions of the great taxpayer's revolt of 1978 is that it taught and continues to teach students of public administration many lessons. California's Proposition 13, in particular, has had a sobering effect on the theory and practice of public administration.

While many explanations have been offered for the passage of Proposition 13 and similar taxing and spending limits in other states and localities,[1] the rationale developed by Kirlin is one of most persuasive:[2] During the late 1960s and throughout the 1970s, the intricately complex political and administrative structure of the public sector became hopelessly beyond the reach of the average citizen through the traditional formal mechanisms of political participation—voting, parties, and interest groups. Taxing and spending referendums like Proposition 13 gave these alienated people an opportunity to express their frustration on a grand issue of public policy while also allowing them the opportunity to act on their disaffection by becoming "idiots" in the original Greek sense of the word, meaning someone indifferent to his duties as a citizen. If citizens could not understand or effect their government, then limiting it and ignoring it became a rational response.

The linkage between citizens and their government has become strained over the past two decades. At a minimum, citizens function as legitimizers of government "to transform power relations into authority relations."[3] In the United States, this legitimacy has eroded substantially under the strain of Vietnam, Watergate, and a host of factors like urbanization, governmental fragmentation, and rapid spatial mobility.[4] While there is little indication that diffuse support for the values that underpin democratic institutions has eroded significantly, confidence in the institutions of our government and for the people who occupy positions in those institutions has declined dramatically.

The contemporary crisis of public confidence in the institutions and leaders of American society is without parallel in this century. Lipset and Schneider capture the significance of this "confidence gap" in the conclusion of their recent extensive analysis of 45 years of public opinion research:

> Although we have pointed to evidence that Americans retain their faith in their social system,
> it would be wrong not to indicate our belief that the situation is much more brittle than it was

at the end of the 1920s, just before the Great Depression, or in 1965, immediately preceding the unrest occasioned by the Vietnam War and the outbreak of racial tension. These two troubled eras, each of which resulted in a decline of faith in institutions, followed periods of high legitimacy. The United States enters the 1980s, however, with a lower reserve of confidence in the ability of its institutional leaders to deal with the problems of the polity, the society, and the economy than at any time in this century. As a result of the strains produced by the experiences of the last fifteen years, our institutional structure is less resilient than in the past. Should the 1980s be characterized by a major crisis, the outcome could very well be substantial support for movements seeking to change the system in a fundamental way. Serious setbacks in the economy or in foreign policy, accompanied by a failure of leadership, would raise greater risks of a loss of legitimacy now than at any time in this century. Although the evidence on the surface seems reassuring, there are disturbing signs of deep and serious discontent.[5]

The decline in trust and support for public administrators has followed this general trend: in the polls, public employees and public agencies are both held in low regard by the American people. Allegations that bureaucrats are generally lazy, untrustworthy, wasteful, and power hungry are widely accepted as fact. The paradox of this situation is that when citizens are asked to evaluate their concrete experiences with public agencies and public employees, they do so in a much more favorable light.

The explanation for this nearly inverse relationship between what Americans believe about their government's poor performances and the satisfaction they report in their day-to-day dealings with government has been fueled by a popular anti-government myth deeply rooted in our culture. According to Goodsell:

> A myth can be so grand only because it is somehow useful [to the enemies of government]. . . . Bureaucracy as an enemy is very dependable because it is never defeated and hence never disappears—thus never terminating its availability as an enemy. In addition, bureaucracy's imputed association with huge size, impersonalness, and mysterious technology, plus its connection with the sovereign power of the state make it particularly ominous and hence as a target of hatred. . . .

> . . . Americans' habitual suspicion of government and corresponding commitment to capitalism make public bureaucracy particularly exploitable: a bureaucratic America stands as the antithesis of a self-reliant, free, and entrepreneurial America. Unfortunate departures from this romantic vision can be blamed on bureaucracy.[6]

The antipathy toward bureaucracy is so pervasive and deeply rooted in our political culture that we cannot realistically begin any discussion of public administration and citizenship without accepting it as a given and perhaps even as a framework that conditions all possible relationships between citizens and the state in the United States. Within this framework, the strategy of "aggressive professionalism" that has characterized public administration for most of the past two decades must be judged as futile, misguided at best, and downright absurd at worst. Although there are numerous examples of excellence and success, relying on neutral competence as a defense against critics and political spoilsmen by sealing off more and more of the technical core of public agencies merely provides more ammunition for critics who charge public administration with being self-serving and unresponsive. Past attempts to remedy this problem by increasing citizen participation largely failed because of the reluctance of "bureaucrat-professionals" to incorporate "citizen-amateurs" on anything more than a marginal basis in agency operations and policymaking. Such arrangements usually collapsed or simply limped along under the weight of widespread citizen apathy and indifference.[7] As a consequence, in the 1980s we find public agencies and public administrators beleaguered by diffuse hostility in the citizenry, vulnerable to increased tinkering by elected officials, and beset by financial stringency.

FISCAL STRESS AND SERVICE DELIVERY ALTERNATIVES

Fiscal stress is an overlay on the anti-government/bureaucracy framework that conditions the relationship between citizenship and public administration. Combining the two sets of constraints highlights two persistent problems of public administration:

1. How can a government build support for taxation to finance public service when citizens do not trust government to produce appropriate services?
2. And, how can governments provide appropriate services if citizens are unwilling to pay for them through collective mechanisms like taxation?

If the answer to both these questions is "it can't," then we can only expect a starved public sector producing low-quality services. But the situation is more complex than that. Until recently, revenues produced through all sorts of indirect means like intergovernmental grants, income tax "bracket creep," and other "fiscal illusions" have provided revenues even when political support for government has been eroding.[8] By the 1980s, however, taxing and spending limitations, tax cuts, and other devices like tax-indexing have reduced the capacity of these mechanisms to produce funds automatically. The link between public support and resources is now more tightly coupled. As a result, either governments somehow are able to develop a new appreciation for the public provision of services or they must find some other way to provide services. In the solution to this dilemma lies a way out of the problems of building a collective appreciation for the public provision of services and, at the same time, rekindling citizenship, at least in a small way.

In their struggle to cope with fiscal stress, governments have chosen a number of avenues to lighten their financial load. The specific tactics are familiar to those who have concerned themselves with alternative methods of delivering services. They include:

A. Privatizing service delivery
    1. Contracting with a private for-profit firm
    2. Franchising services to a private firm
    3. Vouchers
    4. User fees and charges to ration demand for services
    5. Shedding service responsibility to a private firm or non-profit organization
B. Intergovernmentalizing service delivery arrangements
    1. Shedding services to another unit of government or authority
    2. Sharing service responsibility
    3. Sharing functions like data processing, planning, and communications
C. Improving operating productivity
    1. Methods to monitor performance
    2. Methods to maximize output per dollar
    3. Methods to improve financial decision making

        4.   Methods to track costs

        5.   Methods to monitor and manage contracts

D.   Deprofessionalizing bureaucracies

        1.   Civilianizing sworn personnel

        2.   Using volunteers and paraprofessionals

        3.   Using reserves and auxiliaries

E.   Devolving service responsibility

        1.   Neighborhood organization of service delivery

        2.   Self-help

        3.   Coproduction

        4.   Public/private partnerships to solve community problems.

It is important to recognize that for the most part debates over the value of these alternatives have been conducted almost exclusively on the basis of narrow economic and political criteria; i.e., how much money will be saved and how feasible will they be to implement in a political environment composed of people with strong stakes in the *status quo?*[9] Generally ignored in attempts to evaluate these alternatives are their potential contributions to improving citizenship, including: (1) citizen trust in government; (2) citizen efficacy; and (3) a shared conception of the "common good." In other words, their contributions to resolving the gap between disaffected citizens and their government are disregarded.

At the heart of the citizenship issue is the stake citizens have in their community, its government, and its policies. As Norton Long observed well before our current crisis:

> Perhaps the first task of securing citizenship is the development of the sense of *moi commun.* There have to be citizens who feel responsible and they have to have something to feel responsible for. There must be quite literally a public thing with which they identify and which they are concerned to support. . . . Responsibility for something one takes no active part in is difficult to arouse and maintain.[10]

If we accept Long's notion of responsibility as the key to citizen trust in government, efficacy, and a shared conception of the common good, how do the service delivery alternatives governments are now considering and pursuing stack up? And, just as importantly, how do they contribute to reconciling the growing gap between citizens and public employees?

The most radical of these strategies, *privatizing public services,* gives great glee to those who criticize public agencies for failing to meet market tests of efficiency and responsiveness. They argue that if institutional arrangements for the provision of public services are organized along market lines, the consumers of these services will be better off because they will be receiving goods and services that take advantages of the efficiencies derived from competition.[11] Even where government is a monopoly supplier, it can reap efficiencies through the internal economies derived from the bidding of competitive suppliers. In the ideal world of the privatizers, almost everything government does can be put out for bids from vehicle maintenance in the police department to the actual delivery of patrol and security services. Better yet, from the viewpoint of the advocates of privatization, is the situation where governments merely provide a competitive environment where private firms supply services to consumers either with or without a formal contract. In such an arrangement, a city government, for example, can consist "of three persons: the city manager, the city attorney, and a secretary. Their main job [is] administering the contracts under which the various public services [are] provided."[12]

What is the role of the citizen and citizenship in this model? Put simply, citizens are consumers, buying privatized services just as they would buy any other service provided by the private sector. The rights and duties of a citizen in this arrangement would be restricted to buying services and voting in a government that directly provided few services. The high citizenship of Pericles, Aristotle, and Rousseau that requires citizens to be active members of a self-governing community is excused by the advocates of privatization as irrelevant in an age of rational, self-centered private interests.[13] Indeed, privatization affirms the contemporary view of citizenship as passive and legalistic and also the Lockean notion that government is a machine for the furtherance of one's private interests; civic consciousness and commitment are neither something worthwhile in themselves nor part of a citizen's responsibility.[14] This attitude is wholly consistent with the view of the privatizers that the citizen ought to be a consumer, a voter, and perhaps a member of interest groups, nothing more. Public-spirited action has no place in this scheme.

In a similar vein, *intergovernmentalizing* service delivery adds little to providing a structure to support citizenship. Shedding service responsibility to such arrangements simply makes government more complex and more difficult for citizens to comprehend.[15] And, to the extent that local services are transferred to either higher, larger, or more fragmented units of government like the states or special districts, they are likely to be administered by units of government where local interests have difficulty aggregating their influence and accessing decision makers.

The improvement of *operating productivity* has similar drawbacks from the viewpoint of providing citizens an opportunity and incentive to participate in government. Improving the productivity of government operations usually means tightening decision rules, applying technical rationality, and bounding out environmental turbulence—including politics and citizens. By rationalizing the services of government agencies to the most efficient level possible under monopoly conditions, this approach attempts to replicate the efficiencies of the market without market mechanisms. However, government pursuing the productivity panacea will likely discover that after a few noteworthy gains, diminishing returns will set in fairly rapidly and services are bound to deteriorate as budgets contract. Furthermore, there is no place for citizens in this closed, mechanistic conception of public service delivery, except for their indirect role in setting the levels of services through voting and interest group participation and their direct role as service consumers.

More hope is offered by the other two clusters of alternatives—deprofessionalizing bureaucracies and devolving service responsibility. The growing *deprofessionalization* of public bureaucracies is being caused by the need to reduce the high cost of personnel. Examples include civilianizing positions previously occupied by sworn personnel and the use of paraprofessional, volunteer, part-time, reserve, and auxiliary employees. These tactics contribute to saving money on salaries, fringe benefits, and pension costs.

It should be recognized that deprofessionalization runs counter to the trend toward greater professionalization of public employees through specialized selection, education, training, equipment, and technologies. The development of a professional identity and status for public employees has been a mixed blessing. Although professionalization has allowed public employees to claim a legitimate right to define proper conduct with respect to matters concerned in their work, it has also had a perverse outcome: It has promoted the mystification of public work and, consequently, citizen confusion and alienation. In the case of police, for example, Menke, White, and Carey argue:

> We believe police professionalism has at least two consequences that go to the heart of the principles that underlie our society's form of democratic social organization. These consequences include the mystification of the issues of crime and disorder and mystification of the issue surrounding the right of the state (through its agents) to intervene in the lives of the citizenry.[16]

The ethos of professionalism has become so vital to the defense and legitimization of public organizations, their mission, and their decision rules that even when volunteers, civilians, and reserves are vital to meet demand, or simply to save money, they are usually incorporated into the organization with substantial resistance on the part of the full-time staff. Most often they are segregated into special units and treated as marginal employees so as not to "contaminate the professionalism" of the regular staff. Even where this separation breaks down under the most severe conditions of fiscal stress, it usually occurs with great reluctance on the part of managers and often with substantial concessions granted to unionized employees.

An even more promising development for citizenship is the alternative of *devolving service responsibility* to neighborhood organizations, individual service consumers, and public/private partnerships. Some of these activities can be lumped together under the label of "coproduction"; i.e., the joint provision of public services by public agencies and service consumers. The most common example is the carrying out of garbage to the curb rather than having a collector cart it from behind the house. Other examples include parent participation in the educational process by helping their children with homework and the voluntary organization of recreation programs by participants using facilities provided by a local government. Not only is coproduction widespread in our society, it is becoming more so as budgets (and public employee numbers) decline. As Nathan Glazer recently argued:

> A greater degree of voluntarism and of self-help can do a great deal to provide for needs and services that, if provided through the state, require a heavy burden of taxation, high deficits, and a variety of unpleasant and increasingly dangerous economic developments. Certainly the role of the welfare state is still crucial. But it must more and more ponder partnerships with the variety of voluntary, market, non-statutory organizations and mechanisms that we find in each society. Beyond that, the welfare states must ponder the possibility that their own actions undermine these mechanisms. One thing in any case is clear: the problems the welfare state now confronts—economic, fiscal, social, psychological and political—cannot be dealt with by further growth along the lines of the 1950's and 1960's.[17]

Perhaps the most significant thing about Glazer's observation is that he sees voluntarism, self-help, and coproduction as more than a financial panacea for fiscally strapped governments. Indeed, he sees these arrangements as mechanisms for a more continuous day-to-day involvement of individuals and neighborhoods in government. He argues that in a society that has more widespread affluence and education than ever before, the prospects for the successful devolution of service responsibility to citizens from the state increase, and with it a concomitant improvement in the relationship between the public employee and the citizen as they come to share more service and decision-making responsibility.

But despite these optimistic prospects, voluntarism, self-help, and coproduction arrangements by themselves are no guarantee that overall citizen competence and commitment to the common good will be improved. Activities like taking out the garbage, helping one's child with homework, or even serving on a neighborhood patrol will not by themselves necessarily improve a citizen's desire to take an active part in the community. Nevertheless, they are a potential wedge into improved citizenship that is qualitatively superior to the other four alternatives. For example, the private provision of services cannot possibly lead to better citizens—only smarter consumers—while coproduction lays the foundation for a positive relationship between government and citizens by making citizens an integral part of the service delivery process. Through these experiences citizens may build both competence and a broader perspective, a vision of the community and of what it can and should become. As Sheldon Wolin has observed:

Table 5.1

Service Delivery Arrangements, Strategies, and Citizen Roles

Alternative service delivery arrangements	Dominant strategy	Citizen role
(1) Professionalized bureaucracy	Specialization	Client
(2) Privatized service delivery	Contracting out/user fees	Consumer
(3) Intergovernmentalized service delivery arrangements	Shedding and sharing service responsibility	Client
(4) Improved operating productivity	Maximization of output	Client
(5) Deprofessionalized bureaucracies	Use of paraprofessionals/civilianization	Marginal employee
(6) Devolved service responsibility	Coproduction	Coproducer

The specialized roles assigned the individual, or adopted by him, are not a full substitute for citizenship because citizenship provides what other roles cannot, namely an integrative experience which brings together the multiple role-activities of the contemporary person and demands that the separate roles be surveyed from a more general point of view.[18]

The question remains, however, how does one design a system that builds a sense of community responsibility on the foundation of resident involvement in service delivery when that involvement is predicated on narrow self-interest? Some of the answer is provided in the next section of this paper by looking at an example of one such arrangement, community-based crime prevention groups. Before proceeding, the table above [Table 5.1] of alternative service delivery arrangements, strategies, and citizen roles summarizes the argument so far.

COMMUNITY-BASED CRIME PREVENTION GROUPS

Communities always have been concerned about crime. Where effective law enforcement was not developed, citizens have always found ways of apprehending criminals and preventing crime. Citizen activity in modern law enforcement includes activities which can be performed by individuals or groups with or without the assistance or knowledge of the police. In the 1980s, these activities have become a very important deterrent to criminal activities. Yin argues, for example, that "community efforts, far from being a supplementary resource, may actually be the essence of successful crime prevention activities."[19]

As one might expect, there is a wide variety of citizen activity in crime prevention in the United States today. These activities can be roughly divided according to whether they are performed by individuals or groups.[20] Individual activities involve a number of target hardening activities, such as installing locks and alarms. Group activities include education projects and activities which facilitate reporting.[21] Educational projects are aimed at making the public more knowledgeable about crime. Activities include attempts to encourage witness reporting, group presentation projects, membership projects, and home presentation projects about home security and the reporting of suspicious activities. The theory behind these activities is that just being made aware of the scope and magnitude of crime will motivate people to become more involved in activities associated with bringing about its reduction. Educational activities may or may not be provided by law enforcement personnel and may take place in conjunction with other group activities not directly related to law enforcement.

Activities to facilitate reporting provide a means for residents to actually report any information related to criminal activity. These activities include two basic forms: stationary and active. Examples of stationary activities are whistle-stop projects, radio watch projects, and special telephone line projects. Whistle-stop projects involve a whistle alert system used by witnesses and victims of crime. Radio watch projects use people with access to two-way radios and a dispatcher to make crime reporting easier for individuals. Special telephone line projects facilitate anonymous reporting of criminal activities. Active reporting activities include various building and neighborhood patrol programs.

There are a number of important benefits to be derived from these citizen involvement programs. First, resource constraints can often restrict police to providing only arrest and investigation functions. Citizen involvement can supplement these core functions and, in doing so, can extend their role from crime prevention to the actual provision of law enforcement services as well. Second, if citizen groups provide better crime reporting information and are willing to testify, it becomes easier to bring individuals to trial. Finally, and perhaps most importantly, activities that reduce the opportunity to commit crime have been shown to aid the development of a neighborhood's sense of community.[22]

Despite these benefits, there are also a number of problems associated with citizen crime prevention programs. For example, Yin and his colleagues found that groups were susceptible to vigilante behavior when members were recruited on the basis of social compatibility with other patrol members or when group activity became particularly dull. However, one of their conclusions was that vigilantism was only occasionally present in resident patrols, and vigilante behavior can be dealt with through open membership drives and the development of activities to avoid prolonged boredom.[23]

Another problem is "crime displacement," which may occur when a program is successful in preventing crime in an area. Criminals may then move to an area without as successful a crime prevention program or to an area without any program. Crime displacement can be prevented if all areas of a city, or the country for that matter, implement effective crime prevention programs.

A third problem is that of program maintenance. Pomerleau has observed that "a most significant problem with volunteer citizen groups . . . is the maintenance of enthusiasm and active participation."[24] As an example, one frequently given reason for quitting a crime prevention group is boredom, implying that decreased crime provides little to report and little to do. Maintaining community-based crime prevention projects is, therefore, a serious problem for a community and suggests an important avenue toward the development of responsible citizens.

Getting citizens to participate in an organization in the first place is substantially the same problem as that involved in maintaining that participation over time. Five conditions appear to be minimally necessary for the successful development and maintenance of community-based crime prevention groups: skills, incentives, independence, variety, and cooperation.

Though *skills* are usually recognized as important, they are sometimes passed over lightly because they are so basic. For example, there are several important skills involved in reporting a crime or suspicious activity. First, the observer must be familiar with the area involved (e.g., be able to recognize a neighbor's car). Second, the observer must have a definition of crime or suspicious activity to apply to each situation (e.g., an unfamiliar car or van moving slowly through the neighborhood). Third, the reporter must know where to call. And finally, the observer must be able to provide as much information as is available to the police or group dispatcher (e.g., description, color, and license number of vehicle). The police can be particularly helpful in providing training or training materials related to these reporting skills.

Communications skills, while similar to reporting skills, also include the ability to converse with other group members. Salem found that these skills are usually acquired through previous organizational experiences.[25] If this is the case, the longer an individual is an active member of a group, the more likely the skills that person needs will develop.

Leadership skills allow members to direct the group themselves. Experience has shown that dependence on a single individual as a leader can cause a serious problem if the leader leaves the group.[26] The lack of a replacement may cause the group to disband. While it may be important to have a group leader, it may be even more important that a number of members learn leadership skills. This may be accomplished if leadership roles, e.g., chairing meetings, rotate among members of the group.

Finally, some of the technical skills necessary to community-based crime prevention activities are obvious, e.g., the operation of two-way radios or the selection of security locks, and some are less obvious, e.g., first aid or auto safety. In any case, the police can play an important part in providing this technical know-how and assistance.

Long recognized as important for maintaining group solidarity, *incentives* provide the motivation to participate in group activities.[27] In her analysis of citizen participation, Arnstein has observed that you cannot organize a community without such "deliverables."[28]

Monetary incentives include direct and indirect rewards. Direct monetary incentives include payments for salaries of staff, payments for attending meetings or as awards for other participation, and the reimbursement for expenses, such as gas, phone calls, and postage. Indirect monetary incentives include such things as tax credits for "volunteer work" or free day care for the children of participants during activities.[29]

Feedback, the contact with group members by other members or people outside the group to let members know how well they are doing, is an important source of nonmonetary incentive for maintaining organization. Such things as police reports summarizing calls and the results of those calls or an awards ceremony to recognize outstanding accomplishments are examples of feedback. Praise for a job well done on a day-to-day basis is also an important type of feedback. The importance of the police in providing positive feedback to group members cannot be overstressed. Even the tone of voice of the police dispatcher or the response time of an officer answering a member's report can have an effect on a member's participation.

Independence relates to the actual operations of the program and is not meant to imply that there should be lack of contact with police or a larger neighborhood organization, for example. There are three areas of program operations which relate to independence. First, overdependence on an individual member or group of individuals can cause problems when that individual or group is no longer associated with the program and no one else knows what to do. This would include dependence on professional organizers or the police if they helped organize the program. Second, overdependence on outside financial assistance can cause instability. A program which has come to depend on financial assistance (e.g., employed permanent staff) can be destroyed if that funding is eliminated. Finally, dependence on a single issue or some crisis to keep the group organized can threaten program maintenance. While crime is a great issue for getting people organized, it is a poor one for keeping them organized. Instead, getting people together to get to know each other and then making crime prevention one activity of many the group undertakes likely would be a better mechanism for building and maintaining a crime prevention group than a short-term crime crisis.

Variety of task, membership, and funding also are very important aspects in the maintenance of crime prevention groups. Members from various backgrounds bring different attitudes and experiences which can add to the group and can reduce the likelihood of vigilantism. Similarly, the greater number of activities the group undertakes will enhance the probability of attracting and retaining members. There is a fundamental tradeoff between size and variety, however. While

Table 5.2

Program Failure: Some Causes and Solutions

Causes	Solutions
• reporting inconvenient; takes too much time; don't want to bother police; difficulties with police	• simplify reporting; pamphlets on what to report; limit work hours; support from police, positive attitude
• fear of involvement	• anonymous reporting
• no official recognition; no support from police, neighborhood, members, other organizations	• awards, media coverage, ID cards; faster response times by police; community involvement
• novelty wears off; lost interest; don't think important; nothing to do	• other activities; other affiliations; increased responsibilities; show successes
• it's not my job; that's what police are for	• offer tax credits for participation
• loss of community pride; apathy; not important; not seen as effective; no longer need; loss of police support; no sense of security	• develop community support, sense of community, neighborhood unity; contact members frequently; show success; support of and by policy
• boredom; lost interest	• include other issues; redevelop goals
• members do not have time, money for gas, phones, access, etc.	• seek contributions; decrease amount of work by each member; environmental changes
• not well organized; internal conflict; negative purpose	• other affiliations; simplify activities; develop multipurpose, non-crime activity

a small group is likely to enhance the development of participation and group solidarity, it may die of its own success (e.g., if the threat of crime declines). A wider variety of activities may be necessary to sustain and stabilize the group, but this may cause the size of the group to increase and, subsequently, decrease group solidarity.[30] Somewhere during the process of growth and development a balance between the costs and the benefits of small size and diverse functions will have to be found to maintain long-term group effectiveness and solidarity.[31]

Finally, if funding is necessary, it should be attained from a variety of sources to protect the organization from cutoffs and cutbacks from any one source. Similarly, a group's nonmonetary sources of support, e.g., the media and police professionals, also should vary for the same reasons.

Cooperation is an important factor for program maintenance at several levels: with police; between members; and with other groups and organizations. Cooperation between police and private groups and the idea of sharing responsibilities is especially helpful in avoiding police resistance to a community-based crime prevention effort.[32] Similarly, the composition of the group is likely to be especially critical to fostering cooperation. Neighborhood unity or sense of community is likely to be enhanced as members get to know each other. The convergence of social interaction with shared territory, according to Sundeen, is "likely to contribute to the cohesiveness and solidarity of the community marked by gemeinschaft-like social relations among its members, such as mutual aid, cooperation, and wholistic ties. . . ."[33]

To summarize the issues involved in the organization and maintenance of community-based crime prevention groups, Table 5.2 lists some frequently given causes for program failure and proposes some solutions.[34]

THE PROMISE OF COPRODUCTION

Three questions immediately arise about the feasibility of the coproduction concept. The first concerns the utility of using the examples of community-based crime prevention groups to discuss the linkage between coproduction and citizenship; that is, how generalizable is this example to other services that are not so central to citizens' lives or so crisis prone? Second, what are the equity considerations that likely will arise from such administrative reforms? And, third, how does a narrow citizen-based, service-providing group promote the development of such attributes of citizenship as trust in government, citizen efficacy, and a concern for the common good?

Generalizability

Granted, crime and the fear of criminals are more likely to promote citizen interest and involvement than most any other collective problem. Until recently, the fear of crime was strong enough to encourage a steadily growing supply of funds for personnel and equipment for enhanced police protection in nearly every city in the country. Now with funds tight and crime rates high, citizens have stepped into the breech to provide even more support in the form of service coproducton. But crime is not unique in promoting citizen involvement. Enough examples exist of citizens taking and sharing responsibility for service delivery in areas like education, recreation, and social services to suggest that the phenomenon is widespread and deeply engrained in our civil culture.[35]

The challenge for public administrators and elected officials is to recognize the depth and value of these activities and to develop institutional arrangements that allow them to flourish. Before this occurs, however, there will have to be a change of mindset on the part of most public officials. As Sharp has argued:

> The crucial point about the coproduction concept is that it highlights a different understanding of urban service delivery, and of productivity improvement, from that incorporated in the dominant model [i.e., public administrators produce services, citizens consume them]. Here, the assumption is not that government officials perform for citizens, and therefore bear total responsibility for productivity improvements or the lack thereof; rather, the emphasis is upon service delivery as a joint venture, involving both citizens and government agents.[36]

This change of mindsets will not be an easy transition for most public officials, or for that matter, for most citizens. At first, the coproduction concept will strike cords of an older notion anathema to public officials—"community control." Community control connotes a movement to remove authority from professionals and give it to neighborhood-based organizations and, with it, control over public agencies. Insofar as the advocates of coproduction promise to produce these results, they cannot expect to be met with anything other than fierce resistance by public officials who guard their authority jealously. A more moderate—and politically feasible—version of production involves sharing responsibility and authority in service delivery arrangements where the basic authority of public officials over the definition of what constitutes professional staff responsibility is protected and citizen groups work with officials to tailor services to neighborhood needs.

Equity

Coproduction has obvious implications for the equitable distribution of government burdens and benefits. By getting citizens to share some of the burden (in time, money, and effort) of delivering and receiving services, demand for services is likely to decline and along with it, cost. However, where agencies and neighborhoods compete for fair shares of a city's budget and services, there may be resistance to neighborhood assumption of coproduction responsibilities on the grounds that it constitutes a form of double taxation. This is especially likely to occur in communities where some neighborhoods are involved in coproduction and others are not.

The equity problem also can be compounded by social and economic stratification. As Rosentraub and Sharp observe:

> Wealthier, better-educated, or nonminority citizens may be more willing to engage in coproduction activities. To the extent that coproduction raises the quality of services received, it may exacerbate gaps between the advantaged and disadvantaged classes.[37]

Obviously, the capacity of the people in a neighborhood to carry the costs of assuming a greater proportion of service delivery responsibility will be an important consideration in achieving viable coproduction arrangements. When inequities in burdens and benefits are too great in a community, coproduction likely will fail as a means of delivering adequate services. If such serious inequality problems arise, the classic centralization/decentralization cycle described by Herbert Kaufman will occur:

> Decentralization will soon be followed by disparities in practices among the numerous small units, brought on by differences in human and financial resources, that will engender demands for central intervention to restore equality and balance and concerted action.[38]

Bridges to Citizenship

The answer to the question of how well coproduction arrangements serve to help revitalize citizenship lies in the strength of the bridge between government and citizens. At a minimum, such a bridge needs three strands: innovation, participation, and loyalty.

Successful coproduction must involve experimentation and *innovation* in the methods used for making decisions and delivering services. For such an arrangement to work best, a community has to develop a supporting structure for an "experimenting policy"; i.e., a political and administrative climate where citizens, public employees, and public officials are willing to try new methods of delivering traditional public services. Without these innovations, governments are likely to fall back on the limited strategy of trying to tighten their traditional methods of delivering services in order to improve productivity. Experimentation, on the other hand, promotes "learning by doing," where both citizens and public employees learn more about services—and one another—by participating in joint problem solving and service delivery efforts.[39] In such settings, a process of mutual adjustment occurs. According to Whitaker, both the citizen and the public administrator "share responsibility for deciding what action to take. Moreover, each accords legitimacy to the responsibility of the other. The citizen coproducer is not a 'client' in the sense that he or she is not a supplicant seeking the favor of the agency."[40]

This kind of relationship stands at odds with the traditional inclination of public administrators to keep the *participation* of citizens in agency operations at arms length. The warning should be clear: If the use of citizens in service delivery is treated as a marginal activity by public agencies, then we should not expect coproduction to be a very effective instrument for improving the competence or commitment of citizens. In contrast, if agencies can find ways of integrating citizens in their core decision making and service delivery procedures, the likelihood of building lasting attachments will improve. In such cases, the knowledge of citizens about services and service costs will expand; the responsiveness, respect, and appreciation of citizens and professionals to one another will grow; and at least a marginal improvement in citizens' commitment to their community will occur. At a minimum, such changes promise to contribute to arresting the serious erosion of popular support for the institutions of government and their leaders.

The final critical strand in the bridge between coproduction and citizenship is the capacity of a service delivery arrangement to build in citizens a *loyalty* to place, neighbors, and their community. Loyalty develops through face-to-face contact and an investment of energy in the improvement of neighborhoods and communities. Volunteer programs like "adopt a park," "friends of the library," and citizen patrols cannot help but contribute to building loyalty. "Sweat equity" in producing a service or maintaining a physical space promises to build commitment and a more cohesive view of the neighborhood and citizens' role in it.

In sum, the prospects for enhanced citizenship through citizen participation in coproduction arrangements are generally favorable. Where the conditions for coproduction are most favorable (e.g., in homogeneous communities with residential propinquity), we can expect it to flourish—and citizenship to grow. Where conditions are less favorable (e.g., highly stratified communities with scattered housing), other avenues will have to be found to promote *civitas*.[41]

CONCLUSION

Those who believe that citizenship, civic virtue, and "public service" should be an important part of our national culture should be distressed that these features of democracy have come to be regarded as mere myths in a polity that increasingly rewards narrow self-interest. Even those who accept this condition as a natural outgrowth of the characteristics of modern life should be disturbed by our failure to reconcile the growing gap between the roles of citizens and public employees.

For those who wish a more communitarian arrangement of their civic life, coproduction promises a beginning that can be built upon, once working with public employees and with neighbors becomes habitual and an integral part of everyday life. Once this occurs, the prospects for a revitalization of a communitarian spirit rise as they experience the satisfaction of jointly solving problems.

For the public administrator, the lessons are clear: The strategy of coproduction promises to be a powerful tool for resolving fiscal stress and an auspicious start on the road to restoring the trust and support of citizens for their public institutions.

ACKNOWLEDGMENT

I wish to acknowledge the assistance of Barbara H. Seekins, a graduate student at the University of Kansas, and the thoughtful comments on an earlier draft of this paper by Glenn Fisher of Wichita State University and Paul Schumaker and Elaine B. Sharp of the University of Kansas.

NOTES

1. See David O. Sears and Jack Citrin, *Tax Revolt: Something for Nothing in California* (Cambridge, Mass.: Harvard University Press, 1983), especially ch. 3.

2. See John J. Kirlin, *The Political Economy of Fiscal Limits* (Lexington, Mass.: D.C. Health, 1982), p. 10 and ch. 6.

3. Robert A. Dahl, *Who Governs? Democracy and Power in an American City* (New Haven, Conn.: Yale University Press, 1961), p. 133.

4. See Richard Dagger, "Metropolis, Memory and Citizenship," *American Journal of Political Science,* vol. 25, no. 4 (November 1981), pp. 715–737.

5. Seymour Martin Lipset and William Schneider, *Confidence Gap: Business, Labor, and Government in the Public Mind* (New York: The Free Press, 1983), pp. 411–412.

6. Charles T. Goodsell, *The Case for Bureaucracy: A Public Administration Polemic* (Chatham, N.J.: Chatham House Publishers, 1983), pp. 144–146.

7. See Advisory Commission on Intergovernmental Relations, *Citizen Participation in the American Federal System* (Washington, D.C.: U.S. Government Printing Office, 1979).

8. See John Shannon, "The Great Slowdown in State and Local Spending in the United States: 1976–1984" (Washington, D.C.: Advisory Commission on Intergovernmental Relations, 1981).

9. See, for example Robert Poole, Jr., "Objections to Privatization," *Policy Review,* no. 24 (Spring 1983), pp. 105–119; and Martha A. Shulman, "Alternative Approaches for Delivering Public Services," *Urban Data Service Reports,* vol. 14, no. 10 (Washington, D.C.: International City Management Association, October 1982).

10. Norton E. Long, "An Institutional Framework for the Development of Responsible Citizenship," in Charles Press, ed., *The Polity* (Chicago: Rand McNally, 1962), p. 184.

11. See E.S. Savas, *Privatizing the Public Sector: How to Shrink Government* (Chatham, N.J.: Chatham House, 1982).

12. Robert W. Poole, Jr., *Cutting Back City Hall* (New York: Universe Books, 1980). p. 194.

13. See Richard Flathman, "Citizenship and Authority: A Chastened View of Citizenship," *News for Teachers of Political Science,* no. 30 (Summer 1981), pp. 9–19.

14. See Michael Walzer, *Obligations: Essays on Disobedience, War and Citizenship* (New York: Simon and Schuster, 1971); and C.B. Macpherson, *The Life and Times of Liberal Democracy* (Oxford, England: Oxford University Press, 1977).

15. See Edward K. Hamilton, "On Non-Constitutional Management of a Constitutional Problem," *Daedalus,* vol. 107 (1978), pp. 111–128.

16. Ben A. Menke, Mervin F. White, and William L. Carey, "Police Professionalization: Pursuit of Excellence or Political Power," in Jack R. Greene, ed., *Managing Police Work: Issues and Analysis* (Beverly Hills, Calif.: Sage Publications, 1982), p. 98.

17. Nathan Glazer, "Toward a Self-Service Society?" *The Public Interest,* no. 70 (Winter 1983), pp. 89–90.

18. Sheldon Wolin, *Politics and Vision: Continuity and Innovation in Western Political Thought* (Boston: Little, Brown, 1960), p. 434.

19. Cited in J. T. Duncan, *Citizen Crime Prevention Tactics: A Literature Review and Selected Bibliography* (Washington, D.C.: U.S. Government Printing Office, 1980), p. 4.

20. For discussion of this approach see: Frances E. Pennell, "Collective vs. Private Strategies for Coping with Crime: The Consequences for Citizen Perceptions of Crime, Attitudes Toward the Police and Neighboring Activity," *Journal of Voluntary Action Research,* vol. 7, nos. 1–2 (1978), pp. 59–74; Stephen L. Percy, "Conceptualizing and Measuring Citizen Co-Production of Community Safety," *Policy Studies Journal,* vol. 7 (1978), pp. 486–493; and Richard R. Rich, "Voluntary Action and Public Services: An Introduction to the Special Issue," *Journal of Voluntary Action Research,* vol. 7, nos. 1–2 (1978), pp. 4–14.

21. See L. Bickman, P.J. Lavrakas, S.K. Green, N. North-Walker, J. Edwards, S. Borkowski, S. Shane-Dubois, and J. Wuerth, *Citizen Crime Reporting Projects—National Evaluation Program—Phase I Summary Report* (Washington, D.C.: National Institute of Justice, 1976).

22. See, for example, George J. Washnis, *Citizen Involvement in Crime Prevention* (Lexington, Mass.: D.C. Heath, 1976).

23. R.K. Yin, M.E. Vogel, J.M. Chaiken, and D.R. Both, *Patrolling the Neighborhood Beat: Residents and Residential Security* (Santa Monica, Calif.: Rand, 1976).

24. Donald D. Pomerleau, "Crime Prevention," in Bernard L. Garmire, ed., *Local Government Police Management* (Washington, D.C.: International City Management Association, 1977), p. 261.

25. Greta W. Salem, "Maintaining Participation in Community Organizations," *Journal of Voluntary Action Research,* vol. 7, nos. 3–4 (1978), pp. 18–27.

26. See Howard W. Hallman, *Neighborhood Control of Public Programs* (New York: Praeger, 1970).

27. See, for example, James Q. Wilson, *Political Organizations* (New York: Basic Books, 1973), especially ch. 3.

28. Sherry Arnstein, "Maximum Feasible Manipulation," *Public Administration Review,* vol. 32 (September 1972), pp. 377–390.

29. See G.T. Marx and D. Archer, "Citizen Involvement in the Law Enforcement Process," *American Behavioral Scientist,* vol. 15, no. 1 (1971), pp. 52–72.

30. See R. Nanett, "From the Top Down: Government Promoted Citizen Participation," *Journal of Voluntary Action Research,* vol. 9, nos. 1–4 (1980), pp. 149–162.

31. For more on this problem, see Mancur Olson, Jr., *The Logic of Collective Action* (Cambridge, Mass.: Harvard University Press, 1965).

32. See Mark H. Moore and George L. Kelling, "To Serve and Protect: Learning from Police History," *The Public Interest,* no. 70 (Winter 1983), pp. 66–90.

33. Richard A. Sundeen, "Coproduction and Communities: Implications for Local Administrators," unpublished paper, School of Public Administration, University of Southern California, Los Angeles, Calif., 1982; see also Fred Dubow and Aaron Podolefsky, "Citizen Participation in Community Crime Prevention," *Human Organization,* vol. 41, no. 4 (Winter 1982).

34. An earlier version of this table was developed in Barbara H. Seekins, "Maintaining Community-Based Citizen Crime Prevention Groups," field project report, M.P.A. program, University of Kansas, Lawrence, Kan., 1975, p. 28.

35. See Gordon P. Whitaker, "Coproduction: Citizen Participation in Service Delivery," *Public Administration Review,* vol. 40, no. 3 (May/June 1980), pp. 240–246.

36. Elaine B. Sharp, "Toward a New Understanding of Urban Services and Citizen Participation: The Coproduction Concept," *Midwest Review of Public Administration,* vol. 14, no. 2 (June 1980), p. 111.

37. Mark S. Rosentraub and Elaine B. Sharp, "Consumers as Producers of Social Services: Coproduction and the Level of Social Services," *Southern Review of Public Administration,* vol. 4 (March 1981), p. 517; see also Jeffrey L. Brudney and Robert E. England, "Toward a Definition of the Coproduction Concept," *Public Administration Review,* vol. 43, no. 1 (January/February 1983), pp. 59–65.

38. Herbert Kaufman, "Administrative Decentralization and Political Power," *Public Administration Review,* vol. 29, no. 1 (January/February 1969), p. 11.

39. See John Dewey, *Logic: The Theory of Inquiry* (New York: Henry Holt and Co., 1938).

40. Whitaker, "Coproduction," p. 244.

41. For a discussion of the civic education route to citizenship, see H. George Frederickson, "The Recovery of Civicism in Public Administration," *Public Administration Review,* vol. 42, no. 6 (November/December 1982), pp. 501–508.

CHAPTER 6

REINVENTING GOVERNMENT
OR REINVENTING OURSELVES
Two Models for Improving Government Performance

HINDY LAUER SCHACHTER

In this article, I analyze the Bureau of Municipal Research's concept of efficient citizenship as an alternative paradigm to customer-centered public administration. Reinventing government is a powerful buzz phrase these days both in the world of practical politics and academe. (The term emanates from Osborne and Gaebler [1992] and appears in the much-discussed National Performance Review report, *From Red Tape to Results* [Executive Office of the President, 1993], and in Gore [1994]). The aim is a political change to make government work better and cost less (Executive Office of the President, 1993). The strategy is "a new customer service contract" (Executive Office of the President, 1993; i) where administrators give taxpayers the same responsiveness and consideration businesses supposedly give customers.

Frederickson (1994) criticizes the customer-centered model of change for using the wrong metaphor. He argues that citizens are not the customers of government; they are its owners who elect leaders to represent their interests. A customer-centered model puts citizens in a reactive role limited to liking or disliking services and hoping that the administrators will change delivery if enough customers object. Owners play a proactive role; they decide what the government's agenda will be.

Before we accept a customer-centered model, it would be useful to compare it with one that envisions the citizen as owner. This allows us to see if a different way of looking at citizen roles leads to new emphasis on the kind of changes that are necessary to improve government performance. Unfortunately, the major contemporary reform prescriptions tend not to elaborate owner metaphors. Although DiIulio, Garvey, and Kettl called their 1993 book *Improving Government Performance: An Owner's Manual,* the bulk of their analysis hinges on the customer model.

An intriguing variant on the owner model emerged from the New York Bureau of Municipal Research (BMR), a progressive organization incorporated in 1907 to help solve urban political

From *Public Administration Review,* 55, 6 (November/December 1995): 530–537. Copyright © 1995 by American Society for Public Administration. Reprinted with permission.

problems. (For its history, see Dahlberg, 1966.) Its concept of efficient citizenship posited that urban citizens owned their government and as owners had a duty to get involved in city affairs and instruct politicians and public administrators in "shareholder" demands. The implications of this concept emerge from studying the writings of the bureau's founders and from analyzing the organization's miscellaneous publications that appeared under the heading, *Efficient Citizenship* (1908–1913).

The bureau model does not address all of the problems that have been raised in relation to the reinventing government scenario. Another type of analysis would be needed to determine whether the Osborne and Gaebler model undermines bureaucratic accountability to legislatures as suggested by Moe (1994) and Rosenbloom (1993).

Exploring the bureau model is useful for critiquing the scenario's proposed relationship between agencies and the public. It helps modern administrators in two ways. First, the bureau's ideal citizen role contrasts with that offered in Osborne and Gaebler (1992), which models bureaucratic reform on a paradigm of the citizen as customer of public services. Comparing the currently much-debated customer model with the bureau's idea of the citizens as owners shows that the earlier concept provided a more expansive public role and identifies strategies for producing citizens who want to act like owners.

Second, this exercise provides a good example of how historical ideas can illuminate modern issues by throwing a different light on them. While early urban administration and politics textbooks stress the importance of the efficient citizenship concept (e.g., Rowe, 1908; Munro, 1915; and Capes, 1922), the post-World War II literature almost never mentions this metaphor. Examining the bureau's work shows what can be lost by neglecting old ideas—a loss that exists even though most modern readers are likely to find the older literature somewhat naive in its authors' expectations from the average citizen. The point of exploring the model is not to get a contemporary audience to buy the bureau's package in toto, but rather to show a different insight on the relationship between citizens and administrators and how this point of view might contribute to improving government performance.

Several analyses of Progressivism (e.g., Schiesl, 1977; Wiebe, 1967) suggest it was a middle-class movement that tried to diminish the political role of the poor. Because the bureau is associated with the Progressive cause, some people may think it perverse to use the concept of efficient citizenship to argue for a more expansive citizen role. It is important, therefore, to realize that in the 1906–1914 era, bureau leaders often took political stands that opposed what the modern public administration community considers typical Progressive reforms when these recommendations substituted elite decision making for policy determined through normal municipal channels. The bureau insisted that decisions about urban utilities and transportation should be made through city elections rather than by state public service commissions (Bruere, 1908). It favored large, heterogeneous, activist big-city school boards appointed by the mayor rather than small, elite boards that delegated extensively to professional superintendents (Flexner, 1914; 23–24).

As Mosher (1968; 75) notes, the organization had a dual drive to democracy and efficiency. Although, in practice, middle-class people were the prime audience for the bureau's message (as they are the prime audience for books on reinventing government), the BMR writers intended the owner metaphor to apply to every citizen—rich or poor, WASP or ethnic (Allen, 1917; 34–35). The concept is investigated in this article in the expansive mood in which it was conceived.

In this article, I orient the reader by describing the formation of the BMR and the scope of its activities until 1915. I analyze the concept of efficient citizenship and compare the citizen-owner and citizen-customer models.

THE BUREAU OF MUNICIPAL RESEARCH

In 1906, Dr. William H. Allen, general agent for the Association for Improving the Condition of the Poor (AICP), persuaded a group of New York philanthropists, including Andrew Carnegie, R. Fulton Cutting, and John D. Rockefeller, to fund a bureau to develop and disseminate information on city government performance. Cutting, who became the first president of the bureau's board of trustees, asked Allen, Henry Bruere, and Frederick A. Cleveland to serve as co-directors; the three men shared a background as professionals who originally hailed from the Midwest and then received an Ivy League education, at least at the graduate level (Allen, 1949/1950).

Allen held a 1900 Ph.D. from the University of Pennsylvania and had social work experience with the New Jersey state charities Aid Association and the AICP. Henry Bruere had studied economics at the University of Chicago and law at Harvard; he worked under Allen at the AICP for a year before becoming director of the Bureau of City Betterment, a temporary research bureau funded by Cutting during 1906. Cleveland received an 1897 Ph.D. at the University of Pennsylvania, where he met Allen; he had served as a member of the mayor's advisory commission on finance and taxation in January 1905.

Allen (1949/1950; vol. I; 99–100) noted in his memoirs that

> the key idea in starting continuous municipal research was that attacking men as criminals and looking for crime in government . . . gave little if any protection at all to the public. If there really was to be better government, the public must know how governing was done and must help those in power use better methods.

The BMR stressed the importance of establishing standards for city activities so manifestations of worth could be measured against an ideal rather than what might be the incompetence of an average area's performance. Bureau-sponsored studies in New York City resulted in notable administrative changes, including establishment of new accounting methods, reorganization of the Bureau of Water Revenue (increasing collection of water rates by over $2 million a year), and the opening of a child hygiene section in the health department (Gulick, 1928). Many bureau studies focused on helping city agencies improve their internal record keeping.

Beginning in 1909, the bureau also did studies for other local governments and for nonprofit organizations. In 1911, the bureau opened a training school to prepare public management specialists.

The period when the Allen-Bruere-Cleveland triumvirate worked together at the bureau was short. In September 1910, Cleveland took a temporary leave of absence to head President William Howard Taft's Commission on Economy and Efficiency, so there was a hiatus in his bureau service. In January 1914, Bruere left the BMR to serve as chamberlain in the reform administration of New York City Mayor John Purroy Mitchel, leaving Allen and Cleveland as co-directors. Allen resigned in September 1914, and after this date, the efficient citizenship concept was no longer central to the bureau's work. Cleveland left in 1917.

CITIZENS AS OWNERS

In books and articles from the 1906–1914 period, Allen, Bruere, and Cleveland stressed the importance of an active citizenry in spearheading administrative improvement. As a rationale for an enhanced public role, they hit on the metaphor of citizens as owner-shareholders in city corporations and argued that any enterprise needs the careful attention of the proprietor (See, for example, Bruere, 1912a; and Cleveland, 1909 and 1913; 99–112).

In 1909, Cleveland urged New York's citizens to mind their own business—the public business. "In your city," he wrote, "is a great water-producing enterprise. You as citizens pay this water revenue. You, as citizens, have furnished this capital. . . . This is *your* business. Are you *minding your business?*" (pp. 346–347).

Owners with an expectation of improvement, owners willing to work for change, this was the only way to get more efficient city government (e.g., Cleveland, 1913; 454; Bruere, 1912a; 107). Such owners would emerge when the public had information about what the city did and how improved structures or procedures increase accomplishments. Information would produce a movement that would express citizen (rather than official) initiative.

The bureau writers bemoaned the fact that in their era most people got their city-performance information from personal observation, newspapers (which stressed scandals), and a few poorly written government reports (Bruere, 1912a; 121). With these sources, few citizens knew if they were paying too much or too little for street paving, or if they were getting the best milk inspection procedures for lowering infant mortality. The way to get citizens to accept their ownership role was to make more information available to them in a form they could actually use.

The BMR proposed to increase publicly available information in three ways. First, it used common law and statutory right to gain access to public records and make their data available in easy-to-comprehend form, along with analysis on how procedural or structural change might enhance agency performance. Second, it prodded the city to keep clearer, more complete records. Third, it urged citizens to collect information on their own.

A theme that ran through much bureau work was the city's obligation to prepare reports that were useful to a broad range of citizens. Cleveland (1909; 268–275) criticized the fifth annual report of New York City's superintendent of schools for neglecting summary tables and information on evening, vacation, and special classes (information that would have been particularly useful to the poor). Allen (1909) complained that officials obfuscated because they believed the general public had no interest in their reports; he showed people how to read the data that were provided and make comparisons across jurisdictions (Snedden and Allen, 1908).

The assumption was that citizen-owners had the duty to assume an active responsibility for improving government, along with a perfect right to inquire into the affairs of their agents (the public administrators) at any time. Both Bruere and Allen suggested specific ways that citizens might exercise oversight.

In *New City Government* (Bruere, 1912a; 288–290), Bruere tells people how to test police efficiency. They should prepare a precinct map, list the regulations the police are supposed to enforce in the precinct, and note patent violations. They should examine police records to see what the agency had done about such violations, record any arrests made, and trace 200–500 cases through the courts. They should make unannounced visits to police posts to see what the officers are doing (as owners check on their workers) and analyze any complaints that other citizens have made to the precinct. Allen (1909; 29) calls for volunteers to fill out scorecards comparing ventilation, play space, toilets, and so forth in streets and schools in rich and poor neighborhoods.

A BMR bulletin suggested that readers use their vacation time to compare urban services (e.g., police courtesy, street cleanup) in New York and their destination city. When they returned, they could let New York's administrators know about strategies that seem to work elsewhere (*Municipal Research,* 1914).

Both Allen and Bruere insisted that schools must teach children to be efficient citizens. Allen (1917; 50–51) commended a Brooklyn principal who asked students to report why they liked or disliked a particular classroom innovation. The principal collected the information, gave the children feedback on what their classmates reported, and then asked them to suggest ways of making the innovation work, thus giving them practice in analyzing public-sector problems. Allen (1917; 77) also suggested that pupils should learn to get involved in housing issues by going to tenements, noting violations, and reporting them to the authorities; they would become interested in sanitation issues by reporting street-cleaning violations.

Bruere (1912a; 122) wanted children to learn how to read and analyze agency reports and answer questions on health department efficiency based on infant mortality rates or the bacteria count in milk. With such training, people could enter into a life dedicated to municipal improvement.

The bureau's ideas on citizen initiative dominated a series of miscellaneous publications that it produced and mailed to business, professional, and labor organizations under the rubric *Efficient Citizenship* (1908–1913). The first components of this series were postcards, but soon the missives included pamphlets and circulars as well. In his memoirs, Allen (1949/1950; vol. I; 161) noted that he never sent the material in envelopes because he wanted the contents to entice readers.

A few examples give the flavor of the postcards. Publication no. 1 stressed that bureau work was practical and oriented toward bringing city agency techniques up-to-date. No. 45 reminded people that the commissioner of accounts was trying to pinpoint responsibility for defective fire hoses; citizens could bring information to him. No. 143 informed people that the Board of Education's finance committee had recently published a report. Under the title "Plenty of Time to Study the Budget," No. 163 noted when the Board of Estimate and Apportionment would hold public budget hearings, an innovation for which the bureau had fought. No. 495 showed an unclear table on infant mortality produced by a New York City agency and urged people to write the surgeon general in Washington to spearhead a drive for clear, comparative reports on health activities.

An early pamphlet discussed BMR recommendations to improve recordkeeping and promptness in investigating complaints at New York City's Tenement House Department. At least two pamphlets (nos. 386 and 416) compared nonpromotion policies in different school districts. A constant theme was letting people know how they could get public sector information and share their opinions with politicians and administrators. A 1913 pamphlet made the reason for this information exchange clear: "The citizen shirks a large duty if he evades his part of the responsibility for efficient . . . work" (*Municipal Research,* December 1913; 4).

THE ROLE OF THE POOR

One question that can be asked about efficient citizenship is, How inclusive was the concept? Allen (1917; 35) argued that rich and poor were under the same obligation to serve as efficient citizens. He urged everyone to get involved because the city needed all its people. He wanted the parents of poor children to get active in monitoring how New York City's education system treated their children.

Yet, the reality was that bureau activities tended to involve middle-class people. Allen (1907; 198–199) acknowledged as much in one of his most dramatic indictments of injustice when he told his readers to ask themselves:

> Am I doing things which would be considered crimes or misdemeanors if done by residents of the slums? Am I indifferent to wrongs committed by the government? Am I infinitely more interested in suppressing flagrant vice than in preventing flagrant injustice?

Here Allen separated his readers from the slum dweller and urged them to consider whether their acts would not be considered crimes if committed by a poor person. The author admitted that he was talking to people who care about the poor rather than to the poor themselves.

The bureau tried to increase worker participation in politics. It successfully campaigned to hold certain borough board meetings at night to allow more people to come (*Municipal Research,* October 1913). It included unions (as well as business and professional groups) in its "Help-Your-City" campaign where it asked organizations to collect suggestions on government improvement and send them to the BMR (*Municipal Research,* November 1913). Allen considered it disastrous that Mayor Mitchel did not appoint people who were broadly representative of New York's entire electorate (Amberg and Allen, 1921).

Yet the harsh economic demands on a laborer's time precluded most blue-collar workers from becoming involved in the BMR's drive for more citizen concern. Even most business people and professionals lacked the hours or interest to immerse themselves in improving their cities in a time-demanding way.

ANALYSIS

Proponents of reinventing government and efficient citizenship both advocate more efficient and responsive government. Their models use different strategies for reaching these goals because the contemporary model views the public as customers (who react to what a company offers) while the older construct gives the public a proactive role.

To spur change, both sets of reformers use business-world metaphors assuming that private-enterprise efficiency has positive connotations for their audiences. But this practice leaves both models vulnerable to the charge of glossing over important differences between business and government.

Legal rights of possession distinguish business owners who have unique economic rights in the enterprise. (Unlike other stakeholders, they can sell it.) These owners also have the authority to direct the organization's course.

The most fundamental difference between business and citizen ownership relates to economic rights. When ownership is used as a political metaphor, no attention is paid to its pecuniary implications. The bureau writers understood that people do not buy American citizenship or sell it at a profit. The metaphor is clearly intended to relate only to the aspect of ultimate control. The Constitution says that we the people established the central legal document ordaining the government; we the people should have a concern for directing the course of this enterprise.

An assumption that private sector ownership translates into control founders on the difficulties real-world owners have directing their businesses. The owners who invest maximum energy in and make ultimate decisions for enterprises tend to be sole proprietors. Most corporate shareholders have little interest in controlling the companies in which they invest money; they have inadequate time, information, and expertise to get involved in decision making. These shareholders are better models of passive ownership than of active decision making.

Citizen owners have more in common with corporate shareholders than with sole proprietors. Both citizens and shareholders form large, variegated bodies of people who are often ignorant of the identity of their fellow owners and have difficulties coordinating any attempt at control. Because the mass of shareholders and citizens lack time, information, and interest to direct the enterprise over which they have ultimate rights in theory, the ownership metaphor may actually be more useful at explaining why few citizens get involved than in giving them a rationale to do so.

The customer metaphor is equally flawed. In the private market, customers choose among products and services. Although they may not like the range of items businesses offer, they tend to enter transactions voluntarily and prefer getting the car or haircut they purchase to having no car or haircut at all.

Many public agency clients would prefer to have no contact with the bureaucracy. This category of involuntary customer probably contains the owners and managers of many regulated enterprises. It includes most criminal-justice clients (e.g., defendants at trial, prisoners, people on probation or parole). It may well even include some people getting economic benefits from the government (e.g., those on Social Security who would have preferred to invest their retirement funds on their own). Can we use the term customer to refer to people who do not want the services legislation ordains for them?

In addition, strong conflicts of interest exist among people interacting with a given public agency, making it difficult for many departments to identify who their customers are and how they can satisfy customer needs. If food inspection is a bureau's function, who is the agency's customer—Tina, a restaurant owner, or Tom, a consumer of restaurant meals? Tom and Tina may have different definitions of responsive service.

Light (1994) argues that this problem is particularly evident for organizations with stewardship obligations. The Environmental Protection Agency and the Forest Service are supposed to serve one set of clients today while protecting another in the future. The more assiduously these organizations cultivate today's customers, the weaker may be their performance of their stewardship duties.

In the same way that the ownership model scants differences between the control exercised by sole proprietors and corporate shareholders, the customer scenario neglects variations in the treatment clients receive from large and small businesses. The corner grocer may be extremely responsive to the needs of each customer. Health insurers and banks are likely to have bureaucratic structures with many rules and procedures that clients characterize as red rape. The same people who complain about the long line at the motor vehicle bureau are likely to inveigh against the horrendous wait for a teller or a claims agent. If public agencies adopted the interaction strategies large businesses use with the bulk of their individual clients, efficient, responsive service would not necessarily be the norm in all transactions.

We cannot neatly encapsulate government-citizen relations in either the ownership or customer metaphor. Each attempt betrays logical inconsistencies. Yet these loans from private-sector vocabulary engender enough shared meaning so that both phrases have stirred reformer communities. Despite their inability to accurately imply all facets of the object compared, it is important to analyze the two metaphors because each leads to different conclusions about the type of change that is necessary to improve government performance.

Reinventing government centers on how public administrators can satisfy their customers. Administrators are the actors; they survey client attitudes, make services convenient, empower their subordinates, and decide which programs to contract out or decentralize—in many ways acting as owners do in private business. Reform means change in administrative work routines, bureaucratic cultures, and agency procedures to allow various departments to develop entrepreneurs and leaders. Because members of the public are only the recipients of administrative action, little thought is directed toward changing their routines to increase the probability that leaders will emerge from their ranks. The assumption is that changing bureaucratic structures and relationships will yield a more sensitive and responsive public service.

Efficient citizenship assumes citizens act. They monitor agencies and make their preferences known. Reform requires public empowerment through citizenship education and constant information exchange. Although structural change may also be important, the assumption is that government will not work unless citizens get involved in the public arena. (Bruere [1912a; 102–106] argues that a city should worry first about getting information to the public. After this is done, people can debate questions of structural change through citizen initiative rather than official initiative.)

This model develops active citizens as a prerequisite to improving public-agency performance.

It "is the duty of the citizen quite as much as the duty of the officer to assume responsibility for the constructive side of government." (Cleveland, 1909; 352).

Our society does not do an adequate job of developing citizens who want to get involved in public sector issues. Knowledge of and participation in America's political processes is low enough to justify speaking of "a massive state of civic illiteracy" (Chesney and Feinstein, 1993).

A few voices in contemporary public administration argue that agency employees have a responsibility to encourage an actively engaged citizenry (e.g., Gawthrop, 1984; McGregor, 1984). Political philosophers such as Arendt (1958) and Barber (1984) explore the benefits active citizenship brings societies and individuals. But these calls go largely unheeded. Stivers (1990) suggests that our society actually teaches people to regard citizenship as a waste of time—a point of view that achieves credence from the number of people who choose not to vote or serve on juries (two limited, uncontroversial acts of public participation).

Several rationales undergird our lack of attention to promoting citizenship. Some people argue that human nature precludes widespread participation; others see active citizenship as a viable option only in a small, homogeneous society (see the discussion in Stivers, 1990). Public administrators may oppose a wider citizen role if they view it as having a potentially destabilizing effect on "their" agencies (MacNair, Caldwell, and Pollane, 1983).

The bureau literature argues that citizens will act as owners if the proper education and information are available to them. While these conditions alone may be insufficient to get most people to assume the active monitoring role envisioned for them by the BMR, they do seem necessary to increasing interest or participation to any significant degree. Neither is being met.

CITIZENSHIP EDUCATION

Education for citizenship is not built into the education curriculum as the bureau writers had hoped. Schools do not train students to understand and monitor agency work, nor do they impart that any glory might attend involvement in the public scene.

Education for citizenship is important because citizen-owners have to learn to care about the success of an entire enterprise (the public service) rather than focusing solely on how a particular agency responds to their individual demands. Customers care about their own needs; sometimes they register complaints if these are not met. Citizen-owners care about the success of the enterprise in the whole community—although different citizen-owners may have varying definitions of what constitutes success.

When agencies view middle-class citizens as customers, no reason exists to think these clients will care whether the city delivers equal services to rich and poor. This is why a key difference in the owner and customer models relates to the role of private-sector alternatives. The reinventing government paradigm assumes that it is proper for people who are unhappy with public services to seek education or security on the private market. The bureau castigates those who switch. Bruere (1912b; 21) writes

> The most inefficient citizen is one who sends his child to a private school *because* public schools are inefficient, who collects his own garbage *because* public collectors are unreliable, who paves his own street *because* a highway bureau is incompetent, or employs his own watchmen *because* police are undependable (emphasis in the original).

Customers need have no loyalty to any particular merchant; wealthy customers can find their own purveyors and leave the poor to cope with problems in a public education or police protection system. Only when citizens are viewed as owners is the assumption made that they will try to fix the business rather than abandon it.

The Bureau of Municipal Research could ask its predominantly middle-class followers to monitor equal provision of safe schools and streets only because it allotted them an owner's role. Citizenship education facilitates learning why taking such a role matters.

INFORMATION EXCHANGE

The current situation in regard to the availability of information on agency performance is very different from that of the BMR era. Almost all public organizations prepare reports on their activities; the federal and state Freedom of Information Acts mandate that a wide variety of in-house papers are available to anyone who wants to read them. Nonprofit interest groups generate additional reports that are widely available.

Yet the existence of data does not translate into information exchange. People still do not believe they have enough information to participate meaningfully in public debates (see the analysis in Barber, 1984; 154). Often, they do not know which data are available. More fundamentally, many individuals do not understand why they might want to take the trouble to seek such information out. Education has to supply the motive—and education for citizenship is weak. As in the bureau era, the people least likely to seek out the information are the poor, which means that such participation as exists will often be skewed to the middle class. Neither in terms of providing proper education nor in terms of fostering genuine information *exchange* does our society facilitate active citizenship. Whether we view this paucity as a weakness depends on our preferred model of citizen-agency relationship. Do we envision the public as customers or owners of their government? If we envision citizens as owners, then it is a problem that the proprietors lack the psychological and informational resources to mind their own businesses.

FACILITATING CITIZEN DEVELOPMENT

Those people who want to promote a more active citizenry need to focus on enhancing education dedicated to reaching this goal. One step in the right direction may lie in service learning.

Believing that people become active citizens by practicing community involvement, some colleges are creating a connection between service learning and a curriculum aimed at educating democratic citizens. Battistoni's (1994) analysis of the impact of courses that combine community service with reflection on the experience and its relation to citizenship gives room for guarded optimism that these courses can influence student attitudes at least in the short run. Data collected at Rutgers University indicate that students enrolled in service-learning courses had a stronger sense of civic capacity than their peers enrolled in comparison courses. Student journals included such comments as "A citizen must play an active role in his or her community," and "Service is part of my civic responsibility" (p. 9). One path to raising the sense of civic capacity in a broad population may be to implement service-learning programs in elementary and secondary schools to encompass citizens who will enter all occupations and ways of life. While such programs may not affect all the students who participate in them, they may have a positive, incremental impact on citizenship.

CONCLUSIONS

A modern reader may find it strange that the BMR tried to improve agency efficiency by increasing citizen involvement. Creating citizens who initiate action on behalf of the entire community is

relatively unimportant for the reinventing government scenario that posits that outmoded bureaucratic arrangements are the main obstacle to reform. The contemporary model for change wants
to reinvent *government* facilitating the creation of entrepreneurial administrators who gauge the
reactions of citizen-customers and use administrative skills to improve client satisfaction.

The efficient citizenship model challenges the assumption that agency structure and culture
determine performance. This proposal for change suggests that an efficient, responsive government can never emanate solely from reinventing public institutions. The harder task is to reinvent
ourselves as active citizens. We are in trouble to the extent that human nature or the complexities
of our society preclude our taking an ownership role. Without our participation, any attempt at
reform will have at best a very partial success.

REFERENCES

Allen, William, 1907. *Efficient Democracy.* New York: Dodd, Mead and Co.
———, 1909. *Civics and Health.* Boston: Ginn and Co.
———, 1917. *Universal Training for Citizenship and Public Service.* New York: Macmillan.
———, 1949/1950. "Reminiscences." Unpublished manuscript in Oral History Collection, Columbia
    University.
Amberg, Eda, and William Allen, 1921. *Civic Lessons from Mayor Mitchel's Defeat.* New York: Institute
    for Public Service.
Arendt, Hannah, 1958. *The Human Condition.* Chicago: University of Chicago Press.
Barber, Benjamin, 1984. *Strong Democracy: Participatory Politics for a New Age.* Berkeley, CA: University
    of California Press.
Battistoni, Richard, 1994. "Education for Democracy: Service Learning and Pedagogical Reform in Higher
    Education." Paper delivered at the American Political Science Association Conference, New York City.
Bruere, Henry, 1908. "Public Utilities Regulation in New York." *Annals,* vol. 31 (May), 535–551.
———, 1912a. *The New City Government.* New York: D. Appleton and Co.
———, 1912b. "Efficiency in City Government." *Annals,* vol. 41 (May), 1–22.
Capes, William, 1922. *The Modern City and Its Government.* New York: E.P. Dutton.
Chesney, James, and Otto Feinstein, 1993. "Making Political Activity a Requirement in Introductory Political
    Science Courses." *PS: Political Science and Politics,* vol. XXVI (3), 535–538.
Cleveland, Frederick, 1909. *Chapters on Municipal Administration and Accounting.* New York: Longmans,
    Green and Co.
———, 1913. *Organized Democracy.* New York: Longmans, Green and Co.
Dahlberg, Jane, 1966. *The New York Bureau of Municipal Research.* New York: New York University
    Press.
DiIulio, John, Jr., Gerald Garvey, and Donald Kettl, 1993. *Improving Government Performance: An Owner's
    Manual.* Washington, DC: Brookings Institution.
Efficient Citizenship, 1908–1913. Miscellaneous material available at New York City Public Library, Fifth
    Avenue and 42nd Street.
Executive Office of the President, National Performance Review, 1993. *From Red Tape to Results: Creating
    a Government That Works Better and Costs Less.* Washington, DC: U.S. Government Printing Office.
Flexner, Abraham, 1914. *The Educational Activities of the Bureau of Municipal Research of New York: A
    Report to the General Education Board.* Available at the Rockefeller Archives, Tarrytown, New York.
Frederickson, H. George, 1994. "The Seven Principles of Total Quality Politics. . . ." *Public Administration
    Times,* vol. 17 (1), 9.
Gawthrop, Louis, 1984. "Civis, Civitas, and Civilitas: A New Focus for the Year 2000." *Public Administra-
    tion Review,* vol. 44, special issue (March), 101–107.
Gore, Al, Jr., 1994. "The New Job of the Federal Executive." *Public Administration Review,* vol. 54 (July/
    August), 317–321.
Gulick, Luther, 1928. *The National Institute of Public Administration.* New York: National Institute of Public
    Administration.
Light, Paul, 1994. "Partial Quality Management." *Government Executive,* vol. 26 (April), 65–66.

MacNair, Ray, Russell Caldwell, and Leonard Pollane, 1983. "Citizen Participation in Public Bureaucracies; Foul-Weather Friends." *Administration and Society,* vol. 14 (February), 507–524.

McGregor, Eugene, Jr., 1984. "The Great Paradox of Democratic Citizenship and Public Personnel Administration." *Public Administration Review,* vol. 44 (March), 126–132.

Moe, Ronald, 1994. "The 'Reinventing Government' Exercise: Misinterpreting the Problem, Misjudging the Consequences." *Public Administration Review,* vol. 54 (March/April), 111–122.

Mosher, Frederick, 1968. *Democracy and the Public Service.* New York: Oxford University Press.

Municipal Research, 1913–1914. Available at Institute of Public Administration, New York.

Munro, William, 1915. *Principles and Methods of Municipal Administration.* New York: Macmillan.

Osborne, David, and Ted Gaebler, 1992. *Reinventing Government: How the Entrepreneurial Spirit Is Transforming the Public Sector from Schoolhouse to State House, City Hall to Pentagon.* Reading, MA: Addison-Wesley.

Rosenbloom, David, 1993. "Have an Administrative Rx? Don't Forget the Politics." *Public Administration Review,* vol. 53 (November/December), 503–507.

Rowe, Leo, 1908. *Problems of City Government.* New York: D. Appleton and Co.

Schiesl, Martin, 1977. *The Politics of Efficiency.* Berkeley, CA: University of California Press.

Snedden, David, and William Allen, 1908. *School Reports and School Efficiency.* New York: Macmillan.

Stivers, Camilla, 1990. "The Public Agency as Polis: Active Citizenship in the Administrative State." *Administration and Society,* vol. 22 (May), 86–105.

Wiebe, Robert, 1967. *The Search for Order, 1877–1920.* New York: Hill and Wang.

CHAPTER 7

REFRAMING THE METAPHOR OF THE CITIZEN-GOVERNMENT RELATIONSHIP
A Value-Centered Perspective

GERALD E. SMITH AND CAROLE A. HUNTSMAN

One of the prominent paradigms to emerge in recent years is customer-centered public adminis-tration. According to this citizen-customer model, government implicitly enters into a "customer service contract" where administrators give taxpayers the same responsiveness and consideration businesses give customers (Schachter, 1995; National Performance Review, 1993). The customer paradigm has helped reshape the thinking of governments at various levels, from local (Barrett and Greene, 1995) to national (Gore, 1994). Yet, the customer model has been criticized for modeling citizen involvement in terms of passive consumers who like or dislike services and who express their views of government primarily via compliant or satisfaction surveys (Frederickson, 1994).

Schachter (1995) proposes instead that citizens be viewed as owners of government who are proactive in managing the government's scope and affairs. According to this citizen-owner model, "urban citizens owned their government and as owners had a duty to get involved in city affairs and instruct politicians and public administrators in 'shareholder' demands" (Schachter, 1995, 530). However, citizens do not necessarily engage in the affairs of government and may act instead as disenfranchised owners, or even as subjects of the public bureaucracy (Redford, 1969). They do not actively measure or monitor the activities of their government. Few are involved in government service. Many do not vote. They have minimal or no interaction with government. They feel ineffec-tive in dealing with public bureaucracies and bureaucrats (Nachmias and Rosenbloom, 1980).

In this article we propose an alternative perspective to citizens and their relationship to government, a value-centered perspective in which citizens are viewed not as shop-walking proprietors who supervise government employees or as consumers who choose to buy this or that brand of government.

Instead citizens are intelligent investors who coinvest their resources in the community and govern-ment, from which they expect to receive value. They may contribute money to improve a recreational park. They may invest time in serving on a school committee because their children are actively involved in schooling. They may support educational programs long after their own children are grown, because they want to maintain a quality educational environment for their grandchildren.

From *Public Administration Review*, 57, 4 (July/August 1997): 309–318. Copyright © 1997 by American Society for Public Administration. Reprinted with permission.

A value-centered paradigm of citizen involvement may be useful to both public administrators and citizens. The media encourages citizens to ask, What is the *cost* of government? In response, administrators may cut costs, reduce or eliminate programs or services, and make wholesale changes in government. Such actions are directed at only the cost side of government. A value perspective focuses also on the gains and benefits citizens receive from government (Forbis and Mehta, 1981). It encourages citizens to ask, What is the *worth* of government to the citizen?

The worth of government is often lost in the public debate. Such a value perspective encourages public administrators to refocus on the *creation* of value and wealth, rather than simply wealth distribution. A related implication of a value perspective is its potential effect on measurement. Administrators have been encouraged to measure dimensions such as service quality (Zeithaml, Parasuraman, and Berry, 1990), department effectiveness (e.g., timeliness in service delivery), or efficiency (e.g., total number or dollar amount of contracts awarded per department specialist; Kestenbaum and Straight, 1995). However, it is also important to measure citizens' perceptions of the value they receive for the tax investments they make. Do citizens perceive they are getting good value, not only from government in general, but also from specific departments, services, or community assets for which government is trustee?

In this article we explore this value-based perspective of government and the notion of citizens as coinvestors in the community. Is there conceptual merit to such a perspective? Is it useful in practice? We report the results of an exploratory field study of a municipal government that researched citizen attitudes on two specific city services from a value perspective. The results were fascinating and revealing. Citizens were accustomed to thinking of the cost of government. Citizens were unaccustomed to thinking of the value or worth of government. Yet, they engaged in activities and invested in selected government assets and programs that clearly were valuable to them.

THE MEANING OF VALUE

The meaning of value stems from the marginalist revolution in economic thought of the late nineteenth century, which advanced the marginalist theory of value. According to value theory, individuals receive utility by using, holding, or consuming a good. However, the utility derived from each additional unit of a commodity—the marginal utility—is less and less to the individual. The first glasses of water an individual consumes after being deprived of liquid sustenance are far more valuable than the last. Value is a measure of the *worth* of this marginal utility. According to Menger (1871), goods acquire their value because of their ability to satisfy peoples' needs (at the margin) and the importance of the needs they satisfy. Producers compete to create goods that generate *incremental value* for individuals.

Beesley (1992) observes that governments also seek to increase value by the use of ownership rights to run firms, as in government control of nationalized industries; by providing services directly because they have unique abilities to provide them (police protection); or by refereeing market processes by influencing and regulating private business conduct. In summary, a fundamental premise of the value paradigm of economic theory is that individuals are motivated to maximize incremental value, and enterprises (public or private) should be motivated to create incremental value for their constituents.

It is important to note that value as defined here is broader than simply monetary value. Rooke (1991) observed that value may be derived from government activities that provide "social services required by citizens, be they services in support of wealth creation such as the transport infrastructure, or designed purely to improve the quality of life. . . . The arts, music, more esoteric science and the pursuit of knowledge for its own sake are important to all of us here" (31). Moreover, economic value is more than a measure of individual well-being, but also of social and community well-being. According to economic historians, even Adam Smith advocated that one objective of market processes is to realize *social* goals. Field (1994) summarized: "Smith saw humans as fundamentally social (rather than individualistic), and remained fascinated by the . . . institutional environments that could lead us to be virtuous: to experience the pain of another, or consequently, to moderate our expressions of pain so as not to overtax the capability of others to sympathize with our condition" (685).

Nagle and Holden (1994) make an important distinction between actual value and perceived value. Actual value is the true value of savings and benefits gained from using or owning an asset, product, or service. Perceived value is the value buyers *perceive* the product to be worth. "Market value is determined not only by the product's economic value, but also by the accuracy with which buyers perceive that value and by how much importance they place on getting the most for their money" (111). Buyers may inaccurately perceive value because they are unaware of or are not educated about the value of the product or service, or they are not persuaded that the product or service will deliver the value promised by the provider.

There are, of course, many government services and assets that deliver real economic value to citizens as customers, such as police and fire protection, youth programs, education, and elderly services. For some of these, value is tangible and can be calculated and communicated to citizens, such as the savings citizens realize by sending their children to a quality public school instead of a private school. For other city services, value may be intangible and difficult to calculate or articulate, such as the value of police or fire protection, or the value of a conservation or land-use commission. There also may be a gap between the actual value a given government service provides and the perceived value citizens believe the government delivers.

CITIZENS AS CUSTOMERS, OWNERS, INVESTORS

The citizen-government relationship and its impact on the way the public sector works has received significant attention in the literature. One school of thought holds that public administrators act as part of an activist bureaucracy that protects established interests and perpetuates social equity and responsiveness to citizens' concerns. Public administrators are viewed not as bureaucrats, but as public servants who provide stability and continuity in government service (Goodsell, 1988; 1989). Goodsell (1987/1988) cites surveys that report generally favorable views by citizens of their concrete experiences and interactions with government bureaucracy. Moreover, some citizens are not only recipients of public services, but are coproducers with government through voluntary service to agencies and programs (Brudney, 1986). Such service offers symbolic benefits to citizens (Montjoy and Brudney, 1991).

Yet, public perceptions of government bureaucracy are not necessarily so favorable. Rosenbloom and Ross (1994) and Nachmias and Rosenbloom (1980) note that the power of elected officials has diminished relative to that of organizational experts and political staff. Citizens have become suspicious of these passionless, "politically neutral," establishment bureaucrats. Nachmias and Rosenbloom (1980) report that a large majority of citizens perceive that the federal government is too bureaucratic, that elected officials have lost control over bureaucrats, and that the federal government has had either little or negative impact on the quality of life.

The sentiment spills over to state and local government as well, where citizens have placed substantive restrictions on the latitude of public officials, i.e., tax and spending limits, legislative term limits, balanced budget requirements. Thus, while studies of the citizen-government relationship have been instrumental in describing ways in which citizens and government do interact, in fact many citizens are much less confident of and involved in the governing process. Indeed, many citizens fail to participate in the process at all. Only one-half participate in national elections; fewer than one-quarter initiate contacts with local government; even fewer initiate contacts with either state or federal government (Nachmias and Rosenbloom, 1980). Redford (1969) described these silent citizens as "nonleaders" who are subject to the jurisdiction of the bureaucratic state. They feel subjugated rather than served, impotent rather than influential. This then is at least one piece of the problem that the citizen-government metaphor must address: How should citizens and public administrators view their roles within the citizen-government relationship so that citizens feel empowered and motivated to engage in the process of self-government?

The Customer Model

Against this backdrop, market-based and enterprise public administration theories have come forward, including the customer model as embodied in the spirit of the "reinventing" government movement (Osborne and Gaebler, 1992) and the National Performance Review (NPR). The customer model borrows from the total quality management (TQM) and reengineering movements of the American private sector (Kettl, 1994). It assumes fundamentally that public administrators are manufacturers, producers, or suppliers of government services (see Table 7.1). "They survey client attitudes, make services convenient, empower their subordinates, and decide which programs to contract out or decentralize—in many ways acting as owners do in private business" (Schachter, 1995, 534).

President Clinton, in Executive Order 12862, mandated that key agencies identify and survey customers, develop and measure service standards, survey front-line employees, and develop accessible customer complaint systems (Kettl, 1994). The president noted in his introduction of the National Performance Review: "We want to make improving the way government does business a permanent part of how government works . . . asking does it work, does it provide quality service, does it encourage innovation and reward hard work?" (Clinton, 1993)

Ironically, the customer model in practice focuses on production in the operations of government: how well it works, and how well it delivers. Government acts; citizens react. The customer metaphor assumes that citizens are passive consumers of government services, relating to government in much the same way they purchase a routine consumer product. Citizens interact with government primarily through transactions, surveys, or complaints. Moreover, the customer model may have adverse implications for community, since it assumes that citizens are motivated only by self-interest. "Customers may not be good citizens. Encouraging Americans to become more self-regarding individuals may be a poor prescription for civic health. If one's fellow citizen is viewed, not as a member of a common civic union . . . but rather as a potential free rider, then comity and cooperation may be put at greater risk" (Rosenbloom and Ross, 1994, 162).

In his appraisal of the National Performance Review, Kettl (1994) concluded that "the [customer service] notion nevertheless has proven a weak compass for the NPR. The concept is poorly developed, and over-enthusiastic rhetoric has often substituted for clear thinking. If there is something to customer service, that something needs far more careful development" (34) In summary, while the customer model may help galvanize government workers and administrators around a central theme of citizen satisfaction, key limitations remain with respect to how citizens should view their relationship with government.

The Owner Model

Schachter's (1995) model views citizens as being much more proactive, as owners of government (see Table 7.1). The owner metaphor assumes that public administrators are the owners of a public enterprise or business (Frederickson, 1992). Citizens produce revenue and provide capital for the business. Accordingly, citizen-owners have the "duty to assume an active responsibility for improving government along with a perfect right to inquire into the affairs of their agents (the public administrators) at any time" (Schachter, 1995, 532). Studying the Bureau of Municipal Research in New York City, Schachter notes that according to bureau advocates, citizens should inspect police records, note patent violations, make visits to police posts to see what officers are doing (as supervisors check their workers), check on ventilation, play space, and toilets in various neighborhoods, and even use personal vacation time to compare urban services such as police courtesy and street cleanup.

The strength of the owner metaphor is its focus on the role of citizens as owners of government. Citizens are personally empowered to supervise the operations of the government enterprise. They are motivated by duty, responsibility, and concern for the general public interest (Frederickson, 1992).

Ironically, in this model citizens are proactive and drive and direct the relationship between government and citizens. Government workers are reactive. Yet, owners tend to be proprietors; they have individual responsibility for the entire enterprise. They wield unilateral influence and authority within the organization by virtue of their expertise, and their ability to reward, sanction, and exercise legitimate power over employees. Proprietors may hire, fire, supervise, define, and direct the scope and activities of the enterprise. They need not solicit opinion, seek consensus, or defer to group or democratic decision processes. The owner model is consistent with what Van Wart (1995) describes as "traditional" public-sector values that emphasize centralization, non-democratic processes, individual work, hierarchical organization, and simple jobs. These values are internally driven and focus on internal expertise, tradition, and the status quo. There is a top-down managerial focus on supervisors as controllers.

Thus, the owner model, while stressing the moral duty of citizens to accept responsibility for government, seems inconsistent with the practical ability or influence of most citizens. It also suggests a metaphor of citizen involvement that is far more individually oriented, rather than democratically or socially oriented. As Schachter (1995) noted, in communities citizens behave more as shareholders with limited time, information, or expertise to influence government. Thus, citizens may have ownership rights in theory, but citizen-owners may find it difficult to relate to the owner model.

The Value Model

We build on the strengths of these models to propose a third model of citizen-government interaction, in which both parties are proactive and focused on a common goal: creating incremental value for citizens. In a value-centered model, citizens are shareholders of the community enterprise, and government is a trustee, steward, and manager of the enterprise's assets, programs and services that deliver value to its citizen investors (see Table 7.1). The government-as-trustee metaphor embodies important meaning. A trustee is one to whom something is entrusted, to whom property or valued possessions are legally committed in trust. The trustee does not own these possessions; indeed, the trustee's ability to act as an agent of the people is dependent on the public confidence. Character and moral responsibility may be salient. Thus, citizens look to agents in government, not simply as effective managers or administrators, but as respected keepers of the public trust. If trust is compromised or violated, confidence is lost, even though the trustee may be effective at otherwise executing the administrative functions of his or her office.

Table 7.1

Comparative Models of the Citizen-Government Relationship

	Customer model	Owner model	Value model
Conceptual Origins	Total quality management Reinventing government Reengineering movement	Traditional public sector administration Efficient citizenship (Bureau of Municipal Research, New York)	Economic theory Marginalist theory of value
Philosophy	The purpose of government is to produce and deliver quality services to its citizen-customers. Effectiveness is determined by (1) the organization's ability to measure and monitor customer satisfaction, and (2) to deliver quality service.	The purpose of government is to produce efficient services for its citizen-owners. Effectiveness is determined by citizens' supervising, controlling, and managing the delivery of government services.	The purpose of government is to facilitate investment and deliver unique services that preserve and create incremental value for citizens. Effectiveness is determined by governments' ability to identify and create value and wealth for citizens.
Government Roles and Metaphors	Metaphor: Government is producer, manufacturer, and deliverer of quality services. Role: To manage operations, monitor efficiency, enhance delivery, and produce quality services that meet the needs and expectations of customers of government.	Metaphor: Government is a hierarchically organized business run by administrators and task-directed employees. Role: To accomplish job tasks and responsibilities that have been defined by (citizen) proprietors and supervisors; to perform according to job specifications, standards, and requirements.	Metaphor: Government is a trustee, steward, manager of assets and services that deliver incremental value to citizen shareholders. Role: To identify the most important sources of value to constituents; to create incremental value by preserving or investing in community assets; to facilitate wealth creating by coinvesting with citizen investors, and to deliver uniquely valued services to citizens.
Citizen Roles and Metaphors	Metaphor: Citizens are consumers of government services. Role: To make self-interested purchase decisions about city services; to provide continuing feedback to public managers regarding perceived quality and satisfaction with services delivered.	Metaphor: Citizens are individual owners and proprietors of the government enterprise. Role: To measure, monitor, report and supervise employees to ensure that they effectively accomplish and fulfill their responsibilities; to provide capital and revenue for the enterprise.	Metaphor: Citizens are coinvestors and equal shareholders of the public trust. Role: To coinvest with other citizens and government in the creation of incremental wealth consistent with citizen needs; to influence the collective goals and direction of the community enterprise and the common wealth.
Observations and Implicit Assumptions	• Government drives and directs the relationship between citizens and government. • Citizens act as low-involvement, self-interested consumers who passively react and respond. • Though customer focused, primary emphasis is internal, on production and operational efficiency.	• Citizens drive and direct the relationship between citizens and government. • Driven by centralized, nondemocratic, hierarchically structured processes. • Focus is on internally driven processes, internal expertise, tradition, status quo; resistant to change. • Top-down managerial model with supervisors as controllers.	• Citizens coinvest selectively in assets and services that yield greatest incremental value. • Government and citizens share responsibility for wealth creation. • Driven by decentralized, democratic, flat organizational processes. • Focus on externally driven processes, external expertise, market change, and innovation.

The role of government is to create incremental value for citizens, in several ways: (1) by identifying the most important sources of value to constituents; (2) by delivering value and worth with respect to these dimensional sources of value through government services; and (3) by facilitating investment in the capital asset base of the community, e.g., land, parks, facilities, conservation. Sources of value are specific benefits or dimensions along which incremental value is created or preserved for citizens who use, experience, or gain from the services and activities that government provides. For example, a quality public educational system provides an important source of value to many constituents. What is the worth of this source of value? It is at least the savings citizens realize by not sending their children to a private school, say $20,000 for a private boarding school. This is a user-focused conceptualization of value. Citizens do not necessarily receive value just because government is effective at delivering services. They receive value only if it is effective at delivering services that are of significant worth to citizens.

In a value-centered model, citizens are not proprietors, but coinvestors and shareholders in the public trust and common wealth of the community. They grant control, authority, and responsibility to an agent to realize future benefits or advantages. The shareholder metaphor implies a participative and communal form of wealth creation that involves copartnership, coinvestment, common interest, cooperation, and sharing among citizens as co-owners. Citizens are constitutionally granted equal shares of ownership. They therefore have access to equal benefits that flow from the public enterprise, such as public safety or legal protection from discrimination.

As shareholders citizens do not invest in all aspects of government, since that is beyond their scope and ability. Instead they coinvest only in those aspects of government for which they expect to receive reasonable return for their investment. This means they will coinvest: (1) in areas in which they have expertise because they can efficiently make the greatest marginal contribution in these areas for the least marginal effort or cost expended (e.g., a corporate financial manager who serves on a local finance committee); and (2) in areas that are most important or valuable to them because these are areas that yield the most significant personal return for their time or money invested.

Shareholders share in the benefits of wealth creation but only if the total enterprise either preserves or creates incremental wealth for the community. Citizens therefore are motivated to pool their interests and efforts to advocate their positions regarding the direction and focus of the enterprise. They not only vote their opinions, but also collectively work together to ensure that the community enterprise remains properly focused on achieving the collective goals of the shareholder community. The value model is consistent with what Van Wart (1995) describes as "new" public-sector values that emphasize decentralization, bottom-up democratic processes, teamwork, flat organization, and multidimensional jobs. They are externally driven and focus on market change and innovation. Employees are viewed as assets; supervisors, as participative helpers.

FIELD RESEARCH

Our research was stimulated by a change in leadership of Newton, Massachusetts. Newton had recently elected a new mayor, Tom Concannon, after over two decades of leadership by the previous mayor. One of Mayor Concannon's early initiatives was to utilize the resources of a university business faculty located in the area to study the delivery of city services. Newton is a Boston suburb, with a population of 84,000. The largest occupational group in the city is professional and technical, about one-third of the city's inhabitants.

The mayor particularly wanted to understand citizens' perceptions of the city's delivery of services from the perspective of citizens as customers. The city regularly conducts a satisfaction survey in which citizens are asked to rate a variety of city services, ranging from fire protection to park facilities to street lighting, on a scale consisting of good, fair, poor, and don't know. A level of satisfaction is then calculated by dividing the number of good and fair responses by the total number of good, fair, and poor responses. Satisfaction levels on a recent survey exceeded 80 percent on all measures but one, and exceeded 90 percent on most measures. The usefulness of this information was unclear; therefore, the mayor wanted a more robust way to diagnose citizen perceptions at the department level.

We were particularly interested in applying methods of economic value analysis in a government context. These methods have been applied in the private sector (Forbis and Mehta, 1981), and we believed that they might be applicable to the public sector as well.

The mayor designated two pilot areas of city service delivery to focus measurement and analysis efforts: city hall services, such as building and inspectional services; and parks and recreation, including parks, pools, sports, and recreational programs. The city hall services analysis focused primarily on business and proprietor constituents. The parks and recreation analysis focused primarily on residential constituents. Qualitative research methods, specifically depth interviews, were utilized to gather customer data on these two departments. A total of 21 depth interviews were conducted: 11 on city hall services and 10 on parks and recreation. Each interview lasted about 45 to 90 minutes. All questions were open-ended to allow respondents to elicit important sources of value and dimensions of importance. Depth interviews were utilized to allow time and latitude to discuss, probe, and uncover underlying concerns that normally would not emerge from a survey or focus group analysis.

A questionnaire, or interview guide, was developed and followed for all interviews, consisting of three major sections:

1. *Use and Interaction with City Hall:* How do citizens interact with city hall? What is the intensity of usage? What level of experience do they have?
2. *Sources of Economic Value:* What are potential sources of value to citizens, e.g., monetary and nonmonetary savings, gains, and benefits of city services?
3. *Measures of Value:* What is the economic value of these specific sources of value? What are respondents' perceptions of the city's performance in wealth creation with respect to these sources of value?

A sample of potential respondents to interview was provided by the mayor, subject to the following research guidelines. We wanted to ensure that both experienced and inexperienced users of the service were included. We wanted to identify citizens who had recent interactions with the city, since their experiences would most likely be recalled with greater accuracy and detail. We avoided people who were politically connected to the administration to ensure reasonably unbiased opinions.

We share selected exploratory findings from the interviews that illustrate the value perspective. The first set of interviews (on city services) relates to the value of unique services the city provides. The second set (on parks and recreation) focuses on the value of community assets.

FINDINGS

Sources of Value: City Hall Services

A particularly useful insight obtained from the interviews is that there appear to be significant differences in the perspectives of experienced versus inexperienced users of city hall. Our interviews revealed that experienced users of city hall services (mostly business proprietors), on average, spend between 10 minutes and 60 minutes per visit to city hall. However, they also spend approximately five times that amount of time preparing for the visit by filling out forms, obtaining supporting documentation, and engaging in similar tasks. This finding has a fundamental impact on the economic value citizens may receive from city hall. While it may be useful to make actual visits to city hall more efficient, it is even more valuable to identify ways to reduce the preparation required before a user ever arrives at city hall. Therefore, one important source of economic value that emerged from the interviews is the value of time spent preparing to visit city hall.

Time savings while at city hall was another important source of value, particularly for experienced users of city services. Since most of these experienced patrons of city hall were business people or professionals, interactions with city hall translated directly into gains or losses, such as paying a "runner" to spend time at city hall, or paying another employee to cover the office while the principal was at city hall. Addressing this potential source of value, one respondent, a real estate assessor, suggested that the city offer computerized access at the counter to routinely requested information, such as real estate information. He commented:

> [The city has] an elaborate system that nobody else has. They actually have a picture of the property. You can come in and say, "I live on Main Street." They [go to their system and] say, "Is this it?" and they've got a big screen TV up there . . . But at this point, they don't have anything on the desk for [the public] to use. Waltham just went on [line]. Watertown has a computer system. You can just go in and bang in the address and get everything you want.

Evidently, city hall already has the technology to offer significant value to real estate business constituents. Should the city offer such computerized access to real estate information at the counter? To do so would require new investment in computer terminals and cabling, perhaps a computer network contractor. What is the cost of such a project? Is there latitude in the budget?

A value perspective suggests that department employees should ask a different set of questions. What are the sources of value to a real estate assessor of having computerized access at the counter? What is the worth of these sources of value? Given this value, would real estate assessors be willing to coinvest with other assessors and the city to create this incremental value? Are these coinvestments sufficient to warrant community investment in the project?

The inexperienced patrons that we interviewed knew very little about the system at city hall—where to go, whom to see, how to proceed. For these people, the process of interacting with city hall was overwhelming and sometimes discouraging. Success or failure depended on the helpfulness of the particular city employee they happened to encounter. Thus, the most important source of value to these inexperienced patrons was knowledgeable and helpful assistance with the process of government, including steering, direction, steps to take, and contacts to make. One new business owner, who intended to start a new business in the town and needed license approval, expressed his frustration as follows:

> I got so discouraged by what I heard that we started looking in other towns and cities for over a year. . . . I mean, the way they talked about the difficulty of getting a license approved and because basically there are already enough food establishments. . . . If I had been more experienced and had taken what the office said with a grain of salt, and just said, "Yeah, yeah, yeah." If I knew it just depended on finding the right location. . . . A year is a long time and someone could have come in and done the same [restaurant instead of us].

Another new business owner, also seeking license approval, had a much more positive experience because the person she encountered at city hall was very helpful:

> I can't think of one bad experience we've had. Honestly, [the city representative] brought us in immediately when I made our first phone call and she just sat down and listened to what we had to do and to see at what point she would help us with what we were doing. . . . She was wonderful.

A customer model would view these experiences from a customer satisfaction perspective: How can the city improve its operations at city hall to facilitate more satisfactory interactions with citizens? An owner model would view these experiences from an employee performance perspective: How can individual employees do their job better to facilitate more productive interactions with city hall? Both of these are useful perspectives. However, a value model asks fundamentally different questions: What are the most important sources of value to these new business constituents? What is the value either created or lost for these business people by facilitating (or failing to facilitate) productive interactions with city hall?

Addressing this source of value may require designating a person at city hall to handle new business inquiries, to consult with, direct, steer, and facilitate proper interactions with city hall departments. The first intuitive response might be to ask about the cost of such a person. Is there latitude in the budget? However, a value perspective would ask about the worth to new business owners of a new business consultant who would guide them through the license approval process, from start to finish. Given that value, would inexperienced proprietors be willing to coinvest to receive that value?

The frustrated new business owner who lost a year investigating locations in other towns commented on the value of having access to a competent city representative to assist with the licensing process:

> You know, you pay your lawyer $150 an hour or $200 an hour to do that, and in Needham [a neighboring town], that's what we spent, $1,500 on our lawyer to start that [licensing] process because we were told that was the only way to do it in Needham. So I guess we would have been willing to pay, you know, up to that much if we thought it was really going to get us somewhere [with licensing].

When asked to estimate the value of having computerized counter access to real estate property information and avoid waiting at city hall, the real estate assessor said:

> [If I could get that information more quickly from the city] you're looking at somebody [who] could do another job a week. We get $250 for an appraisal so, you know, we have a staff of four or five people losing that amount of time. Four or five extra jobs a week is a $1,000 to $1,250, or say, $1,000 to $1,500 worth of gross revenue to everybody.

Thus, if government were willing to facilitate the creation of $1,000 to $1,500 worth of value for these constituents (real estate assessors), how much would they be willing to coinvest in the creation of that value—perhaps some amount per inquiry? The real estate assessor would realize more revenue. The city could realize additional revenue per inquiry. Is there sufficient willingness to coinvest in the creation of value to justify investing in computerized counter access?

Sources of Value: Parks and Recreation

So far we have discussed value creation from the perspective of business owners in the community. When asked to consider the value and worth of parks and recreational facilities and programs, residents had similar reactions, particularly those with families. One parent commented, "We save about $1,500 a year by using city programs and facilities. For example, we don't have to buy a pool membership at a private club. We don't have to pay for private camps in the summer, and so on."

Residents also participated in value creation by coinvesting in community assets. According to one interviewee, in 1994 the city's soccer league raised $50,000 to irrigate, fertilize, and improve four large fields (about 15 acres) of the city's public grounds. The Parks and Recreation Department matched this amount and coinvested with the parents involved with the project. One parent commented: "We found out [a couple of years ago] that some playing fields were just in terrible shape, bordering on unsafe. At that point, some of the parents got together and decided to approach the city with an alternative. That's how this project started, but there are only four improved fields now; some [others] are still unsafe."

Other respondents noted that they, too, had raised money among neighborhood residents to refurbish neighborhood playgrounds and provided the labor to carry these projects out. They also were quick to acknowledge the involvement, commitment, and support of Parks and Recreation employees to help out with these efforts. One respondent commented: "When I started [working] with the [Parks and Recreation] Department to rebuild our community playground, I found that the staff was extremely dedicated. They even came and worked on the project in their spare time and brought their families to help. Needless to say, our community was very appreciative." More than half of the respondents we interviewed about parks and recreation services were willing to coinvest to sustain and improve the quality of the city's parks and recreation facilities and programs.

The metaphor of citizen coinvestment is not limited to high income communities, such as Newton. Eggers and O'Leary (1995) report similar examples. In San Antonio, a family donated land to the city to build a park in a declining area with growing gang problems. Neighborhood families and a civic club cleared the land and planted trees. Local businesses donated facilities, such as a running track and a bridge. At the completion of the project, the park was turned back over to the city, which agreed to maintain it in conjunction with ownership committees comprised of local citizens who were vested with control of certain sections of the park.

Citizen coinvestment is evident in the recent trend toward closing urban streets to improve the safety, security, and quality of neighborhoods. For example, Waterman Place in St. Louis fell victim to suburban flight in the 1950s, leaving behind a poorer, more transient population. In 1974 neighborhood residents petitioned the city to vest them with deeds of ownership of their streets. In exchange, the neighborhood agreed to assume responsibility for public services such as street lighting, sewers, rubbish collection, and augmented security beyond standard police protection. Following the change, the neighborhood stabilized, the quality of life improved, and property values doubled, from $30,000 to $60,000 for a typical owner-occupied house. In 1993 Chicago implemented a city "cul-de-sac" program, where neighborhoods were given authority to close off streets following a public approval process, including a two-thirds vote of approval by neighborhood residents. Similar initiatives have been implemented in Dallas, Houston, Dayton, and Fort Lauderdale.

Citizen coproduction of public services is another example of citizen coinvestment in the community. For example, Eggers and O'Leary (1995) report that a high crime area of Houston has only 13 full-time members of the police force. They are augmented by 200 volunteer deputies. Each volunteer receives full police training, a state license, and authority to carry weapons, and typically works four nights a week in addition to a regular job. Increasingly, private companies are facilitating citizen coproduction by allowing their employees to participate in volunteer work in the community (Hodges, 1995). Communities benefit from volunteers' expertise, experience, and skills. Companies benefit from a positive public image, and their employees develop a better attitude, which improves performance.

The point of each of these initiatives is that citizens feel empowered and motivated because they have been granted (or have demanded) the opportunity to coinvest with other citizens and with government in the creation of incremental value for their communities. Their motivations may derive from individual duty, but it is likely that they are driven more by collective opportunity to transform the quality of life in their communities. They do create monetary value, but more importantly, they create broader individual value, social value, and community value.

ANALYSIS AND IMPLICATIONS

An analysis of depth interviews conducted with citizens of a local community about two areas of city services indicated that citizens may indeed behave in a manner consistent with a value-centered model. They invest both time and money over and above tax dollars in projects or programs that are of particular benefit to them or their families.

The value-centered model builds on ideas that are central to two other models, the customer model and the owner model. The customer model focuses primarily on customer satisfaction and operational performance and efficiency. The owner model assumes that citizens are owners of the public enterprise, and therefore should assume active responsibility to monitor and manage the enterprise (Schachter, 1995; Frederickson, 1992). The problem with both of these models is that they either describe the citizen as uninvolved with government (the customer model), or they normatively suggest that the citizen should be involved in government (the owner model), even though in practice citizens are rarely so involved because the task of owning the enterprise is so large.

A value model suggests that citizens interact with government because they are fundamentally motivated to create value for themselves and for the community. Taxes paid are an investment in the community enterprise; time spent volunteering is an investment in the community's quality of life. As shareholders, citizens work together to influence the direction and focus of wealth creation in the community enterprise, and they expect reasonable value for their investment.

Several implications follow from a value-centered model of citizen-government relationships. One implication of a value perspective relates to citizen awareness. Our discussion encourages public leaders to reframe the public debate about city services by focusing on a leadership theme that is prominent in public discourse—value. Underlying many social issues at the national, state, and local level (e.g., welfare reform, budget balancing, Medicare/Medicaid reform) are concerns over the value citizens receive from the public enterprise. While these concerns may be well-founded, it should be useful to frame many of these issues from a different perspective, one that has been largely lost in the public debate. What is the *worth* of these aspects of government to its citizens, both at the community level and at the level of the individual citizen? This question suggests the need for a fundamental change in attitude among citizens and administrators. As Rooke (1991) observed with regard to the British system: "To my mind the overwhelming need is to generate an understanding of the importance to our future quality of life of efficient wealth creation. . . . A fundamental change in attitude is required—in truth a deep cultural change."

Public administrators should communicate, reinforce, and reestablish in the public debate a consciousness and awareness of the value of government to its citizens and government's role in the creation of value for the community. This may be accomplished through public forums, town meetings, volunteer organizations, or the activities of interest groups. Rooke (1991) recommends changes in the educational curriculum, so that students and future generations are knowledgeable about the link between public-sector value creation and quality of life. Public administrators should measure the value of government services, programs, and assets; develop reporting systems that track changes in value (value creation); and regularly communicate the effectiveness of the community's value creation efforts to citizens.

A second implication of a value perspective is that it suggests a different administrative philosophy to public administrators, one that focuses on the creation of public wealth, not only at the macro level of large government investment projects, but also at the micro level of department service delivery. Should a department privatize some aspects of its delivery system? It depends on whether administrators believe that the private sector can deliver greater incremental value to the community than the public sector. What are the sources of value to commercial patrons of a well-run building inspection services department? What is the economic value of these services? What changes to the department's current delivery system will yield incremental value for these patrons, and what is the worth of these value creation activities?

A third implication of a value perspective is that it suggests a useful model of citizen involvement in the community. Such involvement is practical and logically motivated by citizens' interest in the community's quality of life. As our depth interviews and examples indicated, citizens were willing to coinvest significant financial and personal resources to improve the quality of community assets that would yield benefits both now and in the future. Moreover, they creatively sought innovative ways to accomplish their coinvestment objectives, such as convincing government departments to coinvest with them by requesting funds from government to match dollar for dollar the funds invested by interested citizens.

There are, however, potential drawbacks to the implementation of a value perspective. First, despite carefully scripted communications by public leaders about the worth of government, citizens may be skeptical and virtually reject such appeals as manipulative attempts by public leaders to mask the real problems with government. Even if government made progress in changing the philosophy and focus of delivering city services to make them more value focused, citizens still may be reluctant to believe that fundamental change has taken place.

Another potential problem with value appeals from public officials is that they may be perceived as focusing the public debate mostly on financial and monetary dimensions. Yet, this misses the broader point of value creation. Public value and wealth are created in many ways, such as by protecting or preserving property and community resources from current use, overuse, or abuse. A specific business proprietor may consider a stringent health regulation a nuisance, but there is a greater value to the community in preserving public health. This type of wealth preservation may be difficult to quantify, yet it is common wealth indeed and is part of a community's portfolio of valuable assets. This suggests the need for fundamental education about the meaning of value creation in the community and its applicability to departments of government that deliver less tangible value.

Another potential problem that merits further discussion is the perspective a value model brings with regard to the poor. The examples cited above give anecdotal evidence that both poor and middle-class citizens behave consistently with the value model, whether investing in inner-city neighborhood development or investing in a youth recreational program. Yet, it is important to note that our focus has been on value creation, not value distribution. To be sure, as John Stuart Mill's social philosophy on the role of government in society advocates, income distribution is still necessary because markets do not necessarily allocate wealth equitably. However, in this article we propose that wealth creation and wealth distribution have gotten out of balance in the public discourse and in public administration. There has been much less emphasis on wealth creation, to the point that it has been lost in the public debate about government. As Sir James Ball (1992) noted, "It is always easier to distribute the cake than to bake it."

How then should the poor be treated according to the value model? A strength of the value model is the premise that all citizens are constitutionally granted the right to be equal shareholders in terms of vote and influence (regardless of differences in the economic investments they make in the form of taxes). Therefore, by right, citizens also must be equal in terms of the benefits they receive, such as equal access to employment, education, health care, protection, and security. Where the poor represent a significant voice in the community, the enterprise will necessarily invest to address the needs of this constituent group of shareholders because they will enforce this right by virtue of their number. Where the poor represent a smaller share of the overall social enterprise, it still is in the best interest of the enterprise to invest in the poor, precisely because the marginal benefit to the community is greater than investing in some other more wealthy part of the community. Such investment not only realizes greater returns for the poor, but it realizes greater marginal returns for the community as a whole. The downtown neighborhood that once was considered a blight on the community becomes a vibrant contributor in terms of culture, economic wealth, and property asset value.

CONCLUSION

In summary, there is merit in introducing concepts such as "value" and "worth" into the debate over government and in refocusing the debate on value creation. Citizens may not buy shares of a community or government, but they do invest by choosing to live in a community, by buying property there, and by giving community service. They expect a reasonable return in both the near term and the long term. Similarly, government employees not only deliver city services to their constituents, they create value for them as well. Viewed from this frame of reference, public servants and citizens may begin to view the citizen-government relationship differently, not as one party overseeing the other or as one party working to satisfy the self-interested needs of the other, but as stakeholders who have common interests in increasing the worth of the community.

ACKNOWLEDGMENTS

The authors are grateful to Mayor Tom Concannon, Carol Bock, Richard Robinson, and the city of Newton for their cooperation and assistance on this project; to Frank Campanella and Boston College for funding the project; to Management Task Force members Judith Gordon, Joe Raelin, Gil Manzon, and Ralph Edwards for their helpful insights throughout the project; and to Tom Nagle for his helpful comments on previous drafts of the manuscript.

REFERENCES

Ball, James (1992). "The Economics of Wealth Creation." In James Ball, ed., *Proceedings of Section F (Economics)*. Plymouth, England: British Association for the Advancement of Science, 4–30.

Barrett, Katherine, and Richard Greene (1995). "Capitol of Bad Management: Congress Stacked the Deck Against D.C. Then Ignored Its Plight. Now It Can Share the Blame." *Financial World,* 14 March, 50–71.

Beesley, Michael (1992). "The Government as Market Creator: Participant or Referee?" In James Ball, ed., *Proceedings of Section F (Economics)*. Plymouth, England: British Association for the Advancement of Science, 82–102.

Brudney, Jeffrey L. (1986). "The SBA and SCORE: Coproducing Management Assistance Services." *Public Productivity Review* 10 (Winter): 57–67.

Clinton, William (1993). "Remarks by the President in Announcement of Initiative to Streamline Government." *Weekly Compilation of Presidential Document* 29, 3 March.

Eggers, William D., and John O'Leary (1995). *Revolution at the Roots*. New York: Free Press.

Field, Alexander J. (1994). "Review of *Adam Smith in His Time and Ours: Designing the Decent Society*." *Journal of Economic Literature* 32 (June): 683–685.

Forbis, John L., and Nitin T. Mehta (1981). "Value-Based Strategies for Industrial Products." *Business Horizons* 24 (May/June): 32–42.

Frederickson, H. George (1992). "Painting Bull's-Eyes Around Bullet Holes." *Governing* (October): 13.

——— (1994). "George and the Case of Government Reinventors." *PA Times* 17 (January): 9.

Goodsell, Charles T. (1987/1988). "What Do Citizens Think?" *Bureaucrat* 16 (Winter): 20–22.

——— (1988). "Bureaucrats Are Human Beings." *Bureaucrat* 17 (Fall): 27–29.

——— (1989). "Does Bureaucracy Hurt Democracy?" *Bureaucrat* 18 (Spring): 45–48.

Gore, Al, Jr. (1994). "The New Job of the Federal Executive." *Public Administration Review* 54 (4): 317–321.

Hodges, Catharine (1995). "Training Teams in the Community." *People Management* 11 (November): 34–36.

Kestenbaum, Martin I., and Ronald L. Straight (1995). "Procurement Performance Measuring Quality, Effectiveness, and Efficiency." *Public Productivity and Management Review* 19 (December): 200–215.

Kettl, Donald F. (1994). *Reinventing Government? Appraising the National Performance Review*. CPM Report 94–2. Washington, DC: Center for Public Management, The Brookings Institution.

Menger, Carl (1871). *Principles of Economics*. Translated by J. Dingwall and B.F. Hoselitz, with an introduction by Friedrich A. Hayek, 1981. New York: New York University Press.

Montjoy, Robert S., and Jeffrey L. Brudney (1991). "Volunteers in the Delivery of Public Services: Hidden Costs . . . And Benefits." *American Review of Public Administration* 21 (December): 327–344.

Nachmias, David, and David H. Rosenbloom (1980). *Bureaucratic Government, USA*. New York: St. Martin's Press.

Nagle, Thomas T., and Reed K. Holden (1994). *The Strategy and Tactics of Pricing*. Englewood Cliffs, NJ: Prentice Hall.

National Performance Review (1993). *From Red Tape to Results: Creating a Government That Works Better and Costs Less*. Washington, DC: U.S. Government Printing Office.

Osborne, David, and Ted Gaebler (1992). *Reinventing Government: How the Entrepreneurial Spirit Is Transforming the Public Sector, from Schoolhouse to Statehouse, City Hall to the Pentagon*. Reading, MA: Addison-Wesley.

Redford, Emmette S. (1969). *Democracy in the Administrative State*. New York: Oxford University Press.

Rooke, Dennis (1991). "Some Perspectives of a Simple Engineer." In James Ball, ed., *Proceedings of Section F (Economics)*. Plymouth, England: British Association for the Advancement of Science, 31–49.

Rosenbloom, David H., and Bernard H. Ross (1994). "Administrative Theory, Political Power, and Government Reform." In Patricia W. Ingraham and Barbara S. Romzek, eds., *New Paradigms for Governments: Issues for the Changing Public Service*. San Francisco, CA: Josey-Bass, 145–167.

Schachter, Hindy Lauer (1995). "Reinventing Government or Reinventing Ourselves: Two Models for Improving Government Performance." *Public Administration Review* 55 (6): 530–537.

Van Wart, Montgomery (1995). "The First Step in the Reinvention Process: Assessment." *Public Administration Review* 55 (5): 429–438.

Zeithaml, V.A., A. Parasuraman, and L.L. Berry (1990). *Delivering Quality Service: Balancing Customer Perceptions and Expectations*. New York: Free Press.

PART 3

ARENAS OF DIRECT CITIZEN PARTICIPATION

Direct citizen participation is manifest at all levels of government, although it tends to be more evident locally and regionally due to problems of scale. We find its expression in all policy areas such as education, health[1] and social services,[2] justice and environmental systems,[3] and economic and community development. Citizens also are involved throughout all stages of policymaking—analysis, initiation, formulation, implementation, and evaluation. The articles in Part 3, although not a comprehensive assortment due to space limitations, enable the reader to appreciate the scope and depth of citizen involvement throughout all phases of the policy process.

The articles are divided into two sets. The first set of four articles focuses on direct citizen participation during policy implementation—the initial entry point for federally mandated citizen involvement. The second set of three articles exemplifies direct citizen involvement during the earlier stages of policymaking. Since interventions during the implementation phase were believed to occur too late in the policy process for citizens to have a positive impact (King, Feltey, and Susel 1998), proponents began to recommend opening up citizen involvement during policy analysis, initiation, and eventually budgeting.

Regardless of the arena of direct citizen involvement, the articles acknowledge tension between experts and citizens. The authors note that as society becomes more modern and bureaucratized, professional administrators and experts begin to dominate the policy process. Experts have the education, skills, and time to devote to policy concerns. In contrast, citizens lack the special training and resources needed to be cogent about complex policy problems, especially those involving highly sophisticated technology (Aron 1979; Hadden 1981; Morgan 1984; DeSario and Langton 1984; Cohen 1995; and Zimmerman 1995). As a consequence of these disparities, professionals and experts gain in power, while citizens, unable to participate as coequals, decrease their involvement.

Struggles among experts, professionals, and citizens become an even greater source of tension when experts and professionals are not attuned to the issues of the poor, minorities, or those left out of the policy process. Under these conditions, reformers often call for institutional change (e.g., decentralization of services, enhanced local control, and direct citizen participation) as a means to redistribute power between experts and citizens and to give citizens without voice and representation a chance to be heard. Thus, direct citizenship participation in a democratic society comes to be viewed by many as a major vehicle of social change and transformation (Korten 1980,

119

1981). The extent to which it is espoused and practiced (e.g., Gittell in education) or the extent to which it is opposed or found to be of questionable value (e.g., Myren in policing) appears to depend on the level of citizen dissatisfaction with a particular government service. As we see below, the greater the dissatisfaction among citizens within a policy domain, the louder the calls for direct citizen participation.

POLICY IMPLEMENTATION IN PROGRAMS AND SECTORS

The first article, "Citizen Participation in Community Action and Model Cities Programs" by John H. Strange, reviews the history of citizen participation in Office of Economic Opportunity (OEO) and Model Cities Programs. The Economic Opportunity Act of 1964, which established Community Action Programs (CAPs), required "maximum feasible participation" by area residents (the poor and minorities) in the operation of the Community Action Program.[4] The article provides a good backdrop for the book in summarizing the various meanings of the term *citizen participation* and reviewing the alternative institutional forms through which participation was encouraged. Of particular significance are the restrictions placed on citizen involvement that made it difficult to attain maximum feasible participation. The article also provides an excellent bibliography on case studies and reports written up to that point in time on direct citizen involvement.

Marilyn Gittell's article, "Decentralization and Citizen Participation in Education," explores the important role that citizen participation has had in the shaping of American public education. We learn how various citizen groups have developed local boards of education as the primary means of citizen participation in school decision making. Her argument is that education needs a balance between professionalism and public participation. Systematic exclusion of certain groups (e.g., parents of school children, the poor, and minorities) has produced failure of the educational system. She sees community control, especially the redistribution of power between experts and citizens, as the vehicle for institutional change. "Quality education without the involvement and participation of the consumers" she asserts, "is a contradiction in terms" (p. 160). From her perspective, "the potential for finding solutions to educational problems can only be enhanced by the broader range of alternatives offered by laymen and nonschool professionals" (p. 160).

"Decentralization and Citizen Participation in Criminal Justice Systems" by Richard A. Myren focuses primarily on the policing function of the justice system, where most citizen action has been found. He outlines four ways in which the citizenry can participate in policing: lending various kinds of support to policy agencies; actual assumption of police duties under the direction of regular policy officers; formal evaluation of police performance; and community control and the setting of policy for police operations. He finds some support projects, a few cities in which community members perform police duties, isolated instances of formal citizen evaluation of police performance, and little evidence of direct citizen participation in the establishment of police policies and procedures throughout large U.S. cities. He also notes that most experts of police operations do not advise citizen participation, especially in setting policy. They cite greater opportunities for corruption and favoritism and the lack of protection of civil liberties among suspects and witnesses.

The fourth article by Curtis Ventriss and Robert Pecorella, "Community Participation and Modernization: A Reexamination of Political Choices," uses community development programs as the backdrop to pose a key question in the debates on direct citizen participation: How do we reconcile direct citizen participation with the exigencies of a modern, rational/analytic, technological society? The authors examine two very different community development programs to address this question. The first program follows a model of social action and community development that is less disruptive of the social order and relies on a bureaucratization and professionalization of its own experts (e.g., lawyers, technicians, researchers) to manage the change process. The authors use David Korten's term (1980, 1981), the "blueprint" approach, to describe this effort because its program strategy mirrors governmental agencies by developing corresponding professional, technical, legal, and bureaucratic staffs and procedures. The consequence of this bureaucratization and professionalization is a drop in direct citizen participation. The second model follows what Korten (1980, 1981) has described as "the learning process approach to change"—maximum citizen participation in the development and implementation of community programs and the use of confrontational tactics, when necessary, to pressure the political system. It requires community development programs to learn how to embrace error, plan with community people, and to link knowledge with action. The authors point out that the dilemma between modernization and direct participation may never be resolved, but the success of the social learning approach challenges the assumption that "a decline in participation is an ultimate price of modernity" (p. 202). Although the authors acknowledge there are risks and opportunity costs in both approaches, and tradeoffs have to be made, they conclude that the effectiveness of economic and community development ultimately rests on the development and transformation of the citizen. It is their belief that the social learning approach holds the greatest promise for the citizen's development and, ultimately, for long-term community development.

POLICY ANALYSIS, INITIATION, AND BUDGETING

Peter deLeon's article, "The Democratization of the Policy Sciences," calls for an end of the "elite syndrome" in policy analysis.[5] According to deLeon, policy analysts (e.g., systems analysts, operation researchers, economists) suffer from geographic and bureaucratic isolation. Distant from the public and its concerns, usually working at the national level, these technical experts conduct studies (e.g., cost benefit analysis, economic modeling) for the policymaker, not the public. The separation between policymaker and public produces "two cultures" and results in a "confidence gap" between the rulers and the ruled. The remedy, according to deLeon, is return to the original intent of policy science—the improvement of democratic practice. This can best be done by "policy sharing" between analysts and the public. Citizens have the responsibility to express their opinions in open public policy *fora* so that their values and needs can inform the policy formulation process. In turn, policy analysts have the responsibility of devising and actively practicing ways to recruit and include citizens' personal and political views into policymaking. Although certain policy issues (e.g., education, health care, social welfare, housing), may lend themselves to a more democratic style of policy analysis due to their pervasiveness, importance, and schedule, deLeon believes that policy sharing is essential to sustain democracy and prevent the "tyranny" of policy science.

"Public Deliberation: An Alternative Approach to Crafting Policy and Setting Direction," by Nancy Roberts, uses two cases to illustrate the success of direct citizen involvement during the policy initiation phase. The first documents how a school superintendent invited direct citizen participation to help solve a district's severe budget crisis. The second case shows how a governor and commissioner of education used direct citizen participation to craft state educational policy. In both cases, all interested groups and individuals were invited and did participate in the deliberations. And in both cases, policy decisions were reached that were informed by the views and opinions of the participants. These cases highlight the importance of the participatory process—its leadership, design, facilitation, and decision making—in ensuring successful citizen involvement. We return to this point in Section 4.3, when we address the issue of citizen participation in large groups and the special techniques that have to be developed to accommodate growing numbers of citizens involved in collective problem solving. The budget case in this article also is important because it demonstrates that, even under crisis conditions, citizen participation can be a viable mechanism for making policy choices.

Carol Ebdon specifically examines direct citizen participation and the budgeting process[6] using a 1996 International City/County Management Association survey. Her article, "The Relationship Between Citizen Involvement in the Budget Process and City Structure and Culture," seeks to identify the determinants of greater citizen participation. Ebdon operationalizes three concepts— institutional structure, degree of cultural diversity/homogeneity, and political culture—and corre- lates them with responses from city managers in cities with a council-manager form of government. In this initial exploration between budgeting and citizen participation, she finds variation in direct citizen involvement and in the use of participatory methods. For example, there are higher rates of participation in cities with "moralistic" and "traditionalistic" policy cultures. Larger cities also use greater citizen participation and a greater number of the participatory methods.

NOTES

1. For health services see Howard (1972).

2. For social services see Rein (1972).

3. Citizen involvement in environmental issues has a long history. The following articles offer a sample of some of the cases: Ireland (1975), Kauffman and Shorett (1977), Godschalk and Stiftel (1981), Plumlee et al. (1985), Kraft and Kraut (1985), and Desai (1989). For those focusing on the tensions between the democratic ethic and technology, see: Fiorino (1990), Frankenfeld (1992), Laird (1993), Zimmerman (1995), and Abel and Stephan (2000).

4. Additional articles on citizen participation in programs can be found in Bachelor and Jones (1981), Rosenthal (1984), and Weissman (1978).

5. For additional articles see Kweit and Kweit (1984) and Wagle (2000) on citizen participation and policy analysis. Subsequent studies (Durning 1993; Fischer 1993; Kelly and Maynard-Moody 1993; Haight and Ginger 2000) are examples of actual citizen participation in policy analysis.

6. For additional sources on budgeting, consult Simonsen et al. (1996), Callahan (2002), Ebdon (2002), Miller and Evers (2002), Beckett and King (2002), and Orosz (2002).

REFERENCES

Abel, R.D., and M. Stephan. 2000. "The Limits of Civic Environmentalism." *The American Behavioral Scientist,* 44(4): 614–28.

Aron, J.B. 1979. "Citizen Participation at Government Expense." *Public Administration Review,* 39(5): 477–85.

Bachelor, L.W., and B.D. Jones. 1981. "Managed Participation: Detroit's Neighborhood Opportunity Fund." *The Journal of Applied Behavioral Science,* 17(4): 518–35.

Beckett, J., and C.S. King. 2002. "The Challenge to Improve Citizen Participation in Public Budgeting: A Discussion." *Journal of Public Budgeting, Accounting & Financial Management,* 14(3): 463–85.

Callahan, K. 2002. "The Utilization and Effectiveness of Citizen Advisory Committees in the Budget Pro- cess of Local Governments." *Journal of Public Budgeting, Accounting & Financial Management,* 14(2): 295–319.

Cohen, N. 1995. "Technical Assistance for Citizen Participation: A Case Study of New York City's Environ- mental Planning Process." *American Review of Public Administration,* 25(2): 119–36.

Desai, U. 1989. "Public Participation in Environmental Policy Implementation: Case of the Surface Mining Control and Reclamation Act." *American Review of Public Administration,* 19(1): 49–66.

DeSario, J., and S. Langton. 1984. "Citizen Participation and Technology." *Policy Studies Review,* 3(2): 223–33.

Durning, D. 1993. "Participatory Policy Analysis in a Social Service Agency: A Case Study." *Journal of Policy Analysis and Management,* 12(2): 297–322.

Ebdon, C. 2002. "Beyond the Public Hearing: Citizen Participation in the Local Government Budget Process." *Journal of Public Budgeting, Accounting & Financial Management*, 14(2): 273–94.

Fiorino, D.J. 1990. "Citizen Participation and Environmental Risk: A Survey of Institutional Mechanisms." *Science, Technology, & Human Values*, 15(2): 226–43.

Fischer, F. 1993. "Citizen Participation and the Democratization of Policy Expertise: From Theoretical Inquiry to Practical Cases." *Policy Sciences*, 26(3): 165–88.

Frankenfeld, P.J. 1992. "Technological Citizenship: A Normative Framework for Risk Studies." *Science, Technology, & Human Values*, 17(4): 459–84.

Godschalk, D.R., and B. Stiftel. 1981. "Making Waves: Public Participation in State Water Planning." *The Journal of Applied Behavioral Science*, 17(4): 597–614.

Hadden, S.G. 1981. "Technical Information for Citizen Participation." *The Journal of Applied Behavioral Science*, 17(4): 537–49.

Haight, D., and C. Ginger. 2000. "Trust and Understanding in Participatory Policy Analysis: The Case of the Vermont Forest Resources Advisory Council." *Policy Studies Journal*, 28(4): 739–59.

Howard, L.C. 1972. "Decentralization and Citizen Participation in Health Services." *Public Administration Review*, 32 (October): 701–17.

Ireland, L.C. 1975. "Citizen Participation—A Tool for Conflict Management on the Public Lands." *Public Administration Review*, 35(3): 263–69.

Kauffman, K.G., and A. Shorett. 1977. "A Perspective on Public Involvement in Water Management Decisions." *Public Administrative Review*, 37(5): 467–71.

Kelly, M., and S. Maynard-Moody. 1993. "Policy Analysis in the Post-Positivist Era: Engaging Stakeholders in Evaluating the Economic Development Districts Program." *Public Administration Review*, 53(2): 135–42.

King, C.S., K.M. Feltey, and B.O. Susel. 1998. "The Question of Participation: Toward Authentic Public Participation in Public Administration." *Public Administration Review*, 58(4): 317–26.

Korten, D.C. 1980. "Community Organization and Rural Development: A Learning Process Approach." *Public Administration Review*, 40(5): 480–511.

———. 1981. "The Management of Social Transformation." *Public Administration Review*, 41(6): 609–18.

Kraft, M.E., and R. Kraut. 1985. "The Impact of Citizen Participation on Hazardous Waste Policy Implementation: The Case of Clermont County, Ohio." *Policy Studies Journal*, 14(1): 52–61.

Kweit, M.G., and R.W. Kweit. 1984. "The Politics of Policy Analysis: The Role of Citizen Participation in Analytic Decision Making." *Policy Studies Review*, 3(2): 234–45.

Laird, F.N. 1993. "Participatory Policy Analysis, Democracy, and Technological Decision Making." *Science, Technology, & Human Values*, 18(3): 341–61.

Miller, G.J., and L. Evers. 2002. "Budgeting Structures and Citizen Participation." *Journal of Public Budgeting, Accounting & Financial Management*, 14(2): 233–72.

Morgan, E. 1984. "Technocratic v. Democratic Options for Educational Policy." *Policy Studies Review*, 3(2): 263–77.

Orosz, J.R. 2002. "Views from the Field: Creating a Place for Authentic Citizen Participation in Budgeting." *Journal of Public Budgeting, Accounting & Financial Management*, 14(3): 423–44.

Plumlee, J.P., J.D. Starling, and K.W. Kramer. 1985. "Citizen Participation in Water Quality Planning." *Administration & Society*, 16(4): 455–73.

Rein, M. 1972. "Decentralization and Citizen Participation in Social Services." *Public Administration Review*, 32 (October): 687–700.

Rosenthal, D.B. 1984. "Forms of Local Participation in a Neighborhood-Based Federal Program." *Policy Studies Review*, 3(2): 279–95.

Simonsen, B., N. Johnston, and R. Barnett. 1996. "Attempting Non-Incremental Budget Change in Oregon: An Exercise in Policy Sharing." *American Review of Public Administration*, 26(2): 231–51.

Wagle, U. 2000. "The Policy Science of Democracy: The Issues of Methodology and Citizen Participation." *Policy Sciences*, 33(2): 207–23.

Weissman, S.R. 1978. "The Limits of Citizen Participation: Lessons from San Francisco's Model Cities Program." *The Western Political Quarterly*, 31(1): 32–47.

Zimmerman, A.D. 1995. "Toward a More Democratic Ethic of Technological Governance." *Science, Technology, & Human Values*, 20(1): 86–107.

CHAPTER 8

CITIZEN PARTICIPATION IN COMMUNITY ACTION AND MODEL CITIES PROGRAMS

JOHN H. STRANGE

Although controversy is endemic to politics, the decade of the 1960's may well be remembered as the era when political controversy erupted with unusual intensity. One of the most controversial pieces of domestic legislation of that period was the Economic Opportunity Act (EOA) of 1964, which established Community Action Programs (CAPs), funded by the federal government, yet operated for the most part by private, nonprofit agencies exempt from direct political review or control at the local or state level. This fact alone would have been enough to create severe political repercussions, but insult was added to injury by the requirement that there be "maximum feasible participation" on the part of the residents of the area or of the poor in the operation of the Community Action Program. Because of this single phrase and its implementation in the Office of Economic Opportunity (OEO) and Model Cities Programs, the decade of the 1960's will most likely be remembered as the decade of participation.

The emphasis on direct citizen involvement in policymaking and implementation has had a significant impact on the conduct of government in general and public administration in particular. The OEO programs, Model Cities, community organization efforts such as welfare rights groups or neighborhood protest associations, women's organizations, and student associations have all created unusually urgent demands for a re-evaluation of the basic tenets of public administration. This essay, and those accompanying it, are designed to provide a summary of what has been learned and what questions remain unanswered about public administration and citizen participation. This essay in particular, with its accompanying bibliography, reviews the two federal programs that were primarily responsible for the renewed interest in citizen participation. First, the history of citizen participation in OEO and Model Cities Programs is discussed. Special attention is given to the variety of meanings that have been given to citizen participation, the numerous techniques employed in implementing this concept, and the administrative and political activities that worked together to restrict participation in Model Cities and Community Action Agencies (CAAs). Second, attention is given to the changes in attitudes toward participation that have occurred over

---

From *Public Administration Review,* 32 (October 1972): 655–669. Copyright © 1972 by American Society for Public Administration. Reprinted with permission.

time. Third, the various objectives sought through participation are reviewed, and the success in achieving them is assessed. This discussion is followed by a review of the conditions necessary for successful citizen participation and the techniques available for achieving participation. A final section discusses the probable future of citizen participation. It is hoped that through a review of these issues, this essay will serve as a general guide to the research and writings on citizen participation, particularly in the OEO and Model Cities Programs, and that it will assist in the expansion and modification of the curricula in the field of public administration. It is also hoped that it will provide some sense of the research questions that remain to be answered.

MEANINGS OF CITIZEN PARTICIPATION

It is important to note that the inclusion of the prophetic and important words "maximum feasible participation" in the original OEO legislation was unplanned, and, for all practical purposes, undefined (22) (127) (150) (153) (236) (207). After passage of the EOA legislation and the establishment of the Office of Economic Opportunity, numerous interpretations were given to all of the terms used in the most controversial portion of the legislation: "maximum feasible," "participation," "poor," "residents of the area." Interpretations varied by region, over time, according to individual needs, and in response to personal objectives and interpretations (1) (51) (153) (200) (201) (210). In general, those writing about the experience of the Community Action Agencies have identified important differences in the interpretation of these terms in three specific areas. First there was a continuing debate over what "maximum feasible" meant. Did it mean that *some* residents, poor people, blacks, or others, were to participate, or did it mean that at least one-third of those in decision-making positions should be from these groups? This latter interpretation was officially made a part of the legislation in 1966, when Republican efforts to scuttle the bill with amendments succeeded in adding the one-third representation requirements without causing defeat of the basic legislation (127) (222). Or did it mean that the designated participants were to have majority control?

Second, controversy surrounded the scope of the participation that was mandated. Was it to take place in the decision-making body of the program, or in the staff? Could participation be achieved through advisory boards? Was it also required in agencies/operating programs subcontracted from the CAPs? (8) (10) (157) (200) (202) (210).

Debates over numbers and the scope of participation seemed enough to inhibit the development of CAPs, but they were joined by controversy over who were to be the participants. Were they to be residents of a specific geographical area, members of a specific ethnic or racial minority, individuals below a given income, persons receiving (or eligible for, but not receiving) some specific government service, or "representatives," however that term might be defined, of one or more of the groups listed above? (1) (8) (10) (153) (161) (200) (202).

We have noted that it is generally agreed that the key phrases relating to citizen participation in the EOA were accidentally chosen and that they were not subjected to congressional scrutiny or challenge. Just the opposite is true with regard to the Demonstration Cities Program, which was established in 1966 as a part of the Department of Housing and Urban Development. The Model Cities Program ("Demonstration" was changed to "Model" in the program's name, political gossip reports, because it had unsavory connotations in the White House) sought to limit, rather than maximize, participation of the poor. Complaints of local and state officials, as well as growing fears among national politicians of the political impact of funds being channeled to active citizens' groups which were not "politically responsible," resulted in the drafting of legislation which placed ultimate responsibility for the development of programs and, more importantly, the expenditure of significantly large amounts of money, in the hands of local elected officials (146). In addition, participation (which could not then be abandoned without intense political and social reaction) was to be sought from all sectors of the community rather than one specific group. Participants were not to be just the poor and blacks or residents or young or old, but were also to be businesspeople and public officials, each equally represented (Demonstration Cities Act of 1966). This retreat from an emphasis on participation, as we shall note below, was only partially successful.

IMPLEMENTATION OF CITIZEN PARTICIPATION

The ambiguity of the meaning of participation and related terms was never entirely resolved except through the implementation of the program in specific localities at a specific time. A number of case studies of participation in Community Action and Model Cities activities are now available in addition to a few comparative studies (10) (12) (16) (21) (39) (40) (45) (48) (50) (51) (53) (54) (55) (72) (76) (87) (92) (96) (100) (102) (103) (117) (122) (137) (147) (149) (156) (157) (165) (166) (176) (186) (193) (196) (201) (206) (217) (222). Although there has as yet been no effort to thoroughly compare the results of these separate studies of participation in different localities, several important findings are readily apparent.

First, one senses the great diversity in the institutional form through which participation has been encouraged. The community action efforts of OEO have been implemented almost exclusively through private, nonprofit, nongovernmental agencies, a factor of great importance in explaining the nature and extent of citizen participation and the controversy surrounding it (222). These nongovernmental institutions took different forms in different cities. In some places, such as New York City, community corporations were established amalgamating government and the private sector (87). In most OEO cities, participation was primarily centered in the nongovernmental Community Action Agency. In many cities, participation was concentrated, not in the CAA itself, but in neighborhood centers or program delivery units that operated with varying degrees of independence from the CAA as well as local government.

Citizen participation in the Model Cities Program has taken a different form than that in Community Action Programs. The Model Cities Program placed ultimate local responsibility with elected public officials. Although "widespread citizen participation" was only one of 30 requirements to be met, it was provided that citizen participation structures "must have clear and direct access to the decision-making process," and they must be provided with technical assistance to assure that they have "the technical capacity to make decisions." Nevertheless, private, nonprofit organizations—such as those which administered community action organizations—were not allowed. This "return" of authority to local government, coupled with the emphasis on participation by business and government as well as by "citizens," was intended to drastically decrease the emphasis on and concern with citizen participation, especially when "citizen" was interpreted to mean the poor or ethnic minorities (100) (146) (210).

Few attempts have been made to explain why these different institutional forms arose. Most explanations stress the importance of the local setting and the enormous impact that specific individuals have had on the nature and impact of citizen participation efforts. Even fewer attempts have been made to assess what differences in the quality and results of participation can be traced to the use of the various institutional forms that have been created to encourage participation.

A second general conclusion that can be derived from the case studies is that emphasis was placed on the participation of minority group members in situations where ethnic and racial minorities were present in significant numbers. "Citizens" and "poor" were often interpreted to mean "black" or "Puerto Rican" or "Indian" without regard to income (200) (201).

Third, most OEO programs complied with the mandates of the national office and emphasized participation in board membership and staff positions rather than through advisory bodies. Specific decision-making positions were accorded citizen participants (51) (117) (122).

Fourth, despite the emphasis on participation in "control" positions, only a very few (1–2 percent) of the Community Action Programs were ever substantially controlled or influenced by the poor or by ethnic minorities (222).

Fifth, in the Model Cities Programs there were several forces at work limiting the reduction in participation sought through an attempt to retain ultimate governmental control over the program. Many HUD and federal Model Cities employees sought to maximize the possibilities for citizen participation. Attempts were made to emphasize ethnic and economic minorities in defining "citizen," to institutionalize the mechanisms for participation by "the poor" through the provision of financial and technical assistance to community residents, to further participation by citing the example of OEO, and, where possible, to encourage local Community Action Agencies to support extensive citizen participation in the Model Cities program as well as their own (146). Attempts, a few of which were successful, were also made to allow local governments to delegate their ultimate program authority to citizens' groups (3) (100) (157) (200).

The major difference between the implementation of the participation mandate in the Community Action Program and implementation in Model Cities was that OEO required participation by a specified number or percentage of citizens with little emphasis on a standard process for that participation, while the Model Cities Program sought to insure participation through the establishment of specific procedures for participation with financial and technical support being supplied in an attempt to insure effective citizen participation.

RESTRICTIONS ON CITIZEN PARTICIPATION

Despite the controversy surrounding the question of participation and the fears of elected officials that their political control had been dissipated, numerous restrictions on citizen participation have been identified by observers of the Community Action and Model Cities Programs. The practices of OEO which restricted participation (for an expanded discussion, see 202) included a growing emphasis on development of OEO programs at the federal level, thus negating participation in localities. National emphasis programs were developed without the citizen participation that occurred in some of the local agencies. OEO also restricted the impact of local participation by using its funding authority to establish program priorities, thereby deciding local program content in fact while retaining the form of local program development. Radical expansion of Community Action efforts into 1,000 communities without a corresponding expansion of program funds restricted the importance of citizen decision making. The poor and minority groups were also discouraged from participating as a result of the complex and numerous reports and forms that had to be prepared. Without adequate technical support, participants became lost and discouraged in a sea of documents and a maze of deadlines. A constant redefinition, at both local and national levels, of who participants were to be and how they were to participate also impeded the participation process. In some localities, local agencies (or local branches of federal agencies) successfully blocked implementation of participatory techniques. Participation also suffered where potential participants had a choice of participating in "control" positions without pay or in salaried non-decision-making positions. Low-income participants, understandably, frequently opted for cash instead of influence. In some areas, and in later time periods, participation of new groups was restricted when earlier citizen participants adopted devices to perpetuate their control through the exclusion of new groups. This occurred both in decision-making bodies and professional staffs. All of these activities seriously undermined the impact of citizen participants in Community Action Agencies (146) (202) (210).

The Model Cities Program suffered from many of the same difficulties. Most important was the legislative mandate of the Model Cities Program limiting the emphasis to be placed on participation. Model Cities' concern with a long and detailed planning process also discouraged citizens who sought immediate solutions to their problems. Funding and application procedures were equally as complex as those of OEO.

Finally, recent reductions in funding and explicit mandates from the highest levels of government to undo arrangements which delegated major decision-making responsibilities to citizen groups in a limited number of cities have served to discourage and reduce the extent and impact of citizen participation in the Model Cities Program (146) (157).

CHANGING ATTITUDES TOWARD CITIZEN PARTICIPATION

The attitudes toward and emphasis on citizen participation have varied over time in both the Community Action and Model Cities Programs. Section 103 of the Demonstration City and Metropolitan Development Act 1966 specified that in order for a Model Cities Program to be eligible for assistance, there must be "widespread citizen participation in the program." As only one of a large number of requirements for funding, many hoped that participation would be de-emphasized. For the reasons noted earlier, several communities, including Dayton, OH, Cambridge, MA, and Philadelphia, PA, delegated significant decision-making authority to citizen groups (100) (146) (157). Elsewhere, significant steps were taken to insure that the *process* for participation was firmly established and vigorously supported (37) (97). Recent developments clearly indicate that the emphasis on participation has declined precipitously since May 1969 (200). Specific institutions have been instructed to terminate delegation of authority arrangements such as those in Cambridge and Philadelphia.

The emphasis on participation in OEO programs has followed a somewhat different course. After the passage of the EOA in 1964, early efforts were directed toward involving the poor and minority groups, or their representatives, in staff and board positions. By mid-1965, some of OEO regional directors, especially in the South, began insisting that at least one-third of the boards of community agencies be nonwhite. As noted earlier, the mandate for one-third representation of the poor became law in 1966. The next redefinition of participation came as OEO began to fund organizations completely controlled by the poor to operate program components or to act as an external pressure group for change. As neighborhood centers came to occupy a central position in the program process, requirements were established that neighborhood boards must be composed of a *majority* from the poor community. Finally, a number of Community Action Agencies, after the enactment of Model Cities legislation, became advocates of an enlarged role for citizen participants in the Model Cities Program (8) (22) (35) (55) (91) (117) (128) (146) (172) (201) (202) (210) (222). These efforts were successful in many instances.

As in the Model Cities case, OEO, since 1969, has downgraded the importance of citizen participation. Participation has been neglected as a condition for funding, responsibility for national emphasis programs has been transferred from OEO to other agencies with less interest in citizen participation, research has been emphasized at the expense of participation, funding has been reduced, and a general discouragement of participation has taken place (202) (210).

OBJECTIVES OF PARTICIPATION AND THEIR ATTAINMENT

Numerous arguments have been offered to support the emphasis that had been given participation in the Model Cities and OEO programs. Three basic reasons are offered in support of citizen participation. It is argued that participation is necessary to affect the participants and/or the community in which they live, that it is required in order to shape and direct the Community Action and Model Cities Programs, or it is necessary in order to influence the practices of government in general. Efforts have also been made to assess the extent to which these objectives have been attained (1) (133) (202).

Some have argued that participation is an essential element in the process of social change since it alone provides the opportunity to create a sense of group identity that is essential if one is to effect change. Organization begets power, and power brings changes in benefits. Ethnicity, economic class, use of governmental services, and residency have all been identified as potential bases for organization (6) (8) (37) (55) (71) (76) (146) (157) (179) (201). Evidence has been produced to indicate that this objective has been attained at least in part. It is clear that more blacks and "low-income persons" found more and better jobs in both the Model Cities and Community Action Programs than in any previous federal program. This finding applies not only to jobs but also to positions of influence in decision-making bodies (117) (128) (146) (201) (222).

A different argument, but one which played a major role in the discussions prior to the enactment of the EOA, is that participation by recipients of social services is necessary in order to overcome a sense of powerlessness. Through participation in an important activity, psychic suffering and apathy are reduced. A job, public affirmation of an individual's worth, and a real chance to enhance one's life opportunities are seen, according to these analysts, as the primary reasons for insisting on citizen participation (138).

Participation has also been seen as a means by which citizens could be trained and educated. By engaging in administrative and political activities, the poor and unskilled learn how the government operates and how to maximize individual benefits. As a result of participation, citizens can also acquire general and specific skills, develop new political and administrative abilities, and expand their individual capacities to solve their own problems. Considerable evidence indicates this has occurred (201) (210).

Although not generally accepted, it has also been suggested that participation should be pursued, since the unskilled and the poor, as a result of exposure and training, can have their social behavior altered in such a way that conditions are established which increase effective individual and family life. In its crassest form, the argument is that lower-class individuals can be taught, through participating, to behave as middle-class persons (See 8). Little evidence exists to evaluate whether or not this actually occurs. Some have found, however, that lower-class persons, when given middle-class status, rapidly acquire middle-class prejudices and biases (117).

Participation has also been viewed as an effective device to influence individual behavior by providing a technique for co-opting opponents (150) also see (8) (133) (141) (179). Some students of citizen participation have attempted to analyze conditions affecting the "costs" of co-optation (201). A similar but distinct argument is that participation affects participants by providing an institutional device which encourages compromise rather than conflict. Melvin Mogulof claims that this in fact has occurred (146).

One of the explanations given for inclusion of language such as "participation of the residents of the area involved" in the EOA was to ensure that blacks in the South were hired and received the benefits of the program without having to face a reluctant Congress on this specific issue (22)

(126) (236). As events developed, this language did ensure full participation by minority groups (201).

It was also assumed that the Community Action Programs, if they were actually to deal with and solve the problems of poverty, had to direct their energies toward the real needs of the poor. It seemed to some that there was no better technique for identifying real needs than through self-identification, which flows from participation by the needy. The special insight, needs, and experiences of the poor themselves can best be identified and used, the argument goes, when there is genuine citizen participation (35) (37) (38). No evidence is available to assess these arguments.

The more political advocates of participation saw an opportunity to redistribute political influence and power through the mechanisms of participation. If control of a publicly financed organization could be acquired, a significant redistribution of the rewards and benefits (jobs, prestige, security) of the political and social welfare systems could be attained. Participation here was equated with control (6) (157), see (17).

There are different assessments as to whether this has occurred. Certainly the employment of minority group members and the poor was significantly increased as a result of the emphasis on participation. Nevertheless, citizen participation did not result in the replacement of previously employed persons by minority group members or the poor. Only in areas where new employment opportunities were present did the emphasis on citizen participation affect employment patterns (201).

Minority group members have also been provided access to governmental and community influentials. The act of participating has provided specific individuals with valuable political education, experience, and skills. The leadership structure of the minority community has been altered, primarily through the addition of younger and more militant spokesmen. Minority group members have also obtained some significant control over resources such as jobs, access to information and officials, access to equipment, and opportunities for disseminating information, along with recognition, prestige, and money (146) (201) (210). Some claim, however, that these results are deceptive and more limited than necessary. The explanation is that the emphasis on participation actually diverted resources that might have gone into other constructive activities (150), also see (8) (124). In addition, participation created, in some places, animosities and difficulties within program staffs or decision-making bodies or between these two groups. This in turn caused program delays, frequent shifts in policy, and consequent increased costs. In some situations limited resources were used to effectuate participation rather than to implement substantive programs (51) (117) (128) (222). Some have suggested that the emphasis on minority group participation resulted in distrust of the program on the part of lower-class whites, intense displeasure with the program on the part of local and national political officials, and an increase in racial polarization (124) (150). It is generally agreed, then, that no radical redistributions of influence, power, services, rewards, or other benefits has occurred. In some cases the number of groups participating in the pluralistic contest for power and influence has been expanded. Where jobs, services, and other political outputs have been redistributed, middle-income interests have prevailed over low-income interests and ethnicity has prevailed over poverty (17) (146) (201) (202) (210) (222).

The emphasis on citizen participation did alter policy discussions in both programs in one especially significant way: it forced policymakers to deal with the problems of race. Participation also brought about improvement in and initial provision of inexpensive services such as street lights, playgrounds, and street repairs (201) (205). Some studies have concluded the primary factor in bringing about policy changes and improved services was political pressure exerted through protest action (117). These studies go on to argue that a limited number of people actually engaged in and supported the protests, and that the protest leaders came from the most articulate and prosperous members of the black, poor, or minority community. Most of these activities are said to have taken place outside the Model Cities and Community Action Programs. Ralph Kramer takes this argument one step further and suggests that federal policy has been far more affected by riots than by the more conventional participation of which we speak here (117).

An entirely different argument, which also negates the influence of citizen participation in causing program policy changes, suggests that program policy was altered primarily because new money was available for new programs which therefore had to be developed (146) (210). In order to take advantage of newly available funds, program development and innovation occurred. In addition, it is argued, most institutional change resulted from negotiation and bargaining which took place in a setting where citizen participants could affect the compromises and agreements reached among the professionals (117) (201) (222).

Although civil service was one of the central elements in the reform movement of the early 20th century, numerous analysts today are calling for re-examination, or even elimination, of the civil service system. The requirement that the poor participate, in jobs and in decision making, has been viewed by some as an important step in the re-evaluation of job requirements and the removal of unnecessarily restrictive standards for employment. Changes in this area have occurred as a result of the emphasis on participation.

Emphasis on citizen participation has also been explained as a technique for establishing a group to criticize and evaluate ongoing programs and to encourage real problem solving. Citizen participation has proved to be a useful counter to exclusionary policies which limited program operation *and* evaluation to specific professional groups. As a result of the emphasis on participation, professionals and their programs were subjected to evaluation by new groups using different standards (200). A similar objective was to establish ongoing political support from participants for the continuation and expansion of the Community Action and Model Cities Programs themselves. This objective has been achieved, with limited and varying success, in both programs.

Participation has also had an important symbolic meaning to minority group communities. In part, citizen participation has symbolized concern with minority rights, political influence for blacks and other groups alienated from the political system, and the problems of the poor (124) (146) (201).

Participation has been used as a standard by which other governmental and private activities are evaluated. To the extent that participation is accepted as a legitimate objective of all social welfare activities, it becomes a useful device to force changes in other practices which could not be attacked directly (202).

Failure to meet the criterion of participation, even if not accepted, also provided an opportunity for Community Action and Model Cities Programs to circumvent, negate, or ignore positions taken by other governmental agencies. Competition with other programs became possible since OEO and Model Cities could claim to be doing a better job. The programs could also bypass recalcitrant or unsympathetic groups if they failed to meet participation standards (146) (201) (202).

By insisting on participation in delegated programs, Community Action and Model Cities Programs brought about an alteration in the programs, employment patterns, and, on occasion, the general orientations of other programs and agencies (146) (201).

The participation was also seen as an unusual opportunity to create new inputs to which bureaucracies must respond. In effect, the argument is that participation of the poor provides an opportunity to replace the middle-class values and orientations of bureaucracy with interests of a broader nature (133).

In some program areas, especially education, citizen participation has been seen as a useful inducement or an effective technique for attaining decentralized authority. At times, this has been combined with the argument that participation of all citizens affects government in general the most by increasing "the legitimacy of government and therefore its effectiveness" (146).

Although no one argues that participation has accomplished revolutionary alterations in the operation of government, citizen participation in the Model Cities and Community Action Programs is acknowledged to have had an important impact.

One development which has resulted from the emphasis on citizen participation has been the establishment of precedents for involvement of minority low-income groups in employment and program development. Regular channels of contact between government and citizens not normally consulted by government have been established. New institutions concerned with the needs and problems of minority groups and the poor have been established (146).

The emphasis on citizen participation (but *not* participation in the sense of control) has spread beyond the boundaries of the Model Cities and Community Action Programs. Colleges, health departments, YMCAs, United Funds, welfare boards, and hospitals have all been subjected to increased pressure to open up their staffs, boards, and services to those previously excluded, especially members of ethnic minorities (202).

Another important impact that citizen participation has had in the realm of government was unplanned and unexpected. That is the impact on public administration and administrators. These essays are in large part an attempt to recognize that impact which to date has received minimal attention. One result of citizen participation on administrators can be seen in the policies and activities of professional members drawn from the field of public administration. The International City Management Association, the National League of Cities, the American Society for Public Administration, the International Association of Chiefs of Police, the American Institute of Planners, and numerous other groups have revised their positions on citizen participation, engaged in new programs for minority groups, or altered by-laws and creeds. Minority caucuses have also been formed in many of these organizations—an indirect result of the emphasis on citizen participation in the Model Cities and Community Action Programs. The education of public administrators has also been altered to take account of citizen participation efforts. The access of minorities to administrative positions has been greatly increased. Finally, standards by which administrators are evaluated have been expanded in numerous areas to include their response to and ability to encourage citizen participation.

Some have argued that the reason citizen participation must be pursued is that it is a basic and inalienable *right* of the American people. There is no question, according to this argument, whether there should be maximum participation or not, or even what its effect will be or has been. Rather, the concern must be to establish the institutional mechanisms which will most successfully guarantee the right of participation to all citizens (35) (38).

CONDITIONS NECESSARY FOR PARTICIPATION

Participation in the Model Cities Program was planned and prepared for to a much greater extent than participation in Community Action Programs. Sherry Arnstein and Daniel Fox, in an outstanding paper originally prepared for HUD, thoroughly discuss the conditions necessary to achieve meaningful participation. They identify five possible structures for Model Cities Programs: (1) a coalition policymaking group with representatives from government and neighborhood associations, (2) a central planning group staffed by residents, (3) a resident's advisory or coordinating group to assist a professional planning group, (4) a professional advisory group responsible to the residents that would assist the professional planners of the programs, and (5) planning groups or task forces established according to function, with heavy resident representation (36) (97).

In addition to a specific structure, Fox and Arnstein argue that the representativeness of resident participants must be ensured. To accomplish this, there must be a specific selection procedure, and there must be methods for maintaining accountability to constituents. They offer four suggestions: (1) specific times for the selection or election of representatives (known well in advance) (2) open meetings of deliberative bodies, (3) regular reports to constituents, and (4) recall procedures (97).

Five other necessities are identified by these two authors. Information must be available in sufficient detail and in plenty of time to allow residents to evaluate alternatives and make choices. There must be a clear set of rules governing participation, including tangible benefits. Technical assistance must be available. Finally, financial assistance is required in several forms: (1) payments for meeting attendance (debated), (2) funds available for technical assistance, (3) simple and quick expense reimbursement procedures, and (4) multiple-year program funding (97).

Fox and Arnstein based their recommendations, in part, on their experiences in the Community Action efforts to maximize participation. There is no evidence of similar concern among OEO officials with the conditions necessary to ensure participation in Community Action Programs. Several arguments were made, from time to time, that elections, or mandated membership on boards, or community organizations were essential to participation. In general, however, OEO lacked a detailed plan such as was available to Model Cities (124) (146).

TECHNIQUES OF PARTICIPATION

When speaking of citizen participation, it is common to think only of participation in decision-making procedures. This is, of course, a most important technique of participation. Membership on the governing board, on the policymaking body, is a much-emphasized technique of participation in both the Model Cities and Community Action Programs. Selection procedures for these participants have differed in various localities. In the early days of OEO, government officials selected the "representatives of the poor." Groups, such as neighborhood councils, have also selected and been represented by participants. In some areas, elections have been used, while Model Cities has often emphasized selection in convention.

One advocate of citizen participation (124) has suggested the use of sample surveys in order to identify resident desires and opinions. Others have stressed employment of the poor, or the establishment of advisory bodies. OEO has emphasized the organization of the poor into independent groups. This has been accomplished in several ways: around the provision of services; through the financial support of pre-existing organizations; and by organizing around particular issues or ethnic, religious, occupational, or residential affiliations. Organization has also been accomplished by establishing functional, nonprofit organizations such as cooperatives or credit unions. In some areas, coalitions of existing organizations have been united into councils or federations.

PARTICIPATION—WHAT LIES AHEAD?

Recent commentaries concerning citizen participation in Model Cities and Community Action Programs note the continued decline in the importance of participation in both of these programs. Since the programs themselves are being de-emphasized, opinion is divided about the future importance that will be attached to citizen participation. Some argue that, as a goal, participation is here to stay (124). Others claim it will rapidly fade in importance. Whatever the opinion about its vitality, all agree that if participation of the poor, of minority groups, of deprived urban residents is to continue without a concomitant growth of hostility, cynicism, and apathy, there must be a massive infusion of funds to accomplish at least a portion of the objectives of the citizen participants. Frances Fox Piven argues the point this way: "Sustained and effective participation will finally depend on the allocation to those communities of the social and economic benefits that are the resources for participation and influence in a complex society" (172). Ralph Kramer puts it slightly differently: "The community development process is no substitute for that massive commitment of national resources required to eliminate poverty by rebuilding the ghetto and restoring full citizenship to minorities, although it may be able to mobilize support for those policies" (117).

REFERENCES

1. Advisory Commission on Intergovernmental Relations, *Intergovernmental Relations in the Poverty Programs,* Report A-29 (Washington, D.C.: U.S. Government Printing Office, April 1966).
2. Robert A. Aleshire, "Model Cities and Anti-Poverty Programs—Will They Be Friends or Foes?" *The Journal of Housing,* Vol. 25, No. 5 (May–June 1968), pp. 236–237.
3. ———, "Planning and Citizen Participation: Costs, Benefits and Approaches," *The Urban Affairs Quarterly* (June 1970).
4. ———, "Power to the People: An Assessment of the Community Action and Model Cities Experiences," *Public Administration Review,* Vol. 32, Special Issue (September 1972).
5. Saul Alinsky, "The War on Poverty: Political Pornography," *Journal of Social Issues,* Vol. 21 (January 1965).
6. Alan A. Altshuler, *Community Control* (New York: Pegasus, 1970).
7. Stanley Arnovitz, "Poverty, Politics and Community Organization," *Studies on the Left* (Summer 1964).
8. Sherry Arnstein, "Ladder of Citizen Participation," *Journal of the American Institute of Planners,* Vol. 35, No. 4 (July 1969), pp. 216–224.
9. David Austin, *Citizen Participation and Participation of the Poor: A Comparison of Administrative Discretion by Federal Agencies in the Application of Two Roles,* mimeo. (Harvard University, May 20, 1966).
10. ———, *Community Representation in Community Action Programs,* Office of Economic Opportunity Grant Number CG 68–9499 A/2, Report #2 (August 1968).
11. ———, *Resident Participation, Political Mobilization or Organizational Cooperation?"* (Florence Heller Graduate School for Advanced Studies in Social Welfare, May 1970).
12. R.W. Avery and H.A. Chesler, *A Community Organizes for Action: A Case Study of the Mon-Yough Region in Pennsylvania* (The Pennsylvania State University Institute for Research on Human Resources, June 1967).
13. Richard F. Babcock and Fred P. Bosselman, "Citizen Participation: A Suburban Suggestion for the Central City," *Law and Contemporary Problems* (Winter 1967), pp. 220–231.
14. Peter Bachrach and Morton S. Baratz, *Power and Poverty: Theory and Practice* (New York: Oxford University Press, 1970).
15. Edward S. Banfield, *The Unheavenly City* (Boston: Little Brown, 1970).
16. Reitzel Barass and Associates, Incorporated, *Community Action and Institutional Change: An Evaluation* (Cambridge, July 1969).
17. ———, *Evaluation of CAP Impact on Organizations* (Cambridge, June 1969).
18. D. Bell and V. Held, "The Community Revolution," *The Public Interest,* No. 16 (Summer 1969).
19. Warner Bloomberg, Jr., and Florence W. Rosenstock, "Who Can Activate the Poor: One Assessment of Maximum Feasible Participation," paper presented to the annual meeting of the American Sociological Association (August 29, 1967).
20. ———, and Henry J. Schmandt (eds.), *Power, Poverty and Urban Policy* (Beverly Hills: Sage Publications, 1968).
21. Richard Blumenthal, "The Bureaucracy: Antipoverty and the Community Action Program," in Allan P. Sindler (ed.), *American Political Institutions and Public Policy* (Boston: Little Brown, 1969), pp. 128–179.
22. Richard W. Boone, "Reflections on Citizen Participation and the Economic Opportunity Act," *Public Administration Review,* Vol. 32, Special Issue (September 1972).

23. A. Donald Bourgeois, "Citizen Role in St. Louis Model Cities Program Described," *Journal of Housing,* Vol. 24 (December 1967), pp. 613–617.
24. G.A. Brager and F.B. Purcell, *Community Action Against Poverty* (New Haven: Yale University Press, 1967).
25. Harry C. Bredemeier, "The Politics of the Poverty Cold War," *Urban Affairs Quarterly* (June 1968), pp. 3–35.
26. Christopher Breiseth, "CAP and the Democratic Process," in Cahn and Passett (eds.), *Citizen Participation: A Case Book in Democracy* (New York: Praeger Publishers, 1969).
27. Ronald L. Brignac, "Public Housing Official Reacts to Citizen Participation—Messages with One-Man Drama," *Journal of Housing* (November 1969), pp. 69ff.
28. Charles B. Brink, *Social Change Evaluation Project* (Seattle: Washington University, 1969).
29. M.P. Brooks, "Community Action Programs as a Setting for Applied Research," *Journal of Social Issues* (January 1965).
30. P. Bullock, "On Organizing the Poor: Problems of Morality and Tactics," *Dissent,* Vol. 15, No. 1 (January–February 1968).
31. Edmund M. Burke, "Citizen Participation Is a Necessity—How Can We Make It Work?" *Journal of Housing* (November 1969).
32. ———, "Citizen Participation Strategies," *Journal of the American Institute of Planners* (September 1968), pp. 287–294.
33. ———, "Have the Poor Wrecked Johnson's War on Poverty?" *Antioch Review* (Winter 1966–67).
34. W.E. Butler and H. Pope, *Community Power Structures, Industrialization and Public Welfare Programs* (Chapel Hill: University of North Carolina, August 1966).
35. Edgar S. Cahn and Jean C. Cahn, "Citizen Participation," in Hans B.C. Spiegel (ed.), *Citizen Participation in Urban Development* (Washington, D.C.: Center for Community Affairs, NTL Institute for Applied Behavioral Science, 1968).
36. Edgar S. Cahn and Barry A. Passett (eds.), *Citizen Participation: A Case Book in Democracy* (New York: Praeger Publishers, 1969).
37. E.S. Cahn and J.C. Cahn, "The War on Poverty: A Civilian Perspective," *The Yale Law Journal,* Vol. 73, No. 8 (July 1964), pp. 1317–1352.
38. ———, "Maximum Feasible Participation," in Cahn and Passett (eds.), *Citizen Participation: A Case Book in Democracy* (New York: Praeger Publishers, 1969).
39. A. Carter, S. Jett, and E. Vargah, *An Evaluation of the McDowell County CAP* (Morgantown, W.Va.: Human Resources Research Institute, January 1969).
40. Everett F. Cataldo, Richard M. Johnson, and Lyman A. Kellstadt, "The Urban Poor and Community Action in Buffalo," paper presented at Midwest Political Science Association Meeting (May 2–3, 1968).
41. Central Piedmont Regional Council of Local Governments, *Citizen Participation,* Clearinghouse No. PB 191 721.
42. Chamber of Commerce of the United States of America, *Task Force on Economic Growth and Opportunity* (Washington, D.C., 1965).
43. A. Alexander Chauncy and Charles McCann, "The Concept of Representativeness in Community Organization," *Social Work,* Vol. 1 (January 1956), pp. 48–52.
44. *Citizen Involvement in Urban Affairs* (New York: New York University Graduate School of Public Administration, April 1969), Clearinghouse No. PB 183 967.
45. "Citizens' Role in St. Louis Model Cities Program Described," *Journal of Housing,* Vol. 11 (December 1967), pp. 613–617.
46. Richard A. Cloward, "The War on Poverty: Are the Poor Left Out?" *Nation* (August 2, 1965), pp. 55–60.
47. "Community Development Corps: A New Approach to Poverty Programs," *Harvard Law Review,* Vol. 82 (January 1969), pp. 644–667.
48. Community Legal Counsel, *Citizen Participation in Chicago's Model Cities Program: A Critical Analysis* (Chicago, 1968).
49. Community Renewal Society, *The Ford Foundation Model Cities Technical Assistance Project: Year End Progress Report* (Chicago, 1969).
50. Community Representation in CAP's (Waltham, Mass.: Florence Heller School for Advanced Studies in Social Welfare, March 1969), Clearinghouse No. PB 188013.
51. Comptroller General of the United States, *Review of Economic Opportunity Programs* (Washington,

D.C.: General Accounting Office, March 18, 1969). The General Accounting Office also published a number of reviews of the effectiveness and administration of specific Community Action Programs. These were also published in 1969.

52. "Controversy over the Federal Anti-Poverty CAP, Pro and Con," *Congressional Digest,* Vol. 47, No. 2 (February 1968), pp. 35–64.

53. Rowena Courson and Stretch Courson, *Community Organization in Low Income Neighborhoods in New Orleans* (New Orleans: Social Welfare Planning Council, December 1968).

54. Fred R. Crawford, *A Comprehensive and Systematic Evaluation of CAP and Related Programs Operating in Atlanta, Georgia* (Atlanta: Emory University Center for Research in Social Change, June 1969).

55. James Cunnigham, *Participant Observation of Citizen Participation in Ten Community Action Programs,* mimeo. (Pittsburgh: University of Pittsburgh, 1967).

56. R.F. Curtis, *et al.,* "Prejudice and Urban Social Participation," *American Journal of Sociology* (Spring 1967).

57. Belden Hull Daniels, "The Urban Poor vs. the Government," in Frank Smallwood (ed.), *The New Federalism* (Hanover, N.H.: The Public Affairs Center of Dartmouth College), pp. 56–71.

58. S.M. David, "Leadership of the Poor in Poverty Programs," in R.H. Connery (ed.), *Urban Riots: Violence and Social Change* (New York: Columbia University, 1969).

59. R.H. Davidson, "The Politics of Anti-Poverty," *The Nation* (February 24, 1969).

60. ———. *War on Poverty: Experiment in Federalism* (Santa Barbara: Department of Political Science, 1969).

61. ———, and Sar A. Levitan, *Anti-Poverty House-keeping: The Administration of the Economic Opportunity Act* (Ann Arbor: The Institute of Labor and Industrial Relations, the University of Michigan and Wayne State University, 1968).

62. L. Davis, "Syracuse: What Happens When the Poor Take Over," *The New Republic,* Vol. 38, No. 6 (March 1968).

63. Andre L. Delbecq and Sidney J. Kaplan, "The Myth of the Indigenous Community Leader," *Academy of Management Journal* (March 1968).

64. J.C. Donovan, *The Politics of Poverty* (New York: Pegasus, 1967).

65. *Education and Manpower Strategies and Programs for Deprived Urban Neighborhoods: The Model Cities Approach* (Washington, D.C.: National League of Cities, August 1968).

66. George H. Esser, "Involving the Citizen in Decision-Making," *Nations Cities* (May 1968) pp. 11–14.

67. ———, "The Role of a State-wide Foundation in the War on Poverty," *Law and Contemporary Problems,* Vol. 31, No. 1 (Winter 1966).

68. Louis A. Ferman (ed.), *Evaluating the War on Poverty,* Annals of the American Academy of Political and Social Science (September 1969).

69. Richard Flacks, "On the Uses of Participatory Democracy," *Dissent* (November–December 1966).

70. Daniel Fox, "Federal Standards and Regulations for Citizen Participation," in Cahn and Passett (eds.), *Citizen Participation: A Case Book in Democracy* (New York: Praeger Publishers, 1969).

71. Herbert J. Gans, "We Won't End the Urban Crisis Until We End Majority Rule," *New York Times Magazine* (August 3, 1969).

72. Neil Gilbert, *Citizen Participation in the Poverty Program,* unpublished Ph.D. dissertation, University of Pittsburgh.

73. James Gordon (ed.), *Model Cities Consultation* (Chicago: Urban Training Center, 1968).

74. Walter Gove and Herbert Castner, "Organizing the Poor: An Evaluation of Strategy," *Social Science Quarterly,* Vol. 50, No. 3 (December 1969).

75. Lester B. Granger, "Community Organization and Tomorrow's Urbanism," *Ekistics* (February 1966).

76. Polly Greenberg, *The Devil Has Slippery Shoes: A Biased Biography of the Child Development Group of Mississippi* (New York: Macmillan, 1969).

77. D.J. Greenstone and P.E. Peterson, "Reforms, Machines and the War on Poverty," in J.W. Wilson (ed.), *City Politics and Public Policy* (New York: John Wiley and Sons, 1968).

78. Charles F. Grosser, "Community Organizations and the Grassroots," *Social Work,* Vol. 12, No. 4 (October 1967), pp. 61–67.

79. Bill Haddad, "Mr. Skinner and the Savage Politics of Poverty," *Harper* (February 1966) pp. 232–236.

80. Robert Hagedorn and Sanford Labovitz, "Participation in Community Associations by Occupation: A Test of Three Theories," *American Sociological Review,* Vol. 33, No. 2 (April 1968), pp. 767–783.

81. Warren C. Haggstrom, *Prerequisites to the Power of the Poor* (Syracuse: Syracuse University Community Action Training Center, 1966).

82. ———, *The Intent and Outcome of Maximum Feasible Participation of the Poor* (Syracuse: Syracuse University Community Action Training Center, 1966).

83. ———, "The Power of the Poor," in Riessman, Cohen, and Pearl (eds.), *Mental Health of the Poor* (New York: The Free Press, 1964).

84. Howard Hallman, "Annotated Bibliography of Community Action Research," (Washington D.C.: The Center for Governmental Studies, 1970).

85. ———, *Community Corporations and Neighborhood Control,* Pamphlet No. 1 (Washington, D.C.: Center for Governmental Studies, 1970).

86. ———, "Federally Financed Citizen Participation," *Public Administration Review,* Vol. 32, Special Issue (September 1972).

87. ———, *Neighborhood Control of Public Programs: Case Studies of Community Corporations and Neighborhood Boards* (New York: Praeger, 1970).

88. ———, "Some Key Issues in Organizing and Operating Neighborhood Boards," mimeo. (New Haven Conn.: Community Progress, Inc., May 1968).

89. William W. Hamilton, "The Cities vs. the People: Citizen Participation in Model Cities," *Everyman's Guide to Federal Programs Impact,* Vol. 1, No. 2 (1969), available from New Community Press, 3210 Grace Street, N.W., Washington, D.C. 20007.

90. Tom Hayden, "A View of the Poverty Program—'When It's Dry You Can't Crack It with a Pick' " (New York: New York University Graduate School of Social Work, July 1966).

91. Florence Heller Graduate School of Advanced Studies in Social Welfare, *Community Representation in Community Action Programs* (Waltham, Mass: Brandeis University, 1969).

92. Stanley Herr, "Citizen Participation and Planning in the Newark Model Cities Program: The Search for an Elusive Model," (New York: Columbia University Institute of Urban Environment, October 4, 1968).

93. W.J. Hifferman, Jr., "Research Notes on the Conventional Political Behavior of the Poor," *Journal of Human Resources,* Vol. 4, No. 2 (Spring 1969).

94. Arthur Hillman, *Local Community Structure and Civic Participation* (Chicago: National Federation of Settlements and Neighborhood Centers, May 1968).

95. M. Hoffman and J. Mudd, "The New Plantations," *The Nation,* Vol. 203, No. 13 (October 24, 1966).

96. Richard Hoffman, *Community Action: Innovation and Coordinative Strategies in the War on Poverty,* Ph.D. dissertation (Chapel Hill, N.C., University of North Carolina).

97. HUD Guide, *Citizen Participation in Model Cities,* Technical Assistance Bulletin No. 3 (Washington, D.C.: U.S. Government Printing Office, December 1968).

98. HUD Handbook, *Citizen Involvement Workable Program for Community Improvement* (Washington, D.C.: U.S. Government Printing Office, October 1968).

99. HUD Region IV, *Citizen Participation Today: Proceedings of a Staff Conference* (Washington, D.C.: U.S. Government Printing Office, June 3–4, 1968).

100. HUD, *The Model Cities Program: A History and Analysis of the Planning Process in Three Cities— Atlanta, Seattle, Dayton* (Washington, D.C.: U.S. Government Printing Office, 1968).

101. Benjamin L. Huffman, "Political Theory and Citizen Participation in Programs of the United States Department of Housing and Urban Development," unpublished paper (New York: Columbia University Institute of Urban Environment, August 1968).

102. Institute of Labor and Industrial Relations, *The Community Organization Approach to Anti-Poverty Action: An Evaluation of the Willow Village Project* (Ann Arbor: University of Michigan and Wayne State University, 1967).

103. Institute of Public Administration, *Community Action Programs in the Northeastern United States* (New York: The Institute, 1967).

104. Institute of Urban and Regional Development, *Power and Participation in the San Francisco Community Action Program 1964–67* (Berkeley: University of California, 1967).

105. Judson L. James, "Federalism and the Model Cities Experiment," paper prepared for the American Political Science Association, September 1970.

106. Paul R. James "Lessons from the Model Cities Program," *Management Information Service,* Vol. 1, No. L-4 (April 1969).

107. *Journal of the American Institute of Planners* (July 1969).

108. Marshall Kaplan, "Advocacy and Urban Planning," *The Social Welfare Forum* (New York: Columbia University Press, 1968).
109. F.E. Katz, "Social Participation and Social Structure," *Social Forces* (December 1966).
110. H.F. Kaufman, K.P. Wilkinson, and L.W. Cole, *Poverty Progress and Social Mobility: Focus on Rural Population of Lower Social Rank in Mississippi and the South* (Mississippi State University Social Science Research Center, September 1966).
111. Lucy B. Kay, *Handbook for CA in Rural Economic Action: A Research Report* (Washington, D.C.: Nathan Associates, Inc., June 1968).
112. Joseph A. Kershaw, *Government Against Poverty* (Chicago: Markham, 1970), Clearinghouse No. PB 183168.
113. Langley Keyes and Lisa Peattle, *Citizen Participation in the Model Cities First Rows* (Cambridge: Urban Ghetto Study Program, Laboratory for Environmental Studies, MIT).
114. Erwin Knoll, "The War on Poverty: Some Hope, Some Hoopla," *The Progressive,* Vol. 29, No. 11 (November 1965), pp. 11–14.
115. Milton Kotler, *Neighborhood Government: The Local Foundations of Political Life* (Indianapolis: Bobbs Merrill, 1969).
116. R.M. Kramer and C. Denton, "Organization of a CAP: A Comparative Case Study," *Social Work,* Vol. 21, No. 4 (October 1967).
117. ———, *Participation of the Poor* (Englewood Cliffs, N.J.: Prentice-Hall, 1969).
118. Elliott A. Krause, "Functions of a Bureaucratic Ideology: Citizen Participation," *Social Problems,* Vol. 16 (Fall 1968), pp. 129–143.
119. S.L. Kravitz, "Community Action Programs: Past, Present, Future," *American Child,* Vol. 47, No. 4 (November 1965).
120. ———, and Ferne K. Kalodner, "Community Action: Where Has It Been? Where Will It Go?" *Annals of the American Academy of Political and Social Science,* Vol. 385 (September 1969), pp. 30–40.
121. Irving Kristol, "Decentralization for What?" *The Public Interest* (Spring 1968).
122. Jonathan P. Lane, *Efforts at Social Change: The Process and Effects of the Community Action Program, 1965–1970* (Washington, D.C.: The Brookings Institution).
123. P.R. Laurence, "Organizational Development in the Black Ghetto," in R.S. Rosenbloom and R. Marris (ed.), *Social Innovation in the City* (Cambridge: Harvard University Press, 1969).
124. Irving Lazar, "Which Citizens to Participate in What?" in Cahn and Passett (eds.), *Citizen Participation: A Case Book in Democracy* (New York: Praeger, 1969).
125. Helene Levens, "Organizational Affiliation and Powerlessness: A Case Study of the Welfare Poor," *Social Problems,* Vol. 16 (Summer 1968), pp. 18–32.
126. Sar A. Levitan, "The Community Action Program: A Strategy to Fight Poverty," *Annals of the American Academy of Political and Social Sciences* (September 1969), pp. 63–75.
127. ———, *The Design of the Federal Antipoverty Strategy* (University of Michigan and Wayne State University: The Institute of Labor and Public Relations, 1967).
128. ———, *The Great Society's Poor Law: A New Approach to Poverty* (Baltimore: Johns Hopkins Press, 1969).
129. ———, *Programs in the Aid of the Poor for the 1970's* (Baltimore: Johns Hopkins Press, 1969).
130. Little, Arthur D., Inc., *Strategies for Shaping Model Cities* (Cambridge, Mass.: 1967).
131. F.J. Lyden, *A Study of Organizational and Institutional Change: Part II* (Seattle: University of Washington Social Change Evaluation Project, 1969).
132. Seymour A. Mann (ed.), *Proceedings of National Conference on Advocacy and Pluralistic Planning* (New York: Hunter College, January 10–11, 1969).
133. Peter Marris and Martin Rein, *Dilemmas of Social Reform: Poverty and Community Action in the United States* (New York: Atherton Press, 1967).
134. Dale Rogers Marshall, "Who Participates in What? A Bibliographic Essay on Individual Participation in Urban Areas," *Urban Affairs Quarterly* (December 1968), pp. 201–223.
135. "Maximum Feasible Participation. The Origins, Implications and Present Status," *Poverty and Human Resources Abstract,* Vol. II, No. 6 (1967), pp. 5–13.
136. "Maximum Feasible Uncertainty," *Mountain Life and Work,* Vol. 45, No. 9 (September 1969), pp. 10–12.
137. Judith V. May, "Two Model Cities: Political Development on the Local Level," paper presented to the American Political Science Association, New York, 1969.

138. Metropolitan Applied Research Center, Inc., *A Relevant War Against Poverty* (New York, 1968).
139. K.H. Miller, "Community Organizations in the Ghetto," in R.S. Rosenbloom and R. Marris (eds.), *Social Innovation in the City* (Cambridge: Harvard University Press, 1969).
140. S.M. Miller and Warner Bloomberg, Jr., "Shall the Poor Always Be Impoverished?" in Bloomberg and Schmandt (eds.), *Power, Poverty and Urban Policy* (Beverly Hills: Sage, 1960), pp. 565–577.
141. ———, and Martin Rein, "Participation, Poverty and Administration," *Public Administration Review,* Vol. 29 (January/February 1969), pp. 15–24.
142. ———, and Pamela Roby, *The Future of Inequality* (New York: Basic Books, 1969).
143. William Lee Miller, *Politics and the 15th Ward* (Boston: Houghton-Mifflin, 1965).
144. "Minimum Participation: Voting for OEO Representation," *Reporter,* Vol. 34 (March 24, 1966), pp. 17–18.
145. Melvin B. Mogulof, "Black Community Development in Five Western Model Cities," *Social Work,* Vol. 15 (January 1970), pp. 12–18.
146. ———, *Citizen Participation: A Review and Commentary on Federal Policies and Practices* (Washington, D.C.: The Urban Institute, January 1970).
147. ———, "Coalition to Adversary: Citizen Participation in Three Federal Programs," *Journal of the American Institute of Planners,* Vol. 35, No. 4 (July 1969), pp. 225–232.
148. ———, "Federal Support for Citizen Participation in Social Action," *Social Welfare Forum* (New York: Columbia University Press, 1969).
149. D.C. Mosely and D.C. Williams, Jr., *An Analysis and Evaluation of a Community Action Anti-Poverty Program in the Mississippi Delta* (Mississippi State University, July 1967).
150. Daniel P. Moynihan, *Maximum Feasible Misunderstanding* (New York: The Free Press, 1969).
151. ——— (ed.), *On Understanding Poverty: Perspectives from the Social Services* (New York: Basic Books, 1969).
152. ———, "The Professors and the Poor," *Commentary* (August 1968), pp. 19–28.
153. ———, "What Is Community Action?" *The Public Interest* (Fall 1966), pp. 3–8.
154. Russell D. Murphy, *Political Entrepreneurs and Urban Poverty: The Strategies of Policy Innovation in New Haven's Model Anti-Poverty Project* (Waltham, Mass.: Heath-Lexington, 1971).
155. National Urban League, *Guidelines for Community Action* (New York: 1965).
156. Lawrence K. Norinwood, *The Development of Social Welfare Action in a Growing Ghetto: A Study of Block Organization in the Anti-Poverty Program* (Seattle: University of Washington Social Change Evaluation Project, 1969), Clearinghouse No. PB 184528.
157. North City Area Wide Council (as told to Sherry Amstein), "Maximum Feasible Manipulation," *Public Administration Review,* Vol. 32, Special Issue (September 1972).
158. OEO, *As the Seed Is Sown* (Washington, D.C.: U.S. Government Printing Office, 1969).
159. OEO CAP, *First Year Evaluation* (Washington, D.C.: U.S. Government Printing Office, March 1969).
160. OEO CAP, *Organizing Communities for Action under the 1967 Amendments of Economic Opportunity Act* (Washington, D.C.: U.S. Government Printing Office, February 1968).
161. OEO CAP, *Participation of the Poor in the Community Decision-Making Process* (Washington, D.C.: U.S. Government Printing Office, August 1969).
162. "Operation of Poverty Program Under Sharp Attack," *Congressional Quarterly Weekly Report,* Vol. 23 (May 21, 1965), pp. 991–994.
163. Susan R. Orden, James J. Vanecko, and Sidney Hallander, *CAPs, as Agents of Change in the Private Welfare Sector* (Chicago: National Opinion Research Center, August 1969).
164. "Organizing the Unaffiliated in a Low-Income Area," *Social Work,* Vol. 8, No. 2 (April 1963), pp. 34–40.
165. Constance Osgood, *Evaluation of the CAP of Kansas City, Missouri I* (Kansas City: Institute for Community Studies, September 1969).
166. OSTI, *Hartford Model Cities Struggle: A History* (Hartford, 1969).
167. Raymond E. Owne, "The Political Dynamics of Urban Poverty: A Study of Black Community Organization," paper prepared for the American Political Science Association (September 1969).
168. Lawrence F. Parachini, "More Drops of Trickle-Down" (Chicago: Urban Training Institute, December 1969).
169. "Participation of the Poor," *Yale Law Journal,* Vol. 75 (March 1966), pp. 599–629.
170. Lisa Peattie, "Reflections in Advocacy Planning," paper presented to Conference on Radicals in the Professions (July 14–16, 1967).

171. Pennsylvania University for Environmental Studies, *Planning Programs for the Reduction of Poverty* (February 1969).
172. Frances Fox Piven, "Participation of Residents in Neighborhood CAPs," *Social Work,* Vol. 11, No. 1 (January 1966), pp. 73–80.
173. ———, and Richard A. Cloward, *Regulating the Poor: The Function of Public Welfare* (New York: Pantheon, 1971).
174. "Poverty Dynamics and Intervention, *Journal of Social Issues,* Vol. 21 (January 1965), pp. 1–149.
175. Robert J. Pranger, *The Eclipse of Citizenship: Power and Participation in Contemporary Politics* (New York: Holt, Rinehart and Winston, Inc., 1968).
176. Charles B. Pyles and Glenn W. Rainey, Jr., "Administrators View Model Cities: Coordination and De-centralization in the Atlanta Program," paper prepared for the American Political Science Association (September 1971).
177. Martin Rein, "Community Action Program: A Critical Reassessment," *Poverty and Human Resources Abstracts,* Vol. 3 (May–June 1968), pp. 2–8.
178. ———, and S.M. Miller, "Citizen Participation and Poverty," *Connecticut Law Review,* Vol. 1, No. 2 (1968).
179. ———, "Social Action on the Installment Plan," *Trans-Action* (January–February 1966).
180. ———, and F. Reissman, "A Strategy for Anti-Poverty CAPs," *Social Work* (April 1966).
181. Frank Reissman, *Strategies Against Poverty* (New York: Random House, 1969).
182. ———, Martin Rein, and Peter Marris, "The Third Face: An Anti-Poverty Ideology," *American Child,* Vol. 47, No. 1 (November 1965).
183. L.B. Rubin, "Maximum Feasible Participation: The Origins, Implications and Present Status," *The Annals of the American Academy of Political and Social Sciences,* Vol. 385 (September 1969).
184. M. Ruffer, "The Road to Neighborhood Government," *New Generation,* Vol. 51, No. 3 (Summer 1969).
185. Edward Rutledge, "Citizen Participation," *Journal of Housing* (November 1969), p. 603.
186. K. Warner Schaie, *Overview Comments on the CAP in McDowell County* (Morgantown: W. Va.: Human Resources Research Institute, February 1969).
187. L.E. Schaller, "Is the Citizen Advisory Committee a Threat to Representative Government?" *Public Administration Review,* Vol. 24 (September 1964), pp. 175–179.
188. S. Schiebla, *Poverty Is Where the Money Is* (New York: Arlington House, 1968).
189. Robert C. Seaver, "The Dilemma of Citizen Participation," *Pratt Planning Papers,* Vol. 4 (September 1966), pp. 6–11. Reprinted in Spiegel (ed.), *Citizen Participation in Urban Development,* Vol. I: *Concepts and Issues* (Washington, D.C.: Center for Community Affairs, NTL Institute for Applied Behavioral Science, 1968).
190. Murray Seidler, "Some Participant Observer Reflections on Detroit's Community Action Program," *Urban Affairs Quarterly,* Vol. 5 (December 1969), pp. 183–204.
191. B. Sexton, *Participation of the Poor* (New York: Center for the Study of Unemployed Youth, February 1966).
192. A.B. Shostak, "Promoting Participation of the Poor: Philadelphia's Anti-Poverty Program." *Social Work,* Vol. 11 (January 1966), pp. 64–72.
193. ———, "Urban Politics and Poverty: An Analysis of Community Action Programs," paper presented to the American Sociological Association (September 1966).
194. John Sidor, *The Pittsburgh Model Cities Program,* unpublished Ph.D. dissertation (Pittsburgh, 1969).
195. Robert S. Sigel, "Citizens Committees: Advise and Consent," *Trans-Action* (May 1967).
196. J.G.E. Smith, G.M. Sider, F. Blackford, W.H. Kelly, and W. Willard, *A Comprehensive Education of OEO CAPs and Six Selected American Indian Reservations* (McLean, Va.: Human Sciences Research, Inc., September 1966), Clearinghouse No. PB 180164.
197. Hans B.C. Spiegel (ed.), *Citizen Participation in Urban Development,* Vol. I: *Concepts and Issues* (Washington, D.C.: Center for Community Affairs, NTL Institute for Applied Behavioral Science, 1968).
198. ——— (ed.), *Citizen Participation in Urban Development,* Vol. II: *Cases and Programs* (Washington, D.C.: Center for Community Affairs, NTL Institute for Applied Behavioral Science, 1969).
199. ———, and Stephen P. Mittenthal, *Neighborhood Power and Control: Implications for Urban Planning* (New York: Columbia University Institute of Urban Environment, November 1968).

200. John Strange (ed.), "Citizen Action in Model Cities and CAP Programs: Case Studies and Evaluation," *Public Administration Review,* Vol. 32, Special Issue (September 1972).
201. ———, *Community Action in North Carolina* (Durham: The North Carolina Fund, 1967), Clearinghouse No. PB 183167.
202. ———, "The Impact of Citizen Participation on Public Administration," *Public Administration Review,* Vol. 32, Special Issue (September 1972).
203. ———, "Local Strategies for Attaining Community Control," in H. George Frederickson (ed.), *Politics, Administration, and Citizen Participation: The Issue of Neighborhood Control in the 1970's* (New York: Intext Educational Publishers, 1973).
204. ———, "Politics, Poverty and Education: Durham, N.C.," in Nicholas A. Masters (ed.), *Politics, Poverty and Education: An Analysis of Decision Making Structures* (University Park, Pa: Pennsylvania State University, 1968).
205. ———, "A Whole Lot of Protest—And What Do You Get?" in Virginia B. Ermer and John H. Strange (eds.), *Blacks and Bureaucracy* (New York: Cromwell, 1972).
206. Paul Street, *Community Action in Appalachia, Unit I: Introduction and Synthesis: Quality of Life in Rural Poverty Areas* (1968), Clearinghouse No. PB 180–096.
207. J.L. Sundquist, *Coordinating the War on Poverty* (Washington, D.C.: The Brookings Institution, March 1969).
208. ——— (ed.), *On Fighting Poverty: Perspectives from Experience* (New York Basic Books, 1969).
209. ———, "The End of an Experiment?" in J.L. Sundquist (ed.), *On Fighting Poverty: Perspectives from Experience* (New York: Basic Books, 1969).
210. ———, and D.W. Davis, *Making Federalism Work* (Washington, D.C.: The Brookings Institution, 1969).
211. Ralph H. Taylor, "Citizen Participation in the Model Cities Program," in Spiegel (ed.), *Citizen Participation in Urban Development,* Vol. II: *Cases and Programs* (Washington, D.C.: Center for Community Affairs, NTL Institute for Applied Behavioral Science, 1969).
212. J.D. Templeton, "Maximum Feasible Uncertainty," *Mountain Life and Work,* Vol. 45, No. 9 (September 1969).
213. S. Thernstrom, *Poverty, Planning and Politics in Boston: The Origins of ABCD* (New York: Basic Books, 1969).
214. Jon Van Til and Sally Bould Van Til, "Citizen Participation and Social Policy: The End of the Cycle?" *Social Problems,* Vol. 17 (Winter 1970).
215. Kenneth C. Tollenaar, "A Call for Invention," *National Civic Review,* Vol. 58 (November 1969), pp. 457–461.
216. A.K. Tomeh, "Informal Participation in a Metropolitan Community," *Social Quarterly* (Winter 1967).
217. Tracar Incorporated, *A Comprehensive Evaluation of the CAP in Austin and Traer's County, Texas* (December 1969), Clearinghouse Nos. PB 188–328. 188–329, 188–330, 188–331.
218. Tracki, Schubert, Bradshaw, and Shiffer, *An Exploratory Assessment of CAP Evaluation Activities,* Vol. II: *Catalog of Abstracts of Evaluation Studies* (Pittsburgh: American Institute for Research, November 1969).
219. John B. Turner (ed.), *Neighborhood Organizations for Community Action* (New York: National Association of Social Workers, 1968).
220. U.S. National Advisory Council on Economic Opportunity, *Continuity and Change in Anti-Poverty Programs,* Second Annual Report (Washington, D.C.: Office of Economic Opportunity, March 1969).
221. U.S. President's Commission on Juvenile Delinquency and Youth Crimes, *Bibliography on Community Organization for Citizen Participation in Voluntary Democratic Associations* (Washington, D.C.: U.S. Government Printing Office, June 1965).
222. U.S. Senate, Committee on Labor and Public Welfare, *Examination of the War on Poverty* (Washington, D.C.: U.S. Government Printing Office, September 1967).
223. J.J. Vanecko, *Community Mobilization and Industrial Change: The Influence of the CAP in Large Cities* (Chicago: National Opinion Research Center, 1969), Clearinghouse No. PB 185–803.
224. ———, *Community Organization Efforts, Political and Institutional Change and the Diffusion of Change Produced by CAPs* (December 1969), Clearinghouse Nos. PB 188–692, 188–693.
225. Roland L. Warren, "Model Cities First Round: Politics, Planning and Participation," *Journal of the American Institute of Planners* (July 1969), pp. 245–252.
226. ——— (ed.), *Politics and the Ghettoes* (New York: Atherton, 1969).

227. Pat Walters, "CDGM: Who Really Won?" *New South,* Vol. 22 (Spring 1967), pp. 49–64 (also in *Dissent,* May 1967).
228. Michael Walzer, "Politics in the Welfare State Concerning the Role of American Radicals," *Dissent* (January–February 1968), p. 36.
229. Chaim I. Waxman (ed.), *Poverty: Power and Politics* (New York: Grosset and Dunlap, 1968).
230. Clair Wilcox, *Toward Social Welfare: An Analysis of Programs and Proposals Attacking Poverty, Insecurity and Inequality of Opportunity* (Homewood, Ill.: R.D. Irwin, 1969).
231. Preston R. Wilcox, "Selected Principles for Involving the Poor," paper presented to the National Conference of Social Workers (May 25, 1965).
232. Eddie N. Williams (ed.), *Delivery Systems for Model Cities: New Concepts in Serving the Urban Community* (Chicago: University of Chicago Center for Policy Studies, 1969).
233. Walter Williams, "Developing an Evaluation Strategy for a Social Action Agency," *Journal of Human Resources,* Vol. 4 (Fall 1969), pp. 451–465.
234. Charles Z. Wilson and Adrienne S. Bennett, "Participation in Community Action Organizations: Some Theoretical Insights," *Sociological Inquiry,* Vol. 37 (Spring 1967), pp. 191–203.
235. James Q. Wilson, "Planning and Politics: Citizen Participation in Urban Renewal," *Journal of the American Institute of Planners,* Vol. 29, No. 4 (November 1963), pp. 242–249.
236. Adam Yarmolinsky, "The Beginnings of OEO," in Sundquist (ed.), *On Fighting Poverty* (New York: Basic Books, 1969), pp. 34–51.
237. L.A. Zurcher (ed.), "Function Marginality: Dynamics of a Poverty Intervention Organization," *Southwestern Social Science Quarterly,* Vol. 48, No. 3 (December 1967).
238. ———, *The Leader and the Lost: A Case of Indigenous Leadership in a Poverty CAP* (Topeka: Menninger Foundation Social Science Research Division, July 1966).

FILMS

1. *No Handouts for Mrs. Hedgpeth* (30 minutes, color, sound), available from: University of North Carolina, Bureau of Audio-Visual Education, Chapel Hill, North Carolina 27514.
2. *Organizing for Power: Alinsky Approach,* five films in series, available from: University of California, Extension Media Center, Berkeley, California.
3. *The Public Will* (30 minutes, color, sound), available from: National League of Cities, 1612 K Street, N.W., Washington, D.C. 20006.
4. *Resident Participation* (20 minutes, color, sound), available from: University of California, Extension Media Center, Berkeley, California.
5. *Economic Opportunity Act of 1964* (26 minutes, black and white), available from: University of North Carolina, Bureau of Audio-Visual Education, Chapel Hill, North Carolina 27514.
6. *Poverty in Rural America* (28½ minutes, black and white), available from: Motion Picture Service, Office of Information, U.S. Department of Agriculture, Washington, D.C. 20250.
7. *VISTA—A Year Towards Tomorrow* (28½ minutes, color), available from: Sterling Movies, Inc., 43 W. 61st Street, New York, New York 10023.
8. *The War Against Poverty* (10 minutes, black and white), available from: New York Times, Office of Educational Activities, New York, New York 10036.
9. *War on Poverty: A Beginning* (54 minutes, black and white), available from: Encyclopedia Britannica Films, 425 N. Michigan Avenue, Chicago, Illinois.
10. *Beyond These Hills* (22 minutes, black and white), available from: Office of Economic Opportunity, Public Information Office, Washington, D.C. 20506.
11. *Storefront* (40 minutes, black and white), available from: Office of Economic Opportunity, Public Information Office, Washington, D.C. 20506.
12. *A New Focus on Opportunity* (28½ minutes, color), available from: Office of Economic Opportunity, Public Information Office, Washington, D.C. 20506.
13. *The Cities and the Poor* (Parts I and II, 59 minutes each, black and white), available from: Indiana University, Audio-Visual Center, Division of University Extension, Bloomington, Indiana, 47405.

CHAPTER 9

DECENTRALIZATION AND CITIZEN PARTICIPATION IN EDUCATION

MARILYN GITTELL

The major arena in which decentralization and citizen control have been contested is in urban public education. It is appropriate, therefore, to use this experience to understand the complexities of social change demonstrated by that struggle.

During 70 years of American public school education, citizen participation has periodically played an important part in shaping educational policies. Civic groups at the turn of the twentieth century were especially active in supporting highly innovative programs for the new immigrant population. The arrival of these groups placed a tremendous burden on the schools, particularly because of the need to acculturate large numbers of non-English-speaking students (2). Almost immediately, citizen groups were formed to apply pressure for new educational programs. They actively campaigned for such innovations as kindergarten classes, first established for German-speaking children in Wisconsin. Subsequently, many city school systems incorporated kindergarten classes into the lower-school programs, and still others provided visiting teachers to work with children in their homes to supplant school programs (2), Colin Greer's recent study (44), however, indicates that these efforts fall short of success and that the immigrant poor were never effectively dealt with by the public education system.

Indirectly, the expanding school population was also a force in restructuring the school system. School board membership, administrative posts, and teaching positions had been traditionally distributed as political patronage (19). As the inadequacies of patronage in education were exposed, civic groups moved to bring professionalism into school systems (8) (18). There developed two systems of education: one urban, based on civil service and in many ways politically unaccountable; the other suburban and rural, with some measure of accountability through formal elected boards with control over policy (1) (60). A combination of the civic reform movement and scientific management provided the rationale for major changes in school organization in the first part of the twentieth century. One of the major groups organized for this purpose, the Public Education Association (14), acted through its branches in several cities to depoliticize school systems and secure structural reorganization. The citizen groups which provided the thrust for urban reform

From *Public Administration Review,* 32 (October 1972): 670–686. Copyright © 1972 by American Society for Public Administration. Reprinted with permission.

were largely middle class or upper middle class, and their commitment was more paternalistic than democratic. The local board of education was designed to be the primary means of citizen participation in school policymaking. In keeping with the strong reform tradition, local boards of education were to be independent of city government, thus separating education from city functions with which it might compete for resources and removing it from direct political control (25) (48). Periodically, recommendations emerged, particularly from academic sources, to abolish boards of education and establish the education function as a division or department of city government under the mayor. These suggestions were rarely taken seriously because of strong opposition from the professional educators who wanted to insulate the educational system from intruders (21) (39).

THE LOCAL SCHOOL BOARD

Members of boards of education recruited from the middle and upper classes were generally established community leaders who had demonstrated some prior role in educational circles. According to a study by the U.S. Office of Education, these boards were comprised of professionals and business-management people (85). Seldom were board members blue-collar workers, teachers, small businesspeople, or lower-management people. In more recent years, large-city boards included some minority group representation, but their general character remained the same, whether elected or appointed. Thus, in 1964, Goldhammer concluded in his study of school boards that "school board members are predominantly conservative . . . because of the extent to which they represent values harmonious with the most influential elements of the community" (40).

As the chief policymaking organ of the school system, the school board is theoretically responsible for outlining policies to be implemented by the professional staff. Because boards seldom have any appreciable staff of their own, they must rely heavily on the superintendent and other school professionals for information and policy recommendations. The power of school boards may vary somewhat from city to city, but generally, studies of school boards indicate they are preoccupied with details and not policy issues. One author, a former Chicago school board member, noted the frustrations that school board members experience in the face of overwhelming problems and the lack of time and resources to deal with those problems. He notes in particular their inability to deal with important policy matters (70).

THE EXPANSION OF PROFESSIONALISM

With the expansion of professionalization and school bureaucracies since the 1940s, civic groups have tended to become more supportive and less critical of school professionals and city school systems (23). They see their task largely as one of securing ever-expanding fiscal support for education from federal, state, and city governments (1) (9). Parent groups in the schools, on the other hand, concern themselves more with individual school needs and pay little attention to city or system-wide issues (42) (57).

Over the years, school officials have successfully convinced consumers and public officials that their professional expertise qualifies them to control all aspects of educational policy. Budgets, determination of curriculum, personnel, and pupil policy are considered matters of internal school policy, not to be encumbered by what is described as outside "political interference."

Social science research and support for scientific management further bolstered the trend toward increasing the power of bureaucrats and reducing the role of public groups and elected officials. The measurement of policy output was determined always in terms other than discrete public benefit. Total expenditures, gross amounts allocated, or simple per capita calculations ignored the inequity of social programs and policies. The common assumption of researchers and professionals was that increased use of professionals in a program as indicated in higher costs would result in an improved delivery of service (64) (65) (66).

Vast changes in the character of the urban school population in the 1950s and the 1960s (88) served as a catalyst for heightened concerns about the viability of these entrenched and highly bureaucratized professional school systems. Earlier failures with educating an immigrant poor population could no longer be covered by a labor market receptive to blue-collar, unskilled workers. The expansion of credentialing and the shrinkage in jobs caused by automation placed an added burden on the poor and in turn increased their expectations and demands on city school systems. Higher drop-out rates and low reading scores and skills development in ghetto schools became a rallying point for those who challenged the effectiveness of those systems (37) (50) (54) (55).

THE FAILURE OF INTEGRATION

The first thrust for the new education reform movement in the 1950s was for integration. The reasoning suggested that in integrated schools, overt discrimination against blacks, Puerto Ricans, Chicanos, and lower-class groups could not be maintained (6). National, state, and city civil rights groups such as the NAACP, Urban League, and CORE took on the struggle for educational improvement through school integration. Local ad hoc groups also organized around particular integration proposals (35) (74). On the spearhead of integration, the battle for educational reform was forged. The recognition that the politics of education was a reflection of the institutional politics of the society as a whole was immediately impressed upon those who were advocating some adjustment in the system (10). There was almost immediate recognition that professional defense of the system as it was suggested the lack of widely claimed "objective" criteria for educational policymaking. First subtly, and then more overtly and directly, the school officials and their middle-class public counterparts demonstrated their commitment to preserving a system which served their needs. Even those who saw gradual changes or adjustments in the schools as reasonable approaches to fulfilling the court directives on integration were faced with strong resistance. City school boards across the country adopted general policies committed to integration, and looked to their administrative staffs for implementation (17) (74). Little was forthcoming. In several instances, school professionals themselves were the source for inaction. Racism was a good part of the story; however, the issue proved even more complex. It was also a matter of power—the power of the professional to control his own setting (16) (39). Teachers and supervisors who had only recently organized in the large cities were reaping new benefits as a strong political force in the city community. Union contracts and work agreements set the framework for general school policy; personnel requirements and increased salaries established a high percentage of mandatory costs in education budgets. Class size, student-teacher ratios, special personnel requirements, and increased expenditures were defined by these groups as synonymous with better education (4). Although the Coleman Report (15) went a long way in undermining these by-now-accepted standards of educational quality, it did not demolish them sufficiently to prevent continued argument for their support. Organized professional groups continued to use these criteria for evaluating education output and continued to assert that increased school expenditures would produce better education. Mounting evidence contradicted these assumptions (51). As education costs spiraled in the 1950s and 1960s, educational achievement declined, particularly in the cities and particularly in the poor and minority group neighborhoods (13) (30) (79).

More than ten years of integration proposals, including paired schools, open enrollment, bus-ing, intermediate schools, etc., fell by the wayside (81). All of the large cities showed increased residential segregation each year and increased school segregation as well (83). With minor exceptions, in most large- and middle-sized cities, the integration effort was a total failure (3) (37) (84). Public and professional resistance increased as successive proposals were announced, although plans were seldom implemented.

By the 1960s, a decade of activity in attempts to reform urban schools brought a new level of sophistication to the reformers. The civil rights groups had forced city school systems to reveal for the first time reading scores, which showed massive failure (88). People began to look more closely at student achievement as integral to educational output. The professionals' argument that the socioeconomic background of the student determined his success or failure in school appeared to eschew institutional responsibility for output. As integrationists looked at the educational product more closely, they began to question even more directly the role of school professionals and school systems. Could one accept that lower-class children were not educable, as the professionals seemed to suggest, or was it the responsibility of schools to educate children regardless of background? Should they not adjust institutions, policies, and programs to the educational needs of the consumers, or were they to remain middle-class institutions serving only a middle-class clientele (7) (33) (47) (75)?

THE EMERGENCE OF COMMUNITY CONTROL

Recognition of a constantly declining education quality and lack of success in achieving integration in the 1950s and 1960s led to the emergence of the decentralization-community control concept as a new thrust for school reform (11) (29). This was predicated on the realization that the political environment of school decision making was the determinant of quality education. So long as the schools in the ghetto were controlled by people removed from the needs of minority children (and often by those who viewed lower-class children as uneducable) quality education would not or could not be achieved. It was a concept born in IS 201, in New York City, among a group of parent activists who had struggled hard and long for an integrated school (86). Their argument was basic. If they were to be denied integration, they should at least control their own schools and develop the means to quality education. Although dissatisfaction with the schools was based on educational failure, these demands also reflected a general and continuing alienation by the black community from those who ran the system, and a heightened frustration with their inability to influence those institutions which shaped their lives and the lives of their children (11). Although one would assume from the rhetoric that our experience with decentralization is widespread, in fact, it is rather limited. A plethora of government programs starting with the Office of Economic Opportunity (OEO) called for public participation, but few, outside education, involved restructuring the institutions to allow for engagement of citizens in decision making.

In the 1950s Kenneth Clark presciently confronted the political as well as the educational issue in his study of Harlem, appropriately titled, "Powerlessness in the Ghetto." The target was the centralized bureaucratic structure of a large-city school system (11). The power holders were the professional staff and the teachers union who in concert monopolized decision making in the system. The consumers, parents and children, were nonparticipants. A variety of studies over a decade identified this pattern of power in urban school systems in America. The evidence suggested why the opposition was mounting and strenuous efforts at reform within the local community were growing.

Earlier studies (13) (46) (67) had intermittently identified the problem of large-scale bureaucracies which were not responsive to local needs; however, those studies were more concerned with the need for *administrative* decentralization of the school system. They did not view the failure of the schools as in any way connected to the lack of client involvement. This distinction between administrative decentralization and community control becomes particularly important to later developments in the school reform movement.

In the summer of 1966, having failed to achieve their goal, the IS 201 parents demanded that the New York City Board of Education give them a direct voice in the operation of their school (29). They provided the major impetus for the creation of the three "demonstration districts" in New York City. They used the phrase "community control" of those districts in their negotiations with the mayor and the superintendent of schools. Many of these community activists and parents in Harlem were trained in Community Action Programs funded by OEO and were familiar with the concept of community participation. Recognizing the limits of non-policymaking participatory roles for community people, they advanced that concept to one of community control. More middle-class and professional reformers joined them in their struggle, espousing the need for decentralization of city school systems to make them more responsive to community interests (82). This new reform movement was not abandoning integration as a cause; it merely established a prior claim for quality education and accepted the reality of a declining opportunity for integration to serve as a means to that end. What they did not fully perceive was that both efforts, integration and decentralization-community control, attacked the same institutional core—a status-oriented school system devised to protect middle-class professional interests. Both reforms tampered with the distribution of power which concentrated control in the hands of school professionals who were threatened by any change in the structure. It was not an accident that the alignment of forces on both issues was the same. Those who opposed integration opposed decentralization; those who long supported integration were in the forefront of the movement for local neighborhood control of the schools.

In the fall of 1967, a plan for community participation and school decentralization emerged from the Bundy Plan (62) prepared for the New York City public school system. Important elements of this plan were largely contained in legislation recommended by the New York State Board of Regents in the 1968 legislative session.

Both the Bundy and the Regents' plans called for the election of *local* boards of education in districts throughout New York City (the Bundy Plan called for 30–45 districts; the Regents' legislation, 10 large and 20 smaller special districts). These proposed local boards would have some budget, personnel, and curriculum powers. Both plans provided for retention of a central-city education agency to set standards, control capital budget expenditures, and provide other central services. The City Board of Examiners, the Board's professional credentialing agent, would be eliminated, making appointment and promotion procedures more flexible.

THE BUNDY PLAN

Recommendations dealt with four main problems: the nature of community voice in educational policy, the composition and selection of community boards of education, relations between community boards and higher authorities, and reform of the personnel system.

To guarantee that community school districts would have flexibility in the way they spent their funds, the panel proposed that they receive lump-sum allocations from the board of education. This would eliminate line-item restrictions, so that the community boards could determine their own priorities. Only through lump-sum allocation would community school boards have effective power to make their own decisions on pupil-teacher ratios, the functions of personnel, the number and kinds of books and other instructional materials, the conduct of experimental programs, and a host of other needs and educational strategies.

To ensure that districts with special needs would receive their fair share, the panel proposed that these lump sums be allocated by a formula that would go beyond per-capita allotment and take into account such factors as income levels, unemployment rates, and the presence, in particular districts, of either non-English-speaking children or gifted children. To ensure against misuse of funds, the panel outlined a number of auditing and reporting procedures and other safeguards.

The choices open to the Bundy Panel in the difficult decisions regarding composition of community boards included community-wide representation, parent-only representation, and arrangements that would include professional representation. The panel decided on a parent-based system, which, it felt, would be most responsive to the needs and interests of children attending the public schools and would prevent a takeover by organized party or church interests.

Seeking to encourage maximum parent participation in the selection process, the Panel recommended that a prescribed proportion of eligible parents—"at a level sufficiently substantial to constitute an effective participatory process"—be established, below which elections would not be valid. In such cases, it proposed that a new election or alternative methods of obtaining parental representation should be employed. (The legislation passed in 1969 carried no such provisions, and, as it turns out, only 15 percent of the eligible voters participated in the initial elections in March 1970.)

The Panel proposed a two-stage process for selection of the parent members: representatives of individual schools would be chosen by an assembly of parents; these representatives, in turn, would select board members on a basis proportionate to the pupil population of each school.

In fixing on a parent-only majority, the Panel sought to avoid the danger that these local boards might be dominated by political clubs, by majorities of residents who were not parents, or by sectarian groups that might not hold the interest of public education uppermost. (The 1969 decentralization law did not limit voting to parents, and in the first elections fears that such organized interests as sectarian groups, the United Federation of Teachers (UFT), and political parties would prevail were borne out in many districts.)

The Panel leavened its recommendations favoring parents, however, with a provision that five of the 11 community board members be appointed by the mayor. This provision reflected a concern for minorities within districts marked by a strong racial or ethnic character—particularly Puerto Ricans in largely Negro neighborhoods. Thus, the report declared:

> It is a real possibility, especially in the early years of the reorganized school system, that a parentally chosen district panel might wholly exclude representatives of minority groups in that district. While we do not hold with proportional representation on Community School Boards, we do believe that total exclusion of minority representation would violate the spirit of community participation in the educational process.

The Panel decided on the mayor as the agent for choosing the centrally selected members because of his citywide purview and his prior responsibility for the city's schools, notably in the allocation of the school budget from the total municipal budget. Another consideration was to help insure a broadly based representation. Recognizing that this decision would unleash charges of political domination (such charges did develop), the Panel nonetheless argued that there were now strong reasons for breaking down the supposed wall between a city's highest political office and its public school system. Nationwide recognition of the urban crisis and its educational component was growing, and traditional strictures maintaining a separation between political and educational authority were weakening.

Both by admitting parents to a more active role in the educational process and by building a closer link to elected government, the Panel sought responsibility and accountability—a school system so organized as to be more responsive to the needs of the citizens. It was also hoped that, through closer ties with city government, the schools would be able to coordinate their programs with other city agencies, such as its 60 existing planning districts and its recreation, health, and antipoverty efforts.

Without diluting the essential independence and decision making of the community boards, the Panel proposed that the community boards have a number of ties with the central education agency (the NYC Board of Education). These ties would include the latter's authority over pupil transfers (to ensure optimum utilization of school buildings throughout the city), over negotiations of the union contract, and—of crucial importance—over integration policy.

Anticipating charges that a federated school system might lead to sectarian pockets—black power districts on the one hand, or ultra-conservative or segregationist districts on the other—the Panel proposed that the central agency be empowered to overrule any actions by a community school board "that are judged to be inimical to a free and open society." But the Panel said this power ought to follow guidelines established by the state commissioner of education. It further cautioned that the central power to curb parochialism or sectarianism should not be interpreted to exclude a reasonable curricular emphasis upon the cultural background of groups that were a large element in a given school—an obvious reference to frequent demands in the ghettos for attention to Negro history and Hispanic and Afro-American studies. Personnel power which was to be delegated to the community boards would include the right to hire a community superintendent of schools. While preserving tenure and centralized collective bargaining, the Panel proposed to place hiring and the granting of tenure at the community level. Its single most important—and controversial—personnel recommendation called for elimination of the central citywide examination system and its venerable Board of Examiners, established in 1898.

This recommendation was intended to ensure a wider pool for recruitment of personnel and a more flexible promotion system. In New York State, only two school systems, New York City's and Buffalo's, required examinations for teacher certification beyond the state standards. The centralized examinations were thought to have conflicted with the requirements of effective decentralization. The examination system had also produced an inbred leadership structure that discouraged flexibility and change. The Panel called, instead, for "a broadening of the concept of merit and qualification leadership, opening the system to more talents and ability, both from within and without the system."

New York City school officials were alarmed by the prospects of these changes. The president of the Board of Education, the sole dissenting member of the Bundy Panel, sharply criticized the Bundy report: "Serious problems must arise in re-casting, in one single stroke, the largest educational system in the world." The professional groups joined in the charge of a "balkanization" of the city system, arguing that the plan would also impede school integration and would be a substitute for needed government spending in the schools. Neither the union nor its new colleague, the CSA (Council of Supervisory Associations), spared expense in their attempts to defeat the passage of a decentralization bill based on the Bundy Plan.

THE OCEAN HILL-BROWNSVILLE EXPERIMENT

Since the fall of 1968, school reformers throughout the United States preface their commitment to educational change with the qualifying phrase, "but we don't want another Ocean Hill-Brownsville. (Ocean Hill-Brownsville was one of three demonstration districts created by the New York City Board of Education in 1967.) This is not unlike the historical search of philosophers and social scientists for a theory of institutional change which is gradual and nondisruptive. As much as they profess change, their priority is stability, and, on balance, there are few changes worthy of an open confrontation with the system. Although the circumstances of the confrontation in Ocean Hill-Brownsville, surprisingly, did not involve violence during a 36-day strike of the city school system, it did openly challenge the power and vested interest of the system sufficiently to be judged by some as revolutionary.

In fact, community control (and the IS 201 and Ocean Hill-Brownsville experiments as forerunners in that struggle) is true to the reformist tradition of urban movements. The concept of community control represents an effort to work within the system, adjusting it to new circumstances and needs. It seeks a balance between public or citizen participation with professional roles in the policy process. It prescribes shared responsibility. It is reformist and not revolutionary in that it does not seek the destruction of the system. The experience of the New York City demonstration districts is particularly relevant, therefore, to any consideration of the potential for community participation as a vehicle for institutional change in urban school systems.

Some of the participants in the particular setting of the Ocean Hill-Brownsville controversy obviously saw the impact of the demands of this experimental school district as a possible catalyst to a major transformation of public education systems over a period of time. At first glance, this may seem extraordinary: that a single school district of eight schools and less than 8,000 students should threaten the whole fabric of public education not only in New York City but throughout the country. Certainly the creation of the district on an experimental basis and the reluctant delegation of minimum authority to it by a central lay board of education in the spring of 1967 did not foreshadow the deep implications of that gesture.

None of the community leaders involved had any illusions about the fact that they were being placated by the creation of demonstration districts. They were not offered integrated schools and they were not offered citywide reform. It was merely a question of how much they could get, and was the package worth agreement.

The negotiations and determination of final plans for the creation of the districts were conducted in the winter of 1966, continuing into the spring of 1967. By April the plans were set. The districts created as experiments by the New York City Board of Education were to test the concept of community participation (36).

In the fall of 1967 the Ocean Hill-Brownsville district's planning board changed the circumstances of the experiment (63). The district took immediate action in running off an official election; it appointed a unit administrator and stated its commitment to seek appointment of a special category of demonstration school principal. Clearly the local leadership was bent on confronting the system at its core. They were not willing to accept the traditional personnel selection system. They had begun to translate community participation into community control. It was a natural evolution. It is not certain that the community leadership seriously planned a strategy of confrontation politics, or whether they conceived their efforts in those terms, but that was the impact (26) (61).

At first, the mayor and Ford Foundation officials (Ford funded some of the district's new programs) viewed the districts and their plans as a reasonable adjustment in the system, which it must be said, cost them nothing in the way of power. What they failed to appreciate and what quickly became evident was their own lack of power in this particular political subsystem (the school system) and their inability to force compromises of any kind from those who held power—the school professionals. The circumstances reflected, again in microcosm, the diminishing power of the traditional city leadership and their ineffectiveness in achieving an adjustment in the system. Ultimately, the reality forced both the mayor and the foundation to back down when challenged by the teachers union and professional power, thus abandoning support for the districts and the experiment.

How fundamental was this effort at institutional change? At a minimum it attacked the structure on the delivery of services and the allocation of resources. At a maximum it potentially challenged the institutionalization of racism in America. It seriously challenged the "merit" civil service system which had become the mainstay of the American bureaucratic structure. It raised the issue of accountability of public service professionals and pointed to the distribution of power in the system and the inequities of the policy output of that structure. In a short three years, the Ocean Hill-Brownsville districts and IS 201, through such seemingly simple acts as hiring their own principals, allocating larger sums of money for the use of paraprofessionals, transferring or dismissing teachers, and adopting a variety of new educational programs, had brought all of these issues into the forefront of the political arena. If these seemingly simple acts had not been such a serious threat to the system, it would be unlikely that they would produce such a strong and immediate response (36).

ANTI-SEMITISM AND RACISM

Perhaps the most disturbing effect of the strike was the polarization of black and white, in particular, black and Jew. Most studies indicate less anti-Semitism among blacks than among whites, but the strike significantly increased black hostility to the Jewish community. It did not create black anti-Semitism but crystallized it in New York. As Jews have increasingly gained acceptance in American society, their reformism has tended to diminish. Black resentment at the lessening of the traditional reformism of their Jewish allies has been growing stronger for some time. Only half the city's Jews supported the proposed civilian review board, and some Jews opposed the building of low-income housing for blacks in Jewish neighborhoods. Still Jewish reformism persists; a recent poll revealed that Jews are the largest white group supporting school decentralization in New York.

In part, the racial tension can be viewed merely as the result of an out-group's resentment of those in power. In New York, both the teaching and the supervisory staffs are predominantly Jewish. Their interest in maintaining the status quo was seized upon by black extremists who produced leaflets attacking not the staff or teachers but the Jews. In turn, the UFT and the CSA distributed copies of those leaflets in an attempt to gather support for their own positions. At this point, the leadership of the Jewish community overreacted.

Black anti-Semitism was not the product of community control. The Ocean Hill board and unit administrator clearly disavowed anti-Semitism, and the board pointedly noted that it had hired a predominantly white, predominantly Jewish teaching staff to fill the classrooms of striking teachers. These new teachers, estranged from the union because of the decentralization issue, eventually took out a newspaper advertisement in order to deny publicly the existence of anti-Semitism in the district's schools.

The racial antagonisms unleashed by the strike made it the most racially polarizing event in the city's history. The extent of black anti-Semitism and anti-white feeling is an indication that urban school reform efforts to transfer power face hard-core opposition (35) (86). So long as community roles were supportive of the system, they could be countenanced; this was true of the traditional parent association roles and even the efforts of the citizen education interest groups. Effective community action, oriented to institutional change, was another matter. If decentralization involved a redistribution of power, the resistance would be immediately manifest.

EVALUATING DECENTRALIZATION AND COMMUNITY CONTROL

Further experience with citywide decentralization plans in New York City, Detroit, Philadelphia, Boston, and Los Angeles supports the conclusion that any effort to reorder school systems through a change in the distribution of power, giving local communities control over school policy, would be met by a coalition of opposition in city and state legislatures. Most noteworthy was the failure of the Bundy Plan in New York City which called for rather fundamental change in the role of parents in the policy process (29).

From 1967 to 1972, the urban school reform movement has been concentrated on increasing community control of the schools through expanded citizen participation in the decision process combined with a breaking down of large-city school systems to the local neighborhood level. The extent of local power sought for neighborhood school boards varies according to particular plans (34, 68). The rhetoric, however, far exceeds action, and we have few models of effective decentralization and community control. It is easy to espouse support for the concept of decentralization, as many do, while at the same time denying the concept of local control. In fact, at least six large cities adopted what they describe as school decentralization plans—they are arrangements for administrative decentralization, but make no provision for increased local community roles. They do not seek to include any new public voice in the policy process to balance professional control of the system. The plans call for dividing the city into districts and assigning district superintendents to field positions. In some cities, even these field superintendents are maintained at headquarters and have little contact with the local community.

In 1969–70, two large cities adopted citywide decentralization plans under state legislation. In Detroit and New York City, the school decentralization plans called for election of local school boards which had the power to choose their own superintendents under traditionally prescribed standards for qualification. In both cities, the size of the districts, boundaries, and election procedures reduced the effective role of local communities under the plan. The results of local board elections in the cities are reflective of this. (See Table 9.1 and 9.2). Minority representation on local boards in both cities has been minimal—less than it has been on citywide boards. The intended goal of local election of local boards—increased representation of the minority population—was successfully thwarted by how boundaries were set and election procedures. There are some who, now pointing to these results, argue against the effectiveness of decentralization, ignoring that the content of the plans produced the undesired results (72). Election of local boards is not a guarantee there will be a distribution of power. Local elections with well-planned districting can easily maintain the existing power structure, as it did in New York City and Detroit. Large districts and complex election procedures are useful tools in controlling results.

The New York law gave the semblance of decentralizing educational decision making but essentially preserved the status quo. It denied local boards any substantial authority over personnel, budget, and educational programs (36).

But if the law was a setback to those groups seeking a voice in making school policy, the elections themselves proved a further disaster. The Institute for Community Studies conducted a one-year study of the elections and the election procedures. It found that the proportional representation system had a "built-in tendency to pit well-organized groups against those that are less organized" (24). The board members elected from these elections were the opposite of that intended. The typical board member was a white male Catholic, professionally trained, with two children, and living in his district for about nine years with his children in parochial school.

The study showed that 63.8 percent of these new board members are middle-class professionals. And, most importantly, 53.2 percent of these board members have children in parochial, not public, schools. This in a school system that is 57.2 percent black and Puerto Rican, many of whom are children of a client poor. Of 279 members elected, only 47 are black (16.8 percent) and 30 are Puerto Rican (10.8 percent). Of 12 districts with 85 percent of their pupils black or Puerto Rican, there are six which have boards with a majority of black and Puerto Rican members.

153

Table 9.1

Comparative Profile of Local School Board Members (averages in percent)

Area represented	Occupation						Education			Public school parents
	Board members in professional, technical, or managerial positions	Board members employed as paraprofessionals or by poverty agencies	Members in the clergy	Members who are homemakers	Members who are laborers or mechanics	Other	H.S. or grade school	B.A. or M.A.	Professional	
NYC under Decentralization (1970)	63.8	10.3	5.3	16.6	4.0	10.0	33	56	23	46.8
Detroit under Decentralization	61.3	—	3.2	12.9	22.6	—	50	44.1	5.9	67.6
Demonstration Districts NYC	16	44	9	22	3.3	6	78	6	15	85

Table 9.2

Comparison of Ethnic Backgrounds of Local School Board Members (averages)

Area Represented	% Pupil population non-white	% School board members non-white
NYC under Decentralization (1970)	34.4	17
Detroit under Decentralization	63	30
Demonstration Districts NYC (Lay Members)	56	61

And it is on these six boards that 44 of 87 citywide minority members sit. Ten districts elected all-white boards in areas where the black and Puerto Rican school population ranged from 11 to 66 percent. The Institute study concluded: "To achieve political effectiveness by activating large numbers of people, especially lower-class citizens, necessitates a substantial command of time, manpower, publicity, organization, legitimacy, know-how and the ingredient that often determines the availability of others, money" (24).

The New York experience was duplicated in Detroit, the other major city to institute school decentralization. Although Detroit created only eight regional boards instead of New York's 31, only 30 percent of their members are black in a city whose school population is 63 percent black. Moreover, 61.3 percent of the local boards' members are middle-class professionals.

Critics of decentralization have also pointed to the low voter turnout in the New York City local board elections as evidence of its failure to secure participation. A black and Puerto Rican boycott of the election, dissatisfaction with the plan, as well as the complexities of proportional representation voting are a partial explanation of the limited turnout; but more important is the recognition that change cannot be expected to occur immediately. A more accurate measure will be the extent of participation in local communities over the next several years and in succeeding elections.

Can school decentralization be judged a failure based on experiences in these cities? Not exactly. First, as has been noted, procedures forced the results, and these can be adjusted to secure more meaningful representation. Second, even with minimal legislative mandate, local school boards may expand their roles by broad interpretation of their powers. In a two-year evaluation of the New York City districts, it became evident that about one-fourth of the local boards are moving towards increased policy roles (77), and pressure has been brought to bear on the legislature to revise the law, to further expand local board powers.

Further evidence must be developed in evaluating New York City and Detroit before final judgments are made. In the evaluation of the New York City experience, several conclusions are relevant to an appreciation of the basic issues likely to arise in any effort to achieve effective decentralization.

Most community school board members interviewed in New York City identified personnel as one of the most important issues with which they deal. Their judgment affirms the projection of several of the analysts of decentralization, that "the effectiveness of the local school board in changing the schools will depend to a great extent on the cooperation and proficiency of the school staff in carrying out such changes" (77). One can argue, furthermore, that "if the local district is bound by existing personnel practices [that is, central examination and assignment of staff] . . . it will not have broadened its own power base in the vital area of control over jobs" (particularly in the districts with low achievement). Thus, some districts have sought to gain power in the area of

personnel by hiring acting principals. Doing so enables them to bypass the civil service requirements for principals. They have done so in the belief that civil service examinations are predicated
not on performance but on conformity to professional standards (77).

Only recently has the validity of those examinations been challenged. In a recent court decision
in New York City, a federal judge (Mansfield) noted that the examination procedure for selection
of principals of the New York City Board of Education has never been validated. He noted that the
Board of Examiners (the credentialing agent of the Board of Education) has never even attempted
to prove that their examination selects the best performers. He argued further that the criteria for
principals' performance could not be efficiently translated into a written examination (12).

The local boards in New York City have been able to develop new procedures for the selection
of principals under this decision. Noteworthy is the fact that those districts having the greatest
parent participation not only experienced the greatest change in personnel selection methods,
they also seemed to differ from their counterparts in the types of people chosen and preferred.
These districts generally sought to hire and maintain a level of minority personnel more closely
related to the composition of the pupil population of the district. This would suggest that even
under a plan which did not call for direct community roles, local boards can effectively delegate
their powers to parent groups in schools and achieve more direct participation. It further suggests
that where increased participation is encouraged, more changes in procedures and policies are
likely to occur.

The New York City experience over the last two years demonstrates that pressure for increasing
local roles comes primarily in the lower-class neighborhood, but several middle-class areas have
also developed procedures for encouraging parent involvement and are seeking broader delegations
of power from the central board and/or revised legislation. Although there has been little progress in
the area of local discretion over school budgets, particularly because of the mandatory expenditures
which result from the union contact, some signs of pressure this area are also developing. Greater
local involvement in the determination of Title 1 expenditures has been achieved in a majority of
the 31 districts, and some reallocation of expenditures and priorities have been made in several
districts. Experimentation with new educational programs seems to be more accepted by the local
boards, although results cannot be measured. This rundown suggests that progress has been made
in the local school districts and, given adjustments in the law, more can be anticipated.

Another source of evaluation of community control relates back to the experience with the
demonstration school districts in New York City from 1967 to 1969, although they were abolished
under the 1969 legislation. These experiments were closer to concepts of local control, although
their powers were never clearly defined.

For one thing, the three districts enlisted new participants, board members who were black or
Puerto Rican, many poor, who were dedicated to school reform. The typical community school
board member was a poor, black female with some poverty program experience and with children
in the public school. More than 25 percent of the normally apathetic community people voted
in these elections, compared with the average 10 percent voting in the citywide decentralization
election of 1970. Most of these board members with children in the schools felt that public schools
had failed and that something had to be done to improve the schools. They were reform-minded,
seeking visible and immediate change in the schools (36).

These members affected personnel policy. They brought in more minority supervisors, the first
black, Puerto Rican, and Chinese principals, and the first black community superintendents. They
enlisted more energetic and dedicated teachers in the slums. And they created a highly innovative
education climate. In Ocean Hill-Brownsville, the alienation between parents and urban schools
was reduced. A study of parents showed that 36 percent of those sampled belonged to a Parent As-

sociation and an overwhelming 86 percent of the parents visited a school. Four-fifths of the parents believed that they had more influence in the running of the schools, and three-fifths felt their schools were better or the same. And although they felt they had some influence, they wanted more (41).

There were more experimental programs adopted by these boards composed of the urban poor than the most affluent educational districts in the country. Ocean Hill had many programs, including a British Open Integrated Day, the teaching of reading first in Spanish, then in English, a Montessori school, a Bereiter-Engelmann school, and on and on. The sheer variety of programs attested to the educational principal that each child is different and learns at different paces and in different methods.

A study of IS 201 shows the pupils did better academically than the rest of the city in percentage terms; they improved at a time when the rest of the city pupils declined because of the long strike. In one school where a new experimental method was employed, the Caleb Gattegno method, the results were dramatic. The 1970 test score results produced at least a one-year advance in reading scores. And the study links that academic success with feelings of efficacy and self-control that these Harlem pupils experienced in a true locally controlled urban school district (45).

The experiment was too short to appraise the long-range educational effects of the program; most important, these besieged districts were under constant attack from professional school interests. Nevertheless, there is sufficient indication to suggest the educational promise of a truly decentralized school system (87). Some commentators have looked at low reading score results in later years, after the districts were abolished, and concluded that the educational output was negative (72, 49). Certainly there is no hard evidence that reading scores will improve under community control. Such evidence would only be available if some experiment over time allowed for such an evaluation to be made.

URBAN SCHOOL REFORM IN THE 1970S

More along the lines of the demonstration districts, alternate community schools and districts within city school systems have been established in several cities, and they continue to gain support. The Adams-Morgan School and the Anacostia District in Washington, D.C., were experiments of that kind. More recently, the city of Newark, New Jersey, has announced the creation of an Experimental School System with financial support from the Office of Education. Under the program, community groups and parent organizations in the city will design, develop, and operate schools for 5,000 students from kindergarten through high school. The plan will permit a Federation Community Schools with independent operation in many areas currently under control of the Board of Education. Essential to the program is community and parental participation (58).

Support is growing outside of school circles for decentralization of the large-city systems and balancing professional bureaucratic roles with parent, student, and community participation. Many of the peripheral groups have also sensed the movement and see in it greater advantage to themselves in a setting unfettered by bureaucratic constraints. Plans call for citywide arrangements and/or optional experimental plans for special districts or community schools within the system.

Administrative decentralization must be distinguished from political decentralization particularly because compromise arrangements often call for administrative decentralization as if it could answer the demands of those seeking an increased community role in school decision making. Administrative decentralization means a shuffling of the bureaucratic and professional staff to provide for more direct field contact—this may involve the creation of field offices or merely the creation of field titles. Political decentralization, on the other hand, requires a shift in power from professionals to the community.

Often administrative decentralization attempts to forestall real local control or compromises between community pressure for policy control and professional defense of the status quo. In Los Angeles, the school board and the professionals twice defeated state legislation for a study of effective political decentralization of the Watts district and instead encouraged administrative decentralization of the school system. In other cities, mounting community interest and pressure for local control was responded to with plans which call for dividing the city school system into districts or regions and assigning district superintendents to these field positions. None of these plans include a new role for the community or a balancing of professional power with citizen participation.

In Philadelphia, Boston, and Los Angeles, the professional school associations and/or the union were instrumental in defeating efforts to move toward delegation of policymaking powers to the local communities. In several cities like Houston and Milwaukee, administrative decentralization was a reaction to pressure from local community groups. Neither plan provided for increased community participation. State studies of political decentralization have been conducted in California and Massachusetts, and currently studies are under way in Illinois and Wisconsin, but there appears to be little evidence that professional pressures opposing political decentralization can be avoided even at the state level. The results in California and Massachusetts suggest that the outcome in most states is more likely to be a plan for administrative decentralization of the city school system.

Reform of the school system from the top, through its administrative structure, has been suggested by some reformers as a desirable alternative to immediate plans for local control. This usually involves bringing in a superintendent committed to rehauling the system. Philadelphia was a good example of an all-out central reform effort; it had the full support of the Ford Foundation and the Office of Education in extensive new funding. Two recent books on the Philadelphia system written by people involved in that struggle have labeled it a failure. In a Philadelphia decentralization study which was prepared in 1970 by a commission on which the various school interests were represented, agreement could not be reached to delegate any power to local boards. The union and supervisory representatives dissented from even minimal proposals for decentralization of decision making. Management and financial studies and plans adopted to modernize school reporting and increase public accountability have also fallen far short of their goals. Experimental programs widely publicized have since been abandoned. These were programs imposed from the central office.

Washington, D.C., is another city in which central reform and circulation of top leadership have been touted as the means for change. Some effort was made under a special projects division to establish some policy power in local boards in Anacostia and in the Adams-Morgan School. The Adams-Morgan School experiment was one of the earliest efforts to establish a local board to run its school. All early evaluations of Adams-Morgan were very positive, although the lack of board control over budget was viewed as a major problem. The Anacostia district, set up with OE support, fell far short of its goal of community control and got bogged down in District politics. Some attribute the failure of Anacostia to minimum funding and limited support.

If the evidence of the vital role of teacher and student attitudes as the major input to educational output is seriously regarded, then minimal programs and/or central system adjustments can never work. Long-range programs and more selective staff recruitment are essential. Changing attitudes can only come from a major shift in the political and social environment of the schools—genuine community control might achieve such results if given a chance.

In any plan for decentralization which is committed to go beyond administrative restructuring, the extent of community participation in policy development can be viewed in several stages. The first consideration is the preparation of the plan; this is probably the most crucial and the most difficult stage at which to involve the public. The planning phase is generally viewed by professionals as solely theirs, and dependent upon professional expertise. There may also be concern that early public participation can endanger or cause undue delay. There is increasing awareness, however, that the early involvement of community representatives is likely to result in the development of more realistic plans, supported by the community at critical stages. Early public participation can also be an effective means of broadening the base of participation in subsequent implementation. Engagement in the process of planning assures fuller appreciation of the intricacies of a function. In the Fort Lincoln project and Anacostia district in Washington, D.C., community groups were involved in the planning period (28).

The content of plans for decentralization provides another basis for evaluation of community roles and potentially provides the measure for its effectiveness. The extent of balancing both community and professional roles, along with central and local power, are the key issues. The major policy questions in any plan will be the setting of local boundaries, the system of representation and governance for the local agency, and the division of personnel and budget power between the central and local agency. Clearly, the size of districts and their constituency can influence the extent and character of community participation, as evidenced in the New York City and Detroit plans.

The division of responsibility for policy between the central and local boards relating to personnel and budget will directly affect the extent to which new local units with new participants can achieve institutional change. If civil service, contract and/or budget constraints so completely delimit local policy roles as to make them nonfunctional, there is little reason to anticipate meaningful local participation. Much of the evidence suggests that if a central authority is retained close to its previous roles and new local decentralized units have little or no power, there will be no inducement to participation. The citizenry will quickly measure the investment of time in terms of ability to effect policy.

If the purpose of decentralization is to effect institutional change, shared responsibility between professionals and clients requires a redistribution of power. The division of responsibility between central and local agencies and the extent of control of local representative bodies, as well as the mechanism for broad participation as reflected in the plan, will determine the potential for these results. When central agencies are abolished or diminished in size, these can be indications of significant potential shifts in roles beyond the specific delegations of power to local agencies. Such provision can be included in legislation of formal plans.

The final stage for evaluation of decentralization would be in the implementation of a plan. Even a limited delegation of power can be broadened in practice as indicated by the experience in Ocean Hill-Brownsville. Conversely, broad grants of power may not be fully utilized for various reasons. In the case of the three demonstration school districts in New York City, no specific power was delegated, but local strategists used harassment, pressure, and open confrontation to broaden their roles. The greater the direct involvement of community in the two earlier stages, the more likely it will be that local units will take on policy roles in the implementation. The broader the base of participation, the more highly organized the community is, the more probable that concern will be with local control over policy. The output of policy change is also more likely to result under the above circumstances. On the other hand, those programs centrally established, with very limited or no local community participation, will generally produce little community interest or involvement at any stage. Needless to say, the chances for institutional or policy changes are also nil.

ALTERNATIVE SCHOOLS

Even in the light of what appears to be some promising developments in the decentralization of urban school systems, there are a large number of people who consider these too gradual and too minimal to warrant optimism or support.

Another phase of the movement for community schools has developed outside and as an alternative to the public school system. It reflects the frustration encountered by those who have attempted to reform the public system without success. In Boston and Milwaukee, federations of community schools have been developed. In both cities, these schools are in ghetto communities servicing their needs; they are run by local parent boards. In other cities, individual community schools have been established. Although they are faced with constant financial crisis, alternative community schools can avoid the hard-core problems attached to trying to change an established system. They can develop their own personnel policies under broad state requirements, and they have full control over their budgets, determining their own priorities in the allocation of resources. These are relatively new experiments and their impact on educational output cannot yet be judged. All that can be observed is the greater sensitivity and interest in achieving quality education, the willingness to experiment with new educational ideas, and an openness with children, parents, and residents which suggests a more positive attitude toward schooling. In these schools, there has been a considerable community involvement in the selection of personnel (56).

A National Association of Community Schools was organized in 1970 to bring together the wide variety of community school districts and individual schools which are cropping up around the country and share common problems and interests. One of the primary efforts of the association is to devise more satisfactory means of funding these alternatives to the public school system.

Community-controlled schools which are mushrooming throughout America have demonstrated in their short lifetimes that the various communities can be effectively involved in the development of a positive educational environment. Although small in number, they are the source of significant experimentation and have as a group adopted a more humanistic approach to learning. They have challenged the kind of professionalism which internalized school politics and closed off the views of those who may have the most to offer in the way of educational change. They have rejected conformity and are dedicated to meeting the needs of their consumers through a balance of interest.

CONCLUSION

Restructuring the governance of American education offers the possibility of creating an environment in which priorities can be reordered and responsiveness to the various communities of interest assured. The dynamic of a viable social system, if it is to be functional, requires a constant reappraisal and adjustment of its institutions.

Those who control the schools have been unable to produce acceptable results; they have excluded the public and the students from a meaningful role in the policy process. The structure of schools must be adjusted to encourage the involvement of all interested parties and to give the community greater control over educational institutions (59). Participation in itself provides an involvement with the system which can diminish alienation and also serve to stimulate educational change, it is itself an educational experience. This new role for the community is not conceived as an abandonment of professionalism, but rather an effort to achieve a proper balance between professionalism and public participation in the policy process (69). Community control implies a redistribution of power within the educational subsystem. The definition of "community" includes not only parents of school children, but also segments of the public which have been excluded from a role in public education. It is directed toward achieving a mechanism for a participatory system which can deal with the political failure of educational systems. Community control is intended to create an environment in which more meaningful educational policies can be developed and a wide variety of alternate solutions and techniques can be experimented with. It also seeks to achieve a more equitable allocation of resources as a result of the redistribution of power. It seems plausible to assume that a school system devoted to community needs, which serve as an agent of community interests, will provide a more conducive environment in which children can learn. This conclusion is based on research that shows child and teacher attitudes are the major influence in education performance. In the community school environment, there is a far better opportunity to achieve the more positive and sympathetic attitudes which will lead to a better performance and educational achievement.

Properly instituted, community control is an instrument of social change. The redistribution of power is in itself an aspect of that change. If adequate provision is made for the technical resources to carry out this new role, community participation has the potential for providing new insights into our concept of professionalism as well as our general theories of educational expertise. If community boards have the resources to engage a variety of professionals in the policy process, institutional changes of all kinds can be anticipated.

In Crozier's book *The Bureaucratic Phenomenon,* he identifies the need to check the power of the experts and the pseudo-experts (20). He concludes that a dynamic equilibrium system is far more favorable to change but recognizes that public bureaucracies tend to be static rather than dynamic. The static model is a system in which management is closed and narrow in its perspective, with little bargaining between groups. The dynamic model involves constant shifting in the bargaining, possible only in a bureaucratic structure in which subordinates participate in the decision-making process. Urban school bureaucracies are of the static variety, and decentralization and participation in the policy process provide the only opportunity to move toward a more dynamic model.

Quality public education without the involvement and participation of the consumers is a contradiction in terms. Basic reform of a public institution does not simply consist of apparent improvements in the quality of its professional functions; it depends on the strength of the process through which the institution is governed and its responsiveness to educational needs (53). It depends on the variety of sources which can make contributions to that system. A closed structure is by its nature static. The failure or short life of many purely pedagogical reform movements in public education in America may in fact be traced to the absence of participation by parents and the larger community. The potential for finding solutions to educational problems can only be enhanced by the broader range of alternatives offered by lay people and nonschool professionals.

REFERENCES

1. Stephen K. Bailey *et al., Schoolmen and Politics: A Study of State Aid to Education in the Northeast* (Syracuse: Syracuse University Press, 1962).
2. Selma Berrol, "The Schools of New York in Transition: 1898–1914," *The Urban Review,* Vol. I (December 1966), pp. 15–20.
3. Maurice R. Berube, "White Liberals, Black Schools," *Commonweal* (ct., 1966).
4. ———, "Problems of Teacher Unionism," *New Politics,* Vol. IV (Fall 1965), pp. 37–42.
5. Maurice R. Berube and Marilyn Gittell, *Confrontation at Ocean Hill-Brownsville* (New York: Frederick A. Praeger, 1969).
6. *Brown v. Board of Education of Topeka,* 347 U.S. 483 (1954).
7. Jerome Bruner, "Culture, Politics and Pedagogy," *Saturday Review,* Vol. 51 (May 18, 1968).

8. Raymond E. Callahan, *Education and the Cult of Efficiency: A Study of the Social Forces That Have Shaped the Administration of Public Schools* (Chicago: University of Chicago Press, 1962).

9. Ronald F. Campbell, Luvern L. Cunningham, and R.F. McPhee, *The Organization and Control of American Schools* (Columbus: Charles E. Merrill, 1965).

10. Stokely Carmichael and Charles Hamilton, *Black Power: The Politics of Liberation in America* (New York: Vantage Books, 1967).

11. Kenneth B. Clark, *Dark Ghetto* (New York: Harper and Row, 1965).

12. *Boston M. Chance and Louis C. Mercado v. The Board of Examiners and the Board of Education of the City of New York,* 70 civ. 4141 United States District Court Southern District of New York, 1971 (mimeo).

13. Citizens' Advisory Committee on School Needs, *Findings and Recommendations* (abridged) (Detroit: Citizen's Advisory Committee, 1958).

14. Sol Cohen, *Progressives and Urban School Reforms* (New York: Bureau of Publications, Teachers College, Columbia University, 1964).

15. James Coleman, *et al., Equality of Educational Opportunity,* U.S. Office of Education (Washington, D.C.: U.S. Government Printing Office, 1966).

16. James Conant, *Slums and Suburbs: A Commentary on Schools in Metropolitan Areas* (New York: McGraw Hill, 1961).

17. Robert L. Crain and David Street, "School Desegregation & School Decision Making," in Marilyn Gittell (ed.), *Educating an Urban Population* (Beverly Hills, Calif.: Sage Publications, 1967).

18. Lawrence A. Cremen, *The Transformation of the School* (New York: Vintage Books, 1961).

19. Joseph M. Cronin, *The Board of Education in the Great Cities, 1890–1964,* doctoral dissertation (Palo Alto: Stanford University, 1965).

20. Michel Crozier, *The Bureaucratic Phenomenon* (Chicago: Phoenix Books, University of Chicago Press, 1967).

21. Ellwood Cubberly, *Public Education in the United States,* revised edition (Boston, 1934).

22. Luvern L. Cunningham, "A School District and City Government," *The American School Board Journal,* Vol. 141, No. 6 (December 1960), pp. 9–11, 37.

23. Robert A. Dahl, *Who Governs? Democracy and Power in an American City* (New Haven: Yale University Press, 1961).

24. Boulton H. Demas, *The School Elections: A Critique of the 1969 N.Y.C. School Decentralization.*

25. Thomas H. Elliot, "Towards an Understanding of Public School Politics." *Teachers College Record,* Vol. LXII (November 1960), pp. 118–132.

26. Jason Epstein, "The Real McCoy," A Review of the Teachers Strike by Martin Mayer, *New York Review of Books,* Vol. 12, No. 5 (March 12, 1969).

27. *Equal Educational Opportunity—1971,* Hearing Before the Select Committee on Equal Educational Opportunity of the United States Senate, 92nd Congress, Washington, D.C. (December 1, 2, 3, 1971).

28. Mario D. Fantini, Milton A. Young and Frieda Douglas, *A Design for a New & Relevant System of Education for Fort Lincoln New Towns* (Washington, D.C.: School District, 1968).

29. Mario D. Fantini, Marilyn Gittell, and Richard Magat, *Community Control and the Urban School* (New York: Praeger Publishers, 1971).

30. Mario D. Fantini and Gerald Weinstein, *The Disadvantaged: Challenge to Education* (New York: Harper & Row, 1968).

31. Joseph Featherstone, "A New Kind of Schooling," *New Republic,* Vol. 58 (March 2, 1968).

32. David J. Fox, *Expansion of the More Effective School Program* (Center for Urban Education, September 1967).

33. Edgar Z. Friedenberg, "Requiem for the Urban School," *Saturday Review,* Vol. 50 (November 18, 1967).

34. Marilyn Gittell, "School Decentralization Today," *Community Issues,* Vol. 3, No. 1 (Flushing, N.Y.: Institute for Community Studies, Queens College, November 1971).

35. ———and T. Edward Hollander, *Six Urban School Districts: A Comparative Study of Institutional Response* (New York: Praeger, 1968).

36. ———, *et al., Local Control in Education: Three Demonstration School Districts in New York City* (New York: Praeger Publishers, 1972).

37. ———and Alan G. Hevesi (eds.), *The Politics of Urban Education* (New York: Frederick A. Praeger, 1969).

38. ———(ed.), *Educating an Urban Population* (Beverly Hills, Calif.: Sage Publications, 1967).
39. ———, *Participants and Participation: A Study of School Policy in New York City* (New York: Praeger Publishers, 1968).
40. Keith Goldhammer, *The School Board* (New York: The Center for Applied Research in Education, Inc., 1964), p. 97.
41. Frances Gottfried, "A Survey of Parental Views of the Ocean Hill-Brownsville Experiment," *Community Issues,* Vol. 2, No. 5 (Flushing, N.Y.: Institute for Community Studies, Queens College October 1970).
42. Grace Graham, *The Public School in the American Community* (New York: Harper & Row, 1963).
43. William R. Grant, "Community Control vs. School Integration in Detroit," *The Public Interest,* Vol. 24 (Summer 1971), pp. 62–79.
44. Colin Greer, *The Great School Legend* (New York: Basic Books, 1972).
45. Marcia Guttentag, unpublished manuscript, available at Harlem Research Center of the City University of New York.
46. Robert J. Havighurst, *The Public Schools of Chicago* (Chicago: The Board of Education of the City of Chicago, 1964).
47. ———, *Education in Metropolitan Areas* (Boston: Allyn & Bacon, 1966).
48. Nelson B. Henry and Jerome G. Kerwin, *School and City Government,* (Chicago: University of Chicago Press, 1938).
49. Nat Hentoff, "Mugging a Corpse," *The Village Voice,* March 2, 1972.
50. ———, *Our Children Are Dying* (New York: Viking Press, 1966).
51. *High School,* film produced by Frederick Wiseman (1969), available on rental basis from Zipporah Films, Inc., 54 Lewis Wharf, Boston, Mass. 02110.
52. Lawrence Iannaconne, *Politics in Education* (New York: The Center for Applied Research in Education, Inc., 1967).
53. Michael B. Katz, *Class Bureaucracy and Schools: The Illusion of Educational Change in America* (New York: Praeger Publishers, 1971).
54. Herbert Kohl, *21, 36 Children* (New York: New American Library, 1967).
55. Jonathan Kozol, *Death at an Early Age* (New York: Bantam Books, Inc., 1968).
56. ———, *Free Schools* (New York: Houghton Mifflin, 1972).
57. William C. Kvaraceus, "P.T.A. The Irrelevant Giant," *The Nation* (October 5, 1963), pp. 200–201.
58. Henry M. Levin (ed.), *Community Control of Schools* (Washington, D.C.: The Brookings Institution, 1970), p. 289.
59. Rod Lewis, "Indian Education Legislation," *Inequality in Education,* Vol. 10 (December 1971), pp. 19–21: Dan Rosenfelt, "New Regulations for Federal Indian Funds," *Inequality in Education,* Vol. 10 (December 1971), pp. 21–25.
60. Roscoe Martin, *Government and the Suburban School* (Syracuse: Syracuse University Press, 1962).
61. Martin Mayer, *The Teachers Strike* (New York: Harper and Row, 1969).
62. Mayor's Advisory Panel on Decentralization of the New York City Schools, *Reconnection for Learning: A Community Schools System for New York City* (New York: Praeger Publishers, 1969).
63. Rhody A. McCoy, "The Formation of a Community Controlled School District," in Henry M. Levin (ed.), *Community Control of Schools* (Washington, D.C.: The Brookings Institution, 1970).
64. Jerry Miner, *Social and Economic Factors in Spending for Public Education,* The Economics & Politics of Education Series (Syracuse: Syracuse University Press, 1963).
65. Paul R. Mort, "Cost-Quality Relationships in Education," in R.L. Johns and E.L. Morphet (eds.), *Problems and Issues in Public School Finance* (National Conference of Professors of Educational Administration, 1952).
66. ———, *Fiscal Readiness for the Stress of Change* (Pittsburgh: University of Pittsburgh, 1957).
67. William R. Odell, "Educational Survey Report for the Philadelphia Board of Education" (Philadelphia: The Board of Public Education, 1965).
68. Tim Parsons, "The Community School Movement," *Community Issues,* Vol. 2, No. 6 (December 1970), Institute for Community Studies, Queens College, City University of New York.
69. Harry A. Passow, *Towards Creating A Model Urban School System: A Study of the Washington, D.C., Public Schools* (New York: Teachers College, Columbia University, 1967).
70. Joseph Pois, *The School Board Crisis: A Chicago Case Study* (Chicago: Educational Methods, Inc., 1964).

71. Public Education Association, *The Status of Negro and Puerto Rican Children and Youth in the Public Schools* (New York: Public Education Association, 1955).
72. Diane Ravitch "Community Control Revisited," *Commentary,* Vol. 53, No. 2 (February 1972), pp. 69–74.
73. Donald H. Ross, *Administration for Adaptability* (New York: Metropolitan School Study Council, Teachers College, Columbia University, 1951).
74. David Rogers, *110 Livingston Street: Politics and Bureaucracy in the New York City School System* (New York: Random House, 1968).
75. Robert Rosenthal and Lenore Jacobson, *Pygmalion in the Classroom: Teacher Expectations and Pupil Intellectual Development* (New York: Holt, Rinehart & Winston, 1968).
76. Robert H. Salisbury *et al., State Politics & the Public Schools* (New York: Knopf, 1964).
77. *School Decentralization and School Policy in New York City,* A Report for the New York State Commission on the Quality, Cost and Financing of Elementary and Secondary Education (Flushing, N.Y.: Institute for Community Studies, 1971).
78. Scope (School & Community Organized for Partnership in Education), *Bulletin* (New York, 1969).
79. Patricia Cayo Sexton, *Education & Income* (New York: Viking Press, 1961).
80. Albert Shanker, "Where We Stand," *New York Times,* February 13, 1972.
81. Eleanor B. Sheldon and Raymond A. Glazer, *Pupils and Schools in New York City: A Fact Book* (New York: Russell Sage Foundation, 1965).
82. Adele Spier, "The Two Bridges Model School District," *Community Issues,* Vol. 1, No. 3 (February 1969), Institute for Community Studies, Queens College, City University of New York.
83. Karl E. Taeuber and Alma F. Taeuber, *Negros in Cities* (Chicago: Aldine Publishing Co., 1965).
84. Urban League of Greater New York, *A Study of the Problems of Integration in New York City Public Schools Since 1955* (New York: Urban League of Greater New York, 1963).
85. Alpheus L. White, "An Analysis of School Board Organization: Trends and Developments in School Board Organizations and Practices in Cities with a Population of 100,000 or More," *American School Board Journal,* Vol. CXLVI (April 1963), pp. 7–8; *Characteristics of Local School Board Policy,* Manuals (Washington, D.C.: U.S. Department of Health, Education, and Welfare, Office of Education, 1959); *Local School Boards: Organization and Practices* (Washington, D.C.: U.S. Government Printing Office, 1962).
86. Miriam Wasserman, "The I.S. 201 Story," *Urban Review,* Vol. 11 (June 1969), pp. 3–15.
87. Charles Wilson, "Beginning of a Miracle," *Interim Report* (August 1969).
88. Roger R. Woock and Harry L. Miller, *Social Foundations of Urban Education* (Hinsdale, Illinois: Dryden Press, 1970).

CHAPTER 10

DECENTRALIZATION AND CITIZEN PARTICIPATION IN CRIMINAL JUSTICE SYSTEMS

RICHARD A. MYREN

Criminal justice systems are one of the mechanisms relied on by modern states to establish and preserve that minimal level of internal stability necessary for growth and development. Such systems are formal, legal, and governmental; supplemented by a variety of informal, nonlegal, nongovernmental social control mechanisms.

For the purpose of this essay, a criminal justice system is defined as the aggregate of agencies (police, prosecution, courts with jurisdiction over violations of the criminal law, probation, parole, correctional agencies, and specialized agencies such as New York's Narcotic Addiction Control Commission and Division for Youth) that have responsibility for enforcement of the criminal law. In another context, the criminal justice system would be defined to include the legislative process that produced the substantive criminal law enforced by the system thus defined, the procedural criminal law (including the law of evidence) that governs how that enforcement can proceed, and the charters or enabling acts creating the agencies of the system. Only peripheral mention will be made of these aspects of criminal justice systems in the current discussion.

The criminal justice systems of the United States (as subsystems of federal, state, county, and city governments) are in trouble. The critical literature includes a massive outpouring of governmental reports (1–19, 25–29), a phenomenon paralleled in Canada (20–24). This year (1972) sees yet another massive study on the part of the Law Enforcement Assistance Administration of the U.S. Department of Justice. Administrator Jerris Leonard has appointed a National Advisory Commission on Criminal Justice Standards and Goals which expects to publish its report by September 15, 1972.

Not all of the critical attention fixed on criminal justice has been on the part of government. The journals published by the law schools of the country have dealt extensively with crime problems (30–39). Special issues of other scholarly and popular magazines have also focused on criminal justice (40–46). Films are becoming sufficiently common to merit catalogs (47). Nor has the critical comment been limited to scholarly journals and heavy governmental reports. The popular press too has highlighted problems in all segments of the criminal justice system (48–64).

From *Public Administration Review,* 32 (October 1972): 718–738. Copyright © 1972 by American Society for Public Administration. Reprinted with permission.

Citizen concern with the seriousness of the crime problem has been evidenced in a number of ways. Acting through Congress, the people of the United States have, since 1960, established a number of successive new agencies to lead a nationwide war against crime, culminating in the Law Enforcement Assistance Administration of the U.S. Department of Justice (65). Operating primarily through block grants to the states, the agency has generated a new level of participation in criminal justice planning by requiring that each state administer its share of the funds through a board widely representative of state and local governments and of the public at large. Most states have, in addition, established regional criminal justice planning groups with similar broad representation. Typically, these boards sit as policymaking groups whose decisions are implemented by professional staffs. In addition, some states use a variety of advisory groups that bring into active participation an even broader range of local officials and citizens (66).

Beyond this primary effort in the Department of Justice, crime and delinquency control components have been made part of almost all proposals in the Model Cities Program of the Department of Housing and Urban Development. Less obviously related but with an important impact nonetheless has been the Legal Services Program of the Office of Economic Opportunity. This program brings legal assistance to poor people facing a wide variety of personal and family problems, many of which could, unattended, become criminogenic (67–68).

In addition to acting through their elective officials, private citizens have evidenced their concern through support of private nonprofit agencies, the most prominent of which is the National Council on Crime and Delinquency (69–71). Citizens are also showing their concern through a variety of actions on the local level. One evidence of citizen concern for crime is the political support given to "law and order" candidates in local elections (72). Another is support for and participation in local vigilante-like groups (73–75). A variation on this self-help approach is the growing tendency of cooperative neighborhood associations to hire a protective service to regularly patrol their neighborhood (76, p. 277) (77). One last kind of local expression of concern is the court-watcher program. This kind of citizen's group, established to monitor the performance of various local criminal justice agencies, is spreading (78).

In summary, the criminal justice systems of the United States are in difficulty—and the people know it. The balance of this essay looks at the extent to which decentralization and citizen participation present a viable alternative in meeting that difficulty.

In the discussion, Alan A. Altshuler's definition of the key terms will be used:

> To *decentralize* means to distribute authority more widely—that is, to a greater number of individuals. Decentralization can take many forms. One of the most vital is to substitute decisions by individuals in the marketplace for decisions by governmental officials. We shall be concerned . . . however, with a specific type of decentralization: that within government, from officials at the center of a jurisdiction to those in geographically defined subjurisdictions (i.e., states within the nation, localities within states, and so on).
>
> Within this type, it is of crucial importance to distinguish *administrative* decentralization from *political* decentralization. The former involves delegation from superior to subordinate officials within a bureaucracy. The organizing principle of bureaucracy remains hierarchical. The top officials remain free to revoke the delegation at any time. The subordinate officials remain dependent in numerous ways upon the pleasure of their superiors. Political decentralization, by contrast, involves the transfer of authority to officials whose dependence is upon the subjurisdictional clientele. The assumption must be that such officials will not be manipulable by the former possessors of the transferred authority.

> *Community control* means the exercise of authority by the democratically organized government of a neighborhood-sized jurisdiction. There is no consensus on how neighborhoods should be defined. . . . Nor is there any consensus about the precise amount of authority that such a government would have to possess in any given policy arena for the label "community control" to be justified. What the term does clearly denote is a category of proposed reforms: transfers of authority from the governments of large cities to the governments of much smaller sub-units within them. Such transfers would constitute political decentralization. At the same time, it should be emphasized that they would remain subject to modification by higher levels of government—just as are the charters of cities and suburbs today (70, pp. 64–65).

Altshuler also sets out the claims that motivate the desire for participation: "These claims seem to focus on three values: political authority, group representation in public bureaucracies, and the private income (wages and profits) generated by governmental activity" (79, p. 64). Police departments are one of the primary targets in the criminal justice system for those advocating decentralization and citizen participation through community control.

DECENTRALIZATION AND CITIZEN PARTICIPATION IN POLICE AGENCIES

Police departments can perform at least the following functions: enforcement of the traditional law, enforcement of convenience norms, performance of service activities, suppression of political opposition, and the combating of external aggression. In the United States, the police agencies of our large cities *legally* carry out the first three of these (80). What is sometimes spoken of as the order maintenance function of the police is actually achieved through these three kinds of activity. Other authors have described police functions in other terms (81–83) (19, Vol. 17, pp. 53–71).

Police departments in the United States are organized as classical hierarchical bureaucracies modeled after the military. They are strongly centralized and strenuously resist control by "civilian" officials. Labor is divided into functional specialties, with activities conducted according to standardized operating procedures. Career routes are well established and have a common entry point with promotions based on impersonal evaluations by superiors. Management proceeds through a monocratic system of routinized superior-subordinate relationships. Status among employees is directly related to their positions (jobs) and ranks (83). This theoretical model is actually found among police departments only in a relatively few, generally middle-sized departments with honest civil service systems. Social relationships, political ties, and corruption lead to modification of this centralized ideal.

Decentralization

There are perhaps no more often-quoted paragraphs in the *Task Force Report on Police* of the President's Crime Commission than the two that describe the fragmentation of policing in the United States. After identifying 40,000 separate police agencies in the U.S., the report notes that only 50 of these are federal, 200 state, and that the remaining 39,750 are in local units of government. Of this massive number of local agencies, 3,050 are in counties, 3,700 in cities, and 33,000 are in the boroughs, towns, and villages (9, Vol. 9, p. 7). Some regard this fragmentation of police services as centralization pushed to its units.

In facing the problem of fragmentation of police services, the task force report recognizes that police often work at cross purposes in the investigation of the same or similar crimes. It further states that what is customarily referred to as "close cooperation" is actually no more than "a lack of conflict." As possible paths to improvement, the report explores consolidation and cooperation or coordination. These concepts are defined as follows:

> Consolidation is the merging, in whole or in part, of governmental jurisdiction, or function thereof, with another governmental jurisdiction, or function thereof.
> Cooperation or coordination presupposes a formal agreement between two or more governmental jurisdictions each with defined responsibilities to jointly provide a common service (9, pp. 69–70).

Cooperation or coordination is defined as "the English common law concept of a region (or community) as an area having a commonality of interests is accepted as a definition of a region in this study; thus it is not restricted to defined political boundaries" (9, p. 70). The task force also posits as two basic assumptions underlying its discussion that local government will continue as a vital force despite some consolidation and that as much local governmental control as is reasonable should be preserved while increasing the quality and quantity of service. It then goes on to consider the pros and cons of coordination and consolidation of police staff services, auxiliary services, and selected field services. It also discusses police service in a consolidated jurisdiction and the obstacles existing to coordination and consolidation. The conclusion is reached that there exist many areas in policing in which coordination and cooperation will result in better programs, but that "comprehensive reorganization under a metropolitan-type government offers the best possibilities for fully unifying police services on an area-wide basis" (9, p. 72).

In exploring obstacles to consolidation, the task force recognizes that the most formidable is local home-rule sentiment that leads "even the smallest local governmental jurisdictions . . . to believe that they can provide at least minimal needed police services." It goes on to support broad joint-exercise-of-powers legislation permitting many types of intergovernmental agreements as the most promising authority for accomplishing coordination and consolidation. Policing of one jurisdiction by another under a formal contract is one of the possibilities opened up by such legislation, and is commonplace in California under the "Lakewood Plan."

There appears to have been very little police coordination and consolidation inspired by the report in the four-plus years since its release. On November 18, 1971, Fayette County and Lexington (Kentucky) police departments announced they would merge the two forces by January 15, 1972. Merger of seven major functions (training, records, computerized information systems, fingerprinting and identification, photo-labs, planning and research, and a computerized digital communications system) is also under way for the Jefferson County and Louisville (Kentucky) departments. Both have been aided by Kentucky Crime Commission block grant funds (85). But Lexington is an exception to the basic fact that little consolidation of police work has resulted from the task force report.

Texts on the administration of large-city police departments have, since World War II, stressed the dangers and disadvantages of too much decentralization to precinct stations, the local neighborhood police office (86, p. 90) (87, p. 71) (88, p. 73) (89, p. 122) (90, p. 26) (9, Vol. 4, p. 123).

The reasons given are these:

1. Precinct buildings with their staffs are an expensive fixed overhead cost
2. Precinct stations foster a breakdown in executive control
3. These stations seduce citizen reliance from central headquarters to their own location

4. This decentralization raises special questions of control over functional specialists
5. Modern communication and motorization make local stations unnecessary
6. Transfer of information, instructions, and records, and the custody and transfer of prisoners, property, and evidence is made more complicated
7. Local precinct stations facilitate influence by ward politicians. Such is the conventional wisdom. The textbooks seem to have influenced reality as witnessed by reductions in the use and number of district stations in such scattered cities as Seattle, Chicago, Oakland, and Kansas City (Missouri), and many other places (90, p. 26).

During the same period, beat patrol has been transformed from an officer walking a relatively restricted area to one patrolling a much larger beat while riding in an automobile or on a motorcycle. The *Task Force Report on Police* summarizes well the rationale for this development:

> A decision to use foot patrols should be made only after careful analysis, since it is a highly expensive form of coverage, geographically restrictive in nature, and can be wasteful of manpower. Without transportation at hand, it provides extremely inflexible and rigid close patrol for specifically limited geographical areas, and does not permit the ready reassignment of the personnel to surrounding locations when and where police services may be specifically requested. Moreover, close supervision of foot patrolmen has proven very difficult (9, Vol. 9, p. 54).

It is recognized that motorized patrol has taken the policeman out of touch with the people in the area that he patrols. He must stay in contact with his car radio to be available for dispatch to trouble sites made known to headquarters by telephone.

A number of technological advances have made inroads on this problem. Early devices made it possible to activate the red light or horn of the police car from headquarters to recall the officer to the car and radio. Development of small, compact radio devices that the officer could take with him when out of his car was a recommendation of the police task force. Several such devices are now available. Another task was to equip foot patrolmen with motor scooters as well as the new portable radios. With the latter making communication possible, need for service in a distant part of the beat reachable rapidly with the scooter can be made known to the officer. The best-managed departments today use a mix of patrol styles to achieve a somewhat closer relationship with residents of the beats than in the recent past, while still preserving the advantages of mobility.

Team Policing

Recognition that police agencies, in their push for efficiency, had lost touch with the neighborhoods being served led many law enforcement leaders to attempt to return greater responsibility to those doing the actual policing. These attempts have taken a number of forms, several of which are referred to as "team policing." A concept introduced into this country from Europe (91), team policing has been tried in communities as scattered as Washington, D.C., New York City (92–99), Detroit (100), Syracuse (101–111), Los Angeles (112–114), Palo Alto (115–188), Holyoke (119, 83), Dayton (83), and Louisville (83), and has doubtless spread to others about whose efforts published reports are not yet available. Patrick V. Murphy, commissioner of police in New York City, who has also held similar posts in Washington and Detroit, was one of the early experimenters. His plan for Washington has been implemented as the "Model Precinct Project," for Detroit as the "Beat Commander," and in New York City as "Operation Neighborhood."

This New York version of team policing is based on assumptions common to all: that street patrolmen and their first-line supervisors are capable of shouldering a great deal more responsibility than has been given to them in the past; that support of the citizens living and working in the many discrete neighborhoods of our metropolitan areas, which is absolutely necessary for successful policing, can best be achieved by having a police subunit permanently assigned to each neighborhood; that the personnel of these subunits must get to know the people in the neighborhood through positive efforts to promote continuous dialogue in both formal and informal settings; and that assistance to the people, both in handling their crime problems and in helping them to make contact with the proper agencies to handle the myriad other problems of big city living, is the best means of achieving respect for and support of police operations.

Operation Neighborhood, begun on a small scale in January 1971, has spread rapidly. Most precincts now have experimental teams, and one, labeled as a "model precinct," now operates entirely on a team basis. Used as the training ground for recruits fresh out of the academy, the precinct is also experimenting with female supervisors and patrolmen resident in the areas they police.

Syracuse is experimenting with crime control teams in a project designed with the assistance of the General Electric Company. Based on a strategy of offensive rather than defensive deployment of police resources, Syracuse committed its first team of eight officers and a captain to an average beat in July 1968. Control of crime was made its sole responsibility. Traffic control and general services to citizens for the beat were handled by other units. Investigation of committed crimes is continued only as long as there is a high probability that they will lead to successful conclusions. When success appears dubious, the investigation is turned over to headquarters to be dropped or assigned to some other unit. This policy has been established because a team member, while investigating one crime, is not in a position to deter or intercept other crimes.

On the basis of careful evaluation, the project has been expanded considerably. The judgment of success is based on a comparatively high clearance rate in known cases, coupled with more subjective impressions that the people who lived and worked in the team area thought that they were getting better police service and that policemen on the team thought the new method of operation was contributing more toward achieving police objectives. The project designers point out, however, that the result might be attributable to "using above average policemen, superior leadership, the Hawthorne effect, or a combination of these and other unrecognized factors." Two disappointments were expressed: "the lack of any demonstration of a Team member's ability to pick up the ball and run with it;" and the "failure of the Team to significantly increase the number of interceptions made of crimes in progress." One of the greatest problems encountered was selling the team concept to that part of the police department not involved in the project.

That difficulty was overcome in Los Angeles, which extended its Basic Car Plan to the entire city within six months of initiation. This was facilitated by use of a less rigid "total responsibility" model in which the Basic Car (A unit) is supplemented by other cars (X units) when necessary.

In addition to the familiarity between people and police that comes with placing primary responsibility for policing a specific geographic district on a specific team of police officers, additional mutual understanding is sought in monthly meetings. Criticisms of these meetings center on the fact that they are structured by the police rather than the residents, that they avoid discussion of controversial subjects, and that they draw primarily those residents who have no complaints about police operations.

Chief of Police E.M. Davis seems convinced that crime and disorder have been decreased by the Basic Car Plan. The *Los Angeles Times* concludes that "exactly how—or whether the Basic Car Plan has affected the city's crime rate (up 4 percent for the first 11 months of 1970) is hard to determine."

Still a fourth approach to team policing in the United States is that advocated by John P. Kenney of the Department of Criminology at Long Beach State College and being tried experimentally by the Palo Alto, California, Police Department. Kenney calls his approach the "Colleague Model":

> Essentially the colleague model is based on a team approach to organization. Relationships are circular rather than hierarchical. The top level of organization reflects an assemblage of top management personnel each with particular expertise in a functional or program area working together to provide direction to the organization. The lower levels of an organization are discrete subassemblies for the performance of specific programs. Essential expertise is included in each lower level team (115, pp. 8–9).

Team assignments are functional and temporal rather than spatial. This application of the team concept in policing obviously has little direct relationship to neighborhood control, although it may be an organizational structure more easily adapted to that end than are more traditional policing models.

Democratic Team Model

A fifth adaptation of team policing that probably has greater significance than any other for decentralization and citizen participation in municipal policing is the democratic team model proposed by John Angel (83). His proposal would split the entire police department into general service sections (neighborhood teams) supported by a specialized service section and a coordination and information section. Basic responsibility for crime prevention and control would lie in the general service sections, teams of about 25 officers policing a relatively small area (results in about five people on duty at all times). Supervision lies primarily in the team itself acting democratically, with an elected team representative serving as contact person for the other general service sections and for the support sections. There are no formal ranks or supervisors. Differences in pay come only with team-recognized superior contribution. It is assumed that this would result from native intelligence, education, experience, and dedication leading to maturity and wisdom. Control would be through a system of checks and balances in which some authority lies in the general services section, some in the coordination and information section, and some in the specialized services section. It would be possible for the general services sections to be at the neighborhood level, the specialized service section at the city level, and the coordinating and information section at a county or regional level.

Specialized services would contain those specialized activities currently classified as line units (investigative, juvenile, traffic, etc.), which would be available on call to general service section personnel. Coordination and information would do the "housekeeping" (central records, communication, research, etc.) and coordination for both general and special service.

General service sections consist entirely of police generalists all of equal rank with no formally assigned supervisor. The team would be responsible for all law enforcement and order keeping in the geographic area assigned. Team members would determine who would lead them, with leadership expected to develop situationally as circumstances dictate and to change from time to time. There would be no procedural guidelines imposed on teams except very broad ones designed to prevent extreme behavior. Each team draws up its own guidelines (119). This allows them to adopt goals and policies consistent with the needs and desires of the people and the methods the team believes best to pursue those goals and policies. Registration of the goals, policies, and procedures adopted with coordination and information might be required. Each team maintains a community office as its local headquarters. Teams are expected to hold periodic meetings with members of the community for working out and then continually re-examining the police-community interaction. Specialists from the other two sections are available to the teams as resource persons for such meetings. Team members are also expected to attend intra-organizational meetings for purposes such as communication and training. Evaluation is multifaceted. Each team member evaluates the others and overall team performance. Specialists evaluate team performance in the area of their expertise. The coordination and information section evaluates how well each team is achieving its goals and adhering to its policies. Procedures are not evaluated. The community can also be tapped for evaluation. Survey research techniques can be used to monitor the extent to which the community is free from fear of crime and from fear of the criminal justice system.

The special services section employs a team or teams of various functional specialists to meet the needs of the general service sections. These specialists are on call for assistance and support of the generalists. Policy on their use is established by each team. When called, a specialist serves at the pleasure of the generalist or team calling him. He is responsible for the performance of his specialty to, but free from interference from, the caller, to whom he makes his report. The use to which the report is put is up to the generalist or team.

Education and training of all personnel is primarily pre-service. Supplemental, refresher, and retraining is the responsibility of the coordination and information section. Any specialty for which there is a felt need can be developed.

Among the functions of coordination and information would be the coordination of the general service sections, functional supervision, planning, training, development of ethical standards, detention of prisoners, keeping of central records, and maintenance of area communications. Performance of the coordination function would not include establishment of enforcement policy, but such tasks as definition of the areas to be policed by the various general service sections and assignment of members to those sections. In so doing, an attempt is made to pick generalists with complementary skills and attitudes. Constant monitoring and evaluation of team functioning are designed to alert for assignments not working out. If a team is not functioning properly, it is a coordinating and information section responsibility to break it up, reassign its members, and select a new team for the area.

The chief coordinator is chosen for a term of years. He is eligible for reappointment. He might be chosen by a search committee composed of members of the department, representatives of citizens in the area served, and executive representatives of the governmental units involved. He would be chosen for his ability and expertise in coordinating and managing human organizations. He serves as spokesman for the entire department when one is needed, and as a contact man with other community institutions.

Anticipated advantages of the democratic police team model include more influence for area residents in the making of police policy decisions, greater flexibility and adaptability in policy formulation, improvement in the quality of police-community interaction, elevation of the professional standing and prestige of police careers, provision for lateral entry, and an increase in the effectiveness and morale of all department employees. Among the assumptions underlying the model are that education and training will be primarily pre-service, emphasizing behavioral and social science concepts that lead to better understanding of self and society; that in-service training will be primarily seminar discussion and other high participation types; that salary will be determined by expertise and experience and not by position; that greater trust will be placed by everyone in the police generalist; and that the generalist will be able to accept and deal realistically with the greater responsibility while learning to live with an ambiguous, unstructured, and insecure job situation.

All of these team policing models fall into Altshuler's category of administrative decentralization. About that concept, he has this to say:

> Most whites, liberal and conservative both, today agree that a great deal of administrative decentralization is called for in the nation's big cities, and that a decisive test of good administration is responsiveness to reasonable client desires. What they generally have in mind, however, is the delegation of authority within bureaucracies to field officers . . . who will be instructed to seek "good community relations"—but who, if perchance they "go native," can be slapped down at will by their superiors at central headquarters. There are substantial variations in the degrees of client responsiveness considered desirable, but few indeed seem prepared to make client responsiveness in the big city ghettoes a function of neighborhood authority as opposed to city government grace (79, p. 16).

He goes on to argue that what is needed today is political decentralization, permanent and irrevocable "transfer of authority to officials whose dependence is upon the subjurisdictional electorate, or, more narrowly, a subjurisdictional clientele." This is the difference between the concepts of decentralization and community control through citizen participation.

Citizen Participation

It is possible for the citizenry being policed to participate in the process in at least four ways: the simple lending of support of various kinds to the police agency, actual assumption of police duties under the direction of regular police officers, formal evaluation of police performance, and the setting of policy for police operations.

Residents of a community can support their police agency in a number of ways. They can make it clear to appointed and elected officials who control the budget that they want their police department to have a high level of financial support. This can be done by working on behalf of and voting for candidates for office who agree with their view, appearing and making supportive statements at budget hearings, and writing letters of support to the fiscal authorities and to the mass media. They can cooperate with the department in the actual execution of its duties, assisting police officers at the scene of crimes or other events requiring police action when requested to do so. They can also report suspicious activities and other information of value to the department in its work. They can cooperate in interviews about events they may have seen, agreeing to serve as witnesses in court when the knowledge they possess is deemed relevant and important to a police case. They can take an active part in crime prevention activities and campaigns and urge their friends and neighbors to do likewise.

Since World War II police agencies have done a great deal to encourage this kind of support through the establishment of public relations or, more recently, community relations units. The former sought primarily to let the public know about what the agency was trying to do, how successful it was, and what support it needed. Community relations, in contrast, not only seeks to impart but to obtain information. It attempts to get feedback from the community on whether department policies have community support, what the image of the department is in the neighborhoods, and what it should do differently to meet more effectively the needs and wishes of the community. Police-community interaction literature is far too great to summarize here (9, Vol. 9, pp. 144–207, 221–228) (90, pp. 215–246).

One of the frequent products of police-community relations programs is an attempt to build bridges between the police and the residents of the area in which they work by a variety of means:

giving the beat officers (an area team) both responsibility and time for more face-to-face discussion with residents when encountered on the street; seeking appointments for those officers with residents to talk about area police problems; setting up small group meetings for officers to meet and talk with a group of neighbors on the same topics; and setting up a team that will stay in an area with an area office, in effect becoming a neighborhood police department that draws heavily on neighborhood sentiment in establishing its policies and procedures. Recruitment of young men and women indigenous to a neighborhood for employment as police community service officers in that neighborhood was recommended by the President's Commission on Law Enforcement and Administration of Justice (9, Vol. 9, p. 123). Although a police employee, the community service officer does not possess full law enforcement powers or carry arms:

> The duties of the CSO would be to assist police officers in their work and to improve communications between police departments and the neighborhood as a uniformed member of the working police. He would render certain carefully selected police services to these neighborhoods.

The concept of the community service officer is tailor-made for our largest cities. Having residents of each neighborhood working for the police in the neighborhood is expected to increase citizen knowledge about and support for police operations. But, the community service officer idea connotes that neighborhood employees of the police department are second-class police officers.

Another form of direct citizen participation in police operations is through service in police auxiliary or reserve units. Such units became widespread during World War II when manpower was short. Their effectiveness then led to their continuation or reconstitution after the war (87, p. 445) (9, Vol. 9, p. 23). With sworn officers, civilian police reserves conduct patrol, handle crowds during parades and other special events, assist in search and rescue operations, and direct traffic. In some circumstances, they work alone. This kind of participation in the police role can lead to greater understanding of police problems on the part of the citizens involved. It is not apt to be attractive, however, to those inner-city residents already alienated from the police agency.

Civilian Review Boards and Ombudsmen

Evaluation of police service by the populace being policed is not a common occurrence. Every-day complaints to command officers or other governmental officials might be considered a kind of informal evaluation (120), but the ineffectiveness of this indirect approach led to the next logical step: formulation of civilian review boards. Few innovations in municipal government have resulted in such violent controversy or in such a voluminous literature (120, pp. 170–181). Walter Gellhorn summarizes the work of the only two wholly independent review boards that existed at the height of the popularity of the idea in 1966 in these words:

> Neither of these two boards has had clear sailing. They were at first perhaps inadequately publicized. The Philadelphia board, having no investigators under its own control, necessarily called on the police to make whatever investigations were needed; and this may have raised doubts about its independence. The Rochester [New York] board, confined to dealing with physical brutality, rejected complaints about other types of misbehavior that had galled local residents. Both boards were beset by litigation commenced by policemen's organizations and were at times enjoined from functioning. These and other factors have contributed to the boards' thoroughly unspectacular records (120, p. 180).

After pointing out that supporters allege a deterrent effect arising from the mere fact of the existence of such a board and that detractors allege that a board destroys police morale, Gellhorn states his own conclusion that, although the general purposes of civilian review boards are commendable, it is doubtful if they can achieve the desired results. He concludes that "stronger medicine is going to be needed to cure community ills" (120, p. 181).

Nor does it appear that Gellhorn believes that the ombudsman is that stronger medicine, although Gellhorn is probably the nation's leading authority on the ombudsman. After careful study of the office that originated in the Swedish Constitution of 1908 and spread to Finland, Denmark, Norway, and New Zealand, as well as studies of offices with similar functions in Yugoslavia, Poland, the Soviet Union, and Japan, he concludes that the ombudsman is only a device for making a sound system work better (121). He maintains that a successful ombudsman operation requires a basically effective set of administrative institutions; appointment by officials who believe in the importance of his office and want him to succeed; appointment of an individual with outstanding personal education and experience credentials; and a supportive body of good citizens who will not attempt to corrupt officials to advance their own selfish purposes, who do not balk at paying the taxes the services necessitate, and who do not indiscriminately withhold the respect and appreciation that might encourage faithful public servants.

Whether these required conditions for successful ombudsmanship exist in the federal and state governments of the United States is an open question that may never be answered (122). Agitation for appointment of ombudsmen at those levels seems to have peaked and declined. In New York State, legislative hearings produced almost solid opposition to the proposal from state officials in all departments, not only from those comprising the criminal justice system (123) (124).

One possible evaluative technique that has not been systematically attempted on a jurisdiction-wide basis over time is use of survey research methods to determine the extent to which residents of the jurisdiction are both free of fear of criminal attack and free of fear of suppressive criminal justice system tactics. It would seem possible to blend such an attitudinal survey with a validating survey of community behavioral indicators related to the attitudes check. The results over time should give some indication of criminal justice system health.

Citizen participation in community policing through simple lending of support of various kinds to the police agency, through actual assumption of police duties under the direction of regular police officers, and through formal evaluation of police performance seem to many to be too slow and ineffective to produce needed change in police organization and operations. As a result, some citizens seek to participate through achievement of a voice in setting policy for the local police agency. This is what Altshuler calls community control through political decentralization.

Community Control

One of the early discussions of the wisdom of vesting political control of the police working in a big-city neighborhood in the people of that neighborhood took place at a seminar on violence conducted by the New York State Joint Legislative Committee on Crime, Its Causes, Control and Effect on Society in New York City in July 1968 (67, pp. 142–178). Less than three years later, the arguments of the professors there gathered for quiet discussion were heard again more stridently in a political contest in Berkeley, California—a contest over whether an amendment to the city charter should be adopted that "would re-arrange city government to permit direct control of the police by the people in three administrative (and neighborhood) districts" (125, p. 3). The charter amendment failed at the polls in April 1971, a defeat that leaves the United States without an experiment in community control of segments of a metropolitan police department.

Proponents of the Berkeley charter amendment argued that there was no effective citizen control of the city police department. They alleged that the theoretical authority of the city manager was not in fact exercised, and that, even had the manager been in control, he was insulated from citizen supervision by a requirement of a two-thirds majority in the city council to override his decision. To overcome this situation, they advocated splitting the city into three neighborhoods:

> In the Berkeley community, Jefferson's "wards" are the three distinct areas defined by the Community Control Amendment: the black community, the campus/youth community, and the middle-class Northside/Hill Community. Of course, these are not completely distinct areas. The "black" community defined in the Amendment is actually one-forth white. The "hill" community contains a generation gap. The "campus" community contains students, freaks, and many long-time Berkeley residents. Nevertheless the communities are distinct from each other, each with its common hang-outs, common life-styles, common shopping and recreation areas, common problems (125, p. 3).

Each of the three communities was to be divided into precincts on a population basis. A precinct representative would be elected by the people of that area to sit on a District Police Council. Because of population differences, the black and middle-class communities were each to have two distinct councils and the campus/youth community one. Each district was to comprise 15 precincts, with its council being called the Council of Fifteen. Each of the councils would have elected a commissioner to a five-person police commission for the City of Berkeley. Other duties of the councils would include the following: continual review of all policies of the police department; formulation of recommendations to the police commission for policy changes when the needs or will of the neighborhood they served were no longer being met by the policies; creation and operation of a grievance procedure to hear complaints against police in the 15 precincts of the district; and discipline of members of the police department for violations of law or policy in their district. Each Council of 15 was to be required to meet regularly at times when interested persons could attend. Council members would be subject to recall on petition of 20 percent of those who voted in the last precinct election.

Administrative coordination of the three essentially autonomous neighborhood police departments was to be vested in the five-member police commission, which would have assumed many of the functions of the current police chief. Responsibilities of the commission would include: setting policy for all city police; determining qualifications for employment in the police department; establishing compensation levels for all police employees; meting out punishment to police officers found guilty of violation of law or policy; entering into necessary agreements with other police departments and governmental agencies; and facilitating agreements among the three separate departments for the operation, maintenance, and staffing of facilities of common interest, such as weapons, vehicles, laboratories, and vehicle repair stations. Financing would have continued to be through appropriation by the city council with the budget distributed to the three constituent forces on a population basis. Every police officer would have been required to live in the neighborhood to which assigned for duty (125, *passim*).

Although the Berkeley neighborhood policing charter amendment was defeated at the polls, it is probably only a matter of time before some such scheme of political decentralization of the police department is tried in an American city. Cities with strong team policing under administrative decentralization are likely candidates.

An Assessment

There is little direct citizen participation in the establishment of police policies and procedures in the large cities of the United States. There are some general support projects of a police-community relations nature, some cities in which lay persons perform actual police duties under supervision of regular police officers, and isolated instances of formal citizen evaluation of police performance. But these do not offer promising vehicles for broad-scale citizen participation. When such participation does occur, it will probably be in a city in which administrative decentralization has established a strong tradition of neighborhood team policing coupled with a practice of consulting with neighborhood groups as to how police operations can best serve community needs. A city with that kind of tradition might well opt for politically guaranteed community control. A combination of John Angell's democratic team policing model with a John Kenney colleague model coordination and information section would seem apt for such a trial. Broad policy could be set by an elected neighborhood council, with the team establishing procedures designed to implement the policies. Such an experiment would be well worth trying.

Among serious students of police operations, there is little agreement about the advisability of citizen participation in setting policy. James Q. Wilson sees some advantages in administrative decentralization with central command control, but criticizes democratic decentralization and political decentralization:

> A decentralized, neighborhood-oriented, order maintenance patrol force requires central command to insure a reasonably common definition of appropriate order, a reduction in the opportunities for corruption and favoritism, and the protection of the civil liberties of suspects and witnesses (126, p. 293).

Albert J. Reiss, Jr., seems to come out with the same result:

> There is a substantial risk that local political control will become merely a substitute for central bureaucratic control. Neither central nor local control guarantees or thwarts broad citizen participation in governments or the nature of the accountability of the agency to citizens. . . . In mass democratic societies, the central problem for citizens is how they may be brought closer to the centers of political power that control the acquisition and allocation of resources, not whether administrative control is centralized or decentralized in the bureaucracy (127, pp. 211–212).

An alternative view of complete political decentralization, and its merits, is strongly put forward by Karl Hess:

> Many who oppose decentralization are haunted by a specter of resurgent plantationism in the South. But local power there certainly need not mean Klan power over everyone. Rather, localism could mean a chance for black communities to have the sort of local identity which can defend against depredations by making the black community something more than just a niggertown appended to the white establishment's turf . . .
>
> But it is in the cities that the neighborhoods have been most abused. They have been gobbled up by the urban imperialism of downtown rentiers. They have been insulted as ethnic or racial while the downtown Wasps milked them dry for votes or zoning. And yet they persist—occupied by strange police, harassed by criminals who have more connections downtown than any of the

victims, impoverished by absentee landlords and tax collectors, abandoned by megalopolitan hospitals and treated like Skinnerian mice by visiting school teachers.

They need not take it. They do not need it. They should rise. They should secede (131).

Short of secession, they might at least try on an experimental basis the modified democratic team policing model suggested above. It is probably true that administrative decentralization of bad police operations will not alone lead to improvement. Present policies to which neighborhoods react negatively, particularly ghetto neighborhoods, can be made responsive to neighborhood wishes only through political decentralization, and through citizen participation in setting police policies (132).

DECENTRALIZATION AND CITIZEN PARTICIPATION IN PROSECUTION AND ADJUDICATION

Although decentralization (both administrative and political) of police operations is a burning issue, there is much less discussion of its applicability to court determination. When considering the adjudication of criminal cases, most persons think of the personnel involved as lawyers. And lawyers are prominent as judges, prosecutors, and defense attorneys. But non-lawyer professionals, probation officers, and court administrators are increasingly present. In addition, ordinary citizens have historically played formal roles as grand and trial jurors and as witnesses. Their involvement has become increasingly less frequent, however, as the percentage of convictions based on a plea of guilty rather than based on a trial decision has increased (133). Albert J. Reiss, Jr., points out that the processing of a criminal charge has become largely the work of "pro's with pro's," prosecutors working out settlements with defense attorneys or public defenders later ratified by judges (134).

Decentralization

Adjudication of criminal cases is initiated by prosecutors. Although police officers determine the charge used as a basis for on-view arrests, that charge is invariably reviewed and frequently changed by the prosecutor or an assistant prior to trial. Federal prosecutors (U.S. Attorneys) are appointed, but local prosecutors are elected in all but four states (9, Vol. 4, p. 73). The American Bar Association Project on Standards for Criminal Justice has defined the function of the prosecutor as follows:

(a) The office of prosecutor, as the chief law enforcement official of his jurisdiction, is an agency of the executive branch of government which is charged with the duty to see that the laws are faithfully executed and enforced to maintain the rule of law.
(b) The prosecutor is both an administrator of justice and an advocate; he must exercise sound discretion in the performance of his functions.
(c) The duty of the prosecutor is to seek justice, not merely to convict . . . (19, Vol. 15, p. 25 and Supplement, p. 2).

The report goes on to specify that:

The prosecution function should be performed by a public prosecutor who is a lawyer subject to the standards of professional conduct and discipline (19, Vol. 15, p. 26).

Another section deals with the interrelationship of prosecution offices within a state:

(a) Local authority and responsibility for prosecution is properly vested in a district, county or city attorney. Wherever possible, a unit of prosecution should be designed on the basis of population, caseload and other relevant factors sufficient to warrant at least one full-time prosecutor and the supporting staff necessary to effective prosecution.

(b) In some states conditions such as geographical area and population may make it appropriate to create a statewide system of prosecution in which the state attorney general is the chief prosecutor and the local prosecutors are his deputies.

(c) In all states there should be coordination of the prosecution policies of local prosecution offices to improve the administration of justice and assure the maximum practicable uniformity in the enforcement of the criminal law throughout the state. A state council of prosecutors should be established in each state.

(d) In cases where questions of law of statewide interest or concern arise which may create important precedents, the prosecutor should consult and advise with the attorney general of the state.

(e) A central pool of supporting resources and manpower, including laboratories, investigators, accountants, special counsel and other experts, to the extent needed should be maintained by the government and should be available to all local prosecutors (19, Vol. 15, pp. 26–27).

Against this organizational ideal must be set the reality found by the President's Commission on Law Enforcement and Administration of Justice:

> In larger communities, the prosecutor has a staff of assistants, as many as 216 in Los Angeles County or 153 in Chicago. But the great majority of the country's more than 2,700 prosecutors serve in small offices with at most one or two assistants, and frequently the prosecutor and his assistants are part-time officials. . . . The conception of the prosecutor's office as a part-time position is one of the consequences, as it is one of the causes, of the low salaries paid to prosecutors and their assistants. . . . While direct conflicts of interest between the prosecutor's public office and his private practice are clearly unlawful and, we may assume, rare, there are many indirect conflicts that almost inevitably arise. . . . The high political orientation of the prosecutor's office contributes to the problems of low pay and part-time service. . . . The prosecutors in most cities select a high proportion of their assistants primarily on the basis of party affiliation and the recommendations of ward leaders and elected officials (9, Vol. 4, p. 73).

As the discussion in the report and the new standards makes clear, the trend in organization of prosecution offices, if one exists, is toward full-time offices that may serve a region rather than a single city or county, and towards statewide coordination if not control.

Much the same situation exists in the courts that have jurisdiction to try criminal cases (9, Vol. 4, *passim*). The trend is toward a criminal part of a general trial court with broad subject matter and geographic jurisdiction and away from the separate and independent criminal courts.

Two controversies plague the organization of probation services for courts with jurisdiction over crimes: whether the probation officer should function under the direct supervision of the local judge or as part of an independent probation agency, and whether independent probation agencies should be locally organized or part of a statewide system. It seems clear from the President's

Commission Report that the trend is toward separation from the court and inclusion in statewide systems (9, Vol. 4, pp. 35–37). In fact, there appear to be strong pressures to include probation in the general correctional services unit of the state.

Offices of court administration, designed to relieve judges from administrative and clerical detail, are generally appended to court systems rather than to individual independent courts (9, Vol. 4, pp. 80–96) (46, *passim*). This possibility creates part of the pressure toward unified court systems.

The role of defense counsel in criminal cases is also clearly stated by the American Bar Association Project on Standards for Criminal Justice:

(a) Counsel for the accused is an essential component of the administration of criminal justice. A court properly constituted to hear a criminal case must be viewed as a tripartite entity consisting of the judge (and jury, where appropriate), counsel for the prosecution, and counsel for the accused.

(b) The basic duty the lawyer for the accused owes to the administration of justice is to serve as the accused's counselor and advocate, with courage, devotion and to the utmost of his learning and ability, and according to law.

(c) The defense lawyer, in common with all members of the bar, is subject to standards of conduct stated in statutes, rules, decisions of courts, and codes, canons or other standards of professional conduct. He has no duty to execute any directive of the accused which does not comport with law or such standards; he is the professional representative of the accused, not his alter ego . . . (19, Vol. 16, p. 153).

In addition to devoting one of its reports to providing defense service to those accused of crime who cannot afford them (19, Vol. 6), the standards also contain the following polite urging addressed to private practitioners:

(a) The bar should encourage through every available means the widest possible participation in the defense of criminal cases by experienced trial lawyers. Lawyers active in general trial practice should be encouraged to qualify themselves for participation in criminal cases both by formal training and through experience as associate counsel.

(b) All qualified trial lawyers should stand ready to undertake the defense of an accused regardless of public hostility toward the accused or personal distaste for the offense charged or the person of the defendant.

(c) Qualified trial lawyers should not assert or announce a general unwillingness to appear in criminal cases; law firms should encourage partners and associates to appear in criminal cases (19, Vol. 16, p. 155).

It remains to be seen whether this urging will be sufficiently heeded by the American bar to fill the unmet need:

It is clear that the legal manpower needs as estimated . . . are not now being met. Data furnished by the National Legal Aid and Defender Association show that there are about 900 defenders in the United States, of whom about half are full-time. At the Airlie House Conference it was estimated that there are between 2,500 and 5,000 lawyers who accept criminal representation more than occasionally. Where counsel must be provided as a matter of constitutional or statutory requirement, the need is often met by the appointment of lawyers who are unfamiliar with the criminal process and sometimes who have had no trial experience. In many States, counsel are not appointed for misdemeanor defendants who are unable to retain a lawyer, and in most States counsel are not provided for probation or parole revocation hearings (9, Vol. 4, p. 56).

In summary, there is little indication that further administrative decentralization is likely in the adjudication portion of the criminal justice systems.

Citizen Participation

Because lawyers, as principal participants in adjudication of criminal cases, regard administration of the criminal law as a matter requiring professional expertise, there is little political decentralization of that process. Appointed and elected officials exercise both responsibility and authority with little contact with community residents except at election time. Nor is there much pressure in the United States for such measures as civilian judges without law training. Dissatisfaction with the justice of the peace system has, in fact, resulted in movement to eliminate the remaining lay judges.

One decision point that might possibly be influenced by formal citizen input is the charge determination of the prosecutor. Just as police teams might respect neighborhood policy on how limited enforcement resources should be employed, so prosecutors might respect formally stated community wishes as to how limited prosecution and court resources should be focused.

Another path for citizen participation is through probation volunteer programs:

> The ghost of John Augustus rose again in 1960, looking somewhat different, when Royal Oak, Michigan, began easing into the use of volunteers with misdemeanants. Juvenile courts at Lawrence, Kansas, and Eugene, Oregon, had experimented with this kind of volunteer usage, since the mid-fifties. Judge Horace B. Holmes began using volunteers at the Boulder, Colorado, Juvenile Court in 1961. But not until 1967 did the court volunteer movement really take hold. Today, some 50,000 citizens contribute several million hours of service a year, in 1,000 court probation departments, and at least one new court a day is estimated to be launching its venture into volunteerism (135, p. 12).

Nor is the volunteer movement limited in its functions:

> Thus, in the area of direct contact with probationers, volunteers can offer services such as: (1) support/friendship, sincere warmth; (2) "mediation," facilitation of social-physical environment (get jobs, intercede with teacher, etc.); (3) behavior model, good example; (4) limit-setting, social control, conscience; (5) teacher-tutor of skills, academic, vocational or social; (6) observation-information-diagnosis-understanding (extra eyes and ears (a) on the probationer, (b) on the community, or even, (c) on court operations); and (7) advisory or decision-making participation in formulation or modification of probation plan.
>
> Volunteers can also do many things not primarily involving direct contact with probationers. Among these are: (8) administrative, office work, and related facilitation; (9) help recruit, train, and supervise other volunteers; (10) expert consultant to regular staff; (11) advisor to court, participation in policy-making, formally or informally, the volunteer as a source of ideas; (12) public relations, public education, and related impact on the community; and (13) contributions of money, materials, facilities, or help in securing them from others (e.g., fund raisers) (135, pp. 15–16).

Perhaps some of the growth of the probation volunteer is attributable to the rise of national organizations to serve it. One is the National Information Center on Volunteers in Courts (P. O. Box 2150, Boulder, Colorado), which publishes the *Volunteer Courts Newsletter.* Another is Volunteers in Probation, Inc. (200 Washington Square Plaza, Royal Oak, Michigan 48067) (136) which has just joined forces with NCCD:

> The National Council on Crime and Delinquency, the country's largest voluntary agency in the criminal justice field, and Volunteers in Probation, Inc., the largest volunteer probation program, will merge operations this month. VIP will become a major Part of NCCD's citizen action program (137).

This merger should assure a long-range future for volunteers in probation.

An Assessment

There is little decentralization, either administrative or political, in the adjudicative phase of the criminal justice process. The expertise of lawyers dominates the process of determination of guilt or innocence. Only after the decision is made to leave the convicted defendant in the community on probation is there any appreciable role played by ordinary citizens.

DECENTRALIZATION AND CITIZEN PARTICIPATION IN CORRECTIONS

At least since the publication in 1967 of the final report of the President's Commission on Law Enforcement and Administration of Justice, there has been a growing emphasis on the system aspects of administration of justice. This has led to a realization that the individual agencies (whether police, prosecution, courts, or corrections) do not have separate functional goals but share the one goal given by society to the system: reduction of crime. Despite this emphasis, it has recently been pointed out that there may be system subdivisions that bear separate scrutiny. In discussing how the governor and legislature of a new state might organize its criminal justice system, Richard A. McGee suggested, among other considerations, that they:

> ... Divide the total criminal justice system into three mutually supportive but administratively separate parts and avoid mixing the functions of the three parts just because it may seem expedient or customary. Each part calls for different emphasis, disparate attitudes, different professional training, and occupational skills.
> Logically, these three major criminal justice subparts are (a) the police, (b) the courts, and (c) correctional agencies (138, p. 618).

In defining his terms, the author states that:

> "Correctional services" includes all of those activities designed for the purpose of controlling, managing, counseling, treating, and processing juvenile and adult persons placed in custody or under official supervision after having been charged with or found guilty of delinquent or criminal acts. These functions include detention halls for juveniles, common jails, correctional schools, reformatories, prisons, probation and parole services, and any other programs by whatever name which have like purpose (138, p. 616).

In answer to his own question about the current status of "correctional services" in the United States, McGee suggests the following:

> First, we are obviously in a state of groping for new, more rational, and more efficient ways to organize and support this agglomeration of closely related public services.
>
> Second, it is apparent that the organizational structure for correctional functions, viewed from a national perspective, is passing through a painful period of evolution which so far has produced an almost incomprehensible mixture of organizational patterns, most of which were never really "organized" but . . ."just grew."
>
> Third, no state or major jurisdiction in the nation can yet be said to have devised and implemented a total correctional system which makes full use of what we know about organizational principles and sound correctional practice (138, p. 618).

With these suggestions about the basic nature of the target in mind, discussion now turns to the apparent impact of administrative decentralization on correctional services.

Decentralization

It seems safe to say that there are trends in corrections today toward decentralization of program and toward centralization of organizational structure. These movements lead McGee to suggest for his mythical new state that:

> At the apex of the state system there should be a single authority responsible to the governor for all correctional functions as defined heretofore. . . .
>
> The state government will normally engage in two broad classes of correctional services. First, there are those which are direct operational functions like managing prisons and correctional schools, or supervising state parolees. Second, there are the standard-setting and regulative functions like administering subsidies and inspecting and licensing programs operated by units of local government or by private agencies with which the state or local government have contracted for services (138, p. 619).

The "Directions for the Future" program outlined by the President's Commission on Law Enforcement and Administration of Justice relies heavily on "Reintegration of the Offender into the Community" (9, Vol. 3, pp. 6–7). This is to be achieved largely through increased use of probation in lieu of incarceration (139), and earlier and more extensive use of parole after imprisonment (9, Vol. 3, p. 9). Also envisaged are new kinds of institutions in the home communities that attempt to carry out the resocialization process in the community into which the prisoner is to be reintegrated (9, Vol. 3, pp. 9–11 and 38–45). One of the hopes expressed is that this decentralization will lead to greater involvement of both individuals and organized groups in the community in the rehabilitative process.

Citizen Participation

Paralleling the experience with probation discussed above has been a more general use of volunteers in corrections (140). Vincent O'Leary describes the situation this way:

> Since the latter part of the 1950's, there has been a growing emphasis on bringing more citizens into correctional affairs. And yet, the extent of such involvement is relatively small.

An important reason is a failure to recognize the varying roles which citizens can play in corrections and the different strategies which must be employed to recruit them and maintain their participation. Four key roles can be identified: *the correctional volunteer,* those who work directly with correctional clients; *the social persuader,* persons of influence in the dominant social system who are willing to persuade others to support correctional programs; *the gate-keepers of opportunities,* custodians of access to important social institutions; and *the intimates,* members of offenders' traditional peer groups and their communities. Each of these roles induces supportive and resistant forces within the correctional system. These must be successfully manipulated if widespread citizen participation is to be achieved (141, p. 99).

As the author goes on to point out, no correctional system is doing an adequate job of utilizing citizen talent across this broad spectrum of possible participation.

It is interesting to note that the typology does not include citizens participating through establishment and control of policy in correctional agencies. This may be due to the belief that correctional policy setting is regarded as a professional task in which lay talents are a resource to be used as the specialist sees them fitting in. But it may also be attributable to lack of broad-based citizen interest in corrections. There have not been the citizen campaigns for control of corrections that have arisen for control of neighborhood police and neighborhood schools. This may be because the impact of correctional policy on the community is indirect rather than direct, a failure to realize that a part of what is seen as a police problem of failure to suppress crime on the streets is at least partly a correctional problem of failure to reintegrate former inmates into the society to which they return.

SUMMARY AND CONCLUSIONS

This essay has only begun to explore the broad topic of decentralization and citizen participation in the criminal justice system. Most attention has been given to the impact of these trends on policing in the United States. This seems defensible for a number of reasons. *First,* it is in the police component where most of the decentralization and citizen participation action has been found. This is probably attributable to the fact that police action is painfully obvious to the residents of a neighborhood and its impact felt immediately and directly. It also is a governmental subsystem manned by persons without special pre-service education, which makes the ordinary citizen believe that he is qualified to comment on and participate in police operations.

Second, what happens at the police level determines to a large extent what the balance of the criminal justice system can do. The primary sorting out of "criminals" from "ordinary citizens" is done by the police. Police officers determine, in one way or another, the limits of community tolerance in their exercise of discretion as to how limited resources for enforcement are to be deployed. It is literally impossible for them to enforce all of the law all of the time. Only those arrested by the police can be adjudicated by the courts and "rehabilitated" by corrections.

In our police organizations are found some of the most interesting experiments and social campaigns for both administrative and political decentralization. But there is much less experimentation in both courts and corrections with administrative and political decentralization, although there are definite trends toward the decentralization of programs in corrections. Both of these segments of the criminal justice system may, however, in the future be affected dramatically by decentralization experiments at the system threshold—in police agencies. Only time will tell.

This substantive discussion seems to lead logically, in a curriculum essay, to a question about the role of higher education in the preparation of young men and women for careers in the criminal justice system. There is no doubt that the relatively new field of criminal justice studies is one of the fastest growing in academia (142). Neither is there any doubt that it does not fit neatly into traditional discipline-dominated college and university structures. Criminal justice programs in higher education comprise integrated, interdisciplinary, scholarly teaching and research in the behavioral and social sciences (defined to include law and public administration) focused on a social problem, the problem of crime. As such, they are neither disciplinary nor professional. For this reason, they seem best taught in a separate department, school, or college of criminal justice (143, p. 12).

As a field of study in higher education, criminal justice must concern itself with a least five areas: the nature of crime and its relationship to other kinds of deviance as well as to conformity; the nature of society's reaction to crime, both historically and in the present, which requires exploration of all past and current crime control theories and mechanisms, informal as well as formal, legal, and governmental; in-depth consideration of criminal justice systems as one common social control mechanism; the nature of personal, organizational, and institutional change along with the skills and strategies of achieving such change; and the design of research so badly needed to expand our meager knowledge about crime together with the methodologies most useful for implementation of those designs in a generally inhospitable research setting.

This field of study goes far beyond the scope of traditional criminology as a sub-field in sociology, far beyond criminal law and procedure as one small part of law school curricula, far beyond abnormal psychology as one concern of social psychology, and far beyond public administration with its traditional preoccupation with bureaucratic structure and process.

Professors capable of integrating the insights and approaches of all of these traditional disciplines have not generally been available, but are beginning to emerge from the less than a handful of strong graduate programs created or recreated in the late 1960s. Meanwhile, the difficult problem of integration can best be achieved through interdisciplinary faculties functioning in a separate academic unit. Neither simple joint appointments nor complex consortium arrangements can do the extremely difficult job of building this new field. Schools of public administration and public affairs can best assist through urging a few of their brightest graduates to join such faculties, through helping to build recognition of the need for such new programs in more colleges and universities, and through effective exploration of areas of mutual interest when they come into being. One such area is certainly the utility of administrative and political decentralization in the organization and operation of criminal justice systems.

REFERENCES

References are listed in order of occurrence in the text.
1. National Commission on Law Observance and Enforcement (Washington, D.C.: U.S. Department of Justice, 1931), 14 nos.:
    No. 1.   *Preliminary Report on Observance and Enforcement of Prohibition.*
    No. 2.   *Report on the Enforcement of the Prohibition Laws of the United States.*
    No. 3.   *Report on Criminal Statistics.*
    No. 4.   *Report on Prosecution.*
    No. 5.   *Report on the Enforcement of the Deportation Laws of the United States.*
    No. 6.   *Report on the Child Offender in the Federal System of Justice.*
    No. 7.   *Progress Report on the Study of the Federal Courts.*
    No. 8.   *Report on Criminal Procedure.*
    No. 9.   *Report on Penal Institutions, Probation and Parole.*
    No. 10.   *Report on Crime and the Foreign Born.*

No. 11. *Report on Lawlessness in Law Enforcement.*
No. 12. *Report on the Cost of Crime.*
No. 13. *Report on the Causes of Crime.*
No. 14. *Report on Police.*
2. Attorney General's Conference on Crime, *Proceedings* (Washington, D.C.: U.S. Government Printing Office, December 1934).
3. Attorney General's Survey of Release Procedures (Washington, D.C.: U.S. Department of Justice, 1939), 5 vols.:
     Vol. I.   *Digest of Federal and State Laws on Release Procedures.*
     Vol. II.   *Probation.*
     Vol. III. *Pardon.*
     Vol. IV.   *Parole.*
     Vol. V.   *Prisons.*
4. The American Bar Foundation's Series on the Administration of Criminal Justice in the United States:
     1. Lawrence P. Tiffany, Donald M. McIntyre, Jr., and Daniel L. Rotenberg, *Detection of Crime* (Boston: Little, Brown and Company, 1967).
     2. Wayne R. LaFave, *Arrest* (Boston: Little, Brown and Company, 1965).
     3. Frank W. Miller, *Prosecution: The Decision to Charge a Suspect with a Crime* (Boston: Little, Brown and Company, 1969).
     4. Donald J. Newman, *Conviction: The Determination of Guilt or Innocence Without Trial* (Boston: Little, Brown and Company, 1966).
     5. Robert O. Dawson, *Sentencing: The Decision as to Type, Length, and Conditions of Sentence* (Boston: Little, Brown and Company, 1969).
5. President's Commission on Civil Rights (Washington, D.C.: U.S. Government Printing Office, 1961), 5 vols.:
     Vol. 1. *Voting.*
     Vol. 2. *Education.*
     Vol. 3. *Employment.*
     Vol. 4. *Housing.*
     Vol. 5. *Justice.*
6. President's Committee on Juvenile Delinquency and Youth Crime. (An operational entity rather than a study commission, established in 1961 by executive order, composed of the Attorney General, the Secretary of Labor, and the Secretary of Health, Education, and Welfare; no report issued.) For an account of the work of this committee, see Daniel P. Moynihan, *Maximum Feasible Misunderstanding* (New York: The Free Press, 1969), pp. 61–74.
7. Attorney General's Committee on Poverty and the Administration of Federal Criminal Justice, *Poverty and the Administration of Federal Criminal Justice* (Washington, D.C.: U.S. Government Printing Office, 1963).
8. National Conference on Bail and Criminal Justice, *Proceedings and Interim Report* (Washington, D.C.: Office of the Attorney General, 1965).
9. President's Commission on Law Enforcement and Administration of Justice, "Katzenbach Report" (Washington, D.C.: U.S. Government Printing Office, 1967), 10 vols., 5 field surveys:
     Vol. 1.   *The Challenge of Crime in a Free Society.*
     Vol. 2.   *Task Force Report: Assessment of Crime.*
     Vol. 3.   *Task Force Report: Corrections.*
     Vol. 4.   *Task Force Report: The Courts.*
     Vol. 5.   *Task Force Report: Drunkenness.*
     Vol. 6.   *Task Force Report: Juvenile Delinquency.*
     Vol. 7.   *Task Force Report: Narcotics and Drug Abuse.*
     Vol. 8.   *Task Force Report: Organized Crime.*
     Vol. 9.   *Task Force Report: The Police.*
     Vol. 10. *Task Force Report: Science and Technology.*
     Field Surveys:
     I. *Report on a Pilot Study in the District of Columbia on Victimization and Attitudes Toward Law Enforcement* (prepared under a grant by the Office of Law Enforcement Assistance, U.S. Department of Justice, to the Bureau of Social Science Research, Inc.).

II. *Criminal Victimization in the United States: A Report of a National Survey* (prepared under a grant by the Office of Law Enforcement Assistance, U.S. Department of Justice, to the National Opinion Research Center).

III. *Studies in Crime and Law Enforcement in Major Metropolitan Areas* (prepared under a grant by the Office of Law Enforcement Assistance, U.S. Department of Justice, to the University of Michigan), 2 vols.

IV. *The Police and the Community* (prepared under a grant by the Office of Law Enforcement Assistance, U.S. Department of Justice, to the University of California at Berkeley).

V. *A National Survey of Police and Community Relations* (prepared under a grant by the Office of Law Enforcement Assistance, U.S. Department of Justice, to Michigan State University).

10. First National Conference on Crime Control, *Proceedings* (Washington, D.C.: U.S. Government Printing Office, 1967).

11. National Advisory Commission on Civil Disorders, "Kerner Report" (Washington, D.C.: U.S. Government Printing Office, 1968), 2 vols.:
   Vol. 1.   *Report.*
   Vol. 2.   *Supplemental Studies.*

12. National Commission on the Causes and Prevention of Violence, "Eisenhower Report," (Washington, D.C.: U.S. Government Printing Office, 1969), 15 vols.:
   Final Report: *To Establish Justice, To Insure Domestic Tranquility.*
   Vol. 1.   *Violence in America: Historical and Comparative Perspective,* Part I.
   Vol. 2.   *Violence in America: Historical and Comparative Perspective,* Part II.
   Vol. 3.   *The Politics of Protest: Violent Aspects of Protest & Confrontation.*
   Vol. 4.   *Rights in Concord: The Response to the Counter-Inaugural Protest Activities in Washington, D.C.*
   Vol. 5.   *Shoot-Out in Cleveland: Black Militants and the Police.*
   Vol. 6.   *Shut It Down: A College in Crisis.*
   Vol. 7.   *Firearms and Violence in American Life.*
   Vol. 8.   *Assassination and Political Violence.*
   Vol. 9.   *Violence and the Media, Part I.*
   Vol. 9a.   *Violence and the Media, Part II.*
   Vol. 10.   *Law and Order Reconsidered.*
   Vol. 11.   *Crimes of Violence, Part I.*
   Vol. 12.   *Crimes of Violence, Part II.*
   Vol. 13.   *Crimes of Violence, Part III.*

13. Joint Commission of Correctional Manpower and Training (Washington, D.C.: American Correctional Association, 1969), 15 vols.:
   1. Final Report: *A Time to Act.*
   2. Staff Report: *Perspectives on Correctional Manpower and Training.*
   3. Staff Report: *Manpower and Training in Correctional Institutions.*
   4. Research Report: *Developing Correctional Administrators.*
   5. Seminar Report: *Differences that Make the Difference.*
   6. Seminar Report: *Targets for In-Service Training.*
   7. Seminar Report: *Research in Correctional Rehabilitation.*
   8. Seminar Report: *Offenders as a Correctional Manpower Resource.*
   9. Seminar Report: *Criminology and Corrections Programs.*
   10. Survey Report: *The Public Looks at Crime and Corrections.*
   11. Survey Report: *Corrections 1968: A Climate for Change.*
   12. Survey Report: *Volunteers Look at Corrections.*
   13. Consultant's Paper: *The Future of the Juvenile Court: Implication for Correctional Manpower and Training.*
   14. Consultant's Paper: *The University and Corrections: Potential for Collaborative Relationships.*
   15. Consultant's paper: *The Legal Challenge to Corrections: Implication for Manpower and Training.*

14. President's Commission on Campus Unrest, "Scranton Report," *Campus Unrest* (Washington, D.C.: U.S. Government Printing Office, 1970).

15. Commission on Obscenity and Pornography, *Report* (Washington, D.C.: U.S. Government Printing Office, 1970), with ten technical reports to the commission:

Vol. I   *Preliminary Studies (1971).*
Vol. II   *Legal Analysis (1971).*
Vol. III   *The Marketplace: The Industry (1971).*
Vol. IV   *The Marketplace: Empirical Studies (1971).*
Vol. V   *Societal Control Mechanisms (1971).*
Vol. VI   *National Survey (1971).*
Vol. VII   *Erotica and Antisocial Behavior (1971).*
Vol. VIII   *Erotica and Social Behavior (1971).*
Vols. IX & X   *(not yet released).*

16. President's Task Force on Prisoner Rehabilitation, *The Criminal Offender: What Should Be Done?* (Washington, D.C.: U.S. Government Printing Office, 1970).
17. National Commission on Reform of Federal Criminal Laws (Washington, D.C.: U.S. Government Printing Office):
    1. *Working Papers,* Vols. 1 and 2 (1970).
    2. *Study Draft of Proposed Revision of Federal Criminal Law, Title 18* (1970).
    3. *Final Report* (1971).
18. President's Commission on Drugs (in progress), *Preliminary Report* (Washington, D.C.: U.S. Government Printing Office, 1971).
19. American Bar Association Project on Standards for Criminal Justice (Chicago: American Bar Association), 18 vols.:
    Standards Relating to:
    1. *Fair Trial and Free Press* (Tentative Draft, December 1966; Supplement, includes all Standards, March 1968; approved by the House of Delegates, February 1968, with amendments as shown in Supplement).
    2. *Post-Conviction Remedies* (Tentative Draft, January 1967; approved by the House of Delegates, February 1968, as proposed in Tentative Draft).
    3. *Pleas of Guilty* (Tentative Draft, February 1967; Supplement, includes amendments only, March 1968; approved by the House of Delegates, February 1968, with amendments as shown in Supplement).
    4. *Appellate Review of Sentences* (Tentative Draft, April 1967; Supplement, includes amendments only, March 1968; approved by the House of Delegates, February 1968, with amendments as shown in Supplement).
    5. *Speedy Trial* (Tentative Draft, May 1967; approved by House of Delegates, February 1968, as proposed in Tentative Draft).
    6. *Providing Defense Services* (Tentative Draft, July 1967; approved by the House of Delegates, February 1968, as proposed in Tentative Draft).
    7. *Joinder and Severance* (Tentative Draft, November 1967; Supplement, includes amendments only, September 1968; approved by the House of Delegates, August 1968, with amendments as shown in Supplement).
    8. *Sentencing Alternatives and Procedures* (Tentative Draft, December 1967; Supplement, includes amendments only, September 1968; approved by House of Delegates, August 1968, with amendments as shown in Supplement).
    9. *Pretrial Release* (Tentative Draft, March 1968; Supplement, includes amendments only, September 1968; approved by House of Delegates, August 1968, with amendments as shown in Supplement).
    10. *Trial by Jury* (Tentative Draft, May 1968; Supplement, includes amendments only, September 1968; approved by House of Delegates, August 1968, with amendments as shown in Supplement).
    11. *Electronic Surveillance* (Tentative Draft, June 1968; approved by House of Delegates, February 1971).
    12. *Criminal Appeals* (Tentative Draft, March 1969; approved by House of Delegates, August 1970).
    13. *Discovery and Procedure Before Trial* (Tentative Draft, May 1969; approved by House of Delegates, August 1970).
    14. *Probation* (Tentative Draft, February 1970; approved by House of Delegates, August 1970).
    15&16. *The Prosecution Function and the Defense Function* (Tentative Draft, March 1970; approved by House of Delegates, February 1971).
    17. *Function of the Police* (Tentative Draft, April 1971).
    18. *Function of the Judge* (In process).
20. Committee on Juvenile Delinquency, "Macleod Report" (Ottawa: Queen's Printer, 1967), 1 vol. in French and English.

21. Canadian Committee on Corrections, "Quimet Report" (Ottawa: Queen's Printer, 1969), 1 vol. in French and English.
22. Commission of Enquiry into Civil Rights, "McRuer Report" (Toronto: Queen's Printer, 1970), 7 vols. (see particularly vol. 6: *Justice*).
23. Commission of Enquiry into the Administration of Justice on Criminal and Penal Matters in Quebec, "Prevost Report" (Quebec: Quebec Official Publisher, 1970), 18 vols. in French, 5 vols. in English.
24. Commission of Enquiry into the Non-Medical Use of Drugs, "LeDain Report" (Ottawa: Queen's Printer, 1970, Interim Report; 1971, Final Report in French and English).
25. Kentucky Department of Law, "Law Enforcement in Kentucky: Report to the Committee on the Administration of Justice in the Commonwealth of Kentucky," *Kentucky Law Journal*, Vol. 52, No. 1 (1963), entire issue.
26. Governor Rockefeller's Conference on Crime, *Proceedings* (Albany, N.Y.: Executive Department, 1966).
27. New Jersey Governor's Select Commission on Civil Disorder, *Report for Action* (Trenton, N.J.: Office of the Governor, 1968).
28. New York Governor's Special Committee on Criminal Offenders, *Preliminary Report* (Albany, N.Y.: Executive Department, 1968).
29. New York City Mayor's Committee on the Administration of Justice Under Emergency Conditions, *Report* (New York: Office of the Mayor, 1968).
30. Comments and Research Reports, Yale Kamisar, "Some Reflections on Criticizing the Courts and 'Policing the Police,'" *Journal of Criminal Law, Criminology and Police Science*, Vol. 53 (1962), pp. 453–462.
31. Yale Kamisar, "On the Tactics of Police-Prosecution Oriented Critics of the Courts," *Cornell Law Quarterly*, Vol. 49 (1964), pp. 436–477.
32. Robert J. Bowers, "Nature of the Problem of Police Brutality," *Cleveland-Marshall Law Review*, Vol. 14 (1965), pp. 601–609.
33. Herman Goldstein, "Police Policy Formulation: A Proposal for Improving Police Performance," *Michigan Law Review*, Vol. 65 (1965), pp. 1123–1145.
34. Herman Goldstein, "Administrative Problems in Controlling the Exercise of Police Authority," *Journal of Criminal Law, Criminology and Police Science*, Vol. 58 (1967), pp. 160–172.
35. Ellwyn R. Stoddard, "The Informal 'Code' of Police Deviancy: A Groups Approach to 'Blue Coat Crime,'" *Journal of Criminal Law, Criminology and Police Science*, Vol. 59 (1968), pp. 201–213.
36. Frank J. Remington, "The Role of Police in a Democratic Society," *Journal of Criminal Law, Criminology and Police Science*, Vol. 59 (1968), pp. 361–365.
37. Note, "Grievance Response Mechanisms for Police Misconduct," *Virginia Law Review*, Vol. 55 (1969), pp. 909–951.
38. Note, "The Unconstitutionality of Plea Bargaining," *Harvard Law Review*, Vol. 83 (1970), pp. 1387–1411.
39. Note, "Police Practices and the Threatened Destruction of Tangible Evidence," *Harvard Law Review*, Vol. 84 (1971), pp. 1465–1498.
40. "The Police in a Democratic Society: A Symposium," *Public Administration Review*, Vol. XXVIII, No. 5 (September/October 1968).
41. "The Police and the Rest of Us: A Special Supplement," *The Atlantic*, Vol. 223, No. 3 (March 1969).
42. "The Cops: Nine Inquiries into the Institutions, Traditions and Practices of the Contemporary Police Force," *The Nation*, Vol. 208, No. 16 (April 21, 1969).
43. "Police and Society," *American Behavioral Scientists*, Vol. 13, Nos. 5 & 6 (May/June and July/August 1970).
44. "Symposium on Five Pieces in Penology," *Public Administration Review*, Vol. XXXI, No. 6 (November/December 1971).
45. "Special Police Issue," *Law and Society Review*, Vol. 6, No. 2 (November 1971).
46. "Symposium on Judicial Administration," *Public Administration Review*, Vol. XXXI, No. 2 (March/April 1971).
47. *Police Film Catalog*. A comprehensive listing of available law enforcement training films arranged in four major subject areas: Police and Their Profession, Police and the Law, Police and Society, and Films for the Police. International Association of Chiefs of Police, Eleven Firstfield Road, Gaithersburg, Maryland 20760.

48. Murray Kempton, "Cops" (a review of four books about the police), *New York Review of Books,* Vol. 15 (November 5, 1970), pp. 3–7.
49. David Burnham, "Study Scores City's Police and Courts as Inefficient," *New York Times,* March 14, 1971, p. 1, c. 6.
50. "G-Man Under Fire," *Life,* Vol. 70, No. 13 (April 9, 1971), pp. 39–45.
51. Tom Buckley, "Murphy Among the 'Meat Eaters,'" *New York Times Magazine* (December 19, 1971), pp. 8–49.
52. James Mills, "I Have Nothing to Do with Justice: Brilliant and Cynical, A Legal Aid Lawyer Wins Freedom for Thousands of Muggers, Rapists and Thieves," *Life,* Vol. 70, No. 9 (March 12, 1971), pp. 56–67.
53. "Excerpts from President Nixon's Address to National Conference on Judiciary," *New York Times,* March 12, 1971, p. 18C, c. 1.
54. Jack Star, "Jam-Up: Crisis in Our Criminal Courts," *Look* (March 23, 1971), pp. 32–39.
55. "Improve Justice, Law Expert Asks?" *New York Times,* April 20, 1971, p. 16C, c. 3.
56. Leslie Oelsner, "Rise in Crime Straining Probation System of the Courts Here," *New York Times,* December 6, 1971, p. 43C, c. 1.
57. "The Push to Streamline the Courts," *Business Week* (December 4, 1971), pp. 46–47.
58. Leslie Oelsner, "Prisoner's Rights: What Rights for the 'Slave of the State'?" *New York Times,* December 26, 1971, p. 5E, c. 1.
59. "Prisons: Attica's Legacy," *Newsweek,* Vol. 78, No. 14 (October 4, 1971), p. 23.
60. "Prisons: Attica Aftermath," *Time,* Vol. 98, No. 15 (October 11, 1971), p. 24.
61. Arthur I. Waskow, "I Am Not Free," *Saturday Review* (January 8, 1972), pp. 20–21.
62. "Attica Prison's Bloody Monday," *Life,* Vol. 71, No. 13 (September 24, 1971), p. 26.
63. "Justice on Trial," *Newsweek* (March 8, 1971), pp. 16–46.
64. "Urban Affairs: The U.S. Gets Its First Walled City," *Business Week* (March 6, 1971), p. 28.
65. Law Enforcement Assistance Act of 1965 established the Office of Law Enforcement Assistance (OLEA) in the U. S. Department of Justice. The Omnibus Crime Control and Safe Streets Act of 1968 replaced OLEA with the Law Enforcement Assistance Administration (LEAA) in the Department. Related units dealing with juvenile delinquency have had a similar history in the Department of Health, Education, and Welfare.
66. Orange County (California) Criminal Justice Council, *Criminal Justice: An Integrated Systems Approach,* 1972.
67. State of New York Joint Legislative Committee on Crime, Its Courses, Control and Effect on Society, *Seminar on Violence* (Albany: Committee Document, July 1968), p. 124.
68. American Bar Foundation series on Legal Services for the Poor (1155 East 60th Street, Chicago, Illinois 60637):
Lee Silverstein, *Eligibility for Free Legal Services* (40 pp., 1967).
———, *Waiver of Court Costs and Appointment of Counsel for Poor Persons in Civil Cases* (36 pp., 1968).
Staff of the *Duke Law Journal, The Legal Problems of the Rural Poor* (131 pp., 1969).
Geoffrey C. Hazard, Jr., *Social Justice Through Civil Justice* (14 pp., 1969).
Audrey D. Smith, *The Social Worker in the Legal Aid Setting: A Study of Interprofessional Relationships* (14 pp., 1970).
Geoffrey C. Hazard, Jr., *Law Reforming in the Anti-Poverty Effort* (16 pp., 1970).
Felice J. Levine and Elizabeth Preston, *Community Resource Orientation Among Low Income Groups* (36 pp., 1970).
Staff of the *Denver Law Journal, Rural Poverty and the Law in Southern Colorado* (85 pp., 1971).
Geoffrey C. Hazard, Jr., *Legal Problems Peculiar to the Poor* (16 pp., 1971).
Kenneth P. Fisher and Charles C. Ivil, *Franchising Justice: The Office of Economic Opportunity Legal Service Program and Traditional Legal Aid* (18 pp., 1971).
F. Raymond Marks, Jr., *The Legal Needs of the Poor: A Critical Analysis* (17 pp., 1971).
Dorothy Linder Maddi, *Public Welfare Caseworkers and Client Referrals to Legal Services* (10 pp., 1971).
Dorothy Linder Maddi and Frederic R. Merrill, *The Private Practicing Bar and Legal Services for Low Income People* (21 pp., 1971).
Barbara A. Curran and Sherry L. Clarke, *Use of Lawyers' Services by Low-Income Persons* (1971).

69. National Council on Crime and Delinquency, *Goals and Recommendations: A Response to 'The Challenge of Crime in a Free Society,' the Report of the President's Commission on Law Enforcement and Administration of Justice* (New York: NCCD, 1968); ———, *Citizen Action to Control Crime and Delinquency: Fifty Projects* (1968).
70. "Murphy to Head Law Enforcement Council," *NCCD News,* Vol. 50, No. 5 (November-December 1971), p. 3.
71. Westchester Citizens Committee of the National Council on Crime and Delinquency, *Fact Sheets Concerning Law Enforcement and the Administration of Criminal Justice in Westchester County, New York* (1969).
72. Martin Waldron, "Houston Voters Choose a Mayor," *New York Times,* December 8, 1971, p. 27C, c. 1.
73. "75 Imperiale Supporters Block Debate with Newark Moderates," *New York Times,* January 19, 1971, p. 46, c. 3.
74. J. Anthony Lucas, "Bad Day at Cairo, Ill.," *New York Times,* February 21, 1971, VI, p. 22.
75. Thomas A. Johnson, "Who Killed the 10 Drug Pushers?" *New York Times,* January 23, 1972, p. 55, c. 4.
76. Thomas M. Scott and Marlys McPherson, "The Development of the Private Sector of the Criminal Justice System," *Law and Society Review,* Vol. 6, No. 2 (1971), pp. 267–288.
77. "A Precinct Tries New Team Effort," *New York Times,* December 5, 1971, p. 112, c. 1.
78. Citizens for Law, Order and Justice, *A Laymen's View of the Functioning of Law, Order and Justice in Schenectady (N.Y.): Second Annual Report* (Summer 1971).
79. Alan A. Altshuler, *Community Control: The Black Demand for Participation in Large American Cities* (New York: Pegasus, 1970).
80. Richard A. Myren, *The Role of the Police* (a paper submitted to the President's Commission on Law Enforcement and Administration of Justice, 1967).
81. William P. Brown, *Goal Direction in Police Work* (unpublished working paper), p. 18.
82. Thomas E. Bercal, "Calls for Police Assistance: Consumer Demands for Governmental Service," *American Behavioral Scientist,* Vol. XIII, Nos. 5 and 6 (May-June, July-August 1970), p. 686.
83. John E. Angell, "Toward an Alternative to the Classic Police Organizational Arrangements: A Democratic Model," *Criminology,* Vol. 9, Nos. 2 & 3 (August/November 1971).
84. Gordon E. Misner, "Recent Developments in Metropolitan Law Enforcement, Part II," *Journal of Criminal Law, Criminology and Police Science,* Vol. 51, No. 2 (1960), pp. 265–272.
85. "Two Precedent-Setting Mergers of Principal Law Enforcement Agencies," *Crime Control Digest* (January 7, 1972).
86. V.A. Leonard, *Police Organization and Management* (Brooklyn: The Foundation Press, Inc., 1951).
87. International City Managers' Association, *Municipal Police Administration,* 4th edition (Chicago: International City Managers' Association, 1954).
88. O.W. Wilson, *Police Planning* (Springfield, Ill.: Charles C. Thomas, 2nd edition, 1957).
89. John P. Kenney, *Police Management Planning* (Springfield, Ill.: Charles C. Thomas, 1959).
90. Institute for Training in Municipal Administration, *Municipal Police Administration* (Washington, D.C.: International City Managers' Association, 6th edition, 1969).
91. Samuel G. Chapman, *Police Patrol Readings,* Chapter V, "British Patrol and Team Policing" (Springfield, Ill.: Charles C. Thomas, 1964), pp. 234–276.
92. City of New York Police Department, *Press Release No. 112,* December 30, 1972.
93. "A Precinct Tries New Team Effort," *New York Times,* December 5, 1971, p. 112, c. 1.
94. John T. McQuiston, "Murphy, in Test, Assigns Patrolman to Home Precinct," *New York Times,* January 20, 1972, p. 55C, c. 1.
95. Peter Kihss, "24th Designated the First Model Precinct," *New York Times,* February 3, 1972, p. 35, c. 1–6.
96. Judy Klemesrud, "The Desk Sergeant at 24th Precinct Doesn't Fit Stereotype," *New York Times,* March 6, 1972, p. 38, c. 1.
97. Ralph Blumenthal, "Harassment Drives City's 'Resident Policemen' from Their Home Precincts," *New York Times,* March 13, 1972, p. 31, c. 2.
98. ———, "6 New 'Resident Policemen' Volunteer," *New York Times,* March 14, 1972, p. 47, c. 3–5.
99. John V. Lindsay, "A Plan for Neighborhood Government for New York City" (New York: Office of the Mayor, June 1970), 16 pp., mimeo.

100. Patrick V. Murphy and Peter B. Bloch, "The Beat Commander," *Police Chief,* Vol. 37, No. 5 (May 1970).
101. W. H. T. Smith, R. D. Priest, and J. F. Elliott, "An Exploratory Program of The Syracuse Police Department and General Electric Company in Law Enforcement Problems," *Police,* Vol. XII, No. 3 (1968), p. 92.
102. J. F. Elliott, "The Concept of the Offensively Deployed Police Force," *Police,* Vol. XIII, No. 1 (1968), p. 65.
103. ———, "Random Patrol," *Police,* Vol. XIII, No. 2 (1968), p. 51.
104. ———, "The Crime Control Team," *Police,* Vol. XIII, No. 5 (1969), p. 35.
105. ———, "Project Management Approach to Controlling Urban Crime," *Aerospace Management,* Vol. IV, No. 2 (1969), p. 59.
106. ———, "Crime Control Team," *Event,* Vol. IX, No. 3 (1969), p. 16.
107. ———, "The Police–How Effective Are They?" *Event,* Vol. X, No. 1 (1969), p. 34.
108. ———, J. F. O'Connor, and Thomas J. Sardino, "The Detection and Interception Capability of One-and Two-Man Patrol Units," *Police* (November-December, 1969), p. 24.
109. ———,———,———, "Experimental Evaluation of the Crime Control Team Organization Concept," *Police* (May-June 1970), p. 44.
110. Thomas J. Sardino, "The Crime Control Team," *FBI Law Enforcement Bulletin* (May 1971), p. 16.
111. J. F. Elliott and Thomas J. Sardino, "Crime Control Team: An Experiment in Municipal Police Department Management and Operations" (Springfield, Ill.)
112. Los Angeles Police Department, *Basic Car Plan* (Los Angeles: Office of the Chief of Police, 1971).
113. Robert Rawitch, "Police Basic Car Plan: Review a Year Later," *Los Angeles Times,* February 21, 1971, Sec. C, p. 1, c. 5.
114. E. M. Davis, "The Los Angeles Basic Car Plan," address delivered to the 1970 International Association of Chiefs of Police Annual Conference in Atlantic City, October 6, 1970 (Los Angeles: Office of the Chief of Police, 1970).
115. John P. Kenney, *Team Policing Organization: A Theoretical Model,* working paper (1971), 21 pp., mimeo.
116. James C. Zurcher, *Palo Alto Police Adopt "Team Management/Team Policing" Reorganization Plan,* working paper (1971), 9 pp., mimeo.
117. Leo E. Peart, "Team Management/Team Policing Organization Concept," *The Police Chief Magazine* (April 1971).
118. "Management by Goals Concept Tried in Palo Alto," *Criminal Justice Newsletter,* Vol. 2 (May 3, 1971), p. 67.
119. Holyoke (Massachusetts) Police Department, *Policy and Procedure Manual, Model Cities Police Team Project* (December 1970).
120. Walter Gellhorn, *When Americans Complain: Governmental Grievance Procedures* (Cambridge: Harvard University Press, 1966).
121. ———, *Ombudsmen and Others: Citizens' Protectors in Nine Countries* (Cambridge: Harvard University Press, 1966).
122. "The Ombudsmen or Citizen's Defender: A Modern Institution," *The Annuals of the American Academy of Political and Social Science,* Vol. 337 (May 1968), entire issue.
123. *A Legislative Proposal to Create the Office of Ombudsman, An Ombudsman for the State of New York* (Albany: Senate Finance Subcommittee on the Ombudsman, August 1969).
124. *Subcommittee Report and Recommendations on a Legislative Proposal to Create an Ombudsman for the People of New York State* (Albany: Senate Finance Subcommittee on the Ombudsman, 1970).
125. The Red Family, *The Case for Community Control of Police* (Berkeley: The Red Family, 1971), 49 pp.
126. James Q. Wilson, *Varieties of Police Behavior: The Management of Law and Order in Eight Communities* (Cambridge: Harvard University Press, 1968).
127. Albert J. Reiss, Jr., *The Police and the Public* (New Haven: Yale University Press, 1971).
128. Elinor Ostrom, "Institutional Arrangements and the Measurement of Policy Consequences: Applications to Evaluating Police Performance," *Urban Affairs Quarterly,* Vol. 6, No. 4 (June 1971), p. 447.
129. ———, and Gordon Whitaker, "Does Local Community Control of Police Make a Difference? Some Preliminary Findings," *American Journal of Political Science,* Vol. 17 (February 1973), p. 48–76.
130. ———,———, "Black Citizens and the Police: Some Effects of Community Control," delivered at the 1971 Annual Meeting of the American Political Science Association, Copyright 1971 by the American Political Science Association.

131. Karl Hess, "Breaking Up City Hall: Why Neighborhoods Must Secede," *New York Times,* January 31, 1972, p. 26, c. 41, c. 5.
132. Richard Danzig, *A Complementary Decentralized System of Criminal Justice* (working paper prepared for the Association of the Bar of the City of New York, September 1970).
133. Jerome H. Skolnick, *Justice Without Trial: Law Enforcement in a Democratic Society* (New York: John Wiley, 1966).
134. Albert J. Reiss, Jr., unpublished remarks at the 1972 annual conference of the Academy of Criminal Justice Sciences, Boston, February 24, 1972.
135. Ivan H. Schier, "The Professional and the Volunteer in Probation: An Emerging Relationship," *Federal Probation,* Vol. 34, No. 2 (June 1970).
136. Royal Oak (Michigan) Municipal Court Probation Department. *Concerned Citizens and a City Criminal Court* (1969).
137. National Council on Crime and Delinquency, "Volunteer Probation Organization Becomes Part of National Council on Crime and Delinquency," press release, January 3, 1972.
138. Richard A. McGee, "The Organizational Structure of State and Local Correctional Services," *Public Administration Review,* Vol. XXXI, No. 6 (November/December 1971).
139. Robert L. Smith, *A Quiet Revolution: Probation Subsidy* (Washington, D.C.: U.S. Government Printing Office, Stock Number 1766–0007; DHEW Publication No. (SRS) 72–26011; 1972).
140. Gordon H. Barker, *Volunteers in Corrections* (a paper submitted to the President's Commission on Law Enforcement and Administration of Justice, 1967).
141. Vincent O'Leary, "Some Directions for Citizen Involvement in Corrections," *The Annals of the American Academy of Political and Social Science,* Vol. 381 (January 1969).
142. Richard A. Myren, *Education in Criminal Justice* (report prepared for the Coordinating Council for Higher Education in California, Council Report 70–5, September 1970).
143. National Academy of Sciences and Social Science Research Council, *The Behavioral and Social Sciences: Outlook and Needs* (Englewood Cliffs, N.J.: Prentice-Hall, Inc., 1969).

CHAPTER 11

COMMUNITY PARTICIPATION AND MODERNIZATION
A Reexamination of Political Choices

CURTIS VENTRISS AND ROBERT PECORELLA

A critical issue facing democratic societies is how to integrate the concept of citizen participation with the technocratic nature of modern organizations. The issue of participation in the workplace has a long and controversial history in organizational theory.[1] The nature and extent of citizen participation in governmental organizations, an issue of concern since the formation of Greek city states, takes on added significance under the pressures of modernization.[2] Classic democrats, while acknowledging the complexity of modern society, have concluded that participation is too crucial an element of citizen development to be sacrificed to the demands of modernity.[3] On the other hand, pluralist theorists, while acknowledging the importance of participation in abstract terms, have concluded that the "law of oligarchy" is indeed writ in iron, and elite accountability not mass participation is the optimal form of democratic process attainable in modern society.[4] The issue of participation will not and, given the values at stake, should not go away.

In the 1960s, proponents of "participatory democracy" turned their attention to the urban neighborhood.[5] Neighborhood organizations, spawned by resident reactions against local "pro-growth coalitions" and encouraged by federal programs, were seen as places where citizen participation in local politics was possible.[6] In the ensuing 20 years, however, research on participation within neighborhood organizations had produced disquieting results for "participatory democrats." Generally, analysts have concluded that the very nature of bureaucratic society (Weber's "iron cage") has a decisively negative effect on lay participation in decision making.[7] Neighborhood organizations, according to this emerging consensus, tend to deemphasize participation as they increase their levels of professionalism and bureaucratization, thus becoming very much like the organization with which they interact in the larger society.[8]

This paper focuses on the constraints imposed on the internal decision-making processes of community organizations by the forces of modernization. These constraints arise from the need for community organizations to transform social action into institutional action in order to achieve their basic goals.[9] Such a transformation frequently entails a decline in community participation and a delegitimization of political issues which only reinforces a managerial and instrumental approach to community problems.

The point is not to elaborate on the nature of a bureaucratized society (as tempting as that might be), but to discern a process by which community organizations can continue, as they must, to deal with public agencies, but at the same time delimit the effects of the modernization process. The dilemma facing community organizations, as economists would put it, is a trade-off—an opportunity cost that cannot be avoided. As community organizations increase their effectiveness in coping with complex urban problems, they run the risk of becoming mirror images of the bureaucratic agencies with which they must deal. Conversely, if they limit the influence of these forces, they must sacrifice certain programs of potential benefit to their communities. Admittedly, the issue is not a simple case of either/or. Nevertheless, it represents a tension with which most, if not all, community organizations must grapple.

What we propose is not a wide-ranging "search for the Grail." Generally, panaceas for complex social problems either address uninteresting aspects of those problems or are themselves examples of ideologically tortured logic. Rather, we seek to examine the dilemma facing community organizations from a perspective which acknowledges the firm empirical grounding of the emerging consensus without conceding to it the notion of inevitability. This effort is, in large part, an extension and elaboration on the work of David Korten and his "learning process approach" to organizational behavior.[10]

The paper is divided into three parts. The first part briefly describes the development of two community organizations and how, in one case, the organization's operations and goals were eventually transformed by the exigencies of modernization. The second community organization represents a "learning organization" whose original goals remained basically intact. Part two addresses several of the critical issues raised in Terry Cooper's analysis of the bureaucratization of community organizations. We argue that Cooper avoided important implications of his own findings, which gave us insight into the evolution of community organizations. The third part discusses how Korten's "learning process" offers community organizations an alternative method with which to confront the participation/modernization dilemma.

TWO MODELS OF SOCIAL ACTION: THE COMMUNITY ORGANIZATIONS OF TELACU AND UNO

East Los Angeles is a community plagued by serious urban problems. With a population of over 120,000 (not including illegal aliens), 90 percent of the residents are Hispanic. East Los Angeles has the largest urban concentration of people with Mexican heritage other than Mexico City itself. It is an area with a 20 percent unemployment rate, double that of Los Angeles as a whole. Furthermore, one-quarter to one-third of the residents live below the poverty level. Almost 60 percent of the students do not complete the tenth grade. It is also an area with a serious housing problem. For example, in Boyle Heights, 25 percent of the 21,931 housing units are structurally unsound, and 68 percent are regarded as substandard. Similar figures exist for the unincorporated areas of Lincoln Heights and El Sereno. East Los Angeles also has one of the more serious gang violence problems in the United States. It is a poor community; a community which has felt left out of the political process. It is a community—politically speaking—attempting to be noticed.

The invisibility of this community, however, has been ameliorated somewhat by two large and powerful community-based organizations: The United Neighborhood Organization (UNO) and The East Los Angeles Community Union (TELACU).[11] While both are based in East Los Angeles, they work on programs for the most part independently of each other. Their organizational structures and goals differ dramatically. For instance, UNO is a perfect example of what Janice Perlman[12] calls a direct-action organization, an "Alinsky-style" group which uses political pressure to attain its goals. On the other hand, TELACU is a community development corporation. According to Geoffrey Faux, "community development corporations are business corporations owned and controlled by residents of impoverished communities who are attempting to use business forms and methods to generate revenue and social benefits for their neighborhoods."[13]

UNO is involved with public agencies in a different fashion than TELACU. According to an organizer in UNO, "UNO does not have to play ball with government bureaucracies." This point is by no means subtle. As Marilyn Gittell has argued effectively, community organizations which deal with service delivery are those groups which are "rendered ineffective as change agents and representatives of political interests to the extent that they accept and are accepted by the policy process."[14] What Gittel implies in her analysis (an analysis which was based on data gathered from 16 community organizations in Atlanta, Boston, and Los Angeles) is that community organizations will eventually see their agendas for policy action conform to, or become dictated by, the procedural requirements of government policymaking. Although TELACU clearly falls into this pattern, UNO does not. Before pursuing the analysis, we need to look more closely at the evolutions of TELACU and UNO.

TELACU

TELACU was first established in 1968 by Esteban Torres with the financial backing of the United Auto Workers, the Alliance for Labor Action, the Ford Foundation, and the local Community Action Agency. Although TELACU was conceived as a CDC [community development corporation], Torres felt that it was critical to first organize the community to meet its own pressing needs. If workers could be organized, Torres believed, so could an urban community. With a technical staff of 30 drawn from the local community and $250,000, TELACU began dealing with the citizenry of the area on such diverse issues as poor housing, education, and community revitalization. Results were at best mixed. TELACU found that implementing its plans was a frustrating experience given constant community tension.

This tension was evident when TELACU initiated a multi-million dollar housing project called Maravilla. TELACU realized that explicit community support was required for the project's success. After considerable delay, TELACU finally gathered together the groups to support this program. The frustrations of mobilizing such a politically scarred community left its mark on TELACU. By 1970, the leadership of TELACU sought a more prudent method for planning and implementing goals. As their own literature spells out:

> Dealing with constant community tension left TELACU with little time to focus on improving its management structure. CDC leaders knew that the energy had to be focused more finely if the organization was to live up to its own (to say nothing of the community's) expectations. Despite some early successes—particularly in housing, but also in employment training and programs for the elderly—fragmentation of its development effort had led to soured hopes in the form of shaky ventures and the defunding of a housing program.[15]

This was a decisive turning point for TELACU. For the first time, TELACU decided to concentrate its efforts on economic development. With the assistance of an OEO [Office of Economic Opportunity] grant, TELACU started to "create or strengthen (and, when appropriate, to control) viable business ventures whose operations contribute to the physical improvement of the community."[16] The goal behind TELACU's strategy was to be the "central organization with which all public and private institutions must deal when making decisions that affect the future of East Los Angeles."[17] This goal was illustrated in 1973, when TELACU created the Community Planning and Development Corporation to initiate and carry out broad development activities.

In 1975, under the direction of its new president, David Lizarraga, TELACU developed a master plan, a blueprint to guide the revitalization of the area. The master plan, in brief, was designed to develop four basic programs: the TELACU Investment Program, the Community Corporation and the Community Thrift and Loan, the Business Development Office, and the Banking Investment Strategy. The master plan's focus was to provide equity capital for businesses in the region, to provide training, and to act as a catalyst for economic growth.

It was during this period, however, that citizen participation within the organization began to decline dramatically. One key administrator who had been with TELACU since 1968 commented: "It is impossible to run our kind of organization without lawyers, technicians, and researchers. Citizens cannot be expected, nor should they be expected, to learn about such things. . . . We learned that it is a simple fact of life." In the next breath, he emphasized the real meaning behind declining citizen participation: "You have to realize that the agencies and governmental bodies we deal with have their own language, their own specific procedural manner which most citizens would find frustrating and time consuming without possessing the necessary technical skills."

It is exactly this point that motivated Terry Cooper to draw the following conclusion—that "in order to effectively relate to public agencies which approach a community from professional, technical, legal, and bureaucratic perspectives, a community organization must move away from its lay perspectives and adopt legal, technical, and bureaucratic perspectives. In short, it tends to assume the dominant perspectives of the public agency with which it proposes to work."[18]

Since its inception in 1968, TELACU has grown to an organization which is estimated to be worth $65 million and has a technical staff numbering well over 300 people. The organization's evolution is summarized succinctly, if rather bluntly, by one TELACU official who said, "Who cares about an organization that doesn't maximize citizen participation if in the end the job gets done."

UNO

UNO began in response to what was happening to TELACU. UNO's leaders believed that TELACU was not sufficiently issue oriented; it did not confront the problems of redlining, gang violence, and lack of citizen involvement. The issue was how to organize and maintain effective community involvement (the original goal of TELACU).

During a visit to San Antonio in 1975, Bishop Juan Arzube (who was to become known as the "father of UNO") observed "more than a thousand Mexican-American residents of that city barrio effectively organized to pressure a group of councilmen who had to meet their organization, Communities Organized for Public Service—or as it is known throughout Texas—COPS."[19] As he watched the meeting, he was struck with how the poor could change the political process without violence. Deeply impressed by what he had seen, Arzube began talking to local church leaders in East Los Angeles about starting an alternative community organization based upon political power, citizen education, and moral values. Father Pedro Villarroya, a leading organizer for UNO, stated that "the focus of the organization was to give the community real control over its destiny, to have people help and learn themselves."

The immediate question was whether any community organization could be set up to achieve these goals. In 1976, with a grant of $60,000 from the Catholic Campaign for Human Development, the Inter-Religious Sponsoring Committee (a group formed to do preliminary organizing) hired Ernie Cortes, who had put together COPS in San Antonio. The key to Cortes' strategy was to link the citizen's cultural roots (i.e., the role of the church) to what he called "citizen anger." The process was slow. But through a long series of house meetings and interviews, the organization began to take shape. UNO was finally born in 1976.

Since its inception, UNO has emphasized two basic strategies for political effectiveness: maximizing citizen participation in the development and implementation of its programs and using confrontational tactics, when necessary, to pressure the political process. The key to effectiveness, UNO's leaders felt, was always "learning"—not only as a community or as an organization, but as individuals. Through this process of "learning," UNO has managed to define operationally its organizational commitment to participation, thereby avoiding the goal displacement that occurred at TELACU. Unlike professionalization and bureaucratization, "learning" is not a substitute for citizen participation or confrontational tactics; it is, in fact, a mode of operation conducive to such organizational strategies.

This learning emphasis involves three different approaches: personal interviews, house meetings, and training sessions. The personal interviews were first used to facilitate interest in the community organization. The primary focus of these interviews was (and still is) to identify the major concerns of the community. The interviews involved thousands of families and succeeded in drawing a large number of people into active involvement with UNO. While used less frequently today, personal interviews maintain communication with residents who are unable to involve themselves actively in the organization. The house meetings attempt to organize citizens around their 18 local churches. House meetings complement personal interviews by further building relationships within the community and by providing a forum to bring people to focus on a specific issue. Gloria Chavez, the former president of UNO, stated that "the key aspect of this process is that it links individual and group learning to community learning, providing a forum for experimentation." The training sessions are conducted to educate residents in basic skills in order to maximize their effectiveness in political affairs. Residents learn "basic organizational skills such as research, chairing meetings, negotiating with public officials, administering interviews and house meetings, and other elements of organization."[20] More to the point, these sessions provide citizens with an "analysis of policies and operations of specific industries and governmental departments that affect the community."[21] "We always understand," insisted Father Villarroya, "who we are dealing with and their own power agenda in order to effectively mobilize our own energy for social change."

What does this approach look like in action? One of the best examples can be found in the fight to combat exorbitant car insurance rates.

> A persistent complaint in the interviews was skyrocketing auto insurance rates. Researchers soon discovered the reason. East Los Angeles was redlined by auto insurance companies, which charged drivers hundreds of dollars more than normal because of where they lived, regardless of their driving records. UNO chose insurance rates to be the first major area wide issue, complementing ongoing action on a variety of local neighborhood projects.[22]

The house meetings confirmed that not only was this issue important to the community, but that it should be UNO's top priority. The training sessions provided the community with the necessary information about this issue and how they could pressure the State Insurance Chairman to take immediate action.

UNO, by mobilizing the community, won this battle, obtaining a 37 percent reduction in auto insurance rates for East Los Angeles. UNO has used this same process to obtain funds for housing rehabilitation programs, to implement an experimental program to combat gang violence, to initiate educational reforms in the local schools, to extend health care to undocumented aliens, to pressure local officials for a community investment program designed to upgrade facilities in the area, and to provide social services congruent with the needs in the community.

According to many observers, including TELACU, what is remarkable about UNO is that these victories were accomplished with a meager budget ($160,000 in 1980–1981) and with a full-time paid staff of three community organizers. In addition, the majority of UNO's funds come from private donations and fees received from their local parishes.

UNO and TELACU represent philosophically distinct community organizations. Yet, they each began with the goal of politically mobilizing community residents in East Los Angeles and—although the nature and extent of interaction each organization has with external agents differs—each operates in a larger environment shaped by the forces of modernization. Certain questions, therefore, need to be raised. What in the nature of the modernization process encourages an organization like TELACU to displace its original goal of community participation with goals related strictly to community economic development? How is an organization like UNO able to maintain its original participatory goals and at what price? And finally, what do the distinctions between TELACU and UNO indicate about the political process, i.e., what choices are available given the constraints of modernization? The best manner in which to address these questions is to discuss them within the context of Terry Cooper and David Korten's contributions to the literature.

MODERNIZATION AND COMMUNITY ORGANIZATIONS

Terry Cooper's analysis of modernization, while enriching in its implications for community organizations, is based on the rather straightforward idea that we are embedded deeply in a technical/rational society. The entire emphasis of his study rests on this point:

> This study examines a recurring problem, namely that community organizations which manage to survive and engage public agencies for a prolonged period of time tend to assume the major organizational characteristics of those agencies. They become professionalized and bureaucratized. A concomitant of this metamorphosis is a diminution of their community constituency.[23]

To illustrate his point, Cooper analyzed the evolution of a community organization, the Pico-Union Neighborhood Council (PUNC), over an 11-year period. PUNC moved "from broad-based community participation and militant advocacy to community development and program development carried out largely by professionals."[24] Cooper is careful to point out that this transformation did not result from "crass capturing of leadership nor the creation of direct dependency by the granting of favors and funds."[25] The transformation was instead more subtle, involving "cognitive, structural, and operational changes in the organization and its leadership as it interacted with the Community Redevelopment Agency (CRA)."[26]

PUNC was forced to professionalize itself in order to maintain a relationship with the CRA for two basic reasons. First, for PUNC to be effective, its program had to correspond to the prevailing legal, technical, and bureaucratic perspectives of the CRA. Cooper explains: "Even if PUNC had been able to generate sufficient money drawn from within the community, it would have been drawn into CRA's web or perspectives by the scale of its task, the technical nature of redevelopment planning and CRA's official control of the process."[27] The result of this was a dramatic drop in citizen participation and the displacement of PUNC's original militant goals.

The second reason for PUNC's transformation is linked to the fact that society has been inundated with "massive industrial systems and technological instruments."[28] "As a result," argues Cooper, "interdependence has been created on a national or international scale, transcending the boundaries of traditional communities and leaving them without the means for identifying their problems and effectively engaging governmental structures."[29] PUNC became a victim of its own success.

> PUNC was able to meet the needs of some of its members for political efficacy in relation-ship to modern society, but in so doing neglected the affective and social needs of those who could not or would not participate in the increasingly technical planning process.[30]

Cooper's analysis is Weberian with a twist. Weber refers pessimistically to the "iron cage" which results in part from the ubiquitous spread of functional rationality (rationality predicated solely on calculation and efficiency) in Western society. Cooper believes that community organizations will become "contaminated," to one degree or another, by this pervasive process of modernization. However, in contrast to Weber's future of "specialists without vision, sensualists without heart,"[31] Cooper sees the possibility for ameliorating at least some of the adverse effects of functional rationality on community organizations.

Cooper believes that the new mission for government or private organizations should be "to minimize the professionalizing of these local organizations in order to mitigate the screening out of participation by community residents."[32] He offers specific proposals: First, Cooper contends, there should be a commitment to support the integrity of client communities. "Consequently, careful attention should be given to minimizing the displacement, weakening, or neutralization of community maintenance structures such as block clubs, neighborhood associations, and self-help programs.[33] Second, a "community educator should be incorporated into the mission of public organizations."[34] He supplements this approach with the suggestions that community advocacy units could be created within public organizations. Both of these approaches are, to a large extent, designed to facilitate a more effective interaction of public organizations with community groups without the latter surrendering themselves to professionalization. Finally, public service education classes should be introduced into the public administration curriculum so that students, who eventually become public-sector professionals, will treat communities as clients.

All of Cooper's recommendations are examples of institutional philanthropy, and as noble as his concerns are about the forces he has tried to outline, he does not quite know how to confront them. On the one hand, he resigns himself to the influence of modernization; yet on the other hand, he proposes a momentary truce in the process. There is, if one follows his logic, a crack in the process which if properly opened can offer the needed political space for community organizations to operate in a more participative manner.

In effect, the ultimate trap of modernization is that we are left with an option of merely reform-ing procedures without examining critically the underlying causes of social problems. There are structural, cognitive, and political limits to organizational effectiveness, and those limits are defined not only by program compatibility with the prevailing norms of public organizations, but by the incessant need to regard political issues as merely problems of coordination and management.

Modernization, by reinforcing the managerial tendency (which in turn, defuses potential so-cial conflict) is symptomatic of the overall theory that political problems can only be solved by displacing them. What Cooper perceived as a possible crack in the modernization process may only be an ephemeral aberration: we believe we are improving social conditions by moving, when necessary, the "political furniture" around the room. This managerial maneuvering, however, only distracts attention from "the interests and values at work within the policy process which are shaped by ideologies or dominant belief systems, which, in themselves, are a reflection of the broader power relationships."[35]

The evolution of TELACU is a classic example of this process. TELACU became a victim of modernization, but not solely for the reasons proposed by Cooper. TELACU was transformed not only cognitively and operationally, but more importantly, politically—it became an agent legitimizing the political process and the need for the community to work within it. This is not to imply that TELACU became a mere puppet of government, but rather that it came to be an "institutional carrier" of the importance of managing social problems in accordance with the status quo. TELACU devised a deliberate strategy to integrate itself politically with those who have influence over the policy process. "In order for TELACU to be effective in what it does," one public administrator put it, "it has to be always regarded as a politically safe organization, an organization which is not disruptive to the political order. It lives or dies on making that point clear."

Although it is true that UNO does not deliver services like TELACU, it is involved with the technical and political intricacies of such issues as community planning and development, making it vulnerable to the process of modernization. As UNO began to deal with these broader community issues, there were predictable tensions in the organization about how to maintain its original goals. Tensions notwithstanding, UNO believes that it can be effective on complex urban issues and maintain its community base by striving to be a "learning organization"—an organization which plans with people, links knowledge with action, and evaluates continuously its purposes and goals. There is, of course, a trade-off. UNO will continue to encounter resistance from public agencies. Nevertheless, it sees the necessity to take a political stand against becoming redefined organizationally and politically by the forces of modernity.

One UNO leader emphasized this point when he stated: "If we do not resist these political forces that would change us, we will eventually lose sight of why we are here and what we need to do. We will become actors whose lines are written by someone else. . . . We can never allow that to happen." UNO avoids becoming an actor "whose lines are written by someone else," maintains its original emphasis on participation, and continues as a viable community organization confronting "the system" when necessary through the use of a "learning process approach" to decision making.

A LEARNING PROCESS APPROACH

In order to understand UNO's success in maintaining its community base, it is useful to examine David Korten's distinction between a blueprint and a learning process approach to organizational behavior. In the former, there is an emphasis on project; in the latter, the emphasis is on program. Projects require "detailed, upfront planning, coupled with rigorous adherence to fast-paced implementation schedules and pre-planned specifications."[36] This blueprint approach insures that planning and implementation will reside with "technicians and government bureaucrats neither of whom are rewarded for being responsive to local conditions nor contributing toward the development of local institutional capacities."[37] This approach, embraced by TELACU, not only reinforces professionalization and bureaucratization, it perpetuates a view of citizens as merely the passive beneficiaries of change. In other words, social change is something which just happens (or, more to the point does not happen) not something which citizens can create for themselves.

The program emphasis of the learning process approach, on the other hand, is a course of action conductive to the needs of beneficiaries, needs which are jointly agreed upon and that "fit" the capacities of the assisting organization involved. Korten defines this "fit" in an interesting manner:

Between beneficiaries and the assisting organization, the critical fit is between the means by which the beneficiaries are able to define and communicate their needs and the program by which the organization makes decisions. This may require changes both at the community level—developing a way for the poor to express their needs—and the assisting organization level—developing ways for the organization to respond to such information.[38] (emphasis added)

This fit is not based upon *blueprints,* but upon the facilitation of leadership and teamwork within the community organization. It is only through this approach, Korten concludes, that an organization can hope to learn the nature of beneficiary needs and what is required to address them effectively. "Achieving fit through a learning approach calls for organizations that have little in common with the implementing organizations geared to reliable adherence to detailed plans and conditions precedent favored in the blueprint approach."[39]

The new requirement for organization is to learn how to: embrace error; plan with people; and link knowledge with action.[40] Embracing error implies an awareness of the limitations "of the knowledge of their members . . . and to look upon error as a vital source of data adjustment for making adjustments to achieve a better fit with beneficiary needs."[41] Planning with people means that citizens can contribute to program design—they do have the capacity to learn and change. More importantly, planning with people recognizes that citizens have knowledge of community problems which too often goes unnoticed by researchers who reside outside the community. Linking knowledge to action attempts to integrate what is learned from the two previous steps. Moreover, Korten makes a point worth considering if community organizations are serious about adopting the learning approach. He proposes the development of field-based learning laboratories:

These laboratories [can be] designed not only to produce a program model, but also gradually to build the experience within the broader organization required to make it work. . . . Researchers [can be] involved . . . but only in supporting rather than controlling roles.[42]

This point is crucial. What Korten is trying to emphasize is that the community organization, with the proper assistance, can demystify the social sciences, "making it every person's tool, turning both the agency and the . . . [citizen] into more effective action researchers."[43] To many this is a futile attempt, considering the investment the citizen will have to make. Yet, as should already be obvious, UNO's approach is strikingly similar to what Korten is proposing. UNO created a model of learning which can be depicted in Figure 11.1.

The "learning process approach" as a model of behavior does not, in and of itself, define an organization's goals and purposes. Rather, it provides a framework within which political choices can be made. The value of such a learning model to an organization like UNO is that it does not take the existing power structure as a given, that it does not attempt to initiate programs or provide services without ascertaining beneficiary needs and the effects of services and programs on those needs, and that it does not separate policy formulation and implementation from citizen participation.[44] UNO is able to maintain its original goals—goals displaced by TELACU—because the learning model allows the organization to operationalize its commitment to these goals. It is this commitment coupled with the "learning process approach" which most clearly distinguishes UNO from TELACU.

The learning process is not a panacea for all the difficulties facing community organizations; it is only a process which provides, in the words of David Korten, a creative forum "for skills in building the capacities for action through action."[45]

Figure 11.1   **UNO's Organizational Learning Model**

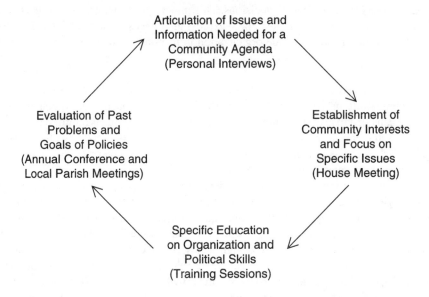

CONCLUSIONS

The dilemma of modernization as it relates to community organizations may never be solved. However, UNO's success in balancing the conflicting pressures involved in dealing with complex social problems and maintaining community participation calls into question the emerging consensus that a decline in participation is an inevitable price of modernity. The pressures of modernization notwithstanding, political choices are available to leaders of community organizations. More to the point, the values embedded in political choices—choices constrained but not determined by historical forces—still form the basis of organizational behavior.

Choices, however, involve costs; a learning organization pays a price for its decision to maintain community participation. Group decision-making processes in a learning organization are inherently time consuming, frequently frustrating, and more than occasionally conflictual. Not only must the distance—in culture, language, and priorities—between professionals and residents be bridged, but conflicts between and among residents must be mediated and a policy consensus developed. The amount of time and effort spent on any one project represents a significant opportunity cost given the number of social problems requiring attention.

On the other hand, an organization like TELACU also pays a price for its decision to embrace professionalism and bureaucratization. TELACU's success in developing a wide variety of programs and funding sources is indeed impressive. The problems with this mode of operation, however, tend to be more long-term in nature. As a research analyst in Los Angeles County put it:

> If economic development implies some sort of need for economic self-sufficiency and control over one's destiny, it cannot be fully effective without the transformation of the citizen itself. Economic development has been unfortunately too narrowly defined and that's why we sometimes have meager results regardless of the money spent. . . . I think we are beginning to understand that economic development is also an integral part of citizen development.[46]

The political decision to resist the pressures of modernization involves both risks and opportunity costs. If UNO remains seriously committed to a learning approach, it will remain an organization in the continual and perhaps often tumultuous state of internal reassessment. However, in spite of—or more to the point because of—this mode of operation, UNO has the potential to generate meaningful social change by raising basic questions. On the other hand, the political decision to accept the forces of modernization should insure for TELACU a certain degree of organizational stability. However, in social terms, this mode of operation is analogous to replacing the horse with the cart—one remains firmly in place.

NOTES

1. The literature in this area ranges from the "human relations" school (Elton Mayo, *The Human Problems of Industrial Civilization*, New York: MacMillan, 1933) through "participative management" models (Chris Argyris, *Integrating the Individual and the Organization*, New York: John Wiley, 1964, and Rensis Likert, *New Patterns of Management*, New York: McGraw-Hill, 1961) to the current interest in "holistic approaches" to decision making (William Ouchi, *Theory Z*, Reading, Mass.: Addison Wesley, 1982).

2. Modernization can be defined as that process by which the values of participation and accountability are supplanted by notions of professionalism and efficiency. Modernization is associated with: the development of large-scale bureaucracies which formalize political relationships; divisions of labor which transform traditional social roles; and economic interdependencies which transcend traditional social boundaries. In the United States, modernization, which began during the Industrial Revolution, continues today in an increasingly technocratic society. The most important effect of modernization for our purposes is the pressure for professionalization and bureaucratization on community organizations.

3. See Carole Pateman, *Participation and Democratic Theory* (Cambridge: Cambridge University Press, 1970).

4. See Robert Dahl, *Polyarchy, Participation and Opposition* (New Haven: Yale University Press, 1971).

5. See Milton Kotler, *Neighborhood Government* (New York: Bobbs-Merrill, 1969); and David Morris and Karl Hess, *Neighborhood Power* (Boston: Beacon Press, 1975).

6. The term "pro-growth coalitions" is borrowed from John Mollenkopf, "The Postwar Politics of Urban Redevelopment," in William Tabb and Larry Sawers, eds., *Marxism and the Metropolis* (New York: Oxford University Press, 1978), pp. 117–152. An in-depth analysis of the potential for citizen participation within neighborhood organizations is contained in Charles Hampden-Turner, *From Poverty to Dignity* (New York: Anchor Press, 1974). For a critical review of modes of participation at the community level, see Sherry Arnstein, "A Ladder of Citizen Participation," *American Institute of Planners* 35 (July 1969): 216–224.

7. See James Davies, "Citizen Participation in a Bureaucratic Society: Some Questions and Skeptical Notes," in G. Frederickson, ed., *Neighborhood Control in the 1970s* (New York: Chandler, 1973); and J. C. Hetherington, "Community Participation: A Critical View," in Richard Weistart, ed., *Community Economic Development* (New York: Praeger Publishers, 1977).

8. See Terry Cooper, "Bureaucracy and Community Organization: The Metamorphosis of a Relationship," *Administration and Society* 11 (February 1980): 411–444.

9. See Max Weber, *Economy and Society: An Outline of Interpretive Society,* 3 vols., eds., G. Roth and C. Wittich, trans., E. Fischoff, et al. (New York: Bedminster Press, 1968), pp. 452–467.

10. David Korten, "Community Organization and Rural Development: A Learning Process Approach," *Public Administration Review* (September/October 1980): pp. 480–511. We must warn the reader that we have only extracted certain aspects of Korten's notion of learning for our analysis. An extensive examination of his ideas was beyond the scope of this article.

11. There is one other group which is as large as TELACU in Los Angeles. That group is run by Ted Watkins, president of the Watts Labor Community Action Committee.

12. Janice Perlman, "Grassrooting the System," *Social Policy* (September/October 1976): 4–20.

13. G. Faux, *CDC's: New Hope for the Future* (New York: The Twentieth Century Fund, 1971), p. 3

14. Richard Rich, "Dilemmas of Citizen Participation in the Neighborhood Movement," *Urban Affairs Quarterly* (March 1982): p. 389. See Marilyn Gittell, *Limits to Citizen Participation* (Beverly Hills: Sage, 1980).

15. "TELACU Community: Development for the Future," p. 6.

16. *Ibid.,* p. 7.

17. *Ibid.,* p. 8.

18. Cooper, "Bureaucracy and Community Organization," p. 434.

19. Frank Del Olmo, "Community Coalition Mobilizing East Los Angeles," *Los Angeles Times,* December 26, 1977, Part II, p. 1.

20. This information was supplied by a UNO pamphlet entitled "The United Neighborhood Organization," p. 3.

21. *Ibid.,* p. 3.

22. Harry Boyte, *The Backyard Revolution: Understanding the Citizen Movement* (Philadelphia: Temple University Press, 1980), p. 66.

23. Cooper, "Bureaucracy and Community Organization," p. 412.

24. *Ibid.,* p. 413.

25. *Ibid.*

26. *Ibid.*

27. *Ibid.,* p. 435.

28. *Ibid.,* p. 437.

29. *Ibid.*

30. *Ibid.,* p. 438.

31. Max Weber, *Protestant Ethic and the Spirit of Capitalism* (New York: Charles Scribner's Son, 1930), p. 182.

32. Cooper, "Bureaucracy and Community Organization," p. 439.

33. *Ibid.,* p. 440.

34. *Ibid.*

35. S. Barrett and C. Fudge, eds., *Policy and Action: Essays on the Implementation of Public Policy* (London: Methuen Books, 1981), p. 262.

36. David Korten, "Community Organization and Rural Development," p. 484.

37. *Ibid.,* p. 484.

38. *Ibid.,* p. 496.

39. *Ibid.,* p. 498.

40. *Ibid.,* p. 498–499.

41. *Ibid.,* p. 498.

42. *Ibid.,* p. 499.

43. *Ibid.,* p. 501.

44. This point is addressed in E. Alexander, "Goal Setting in an Uncertain World: A Case Study of a Local Community Organization," *Public Administration Review* (March/April 1976), pp. 182–191.

45. David Korten, "Community Organization and Rural Development," p. 502.

46. Interview with senior analyst in Los Angeles County government, April 20, 1981 (anonymity requested).

CHAPTER 12

THE DEMOCRATIZATION OF THE POLICY SCIENCES

PETER deLEON

In the past few years, numerous authors have addressed the shortcomings of public policy analysis. Some of these criticisms have been concerned with the subject aspects of the approach, pointing out how many years and multiple megadollars of policy research have not improved American social welfare policies nor corrected the deficiencies of the U.S. educational system. While one can legitimately argue that the problems addressed are extremely difficult—indeed, they might not have a feasible solution—this is little solace when the accountability roll is called. Others have described what they refer to as the internal contradictions of the policy sciences' philosophy and approach.[1] And everybody complains that nobody ever seems to listen, alas, for apparently good cause. Finger pointing rather than the proposition of real remedies appears to be the general order of the day.

There is one aspect of policy research, especially from government or government-sponsored quarters, that many have identified as a pressing source of these troubles—that is, its elite characterization. How can the insulated analyst in Washington know what the recipient in (say) Santa Fe wants, especially if the analyst and the recipient live in and represent vastly different cultures and life experiences? According to this complaint, it is little wonder that the analyst consistently makes recommendations that the recipient finds oddly inadequate or inappropriate; as a consequence, the program flounders and often flunks. Not only has the problem failed to have been corrected but, even worse, the intended recipient now has a revised and probably lower opinion of the government. "Thus, an unintended side effect of policy analysis may be to erect barriers in the way of important ends of participatory democracy" (Jenkins-Smith, 1988, p. 69).

This separation syndrome almost surely contributes to ineffective programs and results. For that reason alone, the dichotomous relationship is troublesome. However, there is a second aspect of the two-culture problem that is even more worrisome to a democratic polity. Namely, a strong bias exists in this arrangement towards recognizing the policymaker as the analysts' legitimate—often, only—client, thus reinforcing the isolation of the analysts. In the analysts' current positions (geographic and bureaucratic), they are effectively sequestered from the demands, needs, and (most

From *Public Administration Review*, 52, 2 (March/April 1992): 125–129. Copyright © 1992 by American Society for Public Administration. Reprinted with permission.

critically) values of the people they are reputed to be helping. As such, they are helping to establish and sustain the gap between the ruler and the ruled. In this environment, they are seemingly indifferent to the form of government. In Dryzek's (1989, p. 98) charge, "most policy analysis efforts to date are in fact consistent with an albeit subtle policy science of tyranny." Policy knowledge in any number of fields is in the exclusive hands of experts, superseding and, hence, undermining the democratic ethos.[2]

This tendency stands in stark contrast to the original conception of the policy sciences. They were initially designed to provide "intelligence pertinent to the integration of values realized by and embodied by interpersonal relations [such as] human dignity and the realization of human capacities" (Lasswell and Kaplan, 1950, p. xii). They were, in Harold Lasswell's (1951, p. 15) seminal formulation, the "policy sciences of democracy . . . directed towards knowledge needed to improve the practice of democracy."

The roots of this discrepancy are not difficult to fathom. In spite of the pioneering work of humanists like Lasswell, Abraham Kaplan, and Robert Merton, most of the early policy research was carried out by technicians, usually systems analysts and operation researchers. Their positivist pursuit of a clearly defined objective function needed little contribution from the recipient. This tendency was subsequently reinforced by economists who predicated their policy recommendations on "objective" economic relationships pursued by rational actors, again requiring little knowledge of the intended client's particular needs and the political climate in which public policymakers, by definition, must operate. Their presumption (some would say arrogance) was pervasive.[3] Applied economics, generally in the guise of benefit-cost analysis, were ascribed talismanic qualities in one of the leading policy texts; e.g., "Benefit-cost analysis is a methodology with which we pursue efficiency and which has the effect of limiting the vagaries of the political process" (Stokey and Zeckhauser: 1978, p. 151). Econometric models achieved great currency in fields as disparate as energy and hospital cost containment without ever having to ask what consumers felt.

However, there is a large literature that has taken the economic (including public choice theory) paradigms to serious task. Without rehashing these arguments here,[4] the basic problem with the economic model was that it could not retain its theoretic rigor and still incorporate personal and political values into its analysis. There was an abiding inability to reconcile rational effectiveness with political palatability. Even benefit-cost analysis was revealed as subjective and manipulable except only in the most mundane exercises (Downs and Larkey, 1986); critical questions of standing were found to be more politically than analytically inspired (Whittington and Macrae, 1986; Trumbull, 1990). In short, it was unable to operate in any political arena where variables other than strictly economic questions arose (i.e., almost nowhere of interest) without further contributing to the elite syndrome and the widening separation between the analyst and the public. This, in turn, led to a confidence gap between the two parties.

One proposed alternative to the perceived shortcomings of the rational actor paradigm is the greater incorporation of citizens' values on an explicit basis into the policy process (e.g., Fischer and Forester, 1987; and Fischer, 1980). No doubt this is an appropriate response but one that has formidable obstacles to being enacted, as we shall see. However, in this case, the candle might be worth the game, for the results would both make policy research more cognizant of the values entailed and reduce the gap between the analysts and the recipient.

THE DEMOCRATIZATION OF POLICY ANALYSIS

Many authors have written about the dilemmas of liberal democracy, as political interest groups intervene between the politician and the citizen.[5] The remedy increasingly prescribed has been greater direct citizen participation in the acts of governance, reflecting what Redford (1969) has termed "democratic morality." Although the form and forum may change,[6] the idea is basically the same. This breed of "strong democracy" (as opposed to "thin democracy") has been defined by Barber (1984, p. 132) as:

> politics in the participatory mode where conflict is resolved in the absence of an independent ground through a participatory process of ongoing, proximate self-legislation and the creation of a political community capable of transforming dependent, private individuals into free citizens and partial and private interests into public goods.

Dryzek (1989, p. 118) seconds Barber's nomination, observing that "political education, participatory action, and successful social problem solving could together help constitute a community fully capable of steering its own course into the future. The distinction between citizen and expert would lose its force" (also see Pateman, 1970; Benello and Roussopoulos, eds., 1971; and Langton, ed., 1978).

This approach has been translated into the language of policy inquiry. According to Paris and Reynolds (1983, p. 260), "the plurality of rational ideologies supports the use of roughly and broadly republican or democratic decisionmaking procedures." Lindblom (1986, p. 361) sets out the reasoning with admirable terseness: "Instead of serving the needs of officials alone, help for the ordinary citizen."

Without questioning these claims towards a "more perfect union," I would like to argue that the realization of participatory democracy, or a variation some call "empowerment," is much more nettlesome than its proposition—maybe unattainable. Even when we accept its ideological rectitude, we must pause at its formidable operational hurdles. How does one ensure an informed citizenry? While this has always been a dicey proposition, it seems to be receding even as Barber and his colleagues base their solutions upon it. A recent survey commissioned by the *Los Angeles Times* (Anonymous, 1990, p. iii) comments on this ebbing of interest:

> From 1941 until 1975, young Americans knew as much about public affairs and public people as did their elders, and they followed most major news events as closely. But from 1975, young people have been much less attentive to news and public affairs. Today, they typically register 20 percent less interest in major news stories than do Americans over 30.

Or an involved citizenry? Americans have consistently demonstrated one of the lowest voting rates among the Western democracies. Lacking these—to say nothing of solutions to the various technical problems, such as how to poll an entire population—the sheen of participatory democracy begins to tarnish. And, lastly, is it functional? Would it work? Decisions, by their very nature, are required when disputes occur; they must be made, and often made expeditiously. But Barber (1984, p. 207) avers that "whenever possible, the strong democrat will try to defer decisions on which there is not yet agreement rather than win a majority decision that leaves behind a legacy of dissatisfaction." He would seem to prefer sclerotic democracy to the thin variety. In short, those scholars who rely on participatory democracy to resuscitate the policy sciences' credibility surely must be a patient body.

But participatory democracy is not the same as a participatory or democratic policy analysis. A democratic policy analysis should make for much more effective policy because it would be operating under the recipients' values and needs hierarchies (i.e., those directly affected by the programs) as opposed to those of the removed (however sympathetic) analyst and policymaker.

Rather than directing our efforts towards the more ambitious (perhaps unattainable) goals of participatory democracy, the realization of a policy sciences of democracy is a more discrete objective, and one with significant advantages for all concerned. The achievement of a participatory policy analysis would not only be beneficial to the policy sciences of democracy *quo* democracy but it would also directly enhance the possibility and credibility of participatory democracy.

POLICY ANALYSIS AND POLICY POLLING

The concept of a democratized policy analysis is relatively straightforward. Instead of involving every citizen in decisionmaking (or "empowerment," e.g., Model Cities), the idea is to increase citizen participation in the articulation and formulation of public policy programs. Rather than having the many engage in the actual policy decision (as one finds in a strong democracy), it asks that policy analysts devise and actively practice ways to recruit and include citizens' personal views into the policy formulation process. This represents a conscious effort to translate and aggregate with fidelity *individual* preferences into *public* policy. In line with March and Olsen (1990), the underlying assumption is that people will have more confidence in a policy in whose development they were consulted, although the final policy does not agree with their particular preference. Even Barber (1984, p. 207) would seem to assent: "But for us to accede to a political judgment that we have helped formulate is less alienating than having to accede to a majority that has outvoted us."

In this usage, the "policy sharing" can be roughly equated with access to planning and policy decisions, and an implied influence over subsequent operational decisions. It does not necessitate that people be particularly well-informed. The key requirement is not that these citizens are sufficiently knowledgeable ("expert") to comment but that they are sufficiently affected that they are willing to express their perceptions in an open public policy forum. The position holds that there are critical policy choices that should be made on information that goes beyond hard numbers and expert fact. A citizen would not have to understand megatons and fratricide to know that the world is held in nuclear peril and would be safer without so many of these weapons (Shubik and Bracken, 1982), a realization that has led to greater citizen participation in the formerly closely held strategic policy debate over the last two decades (deLeon, 1987; Dahl, 1985).

In addition, policy sharing implies that these citizens have some confidence that their individual and aggregated opinion on a specific subject (thus distinguishing it from voting on a ambiguous amalgam of issues in a general election) will be heard and considered within the policy councils. This is the key distinction between participatory democracy and a democratic policy analysis.[7]

This places a new and (to date) unwelcomed burden on government institutions and analysts. They must now seek out, even solicit, public opinion regarding matters under policy consideration; the comfort of isolation and anonymity would be a bygone luxury. Public opinion surveys should only be one of many techniques. In particular, new citizens' forums must be created and located so that the affected parties can make their beliefs known with a minimum of inconvenience. "Citizens' panels," which combine survey techniques and randomly chosen citizens, are one possibility (Crosby, Kelley, and Schaefer, 1986). Information must be provided to these *fora* in as balanced a mode as possible. Then the analysts must somehow aggregate these materials into their analyses and recommendations. Fischer (1980, pp. 49–50) summarizes the new requirements: "Such policy argumentation starts with the recognition that the participants do not have solid answers to questions under discussion, or even a solid method for getting the answer." The very newness of these demands will make their acceptance problematic within the halls of well-practiced governmental routine.

These are scarcely novel concepts. Congressional committees often hold hearings across the country. Environmental impact hearings assume this mode and are commonplace (Bartlett, ed., 1988; Hart *et al.,* eds., 1984). The procedure is widely practiced on local government levels, to widely varying results (Gittell, 1980; and Kweit and Kweit, 1981). The extension to other subject areas should be straightforward. Yet, for all its apparent value, policy sharing conceals any number of potentially lethal snares. What impetus would motivate a government to try these new and problematic procedures or the citizen to participate? Who decides which parties have the relevant voice while avoiding the taint of political bias? Or who will speak for these groups? What criteria will be employed? What are the operating rules of procedure? Majone writes that "The supreme analytic achievement is no longer the computations of optimal strategies, but the design of procedural rules and social evidence." But he gives little indication as to what these rules might be except that they should be "argumentative" and adjudicated in "adversarial settings," somehow overlooking how cumbersome the judicial system (his preferred analogy) has become (Majone 1977, p. 174). How can this newly obtained mountain of data be integrated into the policy process? Will the losers suspect a political charade and refuse to participate in the next round? And so forth.

Likewise, the examination of possible examples or models we have in hand on the national level is not very encouraging. The NEPA-mandated Environmental Impact Statements (EIS), while widespread, have provided little support to the proposal's efficacy, except that the EIS uniformly greatly extend the time frame necessary for a decision, a condition surely not prized when matters are pressing. The widely publicized hearing on solar energy by President Carter's domestic policy review (DPR) staff conscientiously labored to involve hundreds of opinions through scores of hearings that produced pounds of public testimony. But, in the end, these hearings were largely dismissed by the DPR staff who "saw the core of the [solar energy] problem in highly technical terms, and the lay public had nothing to say that could help them solve that problem. . . . Because they lacked a certain rather esoteric knowledge, a group of interested citizens were effectively disenfranchised from a policy debate in which they had an intense interest" (Laird, 1988).

It would seem, then, that a democratic policy analysis is a better idea in concept than it is in practice. As such, it should be sadly but prudently set aside. But this might be a hasty conclusion, one based upon present conditions rather than what might be possible. The EIS procedures have admittedly taken a great deal of time but there is a significant portion of the population who have found the results satisfactory; some (generally of the conservation bent) have even found their dilatory procedures laudable. That is, for those cases in which time constraints can be relaxed, the resulting policy appears to be worth the long gestation. Citizens might be more amenable to such delays if they are assured that they (rather than a distant government) are part of the delay.

The lengthened time requirements are an unquestionable EIS characteristic and, as we have said, there are moments when time is of the essence. Still, this is not a fatal blow to this idea. What it does verify is what we already knew: not all decisions should be treated identically and time is one of the important variables in determining what mode of decisionmaking should be utilized. Criticism of the EIS can therefore be seen as a "glass-half-empty" reading when, to the majority, the glass is half full, certainly a more encouraging perspective towards the democratization of public policy analysis. We can, I propose, select a number of policy issues whose pervasiveness, importance, and schedule would lend themselves to a more democratic style of policy analysis. Issues surrounding health care, social welfare, housing, national security, and infrastructure all could benefit from a more public vetting than is presently the case. The decentralization of school authority currently occurring throughout the nation is an example of policy sharing on a local level, an experience that might become a "natural experiment" for nation-scale policy sharing.

For this to happen, there must be a two-sided learning experience. The first is that government analysts, agencies, and policymakers must create and proliferate the incentives and forums essential for a democratic policy analysis to function. Moreover, they must provide some assurance that these will not be shams, i.e., that the information gathered will be an important component of policy formulation, and that the information not be manipulated or restricted (Jenkins-Smith, 1988, p. 78). The second is that citizens must recognize that it is their responsibility to articulate their opinions.

We as analysts must admit that the partial return of policy formulation to the constituencies does not imply that policy analysts will find themselves out of work. The bureaucratic demands would be just as great, only (as noted above) the requirements would be much expanded and perhaps more difficult given the training of the present corps of analysts; sociology would join economics and public administration in the analyst's preferred disciplinary arsenal; and a more proactive stance would be necessary to promote the process rather than a particular position (Kathlene and Martin, 1991).

CONCLUSIONS

As has been noted above, the design and execution of a democratized policy analysis will not be an easy transition. But given the public perception of its governmental servants and services juxtaposed with the general state of disregard for public policy analysis, it is clear that something radical must be done if the ruled are to retain any faith in the ruler, that is, if governance philosophy and practices to which we subscribe are to continue. At the very least, the idea of policy sharing would reaffirm the profession's dedication to the policy sciences of democracy, one "of the people, by the people, and for the people," an essential symbolism.

NOTES

Prepared for presentation to the Annual Meeting of the American Political Science Association, San Francisco, California, August 30–September 2, 1990. I owe a great intellectual debt to Frank Fischer (Rutgers), Hank Jenkins-Smith (New Mexico), Robert Denhardt (University of Central Florida), and Linda deLeon (University of Colorado-Denver) as well as the anonymous referees who commented constructively on the text.
1. Two of the more articulate critics in this vein are Hawkesworth (1988) and Stone (1988).
2. The best elaboration of this charge is Jenkins-Smith (1989).
3. This evolution is described in deLeon (1989).
4. The most accessible critiques are Bobrow and Dryzek (1987) and Paris and Reynolds (1983).
5. Still one of the most cogent is Dahl (1982); also see Bachrach (1976).
6. See Jenkins-Smith (1988).
7. Elsewhere I have referred to this as "participatory policy analysis" (deLeon, 1990).

REFERENCES

Anonymous, 1990. *The Age of Indifference: A Study of Young Americans and How They View the News.* Los Angeles, CA: Times Mirror Center for the People and the Press, June 28.
Bachrach, Peter, 1976. *The Theory of Democratic Elitism.* Boston: Little, Brown.
Barber, Benjamin R., 1984. *Strong Democracy: Participatory Politics for a New Age.* Berkeley: University of California Press.
Bartlett, Robert, ed., 1988. Symposium on "Policy and Impact Statements." *Policy Studies Review,* vol. 8 (Autumn), *passim.*
Benello, C. George, and Dimitrios Roussopoulos, eds., 1971. *The Case for Participatory Democracy.* New York: Grossman.
Bobrow, Davis B. and John S. Dryzek, 1987. *Policy Analysts by Design.* Pittsburgh, PA: University of Pittsburgh Press.

Crosby, Ned, Janet Kelley, and Paul Schaefer, 1986. "Citizen Panels: A New Approach to Citizen Participation." *Public Administration Review,* vol. 46 (March/April), pp. 170–179.

Dahl, Robert A., 1982. *Dilemmas of a Pluralist Democracy.* New Haven, CT: Yale University Press.

———, 1985. *Controlling Nuclear Weapons: Democracy versus Guardianship.* Syracuse, NY: Syracuse University Press.

deLeon, Peter, 1987. *The Altered Strategic Environment.* Lexington, MA: D.C. Heath.

———, 1989. *Advice and Consent: The Development of the Policy Sciences.* New York: The Russell Sage Foundation.

———, 1990. "Participatory Policy Analysis: Prescriptions and Precautions." *Asian Journal of Public Administration,* vol. 12 (June), pp. 29–54.

Downs, George W. and Patrick D. Larkey, 1986. *The Search for Governmental Efficiency.* New York: Random House.

Dryzek, John S., 1989. "Policy Sciences of Democracy." *Polity,* vol. 22 (Fall), pp. 97–118.

Fischer, Frank, 1980. *Politics, Values, and Public Choice.* Boulder, CO: Westview Press.

Fischer, Frank and John Forester, eds., 1987. *Confronting Values in Policy Analysis.* Newberry Park, CA: Sage.

Gittell, Marilyn, 1980, *Limits to Citizen Participation.* Beverly Hills: Sage.

Hart, Stuart L., *et al.,* eds., 1984. *Improving Impact Assessment.* Boulder, CO: Westview Press.

Hawkesworth, M.E., 1988. *Theoretical Issues in Policy Analysis.* Albany: State University of New York Press.

Jenkins-Smith, Hank C., 1988. "Analytic Debates and Policy Learning: Analysis and Changes in the Federal Bureaucracy." *Policy Sciences,* vol. 21, pp. 169–212.

———, 1989. *Democratic Politics and Policy Analysis.* Pacific Grove, CA.: Brooks/Cole.

Kathlene, Lynn and John A. Martin, 1991. "Enhancing Citizen Participation: Panel Designs, Perspectives, and Policy Formation." *Journal of Policy Analysis & Management,* vol. 10 (Winter), pp. 46–63.

Kweit, Mary Grisez and Robert W. Kweit, 1981. *Implementing Citizen Participation in a Bureaucratic Society.* New York: Praeger.

Laird, Frank N., 1988. "Technocracy Revisited: Knowledge and Power in Technical Decisions." Paper presented at the 1988 Meetings of the American Political Science Association. Washington, D.C.

Langton, Stuart, ed., 1978. *Citizen Participation in America.* Lexington, MA: Lexington Books.

Lasswell, Harold D., 1951. "The Policy Orientation." In Daniel Lerner and Harold D. Lasswell, eds., *The Policy Sciences.* Stanford, CA: Stanford University Press, pp. 3–16.

Laswell, Harold D. and Abraham Kaplan, 1950. *Power and Society.* New Haven, CT: Yale University Press.

Lindblom, Charles E., 1986. "Who Needs What Social Research for Policymaking?" *Knowledge: Creation, Diffusion, Utilization,* vol. 7 (June), pp. 345–366.

Majone, Giandomenico, 1977. "Technology Assessment and Policy Analysis." *Policy Sciences,* vol. 8 (June), pp. 173–176.

March, James G. and Johan Olsen, 1990. *Rediscovering Institutions.* New York: Free Press.

Paris, David and James Reynolds, 1983. *The Logic of Policy Inquiry.* New York: Longman.

Pateman, Carole, 1970. *Participation and Democratic Theory.* New York: Cambridge University Press.

Redford, Emmett S., 1969. *Democracy in the Administrative State.* New York: Cambridge University Press.

Shubik, Martin and Paul Bracken, 1982. "Strategic War: What Are the Questions and Who Should Be Asking Them?" *Technology in Society,* vol. 4, pp. 155–179.

Stokey, Edith and Richard Zeckhauser, 1978. *A Primer for Policy Analysis.* New York: W.W. Norton.

Stone, Deborah A., 1988. *Policy Paradox and Political Reason.* Glenville, IL: Scott, Foresman.

Trumbull, William N., 1990. "Who Has Standing in Cost Benefit Analysis?" *Journal of Policy Analysis & Management,* vol. 9 (Spring), pp. 201–218.

Whittington, Dale and Duncan Macrae, Jr., 1986. "The Issue of Standing in Benefit Cost Analysis." *Journal of Policy Analysis & Management,* vol. 5 (Summer), pp. 665–682.

CHAPTER 13

PUBLIC DELIBERATION
An Alternative Approach to Crafting Policy and Setting Direction

NANCY ROBERTS

General managers face two basic challenges in leading and managing their public bureaus. They are expected to strive for both organizational efficiency and organizational effectiveness. *Webster's Third* (1971, 725) defines efficiency as the "capacity to produce results with the minimum expenditure of energy, time, money, or materials" and effectiveness as "productive of results" (1971, 724). To achieve efficiencies, managers focus on doing things well. They attend to the internal organization and center their energies on routinizing, refining, formalizing, and elaborating on existing knowledge, and on making short-run improvements. "Efficiency thrives on focus, precision, repetition, analysis, sanity, discipline, and control" (March, 1995, 5). On the other hand, to achieve effectiveness, managers must be concerned with doing the right things. Knowing what to do typically comes from an understanding and interpretation of the external environment as it signals what ongoing adaptations are required in organizational technology, knowledge, strategy, and values. "Adaptation thrives on serendipity, experimentation, novelty, free association, madness, loose discipline, and relaxed control" (March, 1995, 5).[1]

Both effectiveness and efficiency are necessary for bureau performance. Each plays an important part, but at the same time each interferes with the other. In the competition for scarce organizational resources, the natural processes of each tend to pit one against the other. Effectiveness thrives on exploration and experimentation, but efficiency attempts to drive them out (March, 1995, 5).

Depending on their pursuit of efficiency and effectiveness, managers have developed four basic approaches to general management: the directive approach, the reactive approach, the generative approach, and the adaptive approach (Figure 13.1). Each approach should be considered as an ideal type that emerges from an interaction among an organization's major elements—its political, technical, social, and economic environment, as well as internal leadership, membership, and design factors. (It is possible to have hybrids that mix elements from each approach, but they will not be developed here.)

After a brief overview of the four approaches, this paper will explore the generative approach

---

Reprinted with permission.

in greater depth, especially its use of public deliberation as an alternative way to establish public policy and set bureau direction. Having observed several of these deliberations to establish public policy, my goal is to distill the essence of their structure and process for the purpose of both improving future practice and building better theory. To this end, two cases will be examined: budget deliberations in a local school district and public deliberations over state educational policy.

FOUR APPROACHES TO GENERAL MANAGEMENT

General managers employing the directive approach (the first quadrant of Figure 13.1) resolve the tension between efficiency and effectiveness by designing bureaus for optimal efficiency and minimal effectiveness. In practice, they pursue efficiency by running their bureaus like well-oiled machines (Mintzberg, 1996a). They avoid questions of adaptation and effectiveness that force a reexamination of current operations. Instead, they focus on maintaining internal order and control. Serving as the locus of decision-making, they set the organization's goals to ensure that all members act in concert. They insist on formalized jobs and standardized work to maintain orderly, reliable, and coordinated activity. Using both budgetary and operational controls to monitor actions, they correct deviations in performance. They oversee uniform policies that cover rights and duties, promotions based on competence and merit, and impersonal role relations to ensure the smooth flow of work. Since change disrupts orderly operations, they minimize it whenever possible. When forced to change, they take on the role of strategic planner and driver of the organizational system by issuing top-down directives to modify organizational routines and standard operating procedures.

Using the reactive approach to management (the second quadrant of Figure 13.1), the general manager relieves the tension between efficiency and effectiveness by reducing the pressure on each dimension. In practice this means that the general manager strives for neither optimal effectiveness nor optimal efficiency and does not make much effort to reconcile the competing demands of the two dimensions. Acting out of concern for effectiveness at one moment and efficiency the next, such managers produce an inconsistent, disjointed pattern of activity in response to the needs of the moment. Without an underlying logic to inform their actions, they fail to provide coherent, integrated policies to guide the organization as a whole. Organizational members emulate such "muddling through" with their own patchwork of poorly coordinated decisions (Lindblom, 1959; 1979). Organizational policies that emerge are the result of partisan mutual adjustments made in response to competing demands in the political context (Lindblom, 1959; 1979). As a consequence of this reactive posture, the general manager is forced to assume the role of "fire fighter" whose function is to put out fires whenever they erupt.

General managers who take the generative approach (the third quadrant of Figure 13.1) are challenged to be managers of organizational tensions and masters of paradox (Handy, 1995). No longer content with trade-offs between efficiency and effectiveness, they search for ways to reconcile what appears to be competing expectations. They seek both efficiency and effectiveness, short-run and long-run perspectives, global and local considerations, individual and collective needs, social and economic concerns, security and freedom, change and stability, diversity and commonality of purpose. The goal of these general managers is to help people find some underlying framework or solution that would enable them to resolve the paradoxes inherent in modern organizations. They begin the search by promoting generative learning—learning that develops people's capacity to create new solutions to old problems—rather than settling for adaptive learning, which only prepares them for coping. Generative learning opens up new ways of looking at the world and encourages a deeper understanding of a system and its underlying dynamics. Such

Figure 13.1 **Four Approaches to Public Sector General Management**

	Low	High
High Efficiency	**1** Directive Approach Role: Strategic Planner, Controller	**3** Generative Approach Role: Steward
Low	**2** Reactive Approach Role: Fire Fighter	**4** Adaptive Approach Role: Champion of Innovation

Effectiveness

learning becomes possible through an open, deliberative process when people are invited to help craft policy and set organizational direction (Reich, 1990). As conveners of public deliberations, these general managers assume the roles of steward, teacher, and designer whose functions are: to establish the creative tension between a vision and current reality, to invite participation in the resolution of that tension, and to ensure a process in which generative learning can take place (Senge, 1990).

Managers pursuing the adaptive approach to general management (the fourth quadrant in Figure 13.1) design their bureaus for optimal effectiveness. Adaptation to the external environment—the principal way to achieve effectiveness—is their major concern; efficiency is of minimal interest. In practice, such general managers take on the role of champion of innovation (Mintzberg, 1996b). As champions, they decentralize decision-making so that it rests on the shoulders of organizational members closest to customers and other important stakeholders in the external environment, substituting stakeholders for bosses as the basis of authority. They rely on members' up-to-date knowledge to signal the adaptations and innovations in products and services that are required to attract and keep stakeholder support. To ensure a continual stream of new ideas and keep the creative juices flowing, they reward entrepreneurship and innovation, and they design organizations around project work and cross-disciplinary teams. Relying on a general vision of the future rather than insisting on specific goals and objectives, they encourage "groping along" rather than planning in the search for new ideas (Behn, 1988). Flexibility, creativity, exploration, and experimentation are far more important to them than rigid adherence to internal order and control.

The directive, reactive, and adaptive approaches have been well-documented in the management literature. The generative approach, however, is just now emerging as a separate configuration as researchers begin in earnest to explore it. Some focus on its philosophical foundations (Fox and Miller, 1995), while others outline the practical techniques and processes necessary to create and sustain it (Weisbord, 1992; Weisbord and Janoff, 1995; Bunker and Alban, 1992). Others examine its implications for leadership (Block, 1993; Bryson and Crosby, 1992), for public participation in policy-making (Roberts and Bradley, 1991; Thomas, 1995), for alternative forms of organizing (Quinn, Anderson, and Finkelstein, 1996; Osborne and Gaebler, 1992), for organizational cultures (Barrett, 1995; Schein, 1993), and for new disciplines to make learning possible (Senge, 1990). These and other issues will open up other possibilities in the future as the political context continues to demand attention to both organizational efficiency, expressed as concern over costs and budgets, and effectiveness, expressed as choice among alternative options of what government should do and be in the future.[2]

The purpose of this article is to explore in greater depth one aspect of the generative approach—public deliberation. I adopt the view that deliberation represents civic discovery—a process of "social learning about public problems and possibilities" (Reich, 1990, 8). The point of deliberation is the "creation of a setting in which people can learn from one another" (Reich, 1990, 7). It is a public consideration "about how problems are to be defined and understood, what the range of possible solutions might be, and who should have the responsibility for solving them" (7). The effort is "iterative and ongoing" (7) and requires communication flow in both directions (8). Although public executives bring certain ideals and values to the process, even specific ideas about what they think should be done, they nevertheless look to the public and to its intermediaries (e.g., press, interest groups, other government officials) as sources of guidance in setting direction. They are expected to be honest and direct about their values and tentative about their goals, while listening carefully to others so that their agendas can be adjusted accordingly as the public responds to them. The deliberative process thus requires public executives "not simply to discover what people want for themselves and then to implement the best means for satisfying these wants. It is to provide the public with alternative visions of what is desirable and possible, to stimulate discussion about them, to provoke reexamination of premises and values, and thus to broaden the range of potential responses and deepen society's understanding of itself" (8). The challenge is to surface a broader repertoire of options and possibilities for the future rather than to be mired in "thoughtless adherence to outmoded formulations of problems. . . . Policy-making should be more than and different from the discovery of what people want; it should entail the creation of contexts in which the public can critically evaluate and revise what it believes" (8).

CRAFTING POLICY AND SETTING BUREAU DIRECTION THROUGH DELIBERATION: TWO CASES

Randall at Rosemount School District

Superintendent Ruth Randall had been in office less than six months when her district, like many others in Minnesota and throughout the country in the early 1980, faced serious budget shortfalls (Roberts, 1985). Over the next two years, she witnessed cuts of 38.3 percent in state aid to education. Unlike her counterparts, however, she was unwilling to rely on additional levies (one had recently passed) or to allow retrenchment to undermine district morale and the quality of its educational programs. Instead, Superintendent Randall decided to begin deliberations with the community and school district personnel to cut $2.4 million from the district's budget.

The design of the deliberation over the budget was complex. Deliberations began in December 1981 and extended over a four-month period. Principals and supervisors first solicited recommendations from 1,500 employees on budget reductions. These recommendations were then categorized and ranked by a special task force made up of teachers, administrators, and support staff. The task force was divided into three subgroups to examine different areas of the budget: staff, programs, and supplies. It was chaired by a teacher who had represented teachers in recent union negotiations with the board of education. Tentative recommendations were prepared and sent back to the 1,500 staff members for their review. In the meantime, the task force chair completed a cost analysis of the various suggestions and put the data in a form to disseminate to the community.

Recommendations were numbered; ranked as either high, medium, or low; and labeled for grade-level impact. Estimates were given on the savings anticipated and the number of students and teachers who would be affected. In addition, information to explain the ranking and suggestions for possible future action were included. Where feasible, dollar amounts were listed for reducing or eliminating a program.

Concurrent with these events, the board of education held workshops to study budget issues. The 13,000 students in the district met in quality circles to offer suggestions on how they could save money. And finally, 101 staff members received in-service training on how to run public meetings. They were to serve as conveners, presenters, and observers during the citizens' meetings on March 24.

The citizens' meetings were held in 10 elementary schools in the district. More than 2,000 people came to speak, listen, and react to the recommendations that had been developed at that point, and to provide their own recommendations for budget reductions.

By April 1982, the 15 building principals and nine district administrators were ready to meet in a two-day session to review suggestions and their implications. After these final deliberations, student, staff, and citizens' recommendations were submitted to the superintendent, who read all 4,000, according to those who worked with her. On April 5, 1982, the superintendent presented the final recommendations to the board of education. With only brief discussion, the board unanimously approved them. Thus, through public deliberation, the district met its targeted cuts, minimized disruptions in its operations, and avoided threats to morale.

Randall as State Commissioner of Minnesota Public Education

Minnesota Governor Rudy Perpich wanted a visionary proposal for primary and secondary education in the spring of 1985. Emerging from a bruising fight with educators during the 1985 legislative session over the issue of public school choice, he was eager to mend some fences. His initiative had gone down in defeat (except for one element of it called the postsecondary enrollment option), so he was eager to find common ground with his opponents. Educators had not liked his ideas for redesigning education. The adversarial legislative debate was unusual in a state known for its consensual politics. Hoping to begin a dialogue with educators, the governor instructed Commissioner Ruth Randall to convene a group to develop a visionary proposal for public education (Roberts and Bradley, 1991).

Commissioner Randall convened the Governor's Discussion Group in August 1985. Familiar with stakeholder management (Roberts and King, 1989), she opened participation to "all interested parties in the state." The discussion group eventually comprised 61 participants representing 24 stakeholder groups. On average, the stakeholder groups had 2.5 participating members, with sizes ranging from three groups with a single participant each, to one group with six participants. Each group designated a representative, and groups with multiple members each designated an alternate. The Governor's Discussion Group met regularly (at least monthly), and by February 1987 had held a total of 22 meetings. Meetings were generally two hours long but increased to three hours as the December 1986 deadline to complete the proposal approached. The commissioner was responsible for chairing and staffing these meetings. Two staff members from the Department of

Education assisted her. The commissioner also had the ultimate responsibility for constructing and mailing out the agenda, for which she actively solicited items.

At their first meetings, the discussion group divided the substance of its task into nine major topic areas. A planning model—including group process procedures and technical guidelines for preparing a policy document—was introduced later to facilitate a more structured approach to the work.

Several formal positions were established: stakeholder group member (representatives and alternates), convener, staff person, facilitator, and observer. Tasks assigned to the members ranged from reading various materials and papers, examining data and reports, and working together in small subgroups to prepare position papers, gather data, and make oral reports of the findings.

Mutually accepted norms and rules generally governed the participants' behavior. For example, the group often expressed a preference to work collectively and resisted suggestions that it split into independent subgroups. Whenever subgroups were formed to address a particular issue, they reported on their work to the entire discussion group at the next meeting.

The Governor's Discussion Group used various decision-making techniques to guide its process: a consensus approach (the commissioner's preferred mode) and voting. The commissioner's initial instructions to the group were to avoid debate and focus the deliberation on developing a consensus on problem definitions. Solutions were to be debated later.

Although the group experienced serious process problems in coming to agreement on their final recommendations to the governor, all group members eventually did sign the recommendations. The governor, in turn, incorporated two major elements of their proposal into his legislative package for the 1987 session: choice for at-risk students—those who had dropped out of school or those who were doing poorly enough to be in danger of dropping out—and the expansion of voluntary open enrollment (parent-student choice) to all public schools. In the following year, Minnesota passed the first public school choice program in the country, enabling all students in kindergarten through 12th grade to attend the public school of their choice by the 1990–1991 school year. The Governor's Discussion Group, said many observers, greased the skids for its passage.

THE STRUCTURE OF DELIBERATION

In both cases, four design elements were important parts of deliberation. Each deliberation began with a *strategic question,* which, if not resolved, would have had serious consequences for the leader and the organization (Bryson, 1996). Deliberation also required *stakeholder collaboration* (Gray, 1989), which gave participants an important, visible forum to address their common concerns as well as their differences. Third, deliberation featured *generative learning* rather than adaptive learning (Senge, 1990) and encouraged participants to move beyond their old assumptions to find new solutions and opportunities for action. Finally, the process was geared toward *executive action* of its authorizing agents, who were expected to follow through on its recommendations for change.

Strategic Issue Identification

Ruth Randall was clear about the strategic issues she faced. For the district it was how to manage the revenue shortfall without damaging the quality of education; for the state Department of Education, it was how to redesign Minnesota education to make it more supportive of the learning needs of children in a changing society. These strategic issues, posed as questions, began the deliberative process in both cases. They were useful devices to focus attention, direct energy, and concentrate organizational resources on matters that were central to their respective mandates and missions. If successfully resolved, they had the potential for leveraging further change. If unresolved, they had the potential for deepening the discord and distrust among the various stakeholders and reducing the willingness to support future deliberations.

Stakeholder Collaboration

The public deliberations in each instance met the necessary and sufficient conditions for collaboration to occur (Roberts and Bradley, 1991). They had a *transmutational purpose* defined as a "shared, goal-directed activity among participants to fashion a set of raw materials (objects, ideas, or social relations) into a developed product" (212). They had explicit and *voluntary membership,* i.e., the parties freely participated, knowing and agreeing upon who was involved and in what capacity (212). They had *organization* since the work was complex and elaborate, and involved a creative, goal-directed effort. The complexity also required them to establish a set of agreed-upon norms and rules to determine direction and action (212). They evolved an interactive process, defined as sustained reflexive interaction among the participants (212). And since both endeavors were creative and fraught with inevitable and unanticipated technical, organizational, and process difficulties, virtually all aspects of their activities were open to reexamination and reevaluation (212). Each collaboration also had a *temporal property* (212). As a temporary social form directed to a particular common end, the voluntary association was dissolved once the goal was accomplished. Each deliberation met the necessary and sufficient conditions for collaboration to occur (Table 13.1).

Generative Learning

Dealing with complex, "messy" problems requires collective learning, especially when information, knowledge, and expertise are no longer the sole province of agency leadership or organizational members. But attracting people with the information, knowledge, and expertise on a particular issue and getting them to work toward a common purpose is a challenging task. Stakeholders have different conceptual maps or mental models (Senge, 1990; Eden, 1989) that frame their issues: "We can protect jobs or the environment, but we cannot do both"; "I am an environmentalist"; "I am an advocate for a growing economy." In adversarial relationships, the natural inclination is for people to defend their positions, consider them as incontrovertible facts, and resist any attempt to treat them as assumptions. Adopting nonnegotiable and rigid stances, they become caught up in defensive routines (Argyris, 1985). But to participate in deliberations, people must be aware of their assumptions and be willing to hold them up for examination. Bohm describes it as hanging your assumptions up in front of you so that you can keep them accessible to questions and observations (Bohm, 1990). Detaching assumptions and thoughts from the person who holds them enables people to become observers of their own thinking and to become aware of the potential incoherence in their thoughts. The point is to hold a position rather than to be held by one (Bohm, 1990). Through this process, people can begin to treat one another like colleagues who are attempting to move toward a greater understanding of an issue. The goal becomes one of creating a common pool of meaning that goes beyond stating and defending one's interpretation of reality.

We see evidence of generative learning in the deliberations described in the case studies. Teachers, administrators, parents, students, and community members learned that in working together on budget reductions, they could avoid the rancor and divisiveness that often plague school districts forced to deal with cuts. Beyond that, they learned that their collective energies could unleash an innovative spirit throughout the district, which in time could produce additional experiments

Table 13.1

Collaboration: Data Summary

Setting Direction in State Educational Policy

Necessary Elements

Purpose
1. The Governor's Discussion Group shared the goal of developing a "visionary proposal" for state education.
2. The group agreed to work together to refashion divergent stakeholder ideas into a cohesive proposal to the governor.

Membership
1. Twenty-four stakeholder groups participated in the discussion group and were identified on the membership list.
2. Membership was voluntary.
3. Membership was open to all interested parties. Although there were some objections to the open door policy, the commissioner permitted all who were interested to attend. Membership was by mutual agreement. No participant was forced to leave the discussion group, and all participants eventually accepted the terms of participation.

Organization
1. Planned meetings were held on a regular basis with prepared agendas and items for future action.
2. Specialized tasks were assigned and performed: gathering data, reading materials, preparation of position papers, presentation of findings and recommendations, and working in subgroups.
3. A differentiated role structure was created with duties and rights assigned to regular group members and alternates, staff, and facilitators. Role assignment was explicit, although there was some ambiguity about whether the commissioner was the group's leader or facilitator. The ambiguity led to role conflicts throughout the deliberations.
4. Mutually accepted norms and rules generally governed participants' behavior, although some norms were occasionally violated. The most critical violation was in the final meeting during the last 30 minutes of the group's discussion. Items were added to the Visionary Proposal to accommodate one member, despite the fact that the group had voted to limit the introduction and discussion of any further materials.
5. Decisions affecting direction were made jointly. Various decision rules were used such as voting and consensus. However, it was sometimes unclear when these decision rules applied. The most serious instance occurred during the group's last 30 minutes of deliberations.

Sufficient Elements

Interactive Process
1. On an ongoing basis, members of the Governor's Discussion Group collectively evaluated what they were doing and how they were doing it. They scheduled retreats, special sessions, and reviews to assess their work.
2. The discussion group refined its ideas on an ongoing basis. They met when needed and were willing to question their assumptions. They changed agendas to reflect participant interest.
3. The discussion group preferred to have all members address each topic as a group. Subgroups did not make decisions, but reported back to the larger group for a discussion of the issues.

Temporal Property
1. The Governor's Discussion Group met for 18 months. The group completed its charge in February 1987.

(continued)

Table 13.1 *(continued)*

Reducing a School District Budget

Necessary Elements

Purpose
1. To deliberate as a community to develop recommendations on how to make budget cuts.

Membership
1. Membership was voluntary and extended to all interested parties.

Organization
1. December 1981—15 principals and 20 supervisors solicited recommendations from 1,500 employees on budget adjustments.
2. January 1982—45 teachers, administrators, and support staff were invited by the superintendent, building principals, and task force chairman to participate in a task force on budget adjustments to categorize and rank recommendations from staff members. Three subgroups were formed: staff, programs, and supplies.
3. January 1982—Tentative recommendations were sent back to 1,500 staff members for review. The task force chairman was charged with doing a cost analysis of the various suggestions and with putting data in a form that could be disseminated to the parents and citizens of the community. The task force was reconvened to prepare a final set of recommendations.
4. March 1982—Board of Education workshops were held to study budget issues. Quality circles were set up in 727 classrooms and suggestions on how to save money were gathered. In-service workshops on running public meetings were held.
5. March 24, 1982—A citizens' meeting produced a packet of recommendations, which included suggestions on reducing or eliminating programs, staff, supplies, and administrators. It was taken to parents and citizens for their reactions and suggestions. Two thousand people participated with 101 staff members serving as conveners, presenters, and observers in 10 elementary schools in the district.
6. April 1982—15 building principals and nine district administrators met in two-day long sessions to review suggestions and discuss implications. All recommendations from students, staff, and citizens went to the superintendent. She received 4,000 written responses to review. The superintendent announced budget reductions to the staff.
7. April 1982—Recommendations were unanimously approved by the Board of Education with minimal discussion.

Sufficient Elements

Interactive Process
1. Iteration of data among employees, task force members, community participants, and students before final recommendations were made to the superintendent and Board of Education.

Temporal Property
1. Deliberation extended over a four-month period from December 1981 through March 1982.

Source: Roberts and Bradley, 1991, 223–224.

and learning (Roberts, 1985). Participants in the state-level deliberations were able to agree on a visionary proposal for state education that signaled a major shift in educational policy, not only for the state, but for the nation as well (Roberts and King, 1996).

Executive Action

Deliberation prepares the ground for action. It sets up an expectation that something will change as a consequence of the group's learning and efforts. As we see in both cases, executive action did follow. The school board unanimously adopted Superintendent Randall's recommendations to reduce the budget in the first case, and Governor Perpich championed the visionary plan of the Governor's Discussion Group in the legislature in the second. The Minnesota legislature passed the first statewide choice legislation in the country, thanks in no small measure to the discussion group's proposal. Both policy changes set the tone and shaped the decisions for the administrative actions that followed.

The Deliberative Process

Crafting policy and setting direction through public deliberation challenge public executives in a number of ways. First is the need to realign expectations among participants and observers of the deliberations. People must understand that the point of deliberation is not to prompt a political debate but to engender learning. The goal is not to establish the superiority of one's views, drown out the opposition, or manipulate people to support one's cause. The essence of public deliberation is the pooling of information, resources, and skills to deal with complex social problems for which there are no right answers. Gathering and assessing information, learning from one another, and making value judgments and trade-offs characterize the effort at its best. Power plays, end runs, and coercive tactics do not. Although many participants and observers will struggle to learn the new rules, others will attempt to subvert them. Setting the norms for a public deliberation is an important first step in the learning process for both observers and participants, and knowing how to deal with the power plays that inevitably surface is the second. Randall's appointment of a union negotiator to organize the school district's deliberations on the budget signaled a cooperative approach to problem-solving. Keeping a union representative at the table when he threatened to leave the Governor's Discussion Group and fight out the differences in the legislature is one of the many ways she prevented end runs of the process.

Public executives are also called on to assume new roles, the first of which is to become better problem-finders (Livingston, 1971). Problem-finding at the executive level should not be confused with problem-finding at other management levels. Bureaus are rich in problems. Top executives must learn to focus on strategic problems central to the agency's mission that are likely to threaten its direction. Finding such problems requires distinguishing between day-to-day events and the underlying dynamics of change. It relies on an ability to see interrelationships and processes, not just things and objects. It means learning where to find the high leverage point so that the executive can take small, well-focused actions to produce significant, enduring changes. Figuring out where one has the leverage is important for making lasting improvements in the system (Senge, 1990).

Randall understood how to find the important problems. As superintendent, she held district meetings and invited noted futurists to alert staff and teachers to the trends and forces shaping education. In-service training then gave personnel the opportunity to explore the implications for education in the district. Exploration, in turn, unleashed an enormous amount of creative activity (Roberts, 1985). As commissioner, and self-proclaimed change agent, Randall launched an effort to help a conservative, bureaucratic state agency redefine and restructure itself. Organized around teams and project groups, it encouraged rather than discouraged innovations occurring in the districts.

Executives such as Randall also take on the role of co-learner as they guide stakeholders through a deliberative process. Gone are the notions of heroic management, when the executive is supposed to know all, be all, and do all. Freed from having to provide the right answers, they understand that a good part of their job is to find the right questions on which to focus agency attention, and invite public participation in the collective learning experience around those questions (Randall,

1987). Relaxing requirements for control, they invite others' viewpoints and trust that some new solutions will surface and learning will take place. Public deliberation requires some humility in dealing with the many tensions of public management.

Such a reorientation in leadership is not without its risks. Randall as commissioner was criticized for not being decisive and not knowing how to run proper meetings. Operating with different models of executive behavior, some participants felt she did not exercise proper control or appropriately use *Robert's Rules of Order.* Furthermore, she irritated some stakeholders by allowing anyone to participate in the deliberations, rather than restricting membership to those who represented "legitimate" groups. Her insistence on a consensus alienated and frustrated those who did not understand the point of deliberation. Other executives have faced similar criticisms. William Ruckelshaus, as head of the Environmental Protection Agency, was chided by the press and the public for the deliberations his agency sponsored in Tacoma, Washington. One area resident accused him of copping out of his responsibilities (Scott, 1990, 165). Another complained, "We elected people to run our government, we don't expect them to turn around and ask us to run it for them" (167). Said another, "These issues are very complex and the public is not sophisticated enough to make these decisions. This is not to say that EPA doesn't have an obligation to inform the public, but information is one thing—defaulting its legal mandate is another" (167).

Executives can survive this criticism, but it is important for them to continuously explain their new role as convener and facilitator of learning to all parties. Unless stakeholders understand that the executive is managing a process, not a solution, they will have inappropriate expectations for executive behavior as well as their own. Setting expectations also includes helping participants develop their own process skills that are compatible with learning—listening, inquiry, self-reflection, conflict management, bringing to the surface and testing mental models, and systems thinking (Senge, 1990). Staff support for this endeavor plays an important part, since it is difficult for executives to be solely responsible for all the tasks associated with the deliberation—teaching, learning, facilitating, and designing. But as staff support grows, so do the costs. According to one source, roughly 30 people from the regional office worked full time for four months on the EPA case in Tacoma, Washington, making the process "terrifically costly and time-consuming" (Scott, 1990, 169). Randall had 101 staff members receive in-service training on how to conduct public meetings so they could serve as conveners, presenters, and observers for just one citizens' meeting (Roberts, 1985). These costs can appear to be especially burdensome when a deliberation produces little agreement, or worse, intensifies gridlock. To keep things in perspective, stakeholders need to be reminded of the hidden costs of not having deliberations, such as increasing alienation and distrust of government and higher costs of "adversarial legalism" with its protracted court battles in defense of stakeholder interests (Kagan, 1991; Kelman, 1992).

Public executives also take on the role of steward for democratic principles and institutions. Deliberations can help people examine the premises and values on which their actions are based and can stimulate the discovery of alternative visions of the future. Such experience broadens society's range of potential solutions to complex issues and thus opens up the potential for learning. From Reich's perspective, "in a democratic form of government, such learning, and the deliberation it implies, is a prerequisite to everything else" (1990, 175). Randall understood the deeper meaning of the processes she set in motion when she asked district members to deliberate on budget reductions and state members to build a vision for the future. More was at stake than a budget crisis and union support for the governor. She was preparing the district and the state to deal with larger questions: What was education? Who should do the educating? How should we educate? When and where should we educate? For what purpose should we educate? (Randall, 1987).

Stewards in a democratic society understand that their job is more than managing an issue, making decisions, and implementing them. Their "role is to manage an ongoing process of deliberation and education—a by-product of which is a series of mutual adaptations, agreements, compromises, and, on occasion, stalemates" (Reich, 1990, 8). They help participants explore where they have come from, where they are going, and how they will get there. They understand that a "public servant is in the business of governing. Democracy is not a constraint on [one's] effectiveness as a public servant; it is an aspect of the job itself. Part of [the] job as effective public servant, therefore, is to sustain, even strengthen, democratic institutions" (Reich, 1990, 6).

CONCLUSION

Public deliberation, as a cornerstone of the generative approach to general management in the public sector, is an emerging form of social interaction used to set direction for government agencies. This paper has highlighted some of its more salient features as reflected in two case studies—one at the local level concerning budget cuts for a school district, and the second at the state level where the issue was setting direction for educational policy.

In both cases, we see the heavy requirements the collective process places on all participants. It asks for patience, trust in self and others, respect for those whose ideas are different, ability to see a whole system and its interdependent parts, and suspension of self-interest for the common good. Whether individuals can rise to the occasion or whether the occasion calls for special kinds of people to make the deliberation successful is an important question. Developmental theory in psychology suggests that not all people have the capacity for thinking in systems terms, appreciating different world views, or dealing with ambiguity, complexity, and paradox (Loevinger, 1976; Kohlberg, 1976). Differences among participants in a deliberative process may make it difficult to share models, participate in collaborative efforts, learn from one another, and develop a common vision of the future. Furthermore, developmental theory suggests that not only do people have different perspectives on life, but those at lower stages of development are unlikely to understand and appreciate the logic and world views of persons half a stage beyond them in the developmental sequence (Loevinger, 1976). Deliberation is a sophisticated form of social interaction. Success may depend on the developmental mix of participants in the process. We need to know whether deliberation is a process that works for everyone or whether its special requirements limit participation to a select few. Each of these questions has far-reaching implications for the future of public deliberations and the civic discovery it champions.

Outcomes of a deliberative process are not always successful; the potential is there for gridlock as well as consensus. Consequently, we should not underestimate the potential costs to executives who take this activist approach. Failure is visible and executives risk public embarrassment (Kaboolian, 1995). Knowing more about the conditions under which deliberations are likely to be successful may make it a more attractive option for executives to pursue. We need to know how to choose participants, what the practical limits of their involvement will be, how to fund participation, and how to protect the public interest if partisan political attacks threaten the process. Research along these lines has begun, but more is needed (Thomas, 1995). Other efforts have gone into designing systems to support group decision-making to assist executives in dealing with messy problems. One such support system, called COPE (Eden, 1989), includes software to help people sketch out what they think about particular issues in such a way that two or more individual "cognitive maps" can be merged to give a picture of the group's thinking about the topic. Decision aids such as these have the potential for supporting the consensus-building process. Given the explosion of information technology, these options may offer great promise in the future.

Ultimately, the use of deliberation rests not on technology, but on will. It draws on the belief that the public has a right to participate more fully in decisions that affect it and that executives have a responsibility to ensure that participation is productive. Moreover, executives may have little choice in the matter. The public is seeking greater participation, and those who oppose that force do so at their peril and the peril of their programs. Executives can use public deliberation as a strategy for inclusion or a strategy for self-protection, but use it they will if the growing number of advocates is any indication of where the public is headed (McLagan and Nel, 1995).

NOTES

1. I am indebted to Bradley and Pribram (1997) for their distinction between efficiency (internal operations) and effectiveness (external adaptation). The terms also are employed to capture managerial concern for bureau performance (Brown and Pyers, 1988), and characterize the debate in public administration over bureaucratic responsibility and responsiveness (Burke, 1986; Cooper, 1990; Kearney and Sinha, 1988; Rourke, 1992; Stivers, 1994). The responsible bureaucrat is an efficient, technical expert who autonomously carries out her duties as a professional. The responsive bureaucrat is effective by being accountable to the public, anticipating its political concerns, and adapting bureau strategies accordingly (Stivers, 1994).

2. The generative approach parallels White's (1989) search for a "third approach" to governance. A comparison between the generative approach and White's third approach is beyond the scope of this paper, but it should be noted that both are concerned with encouraging responsiveness to demands, developing mechanisms to gather information, ensuring that demands and preferences are informed, and learning from those closest to policy outcomes.

REFERENCES

Argyris, C. (1985). *Strategy, Change, and Defensive Routines*. Boston: Pitman.
Barrett, P. (1995). "Creating Appreciative Learning Cultures." *Organizational Dynamics* 24(1): 36–49.
Behn, R. (1988). "Management by Groping Along." *Journal of Policy Analysis and Management* 7(4): 643–663.
Block, P. (1993). *Stewardship: Choosing Service over Self-Interest*. San Francisco: Berrett-Koehler.
Bohm, D. (1990). *On Dialogue*. Cambridge, MA: Pegasus Communications.
Bradley, R.T. and K.H. Pribram (1997). "Communication and Optimality in Biosocial Collectives." In D.S. Levine and W.S. Elsberry, eds., *Optimality in Biological and Artificial Networks*. Hillsdale, NJ: Lawrence Erlbaum Associates.
Brown, R.E. and J.B. Pyers (1988). "Putting Teeth into the Efficiency and Effectiveness of Public Services." *Public Administration Review* 48(3): 735–742.
Bryson, J. (1996). *Strategic Planning for Public and Nonprofit Organizations*. 2d ed. San Francisco: Jossey-Bass.
Bryson, J. and B. Crosby (1992). *Leadership for the Common Good*. San Francisco: Jossey-Bass.
Bunker, B. and B. Alban, eds. (1992). *Journal of Applied Behavioral Science, Special Issue: Large Group Interventions* 28(4): 473–479.
Burke, J.P. (1986). *Bureaucratic Responsibility*. Baltimore: Johns Hopkins University Press.
Cooper, R.L. (1990). *The Responsible Administrator,* 3d ed. San Francisco: Jossey-Bass.
Eden, C. (1989). "Using Cognitive Mapping for Strategic Options Development and Analysis (SODA)." In J. Rosenhead, ed., *Rational Analysis for a Problematic World*. New York: John Wiley & Sons, 21–42.
Fox, C.J. and C.J. Miller (1995). *Postmodern Public Administration: Toward Discourse*. Thousand Oaks, CA: Sage.
Gray, B. (1989). *Collaborating*. San Francisco: Jossey-Bass.
Handy, C. (1995). *The Age of Paradox*. Boston: Harvard Business School Press.
Kaboolian, L. (1995). "Dialogue between Advocates and Executive Agencies: New Roles for Public Managers." Paper presented at the third Public Management Research Conference. University of Kansas, Lawrence, Kansas.
Kagan, R. A. (1991). "Adversarial Legalism and American Government." *Journal of Policy Analysis and Management* 10(3): 369–406.

Kearny, R.C. and C. Sinha (1988). "Professionalism and Bureaucratic Responsiveness: Conflict or Compatibility." *Public Administration Review* 48(1): 571–579.

Kelman, S. (1992). "Adversary and Cooperationist Institutions for Conflict Resolution in Public Policymaking." *Journal of Policy Analysis and Management* 11(2): 178–206.

Kohlberg, L. (1976). *Collected Papers on Moral Development and Moral Education.* Cambridge, MA: Center for Moral Education.

Lindblom, C.E. (1959). "The Science of Muddling Through." *Public Administration Review* 19(1): 79–88.

——— (1979). "Still Muddling, Not Yet Through." *Public Administration Review* 39(6): 517–526.

Livingston, J.S. (1971). "The Myth of the Well-Educated Manager." *HBR* (January/February): 79–89.

Loevinger, J. (1976). *Ego Development: Conception and Theories.* San Francisco: Jossey-Bass.

McLagan, P. and C. Nel (1995). *The Age of Participation: New Governance for the Workplace and the World.* San Francisco: Berrett-Koehler.

March, J.G. (1995). "Should Higher Education Be More Efficient?" *Stanford Educator.* Stanford, CA: School of Education News (Fall): 3,5,12.

Mintzberg, H. (1996a). "The Machine Organization." In H. Mintzberg and J.B. Quinn, eds., *The Strategy Process.* Upper Saddle River, NJ: Prentice Hall.

——— (1996b). "The Innovative Organization." In H. Mintzberg and J.B. Quinn, eds., *The Strategy Process.* Upper Saddle River, NJ: Prentice Hall.

Osborne, D. and T. Gaebler (1992). *Reinventing Government.* Reading, MA: Addison-Wesley.

Quinn, J.B., P. Anderson, and S. Finkelstein (1996). "New Forms of Organizing." In H. Mintzberg and J.B. Quinn, eds., *The Strategy Process.* Upper Saddle River, NJ: Prentice Hall, 350–362.

Randall, R.E. (1987). "The Minnesota Dialogue on Education." *Phi Delta Kappan* (March): 539–543.

Reich, R.B. (1990). *Public Management in a Democratic Society.* Englewood Cliffs, NJ: Prentice Hall.

Roberts, N.C. (1985). "Transforming Leadership: A Process of Collective Action." *Human Relations* 38(11): 1023–1046.

Roberts, N.C. and R.T. Bradley (1991). "Stakeholder Collaboration and Innovation: A Study of Policy Initiation at the State Level." *Journal of Applied Behavioral Science* 27(2): 209–227.

Roberts, N.C. and P.J. King (1989). "Stakeholder Audit Goes Public." *Organizational Dynamics* (Winter): 63–79.

——— (1996). *Transforming Public Policy: Dynamics of Policy Entrepreneurship and Innovation.* San Francisco: Jossey-Bass.

Rourke, F.E. (1992). "Responsiveness and Neutral Competence in American Bureaucracy." *Public Administration Review* 52(6): 539–546.

Schein, E. (1993). "On Dialogue, Culture, and Organizational Learning." *Organizational Dynamics* 2(2): 40–51.

Scott, E. (1990). "Managing Environmental Risks: The Case of ASARCO." In R.B. Reich, ed., *Public Management in a Democratic Society.* Englewood Cliffs, NJ: Prentice Hall.

Senge, P. (1990). *The Fifth Discipline: The Art and Practice of the Learning Organization.* New York: Doubleday.

Stivers, C. (1994). "The Listening Bureaucrat: Responsiveness in Public Administration." *Public Administration Review* 54(4): 364–369.

Thomas, J.C. (1995). *Public Participation in Public Decisions: New Skills and Strategies for Public Managers.* San Francisco: Jossey-Bass.

Webster's Third New International Dictionary (1971). Springfield, MA: G. & C. Merriam Company.

Weisbord, M.R. (1992). *Discovering Common Ground.* San Francisco: Berrett-Koehler.

Weisbord, M.R. and S. Janoff (1995). *Future Search.* San Francisco: Berrett-Koehler.

White, L.G. (1988). "Public Management in a Pluralistic Arena." *Public Administration Review* 48(3): 735–742.

CHAPTER 14

THE RELATIONSHIP BETWEEN CITIZEN INVOLVEMENT IN THE BUDGET PROCESS AND CITY STRUCTURE AND CULTURE

CAROL EBDON

Citizen participation in the governance process is widely encouraged by academics and professional organizations and is a popular conference topic. Key public policy decisions are made during the public budgeting process, so this would appear to be an important opportunity for meaningful citizen participation. Yet, little is known about how and when citizens are involved in the budget process. This study uses a 1996 International City/County Management Association (ICMA) survey to explore the extent to which a variety of participatory mechanisms are used in the budget process in U.S. council-manager cities.

Does citizen involvement have equal value in all cities? Research on city form of government and political culture suggests that government structure and city culture are affected by characteristics of the community. If so, then these factors also might affect the need or desire for citizen participation. Cities with more representative structures (elected mayors or city council members elected by district rather than at large) also might be more inclined toward open decision processes. Heterogeneous cities generally have higher levels of political conflict, so they might benefit more from citizen input to help resolve these conflicts. Elazar's (1994) model of political cultures also implies that citizen involvement is more likely in cities with certain cultures. This study investigates the relationships between these structural and cultural factors and the use of citizen involvement in the budget process.

The next section discusses the literature relating to citizen participation and budgeting, and it develops the hypotheses about the relationship between structural/cultural factors and citizen participation in budgeting. The study methodology is then described, and this is followed by the findings of the analysis. Conclusions are presented in the final section.

STRUCTURE, CULTURE, AND BUDGETING

Scholars are increasingly advocating an expanded role for citizens in the governance process (Box, 1998; King, Feltey, & Susel, 1998; Schachter, 1997; Thomas, 1995). Professional organizations also support this effort; for example, the ICMA *Declaration of Ideals* calls for citizen involvement (ICMA, 1999). The goal is for citizens to have an active role in the process and not just be passive "consumers" of government services. In addition, participation is seen as a way in which to educate citizens about what government does and why.

The literature demonstrates the positive effects of citizen participation and the wide variety of participation mechanisms. Citizens in cities with more participation were found to be less cynical about local government (Berman, 1997). The city of Dayton, Ohio, uses community boards to improve neighborhoods; with their support, the city has not lost a tax election in 20 years (Gurwitt, 1992). Other successful cases include the use of citizen surveys (Watson, Juster, & Johnson, 1991) and citizen panels to address particular issues (Kathlene & Martin, 1991).

Little research has been conducted on the use of participation in the public budgeting process, even though important policy and resource allocation decisions are made in this process. One textbook does address the potential benefits of citizen involvement; Bland and Rubin (1997) state that involvement might make citizens more aware of the complexity and competition inherent in budgeting and also might increase trust in the way in which public funds are used. This is supported by a case in which public deliberation was successfully used to make difficult school budget reductions (Roberts, 1997).

But citizen participation is not necessarily a panacea. It is not always easy to get people involved or to ensure that participants are representative of the community. Also, expert professionals might worry about the results of sharing decision making for complex issues with the public (Thomas, 1995). Officials also might be reluctant to include citizens in the budget process for fear that it will increase spending expectations beyond the affordable level. In addition, competition among participants might make elected officials' decisions more difficult rather than less so (Bland & Rubin, 1997).

The perceptions of city officials, then, regarding the relative benefits and disadvantages of participation might affect its use in the budget process. Use of citizen participation also might be influenced by characteristics of the community. Researchers have suggested that government structure and culture vary among cities due to specific characteristics. These structural and cultural differences might be expected to be related to the extent to which citizen participation is needed or used in the budget process.

Methods of electing mayors and city council members have been changing in cities with the council-manager form of government. Reformers traditionally recommended that these cities appoint a mayor from among the city council and elect city council members at large to represent the interest of the entire community. City council members are increasingly elected by districts, however, to enhance minority representation (Alozie & Manganaro, 1993; Ebdon & Brucato, 2000; Renner, 1987). Mayors in council-manager cities also now frequently are elected at large to increase accountability and leadership (Gurwitt, 1993). These election method changes indicate an emphasis on citizen representation. At the same time, however, they also might lead to increased conflicts among council members representing different districts and between the mayor and city council with separate power bases (Whitaker & Jenne, 1995). Cities with at-large mayoral elections or district city council elections might have two reasons to involve citizens in the budget process more formally than in other cities: as a response to citizens' demands for increased representation and to use direct citizen input to help resolve conflicts among elected officials.

In addition to structural factors, the cultural diversity of the community is expected to be related to the use of citizen participation. Heterogeneity often leads to increased political conflicts due to varying group demands (Protasel, 1988). Larger cities and those with greater racial diversity, for example, would fall into this category. "The more heterogeneous a community, the more importance its citizens will place on representation—both on getting their substantive interests realized and [on] finding access for their views" (Nalbandian, 1991, p. 90). One way in which to obtain this access is through citizen participation mechanisms. Therefore, heterogeneous cities are expected to use participation more than are homogeneous cities.

Finally, participation might vary across regions of the country due to differences in political cultures. Elazar (1972, 1994) identifies three major political subcultures in the United States based largely on migration patterns. According to this model, the accepted roles of citizens in governance vary across the three cultures. Roughly speaking, the northern portion of the country has a *moralistic* culture, which views politics as a positive force for the public good in which all members should be involved. The *individualistic* culture is largely found across the middle portion of the country and is based on the marketplace view of government in which politics is a business and is based on favors. The *traditionalistic* culture is found in the southern portion of the country and is based on a paternalistic approach to government in which only the elite are expected to be active as citizens. Based on this theory, cities with a moralistic culture would be expected to have the highest levels of citizen involvement in budget decisions, followed by the individualistic culture, with traditionalistic cities having the lowest levels of participation.

Elazar's (1994) model has been widely debated. Extensive tests on a variety of topics have had mixed results. Scholars have raised concerns about how well the categories describe these regions and whether they hold over time (see, e.g., Gendzel, 1997; Thompson, Ellis, & Wildavsky, 1990). However, the model continues to be used to explain cross-state variations in areas such as local personnel practices (McCurdy, 1998), voter registration laws and turnout (King, 1994), political party activism (Paddock, 1997), and human service delivery systems (Bielefeld & Corbin, 1996). As with those studies, Elazar's model is used here due to a lack of other models to explain regional variations.

This study looks at the use of citizen participation in the budget process. Although participation is considered important by scholars and professional organizations, little empirical research has been conducted on involvement in the budget process. Based on prior research, perceived demand and need for citizen input can vary across cities based on institutional structure, degree of heterogeneity, and political culture. The next section details the methodology used to test these hypotheses.

METHODOLOGY

The study used a 1996 ICMA survey on roles and relationships of local government officials. The survey was sent to 2,787 managers in cities and counties with the council-manager form of government and had a 47% response rate. The current study deleted responses for counties and for cities with missing data for applicable variables, resulting in a sample size of 1,150 cities.

As discussed earlier, citizen participation in the budget process was expected to vary across cities based on three factors: structure, cultural diversity/homogeneity, and political culture. Structure was measured here as the election method for the mayor and the city council, with higher participation expected in cities with more representative election methods, that is, at-large mayoral elections and district city council elections. Two variables were used to measure homogeneity: population and percentage of the population that is White. Greater use of participation was expected in more heterogeneous cities, that is, larger cities and those with larger proportions of non-Whites. Finally, city political cultures were coded according to Elazar's (1994) model. The highest levels of participation were expected in cities with a moralistic culture, followed by individualistic cities, with traditionalistic cities having the least participation.

Citizen participation in the budget process was determined by answers to two of the survey questions. The first question asked how often the manager uses each of five different methods to develop the recommended budget. The response scale was 1 to 4, with 1 = *never* and 4 = *always*. Two of the listed methods dealt with citizen input:

- Gather community input throughout the year through surveys, citizen committees, or other methods and use that information to determine community needs during budget preparation.
- Hold town or neighborhood-based meetings specifically to solicit citizen input.

A second part of the question then asked which three of the five methods the manager felt are most effective for budget preparation.

The second question asked the manager to describe how often the elected body involves citizens when considering the proposed budget. Again, five options were included with the same 4-point scale. The manager also was asked which three options were the most effective methods of budget consideration. The options were as follows:

- Formal recommendations from citizen groups or committees
- Coordination with local media to highlight the community input process
- Sending special public information materials to residents to explain the budget process while it is being considered by the elected body
- Making the proposed budget document or summary available to the public prior to adoption
- Sending the proposed budget summary to residents for comments during the consideration process

In total, seven methods of citizen involvement were identified in the survey. The response scale was collapsed to create a dichotomous variable representing whether or not the method is used.[1] Relationships between participation and the structural and cultural variables were determined by cross-tabulations, with chi-square tests to determine statistical significance.

The study is somewhat limited due to the use of an existing data set. First, all of the cities surveyed use the council-manager form of government; different results might emerge in cities with other forms of government. Second, other important participation mechanisms might be used that were not included in the survey questions. Third, the response format did not provide any information relative to the reasons for either the use or the perceived effectiveness of these methods. Fourth, the data are a few years old, and the results might have changed during the interim. Despite these issues, these data are useful because so little empirical research is available in this area. This study is an initial exploration into the use of citizen participation in the budget process.

FINDINGS

To what extent do council-manager cities involve citizens in the budget process? Table 14.1 shows the percentages of respondents who use the seven methods of participation detailed in the ICMA survey as well as the percentages that consider the method to be one of the three most effective methods of budget preparation or consideration.

The participation methods are classified according to whether they occur during the budget preparation or budget consideration stage. Within each stage, the methods are listed by the degree of actual citizen input they allow. Holding meetings prior to the development of the budget gives citizens a

Table 14.1

Actual Use and Perceived Effectiveness of Citizen Participation
(percentages of respondents)

	Actual use	Perceived as effective
Budget preparation		
Meetings prior to development	17.7	8.2
Citizen input throughout year	50.1	54.3
Budget consideration		
Formal groups	31.8	40.3
Send budget summary for comments	10.7	8.1
Media coordination of input process	33.3	53.9
Send information to citizens	20.2	30.3
Budget available to public	94.7	87.6

Note: $N = 1,150$ for the study. However, the n for each cell varies slightly due to missing information.

greater chance for dialogue specific to the budget than does receiving citizen input on various issues throughout the year. Most of the methods during the consideration stage primarily involve one-way communication from city officials rather than seeking citizen input. The exception to this is the first method, whereby officials solicit formal recommendations from citizen groups.

Citizen input apparently is not part of the budget preparation process in most of these council-manager cities. Just over one half of the responding cities gather general community input during the year through mechanisms such as surveys, but only 17.7% hold meetings specifically related to the budget process prior to development. An additive index also was calculated (data not shown). In the budget preparation stage, 46.7% of the cities did not use either of the two methods, 38.9% used one, and only 14.3% used both.

Nearly all of the cities (94.7%) make the proposed budget available to the public, but other participation methods during the consideration process are used by one third or fewer of these cities. Formal recommendations from citizen groups, the only budget consideration method involving actual citizen input, is used by only 31.8% of the respondents. The additive index for the budget consideration stage (data not shown) indicates that 41.1% use just one of these mechanisms, with an additional 29.0% using two. Only 9.1% use four or five of the methods.

It is possible that managers are simply constrained from using citizen participation to the extent that they would prefer, but based on the perceived effectiveness of the mechanisms, this does not generally appear to be the case. For example, less than one half of the managers in cities using public budget meetings prior to preparation believe that this is one of the most effective methods. The managers would like to see greater use of the media, however; more than one half of the managers believe that this is an effective method, whereas only one third of the cities currently are using it. Overall, however, the implication is that these cities do not use the mechanisms more because they are not perceived as being the most effective methods for budgeting.

Most of these participation methods are not used widely. Next, we explore whether this use varies among cities based on structural or cultural factors. Table 14.2 looks at differences in participation based on the mayoral selection method.

Cities with mayors elected at large were expected to have higher levels of participation because this method emphasizes representation of the public. This holds true for all methods except for the use of formal group recommendations to the city council. However, the difference is not statistically significant for any of the seven methods, so this hypothesis is not supported by the data.

Table 14.2

Use of Citizen Participation Method by Mayoral Election Method
(percentages of respondents)

	Mayor elected at large	Other mayoral selection method
Budget preparation		
Meetings prior to development	18.4	16.0
Citizen input throughout year	51.4	48.8
Budget consideration		
Formal groups	31.0	33.2
Send budget summary for comments	11.5	9.2
Media coordination of input process	34.1	32.5
Send information to citizens	21.4	18.7
Budget available to public	94.9	94.8
n	759	363

Note: N = 1,150 for the study. However, the *n* for each cell varies due to missing information.

Table 14.3

Use of Citizen Participation Method by City Council Election Method
(percentages of respondents)

	Council elected by district or mixed	Council elected at large
Budget preparation		
Meetings prior to development	19.4	17.0
Citizen input throughout year*	54.5	48.3
Budget consideration		
Formal groups	29.6	32.7
Send budget summary for comments	10.0	11.0
Media coordination of input process	35.5	32.5
Send information to citizens	22.9	19.1
Budget available to public	93.3	95.4
n	348	799

Note: N = 1,150 for the study. However, the *n* for each cell varies slightly due to missing information.
*$p < .10$.

Table 14.3 shows differences in participation based on city council election methods. The cities with district elections were expected to have greater use than those with at-large elections. This is the case for four of the seven methods, but the difference is statistically significant in only one case. District city council elections appear to be related to the greater use of obtaining citizen input throughout the year through surveys and other methods. Interestingly, this input occurs before the budget is submitted to the city council.

Tables 14.4, 14.5, and 14.6 relate to the relationship between participation and cultural factors. The first of these is size, which is a measure of homogeneity. Table 14.4 shows the use of these mechanisms in four different population ranges.[2]

Table 14.4

Use of Citizen Participation Method by Population (percentages of respondents)

	> 100,000	50,000–100,000	10,000–50,000	< 10,000
Budget preparation				
Meetings prior to development**	31.9	19.6	17.1	15.7
Citizen input throughout year***	72.5	60.8	51.1	43.1
Budget consideration				
Formal groups***	53.6	35.3	29.6	30.3
Send budget summary for comments	18.5	12.1	11.1	8.8
Media coordination of input process**	50.7	36.3	32.7	30.7
Send information to citizens***	44.1	29.4	16.9	18.3
Budget available to public	97.1	96.1	94.7	94.2
n	69	102	527	452

Note: $N = 1,150$ for the study. However, the *n* for each cell varies slightly due to missing information. **$p < .05$. ***$p < .01$.

Table 14.5

Use of Citizen Participation Method by Whites as Percentages of Population
(percentages of respondents, $N = 286$)

	< 50% White	50–70% White	70–90% White	> 90% White
Budget preparation				
Meetings prior to development	14.3	23.5	30.3	16.7
Citizen input throughout year	71.4	56.9	65.0	57.7
Budget consideration				
Formal groups	28.6	27.5	42.7	41.3
Send budget summary for comments	14.3	12.2	15.7	7.8
Media coordination of input process	14.3	41.2	43.5	36.5
Send information to citizens	14.3	32.0	25.8	28.8
Budget available to public	85.7	94.1	96.0	97.1
n	7	51	124	104

Larger cities were expected to have higher levels of discord regarding budget priorities. Citizen participation could be used to help work toward consensus, so it was expected to be used more in larger cities. This clearly is the case; larger cities are more likely to use all of the methods, and the differences are statistically significant in five of the seven methods. Council-manager cities with populations greater than 100,000 are twice as likely as cities with populations less than 10,000 to have citizen budget meetings (31.9% vs. 15.7%), to send out budget summaries for comments (18.5% vs. 8.8%), and to send information to citizens (44.1% vs. 18.3%).

Heterogeneity also was operationalized here based on racial diversity. Cities with lower levels of minorities were expected to have lower levels of conflict and, therefore, less need for citizen participation to resolve issues (Table 14.5).

Table 14.6

Use of Citizen Participation Method by Political Culture
(percentages of respondents)

	Moralist	Individualist	Traditionalist
Budget preparation			
Meetings prior to development**	17.2	14.2	21.6
Citizen input throughout year	51.3	45.3	52.8
Budget consideration			
Formal groups*	33.7	26.5	33.9
Send budget summary for comments**	12.6	6.6	11.6
Media coordination of input process*	34.6	28.4	36.0
Send information to citizens**	22.7	15.5	20.8
Budget available to public*	96.0	92.6	94.9
n	508	309	333

Note; $N = 1,150$ for the study. However, the *n* for each cell varies slightly due to missing information.
*$p < .10$. **$p < .05$.

The data related to race were not included in the survey and were readily available only for cities with populations greater than 25,000, so the sample size for Table 14.5 is only 286.[3] There is no clear pattern in the use of the participation methods related to racial composition, and the differences are not statistically significant. Cities with the lowest percentages of White residents are not more inclined to use citizen participation.

The final hypothesis relates to Elazar's (1994) political culture model. Cities with a moralistic culture were expected to have higher use of citizen participation, followed by individualistic cities, with traditionalistic cities having the least use of participation. The results are shown in Table 14.6.

The cities with a moralistic culture do have the highest use of four of the seven methods and are the second highest users of the other three. All but one of the differences are statistically significant. However, the individualistic cities, expected to have the second highest use of citizen participation, actually have the lowest level in all seven cases, whereas traditionalistic participation is higher than expected. This does not appear to be consistent with the theory. This might reflect problems with the theory. It is possible, for example, that culture in traditionalistic cities has changed as many southern cities have been forced to open up their political processes through mechanisms such as district city council elections. Another possibility is that the application of the theory is flawed; individualistic cities might be more likely to rely on individual communications between city officials and citizens rather than on group or formal methods of involvement.

Overall, the findings of the analysis are mixed. Council-manager cities with more representative election methods were expected to be more likely to involve citizens in the budget process, but that was not found to be the case. Perhaps the form of government is more important in this regard than are election methods. For example, Rubin (1992) found that more reformed council-manager cities adopt budget reforms more quickly than do less reformed mayor-council cities. Further research might find differences in participation levels between cities with the council-manager and mayor-council forms.

Stronger relationships were found between citizen participation and cultural factors. Cities with different political cultures had significantly different percentages of use of these participation mechanisms, although the order of use among the three cultures was not entirely as expected. Use of citizen participation was not found to vary with degree of racial diversity, but this might be due to the smaller sample used for this part of the analysis. Population does significantly relate to the use of these budget participation methods, however. Larger council-manager cities are much more likely to use the mechanisms than are smaller cities.

CONCLUSIONS

The use of this preexisting data set limits the conclusions and generalizability of the analysis. The survey was conducted in 1996 and included only cities with the council-manager form of government; although use of citizen participation was not found to vary among cities with different election methods, form of government might be related to participation. In addition, the responding cities might not be representative of the population of council-manager cities. However, the findings do provide valuable insights and raise important questions about the use of participation in the budget process in council-manager cities.

Citizen participation in the budget process does not appear to be alive and well in council-manager cities. For the most part, the methods that are used involve city officials simply providing information to the public rather than encouraging dialogue and citizen input. In addition, managers generally do not find active methods of participation to be the most effective methods for budgeting. The reasons for this are not clear. Are officials unwilling to give citizens the opportunity to share in decision making? Have the methods used in the past simply not been the best ways in which to achieve this? Are citizens uninterested or unwilling to understand the complexities of the budget sufficiently to provide useful input? These questions need to be addressed so as to develop effective citizen participation mechanisms.

Should we expect or recommend that all cities use participation in the same way in their budget processes? This research suggests that the characteristics of communities might be important factors in determining the need for and most effective methods of citizen input. Cities with moralistic and traditionalistic political cultures were found to use participation more than were individualistic cities. Perhaps it is more difficult to solicit participation in a formal group format in an individualist culture; if so, then these cities could enhance participation more through individual rather than group methods. Larger and more heterogeneous cities might find it more useful to involve citizens in the budget process so as to develop consensus about conflictual issues among groups, explaining why participation varies significantly by population. Based on these findings, a "one-size-fits-all" approach to budget participation might not be appropriate. Before borrowing participation methods from other cities, managers should consider how well the mechanisms fit with the needs and cultures of their own cities.

NOTES

1. A response of 1 in the survey meant that the method *never* is used, with a 4 meaning that it *always* is used. Responses of 1 and 2 were combined for this study to indicate that the method *never or seldom* is used, whereas 3 and 4 were combined to show that the method *sometime or always* is used.

2. The survey used seven different population ranges. These were collapsed into four ranges in this study for the sake of simplicity. Results were similar to those when seven ranges were used.

3. Racial data are from Gaquin and Littman (1998). The ranges used here for racial composition were chosen arbitrarily. However, similar results were found when different ranges were used.

REFERENCES

Alozie, N., & Manganaro, L. (1993). Black and Hispanic council representation. *Urban Affairs Quarterly, 29,* 276–289.

Berman, E. (1997). Dealing with cynical citizens. *Public Administration Review, 57,* 105–112.

Bielefeld, W., & Corbin, J.J. (1996). The institutionalization of nonprofit human service delivery: The role of political culture. *Administration & Society, 28,* 362–389.

Bland, R., & Rubin, I. (1997). *Budgeting: A guide for local governments.* Washington, DC: International City/County Management Association.

Box, R. (1998). *Citizen governance.* Thousand Oaks, CA: Sage.

Ebdon, C., & Brucato, P. (2000). Government structure in large U.S. cities: Are forms converging? *International Journal of Public Administration, 23*(12), 2209–2235.

Elazar, D. (1972). *American federalism: A view from the states* (2nd ed.). New York: Thomas Y. Crowell.

Elazar, D. (1994). *The American mosaic: The impact of space, time, and culture on American politics.* Boulder, CO: Westview.

Gaquin, D.A., & Littman, M.S. (Eds.). (1998). *1998 city and county extra* (7th ed.). Lanham, MD: Bernan Press.

Gendzel, G. (1997). Political culture: Genealogy of a concept. *Journal of Interdisciplinary History, 28,* 225–250.

Gurwitt, R. (1992, December). A government that runs on citizen power. *Governing,* pp. 48–54.

Gurwitt, R. (1993, July). The lure of the strong mayor. *Governing,* pp. 36–41.

International City/County Management Association. (1999). *ICMA declaration of ideals.* (Available: http://www.icma.org/abouticma/ideals.cfm).

Kathlene, L., & Martin, J. (1991). Enhancing citizen participation: Panel designs, perspectives, and policy formation. *Journal of Policy Analysis and Management, 10*(1), 46–63.

King, C.S., Feltey, K., & Susel, B.O. (1998). The question of participation: Toward authentic public participation in public administration. *Public Administration Review, 58,* 317–326.

King, J.D. (1994). Political culture, registration laws, and voter turnout among the American states. *Publius, 24*(4), 115–127.

McCurdy, A.H. (1998). Political culture, local government, and progressive personnel practices. *Review of Public Personnel Administration, 18*(1), 23–38.

Nalbandian, J. (1991). *Professionalism in local government: Transformations in the roles, responsibilities, and values of city managers.* San Francisco: Jossey-Bass.

Paddock, J. (1997). Political culture and the partisan style of state party activists. *Publius, 27*(3), 127–132.

Protasel, G. (1988). Abandonments of the council-manager plan: A new institutional perspective. *Public Administration Review, 48,* 807–812.

Renner, T. (1987, November-December). Municipal election processes: The impact on minority representation. *Baseline Data Reports,* pp. 1–11. (Washington, DC: International City Management Association).

Roberts, N. (1997). Public deliberation: An alternative approach to crafting policy and setting direction. *Public Administration Review, 57,* 124–132.

Rubin, I. (1992). Budget reform and political reform: Conclusions from six cities. *Public Administration Review, 52,* 454–466.

Schachter, H.L. (1997). *Reinventing government or reinventing ourselves.* Albany: State University of New York Press.

Thomas, J.C. (1995). *Public participation in public decisions.* San Francisco: Jossey-Bass.

Thompson, M., Ellis, R., & Wildavsky, A. (1990). *Cultural theory.* Boulder, CO: Westview.

Watson, D., Juster, R., & Johnson, G. (1991). Institutionalized use of citizen surveys in the budgetary and policymaking processes: A small city case study. *Public Administration Review, 51,* 232–239.

Whitaker, G., & Jenne, K. (1995). Improving city managers' leadership. *State and Local Government Review, 27*(1), 84–94.

PART 4

MECHANISMS OF DIRECT CITIZEN PARTICIPATION

Citizens have numerous ways to participate in their government (Verba and Nie, 1972; Advisory Commission on Intergovernmental Relations, 1980; Verba, Schlozman, and Brady, 1995). Citizens can make political contributions, write or phone their representatives, and work and vote for political candidates. Citizens also can support and join lobby groups to champion their causes (Weber and Khademian, 1997; Berry, 1981; Gormley, 1981; Schuck, 1977). Reliance on elected officials and lobbyists to represent citizen interests are examples of indirect forms of citizen participation. They have been studied extensively in the political science literature. Our focus here is on the mechanisms that directly involve citizens in problem solving and decision making about issues of public concern.

Conventional mechanisms are many (Burke, 1968; Arnstein, 1969; Langton, 1978). They include such things as serving on juries;[1] attending public hearings;[2] participating in advisory boards, commissions, and task forces;[3] responding to telephone polls and newspaper "clip out" questionnaires; contacting and meeting public officials; and writing letters to the editor expressing interest or opposition to some governmental action. Unfortunately, these conventional avenues tend to involve only a small percentage of the citizenry.[4] Most are one-way transmissions of information from public official to citizen or from citizen to public official rather than citizen engagement in dialogues and deliberations over public policy with fellow citizens and public officials.

This section examines some of the innovative mechanisms designed to facilitate greater deliberation among the citizens. They are grouped by level of analysis. Individual-level participation enables citizens to present their views and preferences directly and interactively to their representatives. Group-level participation involves citizens working in groups ranging in size from three to 75. Large-group participation brings hundreds of citizens together to deliberate about some issue or problem. And electronic participation opens up the possibility of cyber-democracy that enables deliberations online in virtual democratic communities.

The decision to sort mechanisms by level of analysis was done deliberately to underscore the tension surrounding the problems of scale. As citizens directly participate in increasing numbers and in more complex formats, the inevitable question arises: How do we get larger numbers of people involved and yet retain the ideal of deliberation that is best enacted in small, face-to-face groups (Cleveland, 1975)? Deliberation is not "the aggregation of interests." It requires thoughtful examination of issues, listening to others' perspectives, and a coming to a public judgment on what constitutes the "common good." Public judgment differs from public opinion, in the sense of the typical opinion poll. Public opinion is "uninformed, superficial and transient" and not a reliable basis for policy (Yankelovich, 1991). Public judgment comes from people to working together, face-to-face, in a shared search for effective solutions to their community problems. It requires information about an issue and knowledge of the basic elements of a problem, as well as an understanding of the relationships among the elements and the consequences and tradeoffs associated with different policies. The larger the number of people involved in direct participation, the harder it is for public judgment to emerge.

Each article in Part 4 offers an innovative solution to deal with the problems of scale. These solutions differ from earlier attempts in a number of ways. Rather than relying on a subset of the population, they all make efforts to be more inclusive, in some cases drawing random samples of participants from all of the major constituencies, including the poor and minorities. They also provide citizens with extensive information about the nature of the policy problem and attempt to engage them in the same problem-solving context that elected officials experience by using the same rigorous approaches in data collection and analysis.

Careful attention also is paid to process issues, not just the content of citizen deliberations. Process is concerned with questions about who participates and how, sponsorship, facilitation, leadership, decision making, sequencing of activities, timing, support and responsibility for implementation. The more people become involved in problem solving and decision making, the more attention to process is warranted. The topic has become so important that a whole subfield devoted to process issues has developed (Bunker and Alban 1997; Bryson and Andersen 2000).

As we see in the following articles, process becomes even more critical when intractable issues such as growth, allocation of environmental resources, and planning for the future drive the agenda. Recommendations on these topics drawn from public deliberations are more likely to be accepted by the wider public and by elected officials if people have confidence in the process used to produce them. In fact, faith in the deliberative process has enabled some communities to use public deliberations for time-sensitive issues. We find three more cases of deliberations to address community budget problems, challenging the belief that deliberations are inappropriate in crisis situations.

INDIVIDUAL PARTICIPATION

Douglas J. Watson, Robert J. Juster, and Gerald W. Johnson, in "Institutionalized Use of Citizen Surveys in the Budgetary and Policy-making Processes: A Small City Case Study," document the use of citizen surveys[5] as an important tool to "stay in touch" with individual citizens. Citizen surveys gained prominence in the 1970s and 1980s, but these early versions did not allow for systematic evaluation of citizen opinion because the data were not comprehensive or representative of the entire community. Based on a case study of local government, this article demonstrates the utility of using interactive citizen surveys to evaluate basic services, identify service delivery problems, establish citizens' goal preferences in terms of services, set local government priorities, and allocate resources during the budget process. It also identifies survey methods and procedures that have to be followed to ensure that results are valid and reliable. Surveys can offer an effective and efficient framework for citizen participation in the local governing process, and as this case suggests, they also can create a positive linkage between citizen attitudes and city leaders' budgetary and programmatic decisions. If quality can be measured in terms of the absence of conflict, the authors conclude that the citizen survey and local government's response to it did indeed alter the political life of the community.

SMALL GROUP PARTICIPATION

"Emergent Citizen Groups and Emergency Management," by Robert A. Stallings and E. L. Quarantelli, documents how emergent groups of private citizens can participate in government activity. Emergent groups are those that "emerge around perceived needs or problems associated with both natural and technological disaster situations" (p. 256). Defined as newly formed, and lacking in formalization and tradition, they are grouped into two major types: emergent groups at emergency times and emergent groups at non-emergency times. NIMBY (not-in-my-backyard) groups that attempt to prevent or close a neighborhood hazardous waste dump would be an example of a non-emergency group.[6] The authors describe the basic characteristics of both types of groups and note five important implications for public managers and administrators who deal specifically with emergent groups. Emergent groups are "inevitable, natural, neither necessarily dysfunctional nor conflictive, and cannot be eliminated by planning" (p. 262). However, the authors point out that if citizens believe that a problem is not being legitimately dealt with by the agencies that are responsible for serving the public, then citizen anger and hostility can result and turn public officials into "the enemy."

Ned Crosby, Janet M. Kelly, and Paul Schaefer, in "Citizen Panels: A New Approach to Citizen Participation," describe another form of small group participation—the citizen panel.[7] The panel is a new form of citizen participation that is modeled after the jury system. It is small but demographically a representative sample of citizens called together for intensive deliberative processes. As a proxy for the public at large, similar to Fishkin's deliberative polling (1991, 1995) and Yankelovich's public agenda forums (1991), it represents conclusions that the electorate would have been expected to reach if it had had a similar opportunity to deliberate. The article presents a case study of 60 randomly selected individuals in Minnesota who participated in a panel charged with analyzing the impact of agriculture on water quality and making recommendations to project sponsors, including several state agencies. The article identifies six criteria for successful citizen panels: a random, stratified sampling of panel participants; effective decision making; fair procedures; cost-effective processes; a design that is adaptable to different tasks and settings; and a high probability that citizen recommendations would be heeded by government officials. The Minnesota citizen panel made a start in meeting the criteria, but the authors conclude that more work must be done to get the recommendations adopted by those public officials in power.

LARGE-GROUP PARTICIPATION

Lance deHaven-Smith and John R. Wodraska, in "Consensus-Building for Integrated Resources Planning," document how government agencies are beginning to use large-group techniques.[8] These techniques enable multiple agencies and jurisdictions to manage resources collaboratively in order to protect ecosystems as a whole. The article describes an integrated resource planning process used by the Metropolitan Water District (MWD) of Southern California. Since water issues involve both technical and equity concerns, the idea was to bring managers, producers, and consumers together for some joint problem solving and decision making. The case demonstrates the use of the American Assembly process, a model developed by Dwight D. Eisenhower when he was at Columbia University to address issues that were national or international in scope. The process requires a series of steps and procedures: background papers written by experts; participants of diverse backgrounds, associations, and fields of expertise; participants divided into equal-sized groups that are microcosms of the whole; group discussions on a specific policy topic over three consecutive days; and a facilitator and recorder assigned to each group. An overall assembly director prepares a report synthesizing the various findings and recommendations from all the groups. In a final or plenary session, a draft report is presented to all the participants meeting together. It is reviewed section-by-section under the direction of the assembly director and amended by the participants (using parliamentary procedures) to reflect the consensus of the body.

Modifications to the American Assembly process used in this case study included a steering committee to set the agenda, multiple assemblies rather than just one, and six open forums around the region to solicit public input. The authors concluded that the process enabled the MWD and member agencies to move to a higher level of regional cooperation than had been achieved in the past.

"State Strategic Planning: Suggestions from the Oregon Experience," by Gerald R. Kissler, Karmen N. Fore, Willow S. Jacobson, William P. Kittredge, and Scott L. Stewart, describes large-group participation techniques that involve hundreds of citizens in setting the state's direction. Their state model of strategic planning is a comprehensive process that includes: university faculty and students who lead regional information-gathering meetings to collect and analyze data and then draft reports for citizens and policymakers; use of benchmarks or performance measures to determine the progress on state strategic initiatives; a "bottom-up approach" (interviews and questionnaires of community leaders) to gather data; small group meetings and facilitated dialogues at the regional level for the purpose of making recommendations on policy tradeoffs; and incorporation of general public views through citizen polls and commissioned focus groups. The authors conclude this model of state strategic planning can be a valuable process to help the state and its citizens adjust to major economic and social transformations.

Edward C. Weeks, in "The Practice of Deliberative Democracy: Results from Four Large-Scale Trials," describes four community dialogues conducted in Eugene, Oregon; Sacramento, California; and Fort Collins, Colorado—three cities with populations ranging from 100,000 to 400,000. The dialogues in Eugene and Sacramento invited citizens to invest their time and intellectual energy to work through difficult budget problems. The dialogues in Fort Collins and Eugene addressed contentious issues of community growth.

The four dialogues were based on the following model of deliberative democracy: all citizens were invited to participate; all citizens received extensive information about the nature of the policy problem; citizens and elected officials were integrated within the same problem-solving context; and rigorous methods of data collection and analysis were employed. Each community dialogue proceeded through agenda setting, strategy development, and decision-making phases. Four methods supported the dialogues: an informational newsletter to every household in the community that introduced the dialogue and provided comprehensive information about the process; a questionnaire and exercises that enabled citizens to work through policy problems and arrive at their preferred course of action; workshops in which citizens were randomly assigned to work through structured exercises in small groups facilitated by community volunteers; and multiple sample surveys that provided a benchmark against which the results from the questionnaires and workshops were measured. Using four criteria to judge the effectiveness of the community dialogues (broad, informed, deliberative, and credible participation), the author found it was possible to convene large-scale public deliberations to enable local governments to take effective action on pressing community problems.

ELECTRONIC PARTICIPATION[9]

Andrew Kakabadse, Nada K. Kakabadse, and Alexander Kouzmin examine the pros and cons of information technology (IT) in the digital age and its ability to support the democratic process. In

"Reinventing the Democratic Governance Project through Information Technology? A Growing Agenda for Debate," they ask to what extent IT can bypass special interest groups, party politics, and the media and offer a new way to build consensus and common ground by engaging all the citizenry in a cyber-democracy or virtual polis. New forms of civic discourse such as the Citycard, electronic town hall meetings, Santa Monica's interactive computer network, and voter communication vouchers suggest there is potential for virtual communities to form. Yet, there is a downside to electronic democracy, not the least of which are the new divisions among the citizenry between the information rich and the information poor, between those who have access to sophisticated information and communication technology and those who do not. The authors have their doubts about a populist model of electronic democracy for these and other reasons. They recommend that the best use of IT is to promote participatory policy analysis to help educate citizens to make more informed policy choices.

NOTES

1. See, for example, Jacobsohn (1977).

2. For an overview of public hearings, see Checkoway (1981), Cole and Caputo (1984), and Kihl (1985).

3. For examples of citizen participation in advisory boards, commissions, and task forces, see Stewart et al. (1984), Rimmerman (1985), and McShane and Krause (1995).

4. Initiatives, referenda, and recalls are exceptions that can involve large numbers of citizens. However, since the intent of these mechanisms is not dialogical or deliberative, they are not included in this overview.

5. For other examples of using survey research, see Milbrath (1981) and Bacot et al. (1993).

6. See Fischer (1993) and Kraft and Clary (1991) for a fuller description of these NIMBY groups.

7. Also see Kathlene and Martin (1991) and Guston (1999) on the use and evaluation of citizen panels. Renn et al. (1993) also use citizen panels along with experts and other stakeholders in a three-step procedure for planning.

8. For an example of a large-group collaboration among governmental agencies (rather than citizens), consult Andranovich (1995).

9. For additional sources on new information technology and citizen participation, consult White (1997), Deibert (2000), Tesh (2002), and Zavestoski and Shulman (2002).

REFERENCES

Advisory Commission on Intergovernmental Relations. 1980. *Citizen Participation in the American Federal System.* Washington, DC: U.S. Government Printing Office.

Andranovich, G. 1995. "Achieving Consensus in Public Decision Making: Applying Interest-Based Problem Solving to the Challenges of Intergovernmental Collaboration." *The Journal of Applied Behavioral Science,* 31(4): 429–45.

Arnstein, S. 1969. "A Ladder of Citizen Participation." *Journal of the American Institute of Planners,* 35: 216–224.

Bacot, H., A.S. McCabe, M.R. Fitzgerald, T. Bowen, and D.H. Folz. 1993. "Practicing the Politics of Inclusion: Citizen Surveys and the Design of Solid Waste Recycling Programs." *American Review of Public Administration,* 23(1): 29–43.

Berry, J.M. 1981. "Beyond Citizen Participation: Effective Advocacy Before Administrative Agencies." *The Journal of Applied Behavioral Science,* 17(4): 463–77.

Bryson, J.M., and S.R. Anderson. 2000. "Applying Large-Group Interaction Methods in the Planning and Implementation of Major Change Efforts." *Public Administration Review,* 60(2): 143–53.

Bunker, B.B., and B.T. Alban. 1997. *Large Group Interventions: Engaging the Whole System for Rapid Change.* San Francisco: Jossey-Bass.

Burke, E.M. 1968. "Citizen Participation Strategies." *Journal of the American Institute of Planners,* 34: 287–94.

Checkoway, B. 1981. "The Politics of Public Hearings." *The Journal of Applied Behavioral Science,* 17(4): 567–82.

Cleveland, H. 1975. "How Do You Get Everybody In on the Act and Still Get Some Action?" *Public Management,* 57 (June): 3–6.

Cole, R.L., and D.A. Caputo. 1984. "The Public Hearing as Effective Citizen Participation Mechanism: A Case Study of the General Revenue Sharing Program." *The American Political Science Review,* 78(2): 404–16.

Deibert, R.J. 2000. "International Plug 'n Play? Citizen Activism, the Internet, and Global Public Policy." *International Studies Perspectives,* 1: 255–72.

Fischer, F. 1993. "Citizen Participation and the Democratization of Policy Expertise: From Theoretical Inquiry to Practical Cases." *Policy Sciences,* 26(3): 165–88.

Fishkin, J.S. 1991. *Democracy and Deliberation: New Direction for Democratic Reform.* New Haven: Yale University Press.

———. 1995. *The Voice of the People.* New Haven: Yale University Press.

Gormley, W.T. 1981. "Public Advocacy in Public Utility Commission Proceedings." *The Journal of Applied Behavioral Science,* 17(4): 446–61.

Guston, D.H. 1999. "Evaluating the First U.S. Consensus Conference: The Impact of the Citizens' Panel on Telecommunications and the Future of Democracy." *Science, Technology, & Human Values,* 24(4): 451–82.

Jacobsohn, G.J. 1977. "Citizen Participation in Policy Making: The Role of the Jury." *The Journal of Politics,* 39(1): 73–96.

Kathlene, L., and J.A. Martin. 1991. "Enhancing Citizen Participation: Panel Designs, Perspectives, and Policy Formation." *Journal of Policy Analysis and Management,* 10(1): 46–63.

Kihl, M.R. 1985. "The Viability of Public Hearings in Transportation Planning." *The Journal of Applied Behavioral Science,* 21(2): 185–200.

Kraft, M.E., and B.B. Clary. 1991. "Citizen Participation and the NIMBY Syndrome: Public Response to Radioactive Waste Disposal." *The Western Political Quarterly,* 44(2): 299–328.

Langton, S., ed. 1978. *Citizen Participation in America.* Lexington, MA: Lexington Books.

McShane, M.D., and W. Krause. 1995. "Community Corrections Advisory Boards and Commissions: Decision Makers or Decoration?" *Public Administration Quarterly,* 19(1): 58–67.

Milbrath, L.W. 1981. "Citizen Surveys as Citizen Participation Mechanisms." *The Journal of Applied Behavioral Science,* 17(4): 478–96.

Renn, O., T. Webler, H. Rakel, P. Dienel, and B. Johnson. 1993. "Public Participation in Decision Making: A Three-Step Procedure." *Policy Sciences,* 26(3): 189–214.

Rimmerman, C. 1985. "Citizen Participation and Policy Implementation in the Columbus, Ohio, DCBG Program." *Public Administration Quarterly,* 9(3): 328–48.

Schuck, P.H. 1977. "Public Interest Groups and the Policy Process." *Public Administration Review,* 37(2): 132–40.

Stewart, T.R., R.L. Dennis, and D. Ely. 1984. "Citizen Participation and Judgment in Policy Analysis: A Case Study of Urban Air Quality Program." *Policy Sciences,* 17: 67–87.

Tesh, S. N. 2002. "The Internet and the Grass Roots." *Organization and the Environment,* 15(3): 336–39.

Verba, S., and N.H. Nie. 1972. *Participation in America: Political Democracy and Social Equality.* New York: Harper and Row. (Reprinted by University of Chicago Press, 1987).

Verba, S., K.L. Schlozman, and H.E. Brady. 1995. *Voice and Equality: Civic Voluntarism in American Democracy.* Cambridge: Harvard University Press.

Weber, E.P., and A.M. Khademian. 1997. "From Agitation to Collaboration: Clearing the Air Through Negotiation." *Public Administration Review,* 57(5): 396–410.

White, C.S. 1997. "Citizen Participation and the Internet: Prospects for Civic Deliberation in the Information Age." *The Social Studies* (January): 23–28.

Yankelovich, D. 1991. *Coming to Public Judgment.* Syracuse, NY: Syracuse University Press.

Zavestoski, S., and S.W. Shulman. 2002. "The Internet and Environmental Decision Making." *Organization and the Environment,* 15(3): 323–27.

— 4.1 *Individual Participation* —

CHAPTER 15

INSTITUTIONALIZED USE OF CITIZEN SURVEYS IN THE BUDGETARY AND POLICY-MAKING PROCESSES
A Small City Case Study

DOUGLAS J. WATSON, ROBERT J. JUSTER,
AND GERALD W. JOHNSON

Institutionalized citizen participation in the management processes of American cities has become an increasingly important element of municipal government. To some degree, this is the result of federal government mandates for citizen participation in grant programs and state government requirements for open meetings (Sharp: 1990, p. 79). A 1979 report identified 155 federal programs that included a provision for citizen participation (Advisory Commission on Intergovernmental Relations: 1979). A second factor is the recognition by city officials of the need and usefulness, politically and otherwise, to "stay in touch" with the views of the members of the community. Increasingly, this second factor has been addressed through the use of citizen surveys (Brudney and England: 1982, p. 129).

Citizen surveys gained prominence in local government in the 1970s and 1980s because the existing mechanisms for learning citizen views were not reliable. Generally, information was obtained through one-on-one contacts, special interest groups, letters to the editor, and complaints. None of these allowed for a systematic evaluation of citizen opinion because the data were not comprehensive or representative of the entire community (Webb and Hatry: 1973, p. 1). Citizen surveys were recognized for their usefulness in several areas, including obtaining feedback on service delivery and as input into the policy process of resource allocation.

However, citizen surveys are still not widely used at the local level of government and, more specifically, they have not reached their full potential as valuable instruments for urban decision-makers and managers. This article addresses why this is the case and shows how the objectives of increased citizen participation and strengthened municipal management and policy-making can be attained through the use of citizen surveys. The article reviews the uses and methods of citizen surveys and presents a case study that illustrates the institutionalization of citizen surveys in the policy, program, and budget processes of one small city.

From *Public Administration Review,* 51, 3 (May/June 1991): 232–239. Copyright © 1991 by American Society for Public Administration. Reprinted with permission.

USE OF CITIZEN SURVEYS

The use of citizen surveys in local government is generally traced to the pioneering work of several medium to large cities in the early 1970s. Specifically, the Dayton (Ohio) Public Opinion Center (DPOC) began surveying citizens in 1970 on a regular basis on local issues (Webb and Hatry: 1973, p. 11). Dallas and St. Petersburg also regularly used citizen surveys during the 1970s (Stipak: 1980, p. 523). While other cities reported using citizen surveys by the 1980s, case studies analyzing successful citizen survey applications were limited primarily to Dallas and Dayton (Glass: undated, p. 4). And, while a 1982 survey of 1041 cities with populations greater than 25,000 showed that over fifty percent of them used surveys during the previous twelve months, only one-third of the cities reported using general opinion surveys in contrast to single purpose surveys (Glass: undated, pp. 3–4).

Webb and Hatry argue that citizen surveys

> are possibly the most, if not the only, efficient way to obtain information on (1) constituents' satisfaction with the quality of specific services including identification of problem areas, (2) facts such as the numbers and characteristics of users and nonusers of various services, (3) the reasons that specific services are disliked or not used, (4) potential demands for new services, and (5) citizen opinions on various community issues, including feelings of alienation toward government and officials (Webb and Hatry: 1973, p. 1).

Glass points out that "surveys are only one of many participatory techniques" but are clearly the most productive because they "produce higher quality information in greater detail than any other citizen participation technique." (Glass: undated, p. 3). Others caution that surveys are just one form of input for the decision-making process and cannot substitute for other forms nor replace the necessity for sound policy judgments (Stipak: 1980, p. 524).

In spite of a number of attempts to analyze the validity and utility of citizen surveys, the results to date have been ambiguous and unconvincing. As Page and Shapiro state, "We can be confident only that public opinion, whatever its sources and quality, is a factor that genuinely affects government policies in the Unites States" (Page and Shapiro: 1983, p. 189). At the local level, there is limited case study data on the use of comprehensive citizen surveys. In fact, few cities have institutionalized citizen surveys (Webb and Hatry: 1973, pp. 1–2). While many communities may use citizen surveys, as previously cited, most do so on a limited basis. They are not a formal part of the management or policy-making processes. This limited and sporadic use has not allowed the full potential of surveys to be analyzed or realized (Webb and Hatry: 1973, pp. 1–2). Webb and Hatry advocate regular annual citizen surveys in which many of the same questions are repeated, allowing for tracking of citizen attitudes toward city services over an extended period (Webb and Hatry: 1973, p. 2). In this way, decision makers can determine whether their efforts are resulting in improvement or deterioration of citizens' perceptions of city services.

One of the reasons that surveys are not institutionalized is the view that citizens cannot assess objectively the quality of service delivery (Sharp: 1990, p. 83). Stipak, for example, found that citizens' views on services were not "associated statistically with levels of service outputs as indicated by objective measures" (Stipak: 1980, pp. 521–525). Objective measures of local government output include such things as tons of garbage collected, miles patrolled by police officers, and response times for fire trucks and ambulances. Stipak's criticism has been challenged on several fronts. Rosentraub, Harlow, and Thompson argued that the data Stipak used did not support his conclusions (Rosentraub, Harlow, and Thompson: 1979, pp. 302–303). Brudney and England reviewed several studies and concluded that citizen assessments did correspond to objective mea-surements of service delivery. Further, Brudney and England concluded, "In a society committed to democratic norms, the views of the citizenry—no matter how (ill) conceived—are significant in themselves!" (Brudney and England: 1982, p. 129). Importantly, Daneke and Klobus-Edwards found that citizen surveys reflect citizen perceptions of service delivery and have a value to deci-sion makers independent of objective measures (Daneke and Klobus-Edwards: 1979, p. 421; see also Schneider: 1976, pp. 297–305). Fitzgerald and Durant stated, in fact, that "citizen evaluations of public services are expected to be colored, in some degree, by personal, group, and community factors" (Fitzgerald and Durant: 1980, p. 586).

The finding of a wide disparity in the subjective perceptions of citizens and the objective assess-ments of service quality can be, however, a most useful one. It provides city leaders with at least two immediate options and opportunities. One, they can attempt to communicate more effectively what they are doing to the citizenry with the objective being that more and better information will lead to greater understanding and less disparity. Two, substantive steps can be taken to reduce the disparity. As Daneke and Klobus-Edwards illustrated with several examples, citizen views sometimes differ considerably on projects and services from those of decision makers. For ex-ample, they found that in a Virginia city, residents rated the quality of street lighting significantly lower than did the professional staff. Surveys there were used to augment objective performance evaluation and to facilitate "strategic renegotiations of policy within the implementation cycle" (Daneke and Klobus-Edwards: 1979, p. 422). That is, presumably, street lighting was upgraded in that community as result of citizens' perceptions that it was inadequate. Communication by city leaders that the street lighting met recommended standards probably would not have changed the opinions of the citizens.

Beyond their usefulness in identifying service delivery problems, evaluating basic services, influencing budget priorities, and identifying citizen goal preferences, Glass concluded that citi-zen surveys have a further use (Glass: undated, p. 5). They indirectly send a message to residents that the city government is concerned about their opinions. If citizens are informed of how the survey will be used to improve the efficiency, effectiveness, or responsiveness of the government, the city's image will be enhanced through "a more positive view of city government" (Glass: undated, p. 5).

NON-USE OF CITIZEN SURVEYS

While impressionistic and anecdotal evidence suggests that the use of citizen surveys has increased during the past decade, no systematic data on a national scale are available to support this conclu-sion. It has, in fact, been suggested that the lessening of federal pressure for citizen participation, and the rising pressure of fiscal problems have resulted in a waning interest in citizen surveys (Streib: 1990, p. 17). A forthcoming (1991) joint publication of the Urban Institute and the International City Management Association will include an update of the 1977 study and thus sheds some light on the trends in citizen survey usage (Hatry *et al.,* 1977) [see Figure 15.1].

It is clear that in spite of the potential value of citizen surveys, many local governments do not use them at all (Webb and Hatry: 1973, p. 8). Daneke and Klobus-Edwards cite "general parochi-alism," "a fear that surveys will create issues and mobilize heretofore acquiescent publics," and "a lack of expertise" as three prominent reasons cities do not use surveys. They point out that the "ignorance is bliss" mentality does not stop latent issues from surfacing and causing unanticipated changes (Daneke and Klobus-Edwards: 1979, p. 421). For example, in one Alabama city, when negative results from a citizen survey were announced by a university research team to community

Figure 15.1
The Citizen Survey

The initial survey was conducted by the Department of Political Science at Auburn University in 1985. A random telephone survey of 95 local residents was conducted using the monthly customer printout from the Auburn Water Works Board to select respondents. This first survey contained a total of 37 questions including 9 respondent background items; 19 questions eliciting opinions concerning current services; and 9 questions asking respondents to identify their priorities among basic services in relation to the city's budget.

The survey results were distributed to department heads and elected officials and published in the local news media. The results were also used in the preparation of the city's budget for the forthcoming (1987) fiscal year. This initial survey served as a pilot project. It convinced city officials that information of practical value could be obtained within the constraints of limited resources and set the stage for conducting an annual survey.

The second survey was conducted in the Spring of 1987, in time to be part of the preparation of the FY 1988 budget. About 150 permanent residents were interviewed. Since then, the survey has been administered in April of each year, in time for the major budgeting activities which occur in June and July.

In 1988, the organizational arrangements for conducting the survey were changed. While the university class continued to conduct the survey, the city's Planning Department was assigned the responsibility for coordinating the survey and processing the results. There was also a significant addition to the survey's scope. The questionnaire was not only used to survey a random sample of 151 permanent residents, it was also administered to 53 citizens who served on the city's numerous boards and commissions. It was assumed that these "civic leaders" would have more knowledge of the city's operations, and that their perceptions could either confirm or contradict the responses of the citizens.

In 1989, this same organizational arrangement was continued and several special questions were added. As the survey became established as an annual city activity, various department heads realized it could be used to solicit community views about specific departmental concerns. The addition of such questions substantially lengthened the interviews. The 1989 survey included a total of 58 questions, of which 24 were openended. With the lengthened questionnaire, each telephone interview took about 30 minutes to complete and involved a complex set of question formats.

As a result of the experience with the 1989 survey, the 1990 questionnaire was significantly revised. Personal background questions were reduced from ten to five and were asked at the end of the interview rather than at the beginning as in previous years. Questions relating to opinions about current services were reduced from 17 to 12. Budgetary priority questions were increased from ten to twelve. Questions submitted by city officials and relating to current problems and projects were limited. The format for all questions was standardized, and openended questions were eliminated. Survey procedures were also standardized and institutionalized.

In March 1990, 226 permanent residents and 55 civic leaders were interviewed. Their responses were tabulated and analyzed separately.

Just prior to the survey, announcements about it were carried by the local news media. About a week prior to the survey a planner met with the political science class, and discussed the logistics of the survey with the students. Twenty-five students conducted the survey, working in shifts from 5:00 to 7:00 PM and from 7:00 to 9:00 PM on three weekday evenings. While by 1990 the citizen survey had become an annual city activity, it was still conducted by university students. All interviewers identified themselves as students from Auburn University. The interviews of civic leaders were conducted by a single student interviewer employed by the city.

The survey data were coded and processed by the survey coordinator from the planning Department. Tabulations and histograms of the responses were prepared and were submitted to the City Manager. A copy of the complete survey results was sent to each department head, the Mayor, and members of the City Council. A news release was prepared and local newspapers ran feature stories which presented the results of the survey and compared them with those of prior years. They also explained how the survey results would be used in the city's budgetary process.

leaders, numerous excuses and explanations were developed by the leaders. They chose to blame "troublemakers" or the "obvious misinterpretation" of the survey questions for the low scores rather than address the results.

Because of the sensitivity of both elected officials and public administrators to citizen opinions, surveys have been subject to abuse. Webb and Hatry explain:

> The findings themselves also may be used as political communication. To some these results are good, to others, bad. It depends a good deal on whether one is seeking change and reforms or defending the status quo, whether one views controversy and public discussion as challenging opportunities or as bothersome circumstances to be avoided, whether one prefers constituents to be apathetic or involved, and whether or not one tends to have faith in an informed public (Webb and Hatry: 1973, p. 41).

Specific examples of abuses include "poor sampling techniques and administration, ineffective or manipulative questionnaire design, and/or inaccurate tabulation and explanation of results" (Daneke and Klobus-Edwards: 1979, p. 423). Ineffective or manipulative use of survey results also, of course, constitutes an abuse. These abuses, and the perception of, or actual, bias, can be avoided. First, outside expertise can be retained, either from a university or independent research organization (Daneke and Klobus-Edward: 1979, p. 423). In fact, "even those governments that have the technical capability to handle the surveys on their own may have difficulty in gaining public credibility for their findings if they do not use outside experts" (Daneke and Klobus-Edwards: 1979, p. 423). A second recommendation is for an independent survey audit prior to the use of the instrument by outside experts and/or by community groups. The auditors look for any biases or slanted questions in the instrument. The audit not only helps assure government officials that the results are reliable but also gives the survey greater credibility with the public (Webb and Hatry: 1973, p. 42). A third recommendation is to involve citizens' groups in the development of the instrument (Daneke and Klobus-Edwards: 1979, p. 423).

The technical issues of bias in survey methods must be addressed separately. They include issues of survey instrument design, data collection, and sample selection. These issues have been addressed in a number of publications (Glass, undated; Webb and Hatry, 1973; Fitzgerald and Durant, 1980; Wilson, 1983; Brudney and England, 1982: and Daneke and Klobus-Edwards, 1979).

These various issues raise a number of important questions about the reliability, validity, logistics, and usefulness of local government citizen surveys in general and about various types of surveys. One way to address these issues is through a case study. The following presents a case study of one type of citizen survey in one community. The value of the case study is that it addresses citizen survey issues as they apply to a specific and rarely used survey form, a comprehensive institutionalized survey intended to support both policy and management decision making, in a relatively small community.

INSTITUTIONALIZED CITIZEN SURVEY: A CASE STUDY

The City of Auburn, Alabama, a university community with a population of about 35,000, has used a citizen survey for the past five years (see Figure 15.1). During this time the survey has become a major element in the city's priority-setting and budgeting processes.

SURVEY RESULTS

In view of the changes that have occurred in the survey populations, format, and procedures, it is perhaps too early to draw substantial general conclusions from the data. However, some trends and relationships are beginning to emerge because some questions have been repeated annually. For example, each year respondents have been asked to rate individual city services such as police protection, schools, and garbage pickup. Following these comments on individual services, they have been asked: "In general, how would you rate the basic services provided by the City of Auburn: excellent, good, fair, poor, or no opinion?"

As a university community, Auburn experiences a significant amount of population turnover each year. It can, therefore, be assumed that some of the respondents base their answers on comparisons with other places they have lived. Table 15.1 shows that between 1985 and 1989, those persons rating the general level of services either "excellent" or "good" averaged 79 percent of all respondents. The positive responses from civic leaders in 1988 was 94 percent. This is interpreted to mean that most citizens had a relatively high degree of satisfaction with the services being provided. In 1990, the number responding "excellent" and "good" increased to 88 percent for the general population and to 99 percent for civic leaders. It is too early to know or assume that this level of satisfaction will continue into the future. If it does, it could be that there is a growing perception that the views expressed during the survey are having an impact on budgetary and programmatic decisions and ultimately services. In addition, the fact that the survey has become a well-publicized annual event could be reinforcing basic positive feelings about city government and the services it provides.

In a similar fashion, those interviewed have been asked what funding priority they would give each service individually in the upcoming budget. They were then read the complete list of all services and asked which one of them they would give the highest priority. Table 15.2 shows the relative budgetary priorities of the citizens over the five-year period. Expenditures for streets and schools clearly were dominant from 1985 to 1989. In 1990, school expenditures remained the top priority, but funding for street improvements dropped out of the top three priorities. This could reflect the fact that expenditures have produced improvements in street conditions; such improvements are highly visible and have had a significant impact on traffic flow; and citizens feel that other services should now get attention.

Table 15.1

Overall Rating of City Services

	Percent responding excellent and good	
Date of survey	Citizens	Civic leaders
12/85	80	—
4/87	77	—
4/88	81	94
4/89	78	—
4/90	88	99

Note: Respondents were asked—"In general, how would you rate the basic services provided by the City of Auburn: excellent, good, fair, poor, or no opinion?"

Table 15.2

Relative Priorities of Citizens for Budgeting

	Top three priorities		
Date of survey	1	2	3
12/85*	Streets	Sewers	Fire
4/87	Schools	Streets	Intersections
4/88*	Streets	Industrial development	Fire
4/89	Streets, Schools		Police
4/90	Schools	Police	Water

*Respondents were not asked to rate schools in the 1985 and 1988 surveys.

The second place priority given to police protection is an interesting phenomenon, especially if it proves to be a trend. Funding for police services received virtually no mention until 1989, when it appeared as the third priority; in 1990, it moved up to second priority. Clearly, city officials will be observing this change in the future to see if it represents a reordering of priorities; and, if so, what are the underlying causes of this shift.

The long-term emphasis on the need for improving streets, a common concern among urban citizens, appears to have had an impact on capital outlay decisions of the City Council. Table 15.3 shows the city's expenditures for street improvements from 1982–83 through 1988–89. Apart from minor projects funded through the operating budget, the city invested no capital funds in such improvements in the first two years of this period, and only a token amount in 1984–85. For these three fiscal years, the bulk of the funds for street improvements came from external sources—e.g., general revenue sharing and/or the community development program. In 1985–86, this pattern changed drastically. The city committed over half a million dollars of its own funds to street improvements. This accounted for 51 percent of the total spent that year. In subsequent years, no external funds were involved. The city's capital outlays for street improvements increased to almost $1.9 million in 1988–89, about 96 percent of the total capital outlays for this purpose.

Table 15.4 shows the amount budgeted for education (transfers to the school board) for 1982–83 through 1989–90. During this eight-year period, the amount more than doubled. More significantly, there was a change in the source of funds. From 1982–83 to 1984–85, the amount allocated to education was relatively substantial. However, it consisted entirely of general revenue sharing

Table 15.3

Expenditures for Street Improvements:
City of Auburn, Fiscal Year 1983 Through Fiscal Year 1989

| | Source of funds | | | | |
Fiscal year	Revenue sharing	Community development	Gas taxes	Capital funds	Total
1982–1983	50,000	65,797	89,576	—	205,373
1983–1984	40,000	431,599	104,846	—	576,445
1984–1985	—	244,252	115,000	26,749	386,001
1985–1986	—	366,608	138,000	530,691	1,035,299
1986–1987	—	—	96,880	853,906	950,786
1987–1988	—	—	158,532	916,432	1,074,964
1988–1989	—	—	75,889	1,899,944	1,975,833

Table 15.4

Budget Allocations for Education: City of Auburn, Fiscal Year 1983 through
Fiscal Year 1990

Fiscal year	Amount budgeted
1982–1983	$693,900*
1983–1984	691,940*
1984–1985	938,060*
1985–1986	1,035,000
1986–1987	1,190,000
1987–1988	1,334,950
1988–1989	1,273,330
1989–1990	1,356,750

*These were General Revenue Sharing funds.

funds. In 1985–86, the city provided money for education from local revenue, without a school tax increase, and has done so since then. During this five-year period, the amount allocated to education has increased by 31 percent.

Table 15.5 compares the funding priorities expressed collectively by the City Council members with those of the citizens surveyed. Allowing for the changes over the years in the questionnaire, the data show a strong relationship between the two sets of priorities. Funding for streets and schools was the main concern for both council members and citizens from 1985 to 1989. In 1989 and 1990, as noted, funding for police protection was given a high priority by citizens. If the posited relationship between citizen and council priorities is correct, this priority should be reflected in the FY 1991 budget.

The question of interest is if, and how, citizens' responses are related to council budgetary processes and decisions. Since 1982–83, Auburn's City Council has been involved in an annual priority-setting activity. However, in the earlier years the relationship between priorities and budget allocations was at best tenuous. For example, in 1982–83 the council gave a high priority to street improvements but appropriated virtually no money for that purpose. A more systematic linkage between priorities and allocations began to be established in 1983–84. The citizen survey

Table 15.5

Comparison of Council and Citizens' Priorities

Date of survey	Council	Citizen
12/85	Major intersection improvements Street paving School funding	Streets* Downtown parking Library
4/87	Major street improvements Intersection improvements School funding	School funding Street improvements Intersection improvements
4/88	Street improvements School funding Recreation facilities	Street improvements* Industrial development Fire protection
4/89	Airport expansion School funding Streets	Streets and schools Police protection
4/90	Employee salaries** School funding Streets	School funding Police Water system

*Citizens were not asked questions about school funding in the 1985 and 1988 surveys.
**Citizens were not asked questions about city employee salaries in any of the surveys.

was initiated as an integral part of this linkage. Since the process has become institutionalized, it can be plausibly argued that the funding pattern in the budget is related to the views expressed by citizens through the survey.

CITIZEN AND COUNCIL PRIORITIES

It should be noted that the City of Auburn has a council-manager form of government. The council consists of eight members, two elected from each of four wards. The mayor is elected at large and serves as chairperson of the council. This structure has contributed to the successful integration of the citizen survey into the city's policy-making and budgetary processes.

It has been noted that the council-manager form of government tends to operate in a way that emphasizes cooperation and a city-wide approach to public polices and issues (Svara, 1990). While district interests enter the decision-making process in various ways and at various points, the policy-making and budgetary processes are designed to encourage broader concerns. In Auburn, for example, all policy and budgetary questions are reviewed and resolved by the council members meeting as a committee of the whole.

Other cities, large or small, in which the district interests are important, either by structure or custom, may find that the objectives for citizen surveys, and the use of survey data, are substantially different. Theoretically, however, an argument in support of the utility of survey data can be made in either context. A comparative study of surveys in both settings would provide additional and useful insights on this general topic.

The assertion of a causal link between citizen priorities and council budgetary and programmatic decisions was explored through a survey conducted in 1989 of council members' attitudes.

Council members were asked several questions concerning their individual assessments of the value of the citizen survey to them, and the extent to which they used the survey data in setting goals and funding priorities.

Five of the nine council members stated that they used the citizen survey data to influence the setting of priorities in the budgeting process; four stated that they used the data to set priorities. In establishing budget priorities, seven council members stated that they felt the survey data were very important; only two responded "somewhat important." And, in ranking four statements on the utility of the citizen survey, council members gave the highest score to its role in helping the council relate community needs to budget priorities.

Thus, a plausible case can be made that citizen survey responses are reflected in council budgetary and programmatic decisions. However, the relationship is not unidirectional. While the information presented here suggests that the council does react to citizens' views, the council also fulfills a leadership role, and in doing so can influence citizens' perceptions of projects and priorities.

For example, airport expansion has become a major concern of the members of the council. However, it is a project which has yet to be accorded a high priority rating in the citizen survey—21 percent gave airport expansion a high priority, 42 percent gave it a medium priority, 29 percent gave it a low priority, and the remainder felt it should receive no priority at all in the 1990 survey. Also, during the past two years the development of a large tract of land donated to the city as a park has engaged a significant amount of the council's attention. In the 1990 survey, some 60 percent of the respondents indicated that they were not aware of the project; and only 17 percent gave it a high priority for development. Since the survey, there has been considerable publicity about both the airport and park projects, essentially placing them on the public agenda. It is anticipated that the 1991 survey will reflect this increased salience and will provide further evidence on the interplay between public and council priorities.

CONCLUSIONS

Auburn's use of citizen survey data illustrates the value that this approach to citizen participation can have for local policymakers. A strong consensus exists among elected officials that survey data are valuable to them as they establish priorities for the city budget. The results suggest that, if properly conducted, citizen surveys can be an efficient and productive linkage mechanism between public officials and citizens. More importantly, the case study illustrates how citizen surveys provide a framework for citizen participation in local government policy and management processes. The key appears to be the institutionalization of the citizen survey program, including the linkage of survey results to the formal budgetary process. On a more qualitative level, the citizen survey program seems to have contributed to the development of a more positive attitude in the community toward both the role of the citizenry and its government.

The data support the Webb and Hatry findings that citizen surveys are efficient ways to secure data important both to the policy process and to citizen participation. The data in the Auburn case also confirm the Webb and Hatry finding on the value of repetitive annual surveys, and the Glass conclusion that citizen surveys can provide high-quality data. Further, the data address the Stipak concern over the relationship between citizen-provided opinion data, specifically on budgetary priorities and judgments that elected policymakers have to make.

In summary, this study supports the conclusion that citizen surveys can provide a productive mechanism to incorporate citizen participation efficiently and productively into local governing processes. The study identifies organizational structures, survey methods, and procedures that make citizen surveys applicable to small communities. While not conclusively demonstrated, the survey and fiscal data appear to confirm a linkage between citizen attitudes and evaluations and leadership budgetary and programmatic decisions. This perception has substantially altered the quality of political life in the community, if quality can be measured in terms of the absence of public conflict. In 1980, town and gown, student and permanent resident, and factional council politics characterized the community. While change in leadership, including the Mayor and City Manager, have certainly contributed to the change in political climate, the role of the citizen survey and its incorporation into the city's policy and management processes suggest that some important and positive linkages between citizen and policy maker have been established.

REFERENCES

Advisory Commission on Intergovernmental Relations, 1979. *Citizen Participation in the Federal System.* Washington, D.C.: Government Printing Office.

Brudney, Jeffrey L. and Robert E. England, 1982. "Urban Policy Making and Subjective Service Evaluations: Are They Compatible?" *Public Administration Review,* vol. 42 (March/April), pp. 127–135.

Daneke, Gregory A. and Patricia Klobus-Edwards, 1979. "Survey Research for Public Administrators." *Public Administration Review,* vol. 39 (September/October), pp. 421–426.

Fitzgerald, Michael R. and Robert F. Durant, 1980. "Citizen Evaluations and Urban Management: Service Delivery in an Era of Protest." *Public Administration Review,* vol. 40 (November/December), pp. 585–594.

Glass, James J., undated. *Citizen Surveys: Powerful Tools for Public Managers.* Auburn, AL: Center for Governmental Services.

Hatry, Harry P., Louis H. Blair, Donald M. Fisk, John M. Greiner, John R. Hall, Jr., and Philip S. Schaenman, 1977. *How Effective Are Your Community Services?* Washington, D.C.: The Urban Institute.

Page, Benjamin I. and Robert Y. Shapiro, 1983. "Effects of Public Opinion on Policy." *American Political Science Review,* vol. 77 (March), pp. 175–190.

Rosentraub, Mark S., Karen Harlow, and Lyke Thompson, 1979. "In Defense of Surveys As a Reliable Source of Evaluation Data." *Public Administration Review,* vol. 39 (May/June), pp. 302–303.

Schneider, Mark, 1976. "The Quality of Life and Social Indicators Research." *Public Administration Review,* vol. 36 (May/June), pp. 297–305.

Sharp, Elaine B., 1990. *Urban Politics and Administration.* New York: Longman.

Stipak, Brian, 1980. "Local Governments' Use of Citizen Surveys." *Public Administration Review,* vol. 40 (September/October), pp. 521–525.

Streib, Gregory, 1990. "Dusting Off a Forgotten Management Tool: The Citizen Survey." *Public Management,* vol. 72 (August), pp. 17–19.

Svara, James H., 1990. *Official Leadership in the City.* New York: Oxford University Press.

Webb, Kenneth and Harry P. Hatry, 1973. *Obtaining Citizen Feedback: The Application of Citizen Surveys to Local Governments.* Washington, D.C.: The Urban Institute.

Wilson, L. A., II, 1983. "Preference Revelation and Public Policy: Making Sense of Citizen Survey Data." *Public Administration Review,* vol. 43 (July/August), pp. 335–342.

CHAPTER 16

EMERGENT CITIZEN GROUPS AND EMERGENCY MANAGEMENT

ROBERT A. STALLINGS AND E.L. QUARANTELLI

INTRODUCTION

The following example describes something seldom envisioned in planning for community emergencies: groups of private citizens carrying out important disaster tasks. This particular disaster is a brush fire in Southern California, but it could have been any type of emergency anywhere in the United States.

> Abetted by drought, arsonists, and fierce Santa Ana winds, the worst fire in Southern California's history broke out on Friday, September 25, 1970. . . . One of the major fire areas was east of San Diego. On Monday, September 28, this fire moved west and south burning 185,000 acres and destroying about 250 homes. In addition, between 50,000–60,000 people were forced to evacuate the outskirts of San Diego. . . .
>
> On Sunday, September 27, evacuation orders were given to residents east of El Cajon, California and south of a 30-mile stretch of Highway 80—this area lies east of San Diego. Evacuees were requested to report to the San Diego County Civil Defense Headquarters for registration and assistance. Swamped with mobilizing and coordinating resources from local, state, and federal agencies, civil defense had neither the time nor personnel to handle evacuee registration adequately and thus turned to the local community for assistance. Volunteers responded to this request by developing an organized effort to handle evacuee registration and support activities for firefighters. This group was separate from civil defense, developing its own independent leadership and making its own decisions; hence, it is viewed as not an extension of civil defense operations but rather as an autonomous operating group.
>
> Mrs. B., vice president of a local women's club, heard from a friend of the need for volunteers to assist in registering evacuees. Accompanied by her husband, she arrived at civil defense headquarters (CDHQ) Sunday afternoon to find that several others present had

---

From *Public Administration Review,* 45 (January, Special Issue 1985): 93–100. Copyright © 1985 by American Society for Public Administration. Reprinted with permission.

already begun to set up tables and card files to help process incoming evacuees. Evacuees began to stream into the building late Sunday afternoon, filling corridors and creating a general state of confusion. At this point, Mr. B. jumped onto a table and asked the crowd to line up behind tables so that an orderly registration could proceed. From this point on, Mr. B. was consulted for directions and decisions.

As evacuation orders were issued over radio and television, individual citizens began telephoning CDHQ volunteering to take animals (primarily horses) and to provide shelter, food, and other supplies for fire victims. The contents of these calls were recorded on cards noting the donor's name, address, telephone number, and nature of donation. It shortly became apparent that more telephones were needed, and four additional lines were immediately installed. In addition to these calls, food, clothing, medical supplies, blankets, and personal items (toothpaste, soap, shaving equipment) began arriving at CDHQ. A number of young men volunteered to unload these items from trucks and cars and to stock them in the designated storage area in the building. It was felt that all items should be inventoried, recording name, address, and telephone number of the donor.

By Sunday evening evacuees had stopped coming in and those present had a breathing spell. This time was further spent organizing activities and making specific task allocations. Mr. B. felt that he needed assistance and called upon a close friend, Mr. R., to see if he would volunteer his time. Mr. R., an insurance salesman with flexible working hours, agreed. He arrived and was briefed by Mr. B. regarding the operation and problems. The greatest problems at this time were answering and recording telephone calls and processing the continuous influx of resources. Working together, Mr. B and Mr. R. began assigning workers who seemed dependable and efficient to specific tasks, e.g., developing and organizing a supply room, an emergency medical area, a home referral system, and a system of food runs to transport sandwiches and coffee to firefighters. An agreement was reached that Mr. B. would become night coordinator while Mr. R. would supervise daytime activities.

On Monday, the demands placed on the group began to change. Instead of handling evacuation registration, firefighters began arriving for food and a place to rest. The whole internal structure was reorganized to meet this demand by acquiring cots and personal toiletries, maintaining a kitchen, and developing a system to launder firefighters' clothing while they slept. A volunteer was assigned to gather and bag clothing and to work out a system to transport it to and from Laundromats where volunteers from local women's clubs would wash them.

By Wednesday, the group organization began to take definite form. Departments were set up to take care of specific task areas. Five basic activities crystallized: general support and assistance; providing food and clean clothing for firefighters; stockroom to receive, record, and dispense all material resources; a food and coffee relay system, which operated between CDHQ and the firefighters; and lastly, a communications department which received, sent, and recorded all incoming and outgoing telephone calls. Mr. R. and Mr. B coordinated and integrated the activities of the various departments. Fifteen persons were present at all times to staff the operation.

One week from the day it began, the decision was made to close down the San Diego support operation. The fire had been contained, and residents had returned to their homes. Material resources, gathered throughout the emergency, were dispensed to other organizations and agencies who would continue to assist fire victims.[1]

EMERGENT CITIZEN GROUPS IN DISASTERS

Dealing with organized groups of citizens is part of the daily experience of many public officials. These groups represent the interests of constituencies such as the elderly, ethnic minorities, parents of school children, and the like. Often neighborhood-based, such groups are part of a long tradition of grass-roots political organization in the United States. About them, much has been written.[2]

Less well-known are groups of citizens such as in the preceding case example that emerge around perceived needs or problems associated with both natural and technological disaster situations. We as sociologists call them "emergent groups" to highlight their newness, absence of formalization, and lack of tradition. They range, for example, from ephemeral teams of neighbors attempting search and rescue, to community residents organizing themselves to force removal of potentially hazardous waste sites or nuclear plants, to disaster victims getting together to pressure officials to take preparedness and mitigation measures for probable reoccurrences of the floods and landslides they have just experienced.

Such emergent groups seem to imply that no public organization exists to respond to the situation or that existing ones will not act in potential or actual emergencies. Partly because of this perceived implication of failure, the appearance of such groups is frequently controversial. Public officials often do not take them into account in community emergency management planning and misunderstand both the reasons behind their emergence and the roles they play in disaster-related community problems. This is especially unfortunate because these kinds of emergent citizen groups are likely to be even more prominent in the future than they are at present. In addition, there is increasing attention to integrated emergency management emphasizing commonalities in disasters occasioned by human, technological, and natural disaster agents, as well as common elements cutting across mitigation, preparedness, response, and recovery activities. Because emergent citizen groups become even more salient when emergency management is viewed in this way, it is important for public officials to know about these groups in order to deal with them more effectively. In this paper we will address three principal questions: (1) What are the characteristics of these emergent groups? (2) What roles do they play in the various phases of the emergency management process? and (3) What implications do such groups have for emergency management policies and procedures?

Our observations are drawn primarily from research by the Disaster Research Center (DRC) on emergent social groupings in actual or potential disasters,[3] supplemented by our own interpretation of selected empirical studies of others.[4] We exclude from this discussion the extensive studies done on established citizen or public interest groups, such as those that are a part of the environmental or anti-nuclear movements,[5] because our interest is in newly formed or forming groups rather than formal organizations or clearly institutionalized voluntary associations. Also, because they are more numerous and prominent, almost all of our remarks are about emergent citizen groups at the local community level.

CHARACTERISTICS OF EMERGENT GROUPS

Emergent groups can be thought of as private citizens who work together in pursuit of collective goals relevant to actual or potential disasters but whose organization has not yet become institutionalized. As such they are less than public bureaucracies but more than independently acting, isolated private persons converging on the same problem. Such groups are considered emergent in two respects: the relationships among the individuals pursuing the collective goals are new (the group has an internal structure that did not exist before) and the tasks being undertaken in pursuit of these goals are new for individuals so joined. In its purest form an emergent group has a new structure (i.e., social relations) and a new function (i.e., goals or tasks).[6]

Emergent citizen groups appear in both the emergency phase of disasters, as well as during the less crisis-like preparedness and recovery phases. Because these two types of settings are somewhat different, features of emergent groups arising in these two contexts will be described separately.

Emergent Groups at Emergency Times

It is possible to identify at least three distinct types of emergent groups in the emergency phase. The first type has been labeled "damage assessment groups"; this is because they often provide public officials with their first information about the actual extent and location of disaster damage. This type is illustrated by groups of citizens performing search and rescue immediately after impact, or attempting to ascertain which facilities and buildings had been damaged, or drawing up lists of missing persons in the later stages of an emergency period. A second type has been designated "operations" groups. Examples include emergent groups that form to collect and distribute food and clothing to disaster victims, or those that undertake street and debris clearance right after impact, or that transmit messages through ham or citizen band radio networks. Sometimes in catastrophic disasters with very extended emergency-time periods, a third type of emergent group appears: so-called "coordinating" groups which sometimes take the form of impromptu citizen committees. These have less to do with immediate assessment or operational activities and more with setting direction, resolving domain disputes, and assuming responsibility for certain communitywide problems.

The three types of emergency phase emergent groups share the following characteristics. Although group size can vary considerably with numbers ranging in the dozens or more, most involve only a handful of people at any given time. There tends to be a core of continuing members with other individuals participating fitfully and irregularly. While there almost always is a sense of "we-ness," or working together as a group, the entity usually does not acquire a name. Member involvement seems partially affected by unique situational factors (e.g., being present where the necessity for search and rescue or debris clearance is apparent) and partially by prior experience, knowledge, or skill (e.g., knowing how to cook for large numbers, handle radio equipment, contact public officials). Therefore, group composition especially as to age, sex, race, and life style varies considerably from group to group.

Structurally these groups tend to be relatively undifferentiated. That is, they have a flat hierarchy with little distance between the top and bottom. There is usually a division of labor, but roles are ordinarily not highly specialized. There are few, if any, symbols of office, and seldom are there clearly designated leaders. Nor is there likely to be a formally assigned liaison or boundary person for dealing with other organizations. Among other things, these structural properties make it difficult for those outside the group to develop relationships with it.

The structure of these emergent groups is closely tied to the tasks they undertake. For example, if the group is involved in taking telephone requests for aid, the structure might consist only of individuals answering telephones, those collating the information received, and one or two individuals loosely overseeing the entire operation. Such groups typically have an almost non-existent administrative structure with proportionately more time and other resources devoted to "line" activities than in established organizations. As a corollary, these groups lack practically all formal elements of organization: while there are clear norms of conduct, there rarely are written rules or organization charts; since almost all participants are volunteers, there are no formal job specifications or formal training; equipment and goods are obtained and used, but seldom are written records kept and archived; policies and tasks are assumed and dropped, but as a result of *ad hoc* decision making rather than long-range planning. In short, emergent groups at emergency times are informal organizations with notably new structures and functions.

Many emergent citizen groups exist for only short periods of time—hours or maybe a few days. Recognition of their efforts by other organizations seems to be a major impetus to their continued existence. Such recognition provides not only visibility for the group but more importantly serves to legitimate the group's function. Persistence is also facilitated by certain internal changes, such as crystallization of a formal structure and delineation of boundary roles. These changes seemingly make the emergent group better suited to the more stable conditions of the non-emergency context. However, while some emergency time emergent citizen groups provide the seed for new organizations in the post-impact phase of disasters, very few directly evolve in such a fashion. Most cease to exist when the immediate emergency time tasks are no longer urgently needed.

Emergent Groups at Non-Emergency Times

Non-emergency time emergent citizen groups tend to focus on a variety of actual or potential disaster-related problems. Current DRC research has already studied about 50 such groups.[7] In the course of doing this work, we have found citizens attempting to organize themselves with respect to the following kinds of matters, among others:

- to plan local evacuation in case of a hurricane;
- to oppose the development of a hazardous chemical waste dump site;
- to help a community rebuild after a tornado;
- to train and prepare a neighborhood for responding to an earthquake;
- to prevent, after a flood, further housing development in a flood plain;
- to obtain reimbursement for homes damaged by landslides;
- to help develop an area's emergency plan;
- to inform a community about the possible dangers if a nuclear power plant were allowed to start up;
- to develop a high tide/flood warning system;
- to have homes physically moved out of a flood plain;
- to plan household and family responses to hurricanes;
- to work on mitigation and preparedness measures for landslides;
- to object to certain post-disaster housing policies;
- to ensure that tornado victims obtained the benefits due them;
- to prevent the pollution of a creek;
- to have a dike built to prevent future flooding;
- to make a community aware of an earthquake threat;
- to replant trees destroyed in a tornado;
- to close down an operative nuclear plant;
- to prepare for expected eventual flooding;
- to have a toxic waste dump site removed;
- to work on a flash flood warning system; and
- to bring actions against community officials for not preventing a disaster.

It is possible to identify two major types among pre- and post-disaster emergent citizen groups. In terms of their overall emphasis, some groups are oriented to specific goals, while others are general in goal orientation. The former involve citizens who come together to deal with specific disaster-related problems in particular localities and where major concern is with clearly identifiable personal and family stakes in the outcome. This type of group is exemplified by attempts to close a neighborhood hazardous waste dump site or to obtain specific information that will maximize recovery among those affected by a landslide. Tasks and contacts tend to be rather specific because of "this danger in our back yard" or "our damaged homes." In contrast are the more frequent general goal emergent citizen groups. These are citizens collectively organized to deal with general disaster problems which actually or potentially affect the entire community but where a case must be made that an actual threat or impact really exists. Examples include earthquake preparedness groups and anti-nuclear plant groups. Objectives and relationships tend to be more general in these groups, but the potential for community controversy and conflict with public officials is present in both general-goal and specific-goal emergent groups.

Emergent citizen groups involved in the preparedness/mitigation and in the restoration/recovery phases of natural and technological threats and dangers usually have the following properties. These groups also tend to be small, with an average overall membership of about 100 but with an active core of only a half dozen or so. Since membership is mostly informal, there are many nonmember participants—persons who take active roles in group activities but who do not identify themselves as members, such as technical experts or mass media reporters who provide information, advice, and other resources because they sympathize with the group's goals. Even though its boundaries tend to be rather fluid, the typical group usually acquires a name early in its career (there is a strong leaning toward acronyms such as H.E.L.P.). A majority of members, especially of the active core, are women. Members, in general, are from white, middle-class backgrounds with many in the 30-to-40 age range. There seldom is racial and ethnic representation even if minorities are prominent in the community at-large.

Structurally these non-emergency time groups are also relatively flat and not very complex. Most have a three-tier or circular structure with a handful of active members in the central core supported by an outer core of less active members who can be mobilized for specific tasks with the remainder of members at the periphery who sign petitions, pay dues, receive a newsletter, or attend an occasional meeting or demonstration. The core of these emergent groups almost always involves a division of labor, often in terms of the particular personal skills of core members. The division of labor is, therefore, frequently sharp because roles are not easily interchangeable. This may account for the fact that there is relatively little turnover of core members, who often devote large blocks of time to the work of the group even though there are no paid positions.

Although there may be a formal hierarchical order resulting from the establishment of formal offices such as chairs or presidents, there seldom is any actual operative hierarchy in the core. In fact, core group decision making is almost always informal and highly democratic, except in some instances where there is a charismatic leader who typically had been one of the group's founders. While larger group meetings are used primarily to ratify core decisions, concern over obtaining larger group approval is genuine. However, even though specific core members are often appointed or designated as boundary personnel with other organizations, the mixture of formal and informal structure sometimes baffles those who have to deal with the emergent group.

Among major activities are attempts to mobilize resources and establish new social linkages. Resource mobilization includes usually unsystematic recruiting of new members; holding irregular meetings for group members; publishing newsletters; and obtaining non-material resources—money being far less important as a group resource than information, specialized knowledge, and access to key persons. Establishing new social linkages involves attempts to identify the organizations that might be able to do something about the perceived problem, actually contacting what are taken to be the relevant governmental officials, and joining in common efforts with other similarly oriented citizen groups; but this most often takes the form of establishing coalitions across, rather than within, communities.

Initially most groups are quite ignorant about how public policies are made and carried out. Often their first efforts take the form of a shotgun approach with many and varied public agencies being contacted, especially the more visible public officials at different levels of government. Actually, the help sought in this shotgun approach is often unclear and undefined, since most emergent citizen groups initially have only very broad and vague goals such as "being able to live in a safe place" or "recovering from the disaster." But an unwillingness to answer questions or to indicate sympathetic interests by those organizations and officials approached is often perceived by the emergent groups as an attempt to deny legitimate citizen concerns or as a cover up of possibly inept, negligent, or illegal actions. Perceptions that the group is being stonewalled or not being given a fair hearing almost always lead to an intensification of effort. This includes attempts to clarify group goals and to develop appropriate strategies and tactics more clearly. The vast majority of emergent citizen groups consciously and deliberately try to avoid identification with the traditional and established political parties in their communities; but to the extent that the groups see themselves as rebuffed, they are likely to start making demands and taking political action in the broad sense of the term.

When emergent groups reach this point, they start to shed some of their emergent qualities and, as such, are beyond the scope of this paper. Actually few emergent groups develop in linear fashion in terms of greater specificity of goals, complexity in division of labor, or formalization through legal incorporation. But to the extent that there is movement in such directions, they come to resemble, if not to be, what is more familiarly known as pressure groups, voluntary associations, or public interest groups.

OTHER TYPES OF EMERGENCE

We noted earlier that two distinguishing features of emergent citizen groups were the development of new structural arrangements among members and the undertaking of tasks that were new to the group. Only those collectivities characterized by both features are properly referred to as emergent groups. We pointed out that not all such groups are comprised exclusively of private citizens. We want to expand on this point, because much emergence takes place within and among organizations in the public sector rather than just among private citizens. There also is much emergent behavior that does not manifest itself in group form. So while the focus of this paper is on emergent groups, it is important to recognize that they are only a part of the full range of emergent phenomena to be expected before, during, and after disaster threats and impacts.

Sometimes private citizens organize new groups in terms of their established work or occupational roles rather than merely as members of the community. For instance, within hours after Wilkes-Barre, Pennsylvania, was severely flooded by Tropical Storm Agnes:

> three prominent civic leaders, a banker, a construction company executive, and a judge, toured the area by helicopter and immediately called an emergency meeting for 13 chief financial institution representatives. . . .

Out of that meeting an informal group was created and an informal leader agreed upon.

The immediate goals of the group, still informal and unnamed, were largely economic, for the financial institutions held mortgages and other notes on apparently worthless homes, automobiles, and businesses. . . .

Since few local residents had flood insurance, a retroactive insurance plan to restore equity or the pre-flood value of property was devised and to treat victims as if they had had flood insurance.

After several meetings with major private insurance company executives . . . as well as federal and state governmental leaders, the group realized that the plan was not feasible. It was then decided to urge unprecedented federal and state assistance through established recovery agencies. . . . [8]

Out of this there eventually evolved another group, the Flood Recovery Task Force, which engaged in a massive lobbying campaign for passage in the U.S. Congress of the 1972 Agnes Recovery Act and worked behind the scenes on community redevelopment of the devastated downtown area of Wilkes-Barre. While many emergent groups composed of citizens in their work roles do not develop in as complex or covert a way as illustrated in this example, there are such groupings in disaster situations alongside the "purer" emergent citizen groups.

There are also emergent groups composed exclusively or primarily of public officials. In the emergency time period damage assessment groups are most often composed of private citizens, but in the Alaska earthquake the first and most systematic team to evaluate building damage consisted of three officials from three different public agencies and one private citizen. Operations groups may have mixed compositions, but often they are likely to be made up of either private citizens or personnel carrying out regular or planned disaster job roles in private or public emergency organizations; for example, in one disaster we found one evacuation center manned exclusively by private citizens who had spontaneously organized to create it and another established and directed by personnel from community emergency agencies and the Red Cross. It is rare, although not uncommon, for emergent coordinating groups to have private citizen composition. Far more often this type of emergent group comes out of newly established relationships among personnel from agencies in the public sector, although in small communities there often is not a clear line between persons acting as private citizens and in their roles as public officials. As one example, in an effort to avoid jurisdictional disputes, an informal coordinating committee was created after the Indianapolis Coliseum explosion which consisted of the city fire chief, the county coroner, the sheriff, the civil defense director, and a representative from the state police.

Finally, there is much quasi-emergent behavior, especially during the emergency time phase of disasters. There are numerous instances where existing public organizations find themselves undertaking new, unexpected tasks but performing them with existing structures; e.g., in a recent flood the city police department opened and initially operated two evacuation shelters until the Red Cross, which by tradition and by plan should have set up the shelters, could arrive and take over. There are also instances in which traditional organizational tasks must be carried out with innovative and unplanned structural arrangements, such as when a weather service office which had lost all its telephone lines asked an amateur radio club to come in and set up a communication network with other weather station offices. An example of a combination of both task and structural emergence took place within a public works department when an emergency staff headed by the chief engineer was informally created to take charge of disaster-related operations during a flood.[9] In these and similar cases no new groups emerge. There is emergence in either the structures or the functions of established public organizations, but these alterations are not the result of previous undertakings or of any kind of planning.

IMPLICATIONS FOR EMERGENCY MANAGEMENT

Given what we have said here about emergent citizen groups and related emergent behavior, what are the implications for public managers and administrators involved in the emergency management process? There are at least five points that can be made concerning how emergent phenomena should be viewed; namely, they are inevitable, natural, neither necessarily dysfunctional nor conflictive, and cannot be eliminated by planning.

First, emergence is inevitable before, during, and after disasters. There are deeply rooted reasons for its pervasive appearance. One necessary condition for the emergence of citizen groups during the emergency time period is a perceived need or demand which requires immediate action. Similarly, emergent citizen groups in pre- and post-disaster periods are stimulated by the perception that a problem or issue is not recognized or acknowledged by others. Perception—whether justified or not—should not be dismissed carelessly, for in the words of a famous social psychological principle, "if people define a situation as real, then it is real insofar as consequences are concerned." In large-scale emergencies such perceived needs arise if there are severe problems of interorganizational coordination, momentary lapses in the assumption of overall authority, or where key organizations confront disaster demands far in excess of their routine capabilities. In non-emergency times, emergency management has come to incorporate certain hazards such as toxic wastes, nuclear energy, dam construction, and flood plains, all of which involve competing and contradictory social values. As such, they are almost necessarily controversial. Thus, in the case of both emergency and non-emergency times, there will always be discrepancies between what some citizens see as what is and what they think should be. Such perceptual discrepancies almost assure the presence of one of the necessary conditions for group emergence.

Second, emergent citizen groups are the outcome of natural social processes; they do not represent a deviational or abnormal pattern. Emergent groups are sometimes viewed disparagingly because they lack many of the properties of more "normal" organizations such as a clear-cut chain of command and a well-defined division of labor. Judged by everyday standards, emergent groups do sometimes appear to be inefficient or ineffective, or both. But such traditional models of organization have never proven helpful in understanding group functioning in disaster, even of the actions of established agencies. Actually their looseness is one of the real strengths of emergent groups. Lacking most of the formal features of traditional organizations, new groups have much greater flexibility which is an important characteristic in suddenly altered or high-demand environments. Compared to existing disaster-relevant organizations, emergent groups have far fewer resources devoted to administrative or management activities. They are not constrained from undertaking new tasks or moving in different directions by established procedures or rules (including laws). They generally have greater proportions of uncommitted resources, such as donated items and volunteer labor, to bring to bear on a perceived need. In other words, some of the apparent disadvantages of emergent groups can provide real coping advantages in fluid and unusually demanding situations. Overstated, disaster-related emergent citizen groups represent normal responses to abnormal settings.

Third, emergent citizen groups while not always functional are not necessarily dysfunctional either. While a perceived gap calling for immediate action may be necessary for the emergence of these groups, it is not sufficient. In the absence of certain situational factors including knowledge and resources, initial, *ad hoc* efforts may not lead to any concerted action. For example, a search and rescue team may form, but if heavy duty equipment needed to raise debris is unavailable the effort is likely to be abandoned. Emergent citizen groups may not always succeed or use the most appropriate means for their objectives, but then neither do established bureaucracies. So while emergence may not be the best solution, it does represent an attempt at resolution of a perceived problem and should be recognized for that fact alone. As such, the appearance of emergent citizen groups is less of an implication of failure by established organizations—as discussed very early in this paper—and more an indication that there are always alternative possibilities for dealing with problems.

Fourth, emergent citizen groups are not inherently in opposition to public authorities. It is true that in the later stages of development of such groups, especially those in pre- and post-impact time periods, there often is conflict and a mutual we-they attitude on the part of community officials and group members. However, the great majority of groups start out with the notion that public officials will be on their side once their attention is called to the issue or question bothering the group. Most citizen groups are also initially very reluctant to engage in open confrontations with community officials, for there are very strong internal normative pressures not to appear to outsiders as being radical in any way. It takes the spread of a belief that some heretofore unrecognized problem is not being legitimately dealt with by the agencies that are responsible for serving the public to create anger and hostility and an increasing definition of public officials as the enemy. In turn, viewing emergent citizen groups in a positive rather than negative light can be difficult for public officials who see themselves defined as the opposition in some conflict over what has become a controversial matter. Rarely is the quality of emergency management the central issue in these controversies, but the us-them nature of conflict usually makes it seem like this is the case. Advantage should be taken of the initially neutral or positive views that citizens generally have of public officials rather than later trying to undo a conflictive or hostile relationship.

Fifth, emergent phenomena cannot be eliminated by prior planning. Several years ago one of us implied that much of group emergence could probably be forestalled through disaster planning. Taken out of context, this sounds like another version of the incorrect criticism that emergence represents the failure of planning. There is a relationship between planning and emergence in the sense that if group emergence is fostered by a perceived need or gap, and if planning or previous disaster experience can reduce that gap, then effective planning may weaken one of the necessary conditions underlying emergence. However, emergencies, especially those largest in scale, always present some unique demands that can never be anticipated. Viewed from the level of the community system, group emergence is one of the ways communities adjust to the uncertainties in their environments. At the organizational level, we might add that not everything that organizations will confront can be anticipated either. Thus, it is unrealistic to expect that any kind of planning could abort all disaster-related emergent phenomena.

Notwithstanding, planning ought to take into account the inevitability and pervasiveness of emergent groups and behavior. For emergency and post-impact times there might be a policy of trying to link emergent citizen groups into the network of emergency management organizations. Such linkages will undoubtedly have the effect of prolonging their life span, but this linking process (some might use the term cooptation) provides a way to try to achieve coordination among all the groups and organizations involved in the disaster response.

For pre-impact times, consideration might be given to what forms of emergent behavior public officials might actually want to facilitate. We do not mean to imply that the generating conditions are so well understood that the desired form of emergence can be guaranteed. But it is possible to encourage existing citizen groups to add an emergency capability or to consider performing a relevant function in an emergency context. A key to this process is legitimization produced by the public recognition of such a group by those in positions of authority. When successful such efforts allow emergency agencies to deal in a pre-planned way with organized groups of citizens in a crisis rather than with isolated individuals or independently operating private groups.

As one example, we conclude by mentioning some of the assumptions underlying current earthquake preparedness efforts in Southern California. The emphasis has shifted from one in which disaster-relevant agencies assumed complete responsibility to a partnership in which these agencies are now also facilitating the community's effort to be more self-reliant. A key planning assumption is that, in the event of overwhelming damage from a major earthquake, neighborhoods may be on their own for up to the first 72 hours after impact.[10] Many police departments have added an earthquake preparedness component to their regular neighborhood crime watch meetings and newsletters. Such strategies represent deliberate attempts to facilitate emergent citizen groups and quasi-emergent behavior.

Finally, to the extent we have greater knowledge and the resulting observations are applied to disaster planning, the more we are preparing for other kinds of community emergencies. Studies made of emergent groups in riots and civil disturbances in American society indicate that there are some differences between such dissensus community crises as compared with the consensus crises of natural and technological disasters.[11] However, there are more similarities than there are differences for most purposes. So, to know about and to plan for disasters is also to have some implicit knowledge and to be doing some latent planning for conflictive types of community emergencies as well.

ACKNOWLEDGMENTS

Data for this report were obtained through funding by grant Number CEE-8113191 from the National Science Foundation (NSF) and by contract EMW-K-0881 from the Federal Emergency Management Agency (FEMA) to the Disaster Research Center. However, all statements made represent the views of the authors and not necessarily those of NSF or FEMA. The authors would also like to acknowledge the comments on earlier versions of this paper by Ross Clayton and David Mars and by three anonymous referees.

NOTES

1. This account is taken almost verbatim from Thomas E. Forrest, *Structural Differentiation in Emergent Groups* (Columbus, Ohio: Disaster Research Center, Ohio State University, 1974), pp. 15, 17–19.

2. For an introduction to this literature, see John D. Hutcheson, Jr., and Jann Shevin, *Citizen Groups in Local Politics: A Bibliographical Review* (Santa Barbara, Calif.: Clio Books, 1976).

3. See the two recent reports from the center: E. L. Quarantelli *et al.*, *Emergent Citizen Groups in Disaster Preparedness and Recovery Activities: An Interim Report* (Columbus, Ohio: Department of Sociology, Disaster Research Center, Ohio State University, 1983); and E. L. Quarantelli, *Emergent Behavior at the Emergency Time Period of Disasters: Final Report for the Federal Emergency Management Agency* (Columbus, Ohio: Disaster Research Center, Ohio State University, 1983); see John Bardo, "Organizational Response to Disaster: A Typology of Adaptation and Change," *Mass Emergencies* 3 (1978); Sue Blanshan, "Disaster Body Handling," *Mass Emergencies* 2 (1977); see also a series of preliminary papers (Nos. 77–79, 83–87, 90) issued by DRC from its current study of emergent citizen groups in actual and potential disaster situations; also Thomas R. Forrest, "Needs and Group Emergence: Developing a Welfare Response," *American Behavioral Scientist* 16 (January-February 1973), pp. 413–425; Thomas R. Forrest, "Group Emergence in Disasters," in E. L. Quarantelli, ed., *Disasters: Theory and Research* (Beverly Hills, Calif.: Sage Publications, Inc., 1978), pp. 105–125; see also G. Alexander Ross, "The Emergence of Organization Sets in Three Ecumenical Recovery Organizations: An Empirical and Theoretical Exploration," *Human Relations* 33 (1980), pp. 23–29; Arnold R. Parr, "Organizational Response to Community Crises and Group Emergence," *American Behavioral Scientist* 13 (January-February 1970), pp. 424–427; and G. Alexander Ross and Martin H. Smith, *The Emergence of an Organization and an Organization Set: A Study of an Interfaith Disaster Recovery Group,* Preliminary Paper No. 16 (Columbus, Ohio: Disaster Research Center, Ohio State University, 1974). For more theoretical

discussions, see a summary of propositions, Robert A. Stallings, "The Structural Patterns of Four Types of Organizations in Disaster," in E. L. Quarantelli, ed., *Disasters, op. cit.,* pp. 87–103; Russell R. Dynes and E. L. Quarantelli, "Group Behavior Under Stress: A Required Convergence of Organizational and Collective Behavior Perspectives," *Sociology and Social Research* 52 (July 1968), pp. 416–429; Russell R. Dynes and B. E. Aguirre, "Organizational Adaptation to Crises: Mechanisms of Coordination and Structural Change," *Disasters* 3 (1977), pp. 71–74; and Russell R. Dynes and E. L. Quarantelli, "Helping Behavior in Large Scale Disasters," in David Horton Smith and Jacqueline Macaulay, eds., *Participation in Social and Political Activities* (San Francisco: Jossey-Bass, 1980), pp. 339–354.

4. In particular, Thomas E. Drabek *et al., Managing Multi-organizational Emergency Response* (Boulder, Colo.: Institute of Behavioral Science, University of Colorado, 1981); Edward J. Walsh, "Three Mile Island: Meltdown of Democracy?" *Bulletin of the Atomic Scientists* 39 (March 1983), pp. 57–60; Louis A. Zurcher, "Social-Psychological Functions of Ephemeral Roles: A Disaster Work Crew," *Human Organization* 27 (Winter 1968), pp. 283–287; William H. Form and Sigmund Nosow, *Community in Disaster* (New York: Harper and Brothers, Publishers, 1958), pp. 37–39; Ronald W. Perry *et al.,* "System Stress and the Persistence of Emergent Organizations," *Sociological Inquiry* 44 (1974), p. 112; and Charles E. Fritz *et al., Behavior in an Emergency Shelter: A Field Study of 800 Persons Stranded in a Highway Restaurant During a Heavy Snowstorm* (Washington, D.C.: Disaster Research Group, National Academy of Sciences, National Research Council, 1958).

5. As examples of this literature, see Steven Ebbin and Raphael Kasper, *Citizen Groups and the Nuclear Power Controversy* (Cambridge, Mass.: MIT Press, 1974); and Philip Lowe and Jane Goyder, *Environmental Groups in Politics* (London: George Allen and Unwin, 1983).

6. For discussions see Russell R. Dynes, *Organized Behavior in Disaster* (Columbus, Ohio: Disaster Research Center, 1974), p. 138; see also E. L. Quarantelli, "Organization Under Stress," in Robert C. Brictson, ed., *Symposium on Emergency Operations* (Santa Monica, Calif.: System Development Corporation, 1966), pp. 5–7; and Jack Weller and E. L. Quarantelli, "Neglected Characteristics of Collective Behavior," *American Journal of Sociology* 79 (November 1973), pp. 676–681.

7. E. L. Quarantelli *et al., Emergent Citizen Groups in Disaster Preparedness and Recovery Activities, op. cit.*

8. This series of direct quotes is taken from Robert P. Wolensky, "Power Structure and Group Mobilization Following Disaster: A Case Study," *Social Science Quarterly* 64 (March 1983), pp. 104–106; see also Robert P. Wolensky, "How Do Community Officials Respond to Major Catastrophes?" *Disasters* 1 (1977), pp. 272–274; and Robert P. Wolensky and Edward J. Miller, "The Everyday Versus the Disaster Role of Local Officials: Citizen and Official Definitions," *Urban Affairs Quarterly* 16 (June 1981), pp. 483–504.

9. John R. Brouillette and E. L. Quarantelli, "Types of Patterned Variation in Bureaucratic Adaptations to Organizational Stress," *Sociological Inquiry* 41 (Winter 1971), pp. 39–46.

10. *Neighborhood Self-Help Program Planning Guide* (Van Nuys, Calif.: Southern California Earthquake Preparedness Project, 1983), p. ix.

11. For a discussion of the differences between consensus and dissensus type crisis situations, see Robert A. Stallings, "The Community Context of Crisis Management," *American Behavioral Scientist* 16 (January–February 1973), pp. 312–325; see also E. L. Quarantelli, "Emergent Accommodative Groups: Beyond Current Collective Behavior Typologies," in Tamotsu Shibutani, ed., *Human Nature and Collective Behavior: Papers in Honor of Herbert Blumer* (Englewood Cliffs, N.J.: Prentice-Hall, Inc., 1970), p. 114. For studies of emergence in riots, see Thomas R. Forrest, "Emergent Communal Response," in Leonard Gordon, ed., *A City in Racial Crisis: The Case of Detroit Pre- and Post- the 1967 Riot* (Dubuque, Iowa: William C. Brown, 1971); Thomas R. Forrest, "Needs and Group Emergence," *op. cit.;* Thomas R. Forrest, "Group Emergence in Disasters," *op. cit.;* and William Anderson, Russell R. Dynes, and E. L. Quarantelli, "Urban Counterrioters," *Society* 11 (1974), pp. 50–55.

CHAPTER 17

CITIZENS PANELS
A New Approach to Citizen Participation

NED CROSBY, JANET M. KELLY, AND PAUL SCHAEFER

Discouragement over modes of political participation seemed matched in the 1960s–70s by a hope that new and viable forms of participation might be found. Disillusionment with the political process was summed up in the statement that "participation through normal institutionalized channels has little impact on the substance of government policies."[1] Several observers concluded that this disillusionment translated into a "society wide uprising against bureaucracy and a desire for participation."[2] This desire for direct participation was furthered by the attempts of the federal government to mandate participation at the local level (starting in 1964 with the Equal Opportunity Act's call for "maximum feasible participation").

The result was a considerable growth in citizen participation at the local level. Federally mandated aspects of this development have been enumerated (around 150 by an Advisory Commission on Intergovernmental Relations count);[3] the movement aspects have been praised by many;[4] and the phenomenon as a whole has been studied in considerable depth.[5] The findings are not especially encouraging:

1. Lack of representativeness of the participants is a real shortcoming of those programs which appear to be more successful.[6]
2. The most successful citizen inputs are found in programs which seem to require the least expertise.[7]
3. Overall, the impact of citizens groups has been limited.[8]
4. Most participatory programs are geared to intervention at the local administrative or delivery level, leaving the vast reaches of agenda-setting and policy prescription relatively untouched.[9]

Since 1974 a small group has been working at the Center for New Democratic Processes to develop a new form of citizen participation which can overcome some of the above problems. Built on analogy with the jury system, the process is simply called a "Citizens Panel," with capital letters being used to set it apart from other participatory methods. We have been encouraged in this

From *Public Administration Review,* 46, 2 (March/April 1986): 170–178. Copyright © 1986 by American Society for Public Administration. Reprinted with permission.

effort by the comments of Robert Dahl that political scientists "need to give serious and systematic attention to possibilities that may initially seem unrealistic, such as . . . creating randomly selected citizen assemblies . . . to analyze policy and make recommendations."[10]

Interestingly, a group of German scholars has worked independently over the same time period to create a similar process. Led by Peter C. Dienel at the Institute for Citizen Partici- pation and Planning Procedures at the University of Wuppertal, this group has conducted seven randomly selected panels on topics ranging from city planning to a nationwide project which used 24 panels in seven cities to do some long range planning on Germany's energy needs.[11]

This paper is organized in three parts. The first describes a set of criteria which can be used to evaluate the success of any citizen participation method. These criteria are derived from the research findings cited above and from a decade of experience at the Center for New Democratic Processes. That part is followed by a description of a Citizens Panel project on the impacts of agriculture on water quality which was run by the center in 1984. The third part of the paper evaluates the project in light of the criteria identified in the first part.

CRITERIA FOR SUCCESSFUL CITIZEN PARTICIPATION

At the outset it is important to distinguish between successful methods of citizen participation and successful citizen lobbying efforts. The latter are attempts to change public policy by get- ting large numbers of people to contact the appropriate public officials. The assumption is that a particular view is correct and the aim is to get as many supporters as possible to express this view to the public officials. Citizen participation, as discussed here, is an attempt to do the reverse: to start with a diverse group of people, inform them on the topic, and then get them to recommend that policy option which they find most appropriate. It is an effort to put a representative group of the public in dialogue with public officials so that the officials get the reactions of "the people themselves" on a particular subject, rather than simply getting the views of those who are lobbying from a particular point of view or interest.

Six criteria are suggested for a successful citizen participation method: (1) the participants should be representative of the broader public and should be selected in a way that is not open to manipulation; (2) the proceedings should promote effective decision making; (3) the proceedings should be fair; (4) the process should be cost-effective; (5) the process should be flexible; and (6) the likelihood that the recommendations of the group will be followed should be high. These criteria contain many normative statements and therefore cannot be justified *simply* by appeal to social science standards.[12] The justification for the particular mix of normative and empirical statements found here goes beyond the confines of this article. The center believes, however, that the criteria suggested are sufficiently close to common procedures in the courts and legislatures that they will not strike most readers as controversial.

Participant Selection

Participants must represent the broader community and must be selected in a way which is not open to manipulation. The standard of selection held by many participatory democrats is that anyone who wants to participate should be allowed to do so. But this criterion is much more acceptable in theory than in practice. If indeed large numbers of people show up in order to take advantage of their right, this makes an effective job of decision making virtually impossible. If only a select group shows up, then the question must be raised as to who they really represent.

A commonly used method to correct for this is through the appointment of participants by elected officials, with an attempt to ensure that the significant groups in the community are represented. This approach may be an improvement on the above, especially if respected community leaders are chosen, but it still has drawbacks. If the group is selected to represent different interests in the community, according to what criteria does one conclude that an interest or a group is properly represented? If one group is twice the size of another, should they receive twice the representation? What should be done if many people belong to more than one group? Finally, how do we know that those selected really represent the groups to which they belong, as opposed to being beholden to the official who appointed them?

What is needed is a method of participant selection which is not open to manipulation either by special interests or by elected officials and which yields a group which clearly represents the broader public. The center argues that a process of stratified random sampling meets this goal. This is discussed in more detail below. It is interesting to note that the history of the franchise for voting in the United States is one of a movement toward methods which are not open to manipulation. If more direct methods of citizen participation in the policy-making process are to gain wider acceptance, they must move in this direction as well.

Effective Decision Making

The aim of general citizen participation, as opposed to lobbying by the committed few, means that emphasis on an effective job of decision making is necessary. Since there are no widely accepted criteria for judging the correctness of a policy choice, this criterion is stated in terms of a process rather than a particular result. Two aspects of the decision-making process can be evaluated for effectiveness: the way the decision was structured for the citizens and the way they performed within the structure. A standard criticism of citizen participation is that average citizens are not capable of making decisions on complex public policy matters. The position of the authors is that average citizens can do an effective job of decision making if the hearing format is properly structured for them.

One of the most obvious requirements is that the citizens be provided with accurate and meaningful information. The absence of this is one of the main reasons why average citizens find themselves at a disadvantage with lobbyists in dealing with public officials. Daniel Bell[13] has noted how the rise of the "knowledge society" has contributed to a low sense of efficacy among many citizens, which in turn has led to class biases among those who choose to participate.[14] The information presented not only should be accurate and relevant but should also be organized and presented in a way which is meaningful, without being patronizing.

Other requirements for promoting effective decision making are also important. Time must be sufficient for participants to learn the information and to reflect on the values and goals relevant to the decision. The group making the decision must be of appropriate size; its agenda must be planned so that the important material is covered in an orderly fashion; the person leading the group must facilitate the discussion; and the views of the participants must be given adequate recognition. A large body of academic and applied work is available on small group decision making, and numerous facilitators are skilled in the art of running meetings.[15] Note that it is this criterion which requires that a successful method of citizen participation include some sort of hearing format for the participants to learn about the issue and an appropriate deliberative format to help them reach their decision.

Fair Procedures

Obviously this is a criterion supported by those who believe in "good government." But a pragmatic reason also exists for being interested in this. If it appears that someone is manipulating the procedures of a citizen participation effort, it loses credibility. Important segments of the public may conclude that the process is not legitimate and withdraw their support. Public officials are reluctant to follow its recommendations, unless they are the ones doing the manipulating. Certainly the finer points of fairness are open to endless debate, but practical experience demonstrates that a number of requirements are rather obvious.

It is important that the issue at hand not be defined so as to leave out the most important questions. A classic example is where a group of citizens is gathered to make recommendations about where a highway (or a hazardous waste site, power plant, etc.) should be located without letting them discuss whether the project is needed. This makes it tempting to say that the citizens should always be given the opportunity to deal with the important assumptions underlying an issue. This, however, could lead to endless discussions if every participant were allowed to raise what he/she felt were the important prior questions. Probably the best guideline is that if a clear majority of the participants feels that an important underlying assumption needs to be considered, then they should be allowed to deal with it.

Similar considerations arise with the setting of the agenda and the provision of information. If an open process is followed in which everyone is given an equal chance to speak, the process may be fair, but the poor organization of material and the lengthiness of the proceedings can make decision making virtually impossible. If one were interested simply in efficient decision making, one could let the staff organize the entire activity, but that would create unacceptable risks that the biases of the staff would dominate the results. A different solution is to use advocacy presentation as is done in the courts. This can lead to well organized information which represents more than one point of view, but it also may leave out some important points of view and can at times so polarize the participants that they are unable to agree on a solution.

No perfect solution to these dilemmas exists, but a good faith effort at fairness which also considers the needs of decision making should yield a process which is viewed as legitimate by the public and officials alike. Some combination of staff input, advocacy presentation, and an open agenda must be used in order to organize the information sufficiently for decision making while at the same time being fair to the parties involved.

Cost Effectiveness

The citizen participation process should be cost effective. This is a difficult criterion to apply because the value placed upon it can vary greatly. Existing public structures have virtually no guidelines for how much should be spent making a decision. A legislature may spend as much time debating an item which costs $100,000 as it does on a program which costs billions.

Note that the immediate costs of decision making may be low when the decision is made by "insiders," so long as one looks only at the costs of the decision *per se*. Were the same decision made by a group of citizens, the immediate costs might be considerably higher because of the number of people involved, the time it would take for them to learn about the issue, the staff required, etc. The long range costs, however, might by considerably lower if the attention paid to the issue led to a more carefully designed policy. Even if the actual policy costs were the same, the distribution of benefits might be claimed to be so much fairer that any additional decision making costs were deemed worthwhile.

Although this criterion is difficult to apply in a noncontroversial way, it is still important. If one method of citizen participation turns out to cost two or three times more than another, then good reasons must be presented as to why the more expensive method is worth the cost.[16]

Flexibility

The citizen participation method should be adaptable to a number of different tasks and settings. A tendency is to see most participatory mechanisms as best adapted to local and relatively simple issues. Since complex issues on the national level are often the ones which have the most significant impact on our lives, it is important that these be seen as amenable to review by participatory methods as well. If one general participatory method can overcome these perceived limitations, it will result in a significant democratic reform.

Recommendations Should Be Followed

Recommendations from the citizen participation process should have a high probability of being heeded by appropriate public officials. Despite its importance, this criterion has not been well met. Observation of federal social programs led Arnstein to state: "There is a critical difference between going through the empty ritual of participation and having real power."[17] She posits levels of control in a widely cited "ladder" of participation. At the lowest end of the scale is manipulation, followed by therapy, informing, consultation, placation, partnership, and delegated power. Actual citizen control resides at the top of the list. While government officials may be unwilling to give up control, a successful participatory technique would aim toward the top of the ladder.

The likelihood that the recommendations of the citizen participation process will be followed depends to a fair degree on its success in meeting the above criteria. All the criteria (except perhaps flexibility) will be important in getting the public to see the process as legitimate. The more legitimate the process in the minds of the public, the more difficult it will be for public officials to ignore the recommendations. Flexibility of design is important because it allows the process to be adapted to meet the needs of the public officials to whom the recommendations are directed. If these officials are allowed to help design the process, then they have a stake in the results. Here again the fairness of the procedures and the selection of participants is important. If officials believe the process is being manipulated by some interest or ideology, they will be exceedingly reluctant to support the project (unless they happen to share that interest or ideology).

THE CITIZENS PANEL ON AGRICULTURE AND WATER QUALITY

This section of the paper covers the 1984 project of the Center for New Democratic Processes which examined the impacts of agriculture on water quality in Minnesota.[18] The project took well over a year to set up and complete; the results are still being evaluated. In the next section, the project is evaluated according to the criteria for successful participation. To the best of the authors' knowledge, the Agriculture/Water Quality Project was the first official use in the United States of a *randomly* selected group of citizens to study a social or political issue. The center has run four pilot projects on Citizens Panels, starting in 1974, but this was the first statewide project and the first time any government agencies acted as sponsors. The only other use of randomly selected panels of which the center is aware is the work of Dienel *et al.* cited above.

The issue of agricultural impacts on water quality was chosen because of its importance in Minnesota for many years. Minnesota is the "Land of 10,000 Lakes;" its largest economic activity is agriculture. When the latter is polluting the former, the potential for intense political conflict is high. The federal government in the 1972 Water Quality Act set up requirements that each state develop plans for dealing with "non-point source" pollution. Although this led to extensive discussion in Minnesota, culminating in a series of reports, federal cutbacks in the 1980s meant that little was done to implement the plans. It was in this setting that state officials recommended a statewide Citizens Panel on the issue.

The process began in 1983 with the gathering of 11 sponsors for the project: Association of MN Counties, Center for Urban and Regional Affairs of the University of Minnesota, MN Association of Soil and Water Conservation Districts, MN Department of Agriculture, MN Department of Natural Resources, MN Farmers Union, MN Farm Bureau, MN Izaak Walton League, MN Pollution Control Agency, MN Soil and Water Conservation Board, and MN Sportfishing Congress. Each sponsor appointed one representative to the steering committee which oversaw the project and made in-kind contributions of about $2,000 apiece.

Informational Meetings

In January and February 1984, a series of informational meetings were held in seven geographically dispersed rural Minnesota communities. The meetings, attended by a total of 275 people, served to acquaint citizens with the project. They also gave the staff an opportunity to gather regional information on the issue and to meet key local actors. In addition, meeting participants filled out questionnaires regarding the issue. Their responses served as a basis for selecting 24 of the 60 potential panelists (see below).

Statewide Poll

In March, a statewide telephone survey of 623 Minnesotans was conducted to gather standardized information on the attitudes of residents toward both agricultural and environmental issues. A professional agency was hired to use exactly the same procedures employed by the Minnesota Poll. When combined with the survey responses from the informational meetings, the poll data provided a baseline for the random selection of the Citizens Panel participants.

Selecting Panelists

Panel members were chosen on a random basis according to a somewhat unique adaptation of a stratified random sample. Rather than stratify the sample on a demographic basis, the potential panelists were divided according to attitudinal groups. These categories were created on the basis of two scales which were developed using the responses to the survey questions. These two scales were then used to divide the respondents into three equal categories: those who cared more about agriculture than the environment (Favors Agriculture), those who cared more about the environment than agriculture (Favors Environment), and those who appeared to care equally about both (Balanced).

A further modification of pure random selection was that half of each panel was selected from among those attending the informational meetings (except in the Metro Area, where all were selected from the survey). This was done largely for pragmatic reasons. Since farmers make up only about 5 percent of the residents of Minnesota, a pure random selection process would have led to

Table 17.1

Panel Composition (except for Metro Area, which consisted only of survey respondents)

	Favors agriculture	Balanced	Favors environment
From the survey	2	2	2
From information meetings	2	2	2

Six persons were selected across the categories as alternates.

about 3 farmers out of the 60 on the Panels. This was unacceptable to the major farm organizations, without whose participation the project would have been considerably weakened.

Survey respondents and informational meeting participants were divided according to the areas of the state in which they lived, and they were numbered consecutively within each of the six categories in Table 17.1. The point on each list where the selection started was drawn in a public meeting by the chair of the county board for each region. Staff phoned and visited those on the list, explaining the project and seeking their participation. Names on the list were called in succession until each attitudinal category was adequately represented. This was a labor intensive but rewarding process. Those contacted were quite responsive. Among those identified through the survey, the acceptance rate was above 40 percent in rural areas and about 20 percent in the Metro Area. Although a few alternates had to be called at the last minute, of the 60 who started, only one did not attend the full four days of hearings, and that was for health reasons.

Agenda Setting

Held over a period of four days each, the regional panels presented several agenda setting difficulties. The issue of agricultural impacts on water quality is an extensive one covering such problems as nitrates in ground water, phosphates in lakes, sedimentation of rivers and ditches, and the complex and poorly researched question of pesticides. Several sponsors urged narrowing the question, but there was no consensus over which aspect of the problem should be selected. Staff was reluctant to narrow the question lest they become involved in an inappropriate value choice regarding which aspect of the issue was most significant. Therefore the whole panorama was presented to the panelists, allowing them to concentrate on what they thought was most important.

The first day of the regional panels was devoted to staff presentations. The materials used by the staff were prepared in consultation with sponsors and with knowledgeable professionals. To check for the efficacy, accuracy, and bias-free nature of staff presentations, a dry run was held. Sponsor representatives, farmers, environmentalists, and other interested parties attended this session. Several major changes in both style and content of staff materials were made. Subsequent changes were also made as a result of suggestions from panel members.

The second and third day of each regional panel consisted of testimony from witnesses. Potential witnesses were identified by asking all contacts in each region to supply names. People identified were contacted by phone and often visited in person. Those who agreed to serve submitted briefs of their testimony to the staff. These briefs were used to prepare a preliminary agenda which included a description of the staff presentations along with names of witnesses and their proposed topics. The agenda was then mailed to sponsors and all regional contacts, including the witnesses, for review and commentary over a two-week period. A final agenda was prepared in accordance with the revisions suggested. A number of people, including several only peripherally involved, took advantage of the opportunity to modify the agenda.

The statewide agenda was set in two ways. The first three days reviewed possible ways to deal with agricultural impacts on water quality. The agenda was set by the staff and steering committee. Four state agencies judged best able to address the issue were selected to present alternative ways to approach the problem. On the third day, the panelists decided which ideas they liked best and directed staff to make up the agenda for days four through six. Staff came up with several frameworks to guide the panelists in their final three days of decision making.

Running the Panels

The five regional panels were run at one-month intervals in the summer and fall of 1984. Given the time necessary to select participants and set the agenda, staff found itself at any moment running one panel while setting the agenda for the next and selecting the participants for the third. The panels were run on two consecutive Fridays and Saturdays. Panelists were paid $75.00 a day for attendance. As noted above, the first three days of the regional panels were devoted to presentations by the staff and by witnesses. On the fourth day, members were asked to respond as a group with recommendations about the significance of the issue, the need for action, spending provisions, funding sources, and specific actions to be taken by appropriate authorities. Participants also selected three from the panel to go to the statewide panel.

In deliberating over their recommendations, panelists found it difficult to reach conclusions. Two panels strongly resisted the process. The performance of chair-persons (chosen by the panel members) varied from good to very poor, so that staff was tempted on occasion to intervene. While some staff, in the interests of a well-formulated set of conclusions, felt it was appropriate to give panelists considerable guidance in putting together a set of recommendations, others thought that in the interests of avoiding bias and giving panelists a sense of efficacy, panel members should be given free rein.

The statewide panel met for two three-day sessions with a break of 10 days in between. Attendance was 100 percent except for one person who failed to make the first day of meetings and had to be replaced with an alternate. The first three days of presentations by the four agencies and the agenda setting for the last three days went as planned. The last three days were devoted to panel deliberations and the preparation of a plan to address the impacts of agriculture on water quality. Preparing a plan was a process novel to all panelists. This led the staff director to fear that their recommendations would not be well enough organized to be taken seriously by the legislature and the agencies which would review them. As a result, staff prepared several "frameworks" for the panelists to use in formulating their decisions. The participants decided to use these frameworks (in making their last decision, they asked staff to leave the room), but, like the regional panels, they found reaching conclusions difficult.

Panel Conclusion

The statewide panel's plan was issued as part of a project report given to the sponsors and other appropriate organizations, key members of the legislature, and the media. A subcommittee of panelists was invited to testify before two legislative committees. Staff were asked to make presentations before the governing boards of each sponsor and the state's Environmental Quality Board and were asked to speak to a number of farmer and environmental organizations about both the issue and the process. The report stimulated one sponsoring agency to set up a special committee of its board to deal with nonpoint source pollution. It has also served as a stimulus to a major piece of legislation dealing with the "set-aside" of marginal lands.

MEETING THE CRITERIA FOR SUCCESSFUL CITIZEN PARTICIPATION

Participant Selection

The use of random selection greatly reduced the possibility that the choice of the participants for the Citizens Panels could be manipulated by special interests. This was not the case with those selected from the informational meetings. Certainly if some interest had mobilized sufficiently, it would have been possible for them to stack the meetings with its members. The idea of drawing participants from the informational meetings was deemed necessary in view of the importance of gaining support from the agricultural groups. In light of the novelty of the process, this appears to have been a reasonable decision. It is assumed, however, that as the process becomes better known, it will not be necessary to use this deviation from random selection in order to select participants.

Use of the survey to divide potential participants into three categories meant that the panelists were representative of the general public in the state, although the informational meetings led to an overrepresentation of farmers and those with special concerns about the environment. The fact that staff took considerable care to explain the selection process at the outset of each panel and on numerous other public occasions did a great deal to allay suspicion of bias in the choice of panel members.

Effective Decision Making and Fair Procedures

These two categories are considered together since in the planning process one could not be dealt with apart from the other. The agenda-setting method described above, wherein large numbers of people were provided opportunity to influence the proceedings, served as a useful check against staff bias. It also provided the organization necessary for clear presentation of information. At one of the regional panels, a group of people came to the proceedings convinced that the panels were an attempt (by "environmentalists," or worse) to make an end run around farmer opposition to state regulations on tillage practices. By the end of the second day of testimony, however, they had put away their tape recorders and otherwise relaxed their vigilance. As the panel closed on the fourth day, one of their number complimented staff on the fairness of the proceedings.

With regard to the presentation of information, while panelists complained of poor work by particular witnesses, they pronounced themselves satisfied in general with the format which included presentations by both staff and witnesses. The latter included a deliberate mix of professionals, such as chemists and hydrogeologists, and lay persons, such as farmers and those interested in sports.[19] The combination yielded an interesting and useful mix of hard data and anecdotes which served to inform and hold the attention of the panelists. Time spent on presentations generally seemed adequate, although some panel members complained of having to absorb too much information in the three days allotted.

The greatest difficulty encountered with regard to fairness and decision making occurred during the panel deliberations. As noted above, panelists' problems in reaching conclusions, whether in one day (at the regional level) or in three (at the statewide level) resulted in some intervention by staff. A questionnaire filled out by panelists at the end of the meetings reveals that while staff were credited with low bias at the regional panels, such was not the case at the statewide hearings (see Table 17.2). The more staff intervened, the more they were seen as introducing their biases into the proceedings.

Cost Effectiveness

The cost effectiveness of the project is not easy to determine. When compared to the many millions of dollars being spent to address the problem, the $120,000 cost of the project is miniscule. To the degree it begins to correct the problem, it is clearly money well spent. Reactions from state officials and sponsors varied, generally in accordance with how they liked the recommendations. Those pleased with the results thought the sum spent was comparatively small. Those less comfortable with the recommendations were apt also to remark on the project's expense.

The costs can be reduced considerably for projects on the local level. Currently, a way is being designed to use Citizens Panels on the level of rural county government for a cost of $10,000 to $20,000. This would involve training local residents to fill some of the roles which were played by staff in the statewide project.

Flexibility

The Citizens Panel method is clearly quite adaptable to a wide range of tasks and settings. While the project on agriculture and water quality was the first large-scale application of the process in the United States, it has been used here successfully on pilot projects dealing with peacemaking, public health care, and the 1976 presidential election. The experiences in Germany show that it can be used on projects ranging from city planning to long-range, national energy planning.

Three areas of flexibility are particularly important. First, there are a number of ways to combine the use of a survey and random selection processes so that a balanced panel can be chosen in a public way which would be difficult to manipulate. Pragmatic adaptation can be made to meet the needs of cost and the political scene while still meeting goals for participant selection. Second, presentations by staff may be combined in various ways with presentations by witnesses and advocates to meet the requirements of fairness and effective decision making. Balance is difficult to achieve, but the process is rich in possibilities. Third, and perhaps most important, Citizens Panels offer a structure which can be adapted to problems ranging from the local to the national level. The two-tiered approach used in the project showed how the views of panels with good ties to local communities can be combined into a set of statewide recommendations.

The Recommendations Should Be Followed

The project was designed to ensure that the Citizens Panel recommendations would be given a meaningful hearing by the proper officials. Sponsors for the project were chosen because of their ability to influence events in the area of agriculture and water quality. Each sponsor agreed, in signing on to the project, to have its governing board or similar body pay "serious attention" to the panel's recommendations. Furthermore, the choice of the issue itself was a major factor in seeing that the findings were heeded; i.e., because the issue was controversial, and at an impasse, many public officials were eager to see what a group of citizens, including farmers, would recommend be done with the problem. Finally, legislators were informed of panel progress and were invited to participate at appropriate stages.

276

Table 17.2

Responses of Panelists to Final Evaluation Questionnaire

	Very satisfied	Satisfied	Neutral	Dissatisfied	Very dissatis-fied	Totals*
In general how do you feel about your participation in the Citizens Panel?						
Regional Panels	37 (63%)	19 (32%)	2 (3%)	1 (2%)	—	59 (100%)
Statewide	9 (60%)	6 (40%)	—	—	—	15 (100%)
Do you feel satisfied that the staff acted in an unbiased way?						
Regional Panels	41 (72%)	14 (25%)	2 (3%)	—	—	57 (100%)
Statewide	6 (40%)	9 (60%)	—	—	—	15 (100%)
Do you feel satisfied that there was a balanced group of witnesses?						
Regional Panels	26 (46%)	27 (48%)	1 (2%)	2 (4%)	—	56 (100%)
Statewide	7 (47%)	8 (53%)	—	—	—	15 (100%)

*Although there were 60 regional panelists, one was taken ill and did not finish the process, and a few others did not answer some questions.

The center's evaluation of the results is that it is a successful start and can be built into a process which is satisfactory over the long run. The sponsoring agencies did indeed give the recommendations serious review and detailed responses were sent to the center by the heads of the agencies. As already noted, one of the agencies set up a new subcommittee of its board to deal with nonpoint source pollution and added staff to the relevant division of the agency. Also a bill passed the Minnesota Legislature which contained elements of the recommendations, but with no funding to carry them out. All of this is positive, but the bulk of the recommendations of the Citizens Panel were not adopted either by the Legislature or the agencies. In future projects the center staff believe this can be improved.

CONCLUSIONS

Studies cited in this article show that the upsurge of citizen participation in the 1960s-70s had limited impacts on institutionalized structures. The authors believe it is important to differentiate between citizen lobbying efforts and procedures for allowing a broad range of citizens to participate in public policy making. To this end, six criteria are suggested which should be met if citizen participation is to be successful.

The 1984 project described above made a start in meeting these criteria. We believe it made a unique contribution in dealing with the problems of participant selection, broad-based decision making, and fair procedures. It is also a flexible process, well adapted to complex issues on a statewide or even national level. The process was relatively expensive, but clearly costs can be reduced considerably for local projects and kept within acceptable limits for larger ones. The area where the most work remains is in getting the recommendations adopted by those in power. As the public learns about the process and the way it meets the first three criteria, they may view the process as legitimate and may begin to support its use on important public policy issues where other approaches are deemed inadequate.

NOTES

1. Robert Alford and Roger Friedland, "Political Participation and Public Policy," *Annual Review of Sociology,* vol. 1 (1975), p. 472.

2. Daniel Bell, *The Coming of Post-Industrial Society* (New York: Basic Books, 1973) p. 365.

3. Advisory Commission on Intergovernmental Relations, *Citizen Participation in the American Federal System* (Washington: Government Printing Office, 1980). This work identified 150 citizen participation projects.

4. See for example, Harry Boyte, *Backyard Revolution* (Philadelphia: Temple University Press, 1980).

5. For excellent overviews see Marilyn Gittell, *et al., Limits to Citizen Participation: The Decline of Community Organizations* (Beverly Hills: Sage Publications, 1980), and Robert W. and Mary G. Kweit, *Implementing Citizen Participation in a Bureaucratic Society* (New York: Praeger, 1981). Other interesting works include Joan B. Aron, "Citizen Participation at Government Expense," *Public Administration Review,* vol. 39 (September/October 1979); Sherry Arnstein, "A Ladder of Citizen Participation," *American Institute of Planners,* vol. XXXV (July 1969); Roger W. Cobb and Charles D. Elder, *Participation in American Politics: The Dynamics of Agenda Building* (Baltimore: Johns Hopkins University Press, 1983); Richard Cole, *Citizen Participation and the Urban Policy Process* (Lexington: Lexington Books, 1974); Stephen D. Cupps, "Emerging Problems of Citizen Participation," *Public Administration Review,* vol. 37 (September/October 1977); Stuart Langton (ed.), *Citizen Participation in America* (Lexington: Lexington Books, 1978); Kenneth C. Laudon, *Communication Technology and Democratic Participation* (New York: Praeger, 1977); Judy B. Rosener, "A Cafeteria of Techniques and Critiques," *Public Management,* vol. 57 (December 1975), pp. 16–19, and "Making Bureaucracy Responsive: A Study of the Impact of Citizen Participation," *Public Administration Review,* vol. 42 (July/August 1982), pp. 339–345; and Sidney Verba, Norman H. Nie, and Jaeon Kim, *Participation and Political Equality* (New York: Cambridge University Press, 1978).

6. Joseph Falkson, *An Evaluation of Policy Related Research on Citizen Participation in Municipal Service Systems* (Washington: TARP Institute, 1974); Gittell, *et al.,* 1980.

7. Falkson, *op. cit.*

8. John H. Strange, "The Impact of Citizen Participation on Public Administration," *Public Administration Review,* vol. 32 (September/October 1972), pp. 457–470; Milbarth, 1980; Marilyn Gittell, "The Consequences of Mandating Citizen Participation," *Policy Studies Review,* vol. 3 (August 1983), pp. 90–95, and Gittell, *et al.,* 1980.

9. Kweit and Kweit, *op. cit.*

10. Robert A. Dahl, "On Removing Certain Impediments to Democracy in the United States," *Political Science Quarterly,* vol. 92 (Spring 1977), p. 17.

11. The major work on the theory and practice of what Professor Dienel calls "planning cells" is Peter C. Dienel, *Die Plannungszelle* (Westdeutscher Verlag, Opladen, West Germany, 1978). The use of the "planning cells" to explore energy futures for Germany is described in Ortwin Renn, *et al.,* "An Empirical Investigation of Citizens' Preferences Among Four Energy Scenarios" in *Technological Forecasting and Social Change,* vol. 26 (April 1984), pp. 11–46. This description concentrates on the attitudes of the participants and plays down the citizen advisory role which Dienel finds so important. Those interested in the details of Dienel's work can learn what has been published in German by contacting the Center for New Democratic Processes (612–333–5300).

12. This is not meant to imply that the social sciences do not make use of normative standards. The structural-functional approach can be viewed as normative in that certain functions *ought* to be performed if a system is to be maintained. Such an "ought" is not moral, but is justified on the grounds of empirical research which demonstrates that the social system cannot be maintained if the function is not performed. The criteria in this article, however, present a mixture of empirical and moral claims. The requirement of effective decision making can be based on the empirical claim that without it, the recommended policy is unlikely to accomplish its intended goals. The requirements of fairness, however, often must be justified through a normative discourse which is analyzed through the standards of meta-ethics rather than of the social sciences. (Appeals can also be made to empirical data about what promotes legitimacy in the eyes of officials and the public.)

13. Bell, *op. cit.,* p. 14.

14. Verba, Nie, and Kim, *op. cit.;* and Gittell, *et al., op. cit.,* p. 253.

15. Anyone wanting to see the mass of work done on small group decision making should glance through the pages of the *Journal of Personality and Social Psychology.* How helpful this will be for those interested in complex social issues is another matter. Michael Saks, in an extensive review of the literature on complex decision making, concluded that most of the research is not relevant to the sorts of problems faced by jurors in a complex trial (*Small Group Decision-Making and Complex Information Tasks;* The Federal Judicial Center; 1520 H Street NW, Washington, DC 20005; 1981).

16. Robert W. Aleshire, "Planning and Citizen Participation: Costs, Benefits and Approaches," *Urban Affairs Quarterly,* vol. 5 (March 1970), pp. 369–393.

17. Arnstein, *op. cit.,* p. 216.

18. The authors wish to acknowledge the assistance of Carolyn Emerson, Karen Husby, and Mary Kearney for invaluable assistance on the organizational aspects of the project. The participation of panelists and sponsors in the project is gratefully acknowledged, as is financial support through a grant from the Joyce Foundation of Chicago.

19. Lay witnesses provide an essential leavening in the presentation of complex information to panelists, who can be awed by, and simultaneously suspicious of, many professionals. Lay persons also may have information which professionals do not have. Unfortunately, some professionals experience great difficulty in rendering their data for public understanding.

CHAPTER 18

CONSENSUS-BUILDING FOR INTEGRATED RESOURCES PLANNING

LANCE DE HAVEN-SMITH AND JOHN R. WODRASKA

Recently, integrated resources planning (IRP) has begun to be used in evaluating water supply options for large populations experiencing water scarcity. Traditionally employed to make decisions in the energy sector about different energy mixes, integrated resources planning is a technical methodology for forecasting needs, delineating alternative supply options, and choosing among different supply combinations (Goodman and Edwards, 1992; Western Area Power Administration, 1994). When used in water planning, the IRP approach lacks an important component seldom required in energy planning: processes for building a political consensus among water managers, producers, and consumers. The need for consensus-building processes in resources management generally is growing. Agencies at all governmental levels are beginning to manage resources collectively rather than individually so that ecosystems can be protected as a whole (Cortner and Moote, 1994). This shift to ecosystems management requires collaboration between many decision makers (Grumbine, 1994; Slocombe, 1993).

In this article, we describe an IRP consensus process used by the Metropolitan Water District (referred to as Metropolitan or MWD) of Southern California. Metropolitan offers many lessons because it is dealing with a wide array of water issues. In terms of population served, MWD is the largest water management district in the world, and its decision makers represent areas that are diverse geographically and politically. The district invests in local water resource development as well as securing imported water, and its programs include not only supply but also conservation, reclamation, and storage.

THE POLITICS OF WATER

Integrated resources planning needs a consensus-building component because water is typically a much more controversial issue than energy. In the latter, decisions about supply combinations are seldom made by the energy producers themselves. Rather, decision makers are usually in a position of selecting from among several types of energy resources (petroleum, hydro-electric,

From *Public Administration Review,* 56, 4 (July/August 1996): 367–371. Copyright © 1996 by American Society for Public Administration. Reprinted with permission.

etc.) from several producers. In this situation, it is fairly straightforward to determine the most cost-effective resource mix. Admittedly, questions about reliability and other factors still require nontechnical, political judgments, but these judgments are not directly linked to the decision-makers' self-interest.

In contrast, water production and water consumption are usually bound together geographically, economically, and politically. In any given region for which a group of decision makers is providing water, choices about water sources will have differential effects for different parts of the region and different political jurisdictions, depending on their existing water resources.[1] Consequently, consideration must be given not merely to technical questions of cost but also to equity across the region.

Certainly, this was the case with MWD. Metropolitan is an umbrella agency covering southern California from Los Angeles to San Diego, a region that includes over 15 million people, 145 cities, and 94 unincorporated communities. The annual water needs of the region are roughly 4 million acre-feet. Sources of water include investment in local ground water, surface water and reuse of waste water, and importation of water from the Colorado River, northern California, and Owens Valley and Mono Basin.

Metropolitan was formed in 1928 to provide imported water to meet the needs of cities, countries, districts, and other water suppliers serving consumers with retail or wholesale water. Twenty-seven pre-existing suppliers (cities, counties, and special districts), each covering a different geographical area and having a different mix of water resources, came together to establish MWD under state enabling legislation (Metropolitan Water District Act, 1969, chap. 209). Within Metropolitan's governance structure, these water suppliers are called Member Agencies. Funding for Metropolitan is provided mainly through water charges the Member Agencies pay MWD for imported supplies. On average, Member Agencies provide about 40 percent of their consumers' water themselves, either from local water supplies or from imports they obtain without MWD, while Metropolitan imports water from outside the region to come up with the other 60 percent. In addition to Metropolitan's historic role of providing imported water, it has played an important role in fostering conservation and in promoting and funding local water development.

In effect, Metropolitan's decisions are made by the 27 Member Agencies themselves. Each Member Agency has at least one director on the Metropolitan Board. Voting is weighted according to the assessed value of the land within each Member Agency's jurisdiction.

Member Agencies vary in their dependence on Metropolitan. Some buy virtually all their water from Metropolitan, whereas others have local ground or surface water as their primary source and use Metropolitan only as a supplement during periods of peek demand, as a source for groundwater replenishment during periods of moderate demand, or merely as a backup supply. Similarly, some have storage capacity in groundwater basins or surface reservoirs, while others do not.

ISSUES IN THE RESOURCES PLAN

In 1992, Metropolitan recognized the new challenges it was facing: a reduction of half of the available water supply from the Colorado River and the State Water Project as a result of environmental regulations and lawsuits; and the relentless pressures of continuing growth in the region. The Board of Directors developed a revised mission statement and goals that defined the accomplishment of Metropolitan's mission and set forth specific parameters for achieving a reliable supply of high-quality water. Metropolitan then set about the process of developing a strategic plan that would chart the course for accomplishing the goals of the board and fulfilling the district's mission as a steward of water resources.

That plan is organized around seven guiding principles that serve as broad aspirations for the future: water, cost, finance, facilities, environmental, work force, and interdependence. In the water section, Metropolitan developed objectives and commitments that recognized Metropolitan as no longer solely a supplier of a single product—imported water—but rather as a provider of water services.

This new view required two important changes in the planning process. First, although Metropolitan could at one time accomplish its mission largely through unilateral actions because its primary role was water importation, today it must coordinate its actions with Member Agencies because it is promoting water conservation, region-wide water management, waste water re-use, and other programs that must be implemented either by or through the Member Agencies. Second, the realization that regional water services must be provided through a combination of different approaches, and not just water importation, raised fundamental questions. What is the appropriate mix of resources (or functions) to provide the desired level of service to the final consumer at the lowest possible cost? To what extent should the region rely on increasing available supplies from Metropolitan's basic Colorado River and State Water Project's sources? To what extent should the region invest in alternative sources, including water marketing and expanded development of local resources?

The strategic plan set forth the integrated resources planning process as a partnership between the Member Agency managers and Metropolitan management, with the latter developing the technical alternatives. Metropolitan had to select some combination of four different ways to address the water shortfall: increasing conservation; enhancing local supplies through waste water re-use, groundwater reclamation, and water desalination; securing additional imported water supplies by helping to correct up-state environmental problems; and storing seasonally available imported water in surface reservoirs and groundwater basins for use later during droughts and periods of high demand.

Technically speaking, the decision was not particularly difficult. Each of these four approaches would produce relatively cheap water up to a certain point, but beyond that point, water production would have become more and more expensive because the easily accessible water would have been exhausted. For example, water conservation would be fairly inexpensive when it came to altering a few wasteful practices of consumers, but it would become increasingly expensive when it involved the widespread deployment of expensive technology. Similarly, some of the environmental problems associated with importing water could be fixed relatively quickly and inexpensively, but, beyond that, the environmental fixes would become increasingly costly. Therefore, from a cost perspective, the best approach was to use all four alternatives up to the point where each began to have diminishing marginal returns.

In practice, the strategy of combining all resource alternatives entailed a departure from existing MWD policy. It meant building expensive surface water reservoirs to store imported water and also managing groundwater on a regional basis. Both of these actions carried political challenges.

Building reservoirs was problematic because some Member Agencies had little need for stored water. Those with substantial water resources of their own could get by with the modest amount of imported water available from MWD under established arrangements. From the perspective of these agencies, surface water reservoirs were an extravagance.

Regional groundwater management was difficult for similar reasons. Regional groundwater management required that water be taken from the "haves" and given to the "have-nots" during times of scarcity, and yet Member Agencies had control over their groundwater supplies and were under no compulsion to share it.

In short, the IRP process could not avoid a number of sensitive political issues. Each alternative resource mix had to be evaluated with respect not merely to cost and reliability, but also in terms of its implications for equity across Member Agencies and for its practicality in terms of implementation.

THE CONSENSUS-BUILDING PROCESS

The consensus-building technique Metropolitan used was a modification of the American Assembly process. The original American Assembly model was developed in 1950 by Dwight Eisenhower (while he was at Columbia University) to address issues that are national or international in scope. An affiliate of Columbia University, the assembly is a national educational institution incorporated in the state of New York. Since its inception, the American Assembly has sponsored dozens of national, regional, state, and local forums.

The basic model is quite simple. The American Assembly process brings together 65 to 75 participants representing diverse backgrounds, associations, and fields of expertise to discuss a specific policy issue. Prior to the event, experts are retained to write background papers that provide essential data and define the main discussion topics. At the assembly, participants are divided into equal-sized groups, each a microcosm of the whole, for four discussion periods over three consecutive days. Each discussion period is scheduled for about three hours. Assigned to each group are an experienced "facilitator" and "recorder" whose responsibilities are, respectively, to encourage open deliberations and to summarize the conclusions. Each group discusses the same questions at the same time. After the discussions, a drafting committee, which includes the group facilitators, the recorders, and the overall assembly director, prepares a report synthesizing the groups' various findings and recommendations. In a final or plenary session, the draft report is presented to all the participants meeting together, reviewed section by section under the direction of the assembly director, and amended by the participants (using parliamentary procedures) to reflect accurately the consensus of the body. The report is usually rather general, and nobody is specifically responsible for implementation.[2]

With respect to water issues, the main drawback to the standard American Assembly model is that it does not provide a mechanism for deliberations and consensus building prior to the event. In most communities, it is not practical to expect participants to be able to articulate and agree on specific policies when participants are confronted with either a blank slate or abstract issues. If the assembly is to lead to policy recommendations that are clear and directive, then the issues discussed in the small group sessions must lay out the basic options the participants might find acceptable. However—and this is the problem—identifying these options requires a considerable amount of preparatory work.

MWD made three modifications to the American Assembly model for use in its integrated resources planning. First, it expanded the role of a steering committee to decide the assembly details. This included selecting the topics for discussion, drafting the discussion questions, preparing background papers, as well as selecting the participants. The steering committee had representatives from all of the stakeholding sectors of the district (Metropolitan staff, Member Agency Management, and Metropolitan Board Members). The committee met every few weeks over a period of months, and its deliberations were at times quite heated. The background papers and questions were based on the work of the Member Agency/Metropolitan Agency Technical Group. An outside assembly director was hired to help the committee, to maintain an open and balanced process, and to direct the assembly itself.

The second change MWD made to the American Assembly model was to schedule a series of assemblies rather than just one. Early on, discussions by the steering committee made it clear that the district was not prepared to jump immediately into the issues raised by the IRP process, or that the IRP alone would be enough to move forward with a resource mix once selected. Therefore, three separate assemblies were held over a 15-month period.

It is important to note that this was the first time Metropolitan's board, Member Agency managers, and Metropolitan management sat down as equals in a deliberative process. This entailed substantial risks, but it had the potential to generate an unprecedented level of understanding and mutual support among southern California's water management community. Each assembly issued a consensus statement on the issues addressed that provided information to the Metropolitan board as it made decisions on the appropriate regional resource mix and a long-range fiscal plan to set forth funding for the mix's capital projects and programs.

The first assembly addressed fundamental issues of governance and prioritization of criteria for evaluating resource-mix alternatives. As in most complex organizations, questions of turf and resources lurked in the background of any discussion about water-supply options. These underlying agendas had to surface and be dealt with before the IRP issues themselves could be resolved. The first assembly tackled roles of Metropolitan, the Member Agencies, and other water suppliers in southern California. MWD's rate structure, prioritization of the criteria for selecting resource-mix alternatives, and a set of action items for the Member Agency Technical Group to address were set forth in the assembly statement.

The second assembly dealt specifically with IRP processes and the resource mix. The choice presented to the participants was one of emphasizing local water resources, imported water, or a mix. The assembly ratified the investment level in each of the resource categories that was core to all the alternatives and the choice of emphasis for investment in noncore resource-mix elements. Reaching agreement on the core-investment level entailed major capital investment decisions that could not be delayed. Participation in the second assembly was expanded to include representatives of groundwater and retail water agencies in the service area.

Finally, the third assembly took up implementation issues. Once the resource mix was selected, decisions had to be made about how to finance capital investments and water management programs as well as a process to assure region-wide water management.

The third modification MWD made to the American Assembly model was to conduct open forums around the region to solicit input from the public. Six forums of both the public and retail water providers were held between the first and second assemblies, and each attracted between 50 and 100 attendees. Most of the forums used a discussion format involving small groups. The participants at each forum selected a spokesperson to present their recommendations to the assembly participants at the convening session of the assembly. This process was continued for the third assembly.

Central to the success of the assembly process was the equal involvement of all interested and affected parties (Metropolitan, Member Agencies, local retail water providers, and groundwater agencies) and the recognition that the consensus policy decisions reached at each assembly were guidance to the Metropolitan board. Final decision making occurred in the normal board policy approval process.

The Metropolitan assemblies reached agreement on a wide range of issues. The assembly statements are available through MWD. The Member Agencies agreed to continue strengthening MWD's role as a water manager and not just a water supplier; develop a more balanced mix of water supplies; invest significantly in water conservation and surface and groundwater storage; and alter water rates to promote conservation, water storage, and waste water reuse by Member Agencies. These decisions are now being fine-tuned and implemented by the MWD board of directors with the ongoing involvement of Member Agency and Met staff.

LESSONS LEARNED

For those who might want to use a modified American Assembly process to augment integrated resources planning or other decision-making frameworks, we learned several lessons that might be helpful. First, we found it useful to think of our consensus building like a funnel going from very general to very specific issues. The IRP is at the middle of the funnel, and it cannot be addressed meaningfully until even more basic questions are aired. In the case of MWD, this did not lead to any radical changes; participants at the first assembly concluded that the district's structure and authority were sound and reinforced the partnership/relationship between Metropolitan's and Member Agencies' staffs in developing policy alternatives. But the fact that they had the opportunity to discuss these issues prevented the issues from polluting the discussion about the IRP policy alternatives, reaffirmed people's confidence in the decision structure, and assured that no one felt as if discussion had been limited or stifled. Although the importance of addressing organizational issues in resources management has been noted, the need to take up these issues early has not been stressed (Grumbine, 1994; Slocombe, 1993).

A second lesson was that the process was as important as the final decisions concerning the IRP. It would not have been difficult to show, technically, that the best water supply mix for southern California was a specific mix of imported water and regionally managed surface and groundwater, but a technical analysis would not have allowed discursive participation. In fact, as Slocombe (1993) and Kessler and others (1992) have noted, technical analysis without decision-maker participation can feel like manipulation even when the analysis is rigorous, objective, and intended solely to be informative.

Third, the authority of the steering committee must be respected. This may be difficult, because it means that managers and public officials must release control to another group. But the steering committee is what assures all participants that the process is open and fair.

Fourth, the implementation of the public forums and the willingness of the decision makers to seek the counsel of key constituencies was fundamental to the acceptance of the ultimate resource mix and investment plan by the water management community and the public. Slocombe (1993) and Cortner and Moote (1994) are correct to emphasize the importance of public participation in natural resources management.

Finally, it is helpful to have an outside facilitator. Much of the actual work can be handled by the participating organizations, including writing the background papers, sending out invitations, making all arrangements, and so on. But an outsider is needed to serve as a referee in any disputes, to encourage the process along when enthusiasm lags, and to assure an independent voice in crafting the assembly statements.

In conclusion, we believe a consensus-building process may also be appropriate with other planning techniques and decision-making frameworks. One of the criticisms of planning is that it often has little effect on actual operations. By developing participatory processes to involve stakeholders, managers may make their plans more practical, obtain essential political support, and establish a mechanism for ongoing plan-review and adjustment.

NOTES

1. For a discussion of how environmental issues are refracted regionally, see deHaven-Smith (1991).
2. For a lengthier description of the American Assembly, see deHaven-Smith and Horniman (1988).

REFERENCES

Cortner, Hanna J. and Margaret A. Moote, 1994. "Trends and Issues in Land and Water Resources Management: Setting the Agenda for Change." *Environmental Management,* vol. 18 (2), 167–173.

deHaven-Smith, Lance, 1991. *Environmental Concern in Florida and the Nation.* Gainesville: University of Florida Press.

deHaven-Smith, Lance and Sarah Horniman, 1988. "American Assemblies: A Tested Approach for Developing a Growth Management Consensus." In Westi Jo deHaven-Smith, ed., *Growth Management Innovations in Florida.* Fort Lauderdale: FAU/FIU Joint Center for Environmental and Urban Problems, Monograph #88–1, pp. 31–42.

Goodman, A.S. and K.A. Edwards, 1992. "Integrated Water Resources Planning." *National Resources Forum,* vol. 16 (February), 65–70.

Grumbine, R. Edward, 1994. "What Is Ecosystem Management?" *Conservation Biology,* vol. 8 (March), 27–38.

Metropolitan Water District Act, 1969. State of California, Statutes, ch. 209, as amended.

Metropolitan Water District Blue-Ribbon Task Force, 1994. "Final Report." January.

Metropolitan Water District of Southern California, 1994. "Integrated Resources Plan Draft Interim Report." March 23.

Slocombe, D. Scott, 1993. "Implementing Ecosystem-Based Management." *Bio Sciences,* vol. 43 (October), 612–622.

Western Area Power Administration, 1994. *Resources Planning Guide: Integrated Resources Planning Tools for the Future.* Washington, DC: U.S. Department of Energy, pp. 2–6.

Wodraska, John R. and P.E. von Haam, 1996. "Lessons in Water Resource and Ecosystem Regulation from Florida's Everglades and California's Bay/Delta Estuary." In *Engineering Within Ecological Constraints.* Washington, DC: National Academy Press.

CHAPTER 19

STATE STRATEGIC PLANNING
Suggestions from the Oregon Experience

GERALD R. KISSLER, KARMEN N. FORE, WILLOW S. JACOBSON,
WILLIAM P. KITTREDGE, AND SCOTT L. STEWART

Strategic planning "is, very simply, a method for aligning an organization with its environment," according to Meising and Andersen (1991). It is a management tool that has been used in the private sector for years as a systematic process for relating the organization to changes in the environment. Strategic planning processes typically involve assessing strengths and weaknesses, identifying opportunities and threats, determining where the organization should be going, and then establishing goals, strategies, and tactics for getting there.

However, critics have questioned the value of strategic planning (for example, Mintzberg, 1994). Hamel (1996) has argued that strategic planning processes are too costly and time-consuming for today's fast-paced, competitive environment in the corporate world. Strategic planning processes produce plans, not necessarily strategies that make a difference. *Fortune* magazine reports that, by downplaying the planning process, some corporations, such as Nike, Amgen, and Harley-Davidson, have created "killer strategies" or strategic initiatives that led to market dominance (Hamel, 1997). Hamel (1996) suggests that the key is to shift the emphasis from "planning" to "strategizing."

Even if the critics are correct about the limited effectiveness of strategic planning in the private sector, it might still be a valuable management tool in the public sector where the pace of change is slower and where inclusive processes are essential for widespread acceptance. Indeed, Bryson emphasizes the value of strategic planning in public and nonprofit organizations because it "can help facilitate communication and participation, accommodate divergent interests and values, foster wise and reasonably analytic decision making, and promote successful implementation" (1995, 5). On the other side of the issue, Miller, Rabin, and Hildreth (1987) have argued that agreement will not last long enough for planning to be done in the public sector.

In spite of such concerns, most authors have urged the public sector to adopt strategic planning as a rational and future-oriented management technique for improving government agencies (Behn, 1980; Bryson, 1988; Bryson, 1995; Meising and Andersen, 1991; Nutt and Backoff, 1992). In fact, their advice is being followed. Berry and Wechsler (1995) found that six out of the ten government agencies responding to their national survey were doing strategic planning and another one in ten said that it intended to do so in the future. They concluded that strategic planning has been "a successful public sector management innovation."

In addition to the use of strategic planning by public agencies, some governors have initiated processes that produced plans for the entire state. Rather than the Soviet style, ten-year plans or attempts at social engineering on a grand scale, these state strategic plans have provided a general framework for public policy development. Because other states may consider developing their own plans, this article will (1) describe the strategic planning process used in Oregon, one of the leading states, (2) indicate the parts of that process that are most valuable, and (3) offer suggestions for future plans.

HOW WERE OREGON'S STRATEGIC PLANS DEVELOPED?

The state of Oregon has developed two strategic plans over the last decade, using somewhat different processes. In this section of the article we will present the dramatic changes in context that led to the original plan issued in the late 1980s and the update in the mid-1990s.

For most of the twentieth century, Oregon's economy was heavily dependent upon extraction and manufacturing industries. Working in the forests harvesting trees, in the fields loading grain, or in the boats catching fish was the dominant way of life for many Oregonians. Many other jobs in rural Oregon were dependent upon natural-resource-based industries, and even Portland, the state's major metropolitan area, was a distribution hub for goods produced in rural portions of the state. With the downturn in the forest products industry in the early 1980s, Oregon's natural resource-based economy went into a long and deep recession. Incomes fell, statewide unemployment reached double digit levels, and many people left the state.

The Original Strategic Plan

By the mid-1980s, there were signs of modest improvement in Oregon's economy. Even though the unemployment rate was declining, per capita incomes were still about 10 percent below the national average—a particular concern to then Governor Neil Goldschmidt. In order to lift the state out of the doldrums of the early 1980s, Governor Goldschmidt asked more than 150 business and community leaders to help write a strategic plan for the state.[1] The plan they drafted, entitled *Oregon Shines: An Economic Strategy for the Pacific Century,* was released in 1989 (hereafter referenced as *Oregon Shines I*).

The planning process they adopted included some regional meetings but was driven primarily by a series of committees that worked on detailed recommendations in designated problem areas. The plan they created described three strategic initiatives: (1) a superior workforce, (2) an attractive quality of life, and (3) an international frame of mind. In the following year the state legislature adopted several of the plan's recommendations. For example, the legislature addressed its concerns about the workforce by adopting legislation and funding programs in the following areas: the adoption of sweeping school reform, the support of school-to-work transition programs, the creation of a Workforce Quality Council to coordinate retraining programs, and the funding of community college professional/technical programs. The state legislature also created the Oregon Progress Board to monitor benchmarks to determine if the state was moving toward the *Oregon Shines I* vision.

The state of Oregon has received several awards for being one of the early adopters of benchmarking. The National Governors Association featured the Oregon Benchmarks in its 1993 policy paper on the redesign of state government. In 1994 the Oregon Benchmarks system was selected as one of the ten winners of the annual Innovations in Government awards presented by the Ford Foundation and the Kennedy School of Government at Harvard. Oregon has not only been an award-winning leader in the adoption of these innovations, it has also sustained its commitment to the concept through two changes in administration.

In the years following the release of *Oregon Shines I* the state's economy experienced a truly remarkable turnaround. By 1995 the state's industry mix was more diversified, unemployment was at historic lows, and population growth was twice the national average. Oregon's economy was so strong that it did not participate in the 1991 national recession.

Public policy in Oregon changed as a result of its strategic plan, but it would be a considerable overstatement to attribute this remarkable turnaround solely to its public policy choices. In a report prepared for the governor's Oregon Shines Task Force, the Office of Economic Analysis (1996) attributed much of the state's recovery to external factors, such as (1) U.S. monetary policy and (2) the downturn in California's economy.

Oregon's above-average forest products and capital goods sectors contracted in response to high interest rates in the early 1980s and benefited from the more favorable interest rates in the 1990s. California's defense sector ballooned during the Star Wars years and collapsed when the Cold War ended. With California's economy "in the tank," Oregon attracted new businesses and new citizens who moved into the state with a good education and the disposable income to help spur the state's economy.

This economic recovery, however, was not experienced evenly around the state. Some parts of the state, particularly rural communities that were dependent upon the old-style manufacturing and extraction jobs, found themselves unable to recruit new businesses, leaving many in their communities without work (Kissler and Tryens, 1997). In addition, many of the best jobs in the metropolitan areas went to the newcomers from out of state, who were better educated and had more experience than native Oregonians.

An Updated Plan

Recognizing that the economy had turned around and that other things had changed since *Oregon Shines I* was released in 1989, Governor John Kitzhaber formed a 46-person task force in April of 1996 to recommend changes to the state's strategic plan. The strategic planning process used in 1996 (hereafter referenced as *Oregon Shines II*) differed in several ways. It featured: (1) significant university involvement, (2) analysis of Oregon Benchmarks to determine measurable progress toward the state's goals, (3) a bottom-up approach involving ten regional meetings held throughout the state, and (4) the adoption of broad recommendations rather than specific strategies and tactics. After describing these four aspects of the process we will evaluate them and relate our recommendations to them.

University Involvement: One of the goals of the Progress Board has been to involve more faculty and students from the state's universities in its various projects. Examples of these collaborations include research at Oregon State University on the root causes of poverty and the ongoing support for several Progress Board activities provided by the Center for Population Research and Census at Portland State University.

Consistent with its goal of greater university involvement, the Oregon Progress Board asked Professor Gerald Kissler and his graduate students from the Public Policy and Management program at the University of Oregon, the authors of this article, to lead the regional information-gathering meetings, analyze data, and draft much of the governor's task force report. When the work of the task force was presented to the Progress Board near the completion of the project, the executive director indicated that this project had been a model for the incorporation of university faculty and students in state policy work.

Analysis of Oregon Benchmarks: Analysis of progress made towards the three goals in *Oregon Shines I* was a joint effort of the University of Oregon team and the Progress Board staff. Some of the more important economic findings from our analysis of the Oregon Benchmarks and other data included the following:

- Oregon companies have been creating tens of thousands of good professional and managerial jobs but Oregonians are not qualified for them.
- Oregon's economy is more diversified but not in the technology sector.
- Oregon is a net importer of high-end professional services.
- Industry spending on research and development (R&D) as a percent of gross state product (GSP) is well below average and suggests that the state is not well positioned for twenty-first-century competitiveness.
- While rural Oregon has experienced a painful loss of jobs in its natural resource-based industries, this state's experience is not unique. In fact, per capita incomes in rural Oregon continue to be higher than the national average for nonmetropolitan counties in the United States.

A Bottom-Up Approach: Prior to each of the regional meetings, University of Oregon students gathered information about major trends, community issues, and local initiatives by talking to knowledgeable individuals in the region and asking them to complete a short questionnaire. They also scanned local newspapers for relevant stories and reviewed state reports on trends in the region.

A worksheet containing information collected prior to the regional meeting was used to guide a small group process that was the primary information-gathering tool. Participants were asked to (1) modify the information on the worksheet, (2) identify local initiatives that would address trends and issues, (3) suggest statewide strategies and actions, and (4) synthesize their ideas into a new vision for Oregon. Having completed this individual process, participants were engaged in a facilitated dialogue with others at their table. Finally, a spokesperson reported on the group's discussion to the reassembled gathering.

The governor's task force valued the comments and suggestions from the community leaders who attended the regional meetings, but they also wanted to check the pulse of the general public. Therefore, we looked at several polls and commissioned focus groups on what "quality of life" means to Oregonians.

Broad Recommendations Rather Than Specific Tactics: We started the process intending to update an economic plan but the regional meeting participants wanted a broader vision that addressed social issues and environmental concerns. The consensus of these regional meetings formed around three new goals for *Oregon Shines II:* 1) quality jobs for all Oregonians, 2) safe, caring, and engaged communities, and 3) healthy, sustainable surroundings.

Oregon Shines I contained hundreds of specific recommendations, but what endured were the general concepts rather than the specific tactics. Drawing upon past experience, we decided to include only general strategies in *Oregon Shines II* and to relate them to the new economic, social, and environmental goals. For example, the general strategies for the economy were to improve education and training, and to increase the competitiveness of Oregon business in the global economy. The strategies for the social goals were to minimize preventable social costs and build strong communities that support families and help restore hope. In the environmental area, the strategies were to develop a better understanding of the underlying issues and to utilize a cooperative visioning process to work toward consensus in order to avoid confrontation and costly litigation.

IS THE STRATEGIC PLANNING PROCESS VALUABLE?

The governor's task force was in operation for almost one year, and the pace of activities left us with less time than we would have liked for evaluation. In the months following the release of *Oregon Shines II,* we had an opportunity to reflect on our contributions, but admittedly from a biased point of view.

The Process Itself

Even though the Progress Board's staff had continued to speak to service clubs and work with community progress boards since the release of *Oregon Shines I,* Governor Kitzhaber felt that it was time to reinvigorate the process. Oregon has not escaped voter cynicism and the general loss of trust in government. Therefore, one very important function of Oregon's strategic planning process was to demonstrate that state leaders were doing something to address the major issues and concerns of citizens through a participatory process.

In contrast with the 1989 process, this approach included a larger number of citizens from a wider range of backgrounds in more parts of the state. However, our process was less effective in engaging business leaders than its predecessor had been. Still, there has been support for strategic planning and benchmarking from the business community.

The governor's task force was chaired by Fred Buckman, CEO of PacifiCorp—a midsized Fortune 500 company in the utilities industry. Speaking on behalf of the business leadership, Mr. Buckman (1996) remarked at the final governor's task force meeting:

> I want to say just a couple of words about the importance of *Oregon Shines* to the business community. And I want to say it in the context of someone who is a relatively new Oregonian. . . . I admit to being quite enamored by the fact that Oregon was willing to step out and actually write down what it intended to achieve and then to measure its performance against those goals. . . . From a business person's perspective I find it very refreshing and reassuring that in a place we choose to do business that there is on the radar screen fairly hard measures of what it is we are trying to achieve.

The Findings

We believe that the analytical work will lead to better informed public policy if the Progress Board is effective in disseminating the findings. By comparing the information collected at the regional meetings with polling data and focus group results, we concluded that the community leaders were more optimistic than the general public. In short, the average person at the coffee shop knows that the economy is more diversified and that the state will never again be as dependent upon its natural-resource-based industries. However, there is a poor understanding of the role of high-end professional services and the nature of the state's new technology-generating industries. Transformations without a clear vision of the future often lead to confusion and fear.

The text of the final report was intended to help reduce confusion and fear, but it will take years to reach large numbers of leaders and general citizens. The governor's task force disbanded after its report was submitted, but one of the important functions of the Oregon Progress Board is to make presentations to community groups throughout the state. In fact, the executive director was scheduled to make at least one presentation per week for the last six months of 1997 to service organizations, city clubs, chambers of commerce, and local progress boards.

The Recommendations

It is too early to know whether the recommendations in *Oregon Shines II* will be followed or whether they will make a difference. We do know, however, that the reaction from community leaders has been very positive. Their feedback indicates that the new plan contains valuable information in an easily understood format that helps them see the relationships among economic, social, and environmental issues. In addition, state agencies and nonprofits are referencing the new state strategic plan in discussing their programs and initiatives. The reaction from the media and state political leaders has also been very positive. Newspaper editorials have praised the vision. Some politicians who had expressed skepticism about state strategic planning and benchmarking also became strong supporters of the concepts during the legislative session.

Both houses of the state legislature overwhelmingly approved the bill reauthorizing the Progress Board. This bill not only declared that an Oregon Progress Board is needed to encourage the discussion and understanding of critical global and national trends, but it also required the Progress Board to develop "a strategy that addresses the economic, social, cultural, environmental and other needs and aspirations of the people of Oregon." In addition, the Progress Board was directed to develop a series of goals with measurable indicators of attainment and to prepare a report at least once each biennium on Oregon's progress.

WHAT CAN WE OFFER TO OTHER STATES?

We believe that there is considerable value in state strategic planning and that the plan should be updated every five to ten years as changes in the context indicate. For us, it is less a matter of "whether" than "how." Therefore, the suggestions offered below are derived primarily from the changes in the process used for *Oregon Shines II,* the update in 1996.

Include University Faculty and Students to Bring New Ideas at the Cutting Edge

One of the benefits of having university involvement in the state strategic planning process was the background research done by faculty and students on the large forces producing an economic and social transformation at the end of the twentieth century. While every state is different, all are affected by the same large forces. New technologies and global competition are reshaping the economy. There is more stress on families but less trust and support in communities for those in need. Population growth and natural resource limitations have caused more citizens to worry about an erosion of quality of life and have led to confrontation between economic interests and environmental concerns.

During the university/agency drafting of *Oregon Shines II,* we attempted to give equal treatment to the economic, social, and environmental areas but found that there was a much better understanding of the factors underlying the economic issues than the social issues, which in turn were often much better understood than the environmental issues. As a result, it is fair to say that our recommendations had less "punch" as we moved from the economic, to the social, and then to the natural surrounding goals.

Analyze Benchmarks and Other Information to Address Myths and Outdated Beliefs

If strategic planning is a rational approach to realigning the state with changes in its context, then planners and policymakers must have a good understanding of the trends and their impacts. Oregon's many years of experience with benchmarking gave us a good place to begin the analysis of the changes that had occurred since the previous plan was issued.

In the process we discovered that the relationship between economic and social issues is much more complex than the authors of *Oregon Shines I* believed it to be. They knew that social problems, like abuse, had increased in the 1980s and assumed that the rise was caused by a weak economy. They believed that Oregon's social problems would decline if the state's economy turned around. Oregon's economy has turned around in the 1990s but there has been no change in the poverty rate; at the same time, other indicators, such as juvenile arrests and teenage drug use, have risen.

Utilize a Bottom-Up Process to Engage the Public, Increase Awareness, and Generate New Insights

Governor Kitzhaber is committed to the concept of participatory democracy. Therefore, he wanted the 1996 update to be developed with more of a bottom-up approach, relying upon citizen input and the analysis of regional information. As a result, *Oregon Shines II* is a more thorough and thoughtful document than it would have been if it had simply been developed by government policy "wonks." This approach worked well in a state with only three million people but would undoubtedly be much more difficult in a larger state.

In the course of meeting with hundreds of Oregonians from different walks of life in all parts of the state, we came to appreciate many different perspectives. Clearly, the public mood is more positive than it was in the 1980s. Still, many Oregonians are having a difficult time making ends meet and a third are worried about their financial security.

To illustrate the differences in attitude found in different parts of the state we developed Figure 19.1. In a Maslow-like fashion, these stair steps illustrate the way that aspirations rise as the economy improves. When a region experiences a long and deep recession, people simply want more jobs to replace those that have been lost. As unemployment rates decline, the focus shifts to better jobs—higher salaries; insurance, retirement, and other benefits; and better working conditions. When salaries approach expectations, the public interest rises to better lives.

Community leaders in different regions were at different stair steps. In some parts of the state where unemployment was still in double digits, the participants in our regional meetings were still at the first step—trying to diversify the local economy to create new jobs. Most of our regional meeting participants, however, were either on the second or third step. They were concerned about economic issues but were unwilling to sacrifice their quality of life for economic development.

In general, the community leaders at our regional meetings were more optimistic than the general public. Community leaders knew that the economy had improved and were anxious to move up to the next step. Our review of the polling data, which was confirmed by our focus groups, indicated that most people are aware that the state's economy is better but they do not see any improvement in their personal situation.

Our experience with the regional meetings and the Progress Board's other efforts to engage the citizenry indicate that it is very difficult to get them to use data to develop informed recommen-

Figure 19.1 **Aspirations Rise as the Economy Improves**

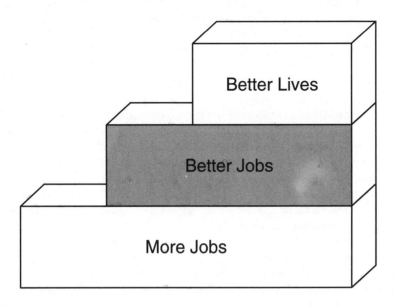

Source: Oregon Shines II.

dations about public policy tradeoffs. However, these forums do provide an important source of information about citizens' beliefs and values. When the process forces them to discuss their views with others around the table, as they did at the regional meetings, they gain a better appreciation for the complexity and interrelatedness of the issues facing the region.

Link Every Major Finding from Research to a Recommendation and Benchmarks to Ensure a More Logical Plan and to Monitor Progress

Other states have strategic plans, but what sets Oregon apart is its considerable experience with benchmarks as measurable indicators of progress toward the state vision. With many years of experience with outcome-based measurements, we were able to write a different kind of strategic plan—one with clear linkages among major research findings, recommendations, and benchmarks.

Oregon's benchmarks report represented a whole new approach to outcome-based assessment and accountability in the early 1990s. However, the benchmarks were developed after *Oregon Shines I* was written in 1989, and there was no way to link the two documents. Now, the benchmarks are incorporated in *Oregon Shines II*. Every major finding is linked to a recommendation and benchmarks for monitoring progress. The result is an approach to state strategic planning that could be helpful to leaders in other states who intend to develop their own plans.

One example of the linked structure relates to the diversification of the economy. It is generally recognized that the technology sector is increasingly important to twenty-first-century competitiveness with the shift to a knowledge-based or information economy (Gilder, 1989; Thurow, 1992;

Toffler, 1980). While the technology sector in Oregon is growing, it is not diversified. Therefore, the governor's task force recommended a shift in public policy from recruiting manufacturing facilities to becoming one of the top ten states in the nation for starting and growing a technology company. The benchmark the Progress Board will be monitoring is total research and development spending by industry as a percentage of gross state product.

CONCLUSION

Some authors have questioned the value of strategic planning in general (Hamel, 1996; Mintzberg, 1994) and its use by government in particular (Miller, Rabin, and Hildreth, 1987). Miller, Rabin, and Hildreth (1987) based their conclusion that "strategists have committed themselves to the road in the public sector that leads nowhere" upon their finding that government financial managers feel vulnerable to a liability suit, are constrained by political concerns, and are less willing to use financial tools with greater associated risk. This conservative, risk-averse behavior by financial managers in the public sector runs counter, they argued, to the values and assumptions of rational decision making and strategic planning.

However, proponents could counter that leaders *should* urge the public sector to adopt strategic planning and other rational decision-making practices *precisely* to override those risk-averse tendencies and thereby make better use of public funds for social purposes. Indeed, the Oregon experience leads us to concur with those who have encouraged the public sector to adopt strategic planning as a rational and future-oriented technique for adjusting to changes in context (Behn, 1980; Bryson, 1988, 1995; Meising and Andersen, 1991; Nutt and Backoff, 1992).

States' strategic planning has been a valuable process in helping Oregon adjust to a major economic and social transformation. And, consistent with Bryson's (1995) views, the process chosen to update Oregon's strategic plan facilitated communication and participation. The regional meetings were useful not only for gathering information from participants but also for "myth busting." Over the next few years we hope that the information in *Oregon Shines II* will increase public understanding and help to reduce confusion and fear.

Even if one grants that the analysis of the benchmarks and the plan's strategies could provide a useful framework for decision makers at the state and local levels, there is still no guarantee that the strategic plan would actually be used. We believe that it will be used for two reasons. First, the original plan led to legislation in the early 1990s and it is happening again with the updated plan. For example, several pieces of legislation were directed at the workforce issue raised in *Oregon Shines I*. Moreover, following the release of *Oregon Shines II,* the legislature called for a plan to reorganize the Economic Development Department to meet the needs of those regions of the state that had not benefited from the economic turnaround. Second, agencies and non-profit organizations are already relating their initiatives to issues raised in the updated plan, as they did when *Oregon Shines I* was released.

Therefore, we conclude that state strategic planning has been a valuable process in Oregon. While each state must tailor its own process, we recommend that state policymakers:

- include university faculty and students because it will bring new ideas at the cutting edge to the public debate;
- analyze benchmarks and other information to address myths and outdated beliefs;
- utilize a bottom-up approach involving regional meetings, because it engages the public, increases awareness of the complexity and interrelatedness of the region's issues, and generates new insights into the status of the state;

- insist that every major research finding be linked to a recommendation and benchmarks because it leads to a more logical plan and a better way to determine whether the state is moving in the right direction.

ACKNOWLEDGMENTS

The authors would like to thank Jeffrey Tryens, Deidre Molander, and Zoe Johnson from the Oregon Progress Board for their assistance in preparing this article. Three other University of Oregon graduate students, Kathrine Richardson, Greg Doss, and Jeff Grieve, were also members of the team that led the regional meetings, analyzed data, and drafted much of the final report.

NOTE

1. Copies of Oregon's state strategic plans and other related materials are available on the web site for the Oregon Progress Board at www.econ.state.or.us/opb/

REFERENCES

Behn, Robert (1980). "Leadership for Cut-Back Management: The Use of Corporate Strategy." *Public Administration Review* 40(6): 613–620.

Berry, Francis Stokes and Barton Wechsler (1995). "State Agencies' Experience with Strategic Planning: Findings from a National Survey." *Public Administration Review* 55(2): 159–166.

Bryson, John M. (1988). *Strategic Planning for Public and Nonprofit Organizations*. San Francisco: Jossey-Bass.

——— (1995). *Strategic Planning for Public and Nonprofit Organizations*. Revised Edition. San Francisco: Jossey-Bass.

Buckman, Fred (1996). "Minutes from the Governor's Oregon Shines Task Force Meeting, September 30, 1996." Salem, OR: Oregon Progress Board.

Gilder, George (1989). *Microcosm: The Quantum Revolution in Economics and Technology*. New York: Simon and Schuster.

Hamel, Gary (1996). "Strategy As Revolution." *Harvard Business Review* 74(4): 69–82.

——— (1997). "Killer Strategies That Make Shareholders Rich." *Fortune* 135(12): 70–84.

Kissler, Gerald R. and Jeffrey L. Tryens (1997). *Oregon Shines II: Updating Oregon's Strategic Plan*. Salem, OR: Oregon Progress Board.

Meising, Paul and David F. Andersen (1991). "The Size and Scope of Strategic Planning in State Agencies: The New York Experience." *American Review of Public Administration* 22: 119–137.

Miller, Gerald J., Jack Rabin, and W. Bartley Hildreth (1987). "Strategy, Values, and Productivity." *Public Policy Review* 43:(11.1): 81–96.

Mintzberg, Henry (1994). *The Rise and Fall of Strategic Planning*. New York: Free Press.

Nutt, Paul C. and Robert W. Backoff (1992). *The Strategic Management of Public and Third Sector Organizations*. San Francisco: Jossey-Bass.

Office of Economic Analysis (1996). *Oregon Shines Update: An Assessment of Oregon's Economy*. Salem, OR: Oregon Department of Administrative Services.

Thurow, Lester (1992). *Head to Head: The Coming Economic Battle among Japan, Europe, and America*. New York: William Morrow.

Toffler, Alvin (1980). *The Third Wave*. New York: William Morrow.

CHAPTER 20

THE PRACTICE OF DELIBERATIVE DEMOCRACY
Results from Four Large-Scale Trials

EDWARD C. WEEKS

INTRODUCTION

There is a familiar lament among politicians, public managers, and ordinary citizens about the gulf of suspicion separating citizens from their government (Dionne 1991; Gore 1994; Grieder 1992; Harris 1994; Harwood 1991; Lipset and Schneider 1987). Citizens are angry with their political leaders, estranged from civic institutions, distrustful of the news media, and pessimistic about the prospect for collective action to solve community problems. At the core of our dysfunctional political culture is the degraded quality of civic discourse—how we talk about public problems.

Many suggest that the cure for the ills of democracy is to more fully engage citizens in the deliberative process of community decision making. Whether called "strong democracy" (Barber 1984), "unitary democracy" (Mansbridge 1980), "discursive democracy" (Dryzek 1990), "civic discovery" (Reich 1988), or "deliberative democracy" (Gutmann and Thompson 1996) the proposed cures share an emphasis on eliciting broad public participation in a process which provides citizens an opportunity to consider the issues, weigh alternatives, and express a judgment about which policy or which candidate is preferred. For the purposes of this paper, "deliberative democracy" is used as the generic term encompassing democratic reforms sharing these features. It is distinguished from ordinary, thin, modes of public involvement by the breadth and quality of participation.

If deliberative democracy is seen as a hopeful way out of the quagmire of civic estrangement—the "din and deadlock" of contemporary civic life—the question of its practical feasibility becomes important (Benhabib 1996; Kirlin 1996). Is it possible to go beyond easy platitudes to actually convene a large-scale public deliberative process? This article addresses that question by reviewing four applications of a model of deliberative democracy based on the metaphor of a community dialogue.

From *Public Administration Review*, 60, 4 (July/August 2000): 360–372. Copyright © 2000 by American Society for Public Administration. Reprinted with permission.

THE ELEMENTS OF DELIBERATIVE DEMOCRACY

Defining deliberative democracy as the "informed participation by citizens in the deliberative process of community decision making" establishes the minimum conditions to be met by any reform claiming that label. That is, deliberative democracy requires that public participation be 1) broad; 2) informed; and 3) deliberative. An additional fourth condition is credibility: if the results of the public process are to be accepted by the general public, by interest groups, and by policy makers, they must be highly credible.

Broad Public Participation

Conventional avenues of citizen involvement, such as public hearings, advisory boards, citizen commissions, and task forces, engage only a small number of citizens and typically involve only those with a particular interest in the specific policy area. Participation by a few citizens with a special interest in the subject matter offers policy makers a skewed representation of the views of the general public and, worse, conveys to citizens the impression of special interest domination of the policy agenda.

If deliberative democracy aspired only to the narrow goal of informing policy makers of the judgment of citizens, participation could be limited to a small, statistically representative sample. For example, Fishkin's (1991, 1995) Deliberative Polling, and Crosby's (1986) Citizen Jury, use small but demographically representative samples for their intensive deliberative processes. The conclusions from these deliberative efforts serve as a proxy for the public at-large. That is, the results from these "trustworthy surrogates" (Dahl 1989) represent the conclusion that would be reached by the electorate if the electorate had a similar opportunity to deliberate.

However, the goal of deliberative democracy requires wider participation. The goal of deliberative democracy is to revitalize the civic culture, improve the nature of public discourse, and generate the political will necessary to take effective action on pressing problems. Without broad participation, the democratic reform will not provide a sufficient number of citizens with the personal experience of public deliberation necessary to affect the local political culture. Broad participation, on the other hand, does not assure representative participation. Oregon's *Health Decisions* involved over 1,000 participants (Nagel 1992) and the Governor's *Conversation with Oregon* included approximately 10,000 participants (Weeks et al. 1992) yet neither could claim to have engaged a group that was representative of the larger population.

Deliberative democracy, then, requires both broad participation and the participation of citizens who are, as a group, representative of the general public. Both conditions are necessary. If participation is large, but unrepresentative, it may fail to accurately reflect the policy preferences of the community. If participation is small, but representative, the results may accurately reflect the policy preferences of the community, but the larger goals of civic engagement will be sacrificed.

Informed Public Judgment

Public opinion, in the sense of the typical opinion poll, does not offer a reliable basis for policy. Ordinary public opinion tends to be uninformed, superficial, and transient. Deliberative democracy is after something stronger. Deliberative democracy depends upon what Yankelovich (1991) terms *public judgment*. Public judgment is informed and, being informed, tends to be consistent and stable. Becoming informed about a policy problem requires a knowledge of the basic elements of the problem, about the relationships among those elements, and about the consequences and tradeoffs associated with alternative policies.

Opportunities for Deliberation

Information is a necessary, but not sufficient condition for public judgment. Judgment requires deliberation. To deliberate is to act on information—it is an application of creative intelligence and normative evaluation that leads ultimately to the formation of personal judgment. The challenge to reformers is to design a process that provides a hospitable environment for the deliberative process.

Yankelovich (1991) cites his experimental work and the work of the *Public Agenda Foundation* to argue that the process of "working through," that is, deliberation, can be accelerated by structured activities that present citizens with options, provide information about their characteristics and consequences, encourage reasoned discussion among peers, and, finally, elicit reflective judgment.

Yankelovich isn't alone in emphasizing discussion among peers as an element of deliberation. Barber (1984, 178–98) places "democratic talk" at the center of strong democracy and ascribes to it nine important functions.[1] Gutmann and Thompson (1996) assert that discussion aids deliberation by increasing the available information, expanding the range of arguments considered and widening the moral frame of reference. Discourse theorists such as Habermas (1996), Dryzek (1990), and Benhabib (1996) simply equate deliberative democracy with face-to-face communication among equals.

While face-to-face discussion can inform and stimulate deliberation, the absence of discussion does not foreclose its possibility. Deliberation is, after all, a fundamentally private, cognitive activity. Any motivated citizen sufficiently well informed about the nature of the public problem, and about the cost, consequences, and tradeoffs associated with alternative solutions is capable of working through the problem to arrive at a reasoned judgment about a preferred course. Face-to-face discussion is a powerful aid to deliberation, but it is not its *sine qua non*.

Credible Results

Any solution to a significant public problem will likely displease some segment of the community. The first line of attack of those opposed to the conclusions of a public deliberative process would be to challenge the quality of the citizen-input data. To meet these attacks, the deliberative process must be methodologically sound. In addition to meeting the usual requirements of methodological rigor, the underlying methods must have a high degree of face validity for public officials, and be easily communicated to the news media and to the public.

A COMMUNITY DIALOGUE: APPLYING THE IDEAS OF DELIBERATIVE DEMOCRACY

The operational requirements of deliberative democracy are daunting. To meet these requirements, a model of deliberative democracy based on the metaphor of a community dialogue has been developed. This community dialogue is broadly inclusive, providing a practical opportunity for all citizens to participate. The dialogue provides citizens extensive information about the nature of the policy problem, engages citizens in the same problem solving context as elected officials, and uses rigorous methods including multiple data sources, multiple measures, and multiple data collection methods. Figure 20.1 presents in graphical form the internal logic and methods of a community dialogue.

Figure 20.1   **Engaging Citizens in a Community Dialogue Based on the Model of Deliberative
Democracy**

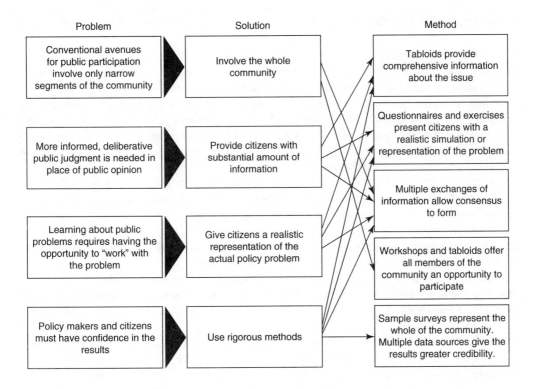

A community dialogue is an iterative process with multiple exchanges as the dialogue proceeds through agenda setting, strategy development, and decision making. The agenda setting round asks the community to define the scope and terms of the dialogue. The strategy development round asks citizens to identify promising options and the decision making round asks citizens to select the preferred course.[2]

Each round of the dialogue is supported by an informational newsletter or tabloid distributed to every household in the community. The tabloid introduces the community dialogue and serves as an information resource approximating the staff briefing a city council receives as it addresses an issue. The tabloid also includes a questionnaire designed to offer a realistic representation of the policy problem, enabling citizens to work through the policy problem to arrive at their preferred course of action.

Community workshops offer citizens an opportunity to work together, face to face, in a shared search for effective solutions to community problems. Participants are randomly assigned to small groups where they work through a structured exercise facilitated by a community volunteer. The workshops are problem-solving sessions that model an invigorated civil society by channeling political animosities into a constructive dialogue about means and ends.

The workshops and tabloids offer an opportunity for all citizens to add their voice to the dialogue. Yet, these respondents and workshop participants represent only a fraction of the community and, as a self-selected group, cannot be expected to be representative of the community at large. Multiple sample surveys provide a benchmark against which the results from the tabloid questionnaires and workshops can be compared. Using multiple survey formats and data collection methods provides an additional check against the confounding influence of methods or measurement artifacts.

FOUR COMMUNITY DIALOGUES

Four community dialogues based on this model of deliberative democracy have been completed. Each dialogue addressed the single most prominent and contentious issue facing the community. Given the high political stakes, the dialogues were not policy experiments in the pure sense where the implementer has full control over the design, operational details, and calendar of the program or policy being tested. Elected officials and appointed executives are unlikely to trust their political and professional fates solely to the discretion of an outside experimenter. Instead, each dialogue was adjusted to accommodate the political and administrative environment.[3] In each instance the municipal government funded the full cost of the community dialogue.

The four dialogues were conducted in three cities: Eugene, Oregon; Sacramento, California; and Fort Collins, Colorado. Eugene, Oregon is a medium-sized university town with a population of approximately 125,000. As is the case with Oregon generally, Eugene has a small minority population. The strong sentimental attachment to Eugene, a well-educated population and the presence of three network television affiliates, a strong daily newspaper and a combative "alternative" weekly combine to produce a particularly active political scene.

Sacramento, California is the state's capital. It has a racially and ethnically diverse population of nearly 400,000. Nearly a quarter of Sacramento's adult population has less than a high school education. Appropriate to its size and its status as the capital city of the largest state, Sacramento has the full complement of media outlets.

Fort Collins shares a number of characteristics with Eugene. The cities are of similar size and demographics, they both are college towns, and both are viewed by their residents as extremely desirable communities (Fort Collins's nickname is "Choice City"). On the other hand, compared to Eugene, Fort Collins has a more passive political tradition. One explanation for the difference in the degree of citizen engagement is the difference in media saturation: Fort Collins is within the much larger Denver media market and has no regular local television news coverage.

RESOLVING A BUDGET CRISIS: EUGENE DECISIONS AND SACRAMENTO DECISIONS

Two of the dialogues, *Eugene Decisions* and *Sacramento Decisions,* focused on resolving the conflict between the public's demand for services and their willingness to pay for them. In neither community were revenues keeping up with the cost of providing municipal services. Both city councils deferred corrective action in favor of less painful temporary fixes such as reduced capital maintenance, salary and hiring freezes, and inter-fund borrowing. When long-term financial forecasts revealed an increasing gap between revenues and the cost of services, the city managers and councils concluded that a lasting solution was needed and that effective action depended upon the public's support for a strategy to balance the budget.

The background of both dialogues highlights a couple of important points. First, the problem of continuing municipal shortfalls persisted in the absence of a political will within the community to take the action necessary to solve the problem. The lack of political will, in turn, was due to the dysfunctional political process. When running for office, council candidates did not address forthrightly either the manner in which revenues would be raised or which services would be cut. Instead, they offered only palliatives such as "increased efficiency," "new leadership," or assorted "reinventing" jargon. During earlier budget hearings, interest groups achieved their ends by making extravagant claims about the benefits of their favored programs or of the consequence of a program's elimination, but offered no alternative solutions. The news media reported the story of financial stress in terms of competing groups and uncritically passed on assertions that there were painless solutions to the city's financial problem.

Eugene Decisions

Eugene Decisions began as a conventional citizen involvement effort which included telephone polls, meetings with community leaders, a public open house, and a newspaper "clip out" questionnaire. The council, hoping to learn which services the public was willing to see reduced, learned instead that most citizens believed that the budget could be balanced through "efficiencies." Moreover, in the face of extreme financial exigency, citizens and community leaders urged the adoption of additional library, public safety, and social services. This dilemma of a citizenry unwilling to accept the discipline of balancing their demand for services with a willingness to pay for them led the council to change course and to adopt a community dialogue based on a model of deliberative democracy.

The next round of what was now intended to be a dialogue included (1) the distribution of a 12-page informational tabloid to all households; (2) community workshops where citizens worked face-to-face in small groups to balance the budget; (3) a budget worksheet distributed with the tabloid; (4) a questionnaire in the form of a budget worksheet sent to a representative sample of registered voters; and (5) two alternate questionnaires sent to independent random samples.

The tabloid provided background information about the city's financial problem and a concise summary of each of forty municipal services, the five new or expanded services identified during the earlier phase, and sixteen revenue sources. The tabloid offered a description of each municipal service, its tax cost and the likely impact of eliminating or significantly reducing the level of service. The tabloid also included a budget worksheet allowing citizens to build their own balanced budget. The tabloid was mailed to each residential address in the city.

The budget worksheet presented the respondent with a template of the municipal budget. It began with the bad news that the city budget was $8 million in the red. The respondent was next given the opportunity to adopt any of the five proposed new or enhanced services with their costs added to the $8 million to become the new projected deficit. The respondent then reviewed the budget amounts for each of 40 services, making reductions where desired. The remaining deficit was to be made up through any desired combination of 16 tax options.

The budget worksheet was included in the tabloid distributed to all households and a more attractively formatted version was sent with the tabloid to a random sample of voters. In addition to the budget worksheet, two alternate survey forms were used. The alternative questionnaires used more conventional, and less demanding, formats.

Over a thousand tabloid budget template questionnaires were returned. The response rates for the sample surveys varied depending upon the level of demand imposed on the respondent. The least demanding format which offered neither cost information nor required the respondent to accept services versus funding tradeoffs has a response rate of 73 percent. The second alternative format, which included cost information but did not require the respondent to trade services for taxes, had a response rate of 70 percent (Figure 20.2). The most demanding questionnaire, the budget worksheet, had a response rate of 53 percent. There was a high degree of consistency among the findings from the several instruments with zero-order correlation ranging from .89 to .98.

Figure 20.2   **Data Collection Methods for Eugene Decisions Strategy Development Board**

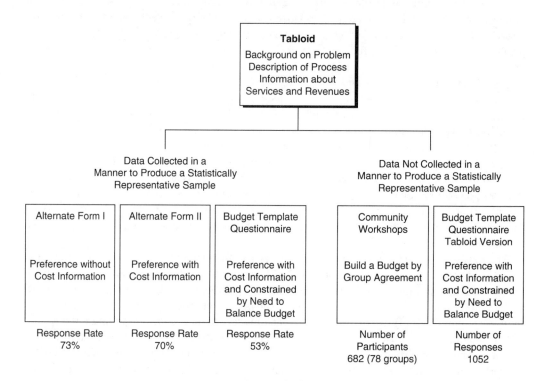

Community workshops provided an opportunity for citizens to work together to develop a solution to their city's budget problem. Workshop participants were randomly assigned to small groups of 7 or 9 people and were given the same task as that confronting the city council. To balance the budget, the group could adopt any combination of service enhancements, service reductions, and taxes. Like the council, they made their decisions by majority vote. Each small group was supported by a citizen volunteer facilitator and by a city staff member serving in a resource role. In addition, department heads and senior staff were available as roving specialists to assist the groups with requested information.

Workshop attendance exceeded expectations. The city had never before had more than a couple of hundred citizens attend a public meeting. Over six hundred and eighty citizens attended the three-hour *Eugene Decisions* workshops.

The first round of public input, including results from the workshops, tabloid questionnaires, and the three sample surveys, was reported to the city council and disseminated throughout the community. Having heard from the public, the Eugene city council met in a series of work sessions to develop specific measures to implement the direction suggested by the public. In addition to 48 specific cost saving measures, the council developed three broad strategies. Each strategy reflected a distinct philosophy. One strategy balanced the budget with $4.4 million in cost savings and $3.6 million in additional taxes. The second strategy added $10.8 million in new services, included $3 million in cost savings, and called for $15.8 million in additional taxes. The third strategy raised no new taxes, balancing the budget solely by cutting expenditures.

The second round of the dialogue sought to assess citizen support for the overall strategies, for the specific cost savings measures, and for a variety of revenue measures. As with the first round, the second round included a tabloid (with embedded budget worksheet) mailed to all households; a more attractively formatted version of the budget balancing questionnaire and two less demanding alternate questionnaires that were sent to independent random samples of voters; and community workshops.

The budget worksheet asked respondents to rank and rate the three broad strategies and to construct their own municipal budget by selecting from among five new or expanded services, 48 cost saving measures (including service reductions and user fees), and 11 tax options with 28 rates. As with the first round, the alternate questionnaire formats used a more traditional, and less demanding, fixed-choice response format.

The community workshops used essentially the same format as that used during the first round. Participants were randomly assigned to small groups which acted as simulated city councils. Their budget deliberations were facilitated by citizen volunteers and supported by city staff serving as information resources. The groups made their budget choices by majority vote.

Participation was expected to decline from the first round. The budget worksheets were more demanding: there were a greater number of more difficult choices to be made and the formatting necessary to prevent logically incompatible choices made the questionnaires more formidable. Additionally, it was thought that the community had tired of the dialogue.

Instead, the response rate for the budget-balancing sample survey increased from 53 percent for the first round to 61 percent for the second round and the number of returned budget worksheets from the tabloid more than doubled to nearly 2,500 returned surveys. Workshop participation declined slightly during the second round, probably because they were scheduled during the televised National Basketball Association championship series in which Oregon's team was playing.

Policy Impact. After receiving the final results, the council began crafting a long-term budget solution. The council carefully built the budget over three evenings when suddenly, in what the news media later termed a "moment of madness," the council reversed course and added $10 million in new services balanced by a municipal income tax—the first in Oregon. These actions were taken on a Thursday evening; on the following Monday the council responded to community anger by withdrawing its earlier decision and enacting a budget plan that mirrored the preferences expressed through the community dialogue. The sustainable changes to the municipal budget included six efficiency measures, twenty user-fee increases, twenty-five service reductions, three transfers of service costs to non-general fund accounts, and three service expansions.

Sacramento Decisions

The success of *Eugene Decisions* demonstrated that ordinary citizens could be brought into a sustained conversation about an important community issue. Most importantly, *Eugene Decisions* revealed that citizens would invest the time and intellectual energy needed to work through a difficult budget problem. There were, however, a number of factors favoring success in Eugene, which limit generalizing that success to other communities. Eugene is a medium-sized city with a well-educated homogeneous population and a tradition of civic engagement. Could a community dialogue succeed in a larger city with a diverse population and with a more typical level of community involvement?

The City of Sacramento struggled unsuccessfully for several years to balance its municipal budget. It had trimmed agency budgets, deferred capital maintenance, raised fees and, where possible, consolidated and eliminated programs. It had, in the words of the mayor, "picked all the low hanging fruit." It was clear that a long-term solution required fundamental choices that would likely be unpopular. With this assessment, the council and city manager concluded that a broad community dialogue was the only course for achieving the sought-after long-term solution.

Sacramento Decisions used many of the same methods used in *Eugene Decisions,* including two rounds of public engagement, community workshops, informational tabloids with a budget-balancing questionnaire distributed to all households, and sample surveys using the budget-balancing questionnaire and alternate formats.

The principal difference in *Sacramento Decisions* was the addition of an extensive outreach effort to enlist the involvement of populations with historically low participation rates. Announcements and dialogue materials were printed in Spanish, Chinese, Vietnamese, Laotian, Hmong, and Russian. Multi-lingual students from the local university conducted meetings at neighborhood cultural centers to discuss the community dialogue and to assist citizens in completing the questionnaire. Community-based organizations (cultural centers, churches and other religious centers, legal aid and other social service organizations) were enlisted to inform their community and to encourage participation. These efforts succeeded in eliciting participation among traditionally underrepresented groups. The characteristics of questionnaire respondents and workshop participants closely paralleled the demographic data on race, ethnicity, and income.

Sacramento Decisions' response rates were lower than Eugene's. The response rates to both the budget worksheet questionnaire and the first alternate form were about 30 percent.[4] An alternative form, using a simple 5-point rating scale, was administered as a telephone survey and had a higher response rate. Workshop attendance, however, was excellent. Attracting a diverse group of 800 participants, workshop attendance substantially exceeded any previous public meeting or set of related meetings.

The low survey response rate is due, at least partially, to the calendar. In October, the city attorney advised the council that the tabloids could be construed as prohibited city-sponsored campaign activity. The council, in turn, directed that data collection be deferred until after the election. This decision meant that most of the data collection would take place during the Thanksgiving through New Year's holiday period.

The city council's and city manager's satisfaction with the first round of *Sacramento Decisions* led to the decision to merge the regular budget process into the community dialogue, creating a single unified process. To that end, the first round budget solution produced by citizens responding to the budget worksheets and workshop exercises became, with small refinements, the proposed municipal budget.

The second round of the community dialogue included a tabloid with an embedded budget worksheet mailed to all households, a community workshop, and a budget worksheet telephone survey. This phase was implemented by city staff and used an approach that mimicked the traditional public budget review process. Instead of asking the respondent to build a budget by selecting from among a range of options, respondents were asked to evaluate the proposed budget and to indicate their agreement or disagreement with each of its elements. Where respondents disagreed, they were asked to suggest alternative budget reductions. The press of time led to the use of telephone interviews for the budget-balancing sample survey. Through a three-stage process, a random sample of residents was recruited to be interviewed, mailed a tabloid and, at an agreed-upon time, telephoned and interviewed.

The second round survey response rates and workshop participation were low. Of the 890 respondents who agreed to be interviewed for the telephone survey, only 400 or 44 percent actually completed the interviews. Workshop attendance dropped to 148 over three sessions and 1,700 completed tabloid questionnaires were returned.

Policy Impact. Merging *Sacramento Decisions* into the current year's budget process assured that the community dialogue would significantly shape the city's budget. California statutes require that a proposed budget be prepared and submitted to the public for comment. The dialogue's first-round results became the city's proposed budget and the second round was the avenue by which public comment was solicited. The public's ratification of the proposed budget led directly to the final budget for the current year and to the city's long-term plan for financial stability.

One issue, in particular, illustrates how a community dialogue empowers elected leaders to make strong decisions. With 80 percent of the city's general fund budget devoted to public safety, any solution which does not severely reduce most other municipal services will include some cuts to police and fire services. Yet, popular political wisdom held that voters would not tolerate cuts to public safety services. Putting the budget into the hands of citizens allowed them to discover the tough reality of the situation, and those who attempted to balance the budget came to the conclusion that they would rather preserve a broader range of services by recommending modest expenditure reductions in police and fire services. With this recommendation ratified through the second round of the dialogue, the final budget included reductions in public safety services.

Managing Community Growth: Fort Collins's City Dialogue and Shaping Eugene's Future

Eugene Decisions and *Sacramento Decisions* focused on a conceptually narrow question for which the budget template offered a reasonable representation of the problem. Is it possible to use a community dialogue to address broader topics with fuzzier boundaries for which there is no simple and comprehensive model? Fort Collins's *City Dialogue* and *Shaping Eugene's Future* offered an opportunity to explore this question.

Growth and its management is the source of conflict in many American communities. Managing growth entails choices about economic development, urban design, environmental quality, transportation, and affordable housing. Addressed comprehensively, growth management shapes the fundamental nature of the community and the quality of life available to its residents.

Debates about growth management take on the character of a moral conflict with organized groups promoting their position and opposing others' views with the exaggerated rhetoric of adversary politics. The vitriolic intensity of the conflict gives political leaders a strong incentive to defer, avoid, or dilute action on growth-related issues. In this manner, the problem persists, positions harden, and a lasting solution becomes even more remote. Eugene, Oregon, and Fort Collins, Colorado, had traveled that debilitating course of political conflict and policy paralysis. In some desperation, the political leadership chose to convene a community dialogue about the future of their city.

Shaping Eugene's Future

Shaping Eugene's Future began with a four-page newsletter mailed to each household. The newsletter introduced *Shaping Eugene's Future* and posed two open-ended questions: "What is it about Eugene that you most value—that you want to be most certain is preserved or enhanced over the next ten years?" and "What is it about Eugene that you feel is most in need of attention over the next ten years? What would be on your 'to do' list?" Nearly 1,500 citizens mailed in a written response, and more responded through an Internet web page or via a telephone voice mailbox.

Concurrently, community workshops were held at area high schools. Upon arriving, participants were assigned randomly to small groups to work through a structured exercise to identify the characteristics of a community that were important to them, and to assess how urgently these issues needed attention in Eugene. Facilitated by community volunteers, these small group discussions offered a rare opportunity for political combatants to meet face-to-face in a problem-solving context. The charged rhetoric and personal invective that had come to dominate political discourse on this topic in Eugene was replaced during these meetings by reasoned discussion and shared problem solving.

The agenda that emerged from the questionnaires and workshops included a list of 34 specific concerns. This agenda was subsequently tested in the community through a telephone poll of a random sample of households. The results from the telephone survey supported the conclusion from the workshops and mail-in surveys.

This first exchange in the dialogue accomplished two important political aims: it did not foreclose any topic from being raised—enabling citizens to set the agenda—and it attracted the participation of citizens outside the activist community. The next exchange required policymakers to respond to the agenda proposed by citizens. This was a closely watched, highly political act. The council concluded that "education" and "health care" are outside their jurisdiction and beyond their influence. The council removed these issues from the agenda and consolidated the remaining ones into eight core topics; 1) land supply and density; 2) development pattern and housing; 3) transportation; 4) infrastructure and its pricing; 5) incentives for jobs; 6) natural environment; 7) parks and open space; and 8) public safety. This agenda was accepted by the general community as well as by the more skeptical activist community.

City staff developed a number of policy options relating to each agenda issue. These options formed the basis for an elaborate set of displays for a week-long community open house. The public comments received during the open house were used by the staff to refine the policy options and by policymakers to choose which options would be brought forward for more extensive public discussion and evaluation.

Ultimately, the council adopted four scenarios describing plausible alternative development paths for Eugene. Titled "Current Trends," "Discourage Growth," "Encourage Growth," and "Recycle Eugene" (emphasizing more intensive development within the core urban area), the scenarios represented four distinct points along the continuum of public discourse in Eugene. Each of these scenarios, in turn, was the product of a set of discrete policy actions addressing each of the eight core areas identified through the agenda setting phase.

The final round of the dialogue involved the preparation of an informational newsletter, the development of a questionnaire that modeled the decision problem facing the city council, and the design of a community workshop to engage participants in a deliberative, problem-solving exercise.

The informational tabloid addressed each of the eight core topics through a format using three elements. The wide middle column of each tabloid-sized page contained a narrative discussion of the topic, employing the device of a hypothetical dialogue among fictional citizens. The left column presented trend and comparative data associated with the issue. The right column summarized the general policy question associated with the topic and presented the key policy options prepared for each topic. Readers were asked to use a numerical scale to rate their preference for each option.

Finally, the tabloid included a detailed description of four growth management scenarios and asked readers to rate their preference for each of the scenarios. The tabloid was mailed to all households in the city (1,500 completed worksheets were received) and was sent separately to a random sample of Eugene voters with a response rate of 55 percent.

The three-hour workshop allowed participants to address each of the eight interrelated topic areas in a meaningful way, provided an opportunity for group deliberation, and allowed for new ideas to be introduced. Small groups (7–9 persons) constructed a synthetic or hybrid scenario out of the 30 policy options which formed the four original scenarios. The work groups were permitted to invent wholly new policy options or revise the city-prepared options if they felt that necessary. All of this work was accomplished through an iterative process of discussion and group voting. The community workshops were attended by about 400 citizens. None of the 42 workshop groups elected to develop new or revised policy options.

Policy Impact. The surprising conclusion of *Shaping Eugene's Future* is the degree of consensus in the community about the preferred course of development. *Shaping Eugene's Future* revealed that there was broad support for a policy of compact urban development emphasizing environmental amenities and alternative modes of transportation. The data from all sources (tabloid questionnaire, community workshops, and sample surveys) told the same story: a preference for carefully managed growth within a compact urban form.

Importantly, the consensus was not purchased at the cost of generality or ambiguity. The agreement was clear and definitive in terms of specific strategies for achieving broader, shared community goals. The specificity of the dialogue simplified the work of the council and made more certain the link between the dialogue and adopted policy. This post-dialogue policy making process took place under the watchful view of activist organizations from all sides and was accomplished without re-igniting community conflict.

City Dialogue

Like *Shaping Eugene's Future,* Fort Collins's *City Dialogue* began with community workshops through which citizens set the agenda for the remainder of the dialogue. More than 500 citizens, including committed activists and ordinary, disinterested residents attended the workshops. Randomly assigned to small groups, they worked together through a structured deliberative process to identify which aspects of community life were most important and most urgently needing attention. The groups produced a list of 42 issues which the City Council subsequently consolidated into 11 key topics. These topics were: 1) local economy and affordable housing; 2) crime and public safety; 3) transportation; 4) planning; 5) environmental quality; 6) cultural opportunities; 7) sense of community; 8) open space, parks and recreation; 9) health care; 10) local government; and 11) education.

To test this tentative agenda in the community, a 20-page tabloid-sized newsletter was prepared and distributed to each residence in Fort Collins. The tabloid summarized and presented comparative and trend data for each issue. For example, for "education" the tabloid reported data on SAT and ACT scores, graduation and drop-out rates, percent of students completing advanced placement courses, student/teacher ratios, percent of teachers with Master's degrees, teacher salaries, and overall and per pupil expenditures by source. The newsletter gave each citizen a reasonably comprehensive picture of the issues identified by workshop participants as important and needing attention.

Included with the tabloid was a four-page questionnaire asking respondents to use a series of paired comparisons to rate the relative importance of each of the issues. An open-ended question similar to that used in *Shaping Eugene's Future* was used to allow respondents to suggest issues not otherwise presented in the tabloid. Over a thousand residents completed and returned the tabloid questionnaire.

Two independent sample surveys were also conducted. One survey used a paired-comparison format and the other used a simpler 7-point Likert-type rating scale. Sixty-one percent of the respondents returned the "paired-comparison" version of the sample survey and about 65 percent returned the simpler questionnaire. There was a high degree of correlation ($r > .9$) between the results from the tabloid questionnaires and the sample surveys.

The tabloid and survey results were to be used to reduce the agenda to a small number of high priority issues and to develop strategies for addressing them. However, the city council, recognizing the high visibility of *City Dialogue* chose not to narrow the agenda. Choosing to go forward with all of the initial issue areas had implications for the "strategy development" phase of the dialogue. Three approaches for developing policy alternatives were considered: (1) the use of city staff and consultant specialists to propose strategies for public consideration; (2) using "stakeholder" groups alone or in combination with staff and consultant specialists to develop policy options; and (3) engaging citizens in directly developing strategy alternatives. The council, honoring the spirit of the community dialogue, directed that strategy development be citizen-based.

A series of workshops offered citizens an opportunity to work together in small groups to devise solutions to pressing community issues. Each small group worked on two issues: one issue selected by the group's members and one issue randomly assigned to the group. The three-hour structured exercise worked through a brainstorming, priority setting, and refinement process aimed at producing a small set of promising strategies. The structure of the brainstorming session encouraged participants to think "outside the box" and to look beyond government action to include actions undertaken by private and not-for-profit sectors and by individuals. In setting priorities, participants considered the feasibility and effectiveness of each proposed strategy. The group then concentrated its attention on two or three strategies selected from among those rated as most effective and most feasible. In refining their proposal, the group was asked to be detailed and specific about who should do what, and to layout a logical causal chain for their proposed strategy.

The workshops were well attended and group discussions were enthusiastic but generally unproductive. Community activists aligned with specific groups or causes were able to sometimes "hijack" their group to advance their cause and favored solution. More often, the group members lacked sufficient knowledge about the underlying issue to fruitfully engage in developing preventive or corrective strategies. Solutions tended to be the conventional wisdom as reflected by recent newspaper headlines.

Policy Impact. The results from the community workshops were organized and presented in fairly raw form to the city council. The results were not rigorously analyzed or even summarized because their primary value seemed to be contained in their actual expression, not in their technical content. The council, in turn, directed that the results be distributed among the appropriate city departments for evaluation and comment. In this manner, the public input was merged into the policy stream of the regular policy process.

The translation of *City Dialogue's* results to policy has been more diffuse and indirect than was the case with the other community dialogues. While there have since been a number of policy decisions that are consistent with the conclusions from *City Dialogue,* the separation in time and the indirect path between dialogue results and policy output renders any claim of policy influence questionable. The ambiguous result of *City Dialogue* is a consequence of designing the second round of the community dialogue such that it yielded only broad policy guidance, making necessary additional staff work to produce specific policy options.

DISCUSSION

This article began by asking if it is practically possible to convene a large-scale public deliberative process. Four criteria were suggested for judging whether a public involvement process rises to the level of deliberative democracy: public participation must be broad, informed, deliberative, and credible. Have these criteria been met by the community dialogues described here? The answer to this question depends, in turn, on the standard used. Against the standard of the *ideal* (e.g., universal participation among completely informed citizens working through a full deliberative process) these efforts fall short. Against a more pragmatic standard of the possible, these dialogues show greater promise.

Broad, Representative Participation

Every adult resident had multiple opportunities to participate in the dialogue by completing the tabloid questionnaires or attending a community workshop. While thousands chose to participate, their number amounts to only a small fraction of the population. Is this an adequate level of participation? In practical terms, this level of participation was sufficient to invest the dialogue with a high degree of political legitimacy which, in turn, empowered elected leaders to take stronger actions than they otherwise thought possible. For example, City of Eugene councilors were able to raise user fees, and reduce, eliminate, or privatize services—actions which, when proposed earlier, had elicited loud protest; the Sacramento city council was able to preserve valued programs by making modest, but politically risky, cuts in fire and police services; and in Eugene the council, with broad public support, adopted a menu of policies for managing growth and shaping the city's development. In short, the dialogue attracted sufficient participation to generate the political will to take effective action on important community problems.

Informed Public Participation

The form and amount of information provided to the citizen participant compares favorably to that which is ordinarily available to the city council. Realizing that every word published will be read by an attentive, skeptical, even hostile audience, the analysis is deeper and more thorough and the presentation is crafted to avoid impermissible advocacy. The careful editing necessary to make efficient use of limited page space in the tabloid and the need to communicate clearly to a lay audience improves the accessibility of the information. Workshop participants have the benefit of detailed briefing books prepared for the support person staffing each group, and small groups have immediate access to department heads and specialized experts in every programmatic area. While a council may inquire more deeply into specific topics and direct staff to prepare special studies, in the main the material provided to citizens is comparable to that available to their elected councilors.

Deliberative Participation

The questionnaires and workshop exercises were designed to put the policy problem into the hands of the citizen in a manner that allows them to experiment with alternatives, judge the consequences and freely construct their own preferred solution. Thus, the budget-balancing questionnaires and workshop exercises used in *Eugene Decisions* and *Sacramento Decisions* enabled citizens to build a budget reflecting their service priorities and tax preferences. The questionnaires and exercises used in *Shaping Eugene's Future* allowed citizens to construct an urban design scheme that suited their values. The community workshops added an important element of face-to-face discussion among community activists leavened by the presence of ordinary, otherwise disinterested, citizens.

An example illustrates how the opportunity for informed deliberation produces a level of public judgment qualitatively different from simple public opinion. During the second round of *Eugene Decisions,* respondents were first asked which of three budget-balancing strategies they favored. Among these was a "no new taxes" strategy. After indicating their most preferred budget-balancing strategy, the respondents turned the page and began crafting their own budget. On average, respondents who selected "no new taxes" as their most preferred strategy constructed a budget that included $3.3 million in new taxes. Why would citizens who initially espoused a preference for no new taxes subsequently construct a budget containing substantial new taxes? The difference lies in the ability to evaluate the consequences of an action. Behind the slogan of "no new taxes" is the consequence of losing valued community services—services for which they are willing to tax themselves.

Credible Results

The use of strong methods, including multiple measures and multiple data collection methods combined with careful pre-testing and straight-forward data analysis produced results that were persuasive to policy makers, the news media, organized interests, and ordinary citizens. In no instance were the results seriously challenged as being inaccurate or as biased in favor of a particular policy outcome.

These trials suggest that it is possible to mount a large-scale public process that meets, if imperfectly, the requirements of deliberative community dialogue. We have seen also how these dialogues break political deadlock and enable strong action on pressing community problems. There remains, finally, the larger question of whether a community dialogue can vitalize the civic culture of the community and raise the quality of public discourse. To address this question it is important to acknowledge that no single instance of a public process will transform a deeply rooted civic culture. At best, change will be gradual as experience with stronger, more participative democratic processes accumulates in the community and in its institutions. At this early point in its history, claims for an impact that extends beyond the immediate policy issue and decision episode rely on anecdotal evidence of incipient changes.

First, experience with a community dialogue appears to have a lasting effect on the host organization. At the conclusion of each dialogue the city council or manager directed that the model become the continuing basis for how the local government "talks" with the public. The clearest example of this is the City of Eugene's return to a community dialogue (*Shaping Eugene's Future*) as the means to resolve the most contentious issue to arise in the community since resolving the city's budget problem using *Eugene Decisions*. The time and expense of a community dialogue limit its use for resolving less important issues or for problems requiring an urgent response. Yet, without exception, city leaders have sought to expand and deepen citizen participation beyond the conventional tools of public hearings, advisory committees, and opinion polls.

The community dialogue also appears to have a lasting effect on the news media. The news media is important for publicizing the dialogue, raising its visibility in the community, and encouraging participation. Surprisingly, the news media has sought a larger role. To support the *City Dialogue,* the Fort Collins *Coloradoan* researched and published a series of articles on each of the priority issues identified during the first round. A television station in Eugene produced and aired an eight-part series on the issues identified during the first round of *Shaping Eugene's Future*. Sacramento's daily newspaper offered to print and distribute the *Sacramento Decisions* tabloid while charging only their direct cost.

In Eugene, the news media's enthusiasm for raising the level of political discourse extended beyond their coverage of the community dialogues. Following *Eugene Decisions,* a consortium composed of the local daily newspaper, a television station, and the public radio station sponsored a large-scale public deliberative process called *Citizens' Agenda*. Each news organization committed itself to using the citizen-developed agenda to focus its coverage of the gubernatorial campaign. The *Citizens' Agenda* concluded with a televised debate in which the candidates were asked questions by members of a panel composed of citizens selected from among those attending the *Citizens' Agenda* workshops. Since then, the news organizations have sponsored a citizen-based deliberative process for each general election.

It is more difficult to document, even anecdotally, changes in public expectations about public involvement in community decision making, support for civic institutions, or style of political discourse. In Eugene and Fort Collins, the judgment of politicians and community activists is that the general public is suspicious of public processes that favor organized groups. Acting on this judgment, for example, the City of Eugene eliminated most standing citizen advisory boards in favor of ad hoc citizen committees with most of its membership randomly drawn from a list of registered voters.

CONCLUSION

Using off-the-shelf social research methods, it is possible to convene a large-scale public deliberative process that enables local governments to take effective action on pressing community problems. These processes serve the goals of tutelary democracy (Durant 1995) to demystify the language of policy debate, making possible substantive public discourse. However, a community dialogue of the sort described here is neither cheap, fast, nor easy. Its application is limited to instances where the issue is critical, the political process is deadlocked, and there remains sufficient time to complete a yearlong public process. Where these conditions prevail, a well-implemented community dialogue is a powerful instrument for creating a public will to act.

Work in developing practical tools for deliberative democracy is in its infancy. This model of a community dialogue joins Fishkin's (1991, 1995) deliberative polling, Crosby's (1986) citizen's jury, and Yankelovich's public agenda forums among the small set of tools available to local governments.[5] Further work will strengthen this model, including: (1) creating more effective strategies for recruiting citizen participation; (2) developing ways to represent policy problems to achieve greater realism and to allow citizens greater flexibility to invent and evaluate options; and (3) finding ways to shorten the interval between exchanges of the dialogue.

The corrosive acids of public cynicism eat away at the foundations of local government. Candidates for public office campaign against the institutions they seek to lead. News organizations reinforce a caricature of local government as inefficient or befuddled and elected officials as foolish or corrupt. In addition, public managers reward the strident expression of a few with a privileged voice in the policy process.

In our enthusiasm for reinventing government, perhaps we have become carried away with the notion of viewing the public as our "customers." The public are not customers and our governments are not markets. These views demean the nature of citizenship and the responsibilities of government. It is time, as George Frederickson (1982, 1991) has urged, to enlarge the sphere of public discourse and restore the voice of ordinary citizens.

NOTES

1. The nine functions of "democratic talk" suggested by Barber include: 1) the articulation of interests; 2) persuasion; 3) agenda-setting; 4) exploring mutuality; 5) affiliation and affection; 6) maintaining autonomy; 7) witness and self-expression; 8) reformulation and reconceptualization; 9) community building as the creation of public interests, common goods, and active citizens.

2. These three rounds are consistent with Yankelovich's (1991) three-stage model of the evolution of public judgment. The agenda-setting phase is comparable to his "consciousness raising" stage where citi-

zens become aware of the issue and of its import. The strategy-development phase shares the objectives of Yankelovich's "working through" stage during which citizens accept the need to act and become engaged in using information to invent and evaluate alternative courses of action. Finally, the decision-making phase is similar to Yankelovich's "resolution" stage during which citizens complete their deliberations and settle upon a particular policy course.

3. While the design and implementation of the community dialogues needed to accommodate the demands of the politically charged environment, local officials did subscribe to an operating agreement specifying roles and responsibilities and acknowledged the experimental nature of the project.

4. While a 30 percent response rate is disappointing and raises questions about systematic bias, it is consistent with the typical response rates obtained for municipal surveys. In a meta-analysis of 261 citizen surveys assessing citizen evaluations of municipal services, Miller and Miller (1992) found an average response rate of 35 percent for mailed surveys. The surveys included in the Miller and Miller analysis employed simple fixed-choice instruments. The challenging nature of the budget worksheet does not seem to have greatly depressed the response rate.

5. Other models based on the use of small-sized citizen panels include Kathlene and Martin's (1991) use of citizen panels for transportation planning in Boulder, Colorado and the multi-phase model developed by Peter Dienel and Ortwin Renn and applied in the United States (Renn et al. 1993)

REFERENCES

Barber, Benjamin. 1984. *Strong Democracy: Participatory Politics for a New Age.* Berkeley, CA: University of California Press.
Benhabib, Seyla. 1996. Toward a Deliberative Model of Democratic Legitimacy. In *Democracy and Difference: Contesting the Boundaries of the Political,* edited by Seyla Benhabib. Princeton, NJ: Princeton University Press.
Crosby, Ned., Janet M. Kelly, and Paul Schaefer. 1986. Citizens Panels: A New Approach to Citizen Participation. *Public Administration Review* 46(2): 170–8.
Dahl, Robert A. 1989. *Democracy and Its Critics.* New Haven, CT: Yale University Press.
———. 1992. The Problem of Civic Competence. *Journal of Democracy* 3(4): 45–59.
Dionne, E.J., Jr. 1991. *Why Americans Hate Politics.* New York: Simon and Schuster.
Durant, Robert F. 1995. The Democratic Deficit in America. *Political Science Quarterly* 110(1): 25–47.
Dryzek, John S. 1990. *Discursive Democracy: Politics, Policy, and Political Science.* New York: Cambridge University Press.
Fishkin, James S. 1991. *Democracy and Deliberation: New Directions for Democratic Reform.* New Haven, CT: Yale University Press.
———. 1995. *The Voice of the People: Public Opinion and Democracy.* New Haven, CT: Yale University Press.
Frederickson, H. George. 1982. The Recovery of Civism in Public Administration. *Public Administration Review* 42(5): 501–8.
———. 1991. Toward a Theory of the Public for Public Administration. *Administration and Society* 22(4): 395–417.
Gore, Al. 1994. Cynicism or Faith. *Vital Speeches of the Day* 60(21): 645–50.
Grieder, William. 1992. *Who Will Tell the People: The Betrayal of American Democracy.* New York: Simon and Schuster.
Gutmann, Amy, and Dennis Thompson. 1996. *Democracy and Disagreement.* Cambridge, MA: Harvard University Press.
Habermas, Jurgen. 1996. *Between Facts and Norms: Contributions to a Discourse Theory of Law and Democracy.* Cambridge, MA: MIT Press.
Harris, Louis. 1994. Changing Trends in American Politics. Paper presented at the Congressional Institute for the Future. Washington, DC.
Harwood Group. 1991. *Citizens and Politics: A View from Main Street America.* Dayton, OH: Kettering Foundation.
Kathlene, Lyn, and John A. Martin. 1991. Citizen Participation: Enhancing Citizen Participation: Panel Designs, Perspectives, and Policy Formation. *Journal of Policy Analysis* 10(1): 46–55.
Kirlin, John J. 1996. The Big Questions of Public Administration in a Democracy. *Public Administration Review* 56(5): 416–23.

Lipset, Seymour Martin, and William Schneider. 1987. *The Confidence Gap.* Baltimore, MD: Johns Hopkins Press.

Mansbridge, Jane J. 1980. *Beyond Adversary Democracy.* New York: Basic Books.

Miller, Thomas I., and Michelle A. Miller. 1992. Assessing Excellence Poorly: The Bottom Line in Local Government. *Journal of Policy Analysis and Management* 11(4): 612–23.

Nagel, Jack H. 1992. Combining Deliberation and Fair Representation in Community Health Decisions. *University of Pennsylvania Law Review* 140(5): 1965–85.

Reich, Robert B. 1988. *The Power of Public Ideas.* Cambridge, MA: Harvard University Press.

Renn, Ortwin, Thomas Webler, Horst Rakel, Peter Dienel, and Branden Johnson. 1993. Public Participation in Decision Making: A Three-Step Procedure. *Policy Sciences* 26(3): 189–214.

Weeks, Edward C., Margaret Hallock, James B. Lemert, and Bruce McKinlay. 1992. *Citizen Participation in Policy Formation: A Review of Governor Roberts' Conversation with Oregon.* Eugene, OR: University of Oregon.

Yankelovich, Daniel. 1991. *Coming to Judgment: Making Democracy Work in a Complex World.* Syracuse, NY: Syracuse University Press.

CHAPTER 21

REINVENTING THE DEMOCRATIC GOVERNANCE PROJECT THROUGH INFORMATION TECHNOLOGY?
A Growing Agenda for Debate

ANDREW KAKABADSE, NADA K. KAKABADSE,
AND ALEXANDER KOUZMIN

INTRODUCTION

In *The Republic,* Plato (1987, 83) characterizes democracy as a "charming form of government, full of variety and disorder" which, ultimately, leads to tyranny. Plato feared that if people were allowed to make decisions collectively, they would simply endorse their own self-interest, resulting in policies that were nothing more than the lowest common denominator of individual greed and desire for personal security (Macpherson 1966, 5). In its Athenian construction, democracy symbolizes rule by and of the people (Dahl 1956; Mayo 1960; Benn 1967, 338).

While Plato (1987) opts for the rule of the "philosopher king," Aristotle (1987) deliberately describes democracy as the rule of the poor in their own interests. Mill (1991, 45) advocates a regulated "rational democracy," one ruled by "an enlightened minority accountable to the majority in the last resort." In contrast, in the American context, de Tocqueville (1994) sees a predicament in integrating democratic political culture with a socially democratic society. He perceives that social democracy does not necessarily lead to political democracy in the sense of self-government. Thus, he opts for the "middle" path and argues that democratic culture should be institutionalized to prevent governance by faceless bureaucracies. Marx (1964), on the other hand, thinks of democracy as the rule of the proletariat (Macpherson 1966; Pateman 1970; Tucker 1970).

The major contemporary justification for participatory democracy is that it serves interests by bringing them into debate and decision procedures: that democratic participation enhances autonomy and, in so doing, democracy is the most efficacious form of government for political equity—it is the natural form for consent through deliberation. Democracy serves welfare, autonomy, equity, access, and agreement, and it tends to diffuse power, which, as a consequence, inhibits the corruption of a highly concentrated power-elite (Mills 1959; Galbraith 1967). Therefore, it is usually less oligarchic and tyrannical than other systems of government. The negative claim for representative democracy is a variant of Winston Churchill's quip: that democracy is the "worst" form of government, compared with all the other known forms, because it always leads to the imposition of the will of the majority on minorities (Spinoza 1951). Hence, democracy is more valuable for what it prevents than it is for what it creates. Democracy is not, in itself, a political paradigm; rather, it is a vehicle for implementing a political paradigm.

This article examines the contemporary conditions of representative democracy, which can be largely attributed to structures of governance and the proposed direct liberal democracy made possible by the development of information technology (IT). The impact of IT on the quality of democratic governance and democratic forms is then discussed. It is concluded that, whichever democratic form is adopted, it is crucial to consider that the role of the elected representative not be undermined by splitting responsibilities from accountabilities and thoroughly utilizing means that give society greater access to the implementation of policy while maintaining elected representatives who are accountable for outcomes.

DEMOCRACY AND INDIVIDUAL RIGHTS

Representative democracy practiced in the last century emerged out of the political philosophy of liberalism (Jones 1991). The concept presupposes a social order based on liberal democracy, where society is simply a collection of "free" and "competing" individuals. The individual is seen as *absolute,* irreducible, separate, and *ontologically prior* to society. Thus, the link between the person and his or her parents, children, extended family, ancestors, community, environment, and nature is not made (Sardar 1996).

The notion of the community and social duties, which was so central to past forms of participatory governance, was abandoned in favor of independence. In this liberal framework, the individual is constantly faced with the paradox of "community" and feeling perpetually and ontologically threatened by the putative drive for independence. The individual's main concern is to keep his or her identity intact, separate from all others, and to preserve boundaries at all costs. Thus, the individual has to make a moral choice between self and society, between the comfort of belonging and the freedom to choose and re-choose different pathways. Therefore, there can never be substantive agreement between the individual and the community as a whole.

The goals of liberal democracy, therefore, focus on providing individuals with all possible avenues to persuade others of what they desire, even at the expense of the community. Therefore, the practice of liberal democracy creates a paradox for government. In pursuing pathways toward communal, social, cultural, economic, or political goals—which would ensure an equal distribution of wealth or provide certain basics such as equal education and health care opportunities for all—government still needs to leave individuals to fend for themselves (Parekh 1993).

This paradox is even more explicit in constitutional democracy, which entails, definitionally, a simultaneous commitment to the principles of democracy and constitutionalism, which are incompatible at the extreme and constitute a presiding tension at best (Holmes 1988). According to the democratic principle, the will of the majority should govern. Thus, to the democrat, limits on majoritarian power are unjustifiable. Unlike that democrat, the constitutionalist is somewhat wary of majorities, particularly the majority's willingness and ability to protect individual autonomy (Croley 1995, 702)—to the point where certain rights possessed by individuals and minorities can override majoritarian will. Thus, democracy affords all qualified members of the political community a voice in political decision making. In practice, however, societies commonly called democracies fall far short of this ideal because of inequalities in wealth, voice, knowledge, and, contemporarily, *access* to communication technology and information, which translate directly into inequality of political power (Dahl 1989). Democracies live by the idea, which is central to the process of gaining the consent of the governed, that the majority has the ultimate power to displace decision makers and to reject any part of their policies (Rosen 1983; Bickel 1986, 27). The identification of democracy with political equality, popular sovereignty, and rule by the majority is promulgated through the history of democratic theory (Dahl 1989, 34; Held 1989).

Constitutional theory, on the other hand, on which many putative democracies rest today, is not simply majority based. The constitution is designed to protect individual citizens and groups against certain decisions that the majority may make, even when that majority acts in what it takes to be the general or common interest (Dworkin 1977, 132). The central purpose of a constitution is to delineate the border between majoritarian power and individual autonomy or between legitimate and illegitimate exercise of majoritarian power (Croley 1995). Among other things, the application of universal rights supports individual autonomy by restricting the powers the majority may exercise—"substantive rights"—or the manner in which the majority may exercise its power—"procedural rights." Thus, majoritarian power loses legitimacy whenever it invades the protected spheres of individual autonomy or otherwise interferes with individual autonomy (Croley 1995, 705). Therefore, "constitutionalism, from a certain perspective, is essentially anti-democratic. The basic function of the constitution is to remove certain decisions from the democratic process; that is, to tie the community's hands" (Holmes 1988). The freedom of "the majority to govern and the freedom of the individual not to be governed, remain forever in *tension*" (Bork 1990, 139, emphasis added). For example, in the information age, the majority's demand for government agencies to make certain information readily available may impinge on the privacy of the individual or minority groups (Balagopal 1989).

ALTERNATIVE MODELS OF DEMOCRACY

Democratic potential is the capacity of citizens to participate effectively and knowledgeably in socially constitutive processes—to exercise power. One can distinguish democratic potential by focusing on the state as the systemic level of interest. It is, however, an identifying feature of contemporary, politically disassociated environments that state affairs are increasingly influenced by processes at the intersystem and individual levels. Part of the task of understanding democratic practice and citizenship is to unravel what these processes mean within the social milieu (Mouffe 1992).

Some theorists link specific information technologies with particular political forms and processes: "voice" to democracy and the city-state; "print" to bureaucracy and the nation-state; and the emergence of the "net," or global information infrastructure, with models of electronic democracy. A variety of democratic modes of governance exist, and each society has its own unique model that reflects its "formative context"—institutional arrangements, cultural values, ethnic tastes, training, historical background, and cognitive frames that shape the daily routines of citizens, express ideology, and formulate objectives (Unger 1987; Korac-Kakabadse, Kouzmin, and Korac-Kakabadse 2000b). However, from the myriad of practices, three models of democracy are identified: Aristotelian-style direct democracy, representative democracy, and electronically facilitated and mediated "direct democracy."

Direct Democracy (Aristotelian)

Aristotle (1987) argued, in the fourth century BC, that democracy could not work in a country larger than a small city-state, such as Athens. One reason is that in a democracy, all citizens should be able to assemble at one place to hear a speaker. Thus, the range of the human voice limited the democracy's size. As late as the mid-eighteenth century, political thinkers argued against the possibility of large-scale democracy, partly because of *communication* limitations. After the United States emerged, a huge democracy by historical standards, such arguments were discarded. The early-nineteenth-century invention of the penny press for printing newspapers made the acquisition of political information by the masses both convenient and affordable. This, in turn, greatly facilitated the extension of political suffrage during that period.

The advent of radio and television increased the media's influence in political elections. The development of mass media, such as newspapers and television, extended the political message not to hundreds or thousands of people within the physical range of voice, but to the tens of millions watching and reading. With the advent of computerized IT, the possibility of *direct* democracy, among other things, emerged. Today, emergent, interactive, direct, and unmediated communication holds the possibility of revolutionizing not only the entertainment industry, but also the nature of public and political discourse. Furthermore, the news media allows vast amounts of information to be processed almost instantaneously while accommodating a broader base of civic access and participation.

Mediated or Representative Democracy

In its simplest form, democracy entails having citizens participate in voting on policy. However, in large states, this is not sensible or even possible, and participation takes place in sequential forms. First, citizens choose representatives, who, in turn, decide on policy. Many critics of direct democracy have argued that the average person does not have the resources, time, ability, or inclination to become an expert on political issues and political candidates. Individual motivation for action is incompatible with collective preferences, even when the latter are well-defined (Downs 1967; Olson 1996). Direct democracy, which inevitably leads to information overload, can, at best, only palliate the political-information problem (Downs 1967).

It is widely believed that different structures for representation produce substantially different outcomes. Hence, there is no simple formula for representative democracy that relates popular preferences to political outcomes in larger political forums. Unfortunately, the technology and institutions of democracy are no longer keeping up with its growth. Many societies continue to have democratic ideals but lack an informed, engaged electorate that can act on those ideals. The result is often a government that neither knows nor implements the public will. Complete failure by certain corporations and public agencies to enforce legal, moral, or safety constraints raises obvious moral problems (Bishop 1991; Korac-Boisvert and Kouzmin 1994). For many individuals who have lost confidence in the ability of both elected representatives and the media to act in their interest, direct democracy, such as the ballot referendum or the town meeting, offers an appealing alternative.

Electronic Democracy

Electronic democracy can be understood as the capacity of the new communications environment to enhance the degree and quality of public participation in government. For example, the Internet can enable certain citizens (namely, those with access to IT) to vote electronically in elections, referendums, and plebiscites. The Internet also can facilitate opinion polling. Therefore, it has the potential to strengthen interaction between government and citizens and between political candidates and voters and affect the changing nature of democratic governance (Edwards 1995, 39–40). The technological innovations that make these activities possible include increasingly sophisticated computer chips, lasers, fiber-optics, low-power television, digital recording, fax, and public and commercial satellite access.

Scholars and researchers began to explore the civic potential of new electronic technology in the 1960s, and phrases such as *teledemocracy, technopolitics, new media, instant polling, satellite politics, video democracy, electronic democracy, cyberdemocracy, virtual polis,* and *couch-potato democracy* have been in common usage for some time (Milward and Snyder 1996). A variety of proposed electronic democracy models exist, but four emerge in the literature: electronic bureaucracy, information management, populist, and civil society.

The *electronic bureaucracy model* refers to the electronic delivery of government services. This model already enjoys increasing success at the federal and state levels in the United States and Australia, where "government online" (electronic information available through the Internet) and "one-stop shops" (the office that handles business of multiple government agencies) are operational. The one-stop-shop concept, as stated in the Green Paper "Government Direct," is receiving consideration in the United Kingdom and in other countries participating in the Organisation for Economic Co-operation and Development (OECD 1996). The goal of this model is to allow for easier, quicker, and cheaper transactions with government on behalf of businesses and citizens and to *reduce,* over time, the size of the public sector. There is sufficient experience with IT-driven restructuring within public-sector agencies and corporations for less sanguine audits of the impact of IT on organizational communicative capabilities and on organizational effectiveness (Korac-Kakabadse, Kouzmin, and Korac-Kakabadse 2000a, 2000c). Mapping the institutional effects of IT communications within "lean" public agencies reveals critical leadership issues for public organizations that are driven by IT and restructuring (Kouzmin and Korac-Kakabadse 2000). Some have argued that the enhancement of service creates inequality between "information-rich" individuals and businesses that can gain access to the technology necessary to use the electronic service, and the "information poor," who cannot (Korac-Kakabadse, Kouzmin, and Korac-Kakabadse 2000b). Many equate service enhancement with differential pricing and regard both as unacceptable. Changing people's attitude toward technology may be a worthy aim, but some consider it more appropriate as an intervention to enhance education and training rather than to use such facilities as a cut-back pricing mechanism.

The *information management model* has more effective communication, bridging individual citizens and decision makers. This model is also receiving some acclaim, with a number of state and federal governments (United States, Australia) providing electronic public services and information at the point of use (Burns 1995; Korac-Kakabadse, Kouzmin, and Korac-Kakabadse 2000a, 2000c). Using multimedia such as touch-screen kiosks in public places (libraries, shopping malls) or personal computers from home, citizens can obtain government information or send messages to their representatives or government agencies. In the United States, the Clinton administration explored this model. Presidential orders, speeches, and other communications were transmitted online, directly to the people, bypassing the news media. The easy access to bills introduced to Congress, as well as to government publications, may result in a more informed citizenry. For example, the ability to circulate government white papers designed to generate political action quickly is a unique phenomenon of IT.

The *populist model* enables citizens to register their views on current issues. It is most often equated with direct democracy. The model received visibility when Ross Perot popularized the term "electronic town hall" in his 1992 presidential campaign, attempting to recreate the spirited gatherings of New England townspeople on a national scale through the medium of interactive technology (London 1994). With the first electronic "town meeting" having taken place in New York State on October 5, 1992, and Santa Monica's interactive computer network PEN (Public Electronic Network) facilitating 24-hour electronic town meetings (London 1994), the age of unmediated communication had emerged, where newspaper editors, the mail carrier, and television journalists are no longer essential intermediaries between citizens and officials. In this manner, the electronic town meeting refers to civic discourse that is quick, direct, interactive, and inclusive (London 1994). Some suggest that such town meetings may be used to educate people about issues or to decide on policies. Considering that politics involves dialogue, not only the dissemination of facts and information, electronic forums can be used to serve both purposes. Electronic referendum fosters the notion that an electronic transaction is an authentic democratic choice. In the United States, numerous projects are under way that suggest electronic town meetings will soon be a regular part of political life. On January 15, 1993, for example, an electronic town hall in Dallas (through the news service CNN) put issues of deficit reduction, campaign financing, and lobbying regulations to the citizens for instant telefeedback.

The *civil society model* refers to the transformation of political culture, and it can be appreciated only within the context of the broader transformations brought about by communication technology. Its goal is to strengthen connections between citizens and promote a robust and autonomous site for public debate. While in the United States, debate has focused on whether an "Electronic Bill of Rights" is needed, citizens in Sweden and Germany are increasingly concerned about the impending age of little or no privacy—in a democracy that is perceived as becoming more of an "electronic tyranny." In addition to the United States, interactive, online systems for everyday use are already available in other polities—such as Canada's Teledon, France's Intelmatique and Minitel, and Japan's Hi-Ovis. Their utilization is limited though, as no one nation is wholly wired with enough fiber-optic cable to accommodate equitable access.

Although all four models have their usefulness and application, the civil society model requires intensive debate. The quality of public dialogue in the future will be influenced by changes in interpersonal relations, employment patterns, and organizational structure, especially in public-sector agencies. The growing cultural and commercial value of information also will be relevant, as will government response to policy issues such as technology, privacy, and regulation. The effects of new technology on policy making hold significant ramifications for participatory democracy. Analysis of such issues will reveal more about the future of democracy than an examination of the technicalities of electronic voting or managing the email deluge. This position is premised on a view of democracy that implies it is more than a mechanism for determining government—rather, it is a genuine opportunity for popular participation, open and accountable government, broad input into the policy debate, and the promotion of informed and critical citizens.

CRITIQUES OF CURRENT MODELS OF REPRESENTATIVE DEMOCRACY

Democratic societies have shown that it is possible to protect human rights, foster citizen participation in the political process, provide economic freedom, protect free speech, and tolerate freedom of the press. However, with the beginning of the third millennium and democracy's global spread, the growing disillusionment with representative democracy has begun to be openly expressed (Gillwald, Sandi, and van Steenbergen 1992). A deep cynicism toward the representative-democracy model is emerging in many democratic societies (Gore 1994). Many disenchanted voters are demanding a shift from "representative democracy" to "direct democracy" (Sardar 1996). The cynicism is created, in part, by democratic processes that foster self-interested groups over wisdom, deviation over tolerance, short-term gain over spirituality, fierce economic competition over collaboration, and community change over stability (Gore 1994). The cynicism is not directed toward democratic principles, but toward the *governance* of democratic processes in a variety of contexts.

Today's liberally-constituted representative democracy, which is defined and structured within the limits set by liberalism, appears to promote rampant individualism (personal and corporate), the breaking of moral taboos, frenzied consumerism, and other absolutes of liberalism that provide fertile ground for the ad hoc morality of liberalism (Carnoy 1984; Sardar 1996). Indeed, liberal secularism in its present form, and as practiced in the West, appears to be unable to deal with any kind of collective identity except that defined by geography (Sardar 1996). With the globalization of markets and capital and the inability of liberal democracies to provide means for enhancing community values, ethical values are coming to the fore.

Liberal representative democracy models appear to have a built-in bias against citizens in disorganized or informal sectors that are not highly focused, in contrast to those driven by single issues. Powerful lobby groups are able to mobilize resources and influence government agendas for their own causes, while groups without resources or a single focus have no mechanism for influencing government policies and process. The imbalance created by lobbying is probably one of the most serious issues confronting current liberal representative democracy models. Political interest lobbying and concern for long-term public policy are often incongruent with each other. Lobbying by corporations, which need access to global markets, plays a key role in U.S. foreign policy and policy in particular directions (Hosenball and Thomas 1997). Lobbying is a controversial, but seemingly accepted, form of competitive political interaction because of its purity of power and winner-takes-all outcome (Sternberg 1990; Tonn 1996).

Some have argued that current democratic processes disable people of wisdom from meaningful involvement in political processes (Tonn 1996). The political process, especially at the national level, values people who have stamina, determination, self-centeredness, the capability to withstand abusive criticism, and the ability to manipulate the media (Tonn 1996, 415). There are no other job requirements beyond getting one more vote than one's opponent, being below or past a certain age, and not being convicted of a felony (Tonn 1996, 415). People of wisdom, on the other hand, are creative, intelligent, insightful, knowledgeable about life, sagacious, open to change, able to deal with uncertainty and conflict, compassionate, mentally flexible, and visionary (Sternberg 1990), holding a strong sense of value (Tonn 1996, 415)—but ill-equipped to cope with current democratic processes.

Others argue that, now more than ever, there is a need for moral leadership in liberal representative democracy (Jearnott 1989, 14), presupposing traits of character and qualities of mind—"self-possessed individuals, possessed of humanity, principles, vision and the craft to make them real" (Jearnott 1989, 35). People of wisdom are not self-selected or self-centered (Sternberg 1990)—they do not normally declare to the world they are the wisest, because that would violate their values (Tonn 1996). Like Socrates, they do not proclaim their wisdom. Furthermore, wisdom is not easily conveyed through 20-second television commercials and bumper stickers (Sternberg 1990). Current political processes tend to drive people of wisdom away from the fore, as many political parties do not hold wisdom as a central characteristic necessary for political office and often are incapable of identifying people of wisdom or nurturing their growth over the years (Tonn 1996, 415). Civic frustrations, political abuse, the ubiquitous Gallop polls, and media saturation require critical attention. This may occur with the onset and excitement of high-tech politics, which hold the potential for vastly increasing direct citizen participation and even the possibility of *enhancing* many processes of government (London 1994).

Many have equated democracy with economic prosperity—economic growth starts to decline and disillusionment with representative democracy shows equally (Sardar 1996). For some, growing disenchantment is partly rooted in the failure of representative democracy to meet economic expectations (Sardar 1996). Others, such as Fukuyama (1992), equate the triumph of the free-market economy with that of representative democracy. However, these views have raised even more questions about the nature and capability of representative democracy. Some question why democratic Russia is facing economic ruin, whereas communist China has a flourishing economy (Sardar 1996).

Others, such as Adonis and Mulgan (1994), suggest that a fundamental weakness of the modern liberal state is the divorce of politics from society, of political responsibility from citizenship, producing low citizen involvement, limited choices, and poor delivery. The governing mechanisms for designing and delivering social policies are not aligned with community needs. Governments often are dominated by elites who offer simplistic and one-dimensional solutions to problems that concern voters (Adonis and Mulgan 1994). Citizen choices are based on the choices of catchall policy programs, which are frequently vague and are often abandoned once political groups achieve power (Depla and Tops 1995). Even in cases where policies are carried out, they are, all too often, seen as ineffective (Adonis and Mulgan 1994). The political system in many democratic states has shown little capability for making difficult decisions under uncertainty (Dror 1987) and even less capability for learning over time (Cutting and Kouzmin 1999, 2000). Weiss (1989) has argued that today's representative-democratic processes (not principles) are not sound enough to sustain societies over the long term, and they are certainly not in a position to meet the challenges of even the most basic obligations to future generations.

DEMOCRATIC GOVERNANCE POTENTIAL THROUGH NEW TECHNOLOGY

The growing literature on the democratic significance of new information technology has focused on its ability to enhance direct citizen participation in the political process. Modern technology is commonly perceived as being of great value in registering the political attitudes and inclinations of the public. New interactive media can accommodate dialogue that flows, in a circular fashion, among interested stakeholders and groupings. This kind of exchange has the potential to return the meaning of "dialogue" to its Socratic usage. In this way, IT promises new ways to build consensus and common ground and to energize the citizenry. Regular dialogue and feedback keep citizens and officials in touch with the ebb and flow of public values and judgments. The value of citizen feedback, combined with new media technologies, has several distinct advantages: It has the capacity to enlarge the scope of political dialogue, and it serves as an educational process that brings issues into public focus and allows them to be defined (London 1994). Besides engaging citizens, feedback also promotes a deeper commitment to and understanding of public policy—and it allows public officials to consider a broader range of policy options on any given issue, based on the real-life concerns and testimonies of everyday citizens (London 1994; Van de Donk and Meyer 1995).

For an example, the Citycard project shows the eventual prospect of the transformation of relations between citizens and local authorities. The main goal is to involve citizens much more in the activities of the local authority, and not just through better dissemination of information. If residents, for example, believe a road-traffic system is not working, Citycard will enable them to communicate views and advice directly to the local authority officers concerned. Still in its pilot phase, the Citycard project is led by two software companies (MARI from the United Kingdom and OMEGA from Italy) in cooperation with Lagotex (Portugal) and the cities of Wansbeck, United Kingdom, and Bologna, Italy. While not exactly the democracy of the Athenian public meeting, this application of IT promises to close the gap between governors and the governed and, in the process, make public officials more accountable to the people they serve (OECD 1987, 1997). There is still more democratic promise to Citycard, because communication will be designed to enable citizens to discuss issues among themselves and then to pass on proposed solutions to local problems. Discussion groups will even have the facility to produce edited documents for passing on to authorities. However, herein also lies the danger and a paradox, as those discussion groups could become new and dysfunctional lobby groups with new and more powerful informational tools.

Technology facilitates new forms of voting and direct participation that are based on theoretically elegant but impractical voting systems (Snider 1994). For example, instead of physically going to the polls, individuals could vote from home. With more convenient and less expensive voting systems in place, individuals could be expected to vote more frequently and on more issues. Ballot referendums and polls could proliferate. Institutional willingness for ballot referendums, a sensitive issue in the United Kingdom, has not shown itself to be so in either California or Switzerland, suggesting that for certain countries, technology may be less important than political and institutional will (Perri, 6 1997).

While instant polling and referendums can render the public as unreflective as legislatures, the potential exists for far more reflective democratic processes. Experiments over the last two decades with televoters have highlighted the potential in this area. A recent senatorial selection in Oregon allowed voting by mail. The voter turnout was 67 percent, almost doubling the national average voter turnout over the last 20 years for senatorial elections in nonpresidential elections (*Washington Post* 1996). Combined with citizen movements toward growing "healthy communities," sustainable development, and enhanced community dialogue, electronic messaging in this arena could be transformative (*The Economist* 1995).

Other benefits of new information technology include improved access to the deliberation of public bodies. In the United States, cable channels already cover House and Senate chambers and congressional hearings, as well as state-level (California House and Senate chambers and legislative hearings) and local-level (city councils, school boards) meetings. In the future, coverage of such meetings at the local, state, and national level is likely to expand dramatically, making government deliberations more accessible to the average person (Snider 1994). Through television, computer, or some synthesis of both, new technology also facilitates electronic town meetings, where citizens are offered direct contact with public officials unmediated by journalists. The idea is to force politicians and the media to talk to the public about important issues that otherwise might escape the political agenda. Combined with televoting, electronic town meetings could significantly improve the ballot referendum—a poor option for fostering deliberation and leading to uninformed voting. Government records also could be made more accessible, an improvement on the cumbersome procedures necessary to gain access to information under the Freedom of Information Act adopted in many Western democracies (United States, Canada, Australia, New Zealand). However, information pertinent to individuals, groups, or security still needs to be protected. The role of electronic communication in political outcomes is growing—from instant opinion polls to chat lines. It is likely that some form of electronic democracy will, among other things, fuel efforts to make technology universally accessible (*The Economist* 1995).

The argument has been put forward that the perceived or assigned shortcomings of liberal representative democracy can be remedied with new information technologies that will simultaneously help to humanize liberal democracy (Sardar 1996). Some claim that technology will enable citizens to have direct access to their representatives, thus bypassing pressure groups, party politics, the media, special interest groups, and other undemocratic channels of opinion formation (Szilagyi 1994; Sardar 1996). Sardar (1996, 846) suggests that elected representatives will perform their function only on people's daily sufferance, which will lead to the loss of the grandeur of parliament and the arrogance of political parties. While Szilagyi (1994) argues that, although the information revolution will change the political system, it also will lead to the collapse of representative democracy as it is known today, replacing it with the "democracy of the information age"—a form of direct democracy. Politicians will be selected according to a free competition of ideas, with a power base that is decentralized, creating a culture where success and status will not depend on the exercise of political power. However, the impact of IT on societal and democratic potential depends on the ever-growing sophistication of information and communication technologies; rules restricting the use of information and communication technologies; and the nature of the entity that makes the rules about the use of information and communication technologies (Braman 1994). It is considered that societies will prosper or falter in the next century depending on their investment in building an information infrastructure (Davis and Davidson 1991).

THE DOWNSIDE OF ELECTRONIC DEMOCRACY

If human knowledge presupposes information, then the collective intellectual abilities of a nation—its human capital—will depend on access to information in electronic form (Crawford 1991). The advancement of IT, such as telecommunication networks, satellites, fiber-optics, and databases, to mention just a few systems, as well as the special nature of computer literacy and process knowledge related to the effective use of information, have promoted the vision of a technological future for many. At the same time, regulation is increasingly difficult to maintain as voices, images, data, and text coalesce into one massive "telematic" network, and as hybrid technologies, such as virtual reality, blur the line and divide speech from action (Fogelman 1994, 295).

Thus, as democracy is about the articulation of common interests and shared concerns between citizens, the broad means of conducting elections represents one downside to electronic democracy. However, digital democracy is mainly about the expression of the individual in front of his or her own computer keyboard. It will be more difficult to aggregate preferences in an acceptable way without institutionalized ways of persuading and ensuring collective action. Furthermore, excessive participation at the wrong time could lead to government paralysis.

Electronic democracy can dangerously overextend the sphere of democratic decision making into what should be the sphere of individual or corporate decision making because the institutional constraints that have been developed in "analogue democracy" do not exist in the digital setting.

For instance, a national electronic town meeting on environmental protection versus economic development could result in interminable debate, little consensus, and no decisions (deLeon 1994, 91). In times of political crisis, the inability to reach a decision could be dangerous. Under normal conditions, open citizen participation in decision making would almost surely present delays (deLeon 1994, 91). Some argue the availability of the instant response provided by interactive technology would discourage deliberation and the thoughtful exercise of democratic choice. Still others suggest that, although much of the technology needed for electronic democracy already exists in a number of societies, no one can really tell whether these technologies will acutely enhance participative democracy or lead to further fragmentation and individualization (Ogden 1994). IT, as it is currently implemented, does not equitably facilitate citizen access to direct democracy: it facilitates such opportunities only to a small, atypical minority group (young, affluent), as they are the only ones who are online.

The very idea of the citizen sitting in front of his or her computer interrogating political representatives takes individualism to a new dimension (Ogden 1994). Information-age direct democracy poses new social segregation challenges for those who are information rich and information poor on an individual and societal basis (Kapor 1992; Korac-Kakabadse, Kouzmin, and Korac-Kakabadse 2000b). Information-poor individuals will not be able to influence political agendas. For example, by 2002, it is estimated that nearly one-fourth of the U.S. workforce will be immigrants, many of whom have a relatively low level of formal schooling and limited English skills (SLCI/IPP 1995).

Furthermore, current IT problems—ranging from internet pornography to online forgery, credit card theft, identity theft, virus attacks, unauthorized access to systems to destroy data, hacking to read email and crack passwords, and taking over accounts—also may erode electronic democracy. Not all technology-related crimes fit the popular definition of "computer crime"—crimes committed using computers and/or telecommunications systems. Some, notably the get-rich-quick schemes, are traditional frauds given new impetus by technology—such as Web pages and email. Although the motivation for computer crime is commercial gain, it is not always the direct benefit. Often, the benefit is seeing the competition destroyed. The use of technology to modify voting patterns may be a new avenue of computer crime. In Australia, for example, the second-most informatized society in terms of computers per capita (the United States being first), computer-crime units are a relatively recent innovation in policing, emerging only since the 1990s (Korac-Boisvert and Kouzmin 1994; Creedy 1997). The number of complaints received for investigation by the crime units has tripled in the last three years. The Australian Institute of Criminology suggests that officially reported computer intrusions represent the tip of the iceberg (Creedy 1997). In increasingly interconnected economies—exemplified by stock exchanges and frontierless capital markets, globalized production and marketing—IT-crime combat and prevention require global policies and cooperation. Moreover, the emergence of regional trading blocs and economic dominance increases the potential for IT crime.

With a growing amount of commerce occurring over the Internet, electronic transactions are becoming the norm. Monitoring and tracking paper exchanges for tax and tariff purposes will become even more complicated as it becomes easier to move a virtual organization's headquarters offshore or to create and issue new electronic media of exchange (Merritt 1995; Korac-Kakabadse, Kouzmin, and Korac-Kakabadse 2000a). The lack of adequate monitoring policies for electronic commerce and electronic money (e-money) taxation may lead to greater difficulties for governments in their attempt to regulate and tax businesses and citizens. Fueled by the current pressure of a growing national debt and socially conservative policy making, leading to an overall shrinking of federal government expenditure on social policies, additional hardship for the underprivileged is almost destined to be a future reality.

Facing pressure to do more with less, government and public and private sectors have turned to IT as a tool for increasing both the efficiency and quality of services. These improvements have been wide ranging, including faster processing and less expensive information storage, quicker responses to information requests, and better integrated information to serve customers (Osborne and Gaebler 1991). However, IT can be a double-edged sword. While IT has enormous potential to increase the efficiency of government operations and the effectiveness of communication, it also may have negative effects if it is not well managed. A poor choice of what to purchase, a badly conceived contract, or inadequately trained staff, for example, can lead to problems such as a restricted ability to communicate, degraded performance, or to the requirement of excessive costs in order to adjust to continuing technological change (Kouzmin and Korac-Kakabadse 2000).

IT advances also raise broader issues about how governments communicate with citizens. Potentially, IT can enhance government accountability and citizen participation in democratic decision making through clearer and more accessible communication and by fostering direct communication between citizens (for example, Internet) in an effort to build public debate dominated neither by political parties nor the news media. However, IT has also a potential downside, as it can isolate individuals, providing better access to information only to the well educated, technologically well equipped, well organized, and those with resources (Perri, 6 1997). Therefore, IT has the potential not only to professionalize lobbying, but also to facilitate lobbying on a large scale.

Electronic democracy and e-governance are emerging global trends and are a part of "operational democracy" (Rosell 1992, 1995). Building an online infrastructure that is accessible to all citizens requires local and regional cooperation, visionary policies, and long-term individual and organizational commitment. There is something in the air or, as Pascal called it, a *je ne sais quoi,* that technology can facilitate improvement of democratic governance processes.

IT IMPACT ON CITIZEN AND REPRESENTATIVE ROLES

Perhaps the most serious problem of electronic democracy arises from its ability to divorce responsibility from accountability, a problem that is twofold. First, although individuals (at least those who can afford technology) will be responsible for influencing the political agenda, they will not be held accountable for their impact on policy implementation (Kapor 1992). The very problem that Plato (1987) feared and wanted to guard against was that of people simply endorsing their self-interest, resulting in policies that were nothing more than the lowest common denominator of individual greed and desire for personal gain or security. Second, elected representatives, driven by an aggregation of electronically derived democratic demands, would be held accountable for policies for which they are not responsible and over which they have little influence. The bargaining power of elected representatives would be undermined and, as such, they would not be able to see through agreements. Furthermore fragmentation and a lack of coherent policy would lead to social vulnerability.

Under current representative liberal democracy, the elected representative is implicitly operating under a social contract obligation, supporting particular principles and being accountable for his or her actions (Shocker and Sethi 1974). In electing representatives, citizens place the onus on the representative to provide an account of his or her actions (Gray, Owen, and Maunders 1987, 2). Representatives' failure to deliver the electorate's expected outcomes leads to dissatisfaction and a change of representation. By defining the relationship between citizens and representatives in contractual or principal—agent terms (Laughlin 1996)—where the agent acts on behalf of the principal under a contract existing between them, which has neither been written nor made explicit (Gray 1983; Tricker 1983; Stewart 1984)—we assume the principal, "society," can be identified along with its concomitant aims, aspirations, and interests (Power 1991, 34). In the implicit contract, the principal—the citizen—typically gives instructions to the agent—the political representative—on what actions are expected from him or her, given certain powers of remuneration from citizens' taxes, power over resources, policy design, and implementation. In so doing, the principal—the citizen—holds the agent responsible and accountable for his or her actions (Gray, Owen, and Maunders 1988).

Using IT to influence the representative's agenda on a daily basis leaves representatives accountable for decisions for which they are not responsible in terms of generating, may not be in agreement with, and for which they may not have had the opportunity to present an alternative case. Such circumstances within an organizational setting are akin to holding a manager accountable for the actions of his or her subordinates while having no control over what they do (Kakabadse 1991). This divorcing of accountability from responsibility leads to the ultimate demise of the implicit contract between the representative and the citizen. The social technology of representative democracy binds agent and principal together, thereby generating a relationship of accountability that is fundamental to the "social contract" of political theory. Being a theoretical construct, social contract theory assumes that "individuals 'choose' to enter and subject themselves to social and political arrangements involving the delegation of authority" (Power 1991, 34). The social nature of the relationship suggests the superiority of an accountability framework over the decision usefulness of operational frameworks such as information technologies (Ijiri 1983; Roberts and Scapens 1985; Williams 1987).

Thus, instead of creating a community based on consensus, unthinking IT applications could easily create states of alienated and atomized individuals who communicate with each other through computer terminals, terrorizing and being terrorized by all those who value conflict or are determined to pursue their own agenda (Ogden 1994; Sardar 1994). For example, in the past two decades, violent crime has increased 200 percent in the United States, and the situation is expected to get worse (Stone 1995). Scientists and leading-edge entrepreneurs are developing interactive technologies to immerse users in a totally convincing illusion. They seek to assemble a "real" and sharable environment within a cybernetic "teleplace"—the synthetic equivalent of a fully "inhabitable" alternate world—in which increasingly alienated individuals will have difficulty distinguishing real affection from "techno-affection." The long-term results of such developments could be socially dangerous. Some research laboratories and arcade virtual reality implementations already enable the user/participant, masked or wrapped in sensory effectors, to walk through unconstructed buildings, feel the pull of molecular gravity, or engage in a high-tech "shoot-out" with a computer or a human operator. Virtual reality peripherals are limited at this time to primitive step-platforms, though data-gloves and bulk head-mounted audiovisual displays, and tactile effectors are already being tested. Systems with tactile effectors, which transcend current definitions of simulation, may for some become a convenient substitute for reality.

For example, tactile effectors such as "remote-intimacy" dimensions have the potential to forever alter the legal and social landscape (Fogelman 1994, 299). Furthermore, the truly persuasive, fully sensory depictions could give rise to a new epoch of high-technology crime and alienation. While with current technology criminals are now able to violate system security by trashing files or spreading obscure viruses, network pirates could someday employ recorded or counterfeit "bit streams" to commit heinous acts of breaking and entering: virtual sexual harassment, information kidnapping, or even remote statutory rape and remote murder (Fogelman 1994, 299; Stephenson 1995). As information becomes increasingly critical to success in both our business and personal lives, the threat of being cut off from information by cyberspace criminals, like being held hostage or being kidnapped, is a very real possibility. Terrorists could cut off communication to an individual, group, community, or entire government and create information agents designed to "mug" consumer information agents as they make electronic transactions (Cetron 1994). If we consider that "telemedicine" will include the automatic transfer of data from consumers to their medical records and that home care will increase (Olson 1996), sending counterfeit bit streams to patients could induce murder. Anarchy, violence, drugs, and other deadly agencies often thwart the good intentions of IT policy. Too often, institutional culture is simply dislocated from the citizen's world (Comer 1988).

The criticism focused on representative democracy and the desire to change it to direct democracy needs to be reevaluated and refocused on examining adopted mechanisms of government and the structure of political parties and adopted philosophies. By 2003, it is projected that industrial workers will make up no more than 13 percent of the workforce in every developed society. Considering that, in the United States alone, knowledge workers will constitute up to 30 percent of the workforce, there is a need for economic policies that are appropriate to a world economy in which knowledge is the key resource. A political philosophy and institutional design for effective democratic governance in a knowledge-based society are long over-due (Drucker 1994; Latham 1998).

Given the centrality of computers to information flow, computer literacy may become the de facto prerequisite for citizenship in the next century if the direct democracy model is adopted. Traditional literacy can be defined not just as the ability to read, but the possession of certain background knowledge, without which the act of reading becomes meaningless (Bransford and Johnson 1972; Hirsch 1987). Computer literacy is as profound as the ability to read, as it requires a range of abstract understandings about how information is accessed, managed, and manipulated—an understanding transcending particular makes and models of computers and software. Computer literacy will provide extraordinary access to information, but only for those who understand the process of information seeking (Paisley 1987, 5). Thus, the distinction between those who have the facility and access to IT and those who do not will become as distinct functionally as the difference between those who can read and those who cannot (Schalken and Tops 1995). The need to redesign the democratic governance project is real. The emerging ethical, legal, and policy ramifications of IT should be politically modeled and critically investigated before they are permitted to personally or physically touch sociopolitical lives (Kagan 1989).

IT IMPACT ON MEDIA, CORPORATE, AND AGENCY ROLES

While the role of government and public-sector agencies is and remains central to the democratic processes of governance in the information society, more and more players—voluntary organizations, interest groups, private-sector think tanks, and the media—have become involved in the process. Communication and IT, the globalization of markets, technology in the workplace, the consumer focus, increased workforce diversity, the changing citizen profile, and the emergence of democracy as the major political framework worldwide are all agents of governance in changing society and organizations (McLagan and Christo 1995; Korac-Kakabadse, Kouzmin, and Korac-Kakabadse 2000b).

There have been recent trends in many political systems to reduce direct state intervention in governance capacities, especially in the workplace. Yet, inasmuch as the state has withdrawn from the delivery of services and benefits, the increased importance of continuing "core" governance functions means that individuals are affected in almost all aspects of their lives by the actions of the state, including a substantial portion of those employed by the state. The role of the state as an employer has become increasingly important in recent years. The greater the importance of even a reduced government as an employer, the more pervasive its influence is likely to be on the way IT developments shape behavior within and without government agencies. Public-sector organizations serve as a model for corporate life in relation to IT usage, and governance issues remain important to public policy and governance debate.

The Role of the Media

Some have argued that people want trustworthy information sources that will do the hard work of gathering and digesting political information—the very task that is putatively being performed by the media, albeit not always reliably. The active role of the media is likely to be replaced by a new type of interactive multimedia characterized by highly specialized media outlets described as "information agents" (Snider 1994). Current reporters work for newspapers whose dominance is based on economies of scale associated with their distribution and propaganda capabilities. Reporters could well become independent information entrepreneurs selling their information wares directly to the public over the telecommunications networks. With the use of IT, these information agents could gather and digest information and disseminate it to clients, just as highly priced consultants do today.

Increasingly, the role of the media and the media's responsibility in helping to revitalize public trust are receiving attention. For example, some argue that journalists have a specific role to play in ensuring that democratic communities continue (Merritt 1995). While the concept that journalists can do more than just transfer information from one point to another may be unsettling for those in journalism, many feel journalists must heed the higher calling of civic journalism (Merritt 1995; Fallows 1996). Further accentuated by the movement of political discourse through new forms of media, such as the Internet, the roles that journalists, as information agents, choose to take in addressing problems in society will go a long way toward defining the final outcomes of such discussion (Fallows 1996). Notwithstanding that existing mass media has attracted vast criticism, the potential for more competitive, diverse, and customized media in the future carries with it new opportunities. For example, traditional self-promotion through television advertisements and by political candidates may become obsolete. Similar repercussions may confront lobbyists and special interest groups who derive their power from the ability to fund a candidate's media campaigns, but who may find themselves undermined when voters buy critical information from independent information agents (Snider 1994). The guiding logic of Ross Perot's "United We Stand" alliance, enabled by "electronic town links" for town meetings, was to facilitate discussion and wide-ranging debates at the grassroots level and not at the lobbyists' level (London 1994).

This alternative assumes universal access to the forthcoming information highways; otherwise, it furthers the gap between those who can purchase critical information from information agents and those who cannot. Furthermore, new IT will make it possible to finance elections publicly in a way that, instead of money going to candidates, money could be given directly to the voters (Snider 1994). Instead of tens of millions of dollars in communication vouchers being given to the U.S. presidential candidates to spend on 30-second television advertisements, money could be given directly to citizens to spend on information about these candidates. Voter-based vouchers are far more democratic than candidate-based vouchers, but such a "democratic" change has not been practical or feasible until present-day developments in IT (Snider 1994, 18).

The Role of Corporations and Agencies

Considering that a contractual (explicit or implicit) relationship exists not only between a business and its shareholders, but also with its employees, customers, creditors, and other stakeholders, corporations and agencies need to be accountable to their constituents (Benston 1982). It is possible for the notion of accountability to be extended beyond a narrow two-party contract to social responsibility, accepting that other parties such as employees, consumers and, even society at large need to be considered (Pallot 1991, 203). Contractual responsibility is likely to encompass others than owners and shareholders. Managing a business exclusively for the shareholders alienates the very people on whose motivation and dedication the modern business depends—the knowledge workers—as the knowledge worker will not necessarily be motivated to make shareholders rich (Drucker 1993, 80).

The demand for public and private organizations to be socially responsible is increasing (Gray,

Owen, and Maunders 1988). Organizations, through social and political pressure, are being tested to accept full responsibility for their impact on communities and society. There is also the concomitant requirement to communicate better corporate actions and intentions to the organization, stakeholders, and society (Mathews 1993, 31; Fox 1994). The disclosure of information is necessary to prevent organizations from what Gross (1978) calls inherently criminal behavior. The consideration that all organizations put a strong emphasis on goal attainment as a measure of performance and effectiveness and operate in environments of uncertainty suggests that, if necessary, such goals will be attained through criminal or illegitimate behavior (Gross 1978; Clegg and Dunkerley 1980). Although this argument represents an extreme position, examples such as the Lockheed bribes scandal in the United States and the Guinness debacle in the United Kingdom suggest there is more than an element of truth in that viewpoint. The poor performance of certain corporations, hostile takeovers, leveraged buyouts, and the acquisitions that created the "bubble economy" that collapsed in a series of financial scandals (Drucker 1993; Hirsh 1994) are examples of irresponsible, if not illegitimate, behavior. The perception is that irresponsible corporate behavior exists, that it is widespread, and that it is not confined to corporate boards, but extends to boards of nonprofit organizations as well (Cadbury 1995; Cutting and Kouzmin 2000; Minkes and Minkes 2000).

THE WAY FORWARD: REINVENTING THE DEMOCRATIC GOVERNANCE PROJECT

Notwithstanding the danger of replacing representative democracy with a new form of cyberdemocracy or virtual polis, there is room for redesigning the project of representative democracy and governance. The focus is not only on the choice between grassroots, participatory cyberdemocracy versus current participatory democracy, but also between top-down, repackaged, and controlled "virtual mercantilism" versus free trade (Rheingold 1993). There is a need for a governance project design that is more responsive to community needs and the needs of the disfranchised in globalizing economies.

Voluntary voting produces elections and policies by referendums, with only a fraction of the population exercising choice. For example, in the United States, after a vigorous and very expensive campaign, 47 percent of the vote is considered a good show at the polls. However, if society adopts compulsory voting, it will help to ensure that elected representatives carry out policies espoused by majorities, and not only those of the espoused majority. Further, the compulsory-voting model would bring citizens to elect representatives responsibly and be held accountable for electing representatives.

To enable representation of minority groups, proportional representation needs to be added to the model. The model of proportional representation has much to offer as it allows small communities to be represented on an equal footing with large ones. When society adopts forms of electronic democracy, with a communications infrastructure available to all citizens, voting patterns could truly represent the will of the majority.

However, much can be learned from the Scottish innovations in "teledemocracy" (Taylor, Bardzki, and Wilson 1995) and from the Swedish concept of local democracy and its relation to central government and, above all, its significance for the individual citizen. The Swedish concept of subsidiarity, closely developing the concept of a "bottom-up" as opposed to a "top-down" approach, provides a guiding design principle for governance in Sweden after possible accession in the European Union (Michalski 1994).

To avoid information overload, which is facilitated by communication technologies (Korac-

Boisvert and Kouzmin 1995) and, at the same time, facilitates government responsiveness to citizens' needs and citizen participation in policy analysis and design, decentralized governance is required. Hence, local issues could be dealt with at the local level, societal issues at the state level, and global issues at the regional and international levels. To improve the quality of democratic governance by making governance more efficient and accessible to citizens, the challenge is a *policy* issue and not an IT issue. The use and application of IT is open to choice and, as such, falls within the domain of public policy and governance (Korac-Kakabadse, Kouzmin, and Korac-Kakabadse 2000b).

The basis of participatory policy analysis is to inform the policy process better and, through direct citizen involvement, to give citizens the opportunity for increased participation in and allegiance to the political system and its processes (deLeon 1994, 88). However, only well-informed citizens can successfully participate in the democratic political process. Making policy information available to all citizens and educating them about how to use communication technology to access information needs to be incorporated in the policy design and implementation processes.

Accomplishing this requires accessibility, equity, and adaptability of policy information. Accessibility means the process is the same for all stakeholders, with multiple and reciprocal pathways for information flow. This may require actively soliciting input from significant stakeholders, not only from lobby groups and institutions, but through creating structures to foster communication. Equity means taking explicit care to balance the potential costs and benefits among all stakeholders and presupposes openness to differing or conflicting perspectives and assumptions (La Porte 1975; Janis and Mann 1977; Brewer 1986).

Adaptability means the willingness and capacity to reevaluate policies continually in light of changing circumstance, new knowledge, and unexpected outcomes (Senge 1990). For example, although many government bodies, regulatory agencies, industries, public interest groups, and individuals are actively developing policies to address environmental issues, only some carry this process with open communication with stakeholders.

If citizen participation is sought for every policy and operational issue in a truly democratic way, there would be very little use for politicians. Instead, there would be a need for administrators who can respond to the demands of the citizen majority on a daily basis. Powerful lobby groups could continue to choose futures that would benefit only a select few. However, the level of citizen participation in policy design and implementation is immensely important. The danger of overextending the shape of democratic policy design and implementation into the desired shape of individual (elected representative) or corporate decision making is more prevalent with electronic democracy (Perri, 6 1997), which, ultimately, leads to the split between responsibility and accountability.

With an appropriate information infrastructure—one that provides universal citizen access—important issues can be debated and voted on in a manner that is more comfortable for citizens (using communication technology from home) and, once the infrastructure is in place, in a significantly more economical and efficient manner—there would be no need for the manual handling of ballot papers. Caution is needed though, as theoretically elegant but practically deceptive voting systems could come into widespread use, possibly leading to information overload, which can, at best, only be a minor palliative to political information problems (Snider 1994). Thus, the main advantages of IT in attempting to improve the Democratic Governance Project are to promote *participatory policy analysis* to better inform the policy process and to educate citizens, through their involvement, so that they can make informed choices. The challenge is to find ways to pool the good judgment and foresight of the public (London 1994). Furthermore, there are non-technology-based approaches for improving democratic governance; for example, instilling a better sense of civic duty in schools and overhauling campaign finance laws to minimize the influence of special interest groups (Snider 1994).

CONCLUSION

While information has always played a key role in democracies, its current role is both expanding and transforming. Multiple models of information transfer are used, not just locally but nationally and internationally. Information transfer and the infrastructures that support them are understood to have profound effects on economic prosperity (Martinez 1994). In the increasingly interconnected and rapidly changing formative context of the information society, traditional ways of organizing and governing, based on more restricted flows of information and limited interconnections in public and corporate organizations and national states, seem to be overwhelmed (Milward and Snyder 1996, 273). Thus, what is becoming increasingly clear in a world of rapid and continuing change, eroding boundaries, multiplying interest groups, and fragmenting institutions and belief systems is the need to invest more time, energy, and attention to developing a shared understanding of the future direction of social changes, but within a more systematic process of agenda setting and, further, within an acceptable and agreed value system.

Hinging on *equitable* access to IT is whether that technology will make society more cohesive and collectively prosperous, or whether it will undermine the bases for democracy and further polarize society into a dispossessed and a wealthy elite—defined not just by investment portfolios, but also by monopoly of information (Martinez 1994). Technology can enhance the learning of conceptual knowledge and the knowledge of process—in particular, enabling forms of information seeking required and engendered by IT. However, technology also can influence the growth of the "knowledge gap" (Paisley 1987). The future of IT influence will require vigilance and a guarantee of access to all to ensure the electronic revolution reconciles society more than it divides it (Schalken and Tops 1995; Korac-Kakabadse, Kouzmin, and Korac-Kakabadse 2000b). The quality of democratic governance is only enhanced by IT if citizens are better informed, but not to the point of information overload.

The realization that what people do really does make a difference requires dramatic changes in governance (Dror 1987). The move toward effective participation is probably the greatest shift of our time. It acknowledges that one lives and works in a highly interdependent world, making complex decisions that have many effects one cannot anticipate. It also reflects the real value of diversity, though it increases the chance of conflict. It also increases the possibility of more creative and sustainable solutions to problems one faces in society, work, or private life. Governments and business are only now discovering the survival advantage of participation. The world has arrived at a moment of immense democratic and entrepreneurial opportunity made possible by IT—and the opportunity should not be wasted. Besides good governance, democracy also requires mechanisms for conflict resolution, a political culture of tolerance and compromise, and the wisdom of leadership. The modern democratic polity requires a large and complex governance capacity because the private sector alone simply cannot provide many vital services such as defense and environmental protection (Snider 1994). New IT, combined with leadership wisdom (Kouzmin and Korac-Kakabadse 2000), can substantially enhance the Democratic Governance Project.

The concept of "cyberspace" or "environment in flux" that coalesces around visions of virtual, community-centered and networked, citizen-controlled "Jeffersonian networks" or autonomous collectives of virtual communities is a concept of a transcendent metacommunity (Rheingold 1993). Individuality without a community orientation leads to further alienation and fragmentation of society and upsets the communitarian balance (Sardar 1996). The shift to community values and needs is necessary and has to take place at the individual and corporate levels. There is a need for a new philosophy that will emphasize the virtue that ensures the continuation of democratic principles and connects the individual with the community. How might—and how should—democratic principles such as rights and freedoms of "new speech" (the many ways of sharing multidimensional worlds of sight, sound, and touch over invisible and ubiquitous "terabyte" highways) be applied in the era of the information superhighway needs to be further examined. Preserving and enhancing democratic principles can be "expensive, dangerous, unpredictable and sometimes ugly and offensive" (Berry 1992, 6), especially in a cyberspace and globalizing context (Robertson 1992; Rosell 1995). As Winner (1987) observes, "political ergonomics" will need to be reinvented in order to design new arrangements for democratic praxis and effective governance in the forthcoming digital age.

REFERENCES

Adonis, Andrew, and Geoff Mulgan. 1994. Back to Greece: The Scope for Direct Democracy. *Demos* (3): 24–31.
Aristotle. 1987. *Politics.* London: Penguin Classics.
Balagopal, K. 1989. Ruling Class Politics and People's Rights. In *Rethinking Human Rights,* edited by Smitu Kothari and Harsh Sethi, 83–92. New York: New Horizon Press.
Benn, Stanley T. 1967. Democracy. In *The Encyclopedia of Philosophy,* vol. 2, edited by Paul Edwards, 338–41. New York: Macmillan/Free Press.
Benston, George J. 1982. Accounting and Corporate Accountability. *Accounting, Organizations and Society* 7(2): 87–105.
Berry, John N. 1992. If Words Will Never Hurt Me, Then . . . ? *Library Journal* 117(1): 6–7.
Bickel, Alexander M. 1986. *The Least Dangerous Branch: The Supreme Court at the Bar of Politics.* 2nd ed. New Haven, CT: Yale University Press.
Bishop, John D. 1991. The Moral Responsibility of Corporate Executives for Disasters. *Journal of Business Ethics* 10(5): 377–83.
Bork, Robert H. 1990. *The Tempting of America: The Political Seduction of the Law.* New York: Free Press.
Braman, Sandra. 1994. The Autopoetic State: Communication and Democratic Potential in the Net. *Journal of the American Society for Information Science* 45(6): 358–68.
Bransford, John D., and Marcia K. Johnson. 1972. Contextual Prerequisites for Understanding: Some Investigations of Comprehension and Recall. *Journal of Verbal Learning and Verbal Behaviour* 11(4): 717–26.
Brewer, Garry D. 1986. Methods for Synthesis: Policy Exercises. In *Sustainable Development of the Biosphere,* edited by William C. Clark and Ted E. Munn, 455–75. Cambridge, UK: Cambridge University Press.
Burns, N. 1995. *Collaborative Computing: What Is It and How Does It Affect Your Business?* New York: Creative Network.
Cadbury, Adrian. 1995. *The Company Chairman.* New ed. Hemel Hempstead, UK: Fitzwilliam Publishing.
Carnoy, Martin. 1984. *The State and Political Theory.* Princeton, NJ: Princeton University Press.
Cetron, Marvin. 1994. The Future Face of Terrorism. *The Futurist* 28(6): 10–16.
Clegg, Stewart, and David Dunkerley. 1980. *Organization, Class and Control.* London: Routledge and Kegan Paul.
Comer, James P. 1988. Educating Poor Minority Children. *Scientific American* 259(5): 42–48.
Crawford, Richard. 1991. *In the Era of Human Capital.* New York: HarperCollins.
Creedy, Steve. 1997. Computer Crimes: Police Get Serious. *The Australian,* February 25, 52–53.
Croley, Steven P. 1995. The Majoritarian Difficulty: Elective Judiciaries and the Rule of Law. *University of Chicago Law Review* 62(2): 689–794.
Cutting, Bruce, and Alexander Kouzmin. 1999. From Chaos to Patterns of Understanding: Reflections on the Dynamics of Effective Government Decision Making. *Public Administration* (London) 77(3): 475–508.
———. 2000. The Emerging Patterns of Power in Corporate Governance: Back to the Future in Improving Corporate Decision Making. *Journal of Managerial Psychology* 15(5): 477–511.

Dahl, Robert A. 1956. *Preface to Democratic Theory: A Formal Analysis of Types of Democratic Theory.* Chicago: University of Chicago Press.

———. 1989. *Democracy and Its Critics.* New Haven, CT: Yale University Press.

Davis, Stan, and Bill Davidson. 1991. *2020 Vision.* New York: Simon and Schuster.

deLeon, Peter. 1994. Reinventing the Policy Sciences: Three Steps Back to the Future. *Policy Sciences* 27(1): 77–95.

Depla, Paul F.G., and Pieter W. Tops. 1995. Political Parties in the Digital Era: The Technological Challenge. In *Orwell in Athens: A Perspective on Informatization and Democracy,* edited by Wim B.H.J. Van de Donk, Ignace th. M. Snellen, and Pieter W. Tops, 155–64. Amsterdam, Netherlands: IOS Press.

de Tocqueville, Alexis. 1994. *Democracy in America.* Edited by J.P. Mayer and translated by George Lawrence. London: Fontane.

Downs, Anthony. 1967. *An Economic Theory of Democracy.* New York: Free Press.

Dror, Yehezkel. 1987. Retro-Fitting Central Mind of Government. *Research in Public Policy and Management* 4: 79–107.

Drucker, Peter. 1993. *Post-Capitalist Society.* New York: Harper Business.

———. 1994. The Age of Social Transformation. *Atlantic Monthly* 274(5): 53–80.

Dworkin, Ronald. 1977. *Taking Rights Seriously.* Cambridge, MA: Harvard University Press.

Edwards, A.R. 1995. Informatization and Views of Democracy. In *Orwell in Athens: A Perspective on Informatization and Democracy,* edited by Wim B.H.J. Van de Donk, Ignace th. M. Snellen, and Pieter W. Tops, 33–49. Amsterdam, Netherlands: IOS Press.

Fallows, James. 1996. Why Americans Hate the Media. *Atlantic Monthly* 277(2): 45–64.

Fogelman, Martin. 1994. Freedom and Censorship in the Emerging Electronic Environment. *The Information Society* 10(4): 295–303.

Fox, Matthew. 1994. *The Re-Invention of Work: A New Vision of Livelihood for Our Times.* New York: Harper.

Fukuyama, Francis. 1992. *The End of History and the Last Man.* London: Hamish Hamilton.

Galbraith, John K. 1967. *The New Industrial State.* New York: Signet.

Gillwald, Katrin, Ana M. Sandi, and Bart van Steenbergen. 1992. Central and East European Futures. *Futures* 24(2): 107–109.

Gore, Al. 1994. The Deadly Age of Cynicism. *Aspen Institute Quarterly* 6(4): 7–21.

Gray, Rob. 1983. Accounting, Financial Reporting and Not-for-Profit Organizations. *AUTA Review* 15(1): 3–23.

Gray, Rob, Dave Owen, and Keith Maunders. 1987. *Corporate Social Reporting: Accounting and Accountability.* Hemel Hempstead, UK: Prentice-Hall International.

———. 1988. Corporate Social Reporting: Emerging Trends in Accountability and Social Contract. *Accounting, Auditing and Accountability Journal* 1(1): 6–20.

Gross, E. 1978. Organizations as Criminal Actors. In *The Two Faces of Deviance: Crimes of the Powerful and Powerless,* edited by Paul R. Wilson and John Braithwaite, 119–213. St. Lucia, Australia: University of Queensland Press.

Held, David. 1989. *Political Theory and the Modern State: Essays on State, Power and Democracy.* Stanford, CA: Stanford University Press.

Hirsch, Eric D. 1987. *Cultural Literacy.* Boston, MA: Houghton Mifflin.

Hirsh, M. 1994. Capital Wars. *The Bulletin,* October 25, 66–70.

Holmes, Stephen. 1988. Pre-Commitment and the Paradox of Democracy. In *Constitutionalism and Democracy,* edited by John Elster and Rune Slagstad, 74–83. Cambridge, UK: Cambridge University Press.

Hosenball, Mark, and Evan Thomas. 1997. A China Connection: How Charges of Clinton Campaign Sleaze Could Turn into a Spy Scandal. *Newsweek,* February 24, 38–40.

Ijiri, Yuji. 1983. On the Accountability-Based Conceptual Framework of Accounting. *Journal of Accounting and Public Policy* 2(2): 75–81.

Janis, Irving L., and Leon Mann. 1977. *Decision Making.* New York: Free Press.

Jearnott, Thomas M. 1989. Moral Leadership and Practical Wisdom. *International Journal of Social Economies* 16(6): 14–35.

Jones, Christopher B. 1991. Eco-Democracy: Synthesizing Feminism, Ecology and Participatory Organizations. In *Advancing Democracy and Participation: Challenges for the Future,* edited by Bart von Steenbergen, Radmila Nakarada, Felix Marti, and Jim Dator, 96–112. Barcelona, Spain: Centre Catala de Prospectova.

Kagan, Shelly. 1989. *The Limits of Morality.* Oxford, UK: Oxford University Press.

Kakabadse, Andrew. 1991. *The Wealth Creators.* London: Kogan Page.

Kapor, Mitchell. 1992. Where Is the Digital Highway Really Heading: The Case for a Jeffersonian Information Policy. *WiReD* 1(3): 47–52.

Korac-Boisvert, Nada, and Alexander Kouzmin. 1994. The Dark Side of the Info-Age: Social Networks in Public Organizations and Creeping Crisis. *Administrative Theory and Praxis* 16(1): 57–82.

———. 1995. IT Development: Methodology Over-Load or Crisis. *Science Communication: An Interdisciplinary Science Journal* 17(1): 57–89.

Korac-Kakabadse, Nada, Alexander Kouzmin, and Andrew Korac-Kakabadse. 2000a. Current Trends in Internet Use: E-Communication, E-Information and E-Commerce. *Knowledge and Process Management: The Journal of Corporate Transformation* 7(2): 133–42.

———. 2000b. Information Technology and Development: Creating "IT Harems," Fostering New Colonialism or Solving "Wicked" Policy Problems? *Public Administration and Development* 20(3): 171–84.

———. 2000c. Information Technology-Enabled Communication and Organizational Effectiveness. *International Review of Public Administration* 5(1): 19–36.

Kouzmin, Alexander, and Nada Korac-Kakabadse. 2000. Mapping Institutional Impacts of "Lean" Communication in "Lean" Agencies: Information Technology Illiteracy and Leadership Failure. *Administration and Society* 32(1): 29–69.

La Porte, Todd R., ed. 1975. *Organized Social Complexity: Challenge to Politics and Policy.* Princeton, NJ: Princeton University Press.

Latham, Mark. 1998. *Civilizing Global Capital: New Thinking Australian Labor.* Sydney, Australia: Allen and Unwin.

Laughlin, Richard C. 1996. Rethinking Models of Accountability: The Influence of Professionalism and "Higher" Principals on Actions and Reactions of "Agents" in the Caring Professions. In *Accountability, Power and Ethos,* edited by Rolland Munro and Jan Mouritsen, 113–21. London: Chapman and Hall.

London, Scott. 1994. Electronic Democracy: A Literature Survey. Paper prepared for the Kettering Foundation, Santa Barbara, CA.

Macpherson, Crawford B. 1966. *The Real World of Democracy.* Oxford, UK: Clarendon Press.

Martinez, Michael E. 1994. Access to Information Technologies among School-Age Children: Implications for a Democratic Society. *Journal of the American Society for Information Science* 45(6): 395–400.

Marx, Karl. 1964. *Economic and Philosophic Manuscripts of 1844.* New York: International Publishers.

Mathews, M. Reg. 1993. *Socially Responsible Accounting.* London: Chapman and Hall.

Mayo, Henry B. 1960. *An Introduction to Democratic Theory.* New York: Oxford University Press.

McLagan, Pat, and Christo Nel. 1995. The Dawning of a New Age in the Workplace. *Journal for Quality and Participation* 18(2): 10–15.

Merritt, Davis. 1995. *Public Journalism and Public Life: Why Telling the News Is Not Enough.* Hillsdale, NJ: Erlbaum.

Michalski, Anna. 1994. Swedish Local Democracy: A Viable Model for Europe. *European Business Review* 94(5): x–xii.

Mill, John S. 1991. *Consideration on Representative Government.* Essex: Prometheus Books.

Mills, C. Wright. 1959. *The Power Elite.* New York: Oxford University Press.

Milward, H. Brinton, and Louise O. Snyder. 1996. Electronic Government: Linking Citizens to Public Organizations through Technology. *Journal of Public Administration Research and Theory* 6(2): 261–75.

Minkes, John P., and A. Leonard Minkes. 2000. The Criminology of the Corporation. *Journal of General Management* 26(2): 1–16.

Mouffe, Chantal, ed. 1992. *Dimensions of Radical Democracy: Pluralism, Citizenship, Community.* London: Verso.

Ogden, Michael R. 1994. Politics in Parallel Universe: Is There a Future for Cyber-Democracy? *Futures* 26(7): 713–29.

Olson, Robert. 1996. Information Technology in Home Health Care. In *Future Care: Responding to the Demand for Change,* edited by Clement Bezold and Erica Mayer, 87–103. New York: Faulkner.

Organisation for Economic Co-operation and Development (OECD). 1987. *Structural Adjustment and Economic Performance.* Paris: OECD.

———. 1996. *Ministerial Symposium on the Future of Public Service.* Paris: Public Management Service, OECD.

————. 1997. Citycard—Opening Channels between the Citizen and Local Government. *Information Society European Style.* Available at http://www.oecd.org/puma/governance.it. Accessed August 17, 2002.

Osborne, David, and Ted Gaebler. 1991. *Re-Inventing Government: How the Entrepreneurial Spirit Is Transforming the Public Sector.* New York: Harper.

Paisley, William. 1987. Many Literacies, Many Challenges. Paper presented at the American Library Association Conference, June 27–July 2, San Francisco, CA.

Pallot, June. 1991. The Legitimate Concern with Fairness: A Comment. *Accounting, Organizations and Society* 16(2): 201–8.

Parekh, Bhikhu. 1993. The Cultural Particularity of Liberal Democracy. In *Prospects for Democracy,* edited by David Held, 127–36. Cambridge, UK: Polity Press.

Pateman, Carole. 1970. *Participation and Democratic Theory.* London: Cambridge University Press.

Perri, 6. 1997. Information Society Symposium: Quality of Democracy Working Group. Email correspondence with Andrew Korac-Kakabadse. October 17.

Plato. 1987. *The Republic.* London: Penguin Classics.

Power, Michael. 1991. Auditing and Environmental Expertise: Between Protest and Professionalisation. *Accounting, Auditing and Accountability Journal* 4(3): 30–42.

Rheingold, Howard. 1993. *The Virtual Community: Homesteading on the Electronic Frontier.* New York: Addison-Wesley.

Roberts, John, and Robert Scapens. 1985. Accounting Systems and Systems of Accountability: Understanding Accounting Practices in the Organizational Context. *Accounting, Organizations and Society* 10(4): 443–56.

Robertson, Roland. 1992. *Globalization: Social Theory and Global Culture.* London: Sage Publications.

Rosell, Steven A. 1992. *Governing in an Information Society.* Montreal: Institute for Research on Public Policy.

————. 1995. *Changing Maps: Governing in a World of Rapid Change.* Ottawa, Canada: Carleton University Press.

Rosen, Frederick. 1983. *Jeremy Bentham and Representative Democracy.* Oxford, UK: Oxford University Press.

Sardar, Ziauddin. 1994. *Muhammed for Beginners.* London: Icon Books.

————. 1996. The Future of Democracy and Human Rights. *Futures* 28(9): 839–59.

Schalken, Kees A.T., and Pieter W. Tops. 1995. Democracy and Virtual Communities. In *Orwell in Athens: A Perspective on Informatization and Democracy,* edited by Wim B.H.J. Van de Donk, Ignace th. M. Snellen, and Pieter W. Tops, 1434–54. Amsterdam, Netherlands: IOS Press.

Senge, Peter. 1990. *The Fifth Discipline.* New York: Doubleday.

Shocker, Allan D., and S. Prakash Sethi. 1974. An Approach to Incorporating Social Preferences in Developing Corporate Action Strategies. In *The Unstable Ground: Corporate Social Policy in a Dynamic Society,* edited by S. Prakash Sethi, 187–92. Melville, California: Melville Publishing.

Snider, James H. 1994. Democracy On-Line: Tomorrow's Electronic Electorate. *The Futurist* 28(5): 15–19.

Spinoza, Benedict de. 1951. *Works of Spinoza.* Vol. 1, 2. Translated by R.H.M. Elwes. New York: Dover.

State and Local Coalition on Immigration, Immigration Policy Project (SLCI/IPP). 1995. *America's Newcomers: An Immigrant Policy Handbook.* Denver, CO: National Conference of State Legislatures.

Stephenson, Neal. 1995. Global Neighbourhood Watch. *Scenarios: 1.01 (WiReD Special Edition),* Fall, 96–107.

Sternberg, Robert, ed. 1990. *Wisdom: Its Nature, Origins, and Development.* Cambridge, UK: Cambridge University Press.

Stewart, John D. 1984. The Role of Information in Public Accountability. In *Issues in Public Sector Accounting,* edited by Anthony Hopwood and Cyril Tomkins, 13–34. Oxford, UK: Phillip Allen.

Stone, Romuald A. 1995. Workplace Homicide: A Time for Action. *Business Horizons* 38(2): 3–10.

Szilagyi, Miklos N. 1994. *How to Save Our Country: A Non-Partisan Vision for Change.* Tucson, AZ: Pallsas Press.

Taylor, John A., Barbara Bardzki, and Caroline Wilson. 1995. Laying Down the Infrastructure for Innovations in Teledemocracy: The Case of Scotland. In *Orwell in Athens: A Perspective on Informatization and Democracy,* edited by Wim B.H.J. Van de Donk, Ignace th. M. Snellen, and Pieter W. Tops, 61–71. Amsterdam, Netherlands: IOS Press.

The Economist. 1995. Democracy and Technology. June 17–23, 21–22.

Tonn, Bruce. 1996. A Design for Further-Oriented Government. *Futures* 28(5): 413–31.

Tricker, Robert I. 1983. Corporate Responsibility, Institutional Governance and the Roles of Accounting Standards. In *Accounting Standard Setting: An International Perspective,* edited by Michael Bromwich and Anthony Hopwood, 27–41. London: Pitman.

Tucker, Robert C. 1970. *The Marxian Revolutionary Idea.* London: Unwin University Books.

Unger, Roberto M. 1987. *False Necessity.* Cambridge, UK: Cambridge University Press.

Van de Donk, Wim B.H.J., and O.M.T. Meyer. 1995. Digitalizing Decision Making in a Democracy: For Better or For Worse. In *Orwell in Athens: A Perspective on Informatization and Democracy,* edited by Wim B.H.J. Van de Donk, Ignace th. M. Snellen, and Pieter W. Tops, 221–30. Amsterdam, Netherlands: IOS Press.

Washington Post. 1996. Postal Voting. January 22, 1.

Weiss, Edith B. 1989. *In Fairness to Future Generations: International Law, Common Patrimony and Inter-generational Equity.* New York: Transnational Publications.

Williams, Trevor A. 1987. *Learning to Manage Our Future.* New York: Wiley.

Winner, Langdon. 1987. *Political Ergonomics: Technological Design and the Quality of Public Life.* Berlin, Germany: International Institute for Environment and Safety.

PART 5

ASSESSMENTS OF DIRECT CITIZEN PARTICIPATION

There are many questions that can be addressed in evaluating direct citizen participation (Chess 2000). Should summative or formative evaluations be employed? Are long-term or short-term impacts better to assess? What should be evaluated—process or outcome variables? Should goals be evaluated or should evaluations be goal-free? Are user-based or theory-based evaluations more appropriate? Who should evaluate—outsiders or participants? What evaluation designs are most appropriate, and should qualitative or quantitative methods be utilized? And what are the uses of evaluation and the implications for agency and citizen use? These and other questions are standard for evaluative researchers to consider (Suchman 1967; Weiss 1972; Herman et al. 1987; Stecher and Davis 1987).

Of the many alternatives open to evaluators, one is particularly important for direct citizen involvement. As we saw in Part 2, administrative theories carry different assumptions about the citizen's appropriate role in a democratic society. The pluralist model, for example, is concerned about the outcomes of participation and the extent to which the benefits and burdens are distributed throughout society. In contrast, the learning model focuses on processes and their educational and psychological effects on participants. Using criteria derived from the pluralist model to judge direct citizen participation based on the learning model would not be appropriate. Not only would we miss what want to measure, we likely would introduce distortion to the results. Failures in direct participation could just as easily be understood as failures in evaluation design.

Along these same lines, evaluators must take care that their own models and views of citizen participation do not cloud their assessments. Administrators have been accused of "cooptation" and "manipulation" because they have given citizens the appearance of delegating authority and responsibility while still retaining control over processes and outcomes (Arnstein 1969, 1972). Alternatively, citizens have been charged with "overdramatization, hyperbole, and shrillness" in their tactics and style. Their "questionable activities, including exploitation and abuse of the mass media" are said to "more closely approximate guerrilla warfare than normal political activity" (Cupps 1977, p. 482).

An alternative interpretation of the above statements about administrative and citizen behavior is that evaluators disagree on the roles that citizens and administrators are expected to play. If one assumes the administrative state model, for example, it is reasonable to believe that administrators are professionals who should retain their authority because of their expertise and their accountability to democratically elected representatives.[1] This point was made by the Reagan administration when it called for a return to the "state model of administrative responsiveness." It believed that federally mandated citizen participation had caused the bureaucracy to become unresponsive to elected officials, and was therefore anti-democratic (Berry et al. 1989, p. 209). Likewise, citizens' use of confrontational tactics as described above could be considered to be consistent with advocacy and interest group politics. In the role of advocate, citizens compete with other interest groups to push their ideas onto the action agenda. Their aggressive behavior could be viewed as appropriate and necessary to promote their ideas in the corridors of power and to win out over competing views.

Thus, evaluation designs, especially given the competing perspectives on citizen participation, need to make clear which administrative model informs their analysis. Otherwise, results can be misinterpreted and the underlying tensions surrounding direct citizen participation can obscure what is really going on. The articles that follow avoid these pitfalls of evaluation research and provide examples of some of the more successful efforts at assessing direct citizen participation. They also employ an impressive array of designs and methodologies that range from surveys to comparative case studies. Most notable are their efforts to build theory by identifying the conditions under which direct citizen participation fails or succeeds.

The first article, "Resident Participation: Political Mobilization or Organizational Co-optation?" by David M. Austin presents findings from the Study on Community Representation in Community Action Agencies (CAA).[2] Central to the study is an assessment of citizen participation, especially as it concerns the congressional mandate requiring one-third of the CAA policy boards be composed of target-area residents. Researchers identified a cross-community randomly selected sample, stratified by region, of 20 CAAs to explore citizen participation and its consequences. In general, due to federal and program constraints, they found that target area residents had little or no part in the initial organization and decisions of the CAAs, and they had very little impact on the major program strategies and mix of programs. Resident participation in 17 out of the 20 CAAs was characterized as advisory, although resident participation in four out of the 17 was able to change the advisory process into a confrontation process within the CAA. Resident participation in the remaining three out of the 20 CAAs had a political function that engaged target-area residents in pluralistic power conflicts in the larger community. Thus, to a large extent, citizen participation was built around a model of advisory and co-opted participation that was shaped by local circumstances. Variations in participation patterns depended on a number of factors: the extent to which there was stability in the social system, accepted patterns of power, the presence of organized political and social movements agitating for community action to benefit low-income or ethnic minority citizens, the percentage of the population that was black or minority, the belief that poverty was a consequence of individual failure, and the city's size.

Erasmus Kloman in "Citizen Participation in the Philadelphia Model Cities Program: Retrospect and Prospect," offers a retrospective evaluation of the Philadelphia program and an appraisal of its future prospects. The Model Cities Program was a congressionally mandated, HUD-implemented initiative that sought to empower inner-city residents and organizations so they could deal better with the problems of urban poverty. The article demonstrates the difficulties of conducting evaluations in highly charged political environments. Disagreements arose over the meaning of citizen participation, on the role of citizens and neighbor associations, on the oversight responsibilities of local and national agencies, and on the criteria to judge policy outcomes. Disputes adjudicated in court between government agencies compounded the difficulties. The article, the first of three in a symposium on the Philadelphia case, illustrates the challenge of reconciling multiple perspectives when conducting an assessment on a contentious topic. The second article in the series offers citizen council members' perceptions in "Maximum Feasible Manipulation" (Arnstein 1972), and the third summarizes public officials' perspectives in "The View from City Hall" (1972).

Judy B. Rosener advocates an approach that she believes avoids some of the major difficulties of evaluation. In "Citizen Participation: Can We Measure Its Effectiveness?" she creates a two-by-two matrix that describes four types of evaluation environments for citizen participation. Quadrant I (the healthiest evaluation environment) finds agreement on participation goals and objectives and whose goals and objectives they are, and agreement on the criteria by which success or failure is measured. In addition, there is knowledge of the cause/effect relationship between a program activity and the achievement of specified goals and objectives. In contrast, quadrant IV at the other extreme has no agreement on goals and objectives, criteria, or the cause/effect relationship between a program activity and the achievement of goals and objectives. Using a case study from the California Department of Transportation, Rosener illustrates how an evaluator can use the matrix to move the evaluation environment from quadrant IV to quadrant I. She also demonstrates how to conduct a program evaluation even when the evaluation has to be "done after the fact" and includes a certain amount of subjectivity in the analysis.

"Making Bureaucrats Responsive: A Study of the Impact of Citizen Participation and Staff Recommendations on Regulatory Decision Making" is an evaluation of citizen participation during public hearings held by the California Coastal Commission. Judy B. Rosener's hypotheses-testing study of 1,816 public hearings found that citizen participation changed commissioners' voting outcomes independent of staff recommendations. Furthermore, when citizen opposition was linked with staff recommendations for denial, the two variables acting together became a strong predictive variable significantly increasing the probability that a commission would deny a permit. In contrast to conventional wisdom, Rosener finds that citizen participation can be effective in public hearings, although she cautions that the relationship among staff recommendations, citizen participation and voting outcomes is complex and needs more study.

Cheryl Simrell King, Kathryn M. Feltey, and Bridget O'Neill Susel in "The Question of Participation: Toward Authentic Public Participation in Public Administration" ask how citizen participation can be improved. Using interviews of subject-matter experts and focus groups (of public administrators, activists and citizens), their study seeks to identify the barriers to citizen participation and strategies for overcoming them. Their findings indicate that effective, or authentic, citizen participation requires dialogue and deliberation.[3] Three barriers to citizen participation are identified: the nature of life in contemporary society; administrative processes; and current practices and techniques of participation. According to the authors, overcoming barriers to citizen participation requires a learning process built on citizen empowerment and education, reeducation of administrators, and enabling administrative structures and processes that change the way citizens and administrators meet and interact.

XiaoHu Wang also searches for a better understanding of citizen participation. In "Assessing Public Participation in U.S. Cities," he reports the findings from a survey of chief administrative officers in U.S. cities with populations greater than 50,000. The officers were asked to identify the types of participatory methods citizens used, where and how much citizen participation occurred in their cities (both in terms of management and service functions), and the extent to which citizens were involved in decision making. He found that a wide variety of citizen participation mechanisms were employed, with a surprising 81.6 percent of the cities using the Internet to communicate with citizens. Some citizen participation appeared to occur in central management functions (e.g., budgeting, personnel, procurement), while a much higher level was reported in service functions (e.g., zoning and planning, parks and recreation, policing and public safety). Citizen participation in decision making did occur, but only about one-third of the respondents agreed or strongly agreed that their cities involved the public in identifying agency goals and objectives. The study also found various causes of increased citizen participation: size of government, political divisiveness, managers' willingness for accountability, and an interesting agenda. Citizen participation had the greatest impact in terms of its ability to meet public needs and build a consensus.

Eran Vigoda explores the relationship between citizen participation and public sector performance in his article "Administrative Agents of Democracy? A Structural Equation Modeling of the Relationship between Public-Sector Performance and Citizen Involvement." Drawing a sample from 260 households in a large Israeli city, he uses five alternative models to test the relationship between public administration performance and citizenship involvement. A structural equation modeling using LISREL VIII reveals the superiority of one model. However, the results were paradoxical, according to Vigoda. Public sector performance was negatively related to citizen involvement. As citizens became more satisfied with performance, they were less inclined to actively participate in political and community affairs. This finding suggests "citizens may become active only when some of their essential needs are not satisfied by public authorities" (p. 434).

NOTES

1. In addition, the congressional mandate "maximum feasible participation" was difficult for administrators to interpret since U.S. Congress could not agree on what participation meant and how it was to be implemented in practice (Cunningham 1972, Strange 1972a and 1972b).
2. See Aleshire (1972) for an overall assessment of community action and model cities programs.
3. See Roberts 2002a and 2002b for an extended discussion of dialogue and deliberation.

REFERENCES

Aleshire, R.A. 1972. "Power to the People: An Assessment of the Community Action and Model Cities Experience." *Public Administration Review* 32 (September): 428–39.
Arnstein, S.R. 1969. "A Ladder of Citizen Participation." *Journal of the American Institute of Planners* 35: 216–24.
———. 1972. "Maximum Feasible Manipulation." *Public Administration Review* 32 (September): 377–89.
Berry, J.M., K.E. Portney, and K. Thomson. (1989). "Empowering Citizens" in James L. Perry, ed., *Handbook of Public Administration*, pp. 208–23. San Francisco: Jossey-Bass.
Chess, C. 2000. "Evaluating Environmental Public Participation: Methodological Questions." *Journal of Environmental Planning and Management* 43(6): 769–82.
Cunningham, J.V. 1972. "Citizen Participation in Public Affairs." *Public Administration Review* 32 (October): 589–602.
Cupps, D.S. 1977. "Emerging Problems of Citizen Participation." *Public Administration Review* 37(5): 478–87.
Herman, J.L., L.L. Morris, and C.T. Fitz-Gibbon. 1987. *The Evaluator's Handbook*. Newbury Park, CA: Sage Publications.
Roberts, N.C. 2002a. "Dialogue and Accountability." *Public Administration Review* 62(6): 658–69.
———, ed. 2002b. *The Transformative Power of Dialogue*. New York: JAI Press.
Stecher, B.M., and W.A. Davis. 1987. *How to Focus an Evaluation*. Newbury Park: Sage Publications.
Strange, J.H. 1972a. "Citizen Participation in Community Action and Model Cities Programs." *Public Administration Review* 32 (October): 655–69.
———. 1972b. "The Impact of Citizen Participation on Public Administration." *Public Administration Review* 31 (September): 457–70.
Suchman, E.A. 1967. *Evaluative Research: Principles and Practice in Public Service & Social Action Programs*. New York: Russell Sage Foundation.
"The View from City Hall." 1972. *Public Administration Review* 32 (September): 390–401.
Weiss, C. 1972. *Evaluation Research*. Englewood Cliffs, NJ: Prentice-Hall.

CHAPTER 22

RESIDENT PARTICIPATION
Political Mobilization or Organizational Co-optation?

DAVID M. AUSTIN

PREFACE

A proposal for this study was developed in early 1966 because of "the central place which citizen participation occupies in the rapidly expanding program of the Office of Economic Opportunity." It was felt that a cross-community evaluative study of the Community Action Program experience could "provide an essential element in the further development of CAP's." In the late spring of 1969, as the final study report was being written, Community Action Programs were contracting and the new OEO Director would soon announce a shift in focus from providing extensive service programs through Community Action Agencies to limited experimental and demonstration programs. The talk in many target areas was not of "participation" but of "community control." The emphasis in this article therefore is not on the significance of the participation experience in 1967–68 for the administration of an on-going program; rather it is on the relation of that experience to the larger and continuing issues of citizen involvement and citizen action in a society that is both democratic and contentious.

THE STUDY ON COMMUNITY REPRESENTATION

The Study on Community Representation in Community Action Programs includes 20 Community Action Agencies (CAAs) in cities with populations from 50,000 to 800,000.[1] These 20 CAAs are a randomly selected sample, stratified by region:

(1) Northeast—Hartford, Providence, Waterbury, Scranton, and Wilkes-Barre; (2) Southeast—Durham, Charlotte, Chattanooga, and Huntington; (3) North Central—Cincinnati, Akron, Cleveland, Flint, Milwaukee, St. Paul, and Lorain; and (4) Southwest-West—San Jose (Santa Clara County), Laredo, San Antonio, and Phoenix. This sample was drawn from among a total group of 60 CAAs in cities in this population range which received OEO grants for local programs, other than Head Start, before July 1, 1965.

The information for the study was gathered from July 1967 to May 1968 by a staff of eight

From *Public Administration Review,* 32 (September 1972): 409–420. Copyright © 1972 by American Society for Public Administration. Reprinted with permission.

full-time researchers, each of whom had responsibility for two or three CAAs. The data-gathering procedures, which were similar for all CAAs, were designed by the central research staff at the Florence Heller School for Advanced Studies in Social Welfare, Brandeis University. The major groups of persons from whom information was obtained included CAA board members, CAA staff personnel including nonprofessional staff persons, presidents of CAA-sponsored target-area associations, and administrators of delegated programs.

The central focus of the study within its definition of participation includes both the activities of target-area members on the CAA policy board and the activities of those target-area associations and advisory groups that were recruited and sponsored by the CAA. Activities related to the direct operation of service programs by a neighborhood corporation are not included since this pattern was found in only a very few instances. The time frame is the period from March 1967 to July 1968, that is, from the date set for the implementation of the congressional requirement that one-third of the policy board be composed of target-area residents to the date when changes were to be made in CAA boards of directors by adding additional public officials to conform with requirements of the Green Amendment of 1967.

Before describing the findings about participation, there are a few general statements which should be made about the organizational context in these CAAs during the 1967-early 1968 period.

1. The basic organizational structure of the CAA, as established in 1964 or early 1965, was essentially the same across all 20 agencies. It was a nonprofit organization, independently incorporated, that resembled a combination of a voluntary social welfare agency and a community health and welfare planning council. Even where the mayor played an active role in its formation, the agency was established outside the political and administrative structure of local government.

2. The operational program of the CAA was tied to geographically defined target areas. In 18 of the 20 CAAs, the program included decentralized service centers and the provision of staff assistance to neighborhood associations or neighborhood advisory councils within these target areas.

3. Every CAA had at least a minimal level of resident participation structure. Residents of low-income target areas constituted at least one-third of the members of the CAA policy board by the first half of 1967. They attended the board meetings and they took part in the decisions made in these meetings. There were also one or more target area associations or advisory councils in every CAA that on occasion reviewed and made recommendations on program and policy issues within the CAA. These associations also served as neighborhood improvement associations and took action to accomplish specific improvements in the environment or in the services available in their neighborhood.

4. The initial structure of the CAA policy board took two forms. One was the administrative board, with up to 20 members, most of whom were delegates from operating agencies, both governmental and nongovernmental, directly concerned with a local war against poverty. The second was the representational board with from 20 to 50 members drawn from a wise variety of agencies and special interest groups that might provide endorsement and support for the CAA. With additional members added to the smaller boards in 1966 and 1967 in order to meet the federal requirement for one-third target-area representation, the differences in board size became less pronounced.

5. The CAA carried responsibility for administering a series of service programs. Most of the programs were funded by federal grants through Title II of the EOA, together with some Neighborhood Youth Corps programs under Title I. The 10 percent local matching effort originally required was largely provided through loans of facilities and in-kind services. The basic program pattern was set in 1965 and 1966. Most of the program operations were delegated to other organizations. Only 20 percent of the $45,850,000 in OEO program funds in 1964, 1965, and 1966 in these

Table 22.1

Characteristics of CAA Board Members, March 1968

	Private board members	Target area board members
White Anglo	80	41
Black	19	53
Male	88	60
Professional, managerial	91	28
Over 45	81	54
College graduate	85	22

Source: Appendix F, Final Report, "Study of Community Representation."
Note: All figures are percentages.

20 cities was used for programs directly administered by the CAA itself. Just under 50 percent went to boards of education, largely for Head Start programs, and just under 25 percent went to voluntary social welfare agencies. Less than 4 percent went to governmental agencies other than the board of education. A study by Stephen Rose of the Florence Heller School which classified these initial programs by program strategy, found that 93 percent of the program funds were committed to service strategy programs, 5 percent to income strategy programs, and 2 percent to institutional change strategies.[2]

GENERAL FINDINGS

The findings from the study fall into two groups. First, there are those general findings which deal with the similarities among the total group of 20 CAAs. Second, there are those findings which deal with the variations among the CAAs. The general findings, which are quite limited, are described first.

Target-Area Participation on the CAA Board

A number of writers have restricted the term participation to the involvement of target-area representatives on the CAA policy board, since this was the issue which attracted the greatest amount of public debate and around which formal legislative and administrative regulations were developed. By early 1967, all 20 CAA boards had at least one-third of their members selected by target-area residents. Most CAAs added target-area members to the board between July 1966 and March 1967. Only two CAAs had as many as one-half of their board members from target areas. In 18 of the 20 CAAs, target-area associations sponsored by the CAA either made the direct selection of the target-area board members or controlled the process by which they were selected. Participation of residents through target-area associations and participation through membership on the CAA board are thus closely related aspects of a common process.

The personal characteristics of the target-area representatives on each board differed markedly from those of the non-target-area members.

In March 1968 the pattern was between the target-area members and the nongovernmental or private, at-large members who constituted two-thirds of the non-target-area segment [see Table 22.1].

Two general findings are important about the role of target-area board members on the CAA board. First, three-fourths of the target-area representatives across all of the CAAs identified themselves as representatives of a specific constituency, either a target area or a target-area association. Only one-third of the non-target-area board members, including both private and governmental appointees, identified themselves as representing a specific constituency. Second, the attendance pattern of target-area representatives at board meetings was very similar to the attendance pattern of non-target-area members on the same boards. This held true for CAAs with a high level of attendance and for those where it was always difficult to get a quorum. The median attendance rate among all of the CAAs for target-area representatives was 56 percent, for non-target-area members, 52 percent.

Target-Area Participation Through Target-Area Associations

The 18 CAAs that had some form of neighborhood organizing program identified some 190 CAA-sponsored target-area associations in the spring of 1968. Information was obtained from the association president and/or staff advisor on 115 of these. The common features of these associations and their activities are as follows:

1. The associations were newly organized by CAA staff. Only 13 percent of the associations existed prior to January 1, 1965.
2. The criteria for membership was residence in a target area. Membership was not restricted to persons from households below the poverty level.
3. Eighty percent of the associations reported an active membership of less than 125 persons.
4. Women constituted half of the membership in 87 percent of associations, and in one-half of the associations women constituted two-thirds of the membership.
5. The associations had very limited operating resources. Only 15 percent of the associations had more than $500 annual income for their own expenses, and a majority had less than $100. The associations had no program or clerical personnel under their direct control, although CAA-funded personnel were assigned to such associations as staff advisors in 14 CAAs.
6. Association presidents and staff advisors identified the three most important action issues acted on by the association during 1967 and the action methods used in connection with those issues. The central finding was that the detailed pattern of issues, methods, and outcomes showed considerable similarity among associations within a particular city and considerable difference across the 20 CAAs. The differences are described below. However, there was a common pattern across all of the CAAs which had target-area associations in the general subjects of action issues. Fifty to 60 percent of all of the issues reported dealt with improvements in either the environment or in service programs other than those of the CAA in a single neighborhood. Ten percent of the issues involved neighborhood self-help projects including tot lots and credit unions. Ten percent involved program or organizational issues with the CAA, and ten percent organizational issues within the association. Ten percent involved issues at a citywide, county, state, or federal level. To a very substantial degree these target-area associations took on the characteristics of neighborhood improvement associations. Very few of the issues with which they were concerned had any direct relation to the economic aspects of the problem of poverty.

Target-Area Participation Through the Employment of Nonprofessionals

The study has little to say about participation through the employment of nonprofessionals because it became evident early in the study that they did not constitute an organized or systematic channel for affecting basic program or policy decisions at the level of the CAA. Fifteen of the CAAs had nonprofessionals on their own payroll, the other five having no program operations under their direct administration. The general characteristics of these nonprofessional employees were identified through 390 questionnaire responses covering two-thirds or more of these employees in 11 of the 15 CAAs. They were residents of target areas (86 percent), women (84 percent), over 35 (median age 38), without education beyond high school (68 percent) and black (67 percent). Less than a fifth reported membership in a civil rights organization (18 percent).

The data from the study suggest that the influence of nonprofessionals on the program of the CAA was primarily through individual actions. Most important was their own involvement with target-area associations. Over 80 percent reported that they met with associations as part of their job, and 56 percent reported that they were a member of such an association. A number of the nonprofessionals had been officers in their associations prior to employment by the CAA. Through the association, these nonprofessional staff members participated in discussions of CAA programs and had contact with target-area members of the CAA board. Seventy five percent of the CAA professional staff members interviewed in 18 CAAs also reported that nonprofessional staff members had made program suggestions leading to program changes or new programs, and cited at least one example of such a change to support their answer. On the other hand, only two instances of group action on any issue by nonprofessional staff members were identified across the total history of all 20 CAAs.

The Impact of Participation

The most general findings about the consequences of participation are negative findings:

1. Target-area residents had little or no part in the initial organization of the CAAs and in the decisions made about organizational structure at that point. These decisions fixed the basic structure of the agency, except for changes to include target-area representatives on the board, until at least 1968. The original ad hoc planning committees, created in 1964 in most instances, were composed of lay and professional representatives of the voluntary social welfare system, the board of education, and county and city government. The initial CAA boards of directors had a similar pattern—governmental representatives, 21 percent; nongovernmental representatives, 73 percent. Target-area participation was negligible in both groups. Demands from black spokesmen for inclusion of black middle-class organizational and professional leaders were acceded to in several cities and reflected in the membership of the initial board, so that there was a range of from 0 percent to 36 percent in black membership by early 1965 (median 19 percent). In the few cities in which groups of low-income persons or advocates of the poor protested the exclusion of explicitly low-income persons in the early development of the CAA, these protests were generally ignored.

2. Target-area residents across all CAAs had very little impact on the major program strategies and mix of programs carried out by the local CAA for several reasons. First, basic decisions about local program strategy, such as the choice between direct administration of programs and delegating programs to existing organizations, were made in 1964 and early 1965 before target-area groups or representatives had any role in program decision making. Second, when target-area residents began to take part in program reviews and budget decisions in 1967 both at the target-area level

and within the board, these CAAs, which were among the first to be funded in the nation, faced severe budget limitations in planning for 1967–68. Federal allocations were sharply below the level necessary for implementing the program proposals developed by CAAs across the country, and the funds available for the older CAAs were reduced to provide funds for more recently organized agencies. Target-area spokesmen did have a role in decisions about eliminating programs, but had little chance to get funds allocated to new types of programs. Third, the major decisions on programs in all CAAs were made outside of the local community. Congressional earmarking, promotion of national emphasis programs by OEO staff, and the establishment of a list of priorities by regional OEO staffs to be used in allocating local initiative funds to individual CAAs all sharply limited the scope of decisions available to the local CAA. Much of the decision making in 1967 and 1968 came down to a choice between applying or not applying for funds for particular packaged programs. Fourth, the complex annual funding system at the federal level with congressional delays in making allocations, reallocations near the end of the fiscal year, and shifting deadlines for funding applications made program planning within the CAA a frantic deadline-beating process. The CAA director was often the only local person with detailed information on funding opportunities and the only source of interpretation as to the federal requirements which applied. Target-area associations and CAA board members were fortunate if they were able to see a program proposal 48 hours in advance of the deadline for their action on it. In a system with so many constraints on program planning and program decisions at the level of the CAA, there would have been little opportunity for resident participation to have a significant influence on programming even under the most favorable local circumstances.

FINDINGS ON VARIATIONS AMONG CAAS

The inclusion of the requirement for participating in the OEO legislation and the implementing guidelines that were prepared by OEO administrators assumed that a single federal policy could produce a common pattern of outcomes in a wide variety of communities across the United States. The findings from this study support a contrary interpretation.

Though federal regulations resulted in a minimal provision of structure for resident participation in all CAAs, the operational pattern of participation which emerged was largely shaped by local circumstances and varied widely among communities. That is, variable local inputs were more powerful than a constant federal input in determining the content of resident participation in the operation of the local CAA.

A corollary to this finding is that there was more variation among CAAs than within CAAs in the operational pattern of participation. There was a common pattern in the behavior of all or most of the target-area representatives on the CAA board within the given community, and a similar pattern of consistency among CAA target-area associations. This made it possible to classify each CAA according to the general characteristics of its pattern of participation. The analysis of the differences among these patterns led to the identification of four types of participation patterns across the 20 CAAs in this study.

Organizational or Political Participation

Most of the national debate about participation has assumed that either in original intent, or by subsequent distortion, resident participation in CAAs was related to larger issues of political participation in planning, decision making, and the management of public programs in a democratic society. There is, however, a long tradition in social welfare and local government of establishing structures for citizen involvement and participation as an adjunct to the administrative operation of service organizations and planning agencies on an advisory basis only. A classic analysis of this procedure was made by Philip Selznick in his study of the voluntary associations sponsored by the TVA in its early years.[3] In this study he used the term *formal* co-optation to describe the process of creating citizen groups as adjuncts to a formal organization, with responsibility but no authority.

The findings of this study are that in 17 of the 20 CAAs the operational definition within the CAA of resident participation emphasized its organizational and advisory functions rather than its political functions. This is not entirely surprising when it is recognized that the most important local forces in the formation of the CAA structures (in these 20 areas) were the community welfare planning council, the board of education, and city hall. Among these 17 CAAs however, there was variation in the ways in which this organizational, advisory approach to resident participation actually worked out. The three major patterns which were found are *limited* participation, *active* participation, and *adversary* participation.

In three of the CAAs the operational definition of participation within the CAA did emphasize its political function. The CAA neighborhood organizing-community mobilization component was used to strengthen the political base of target-area residents in the pluralistic power conflicts of the larger community. However, as described below, the political definition of participation in these three CAAs was not a consequence of either the wording of the federal legislation nor the social philosophy of OEO staff. Rather it emerged as a consequence of specific local conditions.

Limited, Active, and Adversary Organizational Participation

Among the CAAs operating with an organizational definition of participation, there was a clear model implicit in the structural provisions for participation. Participation structure is established to provide orderly channels of communication and in response to formal federal requirements, not because of ideological or political philosophy. A systematic network of neighborhood councils is organized. These councils select target-area residents who will serve on the CAA board. These target-area board members in turn will report back to the target-area councils on issues being acted on by the CAA board. Target-area board members are expected to participate on the board as spokesmen of a single area.

Program and policy decisions are to be recommended to the CAA board on the basis of staff planning and analysis. They are to be voted on by the board with target-area members voting their convictions as individuals, similar to other board members. Most final decisions are expected to be unanimous. Authority for the administration of those decisions is to be clearly lodged in the management staff of the agency. Requests from neighborhoods for adaptations of CAA program or policy and requests made by target-area associations to other community agencies are to be based on an understanding that only minor modifications are possible within fixed frameworks of policy and budget. Target-area participation is expected to produce a variety of criticisms and suggestions that may be incorporated in the recommendations of the staff and in the decisions made by the non-target-area majority of board members, *at their discretion.* Target-area participation is also expected to establish an identity for the CAA within the target areas which will lead to greater utilization of CAA programs and public support for it as an organization.

This implicit model of organization participation was never realized in actual operation in the CAAs with *limited* participation. It was realized to an appreciable degree in those with *active* participation. In those CAAs with *adversary* participation, target-area interests were able to change an advisory process into a confrontation process within the CAA.

Limited Participation—There was a low level of participation by target-area board members in the affairs of the CAA board—low attendance (median 47 percent) and little participation in board discussions. In two CAAs there was no neighborhood organizing component, and in others such components did not get started until 1967. Where there were CAA-organized neighborhood associations, they worked only on short-term projects focused on improvements in their immediate area. They did not have advisory responsibility for target-area service programs. They were involved only sporadically in reviewing CAA program proposals. These associations did not become involved in public controversies around either internal organizational issues within the CAA or external issues involving other community service programs.

At least three factors appear to be important in this limited pattern of organization:

1. A stable social system and a stable pattern of power related to a lack of large-scale in-migration during the 1950s;
2. Absence of organized political or social movements which were agitating for community action to benefit low-income or ethnic minority citizens;
3. Definition by many citizens, including low-income citizens (as indicated by questionnaire responses of both target-area and non-target-area board members), that poverty is a consequence of individual failure rather than a result of discrimination or economic exploitation.

Active Participation—There was a comparatively high level of participation by individual target-area board members in the activities of the CAA board. They attended (median 73 percent), they participated in discussions, and individual target-area representatives initiated alternative proposals to those presented by the CAA staff. The target-area board members did not, however, operate as a distinct voting bloc in board decisions. When target-area members did push a particular issue, they were usually voted down. Target-area advisory councils had a formal advisory role in program planning within their target area, and individual councils on occasion did become involved in controversies with the CAA on budgets and program plans as they applied to a single area. These councils did not become involved in controversies around issues external to the CAA involving other community service operations.

In these CAAs, a decentralized pattern of service centers and/or target-area advisory groups was established early in the CAA operation. The principle of advisory participation was supported by social welfare leaders, municipal leaders, and by spokesmen from ethnically diverse, low-income neighborhoods with previous experience in protecting their self-interests in citywide programs. Consistent with previous local experience, target-area groups did not form a coalition either within the CAA board or across neighborhoods. Without a coalition, the result resembled a traditional pattern of ward politics, with target-area associations and representatives actively promoting the interests of their particular area in competition with other target areas. This resulted in the involvement of the representatives of target areas in a process of bargaining over details with central CAA staff and with the leaders of the CAA board, within basic policy and priority limits over which target-area representatives had no real control.

Adversary Participation—There was a high level of participation by target-area board members in board action. Attendance was high (median 73 percent), and individual target-area representatives frequently introduced and argued for alternatives to the program and budget proposals submitted by the staff. Target-area representatives operated consistently as a voting bloc on contested issues and were able to win on key issues against the opposition of CAA staff and board leadership. A coalition was also organized by target-area association leaders to support common demands on internal issues within the CAA involving budget cutbacks, program choices, and personnel appointments. This coalition and individual associations, however, did not become engaged directly in controversies involving other community service agencies.

In these cities the formation of the CAA coincided with the beginnings of an aggressive civil rights movement among black citizens. The target areas selected for CAA programs were predominantly black or Mexican-American residential areas. Requests were made during the formation of the CAA for substantial representation of black (or Mexican-American) interests. The initial response of elected public officials was based on their recognition that target-area participation can become a base of political power. Representation of target areas in strength on the CAA board and proposals for the organizing of neighborhood associations by CAA staff were resisted on the formal grounds that established governmental bodies and elected officials represent community interests, and that established organizations within target areas should be relied on for program guidance. The unofficial grounds for such objections were that such activities might contribute to the development of a dissident political faction among black citizens or Mexican-Americans.

Target-area response to this opposition became centered on efforts to force the CAA board to include target-area representation and to establish control by neighborhood groups over CAA program and budget decisions within target areas. Substantial representation of target-area interests on the CAA board was achieved by 1967 as a result of both local pressure and pressure from OEO regional staff to force compliance with the legislative requirements for maximum feasible participation. Target-area associations were organized, but with emphasis on their program advisory function.

With target-area representatives on the CAA board, there were a number of bitter conflicts within the CAA over organizational bylaws, allocations of OEO funds, personnel appointments, and also over demands that the CAA board take a position on controversies involving other community organizations. A coalition of neighborhood association leaders served as a caucus to define issues and to provide support for the target-area board representatives on contested issues. The victories which the target-area representatives won on particular issues were made possible by the assistance of some at-large board members and by the frequent absence of some of the public officials and at-large members who would oppose the proposals.

Participation Patterns and City Characteristics

Among the 17 CAAs with basically an organizational approach to participation, eight had limited participation, five had active participation, and four had adversary participation.

There was a pattern of association between certain characteristics of the central cities of the CAA service area and these participation patterns which holds for 12 of the 17 CAAs. The most important factor was city size. Six of eight CAAs with limited participation had central cities with under 150,000 population. Two of nine CAAs above this size had limited participation.

The next most important factor was the proportion of black residents in the central city. Four of the five CAAs with active participation, all of which had central city populations above 150,000, had less than 10 percent black citizens. Three of the four cities with adversary participation had central city populations over 150,000, and of these, two had 10 percent or more black citizens.

Of the five CAAs that are not fully consistent with this model, two of the larger cities with more than 10 percent black population had limited participation. These were Charlotte and Flint, cities with a cohesive power structure and without an aggressive civil rights movement in 1964. One larger city with more than a 10 percent black population, Cleveland, had active participation. It also had a well-developed black political (not just civil rights) movement by 1964–65. One small city, Laredo, and one large city, San Antonio, with large Mexican-American populations but small black populations, had CAAs with adversary participation. In San Antonio, however, the internal conflict was between an official Roman Catholic agency and the white, Anglo-Protestant majority on the CAA board over citywide control of CAA service programs. Target-area representatives served primarily as the advocates of the Catholic agency within the CAA board rather than as spokesmen for a distinctive target-area position.

Political Adversary Participation

In three of the CAAs: Durham, Hartford, and Cincinnati, there was the application of a political definition of participation. In each of these CAAs, most of the basic structure for organizational advisory participation was also present. However, this structure was utilized only to a limited degree, while major attention was placed on the mobilizing of resident associations as action groups around issues involving other community service organizations, both governmental and nongovernmental.

These three situations have certain important similarities. In each of the central cities of the service area, the proportion of black residents was over 10 percent. Two of the cities had more than 150,000 population. In Durham, which had less than 150,000, there were two features that were more characteristic of the larger cities than of other small cities. First, there was a black middle-class leadership group, with an independent financial base in insurance and banking, which had already taken legal action in the early 1960s on school segregation. Second, the key CAA staff member in the neighborhood organizing program component, who was not from Durham, had previous experience in the organization of black protest efforts in large urban areas (Chicago and Cleveland).

In all three situations, there was a demand from the leaders of black organizations for substantial black membership on the original CAA board. In all three cities, there was a pattern of conservative business leadership which had effective political control over the reform-style municipal government, and in particular over the office of the city manager.

In all three situations there was local initiative in developing an action program around the problems of poverty prior to the passage of the OEO legislation. The business leaders who were involved in these initial efforts accepted the demands for black membership, rather than face a public confrontation. The initial CAA board had between one-fourth and one-third of its members who were black citizens, though not low-income citizens. In each situation a staff position directly under the executive director was established early in the development of the CAA with responsibility for neighborhood community development. This staff position was filled by a black professional social worker.

Among these three CAAs there was considerable variety in target-area attendance at board meetings, ranging from 32 percent in Hartford to 88 percent in Durham. Target-area board members did participate consistently in board discussions and decisions. In all three situations there was substantial concurrence between the administrative staff of the CAA, the "liberal" at-large members, and the target-area representatives on the basic program within the CAA. Where there were disagreements and confrontations within the board, it was usually between the majority, including target-area representatives, and "conservative" at-large board members who were opposed to the program plans being proposed. In Durham these confrontations were rather frequent and stormy; in the other two cities they were infrequent. All three CAAs had an internal council or committee made up of target-area representatives to review program proposals before they came to the CAA board, although there were differences in the extent to which these councils were actively utilized by the administrative staff.

The overall program for the development of target-area associations was a responsibility of a central CAA staff person rather than being left to personnel in individual service centers. The target-area associations were not organized as program advisory groups. Within any one CAA the individual associations differed considerably in the extent to which they became involved in decisions about neighborhood or citywide CAA programs. The city target areas were restricted almost entirely to black residential areas (and Puerto Rican in Hartford). The membership and leadership in target-area associations was almost totally black.

Individual associations became involved in controversies involving the school board, city hall, housing authority, police department, and other major community institutions, as well as neighborhood business establishments. In Durham a legal challenge against the Housing Authority initiated by a target-area association eventually resulted in a Supreme Court decision restricting the right of the management to evict tenants without cause. This was one of the very few instances among all 20 of the CAAs in which a lawsuit was used as an action tactic by a target-area association. In nearly all of the public controversies in which individual associations became involved, the issue was defined as a conflict between black or Puerto Rican citizens and a white-controlled, traditional institution. While the issues usually involved low-income citizens, they were defined in ethnic terms much more than in class terms.

When the staff advisor and president of each target-area association was asked to list the three most important issues acted on by the association during 1967, the associations in these three cities stood out in two different ways. First, nearly every association reported at least three issues, and many reported more. Second, a smaller proportion of the three issues listed dealt with decisions within the CAA or problems within the association itself than in the case of other CAAs.

The tactics used to get action on these issues were also different. A higher proportion of the associations in these three cities reported that they had organized educational meetings on issues in its neighborhood, had circulated petitions, and had organized mass attendance at public hearings or committee meetings. Three of the associations in Hartford and Cincinnati reported that they had used such pressure tactics as picketing or mass demonstrations on at least one issue, while in Durham eight associations reported use of such tactics. While their use of such tactics falls far short of the record of more current radical groups, it is also a much more militant pattern than that of the seven CAAs in which there were either no neighborhood associations (two) or in which no association reported any instance of the use of mass pressure.

The leaders of the target-area associations in these three situations formed an independent action coalition across the several target areas. The formation of this coalition was encouraged by staff from the CAA, but the agency provided no formal assistance to it either financially or through the assignment of staff personnel. In each city this coalition became a substantial force in contests between black residents and official institutions. These contests involved such items as the location of a new public housing project within a black ghetto, the membership of a Model Cities board, and police tactics during a major community disturbance. During 1967 and early 1968 these coalitions became major centers of leadership in the mobilization of black citizens as an adversary force in the political system of their cities, quite independently of the CAA. In each city this coalition was successful in forcing at least a public agency to take action on a policy or program affecting low-income citizens.[4]

In all three situations, business leaders, both on and off the board, and the city manager became more and more critical of the CAA during 1967 and early 1968. In the case of Durham and Cincinnati, congressmen from the state made major public attacks on the agency. In these two CAAs the key staff person in the political participation thrust of the agency left just before he would have been forced out.

CONCLUSIONS

The findings in the Study of Community Representation point to general conclusions in three areas. First, the relation of the official federal policy on resident participation to the patterns of participation actually found in local CAAs. Second, the impact of resident participation within the local community. Third, the relation of resident participation under OEO to the general issue of citizen participation in a democratic society.

The discussions within the Task Force on Poverty, the provisions in the federal legislation, and the guidelines written around those provisions had only minimal effect in producing any uniform pattern of resident participation across these 20 agencies. There were no formal political or administrative links and few ideological links between the framers of the federal legislation and those individuals who actually developed the detailed plans for the individual Community Action Agency in each locality. The lack of agreement at the federal level about the meaning of participation added to this problem, but it would have existed even with a much clearer rationale at the federal level.

While the federal program provided some sanctions that could be used to enforce a minimum level of compliance with the structural requirements for participation, it provided few rewards for developing an active pattern of participation. The provisions of the law did establish a principle which could be used by local groups that were already mobilized to support their demands for inclusion of low-income citizens in decision making. Where local interests were not mobilized, the existence of the federal regulations did not prevent a very limited development of participation. To identify the provisions for target-area membership on CAA boards as a substantial step forward in public policy only serves to highlight how thoroughly the model of community decision making by governmental and nongovernmental elites has been rationalized as both right and proper.

Faced with the unevenness of actual resident participation across the country, the response of OEO administrators was to develop a series of guidelines which attempted to specify in more detail the requirements for participation, and also set limits on adversary patterns of participation. While these guidelines had some impact on individual local agencies, it is not all clear that they had any effect in reducing the total amount of variation among CAAs. This study raises a question as to whether federal regulations embodying sanctions but not rewards and that deal with controversial subjects in federally supported locally administered programs can ever bring about consistent and substantive changes in local practices unless supported by organized pressure groups and/or the legal compulsion of a court order.

Within the local community there was a very limited impact from resident participation, particularly in the two-thirds of the situations in which there was neither an organizational adversary pattern or a political adversary pattern in participation. As already pointed out, the basic organizational structure and the basic pattern of service programs at the local level was set before resident participation became a significant factor in most communities. In the development of service programs, the community action agency, as a whole, had limited ability to make significant decisions as a consequence of federal legislative and administrative policies on program allocations and emphases. The general practice of delegating the administration of service programs to existing agencies further reduced the possibilities of significant impact by target-area representatives.

The standard pattern of organizing inclusive neighborhood improvement associations as adjuncts to individual target-area service programs was highly congruent with the pattern of formal co-optation that emerged in at least two-thirds of the CAAs. The reports on the individual agencies suggest that this pattern was adopted, not so much in a deliberate effort to create an image of citizen action rather than the substance of it, but because this was the traditional and accepted pattern within social welfare.

The situations which are an exception to the general finding of limited impact from resident participation are those where the issue of racial confrontation between black citizens and white-controlled institutions was already an issue within the community and where this confrontation either shaped the nature of the issues within the CAA or served to define the thrust of the community mobilization program within the CAA. It is of interest that in the three situations in which a political pattern of resident participation did develop, the key staff person within the CAA in shaping this part of the CAA operation was a professional social worker.

Among the 20 CAAs, it is in those in which there was some form of adversary participation that there appears to have been a link between resident action and changes in institutions outside the CAA. In those with an organizational adversary pattern of participation, this occurred primarily as a result of pressure on the CAA board to take action in a local controversy. In the political adversary CAAs it was generally a consequence of direct action by target-area associations and the coalition of such associations. At best, these impacts were few in number and in most instances limited in scope.

While detailed information is not available about local developments after mid-1968, the information that is available suggests three types of changes. First, that the degree of conflict within the agencies where there had been an organizational adversary pattern declined as some greater degree of trust among target-area and non-target-area interests emerged within the agency. Second, the CAAs in which there was a pattern of political adversary participation became less aggressive in their organizing activities as the price for continued survival. Third, the political and social movements among black citizens that were strengthened through adversary patterns of participation were able to maintain those gains and move forward on an independent basis.

The long-range question is whether resident participation under OEO had any long-range impact on the closed organizational structures, both governmental and nongovernmental, which had developed in American urban areas over the decades of the 1900s. The answers to that question that are suggested by this study do not take into account the experiences with resident participation in the largest cities such as New York, Chicago, Los Angeles, Detroit, and Philadelphia. However, there is not, to my knowledge, any material from those cities to contradict the general answers suggested by this study.

The first answer is that resident participation in the Community Action Agency did *not* institutionalize, as an ongoing operational process, a broadly decentralized process of citizen participation in organizational decision making. It did not create participatory democracy around significant decision making or establish popular sovereignty over the operation of a set of service programs. To a substantial degree the structure of participation and the operation of participation was built around a model of advisory and co-opted participation within the operating constraints of a rather traditional model of the nongovernmental social welfare service agency. If the dynamic of citizen mobilization around the issue of black citizens versus white establishment is separated out, then it is even clearer that the operation of resident participation did not significantly extend the practice of broadly based citizen participation in decision making about public issues and public programs.

The second answer is that the experience of resident participation in the employment of nonprofessional citizen-generalists for the operation of public programs had limited long-range significance. Neighborhood residents without any college education were employed in special job classifications. They were, in general, given little or no specialized training within the agency, and they had little opportunity for upward occupational mobility within the CAA. The employment of nonprofessionals occurred primarily because federal funds were earmarked for that purpose, not as a result of a deliberate creation of an occupational career ladder either within the CAA itself or in the programs delegated to other agencies. With any disappearance of such federal funds, it appeared likely that the job positions would also disappear.

Men and women with some college education who were residents of target areas were employed in middle-range positions that were identified as being part of the "professional" staff system. Most of these persons were black, Puerto Rican, or Mexican-American, and may have had few opportunities for employment in comparable positions in existing agencies. However, once employed by the agency, they either remained for a short time and then moved into a job in a different setting, or they adopted for themselves the professional-technical model of occupations and moved towards specialized civil service appointments or specialized education at the college or graduate level.

These employment positions were important entry jobs for these individuals, but their presence in the agency did not substantially change the general model of seeking technical specialists as top staff persons in the administration of community service programs. If anything, the experience in the CAAs reinforced the model that the route to career advancement and job security is through formal education including graduate professional education rather than through on-the-job training, seniority, and steady promotion within an agency.

The third answer is that in the contest between newly empowered groups of citizens and entrenched political and civic leaders, resident participation did have a significant impact in approximately one-third of the CAAs studied. In these instances, the recruitment and training of young black men and women as staff members, many of whom were also active in political and social movements outside the CAA, the experience of target-area leaders in participating on the CAA board, and the process of community mobilization and conflict in target areas strengthened the organizational network and leadership resources among black citizens. Many of these political gains appear to have continued, although few basic issues in education, housing, employment, urban redevelopment, police practices, etc., have yet been resolved to the satisfaction of black citizens. In the cities in which the dominant target-area group was Mexican-American rather than black, a similar contribution appears to have been made, although the pattern of mobilization appears to lag behind the mobilization in cities with substantial black populations.

It is not yet clear, however, whether the contribution of resident participation to the mobilization and organization of black citizens as a political force will contribute to a general broadening of citizen participation in public decision making. It may only result in limited changes in the pattern of what William Gamson has called "stable nonrepresentation" through the empowering of one new set of pluralistic interests which are also represented by and participate through an elite leadership structure not unlike that of other political forces in our society.[5]

AUTHOR'S NOTE

This article presents findings from the Study of Community Representation in Community Action Agencies, conducted by the Florence Heller Graduate School.

NOTES

1. A detailed description of the Study of Community Representation and its findings is included in reports 1–5 available from the Florence Heller Graduate School for Advanced Studies in Social Welfare, Brandeis University. Report No. 5, in particular, deals with the four distinct patterns of participation which are described later in this article.

2. Stephen M. Rose, "Community Action Programs: The Relationship Between Initial Conception of a Poverty Problem Derived Intervention Strategy, and Program Implementation," unpublished doctoral dissertation, 1970, Florence Heller Graduate School for Advanced Studies in Social Welfare, Brandeis University.

3. Philip Selznick, *TVA and the Grass-Roots: A Study in the Sociology of Formal Organizations.* (New York: Harper and Row Publishers, 1966), chapter VII, "The Voluntary Association at the End Point of Administration," pp. 217–248.

4. Barrs Reitzel and Association, Inc. *Community Action and Institutional Changes,* (Springfield, VA.: Clearinghouse for Federal, Scientific and Technical Information, 1969). Fifty target areas were studied. "In order to summarize the possible multiple relations between community political action, political opinions, and institutional change, target areas were grouped according to the similarity of their militant acts and political alliances. . . . Three groups of communities have been formed. . . . Group III contains eight highly mobilized, politicized and alienated communities. Militant activity is higher on all levels. Young, black, large very active organizations are present. Alliances proliferate, and CAP's place heavy emphasis on community organization. *In this politically hyperactive climate high degrees of institutional change occur in all sectors*" [emphasis added], pp. 1–14.

5. William A. Gamson, "Stable Unrepresentation in American Society," *American Behavioral Scientist,* No. 2 (November–December 1968).

CHAPTER 23

CITIZEN PARTICIPATION IN THE PHILADELPHIA MODEL CITIES PROGRAM
Retrospect and Prospect

ERASMUS KLOMAN

The foregoing scenarios have presented two versions of a single chain of events as seen through the eyes of two sets of beholders. The sharp divergence in the two interpretations of what happened stems from the difference in the vantage point and the differing preconceptions of the two groups of participants. Many other versions could be written from other viewpoints. Many other facets of the story could be displayed. These two accounts point up the width of the gulf separating two viewpoints and the extreme difficulty of reconciling them.

The following discussion presents a retrospective evaluation of the issues and an appraisal of the future prospects for citizen participation in the Philadelphia Model Cities Program. The main purpose of this discussion is not to assess or make judgments on the validity of one or another version. What matters far more than disputes over past history is the ability to learn from the past and to transfer that learning experience to the future. Only if the lessons of the past can be applied to directing the program in the future will programs such as Model Cities begin to achieve their objectives and provide social benefits for the citizenry they seek to reach. Out of a difficult and frustrating experience have come some gains and some losses for the residents of the Model Cities community of North Philadelphia. How can they build on the gains while minimizing the losses in the work to which they have already devoted considerable effort?

PHILADELPHIA'S APPROACH TO CITIZEN PARTICIPATION

Philadelphia entered into the planning for the Model Cities Program six years ago with a belief shared by both officials of City Hall and citizens of the model neighborhood that citizen participation would be critical to the success of the experiment. The program was heralded as a significant breakthrough offering the residents of inner-city poverty areas a new opportunity to help them improve their futures. While officialdom and the new spokesmen for the citizenry may not have seen eye to eye on what participation meant in practice, each began with the belief that community

From *Public Administration Review,* 32 (September 1972): 402–408. Copyright © 1972 by American Society for Public Administration. Reprinted with permission.

involvement was essential to the program's success and each recognized that the program would be a failure unless it produced significant institutional change. In Washington and in other communities the Philadelphia model was widely cited as an example of the fulfillment of the intent of the United States Congress and HUD to establish inner-city programs in which citizens would participate in the reordering of local community political and economic systems no longer serving the interests of inner-city inhabitants.

As in other cities receiving Model Cities planning grants, so in Philadelphia the citizen participation concept aroused considerable interest and anticipation in deep poverty communities which had all but abandoned hope of anything more than handouts from the establishment. Signals from top levels of HUD in Washington seemed to indicate that this was to be a program aimed at treating causes rather than symptoms and that it would help the urban poor and disadvantaged to help themselves. It appeared that HUD sought to create at the grass-roots levels new institutional forms engaging the loyalties of the residents of poverty areas and helping them pull together. Washington, it seemed, was prepared to sanction the setting up of community associations with quasi-governmental authority. The people were to be involved in the decision-making process. Citizens were to have the "right to negotiate" with city administrations. In the words of one of the basic HUD instructions setting out requirements for a Model Cities Program, "citizen participation called for . . . some form of organizational structure, existing or newly established, which embodies neighborhood residents in the process of policy and program planning and program implementation and operation."

These were bold and heady ideas. They intrigued not only certain leadership elements representing the poor but also those in both public and private social agencies who wanted to take meaningful action to deal with the critical problems of urban poverty. Out of this enthusiasm grew the Philadelphia approach to Model Cities. Whatever may have been the flaws in the early plans, they entailed full commitment to citizen participation and to innovation. The idea that there could be an effective working partnership between elected officials and representatives of local communities took hold on both sides.

The implementation of the basic concept suffered gravely from confusion at HUD concerning the meaning of citizen participation. HUD and the administration in Washington had very real problems in providing definitive language to spell out exactly how much authority and power should rest in the hands of citizen groups. Within the Office of Economic Opportunity, citizen participation had already sparked heated controversy over where the line should be drawn between participation and control. Different factions within HUD espoused different views, and neither faction was prepared to yield to the other. To avoid confronting the basic issue head-on, some HUD spokesmen offered the argument that rigid federal guidelines should be avoided for fear they would stymie innovation at the community level. Compromising left citizen participation as a matter for local interpretation. HUD did specify that ultimate program control rested with elected officials, but there were no clear guidelines on how far citizen participation could go up to this point. Until the spring of 1969, City Hall in Philadelphia did nothing to clear the air. It was running scared. It feared to tell the citizen groups that the city had no intention of surrendering ultimate control and decision-making power to the people.

At the community level, people tended to hear whatever interpretation of citizen participation most suited their own outlook. The regional HUD office, headquartered in Philadelphia, favored a liberal interpretation of citizen participation and encouraged the city to provide funds for the Area Wide Council (AWC) to permit recruiting and training professional staff to organize and train area residents. Philadelphia HUD staff, in effect, allied themselves with the AWC as adversaries vs. City Hall.

RACIAL DIVISIONS COME TO THE FORE

The Area Wide Council had begun to take form in the North City area before Philadelphia started planning for the Model Cities Program. AWC had deep roots in the North City and many of its board and officers were area residents. It began as an organization widely representative of the many different ethnic groups living in the North City area. Blacks and Puerto Ricans played leading roles from the beginning, but many white residents were active in the planning activities of the hubs representing their local neighborhoods and in the board for the overall organization. The crossover of racial lines in a communitywide citizens self-improvement endeavor was certainly one of the more hopeful aspects of the AWC in its early stages. A color-blind approach to community development appealed to wide segments of the greater Philadelphia area, particularly white liberals and the leadership of social welfare and civic groups. The history of the AWC, however, revolves in large part around racial polarization and the increasing influence of minority militants.

The question of what is cause and what is effect can be legitimately raised at this point. Was the increasing influence of minority militants a result of environmental change, or did the militants take hold of a situation and create their own environment? The truth probably lies somewhere in between. The facts are that an organization originating as a multiracial representative group with wide involvement of community leaders came to be dominated by its professional staff and particularly its executive director. In accordance with specific instructions from City Hall, the AWC leaders recruited many staff members from outside the model neighborhood. In comparison with a zealous and highly partisan professional staff, the large and unwieldy AWC board of 96 came to have a role of diminishing significance. Despite a standing rule that decisions affecting the organization were to be taken only by the board or its subcommittees, power gravitated to the staff. From then on, the board role appreciably diminished. Within the staff, moreover, there was very little delegation or decentralization. At the same time, the organization came to focus almost exclusively on the problems of black and Puerto Rican minorities in the model neighborhood. This basic change in orientation was partly a reflection of the polarization process occurring in Philadelphia at the time and partly a function of the outlook and views of AWC professional staff as supported by the HUD regional office in Philadelphia.

Gradually emerging under these auspices was a three-part set of goals which came to govern all AWC efforts. These goals were to: (1) redistribute the balance of power between government and community; (2) reorganize institutions, in both the public and private sector, which had failed to serve the community; and (3) reorient the values of citizens in the model neighborhoods as a means of reinforcing and sustaining the total effort.

Although these goals were never formally publicized outside of AWC circles, they were openly announced in AWC meetings with Philadelphia Model City administration staff. While some Model Cities professionals found themselves in sympathy with these objectives, others undoubtedly considered them threatening and beyond the scope and intent of Model Cities legislation. A city administration dependent on political support cannot afford to ignore any community movement which seeks to organize large numbers of people to effect basic change in the power structure. The AWC tried to avoid becoming involved in party political struggles, but the mayor and his advisors could readily see that, if the Area Wide Council were to become a rallying point for North City residents, it would pose a real threat to the Democratic Party of Philadelphia. Fearing the challenge to its power, the city administration employed high-handed tactics, such as holding up on funding and the cancellation of contracts, which caused the citizens groups to question the sincerity and good faith of municipal government.

THE MAYOR AND CITY HALL

On the other hand, as much as any political leader can do so, the mayor tried to avoid the injection of partisan politics into the administration of the program. He consciously maintained a distance between himself and the program's administrators. In the early phases of the program, in fact, he took little or no personal interest in it. Even later, he tended to become personally involved only when its troubles reached the crisis point, as when a change in administrator had to be made. Almost instinctively, however, the mayor, as the leader of a political party, viewed Model Cities Programs in terms of what they could accomplish politically more than in terms of their intrinsic merit. He demonstrated the slant in his perception of the program in his first two appointments of program administrators. Whatever their strengths and capabilities, neither of these appointees had the kinds of background, orientation, and personality which would assure good communications with their constituents in the Model Cities neighborhoods. Both, it should be noted also, were white.

The mayor's persistence in designating new administrators without consulting AWC leadership was another indication of a certain aloofness and unawareness of the true spirit of the program. Finally, the image of the mayor and his administration that began to emerge in an increasingly hostile racial environment was hardly likely to arouse sympathetic understanding among blacks and other minorities who represented a major portion of the city's urban poor. This image was a decidedly negative factor in City Hall-AWC relationships. Any appointee of the mayor was almost automatically suspect in the eyes of minority groups in North Philadelphia, particularly when AWC had been denied any role in his selection.

The Model Cities administration of Philadelphia found itself in a difficult middleman position. Washington insisted that, in order to qualify for Model Cities grants, applications had to be prepared in consultation with, and have the full support of, the citizens groups. Relatively few other cities in the United States had citizens groups which had organized as highly and formulated goals as precisely as the AWC. Moreover, as previously noted, the HUD regional office in Philadelphia had become closely involved in a partisan relationship with the AWC, counseling the staff on how to out-maneuver City Hall.

NOVEMBER 1967 SCHOOL DEMONSTRATION

The incident of the school demonstration of November 1967 probably marks the point at which City Hall doubts about the feasibility of working with the Area Wide Council culminated in the firm conviction that the AWC could not be trusted. An AWC staff member, who served as an assistant field work director, was primarily responsible for the AWC involvement in the incident. He made AWC mimeograph equipment available for duplicating protest leaflets. Having done so, he was fully supported by the AWC executive director. For the two years in which he served on the AWC staff, this AWC staff member continued to engage in such non-AWC organizational activities seeking to help people of the community organize effectively on important civil rights issues. He and his followers represented a relatively small, but highly visible, element of the Area Wide Council. It was the leadership of this element that City Hall feared most and sought unsuccessfully to secure their dismissal from the organization. The executive director and his associates would not yield to City Hall pressure.

After the November 1967 incident, City Hall came increasingly to suspect that the Area Wide Council wanted a good deal more than "equality" in a partnership, that "irresponsible" elements were taking over the organization, and that the partnership principle was too much of a threat to city control. Whether consciously or unconsciously, City Hall policy became a matter of alternating between compliance with HUD grant requirements to meet each new Model Cities deadline and, once a new grant had been awarded, maintaining pressure on the AWC. The pressure took the form of cutting back on the contract, calling for a reduction in staff or making demands for redirection of AWC activities.

CHANGING SIGNALS FROM WASHINGTON

Only in the spring of 1969, after it was apparent that the new Republican administration of Richard M. Nixon in Washington was changing signals and that the Philadelphia grant would be secure, did City Hall make a clear declaration of its intent regarding the limits of citizen participation. In fact, the difficulties City Hall was having with the Area Wide Council were one of the factors taken into account in HUD's redefining of citizen participation. But this redefinition process took place *after* HUD had already specified in written instructions that involvement of citizens in the planning and implementation of programs was a requirement of all Model Cities Programs.

If Philadelphia's city administration was not an example of enlightened democracy at work in the service of its citizens, it was in the company of many other large metropolitan governments. All faced daily crises in their efforts to survive. The problems of urban government had figured significantly in the 1968 elections, and the Nixon administration in Washington was not without its own ideas on the nature and cause of urban problems and how to administer the programs seeking to deal with them.

Not long after the changeover in Washington, it became clear that the Republicans were not going to permit citizen participation the same latitude or the same extent of control as the previous administration. The new HUD leadership was receiving too many reports of trouble from "over-zealous" citizen groups threatening the position of city government to allow the policy direction of the past to go unchanged. As a creature of a Democratic administration, the Model Cities Program was not one of the most welcome members of the new Republican household. Serious consideration was given to discontinuing the program, but that suggestion was dropped, partly because of the political liabilities it would have entailed. The program was to be continued, but on sufferance, and without the highly controversial and potentially "dangerous" turnover of government powers to other citizen representation which had not been duly elected. Philadelphia's City Hall welcomed the signs of change at the national level.

HUD decided to limit the extent of citizen participation in all Model Cities Programs to advisory roles, while specifying that control would remain in the hands of elected officials. The application of this guideline to Philadelphia resulted in the rejection of the proposal for Area Wide Council-controlled corporations to serve as the principal vehicles for carrying out the Model Cities Program. City Hall used this as a means of reasserting its control of the program. It was now in a position to be able to dictate terms to the Area Wide Council in the expectation that they would accept the new conditions rather than risking the loss of further contract funding.

AWC TAKES ITS CASE TO COURT

The AWC, however, felt that too much principle was at stake to accept the new terms. It was convinced of the rightness of its cause, and took its case to the courts. The first decision, at the District Court level, went against the Area Wide Council. On appeal to the Circuit Court, however, AWC won a significant legal battle against both the city and HUD. The Circuit Court opinion ruled that the city had not adequately consulted with the AWC in preparing the June 1969 submission to HUD and that HUD had violated the Model Cities Act in accepting that proposal. After thus reversing the lower court, the Circuit Court remanded the case back to the District judge for further hearings and court action.

At the District level the case went back to the judge issuing the original decision. The AWC had never expected that its case would obtain favorable opinion at this level, believing that the judge was too closely associated with City Hall. Members were therefore not surprised when, in July 1971, the District Court for the second time ruled against the AWC and in favor of the city. Again, the AWC appealed to the Circuit Court.

The issues raised in the appeal, like those asserted when the suit was initiated, were that citizen participation is an important requirement of the law establishing the Model Cities Program, and that HUD and the City of Philadelphia violated this requirement when they amended the basic strategy of the Philadelphia Model Cities Program without the participation of the citizens of the target area. The suit contended that the District Court failed to deal with the basic questions with which it had been charged by the Circuit Court. It requested reinstatement of the Area Wide Council as the citizen participation organization, and agreement by the city to enter into a new contract with the new AWC which would be reconstituted to incorporate the existing citizens organization.

The suit held major implications for the entire issue of citizen participation in the national Model Cities Program. It addressed the basic questions of the real meaning of citizen participation and whether the apparent shift in interpretation on the part of HUD could be defended on legal grounds.

COURT UPHOLDS AWC

In what may become a landmark decision, delivered in February 1972, the Third Circuit Court of Appeals for the second time reversed the District Court, upholding the Area Wide Council and calling for its reinstatement as the citizen participation organization for the Philadelphia Model Cities Program. The AWC was instructed to negotiate in good faith with the existing citizen structure in order to integrate the structure into the AWC. Although HUD and the city sought to take the case before the Supreme Court, the latter refused the appeal and the Circuit Court opinion stands.

After the lapse of two and a half years since the termination of the AWC contract with the city administration, AWC had survived only as a skeletal organization. In fact, its main purpose had been to remain in existence to pursue its case in the courts and be revived in the event of victory. The task of reforming the organization and breathing new life into it remains formidable. Still another change of Philadelphia's Model Cities horses in mid-stream will not be easy, and it is too soon to predict the practical consequences of the Philadelphia decision in terms of impact on the content of the Model Cities Program. Although the Area Wide Council can take satisfaction in being upheld by the American judicial system, it also recognizes that it has lost valuable time in the critical years of a new program. City Hall's Model Cities administration, which had totally severed connections with the remnants of the Area Wide Council, will find it difficult at best to resume a relationship. The Circuit Court judges, in their opinion, expressed the hope that "the passage of time may have sweetened the minds of the parties to this suit." That remains to be seen.

From a juridical viewpoint, the initial concept of citizen participation as incorporated in the Philadelphia Model Cities Program has been sustained, at least for the area in the jurisdiction of the Third Circuit Courts. The opportunity to test this important finding on a wider basis was denied when the Supreme Court refused to hear an appeal which the City of Philadelphia sought to present. HUD has as yet to issue a public statement on the implications of the Philadelphia decision for the national programs. Other similar cases, however, are pending at lower court levels.

ASSESSING THE IMPACT

In comparison with the dimensions of the national task of rehabilitating the inner cities of the nation's major metropolitan areas, the levels of total Model Cities expenditures are modest. Moreover the programs instituted under Model Cities auspices have been running for only brief periods of time. Finally, the system for evaluation of program effectiveness has as yet to be fully applied. Nonetheless, it is reasonable to ask in what way have the people of a model neighborhood, such as North Philadelphia, gained, and how can those gains be measured in relation to the human resources invested?

The significant measures of gains and losses of Philadelphia's North City residents are not to be found in looking at individual programs or statistics on people receiving help, but rather on the broader issue of the meaning of citizen participation. For a brief period, while the Model Cities Program was in its preliminary phases, the officials of City Hall and the Area Wide Council were working together with an apparent understanding of what was meant by citizen participation. Whether the idea ever could have worked in practice may have to remain forever a matter of speculation. If there were other more conclusive examples in other cities of successful experiments, there might be sounder grounds for a conjecture on the possibility of a success story in Philadelphia. What seems so unfortunate in this instance is that the chance for a very worthwhile experiment in citizen participation was abandoned, partly because of the basic insecurity and the tendency to temporize within City Hall and partly because the leadership of the citizens organization was unwilling to continue to work within the system.

The neighborhood councils which displaced the hubs of the AWC were based on a concept which limited citizen participation to an advisory role. That meant taking part in the planning of community programs, and, when those programs were funded through their organization, monitoring the programs to see that they were accomplishing what was intended. Although this role represented a great deal less in the way of operational authority and management control than was first envisaged by the Area Wide Council, it still put more potential power at the grassroots level than was there before the Model Cities Program was initiated.

At first, there seemed to have been little community opposition to the modified concept of citizen participation. Several reasons explain why it was not too difficult to make a transition from one to another concept. The Area Wide Council, though it had started out with wide community support, had stirred up so much controversy and internal friction that some North City residents had no regrets in seeing its departure from the scene. Secondly, the current Model Cities administrator has proven an extremely competent organizer and has won wide respect for the firmness of her conviction and her ability to remain on top of the situation. The people of the North City area may have needed the kind of success symbol she provided. In any event, many seemed to accept what she represents, and the North City area was reorganized into 16 neighborhood councils with a minimum of excitement and turbulence.

Eventually, however, a number of the new councils came into conflict with City Hall's direction of the program. In several instances representatives of the Black Panthers or other militant groups were elected to chairmen or other positions. Where strong anti-white attitudes prevail in various neighborhoods, there is hostility and resentment against City Hall and a Model Cities administrator who is regarded as autocratic and dictatorial. Two councils filed suits against the city alleging that there has been inadequate citizen participation in development of their programs.

The actual programs initiated under Model Cities have had very little tangible or physical impact. A walk through the model neighborhood reveals slight visible evidence of rehabilitation. Most of the Model Cities Programs under way are institutional and social, not physical. Philadelphia is sometimes compared favorably with most other Model Cities Programs around the nation. Perhaps it could be argued that, out of the crisis and conflict of the early Model Cities years, has come a certain creativity. However, some elements of the model community would contend that the Model Cities Program as it has been administered to date represents nothing innovative, but simply more game playing by City Hall.

While the city was the first to renege on its partnership with the citizens, HUD in Washington undermined the chance for significant citizen participation with the changes it initiated early in 1969. Neither HUD nor the city displayed much concern for the impact of their actions on the motivation of their former citizen partners. It was as if people could be turned on and off like water from a tap. But people, unlike water, have memories. They do not forget unfulfilled promises. The effort to change signals on the meaning of citizen participation gave Model Cities residents one more reason to add to their already lengthy list of doubts concerning the commitment of government of whatever level to help them improve their condition. Many of the minority group representatives who worked in the Model Cities Program in Philadelphia remain skeptical as to whether HUD has ever viewed the program as anything but a diversionary tactic or a public relations effort.

TRANSFERRING THE LEARNING EXPERIENCE

The experiment, however, was certainly not without some very significant benefits. Perhaps the most important objective which any citizen participation program can hope to achieve is the education and training of citizens to work in community action programs and to deal effectively with their local government. The people who worked for the Area Wide Council, whether as staff, board members, field workers, or members of the hub organizations, all learned a great deal in the way of very practical lessons. Most of the AWC personnel were members of minority groups either black or Puerto Rican, and they gained a knowledge of the politics of bureaucracy which could serve them well in the future. Many have gone on to use that experience in the political arena. The notable stepping up of black community political activity must be regarded as one of the more hopeful signs on Philadelphia's political horizons.

An outsider looking back at the Philadelphia Model Cities experience might be inclined to think that the AWC personnel would have emerged with such bitter memories that they would no longer be able to work effectively within the system. But that is not the way it worked in Philadelphia. Of course, there is a serious residue of bitterness and racial mistrust, but the bitterness has not prevented many former AWC personnel from continuing to work in constructive ways for their cause. While the AWC professional staff has largely dispersed to other areas than Philadelphia, many of the AWC community-level personnel have continued to work in the ongoing Model Cities Program. Some of the former board members have joined the new neighborhood councils. They provided much-needed continuity to the program. The former executive director of the AWC now serves on the faculty of the University of Pennsylvania School of Social Work and on the technical staff of the City Planning Commission, while also being actively engaged in a number of important civic organizations.

Overshadowing the entire issue of the future of the Philadelphia program is a cloud of uncertainty about the future of the national Model Cities Program. Unless the national program receives vigorous leadership and real commitment from both federal and city governments, it has little chance of realizing the potential for which it was once heralded. It is unfortunate that neither Philadelphia nor any other Model Cities Program stands out as show-window example of the success of the program. But the federal government should look to its own record of policy making and implementation for some causes of failure.

Whatever chance the program had to succeed, it depended on creating a basis for hope among the residents of the model neighborhoods that through citizen participation they would become an effective part of the process by which the quality of life in the inner cities was to be improved. Equivocation and backtracking on the part of HUD and the administration in Washington have done little to nourish hope among the men, women, and children whom the program was designed to help.

The Third Circuit Court decision provides a clear signal that the "very essence of the [Model Cities] Act is participation by the inhabitants of the affected community." Citizen participation is being given another direction but also a new chance in Philadelphia. Is it too late to make the program take hold? What will the Philadelphia revision of citizen participation mean for the national program?

CHAPTER 24

CITIZEN PARTICIPATION
Can We Measure Its Effectiveness?

JUDY B. ROSENER

Debate about the value of citizen participation has greatly increased since the Equal Opportunity Act of 1964 with its well known "maximum feasible participation" clause. Nevertheless, the increased debate has not resulted in consensus about the goals and objectives of citizen participation, or in our ability to evaluate its effectiveness. At best what we have is a growing number of case studies, listings of definitions and techniques, schemes for implementing participation programs, and a few studies which do focus on participation in terms of effectiveness.[1] The issue of participation effectiveness should demand our attention, for while participation mandates have increased, the accumulated knowledge about "successful" and "unsuccessful" participation remains fragmented and unreliable. We seem to assume that more citizen participation will produce "better" public policy. Where is the evidence that "more is better"? It is my contention that evaluation research methodology[2] can provide a conceptual frame of reference which will make it possible to assemble some evidence. The use of such a conceptual scheme will also allow us to generate case studies about citizen participation from which we can generalize, thus improving our ability to understand and predict the effects of involving citizens in the making of public policy.

PARTICIPATION QUESTIONS

By asking the journalistic questions who, where, what, how, and when, the seemingly simple phrase "citizen participation" can be discovered to be, in reality, a very complex concept, and that the lack of knowledge about participation effectiveness is probably related to the fact that so few acknowledge its complexity.

When we ask the question "who," we find there are at least three sets of individuals (political actors) to whom the term citizen participation may have a different meaning: elected officials, public administrators, and citizens.* Each of these groups operates under different kinds of per-

*The term citizens refers to those individuals who do not occupy sanctional governmental decision-making positions.

From *Public Administrative Review,* 38, 5 (September/October 1978): 437–463.Copyright © 1978 by American Society for Public Administration. Reprinted with permission.

sonal, organizational, economic, and political constraints, and each group has different values, expectations, and goals. Even within these groups, there are differences, and the importance of these differences in shaping how individuals or groups view participation cannot be over-emphasized. There should be little doubt that knowing who is doing the perceiving is crucial to any understanding of the effectiveness of citizen participation.

When we ask the question "where," we are talking about goals. Where is it that we wish citizen participation to take us? Are we looking for changes in policy outcomes? Are we looking for changes in our institutions? Are we looking for a more open political process? Are we merely looking for the development of a citizenry with a "democratic character"? In other words, where is the ultimate goal we wish to achieve by involving citizens? Certainly, without knowing this, we cannot determine the effectiveness of participation.

When we ask the question "what," we are referring to objectives, the specific changes or conditions which a program is expected to produce. Put another way, we are asking about the specific function to be performed by any given participation activity as contrasted with the more general statements of intended consequences. Is it the dissemination of information? Is it the generation of alternative options for decisionmakers? Is it the opportunity for those affected by policy decisions merely to review and comment on decisions which have already been made? Or is it a safety valve for citizens so they can vent their emotions? To some citizens, participation means the sharing of decision power; to others it means only expressing an opinion. Unless participation objectives are clear to all of those involved in the participation, assessments of the effectiveness of the participation will be suspect.

When we ask the question "how," we are inquiring into how different kinds of issues relate to participation. Since issues differ in terms of their complexity, duration, scope and intensity they generate different kinds of "participation costs." For example, how does involving the public in a decision to site a nuclear reactor facility differ from the public's participation in a local government decision to make a zone change? How does participation in the development of a state transportation plan differ from participation in the implementation of a local school desegregation plan? It is well known that certain kinds of decisions necessitate the participation of highly trained "experts," while others do not. Certain policy decisions are long term, cover large geographical areas, and affect the lives of thousands of people. Others require no specialized knowledge, are of limited duration, and primarily affect small groups of citizens. In assessing effectiveness, it is dangerous to assume that the costs (in time, money, energy and expertise) of participating are the same for all kinds of policy issues.

As we ask the question "when," we are determining when in the policy process we need or desire participation. Is it during policy formulation? Is it when policy is being implemented? Or is it while the policy is being evaluated? Is it all of these? The participation strategy or technique, and the kinds of participation skills which are needed in the development of a policy are often quite different from those needed while a policy is being implemented. Public administrators often feel that having public input during the development of policy is burdensome, but not so once a policy has been enunciated, and is being implemented. Citizens, on the other hand, might disagree. The question of when citizen participation is needed generally elicits different answers depending on who is being asked.

It is apparent from this simple inquiry that the participation concept is multi-faceted, and if we are to assess the effectiveness of citizen participation in any meaningful manner we will need to acknowledge this complexity. There have been a number of attempts to look at participation in terms of effectiveness.[3] Some of these address the complexity issue. However, for the most part, they do not.

Mazmanian[4] in a study of five Army Corps of Engineers projects conducted an evaluation of participation programs which utilized an assessment model which took into account the many dimensions of the participation concept. He measured the cause and effect relationship between specific participation activities and a clearly articulated set of goals and objectives. The goal was to achieve public support for the Corps. The objective was to achieve public support for specific Corps projects. The participation program involved citizens early and ongoing in the planning of the five projects. Mazmanian made clear in the beginning of his study that he was looking at how the participation activities contributed to the goal and objectives which had been delineated by the Corps. The significance of Mazmanian's study for our purposes is that he evaluated the effectiveness of five specific citizen participation programs using a testable cause and effect hypothesis. He studied the participation programs from the point of view of one identified interested party, the Army Corps of Engineers; he looked at one phase of the policy process, the development of the projects; and he measured the participation programs in terms of a predetermined set of goals and objectives which had been agreed to by the Corps.

As it happened, Mazmanian concluded that the Corps' public participation programs were not effective in achieving their objectives. He found that even though citizens had been involved in the planning of the five Corps projects, they failed to support them. While giving the Corps high marks for involving them in the planning of the projects, the citizens who participated rejected the projects they helped plan. The participation programs were rendered ineffective in terms of the stipulated goals, yet effective in terms of the process. This discovery illustrates the importance of not confusing process goals with product goals in assessing effectiveness.

EVALUATION RESEARCH AND CITIZEN PARTICIPATION

Evaluation research is nothing more than the application of certain kinds of research methods to the evaluation of social programs. Its purpose is to measure the effects of a program against the goals it sets out to accomplish as a means of contributing to subsequent decisionmaking about the program.[5] It is a tool which can be used by decisionmakers and citizens alike. Since any evaluation is basically a judgment about the value of some activity or program, it necessarily involves the value biases of those doing the judging, as well as the values of those being judged. Evaluation research is a "scientific" process which attempts to control as much as possible for the intrinsic subjectivity of the evaluative process.[6] It does not purport to eliminate subjectivity, but rather to acknowledge it, and correct for it as much as possible. Simple as this may seem, it is surprising how few participation programs are judged in this manner.

In order to evaluate citizen participation, using the methodology we propose, it is first necessary to determine whether or not a participation program or activity is perceived as an end in itself (participation for participation's sake), or as a means to an end (as contributing to the achievement of some goal), or a combination of both. In other words, how is the participation valued? If it is seen primarily as an end in itself, it is relatively easy to measure its effectiveness. We can count the number of people participating. We can describe the kinds of people who are participating. We can keep track of the frequency of citizen involvement. We can measure the time invested by individual participants. We can measure participant attitudes about their participation. It is the kind of evaluation which government agencies often employ to show that they have met participation mandates. Most participation mandates are vague and ambiguous, thus sophisticated measures of effectiveness are rarely required, and a counting evaluation is considered sufficient. On the other hand, when participation is viewed as a means to an end, then measurement becomes more difficult. It is important to distinguish between these two kinds of participation, while at the same time recognizing that they are not mutually exclusive, and that focusing on one does not constitute a rejection of the other.

Figure 24.1 **Participation Evaluation Matrix**

Knowledge of a cause/effect
relationship between a participation
program or activity (A) and the
achievement of specified goals
and objectives (B)

Agreement on
program goals
and objectives
(B), whose goals
and objectives
they are, and
the criteria by
which success
or failure will
be measured.

		Complete	Incomplete
Yes		I	II
No		III	IV

The measurement of participation which is viewed as a means to an end requires looking closely at the causal relationship between a participation program or activity and some desired end. This means that at the outset of any evaluation two questions need to be asked. What are the goals and objectives that some specified participation is expected to achieve? (And whose goals and objectives are they: the citizens, the public administrators, the elected officials, or a combination of these?) The second question is how will it be known that there is a cause and effect relationship between what is being proposed as a participation activity and the achievement of the desired goals and objectives?

Thompson,[7] in his analysis of organization assessment, proposes a matrix which helps answer these questions. He uses two variables (each seen on a continuum) which he contends are important in understanding the environments in which different kinds of assessment can take place. These he calls "standards of desirability" (which range from crystallized to ambiguous) and "beliefs about cause/effect knowledge" (which range from complete to incomplete). By using the extreme values of these variables, Thompson describes four possible types of assessment situations. By adopting Thompson's basic idea and modifying his terms, we arrive at a similar type of matrix which can be used to explain possible participation evaluation environments and show how the use of evaluation research methodology can contribute to a "healthy" evaluation environment [see Figure 24.1].

By thinking of participation in terms of this matrix, it is easy to see why a reliable assessment of the effectiveness of citizen participation programs requires more than an "after the fact" determination.

For a participation program to fall in quadrant I (the "healthiest" evaluation environment), there would have to be agreement on goals and objectives, and an indication of whose goals and objectives they were. There would also have to be fairly complete knowledge of a cause and effect relationship between some specified participation program (hereafter referred to as A), and the achievement of the agreed upon goals or objectives (hereafter referred to as B). Most participation programs are not planned so that goals and objectives are articulated or agreed upon prior to the commencement of the participation activities, nor are ways for measuring cause and effect stipulated. For this reason, few participation evaluations are conducted in the most desirable assessment environment represented by quadrant I of the matrix. An example of a quadrant I participation program would be one where the goal (B) is to accommodate handicapped citizens in the public transportation system. The objective (B) is to ensure that the needs of the handicapped are incorporated into transportation policy. The program (A) is a series of workshops where handicapped citizens can express their needs to those responsible for making transportation policy. There would be agreement on the goals and objectives by the citizens and the policymakers, and it would be possible to obtain knowledge about the cause and effect relationship between A and B by seeing whether or not the transportation needs of the handicapped expressed in the workshop were translated into policy.

A participation program would fall into the quadrant II environment if there was agreement on B, but incomplete knowledge that A produced B. In this case, it would be possible for B to have been achieved, but it would not be possible to know whether or not A was partially or totally responsible for producing B. An example of a quadrant II program would be where B is the passage of a statewide citizen initiative proposing a desired policy, and A is the mounting of a coalition of citizen groups to work for the passage of the initiative. If the measure passes, it might be concluded that A contributed to the achievement of B, but it would not be possible to know whether or not the measure would have passed, had the citizen coalition not been formed. In other words, it might have been that A had little or no effect in producing B.

For a participation program to qualify for quadrant III, it would have to be characterized by a lack of agreement on B, while there is reliable knowledge that A produced B. In this case, a program might be perceived as being effective for one group, but not for another. An example of a quadrant III program would be one where a group of senior citizens saw B as their participation on an advisory committee effecting a change in the allocation of revenue sharing monies, but where public administrators saw B as a means of allowing the citizens to merely express their concerns. If the senior citizens did in fact participate as members of the advisory committee, and if they did express their concerns, but their participation did not result in a change in the allocation of the revenue sharing monies, then the public administrators would consider A effective, while the citizens would consider it ineffective. It would not be possible to determine overall program effectiveness because without agreement on B, there would necessarily be debate over whether or not A had been effective.

A participation program would qualify for quadrant IV if there is no agreement on B, and incomplete knowledge of the cause and effect relationship between A and B. In this case, it is not possible to measure effectiveness with any degree of reliability. An example of a quadrant IV program would be one where a traditional public hearing is held because it is perceived by administrators as "citizen participation" and by citizens who feel it is a way to shape policy. There is no agreement on the part of administrators or citizens as to what specific function the hearing is supposed to perform. It would not be clear what constitutes B, and thus it would not be possible to know if A produces B. Under these circumstances, participation is probably considered an end in itself by administrators, and they play the "numbers game." If a large number of citizens turn out for the hearing, the hearing is termed a success. If no one shows up, the hearing is considered a failure. This kind of accounting really tells us very little about the effectiveness of participation. Unfortunately, many participation programs fall into this category.

The value of using the participation assessment matrix in thinking about citizen participation programs is two-fold. First, it forces us to make explicit assumptions which underlie our evaluation of participation programs. We have to make clear what we expect participation programs to accomplish, and who is to be served by the participation. Secondly, it enables us to see how reliably we can assess a participation program given its design and characteristics. Most studies of the impact of participation are conducted as though there is agreement on B, and as though there is knowledge about the cause and effect relationship between A and B.[8] However, in most instances the participation goals and objectives are ambiguous, desired outcomes are rarely specified, and there is very little knowledge about the cause and effect between the two.

If we are honest, we will have to admit that citizen participation is similar to most other complex social phenomena, it is not "obvious and unproblematic,"[9] and assumptions to the contrary are misleading. This situation was confronted in connection with an evaluation of the Public Participation Program employed by the California Department of Transportation (Caltrans) in the development of the California Transportation Plan.[10] Given only two months and limited funds, it was necessary to devise an evaluation scheme in a very short period of time. At the outset it was recognized that the analysis would be forced to rely on existing participation evaluation literature. During the process of reviewing the literature, the lack of linkages between the various participation studies were discovered and the need to develop a scheme for assessing the effectiveness of participation programs was recognized. In retrospect, the Caltrans evaluation experience illustrates an attempt to offer more than a purely subjective assessment of a participation program. It was necessary to organize the information which was available in such a way that it would be possible to judge the effectiveness of the Caltrans participation activities in some systematic manner correcting as much as possible for subjectivity. To do so required a determination of where the goals of the Caltrans participation program were perceived to be, and to relate the participation activities to those goals so that a cause and effect relationship between them could be determined. The Caltrans evaluation experience is cited as an illustration of an attempt to utilize evaluation research in assessing a participation program.

Since the Caltrans program had been planned and operated prior to the evaluation design, the evaluation research methodology was superimposed "after the fact." For this reason, the following description of what transpired should be read with that in mind.

THE CALTRANS PUBLIC PARTICIPATION PROGRAM EVALUATION

The California Department of Transportation (Caltrans) was created in 1973 and was mandated to prepare a Transportation Plan to be submitted to the State Transportation Board early in 1976. The legislation which created Caltrans required public participation in the transportation planning process. The implication of the legislative history was that the purpose of the participation mandate was to make sure that various citizen interests were represented in the plan. However, there were a large number of other Caltrans documents which also had the force of law and some of these defined participation differently.[11] There was no agreement on goals.

Since goals of the participation program were not clear, and since there were no criteria for judging the value of any of the program activities in terms of goals, it was first necessary to develop a set of goals and objectives. This was done, using the legislation and other official transportation documents. Although this "after the fact" method is not recommended, it is one way to develop an assessment capability in the absence of predetermined goals and objectives. In addition to creating a set of goals and objectives, a set of criteria or standards were designated for use in measuring specific participation program activities against the goals and objectives. These standards were also based on legislative and departmental documentation. By clearly articulating the participation program goals and objectives, and by establishing a way for determining a cause and effect relationship between the activities and the goals and objectives, the program moved out of the quadrant IV assessment environment. Obviously, the choice of goals, objectives and measurement criteria represented a value judgment even though it was based on Caltrans documentation. This qualification was noted in the study so that it would be taken into account by those using the evaluation.

There are a large number of evaluation research methodologies available ranging from very weak ones to those with a high degree of reliability and validity. The "one-shot" case study design where observations and measurements are made after the program has been underway is at the bottom of the reliability/validity ladder. This is because there is no baseline data, and no control group.[12] Unfortunately the Caltrans evaluation was in this category. Certainly it is desirable to use evaluation designs which provide the greatest amount of reliability and validity, but in many cases this is not possible. Knowing which evaluation methodology is best suited to the assessment of a particular participation activity is outside the scope of this paper, however it should be noted that there are a variety of possibilities.

In the Caltrans evaluation a goal was defined as a "generalized statement of intended accomplishment; a condition or direction which would result from the successful achievement of the objectives of a program."[13] For example, two of the Caltrans goals were "1) to meet federal, state and regional citizen participation mandates which call for the early and continuous participation of all segments of the public in the planning of the California Transportation Plan," and 2) to make the California transportation planning process more responsive to the expressed needs of the California citizenry.

Objectives were defined as "specific changes or conditions which the programs' efforts were intended to produce." Objectives were divided into two groups, those relating to participants, and those relating to the planning process. One participation objective was the "involvement of individuals and groups which had not historically played a role in transportation planning, i.e., the young, old, poor, handicapped, ethnic minorities." An example of a planning process objective was the "preparation of reports which would be available to the public with descriptions of transportation alternatives, the date which had been developed by Caltrans, and the Caltrans analysis of the anticipated effects of the proposed alternatives."

Specific program activities were defined as "activities which were created to achieve the objectives." Activities such as a newsletter, listen and learn sessions, a public survey, workshops, a statewide advisory committee, etc., were designated as the program activities. In order to determine whether or not these activities contributed toward the achievement of the objectives it was necessary to create measurement criteria to test for cause and effect between the activities and the objectives.

Evaluation criteria were defined as "standards used in the program evaluation in which a judgement of effectiveness can be made." Examples of criteria used in the Caltrans study: "1) evidence of formalized courses of action"; "2) evidence of funding"; "3) evidence that there was interaction between Caltrans staff and participants"; "4) evidence that citizen input was being used in policy and planning decisions"; and "5) evidence that citizens were involved in problem definition, alternative evaluation and priority setting." It was expected that if the participation activities met the criteria, the objectives would be achieved. (Some Caltrans officials called the activities their participation program. To them, just seeing that these activities were carried out constituted an effective program. In other words, the activities were an end in themselves.)

Data relating to all of the specific program activities were accumulated and each activity was described in terms of how it met the criteria. For example, it might be that one activity met some of the criteria but not all of them. Some activities might meet all the criteria. What emerged was a picture showing how each specific program activity contributed to the achievement of the stated objectives based on a set of clearly articulated measurement criteria. Ultimately the decision had to be made as to how many of the programs had to meet the criteria in order for the overall Caltrans public participation program to be judged "effective." In this sense the evaluation was subjective. Had no goals, objectives and measurement criteria been established, it would have been more subjective.

In the evaluation report, assumptions made about the goals, objectives, measurement criteria and program activities were made clear. The issue of whose goals were being considered was addressed, and qualifications about the reliability of an "after the fact" effectiveness evaluation was discussed. Thus, it was possible to draw conclusions about the effectiveness of the Caltrans program within the limited evaluation framework, and to suggest how future programs could be designed so that a more rigorous evaluation could be conducted.

The significance of the Caltrans study to those interested in citizen participation and its impact on the policy process, is not in its findings, but rather that it illustrates an attempt to evaluate participation strategies using one kind of evaluation research methodology.[14]

CONCLUSIONS

Elena C. Van Meter suggests that "effective citizen participation can be the 'bottom line' for govern-ment."[15] She defines bottom line as an "objective measure which policy makers for business can use to cancel product lines and justify changes in the organization and operation of an enterprise." However, she does not define effective citizen participation. What she seems to be saying is that if public officials are to do their job well, they will need to involve citizens in a way judged to be "effective." The problems, of course, is that calling for effective public participation assumes that there is agreement as to its meaning, which is not the case. There is no widely acceptable scheme for conceptualizing and measuring its effectiveness; and it is, in part, this lack of agreement which prevents us from making effective citizen participation the bottom line for government.

The challenge is to add to our limited knowledge about the effectiveness of citizen participation (both as an end in itself, and as a means to an end) by moving out of the quadrant IV assessment environment, where it is difficult to measure effectiveness, and toward the quadrant I environment, where measurement is possible. Once participation is assessed in terms of how it contributes to the achievement of predetermined, clearly articulated goals and objectives, it will then be possible to compare participation activities. The ability to do this will provide public administrators and citizens with knowledge of what "works" and what does not. Knowing what "works" and what does not should minimize the frustration felt by administrators who are confused about what is expected of them, and at the same time it will minimize the distrust felt by citizens who complain that public participation programs are a charade.

The use of evaluation research methodology in the design of participation programs will mean the exposure of value biases and "hidden agendas"; it will move us from the quadrant IV toward the quadrant I evaluation environment. This will reduce the ambiguity surrounding the participa-tion concept. Ambiguity often serves to protect public administrators and citizens alike from being accountable, thus "going public" with explanations of participation assumptions will prove useful. It will mean that those mandating participation programs will need to clarify their expectations; public administrators will need to be honest about their intentions; and citizens will need to be reasonable in their demands. Most important, the use of evaluation research methodology (the measurement of the effects of an activity against the goals it sets out to accomplish) will provide a useful framework for thinking about the effectiveness of citizen participation.

NOTES

1. Sherry R. Arnstein, "Eight Rungs on the Ladder of Citizen Participation," in *Effecting Community Change*, edited by Edgar S. Cahn and Barry A. Passett, New York: Praeger, 1971. Edmund M. Burke, "Citizen Participation Strategies," in *American Institute of Planners Journal*, September, 1968, pp. 287–294. Edgar S. Cahn and Barry Passett (eds.), *Community Participation: Effecting Community Change*, New York: Praeger, 1971. Dale Marshall, *The Politics of Participation in Poverty*, University of California Press: Berkeley, 1971. Judith May, *Citizen Participation: A Review of the Literature*, Institute of Governmental Affairs: UC Davis, 1971. Lester Milbrath, *Political Participation*, Rand McNally: Chicago, 1965. Melvin B. Mogulof, *Citizen Participation: A Review and Commentary on Federal Policies and Practices*, The Urban Institute: Washington, D.C., 1970. Carole Pateman, *Participation and Democratic Theory*, Cambridge University Press: Cambridge, 1970. *Public Administration Review*, Special Issue on Participation, October, 1973. Hans B.C. Speigel (ed.), *Citizen Participation in Urban Development*, Vol. 1, *Concepts and Issues*, Vol. II, *Cases and Programs*, Washington, D.C. Center for Community Affairs NTL, Institute for Applied Behavioral Science, 1968. Sidney Verba and Norman Nie, *Participation in America*, Harper and Row: Chicago, 1972. Sidney Verba, "Democratic Participation," *The Annals of the American Academy of Political and Social Science, II* (September, 1967), 53–78.

2. H.P. Hatry, R.E. Winnie, and D.M. Fisk, *Practical Program Evaluation for State and Local Government Officials*, The Urban Institute: Washington, D.C., 1973. E.A. Suchman, *Evaluation Research: Principles and Practice in Public Service and Social Action Programs*, New York: Russell Sage Foundation. Elmer L. Struening and Marcia Guttentag (eds.), *Handbook of Evaluation Research*. Sage Publications: Beverly Hills, 1975. C.H. Weiss, *Evaluation Research: Methods of Assessing Program Effectiveness*, Prentice-Hall: Englewood Cliffs, 1972.

3. Richard L. Cole, *Citizen Participation and the Urban Policy Process*, Lexington: Massachusetts, 1974. Daniel Mazmanian, "Participatory Democracy in a Federal Agency," in *Water Politics and Public Involvement*, Harvey Dickerson and John Pierce (eds.), Ann Arbor: Ann Arbor Science, 1976. Walter A. Rosenbaum, "Slaying Beautiful Hypotheses with Ugly Fact: EPA and the Limits of Public Participation," paper delivered at the 1975 American Society for Public Administration (ASPA) Conference, Chicago, Illinois. Judy B. Rosener, *The Caltrans Public Participation Program: An Evaluation and Recommendations*, California Department of Transportation, Sacramento. Elena C. Van Meter, "Citizen Participation in the Policy Management Process," *Public Administration Review*, Special Issue, December, 1975. Robert K. Yin and Douglas Yates, *Street Level Governments: Assessing Decentralization and Urban Services (An Evaluation of Policy Related Research)*, Rand Corporation, Santa Monica, CA, 1974. R—1527—NSF.

4. Mazmanian, op. cit.

5. Weiss, op. cit., p. 4.

6. Suchman, op. cit., p. 11.

7. James D. Thompson, *Organizations in Action*. McGraw-Hill: New York, 1967.

8. Rosenbaum, op. cit. p. 4.

9. Lawrence A. Scaff, "Two Concepts of Political Participation," in *Western Political Quarterly*, September, 1975, p. 448.

10. Rosener, op. cit.

11. *Ibid.*, p. 67.

12. P. Rossi and W. Williams (eds.), *Evaluating Social Programs: Theory, Practice, and Politics*. Seminar Press: New York, 1972, p. 46. N.P. Roos, "Evaluation, Quasi-Experimentation and Public Policy," in J.A. Caporaso and L.L. Roos, *Quasi-Experimental Approaches: Testing Theory and Evaluating Policy*, Evanston, Ill: Northwestern University Press, 1970, p. 350.

13. See R.F. Mager, *Goal Analysis*, Fearon: Belmont, Calif., 1972, for a good discussion on goals and objectives.

14. See Hatry, Suchman, Struening, Roos, Rossi, and Weiss for descriptions of various evaluation research methodologies.

15. E.C. Van Meter, "Citizen Participation in the Policy Management Process," *Public Administration Review*. Special Issue, December 1975, p. 812.

CHAPTER 25

MAKING BUREAUCRATS RESPONSIVE
A Study of the Impact of Citizen Participation and Staff Recommendations on Regulatory Decision Making

JUDY B. ROSENER

Conventional wisdom tells us that participation in public hearings is often ineffective; and that part-time regulators "rubber stamp" the recommendations of their staffs. The implication of this conventional wisdom is that regulators listen to citizens, but take their signals from staff.[1] When this notion is coupled with the private sector cry for less regulation and less citizen participation, it is not surprising that there is a move to minimize both.[2] What is surprising is that while the effectiveness of regulatory requirements has been studied and analyzed, there has been little systematic analysis of the effectiveness of citizen participation in regulatory proceedings.[3] The few studies which have generated reliable data tend to focus on who participates, how many people participate, and why people participate. They monitor participation rather than measure its influence. Similarly, there is very little hard data on whether or not regulators "rubber stamp" staff recommendations.[4] There are some case studies which suggest that they do, and one or two attempts to show that they do, but there is insufficient data to support a theory.

Having served eight years as a commissioner on the California Coastal Commission, a state regulatory agency with far-reaching land use authority, I observed that citizens who participated in public hearings to influence the commission's voting behavior appeared to be effective; that is, they achieved their participation goals. I also observed that the commissioners tended to follow the recommendations of the staff in a selective fashion, i.e., when they recommended approval of permits, but not so when they recommended denial. In an attempt to determine whether or not my personal observations were accurate, I conducted a study of three regional California Coastal Commissions over a three-year period. The purpose of the study was to ascertain in a quantitative manner whether or not citizens who participated in regulatory public hearings influenced voting outcomes, and whether or not there was evidence to support the belief that regulators "rubber stamp" staff recommendations, using the commissions as a test case.

From *Public Administration Review,* 42, 4 (July/August 1982): 339–345. Copyright © 1982 by American Society for Public Administration. Reprinted with permission.

THE CALIFORNIA COASTAL ACT OF 1972 AND
COASTAL COMMISSIONERS

The California Coastal Act of 1972 was created in response to a demand for coastal resource protection. After three years in which the California legislature failed to enact coastal protection laws, citizens circumvented their elected representatives and passed a state-wide initiative which created a strong regulatory agency, the California Coastal Commission. The commission was composed of one state commission and six regional commissions. Commissioners were part-time appointees, and had the responsibility and authority to approve or deny all development projects (from the erection of a fence to the construction of a shopping center) in an area designated as the "coastal zone." They had veto power over all local land-use decisions.[5]

The Coastal Act was written by environmentalists and legislators who had championed the need for coastal resource protection. For this reason, strong citizen over-sight provisions were included in the act. These provisions were designed to serve as a check on the use of the discretionary authority provided the commissioners. One of these provisions required that an individual public hearing be held for each permit which might have an "adverse environmental impact" on coastal resources. It was assumed that citizens would take advantage of opportunities to participate in these hearings, and that they would be able to influence voting outcomes.

Some comments about the commissioners and their staffs are necessary in order to understand the focus of the study which follows. Regional commissions consisted of six locally elected officials (members of city councils and county boards of supervisors) and six "public members," two appointed by the governor, two by the speaker of the State Assembly, and two by the State Senate Rules Committee. This appointment "mix" was written into the act at the request of local officials who threatened to oppose passage of the initiative unless they had equal representation on the commissions with what were expected to be environmentally oriented "public members." The voting behavior of commissioners reflected their concern.[6] The "public members" (who identified with the environmental purpose of the act) voted to deny projects much more often than did the local officials who identified with home-rule.

Each commission had its own staff, whose prime responsibility was to make permit recommendations. The Coastal Act was a unique law. There were no precedents for the kind of decisions being made. Commissioners had wide discretion in deciding what constituted an environmental impact. In addition, the commissions, as noted, were split ideologically. Thus, it is easy to see that developing staff recommendations was fraught with difficulties. For the same reasons, it would not be surprising to find citizen participation influencing voting outcomes. It is the author's contention that participation did influence voting behavior (perhaps because of the discretion granted the commissioners) and that it did so independent of staff recommendations. It is also the author's contention that measuring the influence of citizen participation and staff recommendations in a quantitative fashion enhances our ability to understand the role they play in regulatory decision making.

THE STUDY

The study consists of an analysis of 1,816 development permits for which individual public hearings were held. These permits represent approximately 70 percent of all the permits processed by the six regional commissions, although only three of the six commissions were studied.[7] Moreover, this study does not include permit decisions made on the consent calendars or permits issued on the basis of administrative or emergency action. Each hearing represents one permit application.

The 1,816 hearings constitute the total universe of hearings for the three commissions during the time period between April 1973 and December 1975. The hearing data represent the votes of 36 commissioners. The number of permits processed by the three commissions not included in the study is so small that their inclusion would not materially affect the findings.

The decision environment was as follows: The commission staff would process a permit application, write up an analysis of the project, and make a recommendation for approval or denial. The applicant, interested parties, and commissioners would receive the staff report prior to the scheduled public hearing. Usually one public hearing was held, at which time the staff would make its recommendation, the permit applicant would speak, those in opposition to the permit would speak, the commissioners would ask questions of the staff or participants, and a vote would be taken.

While it is impossible to know who a commissioner may have talked to outside the hearing, it must be assumed that, for the most part, it was the staff recommendation and discussion which took place in the hearing which influenced voting outcomes. The reason for this assumption is that most of the commissioners had regular jobs, and the time they spend outside the meetings on commission business was limited. On an occasional permit, a commissioner might attempt to learn more about a project than he or she might otherwise, but, in general, *ex-parte* communications were frowned upon, and most of the influencing took place in the context of the public hearings. While the ideological predisposition of commissioners to resource protection and citizen participation may have played a part in their decision making, these two factors are considered to be constants, and were not included in the study.

THE HYPOTHESES AND METHODOLOGY

As was noted above, there is a dearth of reliable data on whether, or how, citizens influence voting behavior in the context of the public hearing, and whether or not part-time regulators "rubber stamp" staff recommendations. In order to generate data, the following hypotheses were tested:

1. The denial rate of permits will increase when there is a staff recommendation to deny them.
2. The denial rate of permits will increase when citizens oppose them in a public hearing.
3. The denial rate of permits will increase when citizens oppose them in a public hearing, irrespective of the staff recommendation.

The dependent variable used in the analysis was the percentage of permit denials. A denial or "no" vote was seen as an environmental decision, since the Coastal Act said that a project should be approved *only* if it could be shown that it would not cause an adverse environmental impact under the provisions of the act. Thus, to deny a project meant it would cause an adverse environmental impact.

Although commissioners were given wide latitude in deciding whether or not to deny a permit, and the intent of the Coastal Act was to make sure that no projects were permitted which were not protective of coastal resources, relatively few projects were denied.

Only 25 percent, or 1,816, of the total permits processed by the three commissions studied necessitated an *individual* public hearing, the other 75 percent having been put on a consent calendar or issued as administrative or emergency permits. Of the 25 percent of the permits for which an individual hearing was held (the subject of this study), the denial rate was 18 percent (see Table 25.1). While this may appear to be a high denial rate, it must be remembered that this rate refers

Table 25.1

Staff Recommendations and Commission Decision

		Commission decision		
		Decision to approve	Decision to deny	
Staff recommendations	Approval	93% (1,290)	7% (99)	77% 1.389
	Denial	45% (186)	55% (228)	23% 414
		82% 1,476	18% 327	N = 1,803

Level of Association: phi = .52.
Level of Significance: phi < 0.0001.

only to permit applications which, under the provisions of the Coastal Act, had the potential of having a negative impact on coastal zone resources. Given the purpose of the act, which was to protect these resources, the fact that 82 percent of the permits processed were approved indicates that the denial rate was less than might have been expected.

There are a number of reasons why the denial rate was rather low given the mandate of the act. One reason was that it was difficult for commissioners to tell those applying for a permit in a face-to-face situation that they could not build their dream house or subdivide their land. While it is clear that the voters of California were supportive of the Coastal Act, asking individual property-owners and developers to bear the cost of reaching coastal resource protection goals was not easy. Also the provisions of the act were vague. For instance it was difficult for commissioners in exercising their discretionary authority, to decide what constituted an "adverse impact."

Since it was assumed to be more difficult for commissioners to deny permits than to approve them, attention was focused on permit denials, the rationale being that if participants' influence commissioners to deny projects, they can probably influence commissioners to approve them.

The independent variables used in the analysis were the presence or absence of participation in opposition to permits, and the staff recommendations to commissioners for approval or denial of permits. The rational for choosing them was similar to that used in choosing the denial rate as the dependent variable. Each permit had a supporter (the applicant) who participated in the public hearings. Not every permit had an opponent. Therefore, the variation in participation can most clearly be seen by looking at those who participated in opposition to permits.

Non-parametric statistical techniques were used to test the hypotheses. The test for determining the level of association was phi. Since most of the data used in the analysis was nominal, and because the investigation was exploratory, the author used a conservative measure association.

FINDINGS

Public hearings were mandated under the California Coastal Act because they were required as a condition for receiving funds from the federal government (under the Federal Coastal Zone Management Act), and because the authors of the coastal initiative thought that the hearings would provide citizens with an opportunity to make commissioners and their staffs responsive. It assumed that citizens, particularly environmentalist would take advantage of the opportunity to

Table 25.2

Presence or Absence of Opposition and Commission Decision

		Commission decision		
		Decision to approve	Decision to deny	
Presence or absence of opposition	No opposition	89% (987)	11% (127)	66% 1,114
	One or more in opposition	66% (387)	34% (197)	34% 584
		81% 1,374	19% 324	N = 1,698

Level of Association: phi = .27.
Level of Significance: phi < 0.0001.

participate, and that their participation would remind commissioners of their responsibility. Strong public hearing provisions in the act were to favor the interests of the environmentalists who fought for its passage. This view is consistent with the notion that expanded participation opportunities serve those interested in "public goods."[8] Put differently, it was assumed that given the evidence that regulatory agencies tend to favor the interests of those they regulate (their clients), the opportunity for citizens to influence regulators was needed to prevent "client capture."[9] The findings shed light on these assumptions.

STAFF RECOMMENDATIONS

A casual observer might come away from commission hearings sensing a high correlation between staff recommendations and commission decisions. Indeed, most of the time staff recommendations and commission decisions appear to coincide, and commissioners appear to be "rubber stamps" of their staffs. But is this the case? As Table 25.1 indicates, when the commission staff recommended approval on permits, 93 percent of the time the commissioners approved them. On the other hand, when staff recommended denial, commissioners followed the staff recommendation only 55 percent of the time. So while there was a strong relationship between the staff recommendation and commission decisions when viewed in the aggregate, this is not the case when permit recommendations were "decomposed," with the citizen participation variable included in the analysis (see Tables 25.3 and 25.4).

CITIZEN PARTICIPATION

Data on the relationship between the participation of citizens who opposed permits and the commission denial rate are seen below.

When there was no opposition to permits, the denial rate was 11 percent (see Table 25.2). When citizens participated in opposition to permits, the denial rate went up dramatically, to 34 percent. Viewed in the context of the denial rate of 19 percent, the 34 percent figure seems important. It suggests that participation was effective in changing the voting behavior of commissioners. Because commissioners relied on both the staff recommendation and the effect of participation in making their decisions, however, it is necessary to view participation in terms of specific staff recommendations.

Table 25.3

Presence or Absence of Opposition and Decision, for Permits Whose *Approval* Was Recommended by Staff

		Commission decision		
		Decision to approve	Decision to deny	
Presence or absence of opposition	No opposition	96%	4%	71%
		(876)	(40)	916
	One or more in opposition	84%	16%	29%
		(312)	(59)	371
		92%	8%	N = 1,287
		1,188	99	

Level of Association: phi = .20.
Level of Significance: phi << 0.0001.

Table 25.4

Presence or Absence of Opposition and Decision, for Permits Whose *Denial* Was Recommended by Staff

		Commission decision		
		Decision to approve	Decision to deny	
Presence or absence of opposition	No opposition	56%	44%	49%
		(110)	(87)	197
	One or more in opposition	34%	66%	51%
		(72)	(137)	209
		45%	55%	N = 406
		182	224	

Level of Association: phi = .21.
Level of Significance: phi << 0.0001.

CITIZEN PARTICIPATION AND STAFF RECOMMENDATIONS

One might expect that there would be an association between those permits for which the staff recommended denial and the presence of opponents in the public hearings. It is plausible that the staff would recommend denial on "questionable" permits, and that those would be the same permits which citizens would choose to oppose. Therefore, we need to look at the relationship between opposition to permits while controlling for the staff recommendation. That relationship can be seen in Tables 25.3 and 25.4.

The data in Table 25.3 show that when the staff recommended approval on permits and there was no opposition, the denial rate was quite low. The staff was overruled by commissioners only 4 percent of the time. When the staff recommended approval and there was opposition, the denial rate increased to 16 percent. The staff was overruled four times as often. While the absolute number of permit denials is small in comparison to those permits which were approved, it seems reasonable to assume that the presence of participants did have an influence, given the fact that the total number of denied permits is relatively small.

The data in Table 25.4 show that when the staff recommended denial on permits and there was no opposition, the denial rate was 44 percent. It jumped to 66 percent when there was opposition, indicating that even though there was a tendency for commissioners to overrule the staff on recommended denials and vote approval, they did so much less often when citizens appeared in the hearings to oppose those permits.

DISCUSSION

The data suggest a number of things. They show that most of the time citizens did not participate in public hearings held by the Coastal Commission, although when they did, they were effective in increasing the denial rate. Whether their participation or its influence was desirable in terms of the protection of coastal resources is not at issue here. What is at issue is the fact that citizens, participating in public hearings, influenced voting outcomes, and their influence was measured quantitatively. Should the influence of participation and staff recommendations in other kinds of regulatory hearings be measured in a similar manner, we could begin to accumulate the knowledge needed to evaluate the conventional wisdom about the effectiveness of participation and commission staff recommendations.

The data show that while commissioners followed staff recommendations for approval 92 percent of the time, this was not the case when it came to recommended denials. Almost half the time (45 percent), commissioners overruled staff recommendations for denial. This is an important finding because it indicates that looking at staff recommendations in an undifferentiated manner is deceiving. Yet that is how most researchers have viewed commissioner/staff recommendation relationships.

The data show that participation influenced voting outcomes independent of staff recommendations. It appears that while it may have been difficult for commissioners to say no to permit applicants when there was a staff recommendation for approval, it may also have been difficult to say no to environmentalists when they appeared to plead that permits should be denied. While commissioners overruled staff recommendations for denial 56 percent of the time when there was no citizen opposition, that figure dropped to 34 percent when citizens opposed them. This is an important finding because if the two variables (participation and staff recommendation) had not been analyzed separately, it would not have been possible to show that participation had a force of its own.

Finally, the data show that a recommendation for denial, together with participation in the public hearings, constitute a strong predictive variable. When there was a staff recommendation for denial *and* citizen participation, the denial rate was 66 percent, a far cry from the overall denial rate of 19 percent, as shown in Table 25.2.

How can the findings be explained? The relatively low participation rate (34 percent), which remained constant over the three-year period of the study, is similar to the 32 percent rate found in a study of planning commission decisions in Atlanta, Georgia.[10] The obvious explanation of this finding is that citizens tend to participate only when strongly motivated to do so, and most of the time they are not motivated. In the case of the Coastal Commissions, even though the costs of participation were low, there were costs, i.e., time, baby-sitting, Xeroxing, travel expenses, and so forth. It must be assumed that citizens tended to oppose only those permits perceived as having a major environmental impact. Interestingly, the perception of which permits those were was different depending on who was doing the perceiving. The data show that 49 percent of the time, permits received staff recommendations for denial when there was no citizen opposition, and 29 percent of the time they received recommendations for approval when there was citizen opposition. What this says is that if citizens and staff members did not agree on which permits should be denied, commissioners must also have had problems making up their minds. One commissioner explained the dilemma this way: "When there is no one out there objecting, I think there is nothing objectionable, even though the staff says there is. When there is someone objecting, it makes me think there must be something objectionable, but I have to weigh it against the staff recommendation." The findings seem to suggest that the staff recommendation for denial was a necessary, but not a sufficient condition for a permit denial.

One might ask why, when there was a staff recommendation for denial *and* citizen opposition, did commissioners still approve 34 percent of the permits? One explanation is that commissioners used their discretionary authority to make their job easier, to approve rather than deny permits. (It is always easier to say yes than no.) Another explanation might be that many commissioners (most often the local officials) were not strong supporters of the Coastal Act, and they chose to apply the law "loosely." The two reasons offered are not mutually exclusive, and probably both contributed to the fact that commissioners tended to approve rather than deny permits, even when citizens opposed them and staffs recommended they be denied.

The fact that commission staffs recommended denials on many more permits than were denied suggests that the staff may have been "leading" commissioners. In other words, they recommended denial on more permits than they thought would be denied. Many of the staff members were environmentalists, and consciously or unconsciously they may have hoped to convince commissioners to deny permits which could have gone either way. In this regard, it seems possible that staff members viewed citizen participants as a constituency, and recommended denials based on the anticipation that citizens would support their recommendations. Conversations with staff personnel indicate this was often the case. This possibility is intriguing since it is widely held that regulators tend to become "captured" by their clients. These findings suggest that perhaps the participants "captured" the commission staffs. These data on the influence of citizen participation are similar to findings of Sabatier and Mazmanian in their study of the commissions.[11] While participation was not the main focus of their study, they found it to be a factor in explaining the variance in the voting behavior of California coastal commissioners.

SUMMARY AND CONCLUSIONS

It was postulated at the outset that there is a need to evaluate the influence of citizen participation and staff recommendations on the voting behavior of regulators in the context of public hearings. To do this, three hypotheses were tested using data from California Coastal Commission hearings. The findings support all three hypotheses: (1) staff recommendations influenced the voting behavior of the regulators; (2) citizen participation influenced the voting behavior of the regulators; and (3) citizen participation influenced the voting behavior of the regulators independent of the staff recommendations. Furthermore, the data suggest that the relationship between staff recommendations and voting behavior is more complex than has been assumed; that staff recommendations need to be "decomposed" if a true picture of their impact is to be seen. The data indicate that regulators tend to follow staff recommendations when "yes" votes are called for, and to overrule them when "no" votes are recommended, a behavior pattern which, while easy to understand, seems worthy of further study. The findings also suggest that there may be an association between citizen participation and staff recommendations related to the way staff members "lead" regulators. It seems that the anticipation of participation in opposition to permits may influence the development of staff recommendations for denial.

Perhaps the most important finding is that the combination of a staff recommendation for denial and citizen participation in opposition to a permit significantly increases the probability that a permit will be denied. While this finding may seem to be stating the obvious, it is the first quantitative measurement of the influence of these two factors on the voting behavior of regulators.

Taken together, the findings suggest that the conventional wisdom concerning citizen participation and staff recommendations in regulatory hearings needs to be reexamined. While this study does not provide the data necessary to prove the conventional wisdom incorrect, it does suggest a need for a systematic evaluation of the relationship between citizen participation, staff recommendations, and regulatory decision making in the context of public hearings.

ACKNOWLEDGMENTS

The author wishes to thank Dan Mazmanian and Paul Sabatier for their support and suggestions on the previous drafts of this paper.

NOTES

1. Barry Checkoway, "The Politics of Public Hearings," *Journal of Applied Behavioral Sciences,* Vol. 17, No. 4, 1981. Paul Sabatier and Daniel Mazmanian, "Relationships Between Governing Boards and Professional Staff, Role Orientations and Influence on the California Coastal Commissions," *Administration and Society,* Fall 1981. Irving Schiffman, "The Limits of Local Planning Commissions," Institute of Governmental Affairs, University of California, Davis, 1975. Debra W. Stewart, "Full Time Staff and Volunteer Commissioners: A Comparative Study of Staff-Commissioner Relationships on Local Commissions on the Status of Women," paper delivered at the 1978 Annual Meeting of the American Political Science Association, New York, New York. Aug. 31-Sept. 3, 1978.

2. Many of the provisions for the holding of public hearings are embedded in the regulatory policies and laws of the late 1960s and 1970s which are presently under attack on all levels of government.

3. Nelson Rosenbaum, *Citizen Participation: Models and Methods of Evaluation,* Center for Responsive Governance, Washington, D.C., February 1977.

4. See Sabatier, Schiffman, and Stewart, *op. cit.*

5. Regional commission permit decisions could be appealed to the state commission, however very few of them (8 percent) were appealed, making the regional decisions the most appropriate sample.

6. Judy B. Rosener, "Environmentalism vs. Local Control: A Study of Voting Behavior of Some California Coastal Commissioners." Unpublished manuscript, University of California, Irvine, April 1977.

7. The South Coast Regional Commission processed more permits than all of the other commissions combined. The other commissions included in the study were the San Diego Commission and the North Central Commission. Paul Sabatier, U.C. Davis, collected the data from the North Central Commission files. These three commissioners were representative of the different political cultures of the California coastal area included in the coastal zone.

8. Mark Goldberg, "Small Business and Participation in the Regulatory Process," *Citizen Participation,* July/August 1981.

9. Paul Sabatier, "Social Movements and Regulatory Agencies: Toward a More Adequate—and Less Pessimistic—Theory of Client Capture," *Policy Sciences,* Vol. 1, No. 3, 1975.

10. George Rupnow, "An Analysis of Zoning Problems in Atlanta: Policy Practices and Community Acceptance and Their Problem Solving Applications," Frank X. Stegert, ed. Report prepared for the Department of Housing and Urban Development, March 1972.

11. Paul Sabatier and Dan Mazmanian, *Can Regulation Work? The Implementation of Public Policy,* Goodyear Publishing Company, 1982.

CHAPTER 26

THE QUESTION OF PARTICIPATION
Toward Authentic Public Participation in Public Administration

CHERYL SIMRELL KING, KATHRYN M. FELTEY,
AND BRIDGET O'NEILL SUSEL

The appropriate role of the public in public administration has been an active and ongoing area of inquiry, experimentation, revolution, and controversy since the birth of this nation. The contemporary movement to examine the role of the public in the process of administrative decision making has come about in response to problems in the latter half of this century and as a result of concern on the part of citizens, administrators, and politicians over citizen discouragement and apathy (Box, 1996; Putnam, 1995; Timney, 1996; Thomas, 1995). As both citizens and their leaders have noticed, "participation through normal institutional channels has little impact on the substance of government politics" (Crosby, Kelly, and Schaefer, 1986, 172).

Many citizens, administrators, and politicians are interested in increasing public participation in public decisions. Efforts to do so are currently underway across the country. However, there is considerable evidence to suggest that these efforts are not effective (Crosby, Kelly, and Schaefer, 1986; Kathlene and Martin, 1991; Kweit and Kweit, 1981, 1987; Parsons, 1990). Some efforts appear to be ineffective because of poor planning or execution. Other efforts may not work because administrative systems that are based upon expertise and professionalism leave little room for participatory processes (deLeon, 1992; Fischer, 1993; Forester, 1989; White and McSwain, 1993).

The question of how to engender effective and satisfying participation processes is the central issue in this research. Our findings indicate that effective, or authentic, public participation implies more than simply finding the right tools and techniques for increasing public involvement in public decisions. Authentic public participation, that is, participation that works for all parties and stimulates interest and investment in both administrators and citizens, requires rethinking the underlying roles of, and relationships between, administrators and citizens.

In the first section of this article we examine the question of the necessity or desirability of more effective participation by reviewing the literature in U.S. public administration and identifying the relevant contemporary issues for both administrators and citizens. The current model of the participation process is presented and critiqued in the second section, using the concept of authen-

From *Public Administration Review,* 58, 4 (July/August 1998): 317–326. Copyright © 1998 by American Society for Public Administration. Reprinted with permission.

tic participation as a starting point for moving toward more effective participatory processes. We then turn to identifying the barriers to effective participation as seen by our research participants. Strategies for overcoming the barriers are discussed, and implications for the practice of public administration and citizenship are suggested in the last section. Following a grounded theory model (Strauss and Corbin, 1990), this article is organized around the themes that emerged from the literature review, interviews, and focus group discussions (see Table 26.1).

THE NECESSITY OR DESIRABILITY OF MORE EFFECTIVE PARTICIPATION

The role of participation in public administration has historically been one of ambivalence. Although the political system in the United States is designed to reflect and engender an active citizenry, it is also designed to protect political and administrative processes from a too-active citizenry. It is within this context that participation in the administrative arena has traditionally been framed.

In recent times, interest in public participation in administrative decision making has increased as a result of a number of factors, not the least of which is that a citizenry with diminished trust in government is demanding more accountability from public officials (Parr and Gates, 1989). There is also a growing recognition on the part of administrators that decision making without public participation is ineffective. As Thomas indicates, "the new public involvement has transformed the work of public managers . . . public participation in the managerial process has become a fact of life. In the future, this may become the case for even more managers, since the public's demand for involvement does not seem to be abating" (1995, xi). Thomas suggests that under contemporary political and economic conditions, we can no longer not include the public in public decision making.

Table 26.1

Methodology

The research reported here follows a grounded theory model of research (Strauss and Corbin, 1990) and is based on interviews with subject matter experts and focus group discussions among citizens and public administrators in northeast Ohio. We used qualitative techniques because of our desire for depth in addressing the question of how to make participation efforts more effective for both citizens and administrators. We also wanted to allow issues we may not have considered to emerge from the research.

Subject matter experts are individuals we identified as knowledgeable about participation, either through their research or practice. We conducted hour-long telephone interviews with five subject matter experts; one interview was conducted in person. Subject matter experts include two organizers who are currently engaged in extensive participation projects, one for the Environmental Protection Agency and one for the city of Dayton, Ohio, two former executives from national foundations that focus on increasing the links between citizens and government; a public participation practitioner currently working in nuclear waste cleanup in Idaho; and one established scholar in the field.

(continued)

In the interviews the subject matter experts talked about the meaning of participation, identified the key components of successful participation efforts, addressed the issue of decline in participation, suggested ways to bolster citizen involvement in civic processes, and discussed key theories guiding research and practice in participation. We used the results of the interviews to shape the discussion guidelines for the focused group discussions.

The focus groups included three types of participants in public administration: nonelected administrators in local government, activists, and citizens who had participated in at least one pubic process or event during the previous year. A type of snowball sampling helped us identify group participants. The first few participants were identified through our personal and professional networks; we asked them to recommend other potential participants. Surprisingly, given this technique, our participants were fairly diverse with regard to their experiences and perspectives.

The activists and citizens were similar in terms of their interest in, and commitment to, participation. They differed in that the activists were formally tied to organizations that represent citizen interests and had higher levels of participation than ordinary citizens because of their organization's mission and goals. Citizens who did not participate in public processes were not represented in the focus group discussions.

We convened seven groups in three communities in northeast Ohio, chosen to represent the diversity of communities in the area (large city, medium city, rural/edge city). The focus groups ranged in size from six to eleven members, with three citizen-only groups, one administrator-only group, one activist-only group, and two groups of both activists and administrators. Participants were diverse with regard to demographic characteristics, the focus of their participation efforts, and the organizations they represented, although the administrators were all local (city or county). Participants in the groups responded to four general questions: What does public participation mean to you? What are the barriers to effective public participation? How can effective public participation be achieved, if at all? What advice do you have to give to people studying and attempting to practice effective public participation? Other topics and questions emerged in each group. The facilitators guided the discussions but did not control the direction of the conversations. The discussions lasted for two hours and were recorded verbatim by a courtroom transcriber.

In the first stage of the analysis, we coded the transcribed interviews and discussions individually, using a qualitative form of content analysis (see Strauss and Corbin, 1990). In the second stage of analysis, we synthesized the separate analyses, using a nominal group technique to create the categorical themes discussed in this paper.

It is important to note that, except for administrators, all participants in the focus groups were active in public participation processes. We wanted people involved to give us guidance on how these processes might be more effective. Every group discussion turned, at some point, to the question of nonparticipation. Our participants had a great deal to say about nonparticipation. We have incorporated their views of nonparticipation into the discussion.

Paralleling the increased practitioner interest in public participation, contemporary theorists have increasingly focused on participation in their theories of the role, legitimacy, and definitions of the field in what some call "postmodern" times (Frederickson, 1982; Stivers, 1990; Cooper, 1991; Farmer, 1995; Fox and Miller, 1995; Wamsley and Wolf, 1996). In an attempt to find a way to bridge the problems of traditional models of public administration, some researchers call for shifts in the governance process. Stivers calls these changed relationship "active accountability":

> Administrative legitimacy requires active accountability to citizens, from whom the ends of government derive. Accountability, in turn, requires a shared framework for the interpretation of basic values, one that must be developed jointly by bureaucrats and citizens in real-world situations, rather than assumed. The legitimate administrative state, in other words, is one inhabited by active citizens (1990, 247).

Although there is theoretical and practical recognition that the public must be more involved in public decisions, many administrators are, at best, ambivalent about public involvement or, at worst, they find it problematic. In an increasingly global and chaotic world, administrators are grappling with issues that do not seem to have definitive solutions, while still trying to encourage public involvement (Kettering Foundation, 1989). The issues traditionally facing administrators, "the more malleable problems, the ones that could be attacked with common sense and ingenuity, have in recent decades given way to a different class of problems—'wicked problems'—with no solutions, only temporary and imperfect resolutions" (Fischer, 1993, 172). Administrators need guidance and help in addressing these "wicked problems" but find that the help they seek from citizens often creates new sets of problems. As a result, although many public administrators view close relationships with citizens as both necessary and desirable, most of them do not actively seek public involvement. If they do seek it, they do not use public input in making administrative decisions (as indicated by a 1989 study conducted by the Kettering Foundation). These administrators believe that greater citizen participation increases inefficiency because participation creates delays and increases red tape.

As the Kettering Foundation study shows, an "undeniable tension" exists between the public's right to greater involvement and the prerogative of public officials to act as administrative decision makers (1989, 12). Citizens report feeling isolated from public administrative processes. Although they care about the issues facing their communities and the nation, citizens feel "pushed out" of the public process (Kettering Foundation, 1991). Citizens mistrust public officials and administrators. National opinion polls show that citizens' distrust of government is on the rise: 43 percent of citizens reported a lack of trust in government in 1992 while 70 percent reported distrust in 1994 (cited in Tolchin, 1996, 6). This distrust often leads to citizen cynicism or what Mathews (1994) calls impotence and causes interest in participation to decline (Berman, 1997).

Some citizens feel their concerns will be heard only if they organize into groups and angrily protest administrative policy decisions (Timney, 1996). NIMBYs (Not In My Backyard groups) have challenged administrative decisions on a variety of different issues in recent years (Fischer, 1993; Kraft and Clary, 1991), creating no end of trouble for people trying to implement administrative decisions. Citizens involved in these protest groups are confrontational in their participatory efforts because they believe administrators operate within a "context of self-interest" and are not connected to the citizens (Kettering Foundation, 1991, 7).

The participants of our study, administrators, activists, and citizens alike, agreed that participation is necessary and desirable. One citizen told us that participation was "the necessary opportunity to be a part of something bigger than oneself, a part of our responsibility to our community." An activist said, "it is very important to have an opportunity to influence and to know that your

Figure 26.1   **Context of Conventional Participation**

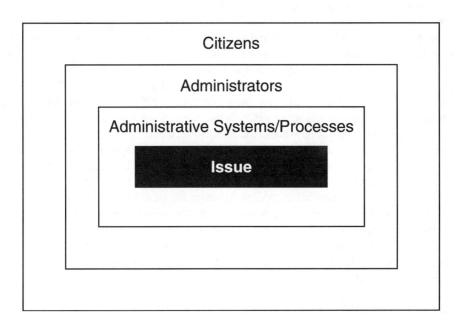

influence has the potential to make a difference." Administrators also stressed the centrality of input: "we *need* input," "we don't make good decisions without it," "it is essential." Our research participants agreed that the main problem with participation as it is currently practiced and framed is that it doesn't work. They believed that finding better ways to engender participation will make it more meaningful for all involved. Administrators recognize the need for participation, but they cannot find ways to fit the public into decision-making processes. Citizens believe that greater participation is needed, but they are rendered cynical or apathetic by vacuous or false efforts to stimulate participation that ask for, yet discount, public input. As a result, citizens find themselves moving from potentially cooperative to confrontational situations that pit administrators against citizens in an adversarial way. Why are we in this paradoxical conundrum? One reason may be the way participation is currently framed, the point to which we now turn.

HOW IS PARTICIPATION CURRENTLY FRAMED?

Public participation processes have four major components: (1) the issue or situation; (2) the administrative structures, systems, and processes within which participation takes place; (3) the administrators; and, (4) the citizens. Participation efforts are currently framed such that these components are arrayed around the issue. The citizen is placed at the greatest distance from the issue, the administrative structures and processes are the closest, and the administrator is the agent between the structures and citizens, as depicted in Figure 26.1.

In the context of conventional participation, the administrator controls the ability of the citizen to influence the situation or the process. The administrative structures and processes are the politically and socially constructed frameworks within which the administrator must operate. These frameworks give the administrator the authority to formulate decisions only after the issue has been defined. Thus, the administrator has no real power to redefine the issue or to alter administrative processes to allow for greater citizen involvement (Forester, 1989).

In the context of conventional participation the administrator plays the role of the expert. White and McSwain (1993) suggest that participation within this context is structured to maintain the centrality of the administrator while publicly presenting the administrator as representative, consultative, or participatory. The citizen becomes the "client" of the professional administrator, ill-equipped to question the professional's authority and technical knowledge. This process establishes what Fischer calls a "practitioner-client hierarchy" (1993, 165). In this falsely dualistic relationship, the administrators is separated from the "demands, needs, and values" of the people whom he or she is presumed to be serving (deLeon, 1992, 126).

Participation in this context is ineffective and conflictual, and it happens too late in the process, that is, after the issues have been framed and most decisions have been made. Therefore, rather than cooperating to decide how best to address issues, citizens are reactive and judgmental, often sabotaging administrators' best efforts. Administrators are territorial and parochial; they resist sharing information and rely on their technical and professional expertise to justify their role in administrative processes. Citizen participation is more symbolic than real (Arnstein, 1969). The power that citizens yield is aimed at blocking or redirecting administrative efforts rather than working as partners to define the issues, establish the parameters, develop methods of investigation, and select techniques for addressing problems.

REFRAMING PARTICIPATION

As defined by the participants of our research, effective participation is participation that is real or authentic. Authentic participation is deep and continuous involvement in administrative processes with the potential for all involved to have an effect on the situation. An activist defined authentic participation as "the ability and the opportunity to have an impact on the decision-making process." According to an administrator, authentic participation is "on-going, active involvement, not a one-shot deal, not just pulling the lever . . . it needs to go out and reach out to every part of your community, however defined." An activist said that good participation has occurred when "people affected by the change are comfortable with the decision made." A citizen explained, "For me, when I change perceptions I know it's a success."

Both citizens and administrators in our study defined the key elements of authentic participation as focus, commitment, trust, and open and honest discussion. As an activist stated, "People need to know that their input is important and will be considered in making that decision." An administrator concurred, "I think one of the keys for effective participation at the citizen and neighborhood level is for decision makers to be interested; to really listen to what the needs are of the people." Another administrator talked about listening and trust: "The first step is to make it clear that you're going to be receptive to their comments. But also I think a critical second step to maintaining their trust is to demonstrate to them that they're being heard . . . and that their ideas are shaping whatever you're developing." To achieve all of this, according to a third administrator, citizens and administrators "need to have a partnership. We do that by being sensitive that other people do have an agenda . . . but everyone should gradually come together."

Authentic participation requires that administrators focus on both process and outcome. In this context, participation is an integral part of administration, rather than an add-on to existing practices. Authentic participation means that the public is part of the deliberation process from issue framing to decision making (Roberts, 1997). As a citizen indicated, "From the very beginning people need to be involved." An administrator told us, "If you go to the community with a

Figure 26.2   **Context of Authentic Participation**

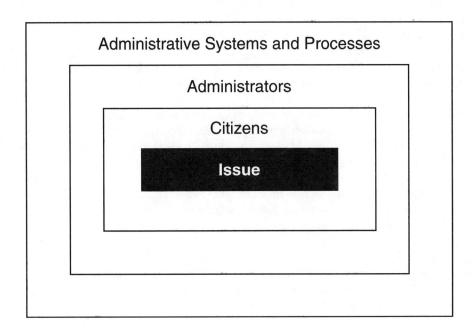

totally preset agenda that doesn't work. Bringing people into the process too late does not work."
An activist concurred, "I think that it is very important that individuals be given the opportunity,
prior to the decision being made, to provide input. [Citizens must have] enough time to process
that information. There is a lot of phony participation going on out there."

Addressing the limitations of current participatory efforts requires that public administrators
become "interpretive mediators." They must move beyond the technical issue at hand by involving
citizens in "dialectical exchange" (Fischer, 1993, 183) and by engaging with citizens in discourse
(Fox and Miller, 1995), rather than simply getting citizens input. Then, the administrator becomes
a cooperative participant, assisting citizens in examining their interests, working together with
them to arrive at decisions, and engaging them in open and authentic deliberation.

A citizen offers a compelling summary of the tensions involved in public participation: "You
have to get in there and ask their opinion. And they will tell you their opinion in the midst of telling you what a lousy job you are doing. And you have to be willing to deal with that, to put up
with it. I think a lot of administrators, like us, don't like criticism. They'll, naturally, avoid it . . .
and forget to go out in the field and get democracy." Getting democracy seems to lie at the core
of why authentic participation is important. Engendering a discourse where all participants have
an equal footing and where one group is not privileged over the other is at the heart of authentic
participation (Habermas, 1975).

The context of authentic participations is very different from the context conventional participation. Authentic participation places the citizen next to the issue and the administrative structures
and processes furthest away. However, the administrator is still the bridge between the two, as
depicted in Figure 26.2. Citizens are central and directly related to the issue; they have an immedi-

ate and equal opportunity to influence the processes and outcomes. The administrators' influence comes from their relationship with the citizenry as well as from their expertise and position. The administrative structures and processes are defined by the relationships and interactions of citizens and administrators.

Authentic participation moves the administrator away from a reliance on technical and expertise models of administration and toward meaningful participatory processes. Table 26.2 summarizes the key differences between unauthentic and authentic participation models. As an activist told us:

> Over the last year, the federal urban development people have put out some strict guide-lines to encourage and mandate participation. And they don't know how to deal with the participation . . . they're intimidated . . . and they [are beginning to realize] that maybe we all can learn better ways of doing this. Their attitudes have always been: we know what's better for the neighborhoods. Maybe they're just beginning to realize that maybe citizens do know something. Maybe they do know what's best for the neighborhood and they're in the process of trying to figure out how to balance what they've been doing all these years with the need for citizen participation.

Processes of authentic participation do not necessarily create more work for administrators. Authenticity does, however, require different kinds of work. In conventional processes, administrators often have to go back and redo projects that citizens block once decisions have been made. One administrator indicated:

> Why not get the citizens in and work these things out before we go with it? Actually, it may seem like it takes a little longer because, in the old way, we make a decision and run with it as far as we can; but then we have to run back and fix it. . . . There's always this arrogance that we know what the people need without their input—our system is set up to keep people away from the decision making.

Authentic participation involves citizens in the making of decisions instead of just judging. As one administrator told us, "There are two ways of participating: making, which includes doing something, and judgment. A lot of us go to meetings where we do nothing but judge. . . . It's the making and the doing that I think we're all wishing more citizens participated in."

Our research shows that the desire for participation is strong, and our participants recognize its importance. The next section examines the barriers to authentic participation.

BARRIERS TO AUTHENTIC PARTICIPATION

The focus group participants and subject matter experts agreed that participation methods and processes pose barriers to participation, but other factors do as well. Three categories of barriers were identified in our analyses: the nature of life in contemporary society, administrative processes, and current practices and techniques of participation.

The Nature of Life in Contemporary Society

The barriers stemming from the practical realities of daily life are tied to the social class position of citizens and include factors like transportation, time constraints, family structure, number of family members in the labor force, child care, and economic disadvantages. Some people express

Table 26.2

Comparison of Authentic and Unauthentic Participation

	Unauthentic participation	Authentic participation
Interaction style	Conflictual	Collaborative
Participation is sought	After the agenda is set and decisions are made	Early; before anything is set
Role of administrator	Expert technician/manager	Collaborative technician/governor
Administrative skills needed	Technical; managerial	Technical, interpersonal skills, discourse skills, facilitation skills
Role of citizen	Unequal participant	Equal partner
Citizenship skills needed	None	Civics, participation skills, discourse skills
Approach toward "other"	Mistrust	Trust
Administrative process	Static, invisible, closed	Dynamic, visible, open
Citizen options	Reactive	Proactive or reactive
Citizen output	Buy-in	Design
Administrator output	Decision	Process
Time to decision	Appears shorter and easier but often involves going back and "redoing" based upon citizen reaction	Appears longer and more onerous but usually doesn't require redoing because citizens have been involved throughout; may take less time to reach decisions than through traditional processes
Decision is made	By administrator/political and/or administrative processes perhaps in consultation with citizens	Emerges as a result of discourse; equal opportunity for all to enter the discourse and to influence the outcomes

a desire to participate more fully in their communities, but the demands of day-to-day life get in the way. As one citizen said, "A lot of people are holding down two jobs and both people work in the family and are too tired . . . [from] trying to survive a day at a time."

The focus group members compared an idealized past where civic participation was common and visible, to the present, where it is nearly impossible to fit participation into an over-crowded schedule. The past was seen as a time of economic security with stable employment where participation in community life was a given. As one administrator explained, "At least in my grandparent's generation they weren't worried if Goodyear was going to be there. They knew they were. They were playing ball, going to Boy Scouts. Now . . . it's unusual if you have a bit of [worry-free] luxury in your life to participate."

According to the older members in the focus group, younger community members are not pursuing an activist tradition. It is a constant challenge to community activists to get younger citizens to participate. One activist said, "We're trying to replace people who were active in the block clubs with people who are from the young families to take over the reins of what the older citizens have been doing for years. That's a hard thing to do."

Citizens, administrators, and activists all agreed that participation is hindered by a lack of education, both informally within families and communities and formally in the schools. One administrator described how early childhood socialization prepared him for a life of participation:

> When I was a kid we would meet at the dinner table . . . and that was the place that almost without fail we'd get around to political and neighborhood and church goings on . . . that would be the basis for learning about and socializing into broader issues in the community. . . . The same thing was true for the neighborhoods. The adults used to gather on the front porches while their kids would play.

The demise of the neighborhood as an organizing and socializing system was described in the following way by one administrator: "People don't talk to each other anymore . . . the neighborhoods aren't neighborhoods . . . they used to be real tight-knit communities." Isolation from others is detrimental to participation.

One subject matter expert suggested that citizen participation is "abysmally low [because] we've taught people not to participate." However, he noted that even if people were invited to participate, "there is still the nature of citizen life itself, we are all very busy, perhaps too busy to participate." He warned against relying on standard indicators to draw conclusions about rates or levels of participation. Traditional participation indicators such as voting, attending civic meetings, or running for city council don't capture the cultural forms of participation that are more likely to involve younger members of the community. However, he also agreed that participatory values have not been reinforced in this "era of privatization and free market economy [where] individuals have a lot of economic pressures without much spare capital."

While day-to-day life keeps people from being more participatory and perhaps inculcates non-participatory attitudes and apathy, many of our research participants felt that current administrative processes are as much to blame for the lack of citizen participation.

Administrative Processes

The second set of barriers identified by our participants consists of those inherent in administrative processes themselves. These barriers are paradoxical. While most people define citizen participation as desirable, any participation seen as challenging the administrative status quo is blocked by the very administrators who desire more participatory processes. As one citizen lamented:

Isn't it a shame [that] one of the obstacles in citizen participation seems to be government. . . . We're talking about grass-roots programs that work *despite* the government, [because they are able to] work around the officials. It seems to me that [elected officials and administrators] should all be wanting to get people to participate . . . not putting up barriers. They only want favorable participation . . . to keep the status quo.

An activist described the barriers in the process as follows:

It seems to me that the political process gets in the way. You can do all the things that should be done, get the citizens together, get them involved, get input. But if the decision has already been made on a different level, it's all [window] dressing. And we have to get past that first. How do you do that when the political process has already made the decision which way it's going to go?

Citizens in our focus groups, like those included in other research, viewed communication in participatory processes as flowing one way—from the administrative professional to the citizen. Citizens in our project felt that information is usually managed, controlled, and manipulated, limiting their capacity to participate. As one citizen explained, "By the time we hear about issues it's too late to affect a decision." Another citizen concurred, "By the time we hear about the issues it is too late in the process. We might hear about it if we read the paper or if someone on your committee is on top of things enough to know what's going on." As a result, citizens talk about administrators as adversaries, as one citizen explained: "I think if we participate . . . we can sometimes beat the administrators to the gun.

Techniques of Participation

One of the most problematic administrative barriers is the techniques used in most participatory processes. As found in other research (Crosby, Kelly, and Schaefer, 1986; Kathlene and Martin, 1991; Kweit and Kweit, 1981; 1987; Parsons, 1990), our focus group participants told us that most techniques used in current participation efforts are inadequate. The most ineffective technique is the public hearing. Public hearings do not work. Low attendance at public hearings is often construed as public apathy or silent approval of the status quo (Kathlene and Martin, 1991). In actuality, low attendance is more likely to be related to the structure of public hearings.

Administrators recognize that the structure of public hearings and public meetings prohibits meaningful exchange. As one administrator said, "The public hearing is not about communicating, it is about convincing." Another explained the limitations of public school board meetings, "When you go to a school board meeting, they get this egg timer, time to grab the microphone and speak. There's no follow-up. You don't even get to ask them questions. . . . There's no give and take." An activist suggested that the public hearing was window dressing, "We have these hearings so they can check off on their list that they've had their citizen participation. . . . It's participation out of the fear that they are going to look bad."

A major problem is the timing of public hearings. They are often held late in the process, when decisions have already been made. As one administrator explained, "I think public hearings are definitely too late. It's a formal process. Citizens know that. They know that and come to public hearings, but they know that it is already too late."

Other common methods of participation are citizen advisory councils, citizen panels, and public surveys (Crosby, et al., 1986; Kathlene and Martin, 1991; Parsons 1990). Limitations of councils and panels include biases in composition, particularly with regard to social class (Verba, et al., 1993). Surveys, on the other hand, document public opinions at one point in time (Kathlene and Martin, 1991) and do not allow for an interactive process or relationship between citizens and administrators.

Administrators in our project were clear that participation techniques need to be improved. One administrator pointed out: "We can't ignore the process of conducting a good meeting. There are many people who get turned off when [meetings aren't run well]. . . . It could be a royal waste of my time and I resent that." Another administrator challenged all administrators:

> Look at alternative ways to get people involved. It isn't just if you can't come to the meeting, you can't be involved. That may be a very interesting challenge for us to think about. What other ways can people feel that they have some say in the process without having to leave their kids and get a baby-sitter and go to a meeting and so forth? Solving these problems may be a tremendous, innovative way to break down some of these barriers.

To move toward authentic participation administrators need to change many of their current practices. One change may be to go where the citizens are rather than asking citizens to come to them. As one administrator proposed, "So imagine if the councilman from your ward called you up and said, you know, I'm interested in meeting with a small group of your neighbors. Can I come to you rather than you coming here?" Another administrator concurred, "We've got to stop doing things the way we've always done them. We can't be having meetings during the daytime and expect people to come. We can't be doing things in a remote place and expect people to come at 8:00 at night. . . . We've·got to go to them."

Accessibility is another important issue. As one administrator outlined, "Another effort in the community is grass-roots leadership. . . . Folks who have been historically excluded from processes of decision making about these scarce resources need to be increasingly included in the processes." Another administrator agreed, "In order to have true participation, those of us who have some authority have to be more active in bringing people who perceive themselves as excluded into the process."

Our research participants told us that they want authentic participation, but many barriers restrict participation. In the final section of this article we suggest how to overcome these barriers in order to move toward more authentic participatory processes.

OVERCOMING BARRIERS TO AUTHENTIC PARTICIPATION

As our findings indicate, people may be more willing to participate if they have a real opportunity to influence both administrative processes and outcomes. Shifting participatory techniques to more effective or authentic practices requires what deLeon (1992) identifies as a two-sided learning process. Both administrators and citizens need to learn.

In order to move toward authentic models, all three components of public participation—the administrative structures and processes, the administrators, and the citizens—must be addressed by those working in, and seeking to understand, public administration. Authenticity cannot be achieved by addressing problems in only one area. For example, citizen empowerment in the absence of administrative transformation is problematic. To develop processes that increase participation without changing the power relations between citizens and administrators is also problematic. Models of authentic participation must take a three-pronged approach, addressing all three components, seeking to (1) empower and educate community members, (2) re-educate administrators, and (3) enable administrative structures and processes. We discuss each of these objectives in the following sections. Table 26.3 provides a summary of practical actions that administrators and citizens can take to overcome barriers to authentic participation in each of these areas.

Empowering and Educating Citizens

Empowering citizens means designing processes where citizens know that their participation has the potential to have an impact, where a representative range of citizens are included, and where there are visible outcomes. The central issue is one of access. According to one subject matter expert, "Creating opportunities for people to participate is the key. . . . It is all about access to skill building and to information."

The education of citizens should focus on teaching specific organizing and research skills. In addition, community members need leadership training. According to a subject matter expert, "democracy schools," much like the Citizenship Schools that fueled the civil rights movement in the South, should be established in local communities "to encourage people to see they can actually make a difference if they get involved." Another subject matter expert recommended learning centers "to provide continued education for elected officials and citizens alike."

Citizens and administrators must work as partners in the establishment of democracy schools or learning centers, and, according to one subject matter expert, "they should be learning the same skills." Educating people, according to one activist, "is having people feel confident and informed . . . directing their energies towards a specific goal instead of sitting there being angry with their situation. . . . Empowerment [comes from] education."

With a shared base of knowledge, citizens and administrators can work together from the very beginning when issues are being defined and framed. Citizens need to be involved from the beginning rather than brought in at the end when questions are already framed in ways that are not amenable to open decision making (e.g., the specific placement of a nuclear waste site versus the question of nuclear waste production and disposal as a community-based issue). In addition, citizens and administrators can work together to develop methods of investigation and select techniques for addressing problems.

Many of the realities of daily life that limit citizens' ability to be involved in public decisions seem almost too big for an administrator to change, especially at the local level. How can we change economies and habits of living that limit people's time, energy, and capacities to participate? Although it is difficult to address the major political, economic, and social issues that limit participation, participants in our research project told us that it is possible to chip away at these big issues. For example, some programs stimulate participation and reduce citizen alienation through the development of alternative economics. Summit County in northeastern Ohio is home of one of the first goods-exchange alternative economies that are now beginning to crop up across the country. People connect with one another through a program called "Summit Dollars," where both the currency and the products are services, hand-produced goods, or hours spent on a project. People barter and exchange their services and goods outside of the regular money economy. Not only are those involved benefiting from this program economically, but participants are also making connections and developing relationships that they may not have made without the program. As a result, alienation is decreasing and connections in the community are increasing.

Summit County also houses a successful program called SHARE, which brings together community members and corporate sponsors to provide $30.00 of groceries a month to each participant willing to pay a reduced amount for the food and donate two hours a month to a community effort. This program is interesting because it brings together participants across class, race, and other

396

Table 26.3

Overcoming Barriers to Authentic Participation: Recommendations for Practice

Barriers	Objectives		
	Empowering and educating citizens	Re-educating administrators	Enabling administrative systems and processes
Realities of daily life	Talk with administrators; establish one-on-one relationships.	Take initiative to talk with citizens; establish one-on-one relationships. Go out and get democracy.	Set up flexible meeting schedules; multiple opportunities.
	Pay attention.	Don't separate yourself from your job; you are a citizen also. Think about your life and plan participation efforts accordingly.	Go to where people are (lunch hour, child care centers, schools, churches, laundry facilities, electronic, etc.).
	Talk to neighbors; form relationships with others in your area (interest or geographical).	Be sure that projects are advertised so that people are informed (flyers in well-attended places, phone calls, mailings, etc.).	Use electronic resources (but don't rely only upon them).
	Strengthen local economies, emphasizing benefits to people versus the economy.		Provide on-site, free child-care; catered meals at a nominal charge for participants, free meals for disadvantaged participants.
	Create opportunities for people to interact with each other.		Seek diversity in representation.
Administrative systems and processes	Teach citizens how to work within the system and to work with the system.	Begin to see citizenry as the fourth branch of government; one can't talk about governance and government without talking about citizens.	Allocate resources for participation efforts.

	Head off antigovernment sentiment by educating citizens about the necessity of government practices (red tape, etc), assuming this is done in a good-faith effort to find ways to work more effectively with citizens.	Shift from majority focus of education on managerial skills to governance skills.	Reward administrators for participation efforts; change job descriptions; participation must be integral to job, not an add-on.
	Place more emphasis on civics and public participation in K–12 (add to 3Rs) as well as in higher education. Educate to participate.	Require continuing education credits for administrators that focus on innovations in practice.	Bring people in before agenda is set; create ongoing project teams that follow project through to completion.
			Shift from emphasis on managerial roles of administration to governance roles.
Participation techniques	Hold workshops with administrators that focus upon discourse skills, meeting skills, and research and statistics skills.	Infuse Master of Public Administration and undergrad curricula with training in the skills below; develop on-site training funded by agencies and local governments: facilitation skills; team-building skills; organizational development skills; discourse skills; interpersonal skills.	Change the way we meet and interact with each other and with citizens: many small meetings; roundtable discussions; outside facilitators; equal participants; no one privileged in group because of position, status, demographic characteristics, etc.
	Hold workshop and training opportunities with administrators prior to beginning project team work.	Require these curriculum changes as part of NASPAA accreditation requirements.	Avoid one-shot techniques like surveys or biased techniques like boards or panels.

boundaries and gives people something tangible in return for their participation efforts. Although the decision to be connected rests with the individual, much can be done to address the barriers that discourage people from being more involved in public decision making.

Re-educating Administrators

Re-educating administrators means changing their roles from that of expert managers toward that of cooperative participants or partners. This task involves shifts at the personal level with regard to inter/intrapersonal skills (Denhardt and Aristigueta, 1996; Stivers, 1994), redefining the role of expertise in public administration, and changing the ways we educate and train public administrators.

Along with the traditional research, budgeting, and management skills that one normally learns in a graduate program in public administration, public administrators also need to be trained in process and interpersonal skills including communication, listening, team building, meeting facilitation, and self-knowledge. In their accreditation reviews public administration programs should be evaluated on the basis of their process-oriented curricula, much in the same way that the National Association of Schools of Public Affairs and Administration (NASPAA) currently evaluates content-oriented curricula.

Administrators need to examine their basic assumptions and practices regarding power. They need to become cooperative participants in the discourse, moving from a self-regarding intentionality where the goal is to protect self, promote self-interests, and hoard power, to a situation regarding intentionality where power and community are grounded in the needs of the issue or situation (Fox and Miller, 1995). The motivation to do so is lacking, of course, when administrators are under pressure from their agencies and institutions to perform in certain ways that serve the institutions, rather than the citizenry. Therefore, examining the basic assumptions about power requires a significant shift in the mainstream values about what it is that administrators do. Administrators typically are expected to manage, not govern (Harmon, 1995; Wamsley, et al., 1990).

Enabling Administrative Structures and Processes

The most difficult things to change are the structures and processes of administration. To shift administrative structures is no small feat. This requires changing institutionalized habits and practices. Without real changes in how bureaucracies function, there will be little movement toward authentic participation and greater cynicism on the part of administrators and citizens. Public organizations must "not only democratize formal institutions and procedures, but also make room for nonbureaucratic discourse and organizational forms" (Tauxe, 1995, 489).

Most of the changes needed in administrative structures will originate with the people involved in administration. Systems and structures are nothing more than the habitual practices of the people involved in the system, or what Giddens (1984) calls recursive practices. If administrators change their practices and start working with citizens as partners, they will begin to shift the way administration is practiced at the microlevel. If changes are made at the microlevel, macrolevel administrative structures and processes will necessarily follow.

Administrators in our study made specific recommendations for changing microlevel practices (see Table 26.3 for examples). Experimenting with a variety of innovative microlevel techniques is a starting point for administrators as they grapple with the problem of how to increase the level of participation in their communities. Some changes must be made or else we risk continuing to hamper our work by practicing participation efforts that, according to a subject matter expert, "are inherently conflictual, discourage public participation, and yield silly outcomes." He added, "In a perfect world, if participation is sought at the first level of the decision rather than at the end, then citizens may be more likely to trust the experts and let them do their jobs. As it stands now, trust will never happen."

It is ironic that the obligation for facilitating change in citizens, administrators, and administrative practices falls on the shoulders of administrators. After all, the administrators have been doing it "wrong" all along. If we assume that a more authentic context of participation allows the administrator to act as facilitator, then it is the responsibility of the administrator to shape the participation process, starting as the initial change agent. It is essential that schools of public administration, as well as those in leadership positions in agencies, create environments within which these change agents can be successful. Such an environment requires appropriate levels of resources and changes in job descriptions for administrators.

We are asking a great deal of administrators and their agencies, but it is clear to us, based on our findings and participation efforts like those in cities such as Cleveland, Seattle, Dayton, and Phoenix (Crislip and Larson, 1994), that the potential is there. In addition, significant reorganization efforts in policy-making bodies, such as the U.S. Environment Protection Agency (King, Stivers, et al., 1998), indicate that it is possible to shift institutional systems so that the policy processes are amenable to collaborative work.

Authentic participation is possible. This study validates previous research, brings together the voices of the people involved in participation at the local level, and suggests a three-pronged approach toward authentic participation. Translating these recommendations into action requires that public administration practitioners and scholars address all three components at the same time, an essential strategy for shifting toward more authentic participation processes in public administration.

ACKNOWLEDGMENT

This article was funded by an inter-institutional grant from the Ohio Board of Regents' Urban University Program. The authors would like to thank Shannon O'Donnell Wolf and Brenda Cox for their assistance in the research. We are also grateful to our reviewers for their contributions.

REFERENCES

Arnstein, S. (1969). "A Ladder of Citizen Participation." *Journal of the American Institute of Planners* 35: 216–224.
Berman, E.M. (1997). "Dealing with Cynical Citizens." *Public Administration Review* 57(2): 105–112.
Box, R.C. (1996). "The Institutional Legacy of Community Governance." *Administrative Theory and Praxis* 18(2): 84–100.
Cooper, T.L. (1991). *An Ethic of Citizenship for Public Administration.* Englewood Cliffs, NJ: Prentice-Hall.
Crislip, D.D., and C.E. Larson (1994). *Collaborative Leadership: How Citizens and Civic Leaders Can Make a Difference.* San Francisco: Jossey-Bass.
Crosby, N., J.M. Kelly, and P. Schaefer (1986). "Citizen Panels: A New Approach to Citizen Participation." *Public Administration Review* 46: 170–178.
deLeon, P. (1992). "The Democratization of the Policy Sciences." *Public Administration Review* 52: 125–129.
Denhardt, R.B., and M.D. Aristigueta (1996). "Developing Intrapersonal Skills." In J. Perry, ed., *Handbook of Public Administration.* 2nd ed. San Francisco: Jossey-Bass, 682–695.
Farmer, D.J. (1995). *The Language of Public Administration. Bureaucracy, Modernity, and Postmodernity.* University, AL: University of Alabama Press.
Fischer, F. (1993). "Citizen Participation and the Democratization of Policy Expertise: From Theoretical Inquiry to Practical Cases." *Policy Sciences* 26(3): 165–187.

Forester, J. (1989). *Planning in the Face of Power.* Berkeley: University of California Press.

Fox, C.J., and H.T. Miller (1995). *Postmodern Public Administration: Toward Discourse.* Thousand Oaks, CA: Sage.

Frederickson, H.G. (1982). "The Recovery of Civism in Public Administration." *Public Administration Review* 42: 501–508.

Giddens, A. (1984). *The Constitution of Society: Outline of the Theory of Structuration.* Berkeley: University of California Press.

Habermas, J. (1975). *Legitimation Crisis,* Boston, MA: Beacon Press.

Harmon, M.M. (1995). *Responsibility as Paradox: A Critique of Rational Discourse on Government.* Thousand Oaks, CA: Sage.

Kathlene, L., and J.A. Martin (1991). "Enhancing Citizen Participation: Panel Designs, Perspectives, and Policy Formation." *Journal of Policy Analysis and Management* 10(1): 46–63.

Kettering Foundation (1989). *The Public's Role in the Policy Process: A View from State and Local Policy Makers.* Dayton, OH: Kettering Foundation.

——— (1991). *"Citizens and Politics: A View from Main Street America."* Report prepared for the Kettering Foundation by the Harwood Group. Dayton, OH: Kettering Foundation.

King, C.S., C. Stivers, et al. (1998). *Government Is Us: Public Administration in an Anti-government Era.* Thousand Oaks, CA: Sage.

Kraft, M., and B.B. Clary (1991). "Citizen Participation and the NIMBY Syndrome: Public Response to Radioactive Waste Disposal." *Western Political Quarterly* 44(2): 299–328.

Kweit, M.G., and R.W. Kweit (1981). *Implementing Citizen Participation in a Bureaucratic Society.* New York: Praeger.

——— (1987). "Citizen Participation: Enduring Issues for the Next Century." *National Civic Review* 76: 191–198.

Mathews, D. (1994). *Politics for the People.* Urbana, IL: University of Illinois Press.

Parr, J., and C. Gates (1989). "Assessing Community Interest and Gathering Community Support." In International City Management Association, eds., *Partnerships in Local Governance: Effective Council-Manager Relations.* Washington, DC: International City Management Association.

Parsons, G.A. (1990). "Defining the Public Interest: Citizen Participation in Metropolitan and State Policy Making." *National Civic Review* 79: 118–131.

Putnam, R.D. (1995). "Bowling Alone: America's Declining Social Capital." *Journal of Democracy* 20(1): 65–78.

Roberts, N. (1997). "Public Deliberation: An Alternative Approach to Crafting Policy and Setting Direction." *Public Administration Review* 57(2): 124–132.

Stivers, C. (1990). "Active Citizenship and Public Administration." In G.L. Wamsley, R.N. Bacher, C.T. Goodsell, P.S. Kronenberg, J.A. Rohr, C.M. Stivers, O.F. White, and J.F. Wolf, *Refounding Public Administration.* Thousand Oaks, CA: Sage, 246–273.

——— (1994). "The Listening Bureaucrat: Responsiveness in Public Administration." *Public Administration Review* 54(4): 364–369.

Strauss, A.M., and J.L. Corbin (1990). *Basics of Qualitative Research: Grounded Theory Procedures and Techniques.* Thousand Oaks, CA: Sage.

Tauxe, C.S. (1995). "Marginalizing Public Participation in Local Planning: An Ethnographic Account." *Journal of the American Planning Association* 61(4): 471–481.

Thomas, J.C. (1995). *Public Participation in Public Decisions.* San Francisco: Jossey-Bass.

Timney, M.M. (1996). "Overcoming NIMBY: Using Citizen Participation Effectively." Paper presented at the 57th national conference of the American Society for Public Administration, Atlanta, GA.

Tolchin, S.J. (1996). *The Angry American: How Voter Rage Is Changing the Nation.* Boulder, CO: Westview Press.

Verba, S., K. Schlozman, M. Brady, and N.H. Nie (1993). "Citizen Activity: Who Participates? What Do They Say?" *American Political Science Review* 87(2): 303–318.

Wamsley, G.L., and J.F. Wolf (1996). "Introduction: Can a High Modern Project Find Happiness in a Postmodern Era?" In G.L. Wamsley and J.F. Wolf, eds., *Refounding Democratic Public Administration: Modern Paradoxes, Postmodern Challenges.* Thousand Oaks, CA: Sage, 1–37.

Wamsley, G.L., R.N. Bacher, C.T. Goodsell, P.S. Kronenberg, J.A. Rohr, C.M. Stivers, O.F. White, and J.F. Wolf, (1990). *Refounding Public Administration.* Thousand Oaks, CA: Sage.

White, O.F., and C.J. McSwain (1993). "The Semiotic Way of Knowing and Public Administration." *Administrative Theory and Praxis* 15(1): 18–35.

CHAPTER 27

ASSESSING PUBLIC PARTICIPATION IN U.S. CITIES

XIAOHU WANG

Public participation is advocated to reduce citizen cynicism toward government, build stakeholder consensus in government, and enhance administrative decision making (Creighton, 1981; King & Stivers, 1998; Langton, 1978a; Sanoff, 2000). Participation theories have been presented and examined in research. Case descriptions or stories in individual governmental agencies are often used to support theoretical assertions. Empirical evidence is needed about participation in government as a whole. Studies involving larger samples of governments can generate more holistic and systematic evidence.

Using survey data, this study focused on three research questions: How much public participation occurs in U.S. municipal governments? What are the possible causes of participation? What are the possible impacts of participation on governmental agencies? This research provides useful information about potential obstacles to participation and ways to enhance participation and performance in government. The Framework section presents relevant definitions and theories.

FRAMEWORK

What Is Participation?

Public participation is defined as citizen involvement in making service delivery and management decisions (Langton, 1978b). Participation occurs when citizens and public officials have participation needs and when participation mechanisms exist (King, Feltey, & Susel, 1998). Traditional participation mechanisms include public hearings, citizen forums, community or neighborhood meetings, community outreaches, citizen advisory groups, and individual citizen representation. Citizen surveys and focus groups, the Internet, and e-mail are also used.

There are two levels of participation. Participation is "pseudo" (Sanoff, 2000) when the purposes of participation are to inform citizens about decisions, placate their complaints, and manipulate

From *Public Performance and Management Review,* 24, 4 (June 2001): 322–336. Copyright © 2001 by Sage Publications, Inc. Reprinted with permission.

their opinions. Genuine participation occurs only when the public is involved in administrative decision making, and citizens are the owners of government and the coproducers of public goods (King et al., 1998; Sanoff, 2000). In genuine participation, citizens are dominant discussants and decision makers, and government's supplementary role is to set goals, provide incentives, monitor processes, and provide information (Gray and Chapin, 1998; Plein, Green, & Williams, 1998).

The participation literature has emphasized two aspects of participation. First, participation appears in various public service functions such as economic development, environmental protection, education, public health, and public safety (Aryani, Garrett, & Alsabrook 2000; Foley, 1998; Iglitzin, 1995; Kovalick & Kelly; 1998; Morgan, 1987; Sanoff, 2000), as well as in management functions such as budgeting (O'Toole and Marshall, 1988; Preisser 1997; Simonsen & Robbins, 2000). Second, participation also occurs in policy making or decision making. In this aspect of participation, the public is involved in goal setting, strategy, policy, capacity determination, and implementation evaluation (Walters, Aydelotte, & Miller, 2000). Participation in decision making is seen as evidence of "genuine" or "meaningful" participation in the literature because it is how "public beliefs and values" can be realized (Lando, 1999; Yankelovich, 1991).

Why Participation?

The public becomes involved in government for various reasons, including external pressures from stakeholders and internal demands from administrators. The size of bureaucracy is associated with public demand for participation. Citizens want to participate more in large governments because they are afraid of losing "personal contact" and control to a large bureaucracy (Creighton, 1981). Political divisiveness among different groups motivates government to involve citizens in decision making to reduce potentially unpopular or questionable decisions (Langton, 1978a, pp. 6–8). Media attitudes influence public participation by making more people aware of problems associated with government (Langton, 1978a, pp. 6–8).

The tension between participation and administration is well-established in the research literature (DeSario & Langton, 1987; Kweit & Kweit, 1987; Simonsen & Robbins, 2000). Evidently, participation is facilitated in an open and accountable administrative system. Public involvement is encouraged by public employees who are willing to be accountable for their operations, efforts, and performance. Sufficient funding and technical assistance are necessary due to the need for personnel and infrastructure to support participation (Cohen, 1995). Organizations that develop agendas that interest the public should have fewer difficulties in initiating and sustaining the momentum for participation.

What Are the Impacts of Participation?

Three impacts of participation on government are anticipated (Creighton, 1981, pp. 11–12; Langton, 1978b, pp. 13–24). First, participation leads to satisfying the needs of the public. The argument is that public needs are not automatically served by a bureaucracy whose main motivation is the maximization of its financial inputs (Niskanen, 1971). The design of representative democracy allows special interest groups with large financial leverages to influence governmental decision making, and the needs of the general public are further compromised (Kaufman, 1969; Lowi, 1969). Public participation provides guidance for bureaucratic production and a balance to the influence of powerful interest groups. The idea is that public participation enhances the communication between the public and government, which allows government to understand what the public wants (Creighton, 1981, pp. 11–12). Consistent citizen involvement also provides government with an opportunity to effectively monitor and respond to the changes in public needs. A good understanding of and prompt responses to public needs result in citizen satisfaction. These arguments are furthered by recent assertions that there is a need to create a market for public service production, which is designed to satisfy the needs of citizens who are also customers (Osborne & Plastrik, 1997; Swiss, 1999).

Second, participation helps build consensus on organizational goals, service priorities, good performance, and fiscal commitment. Stakeholder demands of government vary. As a result, many governmental agencies have multiple and sometimes contradictory goals. Participation allows the public to voice its needs, which provides legitimacy for government to develop publicly supported goals, missions, and service priorities (Langton, 1978b, pp. 13–24). In addition, because there are often no standards for good performance in the public sector due to the lack of market evaluation and the nature of public goods, involving the public in decision making provides a mechanism with which to develop standards and expectations for performance. Participation leads to stakeholder acceptance of organizational goals, performance standards, and decisions (Pateman, 1970).

One enduring task in public management is to resolve the tension between public demands and management reality (DeSario & Langton, 1987). Political conflict, resource availability, management complexity, and impact uncertainty limit governments' capacities to fulfill all public demands. Participation allows the public to reevaluate its demands and better understand these management limitations. It is expected that consensus is built on a mutual understanding between the public and government.

Finally, participation improves public trust of governmental decision making. There has been continuous criticism that government is ineffective in service production, dishonest in decision making, and unfair in service delivery. One reason for this mistrust is the lack of mechanisms with which the public can monitor governmental operations. Consequently, the public becomes alienated. Cases of government mismanagement and efforts to cover it up only aggravate public concerns. Public participation may reduce this sense of alienation. A more open and accountable decision-making process may result in a better understanding of government and improved public trust of government (Creighton, 1981, pp. 11–12).

METHOD

A National Survey

A survey was sent to all chief administrative officers in U.S. cities with populations greater than 50,000 in the late 1990s and early 2000. The list of cities' addresses was obtained from the National League of Cities. The names and addresses were also verified with the International City/County Management Association's (ICMA) (1998) *Municipal Yearbook*. Two hundred forty-nine of 541 surveyed cities returned the survey (a response rate of 46%). Sixty-four percent of respondents were city managers (or chief administrators) or assistant city managers. Fifteen percent were chief finance or budget officers (finance directors or budget directors). Other respondents (21.5%) included senior management analysts, directors of administrations, directors of planning, and other high-level city officials.

To check the nonresponse bias, I examined the population distribution, the form of government, and sample questions of responding cities. First, the population distribution of responding cities was compared with the population distribution of the cities in the ICMA's (1998) *Yearbook*. Except for cities with populations greater than 1 million, of which 7 of 8 responded to the survey (an 87.5% response rate), cities in other population categories exhibited similar response rates: 47.0% for cities with populations ranging from 500,000 to 1 million, 48.7% for cities with populations ranging from 250,000 to 499,999, 51.1% for cities with populations ranging from 100,000 to 249,999, and 41.6% for cities with populations ranging from 50,000 to 99,999. Second, I examined the form of government of the responding and nonresponding cities. Of the cities reporting such information, 179 had a council-manager form of government (52.7% of the 340 council-manager cities in the sample). The response rates for other categories of governmental form were significantly lower (28.7%, 12.5%, and 20.0% for the mayor-council form, the commission form, and the township form, respectively), suggesting that this sample was more representative of the council-manager form of government. Third, telephone surveys were conducted with more than 50 randomly selected city officials who did not respond to the survey (about 20% of nonrespondents). These officials were asked two selected survey questions that included 32 survey items. Their answers were then compared with the respondents' answers. No respondent bias was found by this process. To ensure the validity of the responses, I also conducted follow-up telephone interviews in which respondents were asked to verify their responses through specific examples in their organizations. Few changes were made as a result of these phone interviews.

Several in-depth interviews were also conducted to gain insights about participation practices in governments. The interviewees were survey respondents who had scored high on participation indexes (discussed below). The interviewees were asked about their participation practices and impacts. They were also asked to give specific examples to elaborate their points. The results of these interviews were used to further explore the findings of the mailed survey.

Measurement of Variables

In accordance with the definition of participation outlined above, three dimensions of public participation were measured: the use of participation mechanisms, citizen involvement in service or management functions, and citizen involvement in administrative decision making. First, the use of participation mechanisms was measured. Respondents were asked to assess on a 5-point scale (5 = *strongly agree,* 4 = *agree,* 3 = *neutral,* 2 = *disagree,* 1 = *strongly disagree*) whether their administrations used selected public participation mechanisms (the eight items listed in Table 27.1). These mechanisms are frequently cited in the participation literature (Creighton, 1981, Lindstrom & Nie, 2000, Sanoff, 2000). They include traditional means such as public hearings and citizen advisory boards as well as new mechanisms such as citizen telephone hotlines and the Internet. The Participation Mechanism Index was constructed to include all eight items. The index had a mean of 3.85 and a standard deviation of 0.65. A reliability statistic showed that this index was relatively reliable (Cronbach's alpha = 0.78).

Second, citizen involvement in service or management functions was measured. This dimension concerns the extent of participation in city functions. Survey respondents were asked to identify participation in nine important service or management functions, including policing and public safety, code enforcement, zoning and planning, parks and recreation, transportation and street maintenance, solid waste and garbage collection, budgeting, personnel management, and procurement management (see Table 27.2). In the survey, respondents were asked to assess on a 5-point scale (5 = *strongly agree,* 4 = *agree,* 3 = *neutral,* 2 = *disagree,* 1 = *strongly disagree*) whether citizens on citizen activists in their cities were involved in these functions. An index was then constructed to average the values of all nine items (functions). Because this index measured participation in governmental functions, it was called the Function Participation Index. This index had a mean of 3.14 and a standard deviation of 0.56, and was relatively reliable (Cronbach's alpha = 0.79).

Table 27.1

Use of Participation Mechanisms

	Percent						
Participation mechanism	Strongly agree	Agree	Neutral	Disagree	Strongly disagree	M	SD
Public hearings (*n* = 247)	65.6	31.3	1.2	1.6	0.4	4.60	0.64
Citizen advisory boards (*n* = 245)	40.4	41.2	10.2	5.7	2.4	4.11	0.97
Community or neighborhood meetings (*n* = 246)	43.9	43.5	7.3	2.8	2.4	4.24	0.89
Individual citizen representatives (*n* = 237)	18.1	33.3	27.0	16.9	4.6	3.43	1.11
Citizen surveys (*n* = 238)	23.1	29.8	23.9	18.1	5.0	3.48	1.76
Citizen focus groups (*n* = 241)	18.3	38.2	21.2	17.4	5.0	3.47	1.26
Citizen telephone hotline (*n* = 237)	24.9	28.3	22.8	17.7	6.3	3.47	1.22
Internet (*n* = 244)	39.8	41.8	10.7	7.0	0.8	4.13	0.92
Participation Mechanism Index						3.85	0.65
Cronbach's alpha = 0.78							

Note: Respondents indicated whether their administrations used these participation mechanisms on a 5-point scale (5 = *strongly agree*, 4 = *agree*, 3 = *neutral*, 2 = *disagree*, 1 = *strongly disagree*). Numbers in parentheses are sample sizes. The index was created by averaging the values of all above items.

Third, citizen involvement in strategic processes of administrative decision making was also measured. Nine survey items (listed in Table 27.3) were developed to measure public involvement in goal setting, strategy determination, policy and capacity development, process monitoring, and evaluation. The selection of these items was based on the decision-making and strategic management literature (Bryson, 1995; Thompson & Strickland, 1992). A 5-point scale (5 = *strongly agree*, 4 = *agree*, 3 = *neutral*, 2 = *disagree*, 1 = *strongly disagree*) was used for these survey items. An index consisting of all these items was created. Because it measured participation in decision making, it was called the Decision-Making Participation Index. The index had a mean of 2.56 and a standard deviation of 0.73. Cronbach's alpha (0.91) for this index shows that its reliability is high.

Survey items were also developed to measure the possible causes and impacts of participation. The items used to measure the causes of participation are listed in Table 27.4. They include five items measuring external pressures and six items measuring internal demands and capacities. Respondents were requested to grade these items on a 5-point scale (5 = *strongly agree*, 4 = *agree*, 3 = *neutral*, 2 = *disagree*, 1 = *strongly disagree*).

To measure participation impacts, respondents were asked to indicate on a 5-point scale (5 = *strongly agree*, 4 = *agree*, 3 = *neutral*, 2 = *disagree*, 1 = *strongly disagree*) whether their administrations could identify, assess, or satisfy public need. Four items (Cronbach's alpha = 0.60) were used to measure the identification of public need, including "Our administration can define customers or client needs" and "Our administration can provide services that the public needs." Two items (Cronbach's alpha = 0.78) measured the assessment of public need, including "Our administration frequently modifies goals to respond public demands." Five items (Cronbach's alpha = 0.76) measured the satisfaction of public need, including "Our administration can achieve high citizen satisfaction for public services."

Another participation impact, consensus building, was classified into four dimensions, including consensus building in goals or missions (four items, Cronbach's alpha = 0.87), service priority (one item), expected performance (one item), and fiscal commitment (three items, Cronbach's alpha = 0.68). Respondents were asked to assess the following statements: "Our administration has developed clear goals and objectives for service delivery" (consensus building in goals), "Our administration can achieve consensus on service priorities" (consensus building in service priorities), and "Our administration can increase taxes without strong resistance" (consensus building in fiscal commitments). All assessments were measured using the same 5-point scale (5 = *strongly agree*, 4 = *agree*, 3 = *neutral*, 2 = *disagree*, 1 = *strongly disagree*). Finally, to measure public trust of decision making, respondents were asked to assess citizen perceptions about administrative competency (one item), honesty (two items, Cronbach's alpha = 0.80), and fairness (one item) in their cities.

FINDINGS

How Much Participation?

Cities use a variety of participation mechanisms. Tradition participation mechanisms such as public hearings, citizen advisory boards, and community or neighborhood meetings are widely used (see Table 27.1). Relatively fewer governments use citizen surveys, citizen focus groups, citizen hotlines, and individual citizen representatives. It is surprising that 81.6% of cities (39.8% + 41.8%) use the Internet to communicate with citizens. In the interview portion of this study, one city manager indicated that the residents in her city (Hollywood, Florida) used the Internet to sign up for "civic associations, civic boards, and community groups."

Public participation seldom appears in central management functions (see Table 27.2). Only

Table 27.2

How Much Function Participation? ("In our city, citizens or citizen activists are involved in the following city functions.")

Function	Percent					M	SD
	Strongly agree	Agree	Neutral	Disagree	Strongly disagree		
Management functions							
Budgeting (n = 247)	15.4	30.8	23.1	25.9	4.9	3.26	1.15
Personnel (n = 247)	1.2	5.3	8.5	47.0	38.1	1.85	0.88
Procurement (n = 246)	0.8	0.8	11.4	56.5	30.5	1.85	0.71
Service functions							
Zoning and planning (n = 247)	29.1	64.8	5.7	0.0	0.4	4.22	0.58
Parks and recreation (n = 242)	23.1	64.0	9.5	2.5	0.8	4.06	0.71
Policing and public safety (n = 247)	16.2	56.3	15.4	10.5	1.6	3.75	0.91
Code enforcement (n = 245)	9.0	45.7	24.9	16.7	3.7	3.40	0.99
Transportation and street maintenance (n = 246)	5.3	32.1	26.8	28.5	7.3	3.00	1.06
Solid waste and garbage collection (n = 234)	5.6	24.4	26.5	34.2	9.4	2.82	1.08
Function Participation Index						3.14	0.56
Cronbach's alpha = 0.79							

Note: Numbers in parentheses are sample sizes. The index was created by averaging the values of all above items.

Table 27.3

How Much Decision-Making Participation? ("In our city, citizens or citizen activists are involved in the following processes.")

	Percent						
	Strongly agree	Agree	Neutral	Disagree	Strongly disagree	M	SD
Goal setting							
Identifying agency or program goals and objectives (n = 245)	4.9	29.0	25.3	33.1	7.8	2.90	1.06
Determination of strategies, policies, and capacities							
Developing strategies to achieve agency or program goals (n = 245)	4.5	23.7	29.4	35.1	7.3	2.83	1.02
Developing policy or program alternatives (n = 244)	2.9	27.9	29.9	31.6	7.8	2.87	1.00
Negotiation of agency budgets (n = 245)	0.0	7.3	18.0	54.7	20.0	2.13	0.81
Determining city executive budgets (n = 243)	0.8	4.1	16.5	56.4	22.2	2.05	0.79
Monitoring and evaluating							
Monitoring service delivery process (n = 245)	2.0	20.8	26.5	38.0	12.7	2.62	1.02
Assessing service delivery process (n = 244)	2.0	26.6	25.8	32.4	13.1	2.72	1.06
Auditing service or program achievements (n = 243)	1.2	10.3	20.2	51.4	16.9	2.28	0.91
Evaluating policy or program achievements (n = 245)	1.6	23.7	27.3	37.1	10.2	2.69	0.99
Decision-Making Participation Index						2.56	0.73
Cronbach's alpha = 0.91							

Note: Numbers in parentheses are sample sizes. The index was created by averaging the values of all above items.

a handful of respondents (16 of 247) agreed or strongly agreed that the public was involved in personnel issues such employee hiring and firing in their cities. Even fewer respondents (4 of 246) reported that their cities involved the public in procurement management. Even in budgeting management, where 46.2% (15.4% + 30.8%) of respondents agreed or strongly agreed that the public was involved, few indicated that the public was involved in the negotiation of agency budgets (7.3%) or the determination of city executive budgets (4.9%). On the other hand, participation in service functions was prominent, especially in zoning and planning, parks and recreation, and policing and public safety. More than 70% of respondents agreed or strongly agreed that their cities involved the public in these functions. High participation in these areas is not surprising because citizens are the consumers of these services and also pay for them.

Public participation was very limited in decision making (see Table 27.3). Although about one third of respondents agreed or strongly agreed that their cities involved the public in "identifying agency/program goals and objectives," fewer than 30% of the respondents agreed or strongly agreed that public involvement took place while developing strategies to achieve these goals. Even fewer respondents reported that the public was involved in "monitoring service delivery" (22.8%) and "evaluating policy/program achievements" (25.3%). Respondents scored 2.56 on the Decision-Making Participation Index, significantly lower than their score on the Function Participation Index (3.14; $t = 14.85$, $p < .001$ for a paired sample t test).

This study found that city location is not associated with public participation. Cities in the southern United States scored 3.96 on the Participation Mechanism Index, compared with 3.84 for northeastern cities, 3.75 for north central cities, and 3.82 for western cities.[1] These differences were not statistically significant ($F = 1.05$, $p = .371$ for a one-way analysis of variance test). Cities in the western United States scored slightly higher on the Function Participation Index (3.20) than northeastern cities (2.99), north central cities (3.12), and southern (3.12). However, these differences were also not statistically significant ($F = .948$, $p = .418$ for a one-way analysis of variance test). In addition, southern cities scored 2.62 on the Decision-Making Participation Index, compared with 2.56 for northeastern cities, 2.49 for north central cities, and 2.55 for western cities. Again, no significant differences were found ($F = .335$, $p = .800$ for a one-way analysis of variance test).

This study also found that the form of government did not influence public participation. Council-manager governments scored 3.90 on the Participation Mechanism Index, compared with 3.66 for mayor-council governments and 3.91 for other forms of government. Again, these differences were not statistically significant ($F = 1.78$, $p = .134$ for a one-way analysis of variance test). Also, council-manager governments scored 3.12 on the Function Participation Index, compared with 3.16 for mayor-council governments and 3.20 for other forms of government. Again, these differences were not statistically significant ($F = .310$, $p = .871$ for a one-way analysis of variance test). Finally, council-manager governments scored 2.52 on the Decision-Making Participation Index, compared with 2.62 for mayor-council governments and 2.73 for other forms of government. No significant differences were found ($F = .940$, $p = .442$ for a one-way analysis of variance test).

Why Participation?

The results shown in Table 27.4 support the theory that the size of government influences participation. In this study, the size of government was measured by the number of full-time employees (the median was 939 in this sample). The results shown in Table 27.4 indicate that larger governments tend to have higher participation in service or management functions and decision making. In fact, governments with 939 or more full-time employees scored 3.24 on the Function Participation Index, significantly higher than governments with fewer than 939 full-time employees (3.01; $t =$

Table 27.4

Why Participation?

Association with	Participation mechanisms	Function participation	Decision-making participation
External pressures			
Size of government (number of full-time employees)	0.070	0.131**	0.111*
Much political competition among different groups	0.091	0.100	0.138**
Critical elected officials	−0.036	0.060	0.171**
Cynical media	−0.005	0.104	0.118*
Critical business community	−0.073	0.095	0.134**
Internal demands and capabilities			
Managers' willingness to be accountable	0.222**	0.165**	0.175**
Employees' willingness to be accountable	0.145**	0.210**	0.130*
High ethics among employees	0.160**	0.171**	0.094
Cynical employees	−0.118*	−0.081	−0.004
Budgetary surpluses for new ideas	0.127*	0.013	0.047
Interesting agenda to attract public attention	0.333**	0.153**	0.230**

Note: Except for size of government, which was measured by the number of full-time employees, all variables were measured on a 5-point scale (5 = *strongly agree*, 4 = *agree*, 3 = *neutral*, 2 = *disagree*, 1 = *strongly disagree*). Respondents were asked to use this scale to assess relevant survey items. The measure of association is Kendall's tau-c, which estimates the association between ordinal variables. The statistic ranges from −1 (a perfectly negative association) to 1 (a perfectly positive association).

$*p < .05. **p < .01.$

3.106, $p < .01$ for a t test of the mean difference). Also, governments with 939 or more full-time employees scored 2.69 on the Decision-Making Participation Index, compared with 2.41 for governments with fewer than 939 full-time employees ($t = 2.86$, $p < .01$ for a t test of the mean difference). This result is subject to different explanations. First, it may indicate that the public tends to participate more in large governments because citizens fear losing personal contact or being alienated by the complexity of large bureaucratic operations. Or, it could indicate that large governments have more resources and capacities that can be used to enhance participation.

It appears that the pressures of political competition and stakeholder criticism lead to more public participation in decision making. For example, cities with "much political competition among different groups" ($n = 112$) scored 2.68 on the Decision-Making Participation Index, compared with a score of 2.45 for cities with less competition ($n = 122$). In other words, much political competition may increase participation in decision making by 9.4% (2.68/2.45 − 100%) without consideration of other factors. Similarly, "critical elected officials" may increase participation in decision making by 10.4% and "cynical media" by 5.6% without consideration of other factors. This result supports the argument that political divisiveness motivates governments to involve citizens in decision making to legitimize governmental decisions.

The results in Table 27.4 also suggest that government workers' willingness to submit to accountability increases participation. In the study, respondents were asked to assess their managers' and employees' willingness to expose their activities and job performance to public scrutiny. Cities with "managers willing to expose their activities/performance to public scrutiny" ($n = 112$) scored 3.98 on the Participation Mechanism index, 7.6% higher than the other cities (index score = 3.7, $n = 107$). This willingness may also increase function participation by 5.9% and participation in decision making by 13.8% without consideration of other factors.

Table 27.5

Impacts of Participation

Association with	Participation mechanisms	Function participation	Decision-making participation
Meeting public needs			
Need identification	0.377**	0.202**	0.174**
Need assessment	0.305**	0.133*	0.154**
Need satisfaction	0.254**	0.121*	0.079
Consensus building			
Goals and missions	0.319**	0.129*	0.213**
Service priority	0.246**	0.087	0.146**
Expected performance	0.245**	0.100	0.196**
Fiscal commitment	0.063	0.006	0.042
Public trust of administration			
Competency	0.182**	0.085	0.066
Honesty	0.194**	0.098	0.041
Fairness	0.181**	0.079	0.063

Note: The measure of association was Kendall's tau-c.
$*p < .05. **p < .01.$

The existence of an interesting agenda is also an important variable in public participation. In this study, about two thirds of the respondents (61.4%) agreed or strongly agreed that their administrations had "developed an agenda that interests the public." In these administrations, the scores on the Function Participation Index, the Decision-Making Participation Index, and the Participation Mechanism Index were 3.21, 2.71, and 4.02, respectively, compared with 3.01, 2.32, and 3.52, respectively, for administrations without such agendas. In a follow-up interview, one city manager indicated that his city (Lakewood, Colorado) puts 25 residents through a citizen police academy twice a year. This smaller version of the real police academy allows citizens to "get a flavor of what is like to become a cop and what some of public safety issues are to deal with. . . . These residents in the Citizen Police Academy turn around and become enthusiastic participants [in government]."

Participation Impacts

Table 27.5 shows that the use of participation mechanisms is perceived as effective in meeting public needs, building consensus, and improving public trust. The use of participation mechanisms is significantly associated with all participation impacts. For example, 89.7% of cities using citizen surveys ($n = 126$) agreed or strongly agreed that they could "achieve high citizen satisfaction for public services," compared with 70.5% of cities not using citizen surveys ($n = 112$). In other words, cities using citizen surveys were 27.2% more likely to perceive high citizen satisfaction for public services than cities not using citizen surveys (89.7% / 70.5% − 100%). Also, 84.6% of cities using citizen focus groups agreed or strongly agreed that they could achieve consensus on organizational goals or objectives, compared with 71.4% of cities not using this mechanism. It appears that the use of participation mechanisms is a preliminary and necessary condition to achieve participation goals in meeting public needs, building consensus, and improving public trust.

Table 27.5 shows that function participation is positively associated with meeting public needs. Governments with public involvement in more services and management functions are more able to identify, assess, and satisfy public needs. For example, 70.0% of cities with public involvement in the budgeting function agreed or strongly agreed that they could "define customers or clients and their needs," compared with 59.4% of cities without such involvement. In other words, cities with such involvement were 17.9% more likely (70% / 59.4% − 100%) to "define customers or clients and their needs" than cities without such involvement. Cities with public participation in at least five of the nine city functions listed in the survey (73.2% of the total sample) were 21.0% more likely to "understand citizen needs" than cities with public involvement in fewer than five functions. In sum, it seems that participation advances public needs.

Participation in decision making appears to have significant influence on consensus building (see Table 27.5). Public involvement in goal setting, strategy or policy development, budget determination, and evaluation seems to increase the chance to reach stakeholder agreement on organizational goals, service priorities, and performance expectations. For example, 90.4% of cities involving the public in "identifying agency/program goals/objectives" agreed or strongly agreed that they had "reached consensus on goals and objectives for service delivery," compared with only 72.8% of cities without such involvement. In other words, cities with such involvement were 24.2% more likely (90.4% / 72.8% − 100%) to "reach consensus on goals objectives for service delivery" than cities without such involvement. Also, cities involving the public in "developing policy/program alternatives" were 20.4% more likely to "achieve consensus on service priority" than cities without such involvement. Cities involving the public in "evaluating policy/program achievement" were 16.8% more likely to "achieve consensus on good service performance" than cities without such involvement. Thus, participation is perceived to build consensus.

However, fiscal commitment is not a result of participation (see Table 27.5). No significant relationship was found between participation and a government's capacities in taxation, debt, and budget appropriations. Enhanced public participation does not lead to public willingness to pay for public services. Governments should not expect improved fiscal conditions as a return on participation. Fiscal commitment is influenced by factors other than participation. In fact, only a small number of cities in this sample could raise taxes (12%) and debts (32%) without strong resistance. In the follow-up interviews, several managers described the citizen resistance to any tax measures in their cities.

Participation in functions and decision making does not lead to public trust (see Table 27.5). This study measured perceived citizen assessment of administrative competency, honesty, and fairness. No significant relationship was found between either function or decision-making participation and perceived citizen assessment on these administrative attributes. Public attitudes toward government may not be a result of participation. This result is surprising given that improved public trust is a goal of many participation efforts. Participation may not improve public trust.

CONCLUSION

This study found that cities use a variety of participation mechanisms to involve the public in a wide range of public services. However, the depth of involvement in administrative decision making is limited. The public is not involved in making some critical management and service delivery decisions. The study also found that participation is associated with stakeholder pressure and public employee willingness to submit to accountability. In addition, an interesting agenda also attracts public attention to participation. Finally, the existence of participation mechanisms appears to be a preliminary and necessary condition to achieve participation goals in the satisfaction of public needs, consensus building, and public trust. Participation in decision making leads to better understanding and satisfaction of public needs and the building of consensus on service goals, priorities, and performance expectations.

This study found that participation is limited in two areas. The first is in central management functions (budgeting, personnel, and procurement) where expertise, information, and knowledge are needed. This finding indicates a more important role played by professional managers in these areas, and citizens may not always be interested in the technical issues of management. The second limitation to participation is in decision making. Participation is limited in setting service goals and strategies and in implementing policies. The lack of participation depth in decision making suggests that public involvement in many cities is superficial or "conventional" (King et al., 1998). Participation in these cities remains at the level of offering involvement opportunities and tools. The "authentic" or genuine pattern suggested by the literature is not characteristic of the participation in these cities. Decisions are "administrative," not "public," in these governments.

How is participation enhanced? An interesting agenda attracts the public to participation. In local governments, the issues that concern the well-being and livelihood of the public often include public safety, zoning and planning, and code enforcement. This research found a greater involvement of the public in these areas. Participation is greater in cities with stronger political divisiveness, suggesting that cities are bringing in the public as a force to offset other political influences and legitimize their decisions. Finally, public servants' willingness to be accountable appears to encourage participation. This finding suggests that efforts should be made to educate public servants about the necessities and benefits of participation. Reducing public employees' fear of losing power and control through participation should enhance public involvement.

What can be expected from participation? Participation may lead to the identification of public needs and consensus building on service goals and performance priorities. However, participation in administrative decision making may not lead to public trust toward administrations. Cynical stakeholders may not change their skeptical views toward governments because of participation. This result also implies that public perception of government is a complex variable that could be influenced by numerous political and socioeconomic factors as well as government performance. Simply involving the public in decision making does not do the trick.

In addition, this research found that participation may not lead to fiscal commitment from citizens. The public is not more willing to pay for services simply because it participates more. Governments that expect an improvement in resident fiscal commitment and financial conditions as a result of participation may be disappointed. After all, financial conditions are more a function of economy and financial performance than of participation efforts.

Finally, it is necessary to discuss a limitation of this study. This study surveyed public managers. It measured public managers' perceptions about public participation. It looked at public participation efforts and impacts through managers' eyes. There may be a difference between these perceptions and the reality of public participation that can be determined by surveying managers and the public itself.

AUTHOR'S NOTE

I would like to thank Professors Jerry Gianakis and Ronnie Korosec at the University of Central Florida and two anonymous reviewers for their valuable comments on an early draft of this article.

NOTE

1. Cities were classified according to the states in which they were located. The International City/County Management Association's (1999) classification system was used. Northeastern states include Connecticut, Maine, Massachusetts, New Hampshire, New Jersey, New York, Pennsylvania, Rhode Island, and Vermont. North central states include Illinois, Indiana, Iowa, Kansas, Michigan, Minnesota, Missouri, Nebraska, North Dakota, Ohio, South Dakota, and Wisconsin. Southern states include Alabama, Arkansas, Delaware, Florida, Georgia, Kentucky, Louisiana, Maryland, Mississippi, North Carolina, Oklahoma, South Carolina, Tennessee, Texas, Virginia, and West Virginia. Western states include Alaska, Arizona, California, Colorado, Hawaii, Idaho, Montana, Nevada, New Mexico, Oregon, Utah, Washington, and Wyoming. South states contained 30.9% of the cities in the study, western states contained 35.4%, northeastern states contained 10.8%, and north central states contained 22.9%.

REFERENCES

Aryani, G.A., Garrett, T.D., & Alsabrook, C.L. (2000). The citizen police academy: Success through community partnership. *FBI Law Enforcement Bulletin, 69*(5), 16–21.

Bryson, J.M. (1995). *Strategic planning for public and nonprofit organizations.* San Francisco: Jossey-Bass.

Cohen, N. (1995). Technical assistance for citizen participation: A case study of New York City's environmental planning process. *American Review of Public Administration, 25*(2), 119–135.

Creighton, J.L. (1981). *The public involvement manual.* Cambridge, MA: Abt.

DeSario, J., & Langton, S. (1987). Citizen participation and technocracy. In J. DeSario & S. Langton (Eds.), *Citizen participation in public decision making* (pp. 3–17). New York: Greenwood.

Foley, D. (1998). We want your input: Dilemmas of citizen participation. In C.S. King & C. Stivers (Eds.), *Government is us* (pp. 140–157). Thousand Oaks, CA: Sage.

Gray, J.E., & Chapin, L.W. (1998). Targeted community initiative: "Putting citizens first." In C.S. King & C. Stivers (Eds.), *Government is us* (pp. 175–194). Thousand Oaks, CA: Sage.

Iglitzin, L.B. (1995, Winter). The Seattle commons: A case study in the politics and planning of an urban village. *Policy Studies Journal, 23,* 620–635.

International City/County Management Association. (1998). *The municipal yearbook, 1998.* Washington, DC: Author.

International City/County Management Association. (1999). *The municipal yearbook, 1999.* Washington, DC: Author.

Kaufman, H. (1969). Administrative decentralization and political power. *Public Administration Review, 29*(1), 3–15.

King, C.S., Feltey, K.M., & Susel, B.O. (1998). The question of participation: Toward authentic public participation in public administration. *Public Administration Review, 58*(4), 317–326.

King, C.S., & Stivers, C. (1998). Introduction: The anti-government era. In C.S. King & C. Stivers (Eds.), *Government is us* (pp. 3–18). Thousand Oaks, CA: Sage.

Kovalick, W.W., Jr., & Kelly, M.M. (1998). The EPA seeks voice and role with citizens: Evolutionary engagement. In C.S. King & C. Stivers (Eds.), *Government is us* (pp. 122–139). Thousand Oaks, CA: Sage.

Kweit, M.G., & Kweit, R.W. (1987). The politics of policy analysis: The role of citizen participation in analytic decision making. In J. DeSario & S. Langton (Eds.), *Citizen participation in public decision making* (pp. 19–37). New York: Greenwood.

Lando, T. (1999). Public participation in local government. *National Civic Review, 88*(2), 109–122.

Langton, S. (1978a). Citizen participation in America: Current reflections on the state of the art. In S. Langton (Ed.), *Citizen participation in America* (pp. 1–12). Lexington, MA: Lexington Books.

Langton, S. (1978b). What is citizen participation? In S. Langton (Ed.), *Citizen participation in America* (pp. 13–24). Lexington, MA: Lexington Books.

Lindstrom, M., & Nie, M. (2000, Spring). Public participation in agency planning. *The Public Manager,* 33–36.

Lowi, T.J. (1969). *The end of liberalism.* New York: Norton.

Morgan, E.P. (1987). Technocratic versus democratic options for educational policy. In J. DeSario & S. Langton (Eds.), *Citizen participation in public decision making* (pp. 177–201). New York: Greenwood.

Niskanen, W.A., Jr. (1971). *Bureaucracy and representative government.* Chicago: Aldine.

Osborne, D., & Plastrik, P. (1997). *Banishing bureaucracy: The five strategies for reinventing government.* New York: Addison-Wesley.

O'Toole, D.E., & Marshall, J. (1988). Citizen participation through budgeting. *The Bureaucrat, 17*(2), 51–55.

Pateman, C. (1970). *Participation and democratic theory.* Cambridge, UK: University of Cambridge Press.

Plein, L.C., Green, K.E., & Williams, D.G. (1998). Organic planning: A new approach to public participation in local government. *The Social Science Journal, 35*(4), 509–523.

Preisser, V. (1997, May). Citizen-based budgeting: The Redding, California, experiment. *Public Management,* 18–21.

Sanoff, H. (2000). *Community participation methods in design and planning.* New York: Wiley.

Simonsen, W., & Robbins, M.D. (2000). *Citizen participation in resource allocation.* Boulder, CO: Westview.

Swiss, J.E. (1999). Adopting total quality management to government. In R.C. Kearney & E.M. Berman (Eds.), *Public sector performance: Management, motivation, and measurement.* Boulder, CO: Westview.

Thompson, A.A., Jr., Strickland, A.J. III. (1992). *Strategic management* (6th ed.). Boston: Irwin.

Walters, L.C., Aydelotte, J., & Miller, J. (2000). Putting more public in policy analysis. *Public Administration Review, 60*(4), 349–359.

Yankelovich, D. (1991). *Coming to public judgment.* Syracuse, NY: Syracuse University Press.

CHAPTER 28

ADMINISTRATIVE AGENTS OF DEMOCRACY?
A Structural Equation Modeling of the Relationship between Public-Sector Performance and Citizenship Involvement

ERAN VIGODA

The need continuously to foster democratic values of citizenship participation and involvement is a prominent issue in contemporary political science literature (e.g., Box 1998 and 1999; Frederickson 1982 and 1997; King, Feltey, and Susel 1998; King and Stivers 1998). Barner and Rosenwein (1985) argued that "[d]emocratic values are in essence participatory values. At the heart of democratic theory is the notion that people should get involved in the process of governing themselves . . ." (p. 59). Furthermore, Guyton (1988) suggested that those who do not participate politically are likely to have a highly undemocratic view of the world. To date, studies have been preoccupied with important questions on the nature of these values, their construct and meaning, and their existence and change over time and across cultures (Almond and Verba 1963; Verba, Nie, and Kim 1978; Verba, Schlozman, and Brady 1995). Consensus had also arisen among scholars on the centrality of citizenship involvement in the democratic process, and it has been argued that theory should further suggest better explanations of how democratic values such as high participation and widespread involvement emerge, develop, and transform in an ultradynamic and highly demanding modern society.

Here lies the potential merit of our study, in which we expand on the responsibility of public administration as another agent of citizenship involvement in modern states. We elaborate on several questions: Do public administration outcomes contribute to the expansion of better citizenship involvement and good democratic values among individuals? What is the nature of this relationship, if it exists? Which aspects, if any, of public-sector operation are more important for the improvement of performance that supports democratic values of higher citizenship involvement? Answers to these questions may enlarge our knowledge about the role of public administration in democratic cultures. Participatory democratic theory, as suggested by Pateman (1970)—and more recently (e.g., Peterson 1990; Putnam 1993)—highlights the ways in which institutional arrangements and activities leave their imprint on citizens. If better performance by administrative authorities can lead to more involvement and faith of citizens, specific lessons must be learned

From *Journal of Public Administration Research and Theory,* 12, 2 (April 2002): 241–272. Copyright © 2002 by Public Management Research Association. Reprinted with permission.

regarding the required operative and moral course of public systems. Such lessons may prove to be relevant beyond the simple managerial and financial cost-benefit purposes that are so prevalent in contemporary public management literature. They may justify deeper and farther-reaching demands for effectiveness, efficiency, responsiveness, and morality in the public sector, and they may strengthen the theoretical as well as the practical linkage between outcomes of governmental institutions and a redesign of valuable social norms.

In order to address these questions, our study employed original data collected among Israeli citizens. We empirically tested a hypothesis that public administration outcomes have a generally positive effect on citizens' faith and activism. Several theoretical models were posited and examined to elicit not only general *support* or *reject* conclusion but also to explore the *nature* of relationship among public-sector performance (PSP), faith in citizenship involvement (FCI), and actual citizenship behaviors (ACI) as represented by political and communal participation.

CITIZENSHIP INVOLVEMENT IN MODERN DEMOCRACIES: THIS TIME FROM A PUBLIC ADMINISTRATION VIEWPOINT

While recent decades have witnessed some important explorations of the meaning and nature of citizenship involvement in democracies (e.g., Almond and Verba 1963; Brady, Verba, and Schlozman 1995; Milbrath and Goel 1977; Verba et al. 1995), much work remains to be done. One example is the uncertain knowledge of conceivable relationships between PSP and the emergence of democratic values among citizens. To date, only sparse empirical evidence exists on how public-sector outcomes affect citizens' confidence and trust in government, their willingness to participate in political or communal behaviors, and—most importantly—their tangible involvement in the active democratic process. On the one hand, traditional political science literature frequently concentrates on personal, psychological, or sociological antecedents of citizenship behavior, involvement, and participation (e.g., Carmines 1992; Krampen 1991; Milbrath and Goel 1977; Peterson 1990; Sabucedo and Cramer 1991). Nevertheless, this group of studies usually pays much less attention to outcomes and performances of public organizations, which may serve as additional agents of citizenship involvement. On the other hand, studies in public administration frequently emphasize managerial tools for improving performance in these bodies (Lynn 1996 and 1998; Pollitt 1988; Rainey 1990). These works, like many others, look for better ways to set, implement, and evaluate public policy, and moreover to recognize the valuable contribution of citizenship involvement to these processes. Yet this cluster of studies usually treats PSP and outcomes as dependent variables. Hence much effort has been devoted to better explaining public-sector operation and performance by means of citizens' participation, involvement, feelings of efficacy, and cooperation with government (Box 1998 and 1999).

Surveying these two research lines, we identify a significant scholarly gap waiting to be bridged. Both groups of studies we have outlined seem to have overlooked another possible connection between PSP and citizenship involvement. According to this idea, public-sector operation and performance should be regarded as an additional catalyst for (or, alternatively, an obstruction to) citizens' involvement. In keeping with this argument, Berman (1997) suggested that the literature offered little on the role of public administration in shaping public attitudes. Most studies focus on citizens' roles and better management of citizenship involvement in the administrative process (e.g., Box 1998 and 1999; Rimmerman 1997). However, as with schools, families, peer groups, media, and academia, the special role and responsibility of public-sector organizations in the process of democratic socialization has to be elaborated. Indeed, some studies employed theories of skill and resource transaction between social institutions to argue that citizenship involvement is acquired through a process of political learning (e.g., Pateman 1970; Sigel 1989; Peterson 1990; Sobel 1993; Soss 1999; Verba et al. 1995). Yet while these studies related institutional actions or culture to individual political participation, none of them considered the prospect that public administration *performance* might make an impact on various dimensions of citizen participation. Following this, we suggest that more attention should be turned to the possibility that the administrative system has a meaningful, independent effect on framing and shaping citizenship involvement by its very basic function of providing goods and services to the people. Hence, performance by public-sector agencies may be part of a socialization process that advances democracy among citizens of modern states.

Public Administration and a Strong Democratic Heritage

A well-performing public administration and strong democracies are tightly bound together since they both rely on productive and widespread citizenship involvement. According to this ethos, Woller (1998) indicated that no bureaucracy or democracy can function properly without a minimal input of citizenship activity. Moreover, modern public administration is deeply rooted in a strong democratic heritage. It is democracy that renders legitimacy to the decisions and actions of the public service, and it is democracy again that must check and balance the tyrannical nature of bureaucracies. Yet both bureaucracy and democracy are highly important conditions that make possible the proper running of modern states. No prosperous, free society can long exist without a continual improvement of its administrative bodies, bureaucracy, and public managerial process. Neither can modern societies flourish when democratic values of good citizenship are threatened or spoiled (Verba et al. 1995) or when citizens are apathetic, alienated, or emotionally discouraged from involvement in the process of ruling and being ruled in return.

Therefore, studies in public administration have recognized the advantages of productive reciprocal relationships between citizens and rulers (Box 1998). Ideas first mentioned by Hobbes, Locke, and Rousseau suggest that a hidden agreement, or *social contract,* exists between rulers and citizens. A social agreement between citizens, state rulers, and executives, as formed in modern democracies, constitutes a powerful mechanism with precious collective advantages for societies and individuals. At the same time, it is beset by many difficulties and hindrances that should not be ignored. For example, what happens when governments and public-sector organizations fail to meet citizens' demands? What impact can such a failure have on the legitimacy of government and its image and prestige in the eyes of citizens-clients? Can poor PSP lead to distrust and growing doubt about the democratic process in general? If it can, then how, and how much? These questions are important to all who seek better explanations for the life cycle, stability, and survival of modern democracies. Such explanations will also add to our knowledge of the various impacts of public administration actions in terms of citizenship involvement and orientation toward democracy. Still, in order to provide reliable answers to these questions we must first furnish clear definitions of performance in the public sector as well as a lucid understanding of the essence of citizenship involvement.

Public-Sector Performance and Actions: Several Approaches

Theory has provided many alternatives for the understanding of and the measurement of PSP. Studies have focused on the distinction among public-sector outcomes, outputs, and productivity, and the three big Es of performance: effectiveness, efficiency, and economy (Carter, Klein, and Day 1992; Halachmi and Bouckaert 1995). All indicators have achieved macro- and microlevel recognition, yet such trends have been magnified lately with the upsurge of the new public management (NPM) approach. Despite some serious criticism (e.g., Golembiewski, Vigoda, and Sun forthcoming [2002]; Hood 1991), the NPM perspective has become highly influential and dominant in the current apparatus of public administration. Considerable effort has been dedicated to recognizing and defining new criteria that may help in determining the extent to which public agencies succeed in keeping pace with the growing needs of the public. In contrast to private-sector performance, public-service performance must take into consideration extra criteria such as social welfare, equity and equality, fair distribution of opportunities, and impartial redistribution of public goods to all citizens. Rhodes (1987) and Palfrey et al. (1992) suggested these criteria among the values in addition to efficiency, effectiveness, and economy that characterize market-driven arenas. In practice, one way to test performance of governmental actions is to go to the citizens-clients for their personal evaluations of all these aspects. This approach examines citizens' opinions regarding their consumption of public goods in terms of absolute service, its quality, availability, fairness in distribution, and full orientation to individual needs. According to Stipak (1979 and 1980), despite its limitation because it is a subjective measure of performance, it has advantages that should not be ignored. This measure should be detailed and should refer to various aspects of public outcomes such as productivity, quality of service, quality of operation, equity and equality in distributing goods or services, and general responsiveness to public necessities. Moreover, beyond the significant yet relatively simple and limited evaluation of public administration outcomes by citizens' satisfaction, additional aspects of actions may usefully be examined. Based on a previous framework by Vigoda (2000), we propose several dimensions of public agencies' operation: a personal dimension of *human quality;* an entrepreneurial dimension of *innovation and creativity;* and a normative aspect of *morality and ethics.*

Quality of public personnel is perhaps the most influential and momentous resource of public serving agencies. For example, Parsons (1995, 554) suggests that contemporary literature in public policy "is for the most part concerned with the evaluation of programs and policies. However, in a managerial framework it also encompasses the evaluation of people *qua Human Resources.*" Without doubt, it is important to gain more knowledge about the evaluation of people as opposed to programs and policy. By so doing we improve methods and strategies through which people are better managed. We encourage them to become more committed, competent, and cost effective and also to be in sympathy with the aim of the organization, which is to discharge better services to the citizens (J.L. Thompson 1990, 307).

Another key aspect of public administration operation in modern times is innovation and creativity in individuals as well as bureaucracies. In the last decades scholars have promoted ideas of better flexibility, enterprise, and willingness to adopt creative new opinions. Most importantly, the technological and social environment entered an era of continual change, which has necessitated both the establishment of new standards of operation in the public services of western societies and the transformation of orientations and perceptions of public servants. It has been argued that these alterations may be the right way to relax the tightening strain between democracy and market forces (e.g., Bozeman 1993; Farnham and Horton 1993; Osborne and Gaebler 1992). Scholars have been urged to pursue better macro-and micro-level techniques that make for enduring improvement and adaptability to a rapidly transforming environment, and there has been agreement that a well-performing public sector must rely heavily on creativity and innovation to overcome many of its serious problems and maladies.

In the last decade interest has also increased with regard to issues of administrative morality, ethics, and fairness (deLeon 1996; Lui and Cooper 1997; Gortner 1991; Manzel 1999). Generally, citizens are sensitive to and critical of sharing resources in society despite having almost no opportunity to use their collective opinion in order to influence decision makers. It is expected that citizens as clients increasingly develop independent perspectives on issues such as what kind of moral culture public administration encourages, and how this culture corresponds to general morality in the wider society. We argue in this study that the morality and ethics of public administration agencies and of public personnel may have a momentous effect on perceptions of performance, and in the long run these views may also influence orientation toward democracy, citizenship involvement, and active participation. This argument draws substance mainly from the cognitive approach (Lewin 1936) and the expectancy theory. According to this view, people interpret reality in many ways, one of which is by having an exchange relationship with others (Blau 1964). When an exchange system is unfair or yields no benefits for one side (usually the less powerful) it is only a matter of time until reaction appears. A most serious reaction by citizens to low-performing governments and public agencies may be to lose faith in the democratic process and to turn passive or apathetic (Krampen 1991). When policy agrees with public demands, citizens are more willing to accept administrative actions as responses to their needs and to show more support for the entire democratic process (Vigoda 2000). Accordingly, we decided to include morality and ethics as additional predictors of PSP as well as orientations toward democracy.

Citizenship Involvement: Attitudes Toward Participation and Active Participation

So far we have discussed citizenship involvement as one construct that comprises both attitudes and active participation. Practically, both the positive attitudes of citizens toward the democratic process and their active political participation are essential for the building of strong liberal states and progressive cultures that last. However, in their extensive work, *Voice and Equality: Civic Voluntarism in American Politics,* Verba et al. (1995) argue that "citizen participation is at the heart of democracy" and that "democracy is unthinkable without the ability of citizens to participate freely in the governing process" (p. 1). King and Stivers (1998) and Kramer (1999) further have argued that only by becoming active participants in civic life, rather than remaining passive spectators on the sidelines, can citizens regain trust in democratic ideas of involvement, collective responsibility, self-empowerment, and reconstruction of individuals' creativity and innovation. In light of this, our study distinguished two types of citizenship involvement: attitudes to participation or *faith in citizenship involvement* (FCI), and participation per se or *active citizenship involvement* (ACI). According to Verba et al. (1995) these are separate aspects of the same phenomenon, and in our design each of them was built upon two other factors. FCI comprised faith in citizen involvement and political efficacy, and ACI consisted of political participation and community involvement.

Faith in citizen involvement is an important construct of attitudes toward democracy. It is defined as the extent to which people believe that the average citizen can affect changes in the political system and that by being involved they can influence the political system (Schussler 1982). By this definition, this variable is a good representation of loyalty and trust in the political system. It also reflects an orientation toward politics and an important aspect of citizenship because it helps to shape individuals' understanding of the political world and their place in it (Peterson 1990). People who believe that they can have some say in the political system and are capable of influencing it are also expected to show more active participation under appropriate circumstances. The second facet of faith in citizenship involvement is political efficacy. It reflects individuals' perceptions of their ability to influence political officials and the political system by using personal resources and effort (Barner and Rosenwein 1985; Verba et al. 1995). Milbrath and Goel (1977) argued that political efficacy is part of the sense of mastery that a child acquires during socialization. Moreover, it is possible that political efficacy is later transformed with further events and experiences witnessed during a person's adolescence (Verba et al. 1995). As with faith in citizen involvement, political efficacy also is expected to lead to political participation. A person with high political efficacy will be highly motivated to participate in the political system, be it in national or communal arenas.

In line with this, ACI is represented here by political participation and community involvement. Participation in political activities is a classic construct, one of the most researched in political science (e.g., Almond and Verba 1963; Barber 1984; Brady, Verba, and Schlozman 1995; Peterson 1990; Verba et al. 1995). It deals with people's engagement in such political activities as voting, sending support or protest messages to politicians, political demonstrations, or signing petitions on political issues. The second dimension tested was participation in community activities. Barber (1984) argued that "political participation in common action is more easily achieved at the neighborhood level, where there is a variety of opportunities for engagement" (p. 303). Recent political science and sociological literature has strongly developed the concept of communitarianism as a separate and important dimension of political participation (Etzioni 1994 and 1995). Community activity is considered to be more informal participation than are national activities (Sobel 1993). Certain individual characteristics serve to promote both national and local participation, but other personal and local community characteristics primarily stimulate participation in local politics (Pettersen and Rose 1996). Some people may avoid political activities because they dislike or are indifferent to politics. They may prefer a more personal domain such as the community, which offers membership on a tenants' committee or on a school's parents' committee (Cohen and Vigoda 2000). All in all, both political participation and community involvement evince some of the most elementary constructs of active citizenship involvement.

THE RELATIONSHIP BETWEEN PUBLIC-SECTOR PERFORMANCE AND CITIZENSHIP INVOLVEMENT: ALTERNATIVE MODELS

Five alternative models were posited for the relationship between PSP and perceptual and actual democratic values of citizenship involvement. Each model was subsequently evaluated against all the others for conclusions as to its fit, quality predictability power, and adherence to the theory. In this way, it was possible to obtain some insight into the presumable role of public administration as another agent of democracy, in addition to family, work, media, religious institutions, or the educational system (Peterson 1990). Furthermore, it could provide better understanding of *how* bureaucracies and administrative bodies take part, overtly or covertly, in forming a democratic culture and values of participation. While recent studies have included discussion of some theoretical aspects of this relationship (e.g., Schneider and Ingram 1995 and 1997; Soss 1999), empirical evidence in the field is scarce. The five models presented here elaborate on several substantially distinguished approaches to these questions.

Model 1: A Simple Direct Effect

This model suggests a direct relationship between several constructs of public administration operation and active citizenship involvement. In line with current knowledge (Milbrath and Goel 1977; Verba et al. 1995), a direct effect is suggested between faith in citizenship involvement and active citizenship involvement. This relationship is also included in most of the other models on the assumption that attitudes toward politics and active participation in politics should be treated as separate but related constructs of citizenship involvement (Verba et al. 1995). The simple direct model thus implies that public-sector performance, as reported by citizens' satisfaction, has no effect on patterns of active citizenship involvement. By this rationale, citizens' satisfaction has only a minor relationship with active engagement in citizenship behavior, if any. Quality of public personnel, innovation and creativity, and morality and ethics are proposed to have a direct effect on active participation. Note also that this model portrays the null hypothesis of our study. Support for this model will be in the direction of rejecting the new knowledge (or suggested idea) on the role of public-sector performance and citizens' satisfaction as another agent of citizenship involvement.

Model 2: A Simple Indirect Effect

This model offers a first alternative to the basic simple direct model, where PSP is a mediator between agencies' operation and the two democratic values (faith in citizenship involvement and active citizenship involvement) as they are examined here. The model further suggests no relationship between faith in citizenship involvement and active participation, and it treats both constructs as separate dependent variables. By this model we try to challenge the plausible possibility that attitudes to citizenship involvement and active participation are totally distinguished constructs, each having an autonomous relationship with PSP. Here, for the purpose of comparison, we take to its extreme the notion of Verba et al. (1995) that political participation and attitudes toward participation should be treated separately, and that one should be "concerned with doing politics, rather than with being attentive to politics" (p. 39). According to this model, public administration operation determines performance in the eyes of citizens-as-clients, which in return affects the two types of citizenship involvement.

Model 3: A Complex Indirect Effect

Contrary to the previous model, the complex indirect model redraws a path between faith in citizenship involvement and active citizenship involvement. It relies on the common assumption that political attitudes, beliefs, and confidence lead to political behavior, and that one's active participation must be predominated by faith in the value and advantages of involvement. In their extensive study Verba et al. (1995) advised considering active involvement and attitudes toward involvement as separate constructs, but they also agreed that a relationship exists between the two. In fact, this is the more common approach to the nature of political participation and involvement, supported in other studies. For example, Orum (1989) mentioned several studies that found psychological political involvement positively related to active participation. Feldman and Kawakami (1991) found that those who were more exposed to and interested in political information in the media were more politically active. Other studies by Milbrath and Goel (1977) and Milbrath (1981) also supported this notion. Like model 2, however, this model implies that all other paths remain unchanged, arguing for a mediating effect of PSP in the attitude-action relationship.

Model 4: Faith in Citizenship Involvement Mediates Between Performance and Active Involvement

This model goes a step farther and elaborates on a specific mediating role of faith in citizenship involvement in the relationship between public administration operation and performance, and active political and communal involvement. For the first time, this model proposes that faith in citizenship involvement buffers PSP and actual participatory behavior. This idea is in line with the conception of Brady et al. (1995) on the mediating role of attitudes to politics (e.g., political interest and citizenship) in creating a productive voice and political acts. However, in addition we specify a more imperative role of attitudes and faith in citizenship involvement. In this model, performance of the public sector is described as another antecedent of citizens' faith that in itself may affect political activity. Support for this model may imply that public-sector performance can affect active political and communal participation, but only through the formation of attitudes and perceptions, and perhaps through the re-creation of civic skills and personal resources that are essential for an active role in politics (Brady et al. 1995). According to this model, PSP has no direct effect on political activity of individuals.

Model 5: A Simultaneous Effect of Faith and Performance on Active Involvement

As in the previous three alternatives (models 2, 3, and 4), this model also suggests performance as a mediator between public administration operation and the formation of democratic values. However, instead of faith playing a separate dependent role (model 2) or a mediating function (models 3 and 4), this model proposes that faith in citizenship involvement and public-sector performance have a separate/parallel direct effect on active citizenship involvement; faith in citizenship involvement and public-sector performance are both affected by the independent variables; and public-sector performance has no effect on faith in citizenship involvement. This model also draws substance from the work of Nye, Zelikow, and King (1997), who argued that mistrust in governance is largely affected by factors that are all around us in the cultural and political environment. Among these variables on may well count the administrative-political atmosphere as represented by IC, HQ, and ME. Hence, this model offers a simultaneous effect of faith both in citizenship involvement and in public-sector performance on active political and communal participation. The advantage of this model is its pointing to active participation as determined in parallel by faith in citizenship involvement and public-sector performance. In fact, both variables are described as mediators between public administration operation and active involvement in politics. Thus the model allows a fair comparison of the consequences of these two variables in terms of citizens' behavior or political activity.

METHOD

Sample, Tools, and Procedure

We conducted a survey among 330 residents of six major neighborhoods in a large Israeli city. We collected data during 1998 by a random sample method. Two hundred sixty usable questionnaires (final return rate of 78.78 percent) were appropriate for our needs in this study and were used in the final analysis. Interviewers asked participants to provide information about their attitudes to local municipalities' activities and services. Our questions probed various opinions and perceptions of citizens as to quality of public personnel (managers and employees), ethical image and morality of public servants, and innovation and creativity in the public-service process. An extended separate section of the questionnaires was dedicated to the measurement of public-sector performance by citizens' satisfaction. Participation was voluntary and citizens were assured of full confidentiality of all information they provided. A breakdown by neighborhood showed that 25 percent lived in low-class areas, 33 percent lived in average areas, and 42 percent lived in high-class areas; 54 percent of the sample were female, 45 percent were married, and 66 percent had an income equal to or less than the average salary in Israel. Average age was thirty-five and a half years (s.d. = 14.0); average time of residence in the city was twenty-four years (s.d. = 16).

Fifty-eight percent of respondents held an academic degree; 9 percent more had partly academic or higher education. Note that the demographic characteristics of the sample were quite similar to those of the total population in the city as reported by the city's research and statistics department: average age 35.6; 52 percent female; 46 percent married; 63.1 percent with 13+ school years or some academic degree.

Measures

Dependent Variables

Active citizenship involvement (ACI): ACI was measured by two constructs, political participation and community involvement. According to Verba et al. (1995), political participation refers to "activity that has the intent or effect of influencing governmental action—either directly by affecting the making or implementation of public policy or indirectly by influencing the selection of people who make those policies" (p. 38). Community involvement represents another, more intimate aspect of participation, which focuses on one's attempts to influence and contribute to the community (Milbrath and Goel 1977). As Verba et al. (1995, 460) found, "deep roots in the community are associated with participation in local politics," and this kind of involvement is an indispensable part of general citizenry involvement. ACI was measured by a total of fourteen items (items 1–8 for political participation and items 9–14 for community involvement), based on similar measures developed by Almond and Verba (1963), Milbrath and Goel (1977), and Verba et al. (1995). Respondents were asked to report the frequency of their involvement in the following fourteen political activities:

- keeping informed about politics;
- voting regularly in general elections;
- sending support/protest letters to politicians or to the newspapers;
- being an active member of a public organization (interest group or labor union);
- taking part in demonstrations or political meetings;
- engaging in political discussions;
- being a candidate for public office;
- signing petitions on political issues;
- being a member of a voluntary organization in the community;
- being a member of a tenants' committee;
- voting regularly in local elections;
- being a member of a parents' school committee;
- taking part in community cultural activities;
- writing letters to the mayor, to other local officials, or to local newspapers regarding community affairs.

Respondents were asked to indicate on a three-level scale how active they were in each activity: (1) never was active, (2) active in the past, (3) active today. The overall Cronbach's alpha was .77, which was higher than the separate alpha political participation and community involvement (.64 and .69 respectively).

Faith in citizenship involvement (FCI): This measure included eight items and incorporated two constructs: for items (1–4) of the faith in citizen involvement scale (Schussler 1982) and four items (5–8) of political efficacy (Guyton 1988). Faith in citizen involvement represents attitudes regarding the overall influence citizens may have on political and governmental processes. People with such faith view government as generally accessible to individuals and responsive to their efforts and appeals. Political efficacy was defined as a more personal feeling of one's capability to understand and influence the decision-making process in the political system. The literature usually treats this aspect of efficacy as internal political efficacy (Niemi, Craig, and Mattei 1991) rather than external political efficacy. Each construct was measured by items based on the above studies. The final items were: (1) The public has much control over what politicians do in office. (2) The average person can benefit by talking to public officials. (3) The average person has considerable influence on politics. (4) The government is generally responsive to public opinion. (5) I consider myself to be well qualified to participate in politics. (6) I feel that I have a pretty good understanding of the important political issues facing our country. (7) I feel that I could do as good a job in public office as most other people. (8) I think that I am better informed about politics and government than most people. Responses were made on a 5-point scale, ranging from 1 (strongly disagree) to 5 (strongly agree). Overall, Cronbach's alpha of the full scale was .66.

Independent Variables

The independent variables provided information on PSP as well as three major aspects of local municipalities' operation: human quality (HQ); innovation and creativity (IC); and morality and ethics (ME).

Public-sector performance (PSP): This variable was measured by two different scales of citizen-client satisfaction, satisfaction with service (items 1–6) and satisfaction with operation (items 7–16). Satisfaction with service assembled detailed information regarding citizens' satisfaction with services in the municipal offices. Participants were asked to report on public servants' behavior, ways of handling citizens' requests, and physical conditions in municipal premises. They also were asked to report how satisfied they were with the treatment they received either when they personally visited municipal departments or when they contacted these departments by phone. Items were as follows: (1) How satisfied are you with employees' courtesy and kindness? (2) How satisfied are you about the time required to handle your request? (3) How satisfied are you with the efficiency of public servants? (4) How satisfied are your with the physical conditions in the reception hall? (5) How satisfied are you with the willingness to help you over and above formal requirements? (6) All in all, how satisfied are you with the services you receive in the city offices? Satisfaction with operation referred to a variety of duties for which the municipal authorities were responsible and also to the ways of determining and implementing policy. Participants were asked to report how satisfied they were with the following ten operational fields of the city authorities: roads and infrastructures; cultural and educational services; city decoration and preservation; cleanliness; urban construction planning; ecology and air pollution; initiation of employment programs; parking and traffic arrangements; development of the coast; initiation of outstanding and unique programs. Responses on both scales were measured on a 5-point scale ranging from 1 (not at all satisfied) to 5 (very satisfied). Overall internal reliability of the unified scale was .85.

Human quality (HQ): To assess the quality of public servants we used two constructs: employees' quality (EQ) and leadership and management quality (LQ). Each construct was measured by three items (EQ items 1–3; LQ items 4–6). The final six items of the scale were: (1) Employees of this municipality are professionals and highly qualified. (2) Employees of this municipality show understanding, care, and willingness to serve the citizens. (3) This municipality employs only high quality individuals. (4) Public leadership and senior management in this city are well qualified and have high professional standards. (5) I think that this city is managed appropriately and it is in good order. (6) The leaders of this city have vision and a long range view as to where we are going. Respondents were asked to indicate their attitudes on a 5-point scale from 1 (strongly disagree) to 5 (strongly agree). Internal reliability of the scale was .86, which was higher than the single alpha value of employees' quality and leadership and management quality (.81 and .80 respectively).

Innovation and creativity (IC): This variable represents the degree to which public policy and public personnel in the city were flexible, took initiative, and were willing to adopt new ideas. It was measured by a five-item scale: (1) This municipality comes up with promising new ideas which improve citizens' quality of life. (2) Compared with other cities, this city has a leading position in developing useful projects for the public. (3) I find this city to be run with much creativity. (4) This municipality encourages its employees to take initiative and to suggest good ideas to improve service quality. (5) Advanced technology is involved in improving quality of service in this city. Participants were asked to respond on a scale from 1 (strongly disagree) to 5 (strongly agree). Internal reliability of this variable was .80.

Morality and ethics (ME): This variable described general attitudes to morality and fairness of civic servants. It consisted of three items: (1) In this municipality, most civic servants are neutral and honest. (2) Citizens of this city receive equal and fair treatment from the city officials. (3) In this municipality, exceptions from good moral norms are rare. Participants were asked to respond on a scale ranging from 1 (strongly disagree) to 5 (strongly agree); higher scores represented a more positive (moral and ethical) view of the city public service. Internal reliability of this variable was .75.

Data Analysis

Confirmatory factor analysis (CFA): Prior to the specific evaluation of the five models, we performed confirmatory factor analysis (CFA) to ensure that all the variables included in the models were best represented by the latent constructs as we framed them. This procedure is recommended in the literature to confirm that the tested models include highly coherent constructs that are clearly defined and measured (Joreskog and Sorbom 1994). We compared a large number of models (1- to 12-factor models), which consisted of all latent variables as well as the subscales of employee quality (EQ), leadership quality (LQ), faith in citizen involvement, political efficacy, political participation, and community involvement. For simplicity these results are not included here but they imply that a 6-factor model, which we finally applied, was the most appropriate in terms of fit and coherence with the data.[1]

Path analysis and evaluation of the models: Path analysis with LISREL VIII was used to examine the five models and compare them. We used a covariance matrix as input for the path analysis and examined the variations of relationships in the 6-factor model as arising from the CFA. Note that while the usual approach is to estimate structural relationships among variables that are free of measurement errors we employed another technique that was more appropriate for our case. Bollen (1989) showed that the ratio of the number of observed variables to the sample size should be at least 1:5 in order to allow the common estimation approach. When this ratio is close to or lower than 5 (53:260 or 1:4.9 in our case), or when the ratio between latent and observed variables is higher than 1:5 (6:53 or 1:8.6 in our case), implementation of the common approach of examination is not recommended. A better alternative is to treat the multi-item scales as single indicators of each construct. Accordingly, we also corrected for measurement errors in the models by the following procedure. The random error variance associated with each construct was equated to the value of its variance multiplied by the quantity one minus its estimated reliability (Bollen 1989).

Other studies have successfully implemented this approach in the field of public administration (Cohen and Vigoda 2000). Results of this procedure, however, diverged substantially from the uncorrected single-indicator analysis.

Fit indices: Seven indices were used to assess the fit of the models. The first was the chi-square test, which is the most basic and essential for the nested model comparison. A low and non-significant value of chi-square represents a good fit to the data. The chi-square test is sensitive to sample size, so the ratio of the model chi-square to degrees of freedom was used as another fit index. In this study a ratio up to 2 was considered a satisfactory value. In addition, some other fit indices are also reported as less sensitive to sample size differences and to the number of indicators per latent variable increase (Medsker, Williams, and Holahan 1994). Four of these indices were used in our study: the relative fit index (RFI), the comparative fit index (CFI), the normed fit index (NFI), and the goodness of fit index (GFI). The RFI and the CFI were developed to facilitate the choice of the best fit among competing models that may differ in degree of parameterization and specification of relations among latent variables (Bentler 1990; Bollen 1989). They are recommended as the best approximation of the population value for a single model. The closer their value is to 1 the better the fit. NFI was proposed in earlier studies and is additive for the nested-model comparison (Bentler and Bonett 1980). Its value should be close to 1 to indicate a good fit. The last indicator GFI does not depend on sample size explicitly, and it measures how much *better* the model fits than no model at all. Both these measures should be between zero and 1, and a value higher than .90 is considered very good.

Path coefficients: An attempt to compare several alternative models by structural equation modeling (SEM) must first rely on information provided by a variety of fit indices, as we have described. However, to determine the superiority or domination of one model, one must also consider path coefficients that indicate the quality of the chosen alternative as a correct causal model. Joreskog and Sorbom (1994) defined this as the *plausibility criterion.* This criterion means that the path coefficients in the plausible better-fit model adhere well to the general theoretical conception and to the hypotheses. This adherence should hold in terms of magnitude as well as in the expected directions. Accordingly, a model that fits the data well but that has many theoretical paths that do not support the theoretical arguments cannot be defined as correct. Some balance must be made between the fit indices and the theoretical predictions or hypotheses regarding the relationships among research variables. Hence the accuracy of the theoretical predictions can be tested by the path coefficients in each of the models, as we did in this study.

The percentage of variance explained by the dependent variables: Another important consideration of the quality of the models and their contribution to the theory can be found in analysis of the explained variance of each model. When a low percentage of variance of the dependent variable(s) is explained by a given model, this indicates that the model is not correct (Saris and Stronkhorst 1984). Low explained variance can be a result of measurement errors, omission of important variables from the model, or inaccurate definition of the interrelationships of the variables in the model. Therefore, one should consider the percentage of the explained variance to be another criterion for the correctness of a model.

FINDINGS

Figure 28.1 presents the five alternative models. Path coefficients are displayed in this figure. We will discuss these values later; first let us take a look at some necessary descriptive statistics that may prove to be useful in our analysis.

Figure 28.1 **Five Alternative Models of the Relationship Between PA Performance and Citizenship Involvement**

Model 1: A simple direct effect

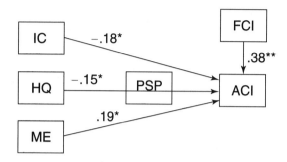

Model 2: A simple indirect effect

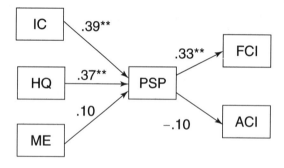

Model 3: A dual pattern effect

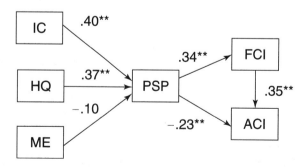

Model 4: FCI mediates between PSP and ACI

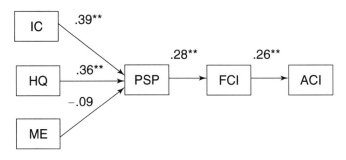

Model 5: A simultaneous effect of FCI and PSP on ACI

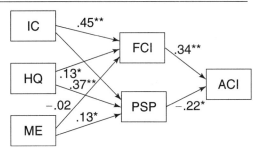

Legend:
HQ = human quality
IC = innovation and creativity
ME = morality and ethics
PSP = public-sector performance
FCI = faith in citizenship involvement
ACI = active citizenship involvement
$*p < .05$ $**p < .01$

Descriptive Statistics and Intercorrelations

Table 28.1 presents descriptive statistics as well as intercorrelations of the study variables. Two important findings are worthy of consideration. First, means, standard deviations, and Cronbach alpha levels were within reasonable limits, which attests to the proper construction of our sample and measures. Note, however, that LISREL reweights variables to maximize the relationship between variables and hence may yield measures that are different from the original. Consequently, Cronbach alpha of the reweighted measures may also be slightly different from those calculated in the conventional way. Despite this, in this study we followed the conventional approach and provided the original alpha values, assuming that they were close to those calculated by LISREL. Cronbach alphas ranged between .66 for FCI and .86 for HQ; all were above the .60 level suggested by Nunnaly (1967) as the minimum required for treating a scale as reliable. Second, with

Table 28.1

Descriptive Statistics and Intercorrelations for the Study Variables
(reliabilities in parentheses)

Variable	Mean	SD	1	2	3	4	5	6
Human quality (HQ)	2.61	.73	(.86)					
Innovation and creativity (IC)	2.71	.71	.60***	(.80)				
Morality and ethics (ME)	2.79	.77	.57***	.47***	(.75)			
Public-sector performance (PSP)	2.72	.57	.60***	.60***	.40***	(.85)		
Faith in citizenship involvement (FCI)	2.87	.59	.17**	.30***	.12*	.22***	(.66)	
Active citizenship involvement (ACI)	1.78#	.35	−.10	−.04	.02	−.15**	.33***	(.77)

N = 260; *P < .05; **P < .01; ***P < .001; # = a scale of 1–3.

Table 28.2

Descriptive Statistics and Intercorrelations for the Inner Factors of HQ, ACI, FCI, and PSP (reliabilities in parentheses)

Variable	Mean	SD	1	2	3	4	5	6	7	8
HQ										
1. Leadership and managerial quality	2.58	.84	(.80)							
2. Employee quality	2.64	.77	.64***	(.81)						
ACI										
3. Political participation#	1.89	.38	−.13*	NS	(.64)					
4. Community involvement#	1.64	.45	NS	NS	.52***	(.69)				
FCI										
5. Faith in citizen involvement	2.48	.72	.35***	.25***	NS	NS	(.67)			
6. Political efficacy	3.42	.71	NS	−.13*	.48***	.15*	.48***	(.79)		
PSP										
7. Satisfaction with service	2.77	.74	.46***	.59***	−.16**	NS	.26***	NS	(.86)	
8. Satisfaction with operation	2.69	.64	.52***	.36***	NS	−.14*	.36***	NS	.40***	(.80)

N = 260; *P < .05; **P < .01; ***P < .001; # = a scale of 1–3.

the exception of the relationships between ACI and the three constructs of public administration operation (HQ, IC, ME), all correlations among research variables were significant, positive, and in the predicted directions. PSP was strongly related to HQ and IC (r = .60; p < .001) and to ME (r = .40; p < .001). FCI was constantly and positively related to all the other variables in the models, most importantly to PSP (r = .22; p. < .001). FCI was positively correlated with ACI (r = .33; p < .001), as was evinced in previous studies (Brady et al. 1995; Milbrath and Goel 1977; Verba et al. 1995). The only exception here was the negative relationship between ACI and PSP (r

Table 28.3

Goodness of Fit Summary for the Research Models

Model/Description	df	X^2	P*	X^2/df	RFI	NFI	NNFI	CFI	GFI
1. A simple direct effect	1	3.27	.071	3.27	.90	.99	.92	.99	1.00
2. A simple indirect effect	7	55.60*	.000	7.94	.75	.88	.77	.89	.94
3. A dual pattern effect	6	13.62*	.034	2.27	.93	.97	.96	.98	.98
4. FCI mediates between PSP and ACI	7	34.52*	.000	4.93	.84	.93	.87	.94	.96
5. *A simultaneous effect of FCI and PSP on ACI*	*4*	*3.76*	*.440*	*.94*	*.97*	*.99*	*1.00*	*1.00*	*1.00*

N = 260
*P = significance

Table 28.4

Explained Variance (R^2) for the Dependent Variables in the Research Models

Model/Description	Public sector performance (PSP)	Faith in citizenship involvement (FCI)	Active citizenship involvement (ACI)
1. A simple direct effect	—	—	.37
2. A simple indirect effect	.65	.10	.02
3. A dual pattern effect	.65	.10	.33
4. FCI mediates between PSP and ACI	.65	.07	.18
5. *A simultaneous effect of FCI and PSP on ACI*	.65	.18	.33

= −.15; p < .01). This relationship somewhat challenged our hypothesis and indicated that better performance by public-sector agencies may cause a decline in active citizenship involvement. In sum, the correlations among the independent variables were quite high; however, none exceeded .70, which indicates the absence of multicollinearity in this study.

To further establish our measures, we also present psychometric properties of the inner factors that were used to create the models' variables. As demonstrated in Table 28.2, these figures further indicated our decision to integrate pairs of factors into four single ones: HQ was constructed of the variables leadership and managerial quality, and employees' quality; ACI was constructed of political participation and community involvement; FCI was constructed of faith in citizen involvement and political efficacy; and PSP was constructed of satisfaction with service and satisfaction with operation. Intercorrelations between pairs of factors were high, between .40 and .64.

Evaluation of Models

Evaluation of the research models relied on three parameters: the path coefficients, which were presented in Figure 28.1; a goodness-of-fit summary for each model, as shown in Table 28.3; and the explained variance parameters displayed in Table 28.4. Together they provided some essential tools for a proper evaluation of the correctness and theoretical adaptability of the five models.

Although the path coefficients of models 2 and 4, as shown in Figure 28.1, were in the predicted directions, these models had a very low fit with the data and had to be rejected. Table 28.3 provides detailed information on the models' fit. The chi-square test produced significant values, indicating that the models did not cohere with the data; chi-square to df ratio (X^2/df) was close to 5 and 8, which exceeds the recommended 2 value. RFI, NFI, and GFI were lower than in all the other models. Furthermore, the explained variance of the dependent variables in models 2 and 4 as presented in Table 28.3 was lower than in most of the other models. The explained variance of FCI was only .10 in model 2 and .07 in model 4, compared with a value of .18 in model 5. The explained variance of ACI was 0.2 in model 2 and .18 in model 4, compared with .33 in models 3 and 5 and .37 in model 1. Consequently, model 2 (the simple indirect effect model) and model 4 (FCI mediates between PSP and ACI) were rejected.

While model 1 (the simple direct effect model) showed better fit indices than the remaining models (model 3, the dual pattern effect and model 5, the simultaneous effect of FCI and PSP on ACI), we had to conclude that it must also be rejected for several reasons. First, some of the central fit indices such as X^2/df and RFI were inferior in this model to those in models 3 and 5. Second, the df value was almost minimal (df=1), which indicates that this model was close to a saturated ineffective model. Nor did model 1 include most of the necessary theoretical relationships between PSP and citizenship involvement, as presented earlier. All these arguments resulted in the rejection of model 1, which also represented the null hypothesis of no relationship between PSP and citizenship involvement in this study.

A comparison between the remaining models (3 and 5) produced more complex findings. Although model 5 appeared much superior in terms of fit indices (nonsignificant chi-square value and better fit in all other indices as well), this model was also less parsimonious than model 3. It had only 4 degrees of freedom, compared with 6 degrees of freedom in model 3, which made the latter more efficient and competent. However, the parsimony criterion was not sufficient to conclude that a model was the correct one; other figures had to be considered. For example, the ratio of number of significant path coefficients to the total number of paths in model 3 was 5/6. The same ratio in model 5 was 7/8, which made this one better in terms of correct path coefficients. In addition, while both models had only one nonsignificant path (ME to PSP in model 3 and ME to FCI in model 5), the accumulative explained variance of the dependent variables in model 5, as presented in Table 28.3, was higher than in model 3. This was mainly due to increase in the explained variance in FCI from .10 (model 3) to .18 (model 5), while the explained variance of PSP and ACI remained stable (.65 and .33 respectively).

Hence despite some weaknesses of model 5, especially its parsimony problem, we concluded that this was the best model among all those we have examined. This model, which represents a simultaneous effect of FCI and PSP on ACI, evinced a very good fit with the data a good magnitude of path coefficients in most of the expected directions, and a sound theoretical adaptability to our conceptual framework. However, none of this meant that model 5 was the only possible correct model or the best conceivable one. A major obstacle to our conclusion that model 5 was the only correct one was the unexpected negative relationship found between PSP and ACI. As shown in model 5, this relationship was moderate, at a value of −.22. This should be noted especially in light of the expected positive relationship found between PSP and FCI, ranging from .28 in model 4 to .34 in models 3 and 5.

Beyond these findings one should also note several other relationships in model 5. According to Figure 28.1, innovation and creativity (IC) as well as human quality (HQ) in the public sector were positively related with FCI (.45 and .13 respectively) and with PSP (.39 and .37 respectively). Morality and ethics (ME) was positively related with PSP (.13) but had no relationship with FCI.

Thus it may be concluded that faith in citizenship involvement was more strongly affected by creativity and innovative orientations of public administration than by other variables such as human quality or morality and ethics. However, these facets were more strongly related with PSP, which served as a mediator to active involvement. In other words, while both FCI and PSP were independent mediators among IC, HQ, ME, and ACI, the nature of this mediating relationship differed across variants of public-sector operation. In addition, the relationship of FCI and ACI was positive and stronger (.34) than the relationship of PSP and ACI (−.22). These findings may indicate that ACI is simultaneously affected by various antecedents, where faith in citizenship involvement plays a central and strong role but not a unique one. Our model shows that performance of public-sector agencies may contribute to the explanation of active involvement and improve its predictive power beyond explanations of resources, psychological engagement, and recruitment networks (Brady et al. 1995).

DISCUSSION

In recent years a considerable number of studies have elaborated on the ample promise of higher citizenship involvement for the reconstruction of healthy public bureaucracies. Scholars have noted that greater citizenship involvement expresses a higher level of collaboration in public domains, where the public is becoming closer to the administrative process (Box 1998 and 1999; Putnam 1993; Rimmerman 1997). According to this reasoning, involvement breeds collaboration and more collaboration improves the effectiveness and performance of bureaucracies. However, we believe that a comprehensive analysis of this collaboration must also embody an opposite flow of influences, which is the effect of administrative performance on democratic values, particularly on perceived citizen trust and on active citizen involvement. The impact of public administration's actions and performance on citizens' perceptions, attitudes, and behavior in terms of democratic beliefs and values should thus be considered more seriously. As Nalbandian (1999) has recently argued, city managers and professionals are frequently seen as community builders and enablers of democracy. Their actions are continually translated by ordinary citizens to reconstruct an image of the public service tightly related to democratic culture. Accordingly, Nalbandian suggests that public-sector performance may affect citizenship values, perceptions, and even actual political or communal involvement. In line with this, our goal in this study was to portray some of the possible relationships between administrative outcomes in local government and democratic premises of citizenship involvement. In general, findings from one Israeli city revealed that this relationship may exist, but its nature is more complex and enigmatic than we might expect.

First and most importantly, the findings quite consistently rejected the null hypothesis on the absence of a relationship between performance of the public sector and citizenship involvement, as represented in model 1. The alternative model 5 (and to a lesser extent model 3) fitted the data quite well, and provided the most rational interrelationships among the study variables. Model 5 further supported our elementary argument on the effect of public-sector operation and performance on different dimensions of citizens' involvement. The implications that can be drawn from this model are threefold:

- Both PSP and FCI are separately affected by the innovation and creativity (IC), by the human quality (HQ), and considerably less by the morality and ethics (ME) of the public service.
- PSP is related to citizenship involvement, yet this relationship is complex.
- FCI is positively affected by PSP while ACI is negatively affected by PSP.

Public-Sector Performance and Citizenship Involvement:
A Paradoxical Relationship

Our findings on the relationship between public-sector performance and citizenship involvement need further elaboration. The relationship may be defined as consistent but paradoxical. Public administration is expected to work effectively, efficiently, and economically for the sake of the public interest. It is designed to bring the best and highest possible outcome to all citizens, thereby nurturing and safeguarding democracy. But Dennis Thompson (1983), challenging this idea, argued that actually "democracy does not suffer bureaucracy gladly. Many of the values we associate with democracy—quality, participation, and individuality—stand sharply opposed to hierarchy, specialization, and impersonality we ascribe to modern bureaucracy" (p. 235). Following this, Kelly (1998) argued that public administration scholars are divided over whether the public bureaucracy or the democratic polity ought to be the starting point of public administration scholarship. A utopian perspective will suggest that the two must go together to create a highly efficient, liberal culture that provides maximum welfare to all citizens. In some respects our findings may offer another look at the odd couple of bureaucracy and democracy. We suggest that performance by the public sector contributes to a healthy development of attitudes and opinions that uphold democracy. Individuals better satisfied with city services and operation are also stronger believers in the democratic process and in their own ability to play a constructive part in these dynamics. If necessary, they express high motivation to be involved in politics and in citizenry actions. Furthermore, they have a sense of being able to make a significant contribution to the manifold expressions of community life. However, the same people admit that feeling satisfied and well treated by official authorities causes them to be less committed to another citizenry duty, namely active participation. These individuals are thus less engaged in *active* political participation and in active community involvement.

How can these paradoxical relationships be resolved? One explanation is that people feel they have a say in politics and administrative agencies, yet at the same time they do not have to use their voice when bureaucracy operates properly and efficiently (and vice versa). This argument relies heavily on the passivity explanation (Soss 1999), which suggests that government assistance and services make recipients appreciative and even dependent, hence politically passive. As suggested by Brady et al. (1995), people do not take part in politics because (1) they can't, (2) they don't want to, or (3) nobody asked. Our analysis seems to accord with the second of these causes: people don't want to take part in politics when there is no pressing need to do so. But we take issue with Brady and his coauthors' argument that "they don't want to" focuses on the absence of psychological engagement with politics—a lack of interest in politics, minimal concern with public issues, a sense that activity makes no difference, and no consciousness of membership in a group with shared political interests. As numerous studies have proposed (Milbrath and Goel 1977; Verba et al. 1995), the sense of being able to influence is not equivalent either to making a decision to become active or to actually becoming active. Citizens may become active only when some of their essential needs are not satisfied by public authorities. Despite feelings of high citizenry influence, motivation to take active part in state-level politics or in community activities diminishes when there is no obvious need for action. Accordingly, *don't want to* rather means *don't need to,* which is also substantially different from *can't* or *not being asked* to be involved, as proposed by Brady et al. (1995). In other words, high performance by the public sector may carry great merit in people's minds but may not necessarily lead people to act. In the long run these may evince with a dangerous threat to democratic action and participation. A calm, stable, and relatively satisfying public arena increases citizens' feeling of welfare and influence, but silently and inexorably it can eliminate their motivation and skills to seek active involvement and control over bureaucracies.

Another explanation for the negative relationship between PSP and ACI may be due to an intervening factor. However, because the LISREL model becomes very complicated and less parsimonious when other demographic variables, potentially intervening ones, are included, we decided not to include these variables in the models. Still, we performed several other tests to examine the possibility of intervening factors. First, we tested the zero-order correlations among a series of variables (gender, age, education, income, years in city), ACI, and PSP. Second, we regressed ACI on PSP and on the demographic variables to test for possible intervening effects. From these findings, we suggest that two variables may be considered intervening: age and education. The zero-order correlation between age and ACI was .31 ($p < .001$) and its standardized Beta value was .32 ($p < .001$). Age also correlated with PSP ($r = -.13$; $p < .05$). In addition, the standardized Beta value for the relationship between education and ACI was .14 ($r < .01$). According to Baron and Kenny (1986), these findings may indicate that age—and to a lesser extent education—may intervene in the relationship between PSP and ACI. Consequently, we recommend that future researchers examine this question more thoroughly.

The Effect of Public-Sector IC, HQ, and ME on Citizenship Involvement

Model 5 showed that different aspects of public-sector operation were positively related to FCI, a relationship that carries several implications. First, our study highlighted the possible effect of innovative public administration on the healthy development of citizens' faith in governance and, through this construct, on the encouragement of active citizenship involvement. Second, this study suggested that innovation and creativity, as well as the human quality of public personnel, may have another indirect positive effect on active involvement, this time through the enhancement of PSP as represented here by citizens' satisfaction. Morality and ethics of public servants may also work in this direction, albeit at a lower magnitude. Thus a major implication might be that public-sector operation exerts competing influences on active citizenship involvement. Some of these influences are positive and some are negative, but they all work simultaneously through FCI and PSP.

CONCLUSION

Consensus seems to exist that unless the ancient hidden social agreement is mutually respected by both rulers and citizens, no bureaucracy can fully justify its existence, and citizens may have the right to ask for better alternatives to democratic regimes. Hence fair transactions between rulers (who hold power and authority) and citizens (who agree to be ruled and governed) constitute the most important condition for governments to conduct, for public administration to manage, and for citizens to support democracy. Governments are committed to providing all citizens with the best services and quality outcomes, which not only maintain their safety in unstable environments but also improve their quality of life, safeguard their liberal rights, and allow them to organize their communities as they see fit. Citizens, on the other hand, are obliged to uphold this system as being genuinely sympathetic and supportive of their needs. According to our findings, however, a paradoxical negative relationship exists between the performance of public administration and the active involvement of citizens. This problem deserves much more elaboration and discussion in future scientific studies as well as in public debates.

Nonetheless, for positive relationships to grow and flourish, there is a need to develop quality public services and renew professional bureaucracies (Woller 1998). High performance of the public sector affects citizens' satisfaction and willingness to play their parts in the social agreement. It is also possible that performance might encourage citizenship involvement and participation in communal and national public lives in ways that are different from what is customary today. This contribution to democracy by routine administrative actions is a covert purpose of public-sector systems. In western democracies public administration bodies have momentous power. It stems from their major role in society, which is equally to serve large populations with heterogeneous needs and to sustain a high level of performance over large areas and lengthy periods. Such functions allow the sound development and healthy progress of democracy. Public organizations should be committed to serve the people to the best of their ability and at the same time to encourage authentic citizenship involvement, which implies less passivity among individuals. It is further suggested that in return, citizens respond by active involvement in the administrative process by sharing ideas, knowledge, and experience with civil servants and with state leaders. Thus citizens and public administrators join in mutual responsibilities and roles aimed at the development of prosperous modern democracies. This study argues that a most important role of public administrators is to develop a sense of partnership and collaboration between rulers and citizens. These alliances must rely on simultaneous improvement of institutional performance as well as greater citizenship involvement by different means. Furthermore, we find the local community level to be a most appropriate habitat for good democratic values and collaboration to grow and prosper.

Our study is not free of limitations, which should be considered and overcome in future research. First, it is based mainly on self-reported data, which are subject to measurement biases such as common method error. While this approach is not uncommon in public-sector analysis, it has its weaknesses as well as its advantages (e.g., Brudney and England 1980 and 1982; Stipak 1979 and 1980). To measure PSP we used subjective evaluations of citizens. As Stipak (1979) noted, such a method involves the danger that "citizens' responses to satisfaction and evaluation questions may not reflect actual service performance" (p. 46). To overcome this problem somewhat, Stipak recommended using more specific subjective indicators than general satisfaction, arguing that this alternative provides greater potential for evaluating service performance. Since our study uses a relatively long, detailed, and specific scale of citizen satisfaction (a 16-item scale) we believe that we largely followed this last recommendation of Stipak without our use of reliable, albeit not objective, measure of PSP. Furthermore, this study generally adopts the cognitive approach to human behavior as framed by Lewin (1936), who argued that people respond to their perceptions of reality, not to reality per se. We believe that this argument is so in our case as well. The actual outcomes and performance of public administration are of immense importance, yet in our case we chose to focus on another relevant question, namely how these outcomes are perceived by citizens and translated into trust and active citizenship involvement. In line with all this, we believe that our subjective measure is appropriate for the present study. Nonetheless, future research on the relationship between public-sector performance and citizenship involvement would definitely benefit from more-objective measures such as an examination of public spending, cost-benefit indicators, or additional measures of innovation, creativity, and quality of public personnel.

A second limitation is that this study examined citizens' perceptions at one point in time; it should be replicated to reveal trends and developments in both public performance and citizenship involvement. Third, the data were collected in an Israeli setting, which is quite different from what a North American or European setting would be. The results might have been affected by cultural and structural factors unique to Israel. For example, the Israeli public sector is more conservative and centralized, and for many years it faced problems typical of relatively new democracies. Hence our conceptual framework would need to be replicated in other settings before firm conclusions could be made.

Despite its limitations, this study provides another look at the relationship of public-sector performance with patterns of citizenship involvement. Until now, most studies have been interested in the opposite flow of influences, which is the contribution of citizenship involvement to the managerial process in bureaucracies. This study also expands on the advantages of using an advanced statistical method (SEM) for better understanding of these relationships. However, more work is needed in order to better explore this arena. Hence the contribution of the study lies in its attempt to suggest a more specific linkage between public-sector performance and the cultivation of democratic values in modern societies.

ACKNOWLEDGMENTS

The author wishes to thank the anonymous reviewers, whose comments significantly contributed to the improvement of this article. A previous version of this article was presented at the 62nd annual conference of the American Society for Public Administration (ASPA), Rutgers University, Newark, N.J., March 10–14, 2001.

NOTE

1. These results are available upon request directly from the author.

REFERENCES

Almond, Gabriel A., and Verba, Sidney. 1963. *The Civic Culture: Political Attitudes and Democracy in Five Nations: An Analytic Study.* Boston: Little, Brown.

Barber, Benjamin. 1984. *Strong Democracy: Participatory Politics for a New Age.* Berkeley: University of California Press.

Barner, Carol, and Rosenwein, Robert E. 1985. *Psychological Perspectives on Politics.* Englewood Cliffs, N.J.: Prentice-Hall.

Baron, Reuben M., and Kenny, David A. 1986. "The Moderator-Mediator Variable Distinction in Social Psychological Research: Conceptual, Strategic, and Statistical Considerations." *Journal of Personality and Social Psychology* 51:6:1173–82.

Bentler, Peter M. 1990. "Comparative Fit Indexes in Structural Models." *Psychological Bulletin* 107:2:238–46.

———, and Bonett, Douglas G. 1980. "Significance Tests and Goodness-of-Fit in the Analysis of Covariance Structures." *Psychological Bulletin* 88:588–606.

Berman, Evan M. 1997. "Dealing with Cynical Citizens." *Public Administration Review* 57:2:105–12.

Blau, Peter M. 1964. *Power and Exchange in Social Life.* New York: Wiley.

Bollen, Kenneth A. 1989. *Structural Equation With Latent Variables.* New York: Wiley.

Box, Richard C. 1998. *Citizen Governance: Leading American Communities into the 21st Century.* Thousand Oaks, Calif.: SAGE.

———. 1999. "Running Governments Like a Business: Implications for Public Administration Theory and Practice." *American Review of Public Administration* 29:1:19–43.

Bozeman, Barry. 1993. *Public Management.* San Francisco: Jossey-Bass.

Brady, Henry E.; Verba, Sidney; and Schlozman, Kay L. 1995. "Beyond SES: A Resource Model of Political Participation." *American Political Science Review* 89:2:271–94.

Browne, Malcolm W., and Cudeck, Robert. 1989. "Single Sample Cross-Validation Indices for Covariance Structures." *Multivariate Behavioral Research* 24:445–55.

Brudney, Jeffrey L., and England, Robert E. 1980. "Public Attitudes toward Community Services: Implications for Policy. *American Review of Public Administration* 14:3:200–05.

——— 1982. "Urban Policy Making and Subjective Service Evaluation: Are They Compatible?" *Public Administration Review* 42:127–35.

Carmines, Edward G. 1992. "Psychological Antecedents of Adolescent Political Involvement: Personal Competence and Political Behavior." *International Journal of Adolescence and Youth* 3:79–98.

Carter, Neil; Klein, Rudolf; and Day, Patricia. 1992. *How Organizations Measure Success: The Use of Performance Indicators in Government*. London: Routledge.

Cohen, Aaron, and Vigoda, Eran. 2000. "Do Good Citizens Make Good Organizational Citizens? An Empirical Examination of the Effects of Citizenship Behaviors and Orientations on Organizational Citizenship Behavior." *Administration and Society* 32:5:596–624.

deLeon, Linda. 1996. "Ethics and Entrepreneurship." *Policy Studies Journal* 24:16:495–510.

Etzioni, Amitai. 1994. *The Spirit of Community*. New York: Touchstone.

———. 1995. *New Communitarian Thinking: Persons, Virtues, Institutions, and Communities*. Charlottesville: Virginia University Press.

Farnham, David, and Horton, Sylvia, eds. 1993. *Managing the New Public Services*. Basingstoke, U.K.: Macmillan.

Feldman, Ofer, and Kawakami, Koichi. 1991. "Media Use as Predictors of Political Behavior: The Case of Japan." *Political Psychology* 12:65–80.

Frederickson, H. George. 1982. "The Recovery of Civism in Public Administration." *Public Administration Review* 42:6:501–09.

———. 1997. *The Spirit of Public Administration*. San Francisco: Jossey-Bass.

Golembiewski, Robert T.; Vigoda, Eran; and Sun, Ben-Chu. forthcoming [2002]. "Cacophonies in the Contemporary Chorus about Change at the Public Worksites, as Contrasted with Some Straight-Talk from a Planned Change Perspective." *International Journal of Public Administration* [25 (1) (February): 111–37].

Gortner, Harold F. 1991. *Ethics for Public Managers*. New York: Praeger.

Guyton, Edith M. 1998. "Critical Thinking and Political Participation: Development and Assessment of a Causal Model." *Theory and Research in Social Education* 16:23–49.

Halachmi, Arie, and Bouckaert, Geert, eds. 1995. *Public Productivity through Quality and Strategic Management*. Amsterdam: IOS Press.

Hood, Christopher. 1991. "A Public Management for All Seasons?" *Public Administration* 69:3–19.

Joreskog, Karl, and Sorbom, Dag. 1994. *Structural Equation Modeling with the SIMPLIS Command Language*. Chicago: Scientific Software International.

Kelly, Rita Mae. 1998. "An Inclusive Democratic Polity, Representative Bureaucracies, and the New Public Management." *Public Administration Review* 58:201–08.

King, Cheryl S.; Feltey, Kathryn M.; and Susel, Bridget O. 1998. "The Question of Participation: Toward Authentic Public Participation in Public Administration." *Public Administration Review* 58:4:317–26.

King, Cheryl S., and Stivers, Camilla. 1998. *Government Is Us: Public Administration in an Anti-government Era*. Thousand Oaks, Calif.: SAGE.

Kramer, Robert. 1999. "Weaving the Public into Public Administration." *Public Administration Review* 59:1:89–92.

Krampen, Gunter. 1991. Political Participation in an Action-Theory Model of Personality: Theory and Empirical Evidence." *Political Psychology* 12:1–25.

Lewin, Kurt. 1936. *Principles of Topological Psychology*. New York: McGraw-Hill.

Lui, Terry T., and Cooper, Terry L. 1997. Values in Flux: Administrative Ethics and the Hong Kong Public Servant." *Administration and Society* 29:3:301–24.

Lynn, Laurence E. 1996. *Public Management as Art, Science, and Profession*. Chatham, N.J.: Chatham House.

———. 1998. "The New Public Management: How to Transform a Theme into a Legacy." *Public Administration Review* 58:3:231–37.

Manzel, Donald C. 1999. "Rediscovering the Lost World of Public Service Ethics: Do We Need New Ethics for Public Administration?" *Public Administration Review* 59:5:443–47.

Medsker, Gina J.; Williams, Larry J.; and Holahan, Patricia J. 1994. "A Review of Current Practices for Evaluating Causal Models in Organizational Behavior and Human Resources Management Research." *Journal of Management* 20:2:239–64.

Milbrath, Lester W. 1981. "Political Participation." In S.L. Long, ed. *The Handbook of Political Behavior*, vol. 4, pp. 197–237. New York: Plenum.

———, and Goel, Madan L. 1977. *Political Participation: How and Why Do People Get Involved in Politics?* 2d ed. Chicago: Rand McNally.

Nalbandian, John. 1999. "Facilitating Community, Enabling Democracy: New Roles for Local Government Managers." *Public Administration Review* 59:3:187–97.

Niemi, Richard G.; Craig, Stephen C.; and Mattei, Franco. 1991. "Measuring Internal Political Efficacy in the 1988 National Election Study." *American Political Science Review* 85:4:1407–13.

Nunnaly, Jum C. 1967. *Psychometric Theory.* New York: McGraw-Hill.

Nye, Joseph S.; Zelikow, Philip D.; and King, David C., eds. 1997. *Why People Don't Trust Government.* Cambridge, Mass.: Harvard University Press.

Orum, Anthony M. 1989. *Introduction to Political Sociology.* Englewood Cliffs, N.J.: Prentice-Hall.

Osborne, David, and Gaebler, Ted. 1992. *Reinventing Government.* Reading, Mass.: Addison-Wesley.

Palfrey, Colin; Phillips, Ceri; Thomas, Paul; and Edward, David. 1992. *Policy Evaluation in the Public Sector.* Aldershot, U.K.: Avebury.

Parsons, David W. 1995. *Public Policy.* Cheltenham, U.K.: Edward Elgar.

Pateman, Carole. 1970. *Participation and Democratic Theory.* London: Cambridge University Press.

Peterson, Steven A. 1990. *Political Behavior.* Thousand Oaks, Calif.: SAGE.

Pettersen, P.A., and Rose, Lee E. 1996. "Participation in Local Politics in Norway: Some Do, Some Don't, Some Will, Some Won't." *Political Behavior* 18:51–97.

Pollitt, Christopher. 1988. "Bringing Consumers Into Performance Measurement." *Policy and Politics* 16:1:77–87.

Putnam, Robert. 1993. *Making Democracy Work: Civic Traditions in Modern Italy.* Princeton, N.J.: Princeton University Press.

Rainey, Hal G. 1990. "Public Management: Recent Development and Current Prospects." In N.B. Lynn and A. Wildavsky, eds. *Public Administration: The State of the Discipline,* 157–84. Chatham, N.J.: Chatham House.

Rhodes, Rod A.W. 1987. "Developing the Public Service Orientation, or Let's Add a Soupcon of Political Theory." *Local Government Studies* (May-June):63–73.

Rimmerman, Craig A. 1997. *The New Citizenship: Unconventional Politics, Activism, and Service.* Boulder, Colo.: Westview.

Sabucedo, Jose M., and Cramer, Duncan. 1991. "Sociological and Psychological Predictors of Voting in Great Britain." *Journal of Social Psychology* 131:5:647–54.

Saris, Willem, and Stronkhorst, Henk. 1984. *Causal Modeling in Non Experimental Research: An Introduction to the LISREL Approach.* Amsterdam: Sociometric Research Foundation.

Schneider, Anne, and Ingram, Helen. 1995. "Social Construction (continued)—Comment/Reply." *American Political Science Review* 89:2:441–46.

———. 1997. *Policy Design for Democracy.* Lawrence: University Press of Kansas.

Schussler, Karlheinz F. 1982. *Measuring Social Life Feelings.* San Francisco: Jossey-Bass.

Sigel, Roberta S., ed. 1989. *Political Learning in Adulthood: A Sourcebook of Theory and Research.* Chicago: University of Chicago Press.

Sobel, Ruth. 1993. "From Occupational Involvement to Political Participation: An Exploratory Analysis." *Political Behavior* 15:339–53.

Soss, Joe. 1999. "Lessons of Welfare: Policy Design, Political Learning, and Political Action." *American Political Science Review* 93:2:363–80.

Stipak, Brian. 1979. "Citizen Satisfaction With Urban Services: Potential Misuse as a Performance Indicator." *Public Administration Review* 39:1:46–52.

———. 1980. "Local Governments' Use of Citizen Surveys." *Public Administration Review* 40:5:521–25.

Thompson, Dennis. 1983. "Bureaucracy and Democracy." In G. Duncan, ed. *Democratic Theory and Practice.* Cambridge: Cambridge University Press.

Thompson, John L. 1990. *Strategic Management: Awareness and Change.* London: Chapman and Hall.

Verba, Sidney; Nie, N.H.; and Kim, Jae. 1978. *Participation and Political Equality: A Seven-Nation Comparison.* Cambridge: Cambridge University Press.

Verba, Sidney; Schlozman, Kay L.; and Brady, Henry. 1995. *Voice and Equality: Civic Voluntarism in American Politics.* London: Harvard University Press.

Vigoda, Eran. 2000. "Are You Being Served? The Responsiveness of Public Administration to Citizens' Demands: An Empirical Examination in Israel." *Public Administration* 78:1:165–91.

Woller, Gary M. 1998. "Toward a Reconciliation of the Bureaucratic and Democratic Ethos." *Administration and Society* 30:1:85–109.

PART 6

BUILDING THEORIES OF DIRECT CITIZEN PARTICIPATION

Theory building is an art, but on the topic of direct citizen participation, not a particularly well developed one. We are in the early stages of theory development. The area is rich in case studies, but there have been no attempts at meta-analysis across cases, as least that we have been able to uncover. Although there is much speculation on what makes direct citizen participation successful or unsuccessful, few definitive statements can be made for all policy arenas, for all stages of the policy process, and for all participants. What works in one situation may not work in another.

The lack of theory development is not surprising given the complexity of the topic. The number of individual, group, and organizational variables, not to mention contextual factors that could be considered, can be overwhelming. One reasonable response has been to reduce this complexity by focusing on one aspect of direct citizen involvement. Sherry Arnstein (1969), for example, categorized various approaches to citizen participation ranging from manipulation to citizen control. Thomas Webler and Seth Tuler (2000) empirically developed a set of "rules," based on Renn and Webler's normative theory of public participation and Jürgen Habermas's concept of ideal speech and communicative competence that they believe should govern interactions between citizens and public officials. Each of these efforts has taken an important first step in theory building, but both require more field-testing in different contexts before they attain the status of a developed theory.

Another technique of theory building is to approach the topic of direct citizen participation by focusing on different levels of analysis. For example, micro-level theory could be developed to account for citizen and administrative behavior during problem-solving and decision-making activities. Mid-range theories could be developed to link the nature of issues being addressed and the type of participation mechanisms being employed. Macro-level theories could be developed to describe how direct citizen participation evolves over time given certain historical and social forces. The three articles selected for this section have taken this approach. They represent the state of the art in theory building for direct citizen participation at the micro, mid, and macro level of analysis.

John Clayton Thomas's article "Public Involvement in Public Management: Adapting and Testing a Borrowed Theory" builds theory at the micro level. He adapts the Vroom and Yetton Model from the literature on small group decision making and tests it against 42 decisions made with varying degrees of public involvement. He finds that the data support the modified theory.

Public administrators have four styles of decision making: modified autonomous managerial; segmented public consultation; unitary pubic consultation; and public decision. Choice of style depends on multiple factors: information available, the structure of the problem, the criticality of public acceptance for implementation success, the public's likely acceptance of the decision if the manager makes the decision alone, the public's acceptance of the agency's goals in solving the problem, and the likely conflict on the preferred solution. Time was not found to be a critical factor in decision-making style, suggesting that managers should either ignore time constraints in deciding how to involve the public or factor in the constraints on both decision making *and* implementation.

At the mid level, Lawrence C. Walters, James Aydelotte, and Jessica Miller offer a model of public involvement based on the purpose of public involvement (discovery, education, measurement, persuasion, and legitimization) and the nature of the issue (well structured, moderately structured, and ill-structured). Creating a purpose-issue matrix, they then position public participation techniques and strategies (*e.g.,* town meetings, focus groups, formal hearings, etc.) within the matrix or order to give public administrators some guidance on which strategies to use under which conditions. A retrospective analysis of two case studies, one that failed and one that succeeded, illustrates the application of the model. Although the model has yet to be empirically verified, the authors believe decision makers and administrators will be able to use it to ensure more successful involvement of the public and improve the quality of the decision.

Eran Vigoda's article "From Responsiveness to Collaboration: Governance, Citizens, and the Next Generation of Public Administration" represents theory building at the macro level. He builds an evolutionary continuum of public administration-citizen interactions based on the role of citizens, governance, and public administration authorities, and their reciprocal interactions. Depending on the historical context, citizens can be viewed as subjects, voters, clients or customers, partners, or owners. Authorities, in turn, can be rulers, trustees, managers, partners, or subjects. Four types of interactions derive from the interactions between citizens and authorities: coerciveness, delegation, responsiveness, and collaboration. Vigoda positions New Public Management (NPM) on the mid-point of the continuum due to its emphasis on responsiveness rather than its willingness to endorse sharing, participating, collaborating, and partnering with citizens. While he considers NPM to be an improvement over earlier classical ideas of administration that viewed citizens as subjects or voters, he still finds that it obscures the importance of citizen participation and collaboration—the essence of democratic civil society. For future public administration, he advocates the next step on the evolutionary continuum—collaborative interactions and partnerships between citizens and authorities. He discusses what collaboration and partnership mean, and whose responsibility it is to forge them. Although his model has not been tested empirically, he speculates that by changing the roles of authorities, citizens, the media, and academia, productive collaborations can be achieved in the future.

REFERENCES

Arnstein, S.R. 1969. "A Ladder of Citizen Participation." *Journal of the American Institute of Planners,* 35 (July): 216–24.
Webler, T., and S. Tuler, 2000. "Fairness and Competence in Citizen Participation: Theoretical Reflections from a Case Study." *Administration & Society,* 32(5): 566–95.

CHAPTER 29

PUBLIC INVOLVEMENT IN PUBLIC MANAGEMENT
Adapting and Testing a Borrowed Theory

JOHN CLAYTON THOMAS

The American public has become increasingly involved in managing public organizations over the past quarter century. By the 1970s, a convergence of new legislative requirements, growing citizen activism, and changing professional values had legitimated citizen roles in programmatic areas as diverse as community development, crime prevention, mass transportation, environmental planning, and hazardous waste disposal (e.g., U.S. Advisory Commission on Intergovernmental Relations, 1979).

This change has raised difficult questions for a generation of public managers. For example, which issues call for public involvement and which do not? How can managers make these determinations as issues arise? These questions have largely gone unresearched as experts have mostly been content to exhort managers to embrace public involvement (e.g., Frederickson, 1972) or driven to warn them of the problems involvement may bring (e.g., Cupps, 1977).

This article reports research designed to answer those questions using a theory borrowed from the literature on small-group decision making. According to the theory (Vroom and Yetton, 1973), the degree of group involvement desirable in making a decision depends on the attributes of the core problem; some problems demand more involvement, others less. The premise of this article is that the same contingency rule may hold for questions of public involvement.

This article first explains the theory and shows how its concepts can be adapted to issues of public involvement. The theory is then tested through a re-analysis of 42 public decisions made with varying degrees of public involvement. That test suggests a modified theory which may be useful to public managers who must plan for public involvement.

THE THEORY

Even a cursory literature survey suggests that the same approach to public involvement does not work equally well in all circumstances. Public hearings, for example, have been praised in some contexts as valuable for both managers and citizens (Kihl, 1985, pp. 198–199) but condemned in others as a vehicle only "to satisfy minimum legal requirements for citizen participation" (Checkoway, 1981, p. 571).

Such conflicting assessments are sometimes characterized as reflecting the different values researchers bring to public involvement (see Checkoway, 1981, p. 578), but that judgment seems premature in the absence of disciplined analysis of specifics of the different cases. Those specifics could explain why what works in one situation fails in another.

Extensive literature on small-group decision making since the work of Mary Parker Follett has suggested the situational specifics which affect how much a group can be effectively involved in making a decision. The Vroom and Yetton (1973) theory summarizing that literature may help to explain when different degrees of public involvement are desirable.

The theory's promise rests on several factors. First, the principal variables in the theory are the same concepts which are central to questions of public involvement. The dependent variable is the "decision and organizational effectiveness" (Field, 1979, p. 249) sought by public managers in their decisions. To explain the impact of involvement on that effectiveness, the theory attempts to resolve the same tension between decision quality and decision acceptability which dominates discussions of public involvement (see, for example, Cleveland, 1975; Cupps, 1977; Nelkin, 1984). Through its concern with acceptability, the theory can also address the questions of legitimacy so important with issues of public policy and administration.

Second, evidence suggests that the theory works in its original private-sector context (see Vroom and Yetton, 1973; Vroom, 1976; Vroom and Jago, 1978). Even one of the theory's early critics (Field, 1979) eventually concluded that the "evidence has accumulated that managers should be aware of the [Vroom and Yetton] normative model and its potential use in decision making" (Field, 1982, p. 532).

Finally, if valid for issues of public involvement, the Vroom and Yetton theory could have practical value by showing "how leaders should use different decision-making methods in different situations to be effective" (Field, 1979, p. 249). That potential assistance for public managers makes this testing more than an academic exercise.

But can the theory work with publics as nicely as it appears to work with subordinates? Vroom and Yetton (1973, p. 40) seem to think so since they argue that the relevant "group" for the theory is "that set of persons or their representatives who are potentially affected by the decision." That definition could fit publics as easily as subordinates.

Applying the theory to public involvement does raise a question of how to define the relevant publics. Those publics can be numerous, diffuse, and much more difficult to define than are the relevant subordinates. For the purposes of this research, the relevant publics on a given issue encompass all organized or unorganized groups of citizens or citizen representatives who (a) could provide information useful in solving the issue or (b) could otherwise affect the ability to implement the eventual decision. Included are traditional interest groups (e.g., business lobbies, labor unions, program beneficiaries), consumer and environmental groups, other public interest groups, residential groups (either organized homeowners associations or unorganized residents who are geographically targeted by a decision), and advisory committees that include representatives of any of these other groups.

The manager should attempt this definition while asking a number of questions posed by Vroom and Yetton (1973, pp. 184–186) about the core problem. Answers to the questions determine the relative needs for quality or acceptability in a decision, leading to a recommendation of how much to involve the group. The questions are easily reworded to fit public involvement issues:

1. Are there any quality requirements such that one solution is likely to be more rational than another? These include professional standards, cost constraints, or any legislatively mandated standards.
2. Does the manager have sufficient information to make a high quality decision? Managers may lack either technical information or information on consumers (i.e., public preferences).
3. Is the problem structured such that alternative solutions are not open to redefinition? Some problems come as predefined choices (e.g., should a facility be built here?) rather than being open ended (e.g., where should a facility be built?).
4. Is public acceptance of the decision critical to effective implementation? For public managers, effective implementation means both successful physical implementation, the concern for Vroom and Yetton, and implementation achieved without public outcry.
5. If public acceptance is necessary, is that acceptance reasonably certain if the manager decides alone? Involvement can be an unnecessary complication if acceptance is already assured.
6. Does the relevant public share the agency goals to be obtained in solving the problem? Agreement on goals gives the manager more reason to share decision-making authority.
7. Is conflict within the public likely on the preferred solution? Conflict within the public may recommend more involvement to focus conflict on the public, not on the manager.

The first three questions and the sixth question speak to the quality dimension: quality requirements, a need for information to enhance quality, any restrictions to predefined alternatives, and any threat to quality from public disagreement with organizational goals. The fourth, fifth, and seventh questions speak to acceptability: acceptance as necessary for successful implementation, need for involvement to obtain acceptance, and public disagreement on what is acceptable.

According to Vroom and Yetton, the manager should use the answers to those questions to choose among five decision-making approaches, varying in the extent of group involvement and potential influence. The options range from (1) autocratic or autonomous decision making, with no group involvement or influence, through (2) consultative decision making, with a limited but significant, group role, to (3) group decision making, with the extensive influence of a decision made jointly by the manager and the public.

To fit cases of public involvement, the assumptions about group influence in consultation must be modified. Vroom and Yetton (1973, p. 13) contend that consultation requires no promise of influence; after consulting, "the manager makes a decision which may or may not reflect the influence of the group." That approach is likely to fail with citizens who, unlike subordinates, are not directly compensated. Other incentives are essential, and the promise of influence is a minimum. With that modification, the Vroom and Yetton options can be restated to fit public involvement questions:

1. *Autonomous managerial decision (A1):* The manager solves the problem or makes the decision alone without public involvement.
2. *Modified autonomous managerial decision (A11):* The manager seek information from segments of the public, but decides alone in a manner which may or may not reflect group influence.[1]
3. *Segmented public consultation (C1):* The manager shares the problem separately with segments of the public, getting ideas and suggestions, then makes a decision which reflects group influence.

Figure 29.1   **Decision Process Flow Chart**

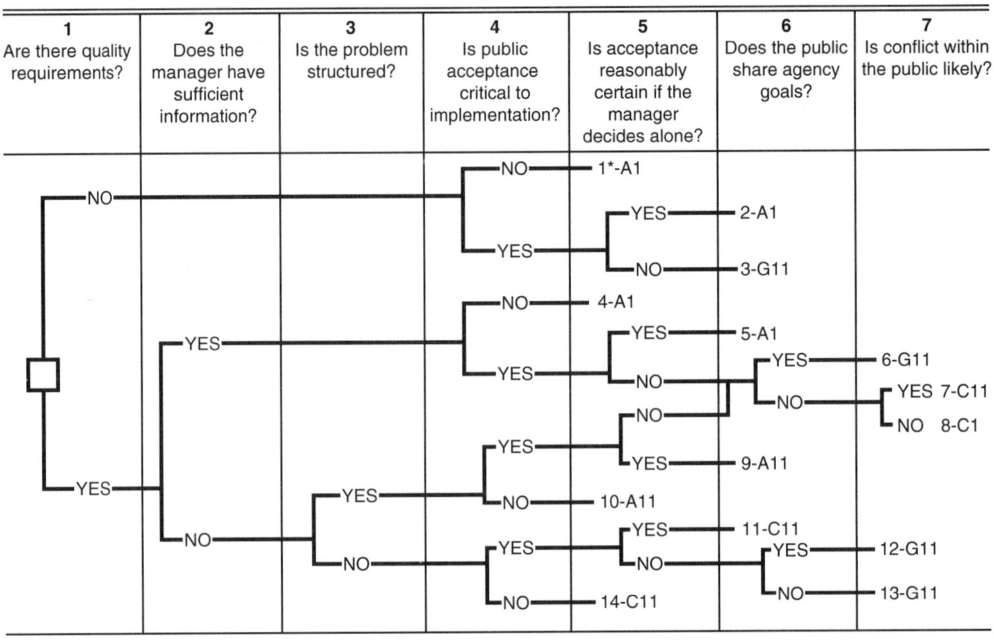

1 Are there quality requirements?	2 Does the manager have sufficient information?	3 Is the problem structured?	4 Is public acceptance critical to implementation?	5 Is acceptance reasonably certain if the manager decides alone?	6 Does the public share agency goals?	7 Is conflict within the public likely?

```
                                              NO------ 1*-A1
          NO----------------------------|
                                        |                 YES------ 2-A1
                                        |--YES-------|
                                                          NO------- 3-G11

                                              NO------ 4-A1
                 YES-----------------------|
                                           |              YES------ 5-A1
                                           |--YES----|                   YES------ 6-G11
                                                        NO----------|
                                                                    NO----|  YES 7-C11
                                                        NO----|            |  NO  8-C1
                                                  YES--|
                                                        YES------ 9-A11
     |                                    YES-----|
     |                                    |         NO------- 10-A11
     |                                    |                   YES------ 11-C11
     YES-----|                            |         YES----|
              NO--------------------------|                 NO---|  YES------ 12-G11
                                          NO------|               |
                                                  YES-------------|  NO------- 13-G11
                                                  NO------ 14-C11
```

*Decision paths are numbered for use in later analyses in this article.
Source: Victor Vroom and Philip Yetton, *Leadership and Decision Making* (Pittsburgh, PA: University of Pittsburgh Press, 1973).

4. *Unitary public consultation (C11):* The manager shares the problem with the public as a single assembled group, getting ideas and suggestions, then makes a decision which reflects group influence.[2]
5. *Public decision (G11):* The manager shares the problem with the assembled public, and together the manager and the public attempt to reach agreement on a solution.

This limited range of approaches may be preferable to the larger number of options suggested elsewhere. For example, Arnstein's "ladder of citizen participation" has eight "rungs," but several (e.g., manipulation) represent involvement without the possibility of influence (see Arnstein, 1969). In addition, as is explained later, the five options can be expanded to a broader choice among specific mechanisms of public involvement.

As Figure 29.1 shows, answering the earlier questions produces a recommendation on which of these approaches to take toward public involvement in resolving a given problem. In general, concerns for quality recommend less involvement, and concerns for acceptability recommend more, but the choice cannot be reduced to a simple additive rule.

According to Vroom and Yetton, two other factors may also affect that choice. Since involving more people in a decision usually lengthens decision making, a time constraint may recommend less involvement than otherwise seems desirable. Or, if a group might be useful for later decisions, the manager may want to nurture its development by inviting more involvement than otherwise seems desirable.

For the theory to be valid for public involvement, consistency with the recommendations of the decision tree must correspond with higher decision effectiveness. But can the effectiveness of public decisions be defined and measured?

There are grounds for skepticism. First, public decisions are often formulated only to satisfy competing interests, to meet the "criteria of consensus and compromise" (Murray, 1983, p. 61), giving no attention to the programmatic goals against which effectiveness might be judged. Failure to define effectiveness at this early stage makes any later definition difficult. Second, even if the goals can be defined, they may prove impossible to measure. As Murray (1983, p. 62) explains, "Many public organizations must deal in social intangibles such as the right to privacy, increased political participation, or improving quality of life. Those are difficult to articulate in any clear, specific way."

The many complaints about the unwanted consequences of public involvement imply, however, that the critics believe they can assess the effectiveness of public decisions. Their criticisms suggest, to begin with, two general dimensions of decision effectiveness: (1) process, how smoothly decision making progresses, and (2) outcome, how well the eventual decision works. Process effectiveness reflects such considerations as: (1) level of antagonism or "unpleasantness" (see Cupps, 1977, p. 482), (2) the time necessary (Cleveland, 1975), and (3) ability to reach a decision. Outcome effectiveness encompasses: (1) correspondence to quality requirements (were they respected?), (2) success of implementation, (3) managerial satisfaction with the eventual decision, and (4) eventual achievement of the intended goals.

METHODOLOGY

The theory is tested using data from previously reported cases of possible or actual public involvement. The author and two graduate assistants identified the cases through an extensive survey of the literature in public administration and related fields. Only published cases were considered in an effort to maximize the quality of the case reporting (i.e., published cases are more likely to have been reviewed and revised).

The cases also had to qualify as the "new public involvement," part of the movement of the last quarter century. That involvement, including most of the cases in this research, has occurred principally on the administrative side of government (e.g., decisions on how Community Development Block Grant funds should be spent, planning to meet water quality standards). A less common form of the new involvement, describing the remaining cases in this research, has occurred as nontraditional policy development (e.g., formulation of policy goals for a community by means of surveys and public hearings). Within these two types, a few cases were included where the public might have been involved but was not, situations also addressed by the Vroom and Yetton theory. In addition, the theory's decision focus dictated that only cases describing decisions could be considered.

Cases meeting these criteria were screened to assure representation of varieties of public involvement and of the range of substantive areas and the expanse of time in which public involvement has been used. These procedures netted 30 cases for study (see Appendix), or 42 actual decisions for analysis (nine cases included two or three decisions).

The cases capture a diverse public involvement history. Of the substantive areas, community and economic development and environmental planning receive the most attention, with 21 percent and 19 percent of the cases, respectively, perhaps reflecting greater actual use of public involvement in these areas. The sample also includes at least two cases each in the areas of housing, school desegregation, crime/police, transportation, nuclear power, and hazardous waste disposal. The dates of the cases show 31 percent occurring in the 1969–1973 period, 48 percent in the

1975–1979 period, and 21 percent in the 1980–1984 period. More recent experience is slighted, as is inevitable in a re-analysis.

Content analysis was used to code the cases on the quality and acceptability questions, decision-making approach, decision effectiveness, and a few other variables. Operationalizations consisted of the author's narrative explanations of the variables along with the coding options. After first reviewing and discussing these operationalizations with the author, a graduate assistant coded each case and provided explanatory notes for each code. The author then independently undertook the same coding process. When both coders completed work on a case, they met to compare results and attempted to resolve differences with the aid of the case notes. The first few cases required extensive discussion between the coders to refine the variables and codes. In addition, with the cases that included two or three decisions, the coders had to reach agreement on the number and nature of the decisions before coding could be completed.

Across all of the cases, intercoder reliabilities, computed as agreements as a proportion of all codes, totaled .762. Many of the disagreements were minor, however, as the results for the decision effectiveness measures illustrate. Using the earlier listing of its possible elements, effectiveness was coded separately for process and outcome as ineffective (0), mixed or uncertain (1), or effective (2). Agreements as a proportion of all codes totaled .729 for both process and outcome, but gamma statistics of agreement, which give less weight to milder disagreements, reached .892 for process and .983 for outcome. To retain unresolvable disagreements, the eventual measures of decision effectiveness were computed as the sum of the two coders' scores.

The structure of the Vroom and Yetton theory also forces attention to cumulative reliabilities. That is, to what extent did the coders agree on all of the problem attributes for each decision, thereby agreeing on the recommended level of involvement? This complete agreement was achieved on 23 of 42 cases. However, if irrelevant disagreements, those which do not affect the Vroom and Yetton recommendation for group involvement, are ignored, the cases with full intercoder agreement increase to 28 of 42 (.667). In addition, two other discordant cases were eventually dropped due to missing data, raising full intercoder agreement on cases actually analyzed to 28 of 40 (.700).

FINDINGS

The cases strikingly embody the quality-acceptability competition which makes questions of public involvement so difficult. As Table 29.1 shows, most of the cases carried both quality requirements and problem structure, and they required acceptance from a public unlikely to accept an autonomous managerial decision. In addition, the relevant publics agreed with agency goals only about a third of the time and disagreed among themselves most of the time. To further complicate matters, those publics usually included both organized and unorganized groups, and a number of other actors were also interested—usually two or more levels of government plus at least five organizations and/or influential individuals.

This complexity probably marks the cases as unlike typical public decisions or public involvement cases, many of which require either no public acceptance or no involvement to assure acceptance and do not interest nearly as many actors. This atypicality may actually enhance the value of the cases for testing the Vroom and Yetton theory. If the theory works to any extent with these cases, it could be more powerful with cases where the quality-acceptability tension is less acute and the burden of complexity less onerous.

Despite this complexity, officials were able to resolve the cases effectively almost half the time, as Table 29.2 shows. Process effectiveness and outcome effectiveness were also closely related (g = .649).

Table 29.1

Characteristics of the Public Involvement Decisions

Characteristic	Qualifying cases: percentage (number)
Problem Attributes:	
Quality requirements	92.9 (39)
More information needed	78.6 (33)
Alternative solutions already defined	61.9 (26)
Citizen acceptance needed	85.4 (35)
Acceptance contingent on involvement	90.5 (38)
Citizens share organizational goals	36.6 (15)
Conflict over solutions likely among citizens	70.7 (29)
Interested Actors:	
Relevant public of both organized and unorganized groups	64.3 (27)
Two or more levels of government	78.6 (33)
Five or more other actors, in addition to decision maker and citizen groups	54.8 (23)

Table 29.2

Effectiveness Ratings of Case Decisions

Rating	Process	Outcome	Overall
Ineffective	21	18	17
Uncertain	2	6	6
Effective	19	18	19
Totals	42	42	42

Combining answers to the quality and acceptability questions on these cases results in high levels of recommended involvement. The median recommended involvement is a unitary public consultation (C11), with 30 of 40 cases having recommended involvements at least that extensive. Actual involvement was much lower, half of the cases using less than a unitary consultation (C1) and almost one-fourth using no public involvement.

If the Vroom and Yetton theory holds, any disparity between recommended and actual involvement should reduce decision effectiveness. To test that proposition, both involvement codes were converted to numerical scores (i.e., A1 = 1, A11 = 3, C1 = 5, C11 = 7, G11 = 9), using two-point intervals to permit coding of a few in-between positions (e.g., involvement between C11 and G11 could be coded as 8). A measure of deviation from recommended involvement was then calculated by subtraction as an absolute difference (i.e., ignoring whether any deviation was toward more or less involvement than recommended).

Consistent with the prediction, this deviation is strongly correlated with the three measures of decision effectiveness. The linkage to process effectiveness is the strongest ($r = -.605$), the linkage to outcome effectiveness the weakest ($r = -.475$). The linkage to the combined effectiveness measure, the principal dependent variable, falls in between ($r = -.571$).

No other measure of involvement performs as well. Correlations with overall decision effectiveness are lower for both (a) the degree of public involvement ($r = .416$) and (b) the number of involvement mechanisms employed (e.g., surveys, advisory committees, public hearings) ($r = .374$).

Assessing the Various Paths

Some branches of the decision tree may be unnecessary to a theory of public involvement. Any branches recommended infrequently or not at all might describe situations which do not arise when public involvement is an issue.

Eight paths, each recommended for no more than one case, could fit this characterization. They have in common no need for involvement as a means to achieve acceptance. With four (paths 2, 5, 9, and 11 in Figure 29.1), acceptance is needed, but involvement is not required. With the others, either only information is needed with acceptance not an issue (10 and 14) or neither information nor acceptance is needed (1 and 4).

Despite their infrequent recommendation, most of these paths describe situations which could face public managers. Consider the case for which path 3 (A1) was recommended, a water quality planning effort by the U.S. Environmental Protection Agency (EPA) in several Texas communities. The enabling legislation stipulated quality requirements and program structure which severely limited the role of public involvement: "It is unlikely . . . that the constraints on the whole 208 process would have allowed for any substantial deviation from what was deemed technically or economically feasible" (Plumlee, Starling, and Kramer, 1985, p. 465). In addition, there was no need for either information or acceptance from the public.

Public managers sometimes face this situation: a program so rigidly constrained by law and so lacking in latitude for public influence that public involvement makes no sense. They need the autonomous managerial decision making (A1) option recommended by the Vroom-Yetton model for that situation.

Or consider the one case following path 10, a 1967 proposal by the Atomic Energy Commission to build a nuclear power plant in Vermont. Here again planners were constrained by quality requirements (e.g., operation without "undue risk to the health and safety of the public") and problem structure (i.e., plant or no plant), but information was needed from the public, if only to satisfy a legal requirement for a public hearing. Public acceptance, however, could be assumed without involvement. Although the same issue would arouse broad public opposition only a few years later, there "was no organized citizen opposition" in 1967; residents apparently viewed the proposed plant as "progress" for the community (Ebbin and Kasper, 1974, p. 93).

This situation, too, may arise occasionally: a problem with many constraints, no need for acceptance, but a need for information from the public. Public managers need the modified autonomous decision-making approach (A11) favored by the model for such cases.

The infrequency of such cases in the sample probably says less about their actual occurrence than about which public involvement cases achieve publication. Cases where public involvement is needed to gain acceptance more often have the visibility and/or controversy conducive to publication. Lacking both, a case may escape attention.

The more attractive candidates for elimination from the model are the paths beginning with *no* quality requirements. For one thing, their elimination would make the model conform better to the common perception that quality requirements are ubiquitous in public management. Fearing the public wrath which can follow even the appearance of malfeasance, policy makers supposedly circumscribe managers' discretion with an "array of laws, procedures, and norms intended to closely control their behavior" (Whorton and Worthley, 1983, p. 126).

Also, an assumption of universal quality requirements affects only a few cases in the sample. Of the paths (1, 2, and 3) beginning with no quality requirement, only path 3 is ever recommended, and that is only for three cases. Moreover, close examination suggests that quality requirements may have been present on those cases. The preferred approach on a community crime prevention

Table 29.3

Effectiveness of Decisions by Choice of Decision-Making Styles

| | Correspondence to style used | | | |
| | Ineffective and uncertain decisions | | Effective decisions | |
Ideal style/path	Wrong*	Right	Wrong*	Right
4 (A1)	1	—	—	—
5 (A1)	—	—	—	1
6 (G2)	2	1	1	3
7 (C2)	9	2	—	2
8 (C1)	3	—	—	2
10 (A2)	—	—	1	—
12 (G2)	—	1	1	3
13 (C2)	1	1	1	4
A1	1	—	—	1
A2	—	—	1	—
C1	3	—	—	2
C2	10	3	1	6
G2	2	2	2	6
Totals	16	5	4	15

*Wrong = deviation of at least two points on the ordinal scale.

case, for example, supposedly depended on what "a community finds comfortable" (Podolefsky, 1983, p. 43), implying no quality requirement, but the eventual choice was between a "social problems approach" and a "victimization prevention" approach, rather than being unrestricted as implied by an absence of a quality requirement.

Finally, an assumption of quality requirements on all cases improves the fit of the model to the data. With the recommended paths modified to reflect that change, correlations with deviation from the Vroom-Yetton recommendation improve for all three measures of effectiveness, moving from −.571 to −.611 for the summary effectiveness measure.

For all of these reasons, public involvement issues probably require only those branches of the decision tree which begin with quality requirements. All data analyses below incorporate this change by recoding the cases originally thought to lack quality requirements. As for managers contemplating public involvement, they should still begin by asking about quality requirements, but the question becomes, "What are the quality requirements?" The answer should constrain the decision but not affect the desirable degree of involvement.

The remaining branches must be further examined to learn if any are ineffective; that is, do any recommend public involvement strategies which produce ineffective decisions? To test for that possibility, data were compiled in Table 29.3 by path and decision-making style for the relationship between use of the recommended (i.e., "right") approach and overall decision effectiveness.

The data give little reason to question the efficacy of any recommendations. For almost every branch and decision-making style, effective decisions mostly follow use of the right approach, ineffective decisions mostly follow use of a wrong approach.

The model even appears to fit the cases where autonomous managerial decision making is recommended, as two of those three cases conform to predictions. In the Texas water quality planning, for example, despite a highly constrained problem with little latitude or need for public involvement, EPA planners pursued a unitary consultation (C11) by creating an advisory committee.

Predictably, "in one way or another every participant . . . indicated that the 208 planning process had been ineffective" (Plumlee, Starling, and Kramer, 1985, p. 460). Citizens were frustrated by involvement without influence; EPA staffers were distracted by needless involvement.

Success does vary depending on the recommended path. Most notably, cases fitting path 7, where unitary group consultation is recommended, were much less likely to end effectively. As Table 29.3 shows, 11 of 21 of the ineffective outcomes—but only 2 of the 19 effective outcomes—occurred on these cases.

That reflects in part the inherent difficulty of path 7 problems, which have the attributes of such an intractable issue as the siting of a hazardous waste disposal facility. In addition to having quality requirements, these problems are structured as either/or: whether to build a disposal facility on a particular site, for example. Public acceptance is needed but unlikely absent public involvement. The public as a whole probably disagrees with the agency's goal (e.g., to build a facility), and segments of the public disagree among themselves on the desirable solution (e.g., "Put it in his neighborhood, not in mine!"). With so much need for involvement combined with such severe quality constraints, these issues are not easily resolved, as the history of hazardous waste facility sitings demonstrates.

But failure on these problems may also derive in part from unwillingness to follow the Vroom-Yetton model. Nine of the 11 ineffective path 7 decisions were made by managers acting autonomously, with the public permitted to provide information at most, a far cry from the recommended unitary public consultation (e.g., Kraft and Kraut, 1985; Moldenhauer, 1986). Confronted with these difficult issues, managers may instinctively prefer the seeming simplicity of a unilateral decision to the inevitably messy process of public consultation. That simplicity can prove short-lived, however, since a dissatisfied public may resist imposition of a managerial decision, creating an even messier, perhaps unresolvable, impasse.

The better choice is to invite the recommended unitary public consultation, as evidenced by the effective decisions on the two path 7 problems where that approach was followed. Quality constraints need not be sacrificed; they can be stipulated to the public as essential constraints, and the manager can still retain final authority for the decision. Full group consultation can then suggest to the manager which alternative has the greatest public support. Consultation should also reveal to the public the disagreements in its ranks, building sympathy for the manager's impossible job of finding a decision satisfactory to all.

The Contingency Factors

The model's recommendations may need to be modified when either of two contingency factors arise. First, Vroom and Yetton argue that a time constraint permits less involvement than would otherwise appear desirable, without endangering eventual decision effectiveness. If so, the data should show the public less involved in effective decisions made under time pressures than in effective decisions made without those pressures. To the contrary, only three of the nine effective decisions made under a time constraint used less than the recommended degree of public involvement, compared to five of the ten effective decisions made without that constraint.

Alternatively, could time constraints affect the rates of effective decisions, not the degree of involvement desirable? Apparently not. Effective decisions were reached as often with time constraints (47% of the cases) as without (48% of the cases).

Explaining these findings requires a better understanding of how time constrains public managers. First, time constraints on the making of public decisions often prove more flexible than they appear, especially if an aroused public resists a quick decision. The manager who then reduces public involvement to save time risks increased public opposition, endangering rather than facilitating an effective decision. Second, public managers face time constraints on implementation as well as on decision making, and the two constraints are inversely related. Time spent to involve more actors in decision making can expedite implementation (i.e., because those involved are likely to support implementation); and time saved by excluding actors from decision making can slow implementation (i.e., because resistance from those excluded must be overcome). With public decisions, as a consequence, managers should either ignore time constraints in deciding how to involve the public or weigh the constraints on *both* decision making and decision implementation.

The data suggest a similar conclusion on the other contingency factor. According to Vroom and Yetton, the desirability of developing a group for use on future decisions justifies *more* involvement than otherwise seems desirable in making a decision. If so, effective decisions where group development appears desirable should feature more involvement than the model recommends. Instead, five of the nine effective decisions where group development appeared desirable used less than the recommended involvement, compared to only three of the nine cases where development did not appear desirable.

Group development probably is never as desirable with external publics as with intraorganizational groups. Too much has been written about the dangers of special-interest groups for public managers to be sanguine about developing external groups which, if potentially helpful, also could become pressure groups hostile to broad community interests. Much as with time constraints, managers should weigh the possible gains from group development against risks before inviting involvement to encourage that development.

CONCLUSION

The Vroom-Yetton contingency theory adapts well to issues of public involvement. It addresses the issues central to that involvement, and its language is easily modified to fit the uniqueness of public decisions. Most importantly, the theory successfully predicts what degree of involvement works best for actual public decisions. Conformity with the model's recommendations for involvement is mostly associated with effective decisions.

The theory even gains elegance when adapted to public involvement. The pervasiveness of quality requirements in public management justifies pruning three branches of the decision tree. Other arguments justify eliminating the contingency factors of time constraints and desirability of group development. What remains is a more parsimonious theory.

A comprehensive theory of public involvement cannot remain so parsimonious, however. It must, at a minimum, also address other possible determinants of decision effectiveness. Any number of factors—e.g., the number of parties interested in the issue, a "NIMBY" ("Not In My Backyard") quality to an issue—could either challenge the Vroom-Yetton theory of decision effectiveness or add to what that theory can explain. A full judgment on the theory must await assessment of those alternative explanations in future research.

Short of that judgment, the theory holds sufficient promise to recommend it to managers as they contemplate public involvement. Anytime a decision appears necessary on planning, implementing, or modifying a program or policy, a manager can employ the revised model shown in Figure 29.2, keeping these cautions in mind:

1. Defining quality requirements—legislative mandates, technical or professional standards, cost constraints—is an essential first step. It can be difficult; the line between a personal preference and a quality requirement is often blurred. Failure to make quality require-

Figure 29.2   How to Determine the Degree of Public Involvement

1 What are the qual- ity requirements?	2 Does the manager have sufficient information?	3 Is the problem structured such that alternative solu- tions are not open to redefinition?	4 Is public accep- tance of the deci- sion critical to effective imple- mentation?	5 If public acceptance is necessary, is it reasonably certain if the manager decides alone?	6 Does the relevant public share the agency goals to be obtained in solv- ing the problem?	7 Is conflict likely within the rele- vant public on the preferred solu- tion?

Figure 29.3   A Matrix Guide to Public Involvement

Style of Decision Making	One Organized Group	Multiple Organized Groups	Unorganized Public	Complex Public**
Modified Autonomous Managerial	Key contacts	Key contacts	Citizen survey	Key contacts/Survey
Segmented Public Consultation	Key contacts	Contacts/Series of meetings	Citizen survey	Citizen survey/Meetings
Unitary Public Consultation	Meeting(s) with group	CAC* or series of meetings	Series of public meetings	CAC* and/or meetings
Public Decision	Negotiate with group	Negotiate with CAC*	Series of public meetings	CAC*/Public meetings

*CAC = Citizens advisory committee
**Complex Public = Some combination of organized and unorganized groups

ments explicit at the outset, however, risks their being compromised in a later process of public involvement, when it will be easier to surrender nonessential requirements than to impose new ones.

2. The structure of pre-defined alternative solutions further constrains decision latitude, adding to the difficulty of deciding with the public (e.g., the path 7 cases). For that reason, managers should attempt to address problems before they become structured as "yes-no" or "all-or-none" choices.

3. As needs for information or acceptance become evident, the manager must identify what segments of the public can satisfy those needs. Overlooking any important group risks later failure if that group mobilizes; focusing on too broad a public, on the other hand, can unnecessarily complicate decision making.

4. Once the appropriate decision-making approach is known, a specific involvement mechanism must be selected. To make this determination, the manager should estimate the number and degree of organization of the relevant publics, then combine that definition with the recommended decision-making style. The matrix in Figure 29.3 shows, in general, what mechanism of involvement should be appropriate for different types of publics and decision-making approaches (see also Thomas, 1987).

The Vroom and Yetton model, as adapted here, may help managers to balance the competing concerns for legitimacy and effectiveness which arise with public involvement. Explicit attention to needs for public acceptance and information assures that the necessary legitimacy of public policies is not ignored. Use of the model could instead improve legitimacy by, as in the cases examined here, inviting more public involvement than public managers might otherwise invite. The model's protections for quality considerations, on the other hand, can help managers avoid the possible "excess of democracy" which Huntington (1975, p. 113) warns can threaten governmental effectiveness.

Bringing the public into public management has proved a difficult challenge. Use of this model could help in meeting that challenge, especially if the alternative is to follow reflexively an autonomous style inappropriate for many contemporary issues which arouse public interest.

NOTES

I thank those who assisted in this research. Partial funding for the research was provided by a curriculum development grant from the National Institute for Dispute Resolution. Erna Gelles and Courtney Waide assisted by identifying the public involvement cases and serving as the first coders of each case. Dick Heimovics helped by suggesting the Vroom and Yetton model and by commenting on earlier versions of this manuscript. The views expressed here, however, are the author's. An earlier version of this article was presented at the 1989 Annual Meeting of the American Political Science Association.

1. The involvement here asks so little of the public—to answer questions in a phone survey, for example—that it may be invited without the promise of influence.

2. Involving the public "as a single assembled group" means that all members of the public have the opportunity to become involved, not that all members of the public actually become involved. Well-advertised public hearings would represent such an opportunity, for example (see Figure 29.3).

REFERENCES

Sherry R. Arnstein, "A Ladder of Citizen Participation," *Journal of the American Institute of Planners,* vol. 35 (July 1969), pp. 216–224.

Barry Checkoway, "The Politics of Public Hearings," *Journal of Applied Behavioral Science,* vol. 17 (no. 4, 1981), pp. 566–582.

Harlan Cleveland, "How Do You Get Everybody In on the Act and Still Get Some Action?" *Public Management,* vol. 57 (June 1975), pp. 3–6.

D. Stephen Cupps, "Emerging Problems of Citizen Participation," *Public Administration Review,* vol. 37 (September/October 1977), pp. 478–487.

Steven Ebbin and Raphael Kasper, *Citizen Groups and the Nuclear Power Controversy: Uses of Scientific and Technological Information* (Cambridge, MA, and London: The MIT Press, 1974).

R.H. George Field, "A Test of the Vroom-Yetton Normative Model of Leadership," *Journal of Applied Psychology,* vol. 67 (October 1982), pp. 523–532.

———, "A Critique of the Vroom-Yetton Contingency Model of Leadership Behavior," *Academy of Management Review,* vol. 4 (April 1979), pp. 249–257.

H. George Frederickson, ed., *Neighborhood Control in the 1970s: Politics, Administration, and Citizen Participation* (New York and London: Chandler Publishing, 1972).

Samuel P. Huntington, "The United States," in Michael Crozier, Samuel P. Huntington, and Joji Watanuki, *The Crisis of Democracy* (New York: New York University Press, 1975).

Mary R. Kihl, "The Viability of Public Hearings in Transportation Planning," *Journal of Applied Behavioral Science,* vol. 21 (no. 2, 1985), pp. 185–200.

Michael E. Kraft and Ruth Kraut, "The Impact of Citizen Participation on Hazardous Waste Policy Implementation. The Case of Clermont County, Ohio," *Policy Studies Journal,* vol. 14 (September 1985), pp. 52–61.

David Moldenhauer, "A Case Study of Victim-centered Political Action: Jackson Township, New Jersey," in David Morell and Christopher Magorian, eds., *Siting Hazardous Waste Facilities: Local Opposition and the Myth of Preemption* (Cambridge, MA: Ballinger Publishing, 1986), pp. 193–231.

Michael A. Murray, "Comparing Public and Private Management: An Exploratory Essay," in James L. Perry and Kenneth L. Kraemer, eds., *Public Management: Public and Private Perspectives* (Palo Alto, CA: Mayfield Publishing, 1983), pp. 60–71.

Dorothy Nelkin, "Science and Technology Policy and the Democratic Process," in James C. Petersen, ed., *Citizen Participation in Science Policy* (Amherst: University of Massachusetts Press, 1984), pp. 18–39.

John P. Plumlee, Jay D. Starling, with Kenneth W. Kramer, "Citizen Participation in Water Quality Planning: A Case Study of Perceived Failure," *Administration & Society,* vol. 16 (February 1985), pp. 455–473.

Aaron Podolefsky, "Community Response to Crime Prevention: The Mission District," *Journal of Community Action,* vol. 1 (September/October 1983), pp. 53–60.

John Clayton Thomas, *Public Involvement in Public Management: A Curriculum Module* (Washington: National Institute for Dispute Resolution, 1987).

U.S. Advisory Commission on Intergovernmental Relations, *In Brief: Citizen Participation in the American Federal System* (Washington: U.S. Government Printing Office, 1979).

Victor Vroom, "Can Leaders Learn to Lead?" *Organizational Dynamics,* vol. 4 (no. 1, 1976), pp. 17–28.

Victor Vroom and Arthur G. Jago, "On the Validity of the Vroom-Yetton Model," *Journal of Applied Psychology,* vol. 63 (February 1978), pp. 151–162.

Victor Vroom and Philip Yetton, *Leadership and Decision Making* (Pittsburgh: University of Pittsburgh Press, 1973).

Joseph W. Whorton and John A. Worthley, "A Perspective on the Challenge of Public Management: Environmental Paradox and Organizational Culture," in James L. Perry and Kenneth L. Kraemer, eds., *Public Management: Public and Private Perspectives* (Palo Alto, CA: Mayfield Publishing, 1983), pp. 126–32.

Appendix 29.1. Public Involvement Cases

Note: Cases are listed by author or, with multiple cases from the same source, by volume editor. Dates refer to year of publication, not case occurrence, and the number of asterisks indicate the number of decisions coded for the case.

* J. Vincent Buck, "The Impact of Citizen Participation Programs and Policy Decisions on Participants' Opinions," *Western Political Quarterly,* vol. 37 (September 1984), pp. 468–482.

* Richard L. Cole, "Participation in Community Service Organizations," *Journal of Community Action,* vol. 1 (September/October 1983), pp. 53–60.

From Paul R. Dommel and Associates, *Decentralizing Urban Policy: Case Studies in Community Development* (Washington: Brookings Institution, 1982).

** John Stuart Hall, "Community Development Block Grant Implementation in Phoenix, Arizona," pp. 47–83.

* Leon L. Haley, "Community Development Block Grant Implementation in Allegheny County, Pennsylvania," pp. 166–194.

* John S. Jackson, "Community Development Block Grant Implementation in Carbondale, Illinois," pp. 195–222.

From Steven Ebbin and Raphael Kasper, *Citizens Groups and the Nuclear Power Controversy: Uses of Scientific and Technological Information* (Cambridge, MA, and London: The MIT Press, 1974).

* "Midland Plant Units 1 and 2," pp. 59–89.

** "Vermont Nuclear Power Station," pp. 90–121.

* "Rule Making Hearings: The Emergency Core Cooling System (ECCS)," pp. 122–138.

* Mark Ferber and Edmund Beard, "Marketing Urban America: The Selling of the Boston Plan & A New Direction in Federal-Urban Relations," *Polity,* vol. 12 (Summer 1980), pp. 539–559.

* Siegrun F. Fox, "Who Opposes Public/Private Financial Partnerships for Urban Renewal? A Case Study," *Journal of Urban Affairs,* vol. 7 (Winter 1985), pp. 27–40.

* Robert S. Friedman, "Representation in Regulatory Decision Making: Scientific, Industrial, and Consumer Inputs to the FDA," *Public Administration Review,* vol. 38 (May/June 1978), pp. 205–214.

From Robert B. Goldman, ed., *Roundtable Justice: Case Studies in Conflict Resolution* (Boulder, CO: Westview Press, 1980).

** Stephen Gillers, "New Faces in the Neighborhood: Mediating the Forest Hills Housing Dispute," pp. 59–85.

** Joel L. Fleishman, "Not Without Honor—A Prophet Even in His Own Country: The St. Louis Tenant Strike of 1969," pp. 87–127.

 * Graham S. Finney, "Desegregating the Schools in Dayton," pp. 181–201.

* Ian M. Harris, "Community Involvement in Desegregation: The Milwaukee Experience," *Journal of Voluntary Action Research,* vol. 9 (nos. 1–4, 1980), pp. 179–188.

From Arnold M. Howitt, *Managing Federalism* (Washington: Congressional Quarterly Press, 1984).

  * Hester Barlow McCarthy and Arnold M. Howitt, "Extending the Red Line to Arlington," pp. 270–295.

  * Arnold M. Howitt and Kay Rubin, "Citizen Participation in Oxford," pp. 303–321.

*** Michael E. Kraft and Ruth Kraut, "The Impact of Citizen Participation on Hazardous Waste Policy Implementation: The Case of Clermont County, Ohio," *Policy Studies Journal,* vol. 14 (September 1985), pp. 170–178.

** Thomas W. Mangione and Floyd J. Fowler, "Reducing Neighborhood Crime: The Hartford Experiment," *Journal of Community Action,* vol. 1 (no. 5, 1983), pp. 49–53.

From Daniel A. Mazmanian and Jeanne Nienaber, *Can Organizations Change? Environmental Protection, Citizen Participation, and the Corps of Engineers* (Washington: The Brookings Institution, 1979).

  * "Project Study III: Flood Control on Wildcat and San Pablo Creeks—A California Showpiece," pp. 103–113.

*** "Project Study V: Flood Control on the Middle Fork of the Snoqualmie River," pp. 132–157.

* Bruce W. McClendon and John A. Lewis, "Goals for Corpus Christi: Citizen Participation in Planning," *National Civic Review,* vol. 74 (February 1985), pp. 72–80.

*** David Moldenhauer, "A Case Study of Victim-Centered Political Action: Jackson Township, New Jersey," in David Morell and Christopher Magorian, eds., *Siting Hazardous Waste Facilities: Local Opposition and the Myth of Preemption* (Cambridge, MA: Ballinger Publishing, 1986), pp. 193–231.

* Adepoju G. Onibokun and Martha Curry, "An Ideology of Citizen Participation: The Metropolitan Seattle Transit Case Study," *Public Administration Review,* vol. 36 (May/June 1976), pp. 269–277.

* John P. Plumlee, Jay D. Starling, with Kenneth W. Kramer, "Citizen Participation in Water Quality Planning: A Case Study of Perceived Failure," *Administration & Society,* vol. 16 (February 1985), pp. 455–473.

* Aaron Podolefsky, "Community Response to Crime Prevention: The Mission District," *Journal of Community Action,* vol. 1 (no. 5, 1983), pp. 43–48.

* Fred Sklar and Richard G. Ames, "Staying Alive: Street Tree Survival in the Inner-City," *Journal of Urban Affairs,* vol. 7 (Winter 1985), pp. 55–65.

* James A. Stever, "Citizen Participation in Negotiated Investment Strategy," *Journal of Urban Affairs,* vol. 5 (Summer 1983), pp. 231–240.

* Thomas R. Stewart, Robin L. Dennis, and Daniel W. Ely, "Citizen Participation and Judgment in Policy Analysis: A Case Study of Urban Air Quality Policy," *Policy Sciences,* vol. 17 (May 1984), pp. 67–87.

** Alan R. Talbot, "The Port Townsend Terminal," in *Settling Things: Six Case Studies in Environmental Mediation* (Washington: The Conservation Foundation and the Ford Foundation, 1983), pp. 78–89.

PUTTING MORE PUBLIC IN POLICY ANALYSIS

LAWRENCE C. WALTERS, JAMES AYDELOTTE, AND JESSICA MILLER

INTRODUCTION

One of the persistent criticisms of policy analysis is that it undermines basic democratic institutions and processes by replacing public participation and debate with esoteric expert analysis. As the criticism goes, policy analysts, decision makers, and other experts hold one or more of the following views regarding public participation in policy discussions:

- Officials and experts see today's problems as too complex for the public to understand (Bell 1973; Brzezinski 1976; Fischer 1995, 12, 190; Prewitt 1983, 51; Mathews 1994, 73). Consider the following observation: "I've heard many times that although democracy is an imperfect system, we somehow always muddle through. The message I want to give you, after long and hard reflection, is that . . . it is no longer possible to muddle through. The issues we deal with do not lend themselves to that kind of treatment. . . . Jeffersonian democracy can not work in the [contemporary] world—the world has become too complex" (John Kemeny [1980], former chair-person of the presidential commission appointed to investigate the Three Mile Island nuclear disaster, as quoted in Fischer 1995, 257).
- Technical experts see the incremental decision making characteristic of democracy as irrational (Sternberg 1989).
- Officials view the public as either uninterested (Mathews 1994, 72), or as pursuing their self-interest rather than the public interest (Fischer 1995, 44; Rein 1976, 98).
- Rational decision making and democratic decision making have different goals, and there is a fundamental tension between the rational pursuit of efficiency and the democratic pursuit of participation (Fischer 1995, 224; Heineman et al. 1997, 25; Rein 1976, 98–101).
- Greater citizen involvement means redefining public officials' roles in the decision making process, an uncomfortable process rejected by many officials. Sharing power is often not appealing to officials (Walsh 1997, 19; Thomas 1995, 5).
- Officials oppose citizen participation because it is more time consuming, expensive, complicated, and emotionally draining (Creighton 1981, 13).

From *Public Administration Review,* 60, 4 (July/August 2000): 349–359. Copyright © 2000 by American Society for Public Administration. Reprinted with permission.

In opposition to these views, those who advocate greater discourse and public participation assert that traditional, scientific, or expert views should no longer be afforded privileged status, allowing a broader range of views and treatments to be considered in decision making (Farmer 1995, 236–7). Others claim that analysts and decision makers have forgotten why the Founders paired rational administration with democratic government. Administration has now become the end rather than the means (Saul 1992, 234). Ultimately, these authors argue that reliance on administrative discretion in decision making is not consistent with democracy or pluralism (Reich 1988).

To be sure, this debate embodies some fundamental differences of opinion. To the extent that decision makers do not wish to open the decision-making process or share power, there is little more to be said. But it appears that many analysts and decision makers shun broader participation due to the cost, uncertainty, and delay often associated with public involvement. Our purpose in writing this article is to suggest that such concerns may be somewhat overblown. We have the sense that decision makers are frequently required to involve the public without incurring additional costs or inefficiency, but do not know how to do so (Thomas 1995). The purpose of this article is to propose a model for the systematic inclusion of public input into relatively complex public policy decisions.

We begin with an overview of two cases from recent Utah history that involved extensive citizen participation. We present a framework for seeking public input and apply it to the two cases as we identify two determinants of success in public participation efforts: the purpose for public involvement and the nature of the issue. Finally, we present a purpose-issue matrix that illustrates appropriate participation techniques given the purpose for including the public and the nature of the issue.

THE UTAH WILDERNESS DEBATE AND THE UTAH GROWTH SUMMIT

The state of Utah recently held a series of public hearings on wilderness designation and growth management. Because these two issues utilized public input differently in the policy development process, they allow us to illustrate our framework in very different situations. While we apply our framework to these cases later in the article, some contextual and historical information is needed to introduce the reader to these issues.

The Utah Wilderness Debate

Utah's wilderness debate centered on one of the most contentious issues in the West—land use. More specifically, how much land should be given the designation of "wilderness." According to the Wilderness Act of 1964, wilderness is defined as " . . . an area where the earth and its community of life are untrammeled by man, where man himself is a visitor and does not remain" (U.S. Code, Title 16, 1995, 213). As part of the review process for wilderness assessment, the Wilderness Act requires public hearings " . . . at a location or locations convenient to the area affected" (U.S. Code, Title 16, 1995, 214).

In 1984, in accordance with the Federal Land Policy and Management Act (FLPMA) of 1976, the Bureau of Land Management (BLM) completed its survey of the Utah lands under its jurisdiction (U.S. Code, Title 43, 1995, 506). It identified 3.2 million acres in Utah that could qualify for wilderness designation (an area somewhat larger than the state of Connecticut) and recommended that approximately two million acres receive the wilderness designation (U.S. Code, Title 43, 1995, 506; Israelson 1994a). While local residents and extraction industries saw the recommendation as being too high, conservationists felt that both the recommendation and the potential wilderness figures were too low (Israelson 1994a). They felt the BLM had improperly excluded some land in its land survey (Spangler 1995). Instead of resolving the wilderness issue, the land survey further polarized the opposing sides.

On January 7, 1995, Utah Governor Mike Leavitt and the Utah congressional delegation announced that by June 1, 1995, Utah would submit a bill to Congress designating an amount of Utah wilderness land (Spangler 1995). The state organized a series of public hearings to determine the exact amount of Utah land to be included in the bill, splitting the process into two phases: county-level public hearings focused on opinions in the counties that encompassed the proposed wilderness land, and regional public hearings. Furthermore, organizers stipulated that: (1) all proposals had to recommend some amount of wilderness land; (2) the BLM inventory of 3.2 million acres of potential Utah wilderness land would stand; and (3) the wilderness bill would have hard release provisions, meaning that land not recommended for wilderness would never again be studied for possible wilderness designation (Spangler 1995).

The county-level hearings were held between January and April 1, 1995 and resulted in a county-commissioner proposal of one million acres of wilderness (Israelson 1995a). In contrast, the regional public hearings recommended 5.7 million acres of wilderness (Spangler 1995; Kriz 1996, 67). The Utah delegation's wilderness bill eventually advocated 1.8 million acres of wilderness which, despite optimistic projections, failed to gain the support necessary for passage into law.

At this writing, the Utah wilderness debate still continues without serious prospect for a broadly accepted resolution. The majority of Utah residents appear to support substantially more wilderness than was recommended in earlier proposals, but not the extreme position of most environmental groups. Local officials and perhaps the majority of residents in rural counties that incorporate these lands favor a minimal designation and hard release of remaining lands. In the end, broadly-based public discussion shed very little light on the issues or potential solutions.

The Utah Growth Summit

In addition to wilderness designation, Utah utilized public hearings to address the issue of growth management. In recent years, Utah has had one of the highest growth rates in the country. Between 1990 and 1997, Utah's population increased by 18.5 percent, from 1.73 million to 2.05 million (Utah Governor's Office of Planning and Budget 1998).

Even more noteworthy than the growth rate, however, is how Utah experiences growth. Seventy-seven percent of Utah's population lives along the western side of the Wasatch Mountain Range, an area referred to as the Wasatch Front (Utah Governor's Office of Planning and Budget 1995a, 75). Running 80 miles along the base of the Wasatch Mountains, the Wasatch Front is limited geographically to an area only 5 to 15 miles wide. As Utah looks to the future, it faces the difficult questions of where to put new residents and how rapid growth will impact the quality of life in the region.

A regional discussion of growth-related issues began when Governor Mike Leavitt proposed a "Growth Summit" in an address to the Utah Legislature in July 1995. (Bernick 1995, 2A). The several meetings of the Utah Growth Summit were eventually scheduled for December 1995. Three working groups—Democratic, Republican, and non-partisan local officials—were to present growth policy proposals at these meetings.

To prepare for the Summit, many communities and interest groups began holding public meetings on growth issues in September. At these meetings, citizens, various interest group representatives, experts, and government officials searched for solutions to the problems associated with growth.

A number of groups were also invited by Utah Lieutenant Governor Olene S. Walker to present their policy proposals in the areas of water, transportation, and open space at public meetings held in November (personal letter 1995). Armed with these proposals, each working group then formulated policies to effectively address the problem of growth in Utah (Utah Governor's Office of Planning and Budget 1996, 3). Two days prior to the Summit, state newspapers devoted one section to articles discussing water, transportation, and open space issues.

The Growth Summit began on December 6, 1995, with a television special on Utah growth issues. Aired by all the television stations and some radio stations in Utah, it was followed by presentations of the three working groups' growth policy proposals. State radio stations subsequently aired call-in shows for citizen response (Utah Governor's Office of Planning and Budget 1996, 9).

The second night, a local PBS station aired a call-in show with Governor Mike Leavitt and other leaders to answer questions and discuss issues raised the night before (Harrie 1995, 1A). On December 8th, the final day of the Growth Summit, Governor Mike Leavitt held an Internet chat session with residents; however, the vast number of responses caused the system to crash (Semerad 1995, 1A).

Overall, the Growth Summit is considered by most participants to have been successful. The public was broadly involved and sensitized to growth issues. Numerous policy proposals were put forward and eventually enacted by the Utah State Legislature (Utah Governor's Office of Planning and Budget 1996, 6). Growth management continues to be an important topic in policy discussions around the state, with both formal and informal groups continuing to develop and discuss potential strategies.

A FRAMEWORK FOR PUBLIC INVOLVEMENT

While both the Utah Wilderness Debate and the Utah Growth Summit relied on non-voting public participation methods, the two efforts were not equally successful in fulfilling their respective purposes. The wilderness hearings sought agreement on the amount of wilderness land that should be protected in the Utah wilderness bill, yet the wilderness hearings did not end the debate over wilderness designation. The Utah Growth Summit, on the other hand, accomplished its more fundamental task of introducing the issue of growth to Utah residents (Utah Governor's Office of Planning and Budget 1995b, 1). The question for decision makers is: what made the difference?

Prior scholarly research recognizes that successful citizen participation depends on the appropriate crafting of citizen participation strategies. To be fully effective, decision makers must appropriately tie the selected strategy to both the purpose for participation and the nature of the issue being considered. We explicate each of these concepts more fully below (Checkoway 1981; Creighton 1981; Hathaway and Wormser 1993; Kathlene and Martin 1991; Kweit and Kweit 1987; Priscoli 1978; Rosenbaum 1978; Rosener 1975; Thomas 1995).

Purpose Tied to the Policy Development Process

Various authors have already noted the need for a careful consideration of the decision makers' purpose for involving the public (Kweit and Kweit 1987; Priscoli 1978). James L. Creighton highlights the purposes of information exchange and legitimization (1981, 57). Additionally, John Clayton Thomas states that decision makers should involve the public to gain information and to exchange public acceptance for influence (1995, 93). He recommends *more* public participation when the acceptance of a decision is important and *less* public participation when the quality of a decision is important (Thomas 1995, 73). The International City/County Management Association and the National League of Cities list community building, public information, deliberation, and decision making as purposes for involving the public (Walsh 1997, 36). Other reasons offered include the venting of emotions or resolution of conflicts (Rosener 1975).

Both Kweit and Kweit and Rosener point out the importance of communicating the purpose to participants. If a purpose is not chosen or not communicated, participants will infer their own purpose and expectations will proliferate without a reasonable means for decision makers to meet them. Citizens hold dear the fact that decision makers serve and represent the people. They soon become dissatisfied with their leaders if they feel decisions have no basis in public opinion. Additionally, without first articulating the purpose, the success of an activity cannot be readily determined (Kweit and Kweit 1981, 37–41; Rosener 1975, 112).

To be helpful though, the observation that purpose is important must be linked to some framework that allows the analyst to understand, organize, and consider alternative reasons for approaching the public. In this light, the purposes for seeking public participation can be organized around the stages of the policy development process. This process is often iterative, but there are relatively well-defined steps that analysts employ in developing an effective public policy. These include:

- Define the problem;
- Identify the criteria to be used in evaluating alternative solutions;
- Generate alternative solutions to the problem;
- Evaluate the alternative solutions based on the evaluation criteria;
- Recommend an alternative
  (Bardach 1996; Dunn 1994; Kweit and Kweit 1987; McRae and Whittington 1997; Patton and Sawicki 1993).

Depending on where the analyst is in the policy development process, the purposes for including citizens will vary. Creighton advocates that decision makers first identify a four-step decision-making process and then set public involvement objectives for each step (1981, 57). More direction is needed, however, regarding what these public involvement objectives should be, as some activities that support the objectives of the policy development process do not require public participation. Additional guidance on when to involve the public is needed. For example, Creighton explains that involving the public simply to fulfill legal requirements, but without an intention of considering their input is often worse than excluding the public all together because it "poisons the agency's relationship with the public and dooms future programs" (1981, 29).

As we see it, the purposes for involving citizens in decision making may be summarized as follows:

1. Discovery—Aid in the search for definitions, alternatives, or criteria.
2. Education—Educate the public about an issue and proposed alternative.
3. Measurement—Assess public opinion regarding a set of options.
4. Persuasion—Persuade the public toward a recommended alternative.
5. Legitimization—Comply with public norms or legal requirements.

These five purposes consolidate and explicate the purposes offered by other scholars. Creighton's purpose of "information exchange" encompasses a broad spectrum of motives for communicating with the public, including our purposes of discovery, education, and measurement (1981, 64–5). We feel that it is more appropriate to list discovery, education, and measurement as discrete purposes for involving the public, along with persuasion and legitimization, because each implies a different type of communication. Furthermore, these distinctions are important in describing why the public is involved at different stages in the policy development process.

Table 30.1

Policy Development Stages and Participation Purposes

Policy development stages	Participation purposes
1. Define the problem	1. Discover—Aid in the search for definitions
2. Identify criteria	1. Discover—Aid in the search for criteria
3. Generate alternatives	1. Discover—Aid in the search for alternatives, and/or 2. Educate—Educate public about issue and/or proposed alternatives, and/or 5. Legitimize—Comply with public norms
4. Evaluate alternatives	2. Educate—Educate public about proposed alternatives, and/or 3. Measure—Assess public opinion regarding a set of options, and/or 5. Legitimize—Comply with public norms
5. Recommend an alternative	2. Educate—Educate public about issue and/or proposed alternatives, and/or 4. Persuade—Persuade public toward a recommended alternative, and/or 5. Legitimize—Comply with public norms or legal requirements

At least one of our five purposes explains the function of public involvement in all of the policy development stages. Table 30.1 outlines where these purposes fit in the policy development process.

As Table 30.1 suggests, discovery is the primary purpose for involving the public in the first two stages of the policy development process. In this context, discovery fills two distinct purposes. First, as Reich (1988) and his coauthors note, it is often the case that people do not have well-formed values and opinions on relatively new public policy topics until there is public discussion and debate. For example, in discussions of growth in Utah prior to the Growth Summit, many participants did not exhibit a particularly rich understanding of the range of growth-related issues facing Utah. Through the Summit process, the public learned about and formed attitudes on these changes and the options for future growth management. They came to understand that growth was more than simply more people; it meant more people on the freeway, increased demand on the water supply, and less open space.

Second, discovery helps develop both a common language for discussing problem definitions and evaluation criteria and a broad perception of the problem being considered. Public policy problems can often be viewed in potentially countless ways depending on a person's interests, background, and experience. Consequently, different participants have different views on exactly how a given problem should be defined, what criteria should be used to identify a good solution, and which alternatives hold the greatest promise for solving the problem. Discovery involves eliciting different problem definitions and evaluation criteria from the public (Creighton 1981, 64), so that a representative problem definition can be formulated. For instance, the Growth Summit began with the growth criteria of water, transportation, and open space; however, through the discovery process, concerns about crime and the viability of communities also emerged. Decision makers, therefore, profit from listening to the public's views on the issues (Creighton 1981, 64).

Furthermore, the representative problem definition narrows the context within which alternative solutions will be generated and evaluated. Without this reference, the rest of the policy development process lacks the agreement necessary to reach a viable resolution. In contrast to the Growth Summit, the participants in the Utah Wilderness Debate never agreed on a problem definition or a set of evaluation criteria. Both sides of the debate realized that the public hearings offered a way to legitimize a single proposal—either one side or the other—and fought earnestly for their side. From the outset, conservationists disagreed with the BLM base and the hard release provisions. They went into the public hearings unsatisfied with what they perceived to be a pre-determined outcome. Had more effort gone into discovery and consensus building, there may have been more room for successful results. As it was, rather than resolving the two views of the problem, the public hearings perpetuated them.

As the analyst seeks to generate alternatives, there are three possible purposes for involving the public: discovery, education, and legitimization. Discovery seeks citizen participation in order to generate more formalized solutions to the problem (Creighton 1981, 64). The public was extensively involved in the development of proposals during the Utah Growth Summit. At the November meetings, various interest and expert groups presented their ideas and proposals to the three working groups.

Public involvement also educates the public on an issue. One major purpose for the Growth Summit was to inform the public about the possible consequences of "unmanaged" growth and the range of options available to governments seeking to influence community development.

Another potential purpose for involving the public in the generation of alternatives is legitimization. High-conflict issues may require citizen participation in the development of alternatives in order for the public to accept the final outcome. Otherwise, groups may see the decision as biased against them or as not reflective of the majority opinion. In the wilderness debate, conservationists criticized the counties' control of the first stage of the public-hearing process. They generally saw the county commissioners as being biased against wilderness designation (Lowry 1993, 48–9). Additionally, key participants refused to legitimize the alternatives without broader agreement on definition and criteria.

As the analysis moves into the evaluation of alternatives, there is still an opportunity to educate the public regarding the consequences of different options. Public involvement informs citizens about the criteria being used to determine success and how well each alternative meets those criteria (Creighton 1981, 65). The preparatory meetings to the Growth Summit educated the participants about alternatives that would and would not work in light of different evaluation criteria.

Analysis of possible solutions also often involves assessing public attitudes and values. A determination of the tradeoffs acceptable to the public defines in part each alternative's political feasibility (Creighton 1981, 65). The political attractiveness of a policy option increases, as does the ease of its administration, if it corresponds to the values of the public. Opinion polls during the wilderness debate had this measurement purpose as citizens were asked to choose between various amounts of wilderness land (Israelson 1994b; Israelson 1995b; Israelson 1995c). It must be noted, however, these polls probably served more as general thermometers of public support for wilderness than as viable indicators of how much land should receive wilderness designation.

As the analysis moves into the final recommendation stage, persuasion often emerges as an important purpose in the policy development process. After evaluating the various policy options, decision makers need to explain the reasons for their decision and build support for their decision. In the Wilderness Debate, the focus was on legitimizing an outcome, and organizers made very little effort to persuade participants that a particular outcome was acceptable if not ideal. In general, building public support for the merits of a recommendation will boost the public's acceptance of any change generated through its implementation.

Table 30.2

The Nature of the Issue Classifications

Characteristics	Well-structured	Moderately-structured	Ill-structured
Degree of Conflict	Consensus	Consensus/conflict	Conflict
Number of Stakeholders	Few	Few	Many
Information Confidence Level	Confident	Confident	Not confident
Number of Alternatives	Limited	Limited	Unlimited
Knowledge of Outcomes	Certain or marginal risk	Uncertain	Unknown
Probability of Outcomes	Calculable	Incalculable	Incalculable

If it is a low conflict issue and the public has not been included earlier in the process, then the education purpose also applies here so that the public understands the issue. In other situations, decision makers are required by law to include the public in the decision-making process. Legitimization can be gained at this stage if it is a low conflict issue. Formal public involvement strategies—such as public hearings, elections, and referendums—fulfill this requirement.

Whatever their actual reasons for including citizens in the policy development process, the method chosen communicates to citizens the degree to which the results will influence future policy decisions. The Utah Wilderness Debate provides an illustration. By using public hearings to involve citizens, decision makers led participants to believe that their input would influence the delegation's proposal. When neither recommendation was chosen, participants became unhappy with the congressional delegation. It is crucial to the success of citizen involvement that decision makers determine in advance how the results will be used.

None of the stages of the policy development process inherently preclude successful public participation. Rather, the purposes for including the public require different forums and approaches to solicit that participation. Using this process of determining a policy's status in the policy development process enables decision makers to narrow the purpose possibilities, which, in turn, provides guidance on when to include the public and the best methods to solicit that participation. Good decisions on citizen participation methods facilitate their success by both managing public expectations and clearly specifying how public input will be incorporated into the analysis.

The Nature of the Issue

The second dimension in designing and appropriately incorporating public participation in policy development is the nature of the issue being considered. Previous research argues that both the desirability of public participation and the appropriateness of participation mechanisms vary with the issue being addressed. Understanding the nature of the issue is, therefore, vital to choosing successful participation strategies (Creighton 1981; Rosener 1975; Thomas 1995).

Past efforts have identified a host of issue characteristics that affect the success of public participation. These characteristics can be effectively grouped by augmenting the description of problem structure set forth by Mitroff and Sagasti (1973; see also, Dunn 1994, 146). In this description, the structure of policy problems is characterized as a continuum from well-structured, through moderately-structured, to ill-structured. Placing a given problem along this continuum requires an understanding and assessment of six clusters of problem attributes, listed here and summarized in Table 30.2.

1. The degree of conflict over the issue.
2. The number of stakeholders.
3. The level of confidence in the information on the issue.
4. The number of alternatives.
5. The knowledge of outcomes.
6. The probability of the outcomes.

These issue attributes significantly affect the success of alternative public participation strategies. The degree of conflict determines when decision makers should include the public in the decision-making process and the amount of consensus building necessary to productively move through the policy development process. In a high conflict issue, public involvement is needed early to encourage consensus and to legitimize the process. Additionally, widespread disagreement about the definition of the problem means that decision makers should utilize participation methods that emphasize compromise in order to establish a common concept upon which the subsequent steps can build. Workshops are often more successful for this purpose than public hearings because they provide an opportunity for dialogue between differing interests, whereas public hearings are frequently more adversarial (Creighton 1981, 77).

Further, because single-issue groups are wholly committed to their issue, they tend to be more resistant to compromise than multiple-issue groups (Creighton 1981, 72; Walsh 1997, 61). Multiple-issue groups have incentives to sacrifice a little on one issue in order to gain in others or overall. When single-issue groups are involved, participation techniques such as small group workshops, advisory committees, or conflict mediation should be used to ensure that their concerns are considered, as well as those of other interested groups.

Utah Wilderness is an issue that has been and continues to be highly divisive. Organizers of the hearings did not acknowledge its contentious nature when they decided on a public-hearings process that provided little opportunity for compromise. The process-strategy decisions also did not ensure a representative sampling of opinion or consensus on the issue definition itself. Rather, the hearings provided a forum for well-entrenched interest groups to become even more entrenched and polarized.

The number of stakeholders and their level of organization is also significant in determining participation mechanisms (Creighton 1981, 78; Thomas 1995, 41; Walsh 1997, 61). If the stakeholders are organized into a few groups, participation can make use of the groups themselves and work through elected political leaders or interest group leaders. Stakeholders recognize the legitimacy of their group leaders; therefore, involving those leaders is often an effective participation strategy (Creighton 1981, 78; Thomas 1995, 57). Examples of methods that involve group leaders are interviews, workshops, and advisory committees as well as focus groups (Creighton 1981, 77; Thomas 1995, 57). The decision maker must carefully ascertain whose interests leaders actually represent and the size of their support, noting always that the most involved groups do not necessarily represent the majority opinion (Thomas 1995, 67; Checkoway and Van Til 1978, 25).

Conversely, if the stakeholders are poorly organized or widely dispersed, and do not have legitimate representatives, methods must be chosen that deal more directly with the stakeholders, such as the media or town meetings (Creighton 1981, 77). Other examples of more direct methods are elections, opinion polls, and public hearings (Thomas 1995, 57).

The level of confidence in the information on any issue influences the amount of issue-education activity that should be pursued. Lack of confidence could be the result of unavailable data or lack of confidence in the source of the data. Thomas stresses that decision makers need to assess whether the information needed to make a quality decision is available (1995, 44). If important information is missing, outdated, or questionable due to its data collection methods, such as the BLM land survey in the wilderness debate, then there will be less confidence in the evaluation of alternative solutions. An explanation of any limitations in the available information should be provided to the stakeholders as well as the impact such limitations may have on the subsequent analysis.

Further, if stakeholders doubt the reliability or objectivity of the source of the information, they may discredit the data and reject any consensus. Analysts should search for corroborating sources. Convincing group leaders of the reliability of the information, perhaps through workshop discussions and presentations, enables group members to hear the information from a source they consider reliable—their leader.

Additionally, some alternatives may be more technical than others or simply less well known. These limitations shrink the number of policy options seriously considered by stakeholders. If there is little understanding about the alternatives or the evaluation criteria, an educational process should be planned to help stakeholders learn about policy options. The Growth Summit and subsequent growth management discussions are excellent examples of this type of participation. One of the important accomplishments of this process has been to sensitize local leaders to a broader range of land use management techniques and concepts.

Creighton suggests the use of an "advisory group that can be thoroughly informed" on technical aspects. Publications might also be used to explain the technical complexities to the stakeholders at large. He prescribes a greater effort to educate other agencies or interest groups than to educate the general public (1981, 77). Again, this approach is consistent with the growth management efforts in Utah. It does not appear to be true of the Wilderness Debate, however.

The number of alternative solutions to be considered also influences participation strategy decisions. As the number of alternatives increases, the probability of achieving consensus around any one alternative decreases. Differentiation between options can become marginal, requiring a more specific measurement of values. Public involvement can become unending as more and more alternatives are introduced. Thus, in terms of citizen participation, the more concrete the alternatives the better. Education efforts can then be more focused and consensus-building activities more productive.

Further complicating many policy problems is the degree to which the outcomes of each alternative are known. When the results are certain or within an acceptable margin of risk, education, measurement, and persuasion efforts can focus on the benefits and risks of the various alternatives. When outcomes are unknown or uncertain, however, participation must be linked to other concepts, such as minimizing the worst outcomes, or incremental improvement. Additionally, when the consequences of policy options are unknown, decisions tend to be based more on principle or value.

The probability-of-outcomes characteristic is interrelated with a knowledge of outcomes. In a well-structured issue, outcomes are either certain or highly probable. The outcomes are knowable, and the probabilities of achieving those outcomes can be calculated. A moderately-structured issue has outcomes that are uncertain and the probability of these outcomes occurring encompasses a wide range. In an ill-structured issue, unknown and unintended outcomes are possible, and attempts to calculate the probability of each outcomes are infeasible.

Again, the Utah Wilderness and Growth Summit processes provide a useful contrast. In the Wilderness debate, county commissioners and local residents of rural counties saw the outcomes of expanded wilderness as highly uncertain. Many of the proposed wilderness areas are rich in coal, oil, and other mineral deposits. Local economic development and job growth are closely tied to the development of extraction industries in the minds of many local residents. In their view, designating these lands as wilderness would preclude development and leave future job growth in these areas highly uncertain and even unlikely. Wilderness advocates, on the other hand, see expanded designation as the only certain way to protect a national trust for future generations. In this view, leaving protection of these lands to developers and local interests is too risky and the potential harms irreparable. This conflict over outcomes argues strongly for a less formal and smaller scale process than the public hearings that were held. Focus groups, working task forces, or town meetings with a clear education agenda, would all have been more effective than the process actually followed.

In contrast, the Growth Summit seemed to reach relative consensus on the likely effects of growth. Most participants saw the outcomes of continued growth under status quo policies as highly probable, although the timetable might be uncertain. Repeated references to southern California probably best typify the image held by most participants. Less certain in the Growth Summit were the alternatives, hence the continued discussions and policy development. In this case, public participation provided a broad forum for establishing consensus on the nature of the problem. Subsequent participation, in the form of smaller working groups and representative task forces, has shifted to the more difficult task of identifying and evaluating alternatives to the status quo.

The continuum described in Table 30.2 links the different issue characteristics together, providing a characterization of an issue for the policy development process. In doing so, it narrows the viable public participation options for decision makers. In our treatment of the policy development process, we argued that regardless of where an issue is in the process, there is an important purpose in seeking public input. In contrast, the nature of the issue can place limitations on the necessity of public involvement and the appropriateness of various participation strategies. Well-structured issues often include the public only to legitimize a recommendation. Decision makers face little, if any, opposition to their recommendation. Moderately-structured issues present more opportunity for involvement but require more care in linking that involvement to the policy development process. As should be expected, ill-structured issues are the issues that require the most care by decision makers in seeking public involvement. Involvement strategies play a crucial role in determining the success of the policy development process; consequently, public participation must be focused and clearly defined so that its success can be measured. We explicate these relationships further in what we have termed the purpose-issue matrix.

The Purpose-Issue Matrix

Table 30.3 visually outlines the effects of purpose and nature of the issue on participation strategy decisions. The issue classification remains constant no matter the purpose; however, the purpose for public participation changes with the policy development process. An empty cell means the public probably need not be involved. Otherwise the cell states the mechanisms that may be used to most effectively involve the public. Thus, different public involvement mechanisms may be utilized at different times in the policy development process as the purposes for involving the public change (Creighton 1981, 79; Walsh 1997, 63).

The timing of public involvement varies according to the classification of the issue. Well-structured issues call for citizen participation later in the policy development process, if at all. Because the few stakeholders agree on the problem and have adequate knowledge about the alternatives, consensus building and educational activities are less necessary. The recommendation may only need confirmation. A stakeholder hearing or vote would accomplish this purpose, depending on legal requirements.

Table 30.3

The Purpose-Issue Matrix

Purpose	Nature of the issue		
	Well-structured	Moderately-structured	Ill-structured
1. Discovery		Interest group forum	Task force Commission Focus groups Neighborhood meetings Internet chat, bulletin board
2. Education		Educational public forum Town meeting Neighborhood meeting News media	Educational public forum Town meeting Neighborhood meeting News media
3. Measurement		Opinion poll Focus groups	Opinion poll Focus groups
4. Persuasion		Persuasive public forum Town meeting Advocacy media	Persuasive public forum Town meeting Advocacy media
5. Legitimize	Elections Referendums Formal hearings as required by law or custom	Elections Referendums Formal hearings Media Task force	Elections Referendums Formal hearings Media Task force

Moderately-structured issues call for greater public involvement throughout the entire process. Once again the stakeholders are few and there is often sufficient knowledge about the issue so that educational and consensus-building activities are less essential. The key here is the uncertainty about the outcomes of the policy options. The utilization of stakeholder group leaders through task forces, issue committees or conferences, or focus groups reflects the increased need for the consideration of stakeholder values due to the heightened uncertainty of the outcomes. A more direct option for discovering values is an opinion poll. A referendum may be necessary to legitimize the recommendation of opinion leaders.

The greatest room for public involvement is with ill-structured issues. These are the most difficult issues because conflict often centers on the basic problem definition and the values inherent in the evaluation criteria. Public educational forums, including Internet chat rooms, provide a means for soliciting public comment on the problem and may be important in the discovery phase of analysis. Often, however, it is participation on a smaller scale that yields important progress on a problem. A carefully selected task force or commission may be able to identify the boundaries of a problem and structure more effectively than testimony in a public hearing. In general, problems that tend to lie further to the right in Table 30.3 (i.e., less structure) will require participation earlier in the policy development process. Public participation will tend to increase in scale as the analyst moves down through the policy development process.

Some policy problems undoubtedly will not fit neatly into these classifications. However, thinking about the policies along these dimensions produces a greater understanding of the problems and potential of public participation.

CONCLUSION

The founders of our country meant for decision making in government to be removed from the direct influence of public passions. Madison thought this arrangement was a good way to avoid the mischief of factions (1987). In addition, governments at all levels face complex and highly technical questions. The public is uninformed on many of these issues: they may not be aware of legal constraints, definitions, or other aspects of a problem that must be understood in order to make an informed decision. Having people serve full time in government positions, whether elected or appointed, allows them to devote their attention to these difficult questions.

As we have tried to illustrate, however, public input has its place in policy analysis. The question then becomes how to balance expertise with public opinion. Public policy requires attention to both technical constraints *and* public preference. Citizens provide guidance to expert analysts about the direction of public policy through their experiences, preferences, and values. Failing to include the public in the decision-making process deprives decision makers of valuable input and compromises legitimacy. Thus, using both issue expertise and public opinion in tandem is more likely to produce good public policy.

An objection could be raised by practitioners who are concerned that laws often dictate the type of public participation required. This could create a problem if the law calls for participation methods that are not ideal in a given situation. While this may be true in some cases, it has been our experience that laws outlining public participation methods are more often than not minimum standards rather than maximums. For example, if a law calls for hearings, as is the case in many environmental policies, practitioners can use the purpose-issue matrix to identify other public participation methods that would be useful. Such additional participation may serve to prepare both decision makers and the public for the eventual hearings, rather than attempting minimal compliance with legal norms. Decision makers and citizens will find the hearings more beneficial with some prior contextual background on the issue.

Introducing a framework to organize public participation suggests that decision makers have a proactive role in the public participation process. The questions addressed throughout this article illustrate some of the complexities of designing a public participation strategy. This framework enables those responsible for directing public participation to approach these questions as design factors rather than unknown quantities that will surface only after the process is underway. Problems associated with public involvement can be anticipated and resolved before the participatory process begins. By working through the framework, questions are matched with answers.

Public participation in the policy process through a variety of mechanisms represents not so much a move toward a more direct form of democracy as much as it does a move toward a better form of representation. Decision makers who use the principles outlined in this article should be able to design and implement public participation strategies that will not only inform the public about substantive policy questions, but also improve the quality of the final decision.

ACKNOWLEDGMENTS

The authors gratefully acknowledge the support of National Science Foundation Grant CMS-9526018. The observations and conclusions presented here are not necessarily representative of either the National Science Foundation or any branch of Utah State government.

REFERENCES

Bardach, Eugene. 1996. *The Eight-Step Path of Policy Analysis: A Handbook for Practice.* Berkeley, CA: Berkeley Academic Press.

Bell, Daniel. 1971. Technocracy and Politics. *Survey* 16.

Bernick, Bob, Jr. 1995. A "mighty oak" of an idea had a rocky start. *The Salt Lake Tribune,* 6 December, 1A-2A.

Brzezinski, Zbigniew. 1976. *Between Two Ages: America's Role in the Technotronic Era.* New York: Viking Press.

Checkoway, Barry. 1981. The Politics of Public Hearings. *Journal of Applied Behavioral Science* 17(4): 566–82.

Checkoway, Barry, and Jon Van Til. 1978. What Do We Know About Citizen Participation? A Selective Review of Research. In *Citizen Participation in America,* edited by Stuart Langton. Lexington, MA: Lexington Books.

Creighton, James L. 1981. *The Public Involvement Manual.* Cambridge, MA: Abt Books.

Dunn, William N. 1994. *Public Policy Analysis: An Introduction.* 2d ed. Englewood Cliffs, N.J.: Prentice-Hall, Inc.

Farmer, David John. 1995. *The Language of Public Administration: Bureaucracy, Modernity, and Postmodernity.* Tuscaloosa, AL: The University of Alabama Press.

Federal Land Policy and Management Act of 1976. 43 U.S.C. seq. 1701 et. seq.

Fischer, Frank. 1995. *Evaluating Public Policy.* Chicago: Nelson-Hall Publishers.

Hamilton, Alexander, James Madison, and John Jay. 1817. *The Federalist, On the New Constitution.* Philadelphia: Benjamin Warner.

Harrie, Dan. 1995. Growth Plan: No Pain, Plenty of Gain. *The Salt Lake Tribune,* 8 December, 1A, 8A.

Hathaway, Janet, and Lisa Wormser. 1993. Working With New Partners: Transportation Decisions With the Public. *Transportation Research Record* 1400 (August): 36–40.

Heineman, Robert A., William T. Bluhm, Steven A. Peterson, and Edward N. Kearny, 1997. *The World of the Policy Analyst: Rationality, Values, and Politics.* 2d ed. Chatham, NJ: Chatham House Publishers, Inc.

Israelson, Brent. 1994a. Issue Remains Untamed as Wilds Act Turns 30. *The Deseret News,* 4 September. Available at *http://www.desnews.com.*

———. 1994b. Wilds Bills: A New Round Begins in the Fight Over Wilderness. *The Deseret News,* 18 December. Available at *http://www.desnews.com.*

———. 1995a. 100 Plead to Keep the Wilds Wild. *The Deseret News,* 13 April. Available at *http://www.desnews.com.*

———. 1995b. Latest Wilderness Poll Shows Bigger Is Better. *The Deseret News,* 20 May. Available at *http://www.desnews.com.*

———. 1995c. Utahns give little support to Wilds Bill. *The Deseret News,* 10 June, 1B-2B.

Kathlene, Lyn, and John A. Martin. 1991. Enhancing Citizen Participation: Panel Designs, Perspectives and Policy Formulation. *Journal of Policy Analysis and Management* 10(1): 46–63.

Kriz, Margaret. 1996. The Wild Card. *National Journal* 28(2): 65–8.

Kweit, Mary Grisez, and Robert W. Kweit. 1981. *Implementing Public Participation in a Bureaucratic Society.* New York: Praeger.

———. 1987. The Politics of Policy Analysis: The Role of Citizen Participation in Analytic Decision Making. In *Citizen Participation in Public Decision Making,* edited by Jack DeSario and Stuart Langton. New York: Greenwood Press.

Lowry, Phillip. 1993. The Utah Wilderness War. Manuscript, Brigham Young University Law Library.

Mathews, David. 1994. *Politics for People: Finding a Responsible Public Voice.* Urbana, IL: University of Illinois Press.

McRae, Duncan, Jr., and Dale Whittington. 1997. *Expert Advice for Policy Choice: Analysis and Discourse.* Washington, DC: Georgetown University Press.

Mitroff, Jan I., and Francisco Sagasti. 1973. Epistemology as General Systems Theory: An Approach to the Design of Complex Decision-Making Experiments. *Philosophy of the Social Sciences* 3 (1): 117–34.

Patton, Carl V., and David S. Sawicki. 1993. *Basic Methods of Policy Analysis and Planning.* 2d ed. Englewood Cliffs, NJ: Prentice Hall.

Prewitt, Kenneth. 1983. Scientific Illiteracy and Democratic Theory. *Daedalus* 112(2): 49–64.

Priscoli, Jerry Delli. 1978. Implementing Public Involvement Programs in Federal Agencies. In *Citizen Participation in America,* edited by Stuart Langton. Lexington, MA: Lexington Books.

Reich, Robert B., ed. 1988. *The Power of Public Ideas.* Cambridge, MA: Ballinger Publishing Company.

Rein, Martin. 1976. *Social Science & Public Policy.* New York: Penguin Books.

Rosenbaum, Nelson M. 1978. Citizen Participation and Democratic Theory. In *Citizen Participation in America,* edited by Stuart Langton. Lexington, MA: Lexington Books.

Rosener, Judy B. 1975. A Cafeteria of Techniques and Critiques. *Public Management* 57(12): 16–19.

Saul, John Ralston. 1992. *Voltaire's Bastards: The Dictatorship of Reason in the West.* New York: The Free Press.

Semerad, Tony. 1995. On-Line Chat Glitch: Growth Summit Ends But Not Without a Few Hitches. *The Salt Lake Tribune,* 9 December, 1A.

Spangler, Jerry. 1995. Utah Leaders Vow to Offer Wilderness Measure by June 1. *The Deseret News,* 8 January. Available at *http://www.desnews.com.*

Sternberg, Ernest. 1989. Incremental versus Methodological Policymaking in the Liberal State. *Administration and Society* 21(May): 54–77.

Thomas, John Clayton. 1995. *Public Participation in Public Decisions.* San Francisco, CA: Jossey-Bass.

U.S. Code. 1995. Washington, DC: U.S. Government Printing Office.

Utah Governor's Office of Planning and Budget. 1995a. *1995 Economic Report to the Governor.* Salt Lake City, UT: Utah Governor's Office of Planning and Budget.

———. 1995b. *Growth Summit Update: Preserving a Century of Quality.* 6 November. Salt Lake City, UT: Utah Governor's Office of Planning and Budget.

———. 1996. *Summary Review of the Growth Summit.* Salt Lake City, UT: Utah Governor's Office of Planning and Budget.

———. 1998. *Utah Projections: Economic and Demographic Summary.* Available at *http://www.governor.state.ut.us/dea/QGET/Homepg.htm.*

Walsh, Mary L. 1997. *Building Citizen Involvement: Strategies for Local Government.* Washington, DC: International City/County Management Association and the National League of Cities.

Wilderness Act of 1964. 16 U.S.C. sec. 1131 et. seq.

CHAPTER 31

FROM RESPONSIVENESS TO COLLABORATION
Governance, Citizens, and the Next Generation
of Public Administration

ERAN VIGODA

INTRODUCTION

Modern public administration involves an inherent tension between better responsiveness to citizens as clients and effective collaboration with them as partners. This tension stems from tangible differences between the nature of responsiveness and the essence of collaboration. While responsiveness is mostly seen as a passive, unidirectional reaction to the people's needs and demands, collaboration represents a more active, bidirectional act of participation, involvement, and unification of forces between two (or more) parties. Moreover, responsiveness is based on the marketplace view of better service for citizens as clients or customers. Answering their needs is seen as vital for government and public administration (G&PA) systems that seek extensive legitimization and high performance. On the other hand, collaboration highlights a moral value of genuine cooperation and teamwork between citizens and G&PAs where each party is neither a pure servant nor the master, but a social player in the theatre of state.

The differences between responsiveness and collaboration/partnership are not merely conceptual or terminological. In fact, they represent an intensifying paradox that emerges in both the theory and the practice of contemporary public-sector management. The paradox increases because of an ongoing consensus on the necessity of both responsiveness and collaboration for moving G&PA systems toward future reforms. Thus, it is quite surprising to find that most of the current theoretical thinking in public administration deals with these values separately, neglecting the mutual benefit of integrating them in a useful manner. An overview of the literature reveals two distinct groups of studies. One group highlights administrative responsiveness to citizens' requests as the most important value of public agencies in a businesslike arena (Chi 1999; Rourke 1992; Stivers 1994; Vigoda 2000). The other group emphasizes partnership between the sides as a premise for cultural revolution in contemporary bureaucracies (Nalbandian 1999; Thompson, Tancredi, and Kisil 2000; John et al. 1994; Hart 1997; Callahan and Holzer 1994). To date, very little literature has consolidated these two prominent themes to illuminate the theoretical as well as the empirical merit of their coexistence (Fredrickson 1982).

From *Public Administration Review,* 62, 5 (September/October 2002): 527–540. Copyright © 2002 by American Society for Public Administration. Reprinted with permission.

The article argues that expanding the orientation of G&PA systems toward responsiveness, as prescribed by New Public Managerialism, is frequently accompanied by lower willingness to share, participate, collaborate, and partner with citizens. This paradox is identified as a theoretical as well as a practical rift in the present array of the New Public Management (NPM) approach. While the article applauds the recent trend in public managerialism that fosters manager-customer relationships in the public arena, it also criticizes such leanings for resting solely on a unidirectional pattern of relationships where citizens are covertly encouraged to remain passive clients of government. The role of "customer" or "client" denotes a passive orientation of citizens toward another party (G&PA), which is more active in trying to satisfy the customer/client's needs. Such a pattern of dependency is likely to create serious obstacles to reforms in public agencies and interrupt the emergence of better public service. The paradox between serving clients and collaborating with citizens needs to be resolved on the way to creating a high-performing type of public organization, one that will work better for societies as well as for individuals in the generations to come.

To promote understanding of the processes that modern societies require and may undergo, I advance in three stages. First, several similarities and differences are presented between the ideas of responsiveness and collaboration as they are developed in recent public administration studies. These discussions make use of various disciplinary sources such as democratic theory, comparative political science, and political economy, as well as theories of administrative reforms. Second, I provide my analysis and view of "one lady with two hats," a metaphor for one continuum connecting two current alternatives of the state of the discipline. In light of this, I finally suggest a discussion that redefines the duties and responsibilities of various players and compares this view and other perceptions of the next generation of public administration.

RESPONSIVENESS AND COLLABORATION: TWO DIFFERENT LADIES, OR ONE LADY WITH TWO HATS?

Responsiveness to Citizens as Clients

Previous work by Vigoda (2000) identifies two approaches to understanding public administration's responsiveness. These approaches can be defined as controversial but also as complementary. They provide distinct views of responsiveness, but in addition, each approach contains checks and balances missing in the other. According to one approach, responsiveness is, at best, a necessary evil that appears to compromise professional effectiveness and, at worst, an indication of political expediency if not outright corruption (Rourke 1992). According to this line of research, responsiveness contradicts the value of professionalism in G&PA because it forces public servants to satisfy citizens even when such actions run counter to the required public interest. In the name of democracy, professionals are almost obliged to satisfy a vague public will. Short-term considerations and popular decisions are put forward, while other long-term issues receive little and unsatisfactory attention. In addition, there is a risk that powerful influences of some may ring out loudly and wrongly pretend to represent the opinions of many. Such influences can result in an antidemocratic decision-making pattern and simply may not represent the true voice of the majority. The other approach to responsiveness suggests that democracy requires administrators who are responsive to the popular will, at least through legislatures and politicians if not directly to the people (Stivers 1994; Stewart and Ranson 1994). This approach is more alert to the need to encourage a flexible, sensitive, and dynamic public sector. It fact, it argues that only by creating a market-derived environment can G&PA adopt some necessary reforms that will improve their performance, effectiveness, and efficiency.

While responsiveness is occasionally considered problematic in the public administration literature, it is undoubtedly critical for politicians, bureaucrats, and citizens alike. A responsive politician or bureaucrat must be reactive, sympathetic, sensitive, and capable of feeling the public's needs and opinions. Because the needs and demands of a heterogeneous society are dynamic, it is vital to develop systematic approaches to understanding it. Undoubtedly, this is one of the most important conditions for securing a fair social contract between citizens and government officials. Hence, scholars and practitioners suggest the elaboration of performance indicators based on public opinion. The opinions of service receivers must be considered good indicators of public policy outcomes (Palfrey et al. 1992; Winkler 1987; National Consumer Council 1986; DHSS 1979). This information can help us to (1) understand and establish public needs; (2) develop, communicate, and distribute public services; and (3) assess the degree of satisfaction with services (Palfrey et al. 1992, 128). Consequently, the NPM approach advocates the idea of treating citizens as clients, customers, and main beneficiaries of the operation of the public sector that is today more oriented toward assessing its performance (Thomas and Palfrey 1996). In essence, the motivation to meet the demands raised by citizens is equivalent to satisfying the needs of a regular customer in a regular neighborhood supermarket. According to this view, responsiveness in the public arena closely complies with business-oriented statements such as "the customer is always right" and "never argue with the clients' needs" that every salesperson memorizes from the first day at work.

But what does responsiveness actually mean? How can we best define and operationalize it for dependable social research? In essence, responsiveness generally denotes the *speed* and *accuracy* with which a service provider responds to a request for action or information. According to this definition, speed may refer to the waiting time between a citizen's request for action and the reply of the public agency or the public servant. Accuracy means the extent to which the provider's response meets the needs or wishes of the service user. Yet while speed is a relatively simple factor to measure, accuracy is more complicated. Beyond the recent trends of analyzing public arenas in terms that are appropriate for the marketplace, public-service accuracy must take into consideration social welfare, equity, equal opportunities, and fair distribution of "public goods" to all citizens (Vigoda 2000). These values are in addition to the efficiency, effectiveness, and service that characterize market-driven processes (Rhodes 1987; Palfrey et al. 1992). To test the accuracy of G&PA endeavors, several methods may be applied:

1. Examining citizens' attitudes and feelings when consuming public services; this can be achieved by using satisfaction measures that indicate the outcomes of certain activities and the acceptance of public administration actions as fruitful, beneficial, equally shared among a vast population, effective, fast, and responding well to public needs.
2. Examining the attitudes and perceptions of others who take part in the process of planning, producing, delivering, and evaluating public outcomes. These "others" include external private and not-for-profit firms, suppliers, manufacturers, and constructors.
3. Comparing objective public outcomes with absolute criteria for speed, quality, and accuracy. The absolute criteria need to be determined in advance within a strategic process of setting performance indicators (Pollitt 1988). Such a comparison is even more effective when it is conducted over time, populations, cultures, and geographical areas.
4. Comparing the distribution of services and goods with moral and ethical criteria set forth by academics and professionals

Subject to several restrictions and balances, responsiveness has a potentially positive effect on social welfare, and it improves the process of modernization in the public sector. Recent managerial positions, such as the NPM approach, also suggest that, as in the private sector, increasing external outcomes (that is, responsiveness of G&PA to citizens' demands) will have a profound impact on internal control mechanisms (Smith 1993). It simply implies that managers and public servants become more sensitive to their duties and highly committed to serving the people.

Collaboration with Citizens as Partners

At first glance, collaboration and partnership between G&PA and citizens seem to contradict the essence of bureaucracy. The ideal type of bureaucracy, as set out by Max Weber, clearly defines organizational characteristics that have remained relevant through the years. Public organizations have undergone many changes in the last century, but they are still based on the Weberian legacy of clear hierarchical order, concentration of power among senior officials, formal structures with strict rules and regulations, limited channels of communication, confined openness to innovation and change, and noncompliance with the option of being replaceable. These ideas seem to be substantially different from the nature of collaboration, which means negotiation, participation, cooperation, free and unlimited flow of information, innovation, agreements based on compromises and mutual understanding, and a more equitable distribution and redistribution of power and resources. According to this utopian analysis, collaboration is an indispensable part of democracy. It means partnership in which authorities and state administrators accept the role of leaders who need to run citizen's lives better—not because they are more powerful or superior, but because this is a mission to which they are obligated. They must see themselves as committed to citizens who have agreed to be led or "governed" on condition that their lives continuously improve.

In support of the above recognition, Thompson (1983) states that "democracy does not suffer bureaucracy gladly. Many of the values we associate with democracy—equality, participation, and individuality—stand sharply opposed to hierarchy, specialization, and impersonality we ascribe to modern bureaucracy" (235). Bureaucracies, like other organizations, constitute a work site that is anything but democratic. According to Golembiewski and Vigoda (2000), bureaucracies embody a firm hierarchy of roles and duties, a vertical flow of orders and reports, accountability to highly ranked officers, fear of sanctions and restrictions, and sometimes even a lack of sufficient accountability dynamics. All of these signal that the "natural state" in public administration is authoritarian.

It seems odd to ask for genuine collaboration between those in power and those who delegate power. In many respects, growing citizen involvement by interest groups, political parties, courts, and other democratic institutions may only bother politicians in office and state administrators. Too broad an involvement, in the eyes of elected politicians and appointed public officers, may be perceived as interfering with their administrative work. The freedom of public voice is thus limited and obscured by the need of administrators and politicians to govern. Consequently, the public lacks sufficient freedom of voice and influence. While mechanisms of direct democracy are designed to show such impediments the door, modern representative democracy lets them in through the rear entrance. Representative democracy frequently diminishes the motives for partnership with governance. Constitutions, legislatures, federal and local structures, as well as electoral institutions are in slow but significant decline in many Western societies. They suffer from increasing alienation, distrust, and cynicism among citizens; they encourage passivism and raise barriers before original individual involvement in state affairs (Eisinger 2000; Berman 1997). Consequently—and as a counterrevolutionary course of action—a swelling current in contemporary public administration seeks to revitalize collaboration between citizens and administrative authorities through various strategies. In fact, such trends are not so new. The need to foster certain levels of cooperation among political government institutions, professional agencies of public administration, and citizens as individuals or groups has been mentioned before and was advanced in several ways. Among these philosophies and strategies, one should mainly consider the following:

1. Greater cooperation with the third sector (Thompson, Tancredi, and Kisil 2000; Gidron, Kramer, and Salamon 1992; Grubbs 2000).
2. Greater collaboration with the private sector and initiation of plans aimed at supporting communities through various services in the fields of internal security, transport, and education (Glaister 1999; Collin 1998; Schneider 1999).
3. Encouragement of state and local municipality initiatives that foster values of democratic education, participation, and involvement among citizens (for instance, the local democratic club established in Culver City, CA [*http://www.culvercityonline.com/*]). This pattern also coheres with the idea of a communitarian spirit that transfers some (but not all) responsibility for civic development from central government to local authorities in states and cities, as well as directly to individual citizens (Etzioni 1994, 1995).
4. Innovation by original citizenry involvement through not-for-profit civic organizations that help to establish a culture of participation and practice of voice (see the examples of "citizens conventions" in Denmark and Israel [*http://www.zippori.org.il/English/index.html*]).

Still, advocates of the NPM approach continue to claim the main instrument to restore ill-functioning G&PA systems is better responsiveness to citizens as clients or customers. According to this line of thinking, which is rooted in political-economy rationality and social choice theory (Kettl and Milward 1996; Hughes 1994), only better compliance with people's wishes can steady the wobbly interface between citizens and rulers in contemporary democracies. But is a market-driven responsiveness really the best answer to crises in governance, or is it only an oversimplification of wider problems in modern society?

Customers or Partners? A Quest for Hats and Ladies

What are the advantages of citizens being treated as clients and customers over their being perceived as equal partners in the process of governance? A metaphor of ladies and hats may prove useful here to examine two competing options: (1) There are two substantially separated faces of government and public administration (two ladies), one that adopts the idea of responsiveness and one that favors collaboration; (2) the discipline of governance and public administration is more coherent (only one lady) than we might think, and at most it changes colors over time (two hats).

Above, I portrayed two themes in current public administration research as separate and dissimilar perspectives. I argued that responsiveness is the essence of NPM, and further suggested that NPM seems detached from the idea of collaboration. Therefore, it may be there are two different types of public administration: Like two ladies, one is attired by the supporters of responsiveness, the other by supporters of collaboration. These two ladies differ substantially because, as explained earlier, they advocate independent views of the roles of G&PA and citizens in the process of running states and societies. Yet it may in fact be only one lady with two hats. One hat, an older styled classic, is more oriented toward bureaucratic tyranny and concentration of power in public agencies. It reflects a situation in which public administration is the right hand of politicians and thus must preserve power through maximum centralization and control over decisions and resources. This hat/attitude implies minimal care for either responsiveness or collaboration because both mean depriving G&PA of its power. The other hat, however, is newer and more receptive and appreciative of de-concentrated managerial ideas, such as better responsiveness and improved collaboration with citizens, that effect a wider process of modernization. This last hat signals a continuous change in public administration systems, and, maturing with time, it implies more citizen participation in the administrative process. A lady of public administration wearing the newer hat is less concerned about bureaucracy losing power and control, but instead favors sharing responsibilities and dialogue with citizens, which may lead to cooperation and partnership on a higher level.

In addition, the "two ladies" version is a more classic approach to the understanding of responsiveness and collaboration in public arenas, so it has received wide scholarly attention over the years. One group of studies has concentrated on the first "lady" of public administration, namely, the idea of responsiveness (Stivers 1994; Rourke 1992), while the other group has focused on the other lady, who represents the idea of collaboration and partnership (John et al. 1994; Thompson, Tancredi, and Kisil 2000; Nalbandian 1999). In fact, hardly any attempt has been made to try to integrate these views or to suggest they may stem from one another. The "two hats for one lady" image inclines to this integration, but it is also less frequently developed and needs more extensive explanation and elaboration. According to this image, responsiveness and collaboration are inherently related. They designate different points on a continuum of G&PA—citizen interaction that are constantly shifting and being reframed with time and social events. Thus, a framework of interaction with citizens is better presented here by one evolutionary continuum (one lady) of public administration. Along this continuum, responsiveness and collaboration are only different "hats" on one line of symmetry.

INTERACTING WITH CITIZENS: AN EVOLUTIONARY CONTINUUM

Figure 31.1 presents an evolutionary continuum of the role of citizens, G&PA authorities, and their reciprocal interaction as it advances with the years. Along this line, citizens may be seen as subjects, voters, clients or customers, partners, or owners. Moving along the continuum, I also observe G&PA as rulers, trustees, managers, partners, or subjects. Stemming from these are five types of interactions between G&PA and citizens. These profiles circle through coerciveness, delegation, responsiveness, collaboration, and back to coerciveness, but this time it is of a different type, namely, citizenry coerciveness. The profiles overlap, indicating the progress and development of interactions are frequently characterized by coexistence of profiles and a gradual decline of the former before the latter (Weikert 2001, 362).

Coerciveness

The old generation of public administration treated *citizens as subjects,* where leaders and administrators held almost absolute power and control over the people. Citizens, for their part, accepted the unlimited tyranny of the state and made only a minimal effort to sound their voices in such an unreceptive environment. The kinds of services delivered to the people were limited and, in any case, absolutely dependent on the government's will and decisions. This type of coercive interaction existed for ages, until the mid- or late-eighteenth century (Fredrickson 1997; Marshall 1950). In many respects, it still predominates in the "popular democracies" or dictatorial states of the second and third world in our era. In both cases, centralized power in governance is accompanied by rigorous bureaucratic structures and is mostly a result of nondemocratic culture. Such a culture imposes a G&PA monopoly on national resources through armed force and dominance of education and socialization systems. The old, orthodox public administration controlled and

Figure 31.1 **An Evolutionary Continuum of Public Administration–Citizen Interaction**

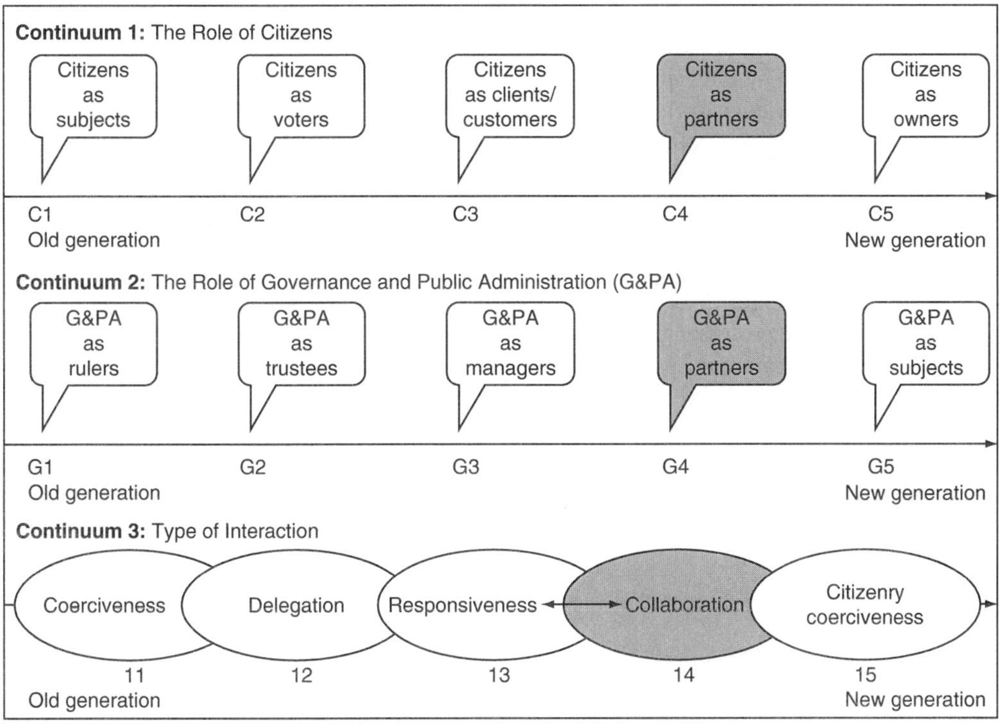

monitored many, if not all, aspects of citizens' daily lives, creating a pattern of coerciveness in the citizen-ruler relationship.

Delegation

The first institutional option for citizens' input into the process of government and society building was through the installation of the voter electoral system, better defined as democratic G&PA or an interaction of delegation. Without a doubt, democracy has created a more equal, fair, open, and flexible coexistence of citizens and rulers and has enabled the former to become active in framing the nature of governance. This is how a *citizens as voters* style emerged, and it has made a tremendous conceptual and practical change in the understanding of citizen–government relationships. Since the end of the eighteenth century, and more robustly toward the late nineteenth century, developing representative democracies of the Western world induced the idea of delegation. In a representative democracy, it was argued, citizens cannot manage their lives but count on the wisdom, experience, and civic goodwill of their representatives. Woodrow Wilson and Dwight Waldo called for a reform of G&PA and for an emphasis on specialization, professionalism, merit-based appointment and promotion, and the application of management sciences in local, state, and federal agencies. Following this, citizens were given the option of voice, but only through representatives and at wide intervals of time (between elections), with no sufficient instruments for an effective in-between influence. Nonetheless, citizens in America and in Europe initiated self-derived attempts to become more involved in administrative actions through interest groups and political parties.

Fredrickson (1997) argues that in the 1950s, "pluralism" emerged as the best term to describe the indirect connection between citizens and governments. Yet with the passage of time, it also became clear that such attempts were too few, too vague, and too slight in their impact on G&PA. The formal "open gate" for citizenry involvement did not mean that a widespread atmosphere of original participation by individual citizens or groups actually matured.

As scientific knowledge has accumulated, the theory of political participation has clarified that there are people who are unable or unwilling to participate in government or political processes, while others are simply not aware of the importance and contribution of this involvement (Verba, Schlozman, and Brady 1995). In fact, representative democracy highly contradicts the promise of vast, spontaneous citizenship involvement. Being remote from decision-making centers, by choice or not, citizens developed increased cynicism toward government and public administration systems. As Eisinger (2000) argues, "over the past decades, scholars, political pundits and elected officials have professed that cynicism has spiraled up and down . . . to the point that it has become an endemic part of the psyche in the 1980s [when] a fog of cynicism surrounds American politics, and that the 1990s are a time of unparalleled public cynicism about politics, which has continued and accelerated to this day" (55). Hence, this simple delegation type of relationship between rulers and citizens drew heavy fire from academics, professionals, public servants, and even politicians. In many respects, the need for an additional change in the nature of state-citizen interaction drove the NPM movement in the following years.

Responsiveness

Citizens as voters was only one step toward the development of the *citizens as clients/customers* model. As Rainey (1990) suggests, the 1960s and 1970s were characterized by the initiation of unsuccessful public policies in Europe and America. Over the years, efforts by governments to create extensive changes in education, welfare systems, health programs, internal security, and crime control were widely criticized for being ineffective and low performing and for misusing public budgets, while responsiveness to the real needs and demands of citizens was paltry. The crisis in practical public policy implementation, together with citizens' increased cynicism toward G&PA, generated rich scholarly activity aimed at creating useful alternatives for improved policy in various social fields as well as in the administrative processes in general (Peters 1999). Voters expressed their dissatisfaction with governors and, hand-in-hand with the academic community, called for extensive reforms in government. This call produced a large number of working papers, articles, and books that portrayed and targeted extensive administrative changes. One of the most inspiring works, Osborne and Gaebler's *Reinventing Government* (1992), is frequently mentioned as the unofficial starting point of such reforms, later known as NPM. According to Peters (1996), Terry (1998), and Weikert (2001), NPM is presently increasing in popularity in North America and across the world, and many governments are adopting ideas and recommendations that have proven beneficial in the continuous implementation of this strategy.

True enough, the NPM approach suggests a different type of interaction between citizens and rulers in democracies. However, the roots of such interactions can be found nearly a century ago. For example, Weikert (2001) asserts that "the ideas behind NPM are not new" and that "NPM builds on a long history of using business practices in government and reflects a resurgence of old ideas about the form and functions of government" (362). During the first years of the twentieth century, reformers and business leaders demanded greater accountability in local government, and many politicians and public officers turned to business principles to improve government activities, invigorate performance, and decrease corruption. However, the vision of NPM is also far different from the old business-guided governance because it aspires to decrease government size and lower its involvement in citizens' lives. NPM relies on the theory of the marketplace and on a business-like culture in public organizations. For example, in an extensive review of NPM literature, Hays and Kearney (1997) find five core principles of this approach: (1) downsizing—reducing the size and scope of government; (2) managerialism—using business protocols in government; (3) decentralization—moving decision making closer to the service recipients; (4) debureaucratization—restructuring government to emphasize results rather than processes; and (5) privatization—directing the allocation of government goods and services to outside firms (Weikert 2001). All of these principles are mutually related, relying heavily on the theory of the private sector and on business philosophy, but they are aimed at minimizing the size and scope of government activities. Integrated with ideas rooted in political economy, they became applicable for public-sector institutions (Farnham and Horton 1995).

Stemming from these above principles, a major belief among NPM advocates is that G&PA encourages a view whereby citizens are clients and customers of the public sector, while G&PA is perceived as managers of large bureaucracies. According to this outlook (Aucoin 1995; Garson and Overman 1983; Pollitt and Bouckaert 2000), the state and its bureaucratic subsystems are equivalent to a large private organization operating in an economic environment of supply and demand. In this spirit, a major goal of government is to satisfy the needs or demands of citizens, namely, to show higher responsiveness to the public as clients. In line with this, Savas (1994) argues that modern states must rely more on private institutions and less on government to satisfy the societal needs of vast populations. Hence, the goal of satisfying the needs of citizens became central to NPM legacy.

Nevertheless, NPM may be criticized for not doing enough to encourage and infuse the idea of collaboration or partnership between citizens and G&PA and for failing to apply these themes in modern managerial thinking (Vigoda and Golembiewski 2001). Unlike traditional public adminis-tration, the NPM movement focuses on citizens as sophisticated clients in complex environments. The principles of NPM cohere with theories of political economy, such as regulative policy by governments or the trend of transferring responsibilities from the state sector to the third sector. As Farnham and Horton (1995) suggest, "these ideas, and the governmental policies deriving from them, challenged the social democratic principles and values" (3) in Britain, America, and many other Western democracies. Public authorities were urged to treat the public well, not only because of their presumed administrative responsibility for quality in action, but also because of their obligation to marketplace rules and economic demands, and above all because of their fear of losing clients in a increasingly competitive, businesslike arena. In fact, while NPM has proved an advance over more classic views of public administration that see citizens as subjects or vot-ers, it is still very limited in fostering the idea of vital collaboration between citizens and G&PA, which is in the essence of democratic civil society.

In line with this, "neo-managerialism" (Terry 1998) places an additional obstacle before pro-ductive partnership that also must be recognized and isolated. According to Terry, neo-manageri-alism fosters the idea that administrative leaders should assume the role of public entrepreneurs. However, "public entrepreneurs of the neo-managerialist persuasion are oblivious to other values highly prized in the U.S. constitutional democracy. Values such as fairness, justice, representa-tion, or participation are not on the radar screen (and) this is indeed, troublesome" (200). In many respects, neo-managerialism and NPM encourage passivity among the citizenry. They impart to citizens the power of *exit* (which was virtually unavailable in the past), but at the same time they discourage use of the original power of *voice* by citizens, who may have much to contribute to their communities (Vigoda and Golembiewski 2001). Hirschman (1970) in fact suggests that exit is an economic choice, while voice is more of a political selection by individuals in and around organizational systems. Exit is also classified as a generally destructive behavior, while voice is a productive one. According to this rationality, NPM restricts and discourages the productive political voices of the people.

Recent developments in the study of NPM have focused on the responsibilities of G&PA in its interaction with citizens, but have paid far less attention to the active roles of citizens and to their obligations in the community. Most of the up-to-date NPM literature favors massive socialization of business management practices in the public sector to provide governments with better tools for policy implementation (Lynn 1998; Pollitt 1988; Pollitt and Bouckaert 2000; Rosenbloom, Goldman, and Ingraham 1994). On the other hand, these orientations and practices so far have not been integrated with another core construct of healthy democracies: genuine collaboration and partnership with citizens founded on equal opportunities for participation and massive involvement in running public life more effectively (Peters 1999). This underevaluation of the idea of partnership and collaboration, at the expense of good responding management, may be deemed a flaw in contemporary NPM theory.

TOWARD COLLABORATION AND PARTNERSHIP: A MULTIDIMENSIONAL PERSPECTIVE

Between Clients and Partners

As I have indicated, collaboration is founded on responsiveness. However, it also reaches decidedly beyond. Moreover, while greater collaboration is not a new idea in public administration, it has never fulfilled its promising potential, partly due to informal competition with businesslike strategies such as NPM. An economic interaction between managers and customers carries some basic deficiencies for modern states. The term *client,* or *customer,* which is so applicable in the private sector (that is, rational-choice theory or agency theory), contradicts the very basic notion of belonging, altruism, contribution to society, and self-derived participation in citizenry actions. When someone is defined as a client, he or she is not actively engaged in social initiatives, but is merely a passive service (or product) consumer, dependent on the goodwill and interest of the owner. While direct democracy suggests that citizens themselves "own" the state, representative democracy adds an interface to this ownership by politicians and administrators. Citizens run their lives through representatives only because they also need a "board of directors" that is professional and capable of making wise decisions for huge communities. An absolute democracy, in which every citizen is equally responsible for every single decision of the state, cannot practically survive and function in growing, expanding, and fast-moving societies (as opposed to the limited nature of the Greeks' polis).

The evolutionary process of G&PA-citizen interactions must be followed by a rational and applicable level of integration across all social players. As Figure 31.2 demonstrates, interrelationships among G&PA, citizens, and other social players are becoming a strategic goal of modern democracies on their way to a new administrative spirit (Fredrickson 1997). The old, orthodox type of public administration was characterized by a triple structure of transactions: (1) a legitimacy-services transaction between G&PA and citizens; (2) a socialization-information and human resources transaction between citizens and other social players; and (3) an authorization-criticism, knowledge, and economic goods transaction between G&PA and other social players. The new, cooperative hat of public administration, however, will be dominated by higher levels of collaboration and partnership that exceed the nature of simple transactions as presented here.

Figure 31.2 **Collaboration among Social Players: An Insight into the Next Generation**

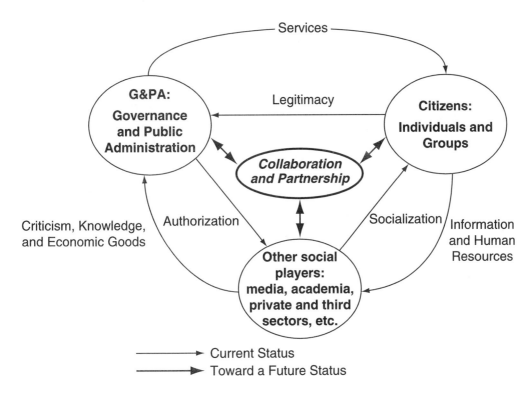

In fact, this is one core challenge for future generations. G&PA must take a step forward, going beyond elementary exchange relationships and responsiveness to demands.

This view seeks to expand on future possible trends in public administration scholarship by renewing the values of collaboration and partnership. I argue that civic society is almost unthinkable in purely rational-economic patterns. Thus, following the dimensions of new governance suggested by John et al. (1994), and somewhat enlarging them for our purposes, the discussion now elaborates on several questions: (1) *What* do collaboration and partnership actually mean? (2) *Where* are they located on the continuum of public administration evolution? (3) *Whose* responsibility is it to make the partnership possible? Consequently, (4) *how* can this productive collaboration between G&PA and citizens be achieved?

The answer to the first question is relatively simple. Three main players are identified. Above all, both G&PA and citizens have core responsibilities in this process. Contrary to the perception of responsiveness, in which G&PA holds almost exclusive power and authority and is expected to navigate among various public demands, the collaborative approach asks for extensive responsibilities and involvement on the part of the public. This can take a form of individual initiatives that seek greater participation in administrative decisions and actions or, alternatively, various kinds of organized citizenry actions (for instance, as represented by semi-organized groups or formed by the third sector). Hence, both parties (citizens and G&PA) must be actively engaged in the process of administrative change and reforms, otherwise the very essence of collaboration is spoiled. Still, in addition to these two central players there is vast room for the operation of other social units. Among these, I have chosen to expand on the role of the media and academia, but other players are relevant here as well (political parties, interest groups, constitutional and electoral institutions, and other bodies of the private sector and the third sector). As will be explained, the role of these institutions is mostly educative and is directed at enhancing socialization for citizen-G&PA collaboration.

The second question—how this collaboration may be accomplished—is more complex. It can benefit from a practical method of studying public organizations, as Golembiewski (1995) suggests. Accordingly, I will try to define and explain various operative goals to be pursued by each accountable party.

The Role of G&PA

The present starting point of G&PA-citizen relationships is not very encouraging. King, Feltey, and Susel (1998) argue that "although many public administrators view close relationships with citizens as both necessary and desirable most of them do not actively seek public involvement. If they do seek it, they do not use public input in making administrative decisions . . . [and] believe that greater citizen participation increases inefficiency, . . . delays, and red tape." Following this, Peters (1999) elaborates on the common belief that public institutions today are structured to prevent effective participation. Given this, the implications for collaboration need no further interpretation; they only emphasize the change and challenge facing modern bureaucracies of our era.

In light of this, the prime responsibility of governments and public administration is to define strategic goals that can enhance partnership with and empowerment of citizens. This partnership also must conjoin with resources that are available in the private and third sectors, which, for diverse reasons, become more willing to engage in actions for the community and for the public. To respond to the demands for effective participation by the public, these institutions may engage in future structural and cultural changes and extensively use the tool of "empowerment" by which collaboration develops. Empowerment may encourage authentic voluntary behavior by citizens that is not manipulated by the state. Governments can only stimulate environmental conditions that are necessary to generate spontaneous behavior by citizens as individuals and groups or as part of organized institutions. Programs of involvement and collaboration need to be governed by citizens and administered by practitioners who understand them. However, public-service practitioners will fulfill their duties by becoming citizens' honest advisers and helpers rather than controllers of public organizations (Box 1998, 1999; Rimmerman 1997). As previous studies suggest, several programs and techniques can be applied to achieve these goals.

First, volunteer programs in the fields of health, welfare services, education, and security need to receive national and federal support (Brudney 1990). Adequate training programs for volunteers as well as volunteer leadership and management need to be developed and implemented by professionals. Second, educational efforts that emphasize the importance of individual-level and organized entrepreneurialism may start in the very first years of school and create awareness in the very young of the high values of citizenship involvement. Without such an extensive educational effort, long-term initiatives will remain limited and incomplete. Governments will also be responsible for coordinating cooperation among different voluntary groups and institutions. This coordination may increase the efficiency of volunteer groups and third-sector organizations to get more value for effort. However, G&PA's role must not be coercive, but must remain consultative. Using their delegated authority, governments can establish public volunteers' committees to coordinate voluntary activity at the local and national levels. G&PA will maintain its advisory position, providing citizens with sufficient conditions and experience to work out their spontaneous ideas.

Public administration may become more active and entrepreneurial in the initiation of partnership between public servants and citizens. In some countries (Britain, Germany, and Australia), public servants—in contrast to governments and elected politicians—usually enjoy a less political image in the eyes of citizens, so they may gain more public trust and participation than politicians. In other countries, such as the United States, public trust can be gained differently, perhaps through higher transparency of G&PA, more involvement of the media, and communal administrative ventures that bring citizens closer to the daily administrative process. The focus of New Public Management in collaborative spheres will benefit from adjusting more vigorously to include transformation of "goodwill" into "effective operations." Public administration, through its professional cadre, can lead the operative involvement of citizens by improving the partnership between government and citizens. Investment in the spontaneous behavior of the people is low cost and economical compared with other reform efforts and thus must be encouraged (Brudney and Duncombe 1992). Another responsibility of public administration is the function of evaluation. All programs of citizens' involvement will benefit from obtaining continuous evaluation by unbiased professionals. These can be found in academia or in the private sector.

The Role of Citizens

First, it is important to define who are the citizens that are requested to join leaderships in taking progressive initiatives for the public good. Box (1998, 73–74) identifies three types of citizens, classified along a continuum of their desire to affect rulers' actions and public policy processes. (1) "Freeriders" are considered consumers of public services who receive public goods gratis and let others do the work of citizenship; (2) "activists," by contrast, are deeply involved in public life and in citizenship actions for the community; and (3) "watchdogs," in the middle of the continuum, are involved only in key issues that are relevant to themselves personally. According to this classification, Box (1998) further suggests that public administration of our time denotes partnership with citizens. Practically and theoretically, G&PA mostly encourages the freeriders and perhaps some of the watchdogs. They do not, however, elaborate on the significance of activists, who are the most natural partners in launching high-quality administrative endeavors. Nonetheless, activists are few in modern societies. Even the most optimistic estimates by scholars in the field of participatory democracy affirm that their proportion is less than 10 percent of the population (Almond and Verba 1963; Verba, Schlozman, and Brady 1995). Still, the political and social influence of this relatively small group is immense and must not be underestimated. Practically and ideologically, this vanguard paves the way for potential social changes, whatever these may be. Collaboration of G&PA with these people, as individuals or as groups, may also lead others to join. The growing activity of the third sector is perhaps one positive signal in this direction. According to O'Connell (1989), voluntary organizations and the third sector constitute about 10 percent of the economic volume of all governmental activities in the United States, and these numbers (including numbers of volunteers) continue to grow.

Supported by rapidly growing academic interest and practical ventures, the promising potential of reciprocal linkage and collaboration between G&PA and citizens can be further developed. In this linkage, citizens have several roles. The most elementary is active participation in running their lives and managing their communities. This role is momentous, so it should not be left solely in the hands of politicians or even professional public servants. It can be accomplished on several levels: individual, group, or institutional (Vigoda and Golembiewski 2001). Participation in neighborhood associations or voluntary groups to aid the young, the elderly, or other sections of the population; active involvement in citizens' committees; involvement in parents' committees at schools; donating money, time, or effort for charity or equivalent social goals; development of community services in various manners; and encouraging others to take part in such activities—all are worthy missions that allow continuous partnership among the people in administrative processes. In addition, citizens have a duty to voice constructive criticism of the public system to encourage a culture of accountability and to provide feedback for politicians and public servants, thereby increasing their responsiveness and sense of responsibility. This can be achieved through original civic journalism, letters to newspapers, public officials, and politicians, radio and television programs, and use of computerized media to spread knowledge and attitudes. The educational system has the power to teach the youngest to become more involved and to use these methods more extensively. This way, civic involvement may resound when children grow up and become adult citizens with formal rights and duties. Thus, citizens, like other social players, serve as socialization agents of partnership. They have an educational mission to contribute increased motivation and furnish values of involvement in future generations. It is well within their power to promote understanding of shared responsibilities within social life.

Lastly, it would be naive to seek large-scale political participation (Almond and Verba 1963; Verba, Schlozman, and Brady 1995) and vast self-derived mobilization by citizens without creating the necessary conditions for such involvement. People have a duty to become engaged in collaborative activities with G&PA but, as mentioned earlier, G&PA has the greater duty to create conditions for such involvement by all available means. Moreover, the voyage to increased collaboration between citizens and G&PA can become calmer and much more effective when the media and academia join in the effort.

The Role of the Media and Academia

Fox and Miller (1997) suggest that "public policy discourse has entered an era of media-driven hyperreality, becoming detached from the lived experience of the polity" (64). The media in free democracies bear responsibility for promoting accountability to citizens. To achieve this goal, the media seek increased transparency of governmental institutions. This important task advances a legitimate debate between citizens and government about how public resources are spent and whether responsibilities are properly shared to increase the public good. Despite its considerable limitations, the positive elements of "loop democracy" (Fox and Miller 1995) cannot be realistic without active, independent, and responsible media.

However, the media have other roles as well. Their primary responsibility is to serve as an effective and reliable communication channel between citizens and governments, one that promotes collaboration and partnership. The media are a powerful tool exercising immense influence over people's attitudes and opinions. This power can be used to encourage citizen involvement and participation in a variety of ways, but also to extend administrative willingness to consult citizens on relevant policy decisions. The promotion of this goal on public television and radio channels as well as computerized networks is subject to policy makers' decisions. Citizens who are aware of their power may demand greater involvement by the public media in covering entrepreneurial actions and in generating favorable public opinion about supportive community activities. The media may also encourage public recruitment to collaborative activities by means of educational programs. Regarding private media, newspapers, and computer networks, citizens' power may be aimed directly at the business telecommunication firms, using the collective strength of consumer groups and general public opinion. This is an important way in which responsiveness can work in the service of collaboration.

Another important player in these processes is academia. The contribution of the management and administration sciences to G&PA-citizen collaboration and partnership is twofold. First, by pointing out theoretical considerations, conceptual grounding, and practical means for cooperation, managerial science promotes the understanding of mutual social efforts. This knowledge is crucial for isolating and cultivating the benefits of partnership. It also highlights its advantages over a simple state of competition, which is a major construct of economics-based systems or a responsiveness-based interaction. Second, when reconfirmed by the power of science, the discussion on collaboration takes priority over other issues in social affairs. The public agenda becomes more sensitive to issues of partnership and their growth value. This way, the managerial and administrative sciences also promote legitimization of cooperation and encourage more individuals to participate in public management enterprises. Scientific confirmation of the actual benefits of collaborative actions fosters their acceptance in the eyes of both citizens and rulers, which, in the long run, may establish them more solidly in state culture.

THE NEXT GENERATION: COLLABORATION—ONE STEP BEYOND RESPONSIVENESS

Looking toward the future of G&PA, Ott (1998) argues that "traditional bureaucracy is not an adequate form of governmental organization" and that "the questions now are not whether government bureaucracies should be reformed but whether it is possible to govern through traditional bureaucratic government structures, whether traditional bureaucratic structures can be reformed enough so that we could govern through them and, which of the many alternative models being proposed would be best suited to governing the United States" (540). This article suggests that traditional structures of G&PA face reforms that are based on an evolutionary continuum. Such reforms will create a different and more flexible model of governing that combines responsiveness, collaboration, and the ideal type of citizens' ownership.

So far, treating citizens as clients of the public system has definitely worked for the benefit of bureaucracies by illuminating some neglected dimensions in G&PA-citizen relationships. Among these improvements are (1) the assumption of greater responsibility by G&PA toward citizens; (2) accountability in and transparency of the public-sector operation; (3) the idea that governments' actions must be continuously monitored to ensure high efficiency, effectiveness, and better economic performance; and (4) recognition that the government's power must depend principally on citizens' support, voice, and satisfaction with the services they receive.

However, in this article, it is argued that some adjustment must be made in the process of running modern states by the new generation of public administration. In fact, this view is much in line with the discourse theory of Fox and Miller (1995). In their stimulating book *Postmodern Public Administration: Toward Discourse,* these authors develop an alternative philosophy for both the institutionalist/constitutionalist and communitarianism approaches to G&PA-citizen relationships. Instead, they render a synthetic (not analytic) idea that the public sphere is an energy field in which mixed interests and explanations of reality coexist despite deep contradictions. According to Fox and Miller (1995, 101), the discipline of public administration, in theory and in practice, is facing a *paradigm shift* from bureaucracy (the orthodox type) to public energy fields (the future "new" type). The discourse theory is built on the public energy explanation, which paves the way for a new model for public administration and policy.

Moreover, while according to Fox and Miller (1995), representative democracy is neither representative nor democratic, it is definitely here to stay. In such a system, citizens cannot and do not want to be in the position of owners in a citizenry coerciveness type of interaction. Citizens give up ownership of G&PA because of restraints impelled by the structure and culture of modern states. Thus, citizens as owners, defined on my continuum as "citizenry-coerciveness" interaction, is an "ideal type of democracy," one that must remain *ideal* but can never be implemented practically. Citizens are unwilling—perhaps incapable—of becoming practical owners of the state even if they are the real owners by all democratic and business criteria. Still, they resist being treated as subjects or even as simple voters, as is usually accepted in the old, orthodox type of G&PA. They generally seek practical flexibility between the role of clients and customers and the position of equal partners. G&PA, at the other extreme, moves between the roles of manager and the proposed mission as citizens' partners. In the last decade, many G&PA systems in America and abroad have gladly adopted the role of managing citizens' lives, and they do so from a businesslike standpoint. In the coming decades, they are likely to face citizens' demands to treat them as equal partners. This shift forward is expected to be less readily adopted by G&PA.

The suggestion, then, is that a better definition of the G&PA-citizen relationship must rely on the conception of collaboration and partnership, if not citizenry ownership and control. Put another way, "government will continue to govern . . . but the more authentic the encounters with citizens will be, the less will government be 'they' and the more will it be 'we'" (Fox and Miller 1995, 128). Hence, this article has attempted to fill a conceptual and practical gap between perceptions of responsiveness and the quest for productive partnership by citizens, state administrators, politicians, and other social players such as the media and academia. I portrayed a normative possible interaction among these players in an evolving marketplace arena that will become even more turbulent in the future. The administrative-democratic turmoil will lead to growing and serious risks of citizens' alienation, disaffection, skepticism, and increased cynicism toward governments. Such trends are already intensifying, and only a high level of cooperation among all parties in society may guard against these centrifugal forces. Thus, the new generation of public administration will need a different spirit, perhaps a combination of communitarianism, institutionalism, and energism—but in any case, one that successfully fosters *mutual effort*. This movement from a "they" spirit to a "we" spirit is perhaps the most important mission of public administration in our era.

ACKNOWLEDGMENTS

The author wishes to thank three anonymous reviewers for their helpful comments and suggestions.

REFERENCES

Almond, Gabriel A., and Sydney Verba. 1963. *The Civic Culture: Political Attitudes and Democracy in Five Nations: An Analytic Study.* Boston, MA: Little, Brown, and Co.
Aucoin, Peter. 1995. *The New Public Management: Canada in Comparative Perspective.* Montreal, Quebec: IRPP, Ashgate Publishing Company.
Berman, Evan M. 1997. Dealing With Cynical Citizens. *Public Administration Review* 57(2): 105–12.
Box, Richard C. 1998. *Citizen Governance: Leading American Communities into the 21st Century.* Thousand Oaks, CA: Sage Publications.
———. 1999. Running Governments Like a Business: Implications for Public Administration Theory and Practice. *American Review of Public Administration* 29(1): 19–43.
Brudney, Jeffrey L. 1990. *Fostering Volunteer Programs in the Public Sector: Planning, Initiating, and Managing Voluntary Activities.* San Francisco, CA: Jossey-Bass.
Brudney, Jeffrey, and William D. Duncombe. 1992. An Economic Evaluation of Paid, Volunteer, and Mixed Staffing Options for Public Services. *Public Administration Review* 52(5): 474–81.
Callahan, Kathe, and Mark Holzer. 1994. Rethinking Governmental Change: New Ideas, New Partnership. *Public Productivity and Management Review* 17(3): 201–14.
Chi, Keon S. 1999. Improving Responsiveness. *Public Administration Review* 59(3): 278–80.
Collin, Sven-Olof. 1998. In the Twilight Zone: A Survey of Public—Private Partnership in Sweden. *Public Productivity and Management Review* 21(3): 272–83.

Department of Health and Social Security (DHSS). 1979. *Patients First.* London: Her Majesty's Stationary Office.

Eisinger, Robert M. 2000. Questioning Cynicism. *Society* 37(5): 55–60.

Etzioni, Amitai. 1994. *The Spirit of Community.* New York: Touchstone.

———. 1995. *New Communitarian Thinking: Persons, Virtues Institutions, and Communities.* Charlottesville, VA: Virginia University Press.

Farnham, David, and Sylvia Horton, eds. 1995. The Political Economy of Public Sector Change. In *Managing the New Public Services,* edited by David Farnham and Sylvia Horton, 3–26. Basingstoke: Macmillan.

Fox, Charles J., and Hugh T. Miller. 1995. *Postmodern Public Administration: Toward Discourse.* Thousand Oaks, CA: Sage Publications.

———. 1997. The Depreciating Public Policy Discourse. *American Behavioral Scientist* 41(1): 64–89.

———. 2001. The Epistemic Community. *Administration and Society* 32(6): 668–85.

Fredrickson, H. George. 1982. The Recovery of Civism in Public Administration. *Public Administration Review* 42(6): 501–09.

———. 1997. *The Spirit of Public Administration.* San Francisco, CA: Jossey-Bass.

Garson, David G., and Samuel E. Overman. 1983. *Public Management Research in the United States.* New York: Praeger.

Gidron, Benjamin, Ralph M. Kramer, and Lester M. Salamon, eds. 1992. *Government and the Third Sector.* San Francisco, Ca: Jossey-Bass.

Glaister, Stephen. 1999. Past Abuses and Future Uses of Private Finance and Public—Private Partnership in Transport. *Public Money and Management* 19(3): 29–36.

Golembiewski, Robert T. 1995. *Practical Public Management.* New York: Marcel Dekker.

Golembiewski, Robert T., and Eran Vigoda. 2000. Organizational Innovation and the Science/Craft of Management. In *Current Topics in Management,* vol. 5, edited M.A. Rahim, R.T. Golembiewski, and K.D. Mackenzie, 263–80. Greenwich, CT: JAI Press.

Grubbs, Joseph W. 2000. Can Agencies Work Together? Collaboration in Public and Nonprofit Organizations. *Public Administration Review* 60(3): 275–80.

Hart, David. 1997. A Partnership in Virtue among All Citizens: The Public Service and the Civic Humanist Tradition. *International Journal of Public Administration* 20(4,5): 967–80.

Hays, Steven W., and Richard C. Kearney. 1997. Riding the Crest of a Wave: The National Performance Review and Public Management Reform. *International Journal of Public Administration* 20(1): 11–40.

Hirschman, Albert O. 1970. *Exit, Voice and Loyalty.* Cambridge, MA: Harvard University Press.

Hughes, Owen, E. 1994. *Public Management and Administration.* London: Macmillan.

John, Dewitt, Donald F. Kettl, Barbara Dyer, and Robert W. Lovan. 1994. What Will New Governance Mean for the Federal Government? *Public Administration Review* 54(2): 170–76.

Kettl, Donald F., and H. Brinton Milward, eds. 1996. *The State of Public Management.* Baltimore, MD: Johns Hopkins University Press.

King, Cheryl S., Kathryn M. Feltey, and Bridget O. Susel. 1998. The Question of Participation: Toward Authentic Public Participation in Public Administration. *Public Administration Review* 58(4): 317–26.

Lynn, Laurence E. 1998. The New Public Management: How to Transform a Theme into a Legacy. *Public Administration Review* 58(3): 231–37.

Marshall, Thomas H. 1950. *Citizenship and Social Class and Other Essays.* Cambridge, UK: Cambridge University Press.

Nalbandian, John. 1999. Facilitating Community, Enabling Democracy: New Roles for Local Government Managers. *Public Administration Review* 59(3): 187–97.

National Consumer Council. 1986. *Measuring Up: Consumer Assessment of Local Authority Services.* London: National Consumer Council.

O'Connell, Brian. 1989. What Voluntary Activity Can and Cannot Do for America. *Public Administration Review* 49(5): 486–91.

Osborne, David, and Ted Gaebler. 1992. *Reinventing Government.* New York: Plume.

Ott, Steven. 1998. Government Reform or Alternatives to Bureaucracy? Thickening, Tides and the Future of Governing. *Public Administration Review* 58(6): 540–45.

Palfrey, Colin, C. Phillips, P. Thomas, and D. Edward. 1992. *Policy Evaluation in the Public Sector: Approaches and Methods.* Hants: Avenbury.

Pateman, Carol. 1970. *Participation and Democratic Theory.* London: Cambridge University Press.

Peters, B. Guy. 1996. *The Future of Governing: Four Emerging Models.* Kansas City, KS: University Press of Kansas.

———. 1999. *American Public Policy: Promise and Performance.* New York: Seven Bridges.

Pollitt, Christopher. 1988. Bringing Consumers Into Performance Measurement. *Policy and Politics* 16(1): 77–87.

Pollitt, Christopher, and Geert Bouckaert. 2000. *Public Management Reform.* Oxford: Oxford University Press.

Pollitt, Christopher, Xavier Girre, Jeremy Lonsdale, Robert Mul, Hilkka Summa, and Marit Waerness. 1999. *Performance or Compliance?* Oxford: Oxford University Press.

Rainey, Hal. 1990. Public Management: Recent Development and Current Prospects. In *Public Administration: The State of the Discipline,* edited by Naomi B. Lynn and Aaron Wildavsky, 157–84. Chatham, NJ: Chatham House.

Rhodes, R.A.W. 1987. Developing the Public Service Orientation, or Let's Add a Soupcon of Political Theory. *Local Government Studies* 13(3): 63–73.

Rimmerman, Craig A. 1997. *The New Citizenship: Unconventional Politics, Activism, and Service.* Boulder, CO: Westview Press.

Rosenbloom, David H., Deborah D. Goldman, and Patricia W. Ingraham, eds. 1994. *Public Administration.* New York: McGraw-Hill.

Rourke, Francis E. 1992. Responsiveness and Neutral Competence in American Bureaucracy. *Public Administration Review* 52(6): 539–46.

Savas, Emanuel S. 1994. On Privatization. In *Current Issues in Public Administration,* edited by F. Lane, 404–13. New York: St. Martin's Press.

Schneider, Anne L. 1999. Public-Private Partnership in the U.S. Prison System. *American Behavioral Scientist* 43(1): 192–208.

Smith, Peter. 1993. Outcome-Related Performance Indicators and Organizational Control in the Public Sector. *British Journal of Management* 4(3): 135–51.

Stewart, John, and Stewart Ranson. 1994. Management in the Public Domain. In *Public Sector Management,* edited by D. McKevitt and A. Lawton, 54–70. London: Sage Publications.

Stivers, Camilla. 1994. *Gender Images in Public Administration: Legitimacy and the Administrative State.* Thousand Oaks, CA: Sage Publications.

Terry, Larry D. 1998. Administrative Leadership, Neo-Managerialism, and the Public Management Movement. *Public Administration Review* 58(3): 194–200.

Thomas, Palfrey, and Colin Palfrey. 1996. Evaluation: Stakeholder-Focused Criteria. *Social Policy and Administration* 30(1): 125–42.

Thompson, Andres A., Francisco B. Tancredi, and Marcos Kisil. 2000. New Partnership for Social Development: Business and the Third Sector. *International Journal of Public Administration* 23(5–8): 1359–85.

Thompson, Dennis. 1983. Bureaucracy and Democracy. In *Democratic Theory and Practice,* edited by Graeme Duncan, 235–50. Cambridge: Cambridge University Press.

Verba, Sidney, Kay L. Schlozman, and Henry E. Brady. 1995. *Voice and Equality: Civic Voluntarism in American Politics.* London: Harvard University Press.

Vigoda, Eran. 2000. Are You Being Served? The Responsiveness of Public Administration to Citizens' Demands: An Empirical Examination in Israel. *Public Administration* 78(1): 165–91.

———, and Robert T. Golembiewski. 2001. Citizenship Behavior and the Spirit of New Managerialism: A Theoretical Framework and Challenge for Governance. *American Review of Public Administration* 31(3): 273–95.

Weikert, Lynne A. 2001. The Giuliani Administration and the New Public Management in New York City. *Urban Affairs Review* 36(3): 359–81.

Winkler, Fedelma. 1987. Consumerism in Health Care: Beyond the Supermarket Model. *Policy and Politics* 15(1): 1–8.

PART 7

DIRECT CITIZEN PARTICIPATION: COMING OF AGE

> The citizen wishes . . . only to act rightly, not to know for certain; only to choose reasonably, not to reason scientifically; only to overcome conflict and secure transient peace, not to discover eternity; only to cooperate with others, not to achieve moral oneness; only to formulate common causes, not to obliterate all differences. Politics is what men do when metaphysics fails; it is not metaphysics reified as a constitution.
> —*Benjamin Barber, 1984*

Direct citizen participation is pervasive. We find examples in arenas from education to the environment, in policy processes from policy initiation through budgeting and implementation, and at all levels of government from the local to the federal. Its growth has been explosive, thanks in no small measure to the federal legislation that mandated it and the practitioners and scholars who have developed innovative techniques to accommodate it. Interactive surveys and statewide collaborative projects are just two of the new techniques that have been used successfully to enable more people to come to public judgment about the common good. Given people's inventiveness and ingenuity, there is good reason to expect that other social inventions will follow in the future.

Despite the pervasiveness and growth of direct citizen participation over the last fifty years, tensions remain. We return to those outlined in Part 1 in order to gauge how much progress has been made in dealing with them.

CHALLENGES OF DIRECT CITIZEN PARTICIPATION

The dilemma of size. Size continues to be a factor in direct citizen participation, although we find very important advances in reducing some of its drawbacks. New *social technology* has been invented that enables more citizens to be directly involved in large-group problem solving and decision making. As reviewed in Part 3, citizen collaborations now can accommodate thousands of people at one point in time. At this juncture, no upper limit to the numbers involved appears to have been reached. Careful attention to design and process issues have improved chances for success, as have new patterns of leadership and decision making. Revolutionary forms of connectedness—media, new adaptations of information and computer technology, the Internet, and the World Wide Web—are now being utilized to support the deliberative process.

One very famous example, which used some new technological advances, is the electronic town meeting for World Trade Center site planning. On July 20, 2002, as part of the civic initiative called Listening to the City, 4,300 people came together to shape the future of Lower Manhattan. New Yorkers from every walk of life participated in reviewing the six plans that had been developed for the reconstruction of the World Trade Center site. The nonprofit AmericaSpeaks designed the format, called 21st Century Town Meeting, to accommodate over 4,000 people who sat in groups of ten, with a facilitator and a laptop computer at each table, and an electronic polling keypad for each person (Lukensmeyer and Brigham, 2002). Nearly 1,000 staff and volunteers supported the event. They came from every state in the union, as well as five countries, to volunteer their services. As part of the design, participants heard presentations about the six plans and then deliberated with their table group about what they had heard. Facilitators worked with each table to ensure participants listened and learned from one another. Each table then submitted its views through a wireless laptop computer that was linked to others in the room. Neutral analysts, called the "theme team," reviewed the comments from the hundreds of tables and identified the strongest themes coming from the deliberations. The theme team, in a matter of minutes, reported back the results of the deliberations to the participants in the meeting room on a dozen large screens. Participants then used their polling keypad to prioritize the themes and to give feedback to the theme team and the public officials. A two-week online dialogue with 818 people in 26 small groups followed, allowing people who could not attend to discuss the issues and review proposals. The results of this innovative program, Listening to the City, had a profound impact on the rebuilding process. Public officials rejected the original six site plans, went back to the drawing board, and identified six new design teams who were charged with developing plans based on criteria set forth by participants. Thus, with this very important example, we see how dialogue and deliberation can be married with computer and information technology to deal with the serious problems of scale.

The dilemma of excluded or oppressed groups. Federal legislation gave some voice to excluded and oppressed groups in the 1960s, but for many, the involvement was short-lived due to changing mandates and regulations that reduced the level of their initial participation. These groups were further disadvantaged because they lacked the resources that would enable them to take time off to join deliberations with more affluent citizens. To bridge the economic divide, at least during regulatory hearings, some assistance was provided in the way of financial aid to help defray the cost of obtaining legal counsel, expert witnesses, necessary documentation, and the actual reimbursement of participation expenses (Paglin and Shor, 1977; Aron, 1979), although these efforts were not widespread throughout government. As noted in Part 3, there has been some success in bringing disadvantaged groups into public deliberations with public officials through the use of interactive surveys that draw random samples of the population. But as society becomes more reliant on information and computer technology to conduct these surveys, it will be important to guard against other divides—those between the information rich and the information poor, between the computer literate and the computer illiterate. The educational divide among citizens also continues to be a source of concern. Many citizens feel intimidated and discouraged from participating because they lack the information and knowledge to consider complex policy issues. Inviting everyone to the table as coequals in a learning process, and giving them the tools and resources they need to be successful, is one of the greatest challenges of direct citizen participation.

A very encouraging demonstration of how social technology could be utilized as a leveling device is the World Trade Center deliberation on reconstruction. When advance registration numbers revealed under-representation of certain demographic and geographic groups, organizers of the 21st Century Town Meeting were able to increase the numbers by directly contacting community neighborhoods and encouraging people to participate. The result was roughly an equal representation of men and women, and a good mixture of age groups, with the exception of youth. (The youth had a much higher participation rate in the online dialogue that followed the event.) Although racial diversity did not match the regional census, it was notable: 14 percent of participants identified themselves as "mixed racial heritage" or "other," 12 percent as Asian, 10 percent as Hispanic, 7 percent as African American, and 67 percent as Caucasian (Lukensmeyer and Brigham, 2002). Equally important, the expert facilitation at each table leveled the playing field by ensuring that all participants had the same information, the same access to subject matter experts who were present to answer their questions, and the same opportunity to be heard.

The dilemma of risk. The risks from complex technology are grave. Direct threats from our technology (*e.g.,* nuclear power and recombinant DNA) and indirect threats from the by-products of the technology (*e.g.,* pollution, environmental degradation) pose hazards to everyone. As Jack DeSario and Stuart Langton (1984) point out, "Never before has mankind had the imminent capability to achieve such radical constructive and destructive alterations of society" (p. 223). However, setting up the incentives and decision processes so that these issues can be dealt with equitably has been a subject of much debate. Early direct citizen participation efforts tended to focus on social issues such as civil rights, housing, urban renewal, education, and social services. It was only in the 1970s with the environmental and consumer movements that direct citizen participation began to collide with technological establishment over issues of risk and the distribution of hazards. The NIMBY opposition got its start in these encounters and continues unabated today, although the oppressed and excluded groups have not been heavily represented in these movements. One mechanism that could be utilized in the future is Paolo Freire's (1970) *conscientizaco,* or "critical consciousness," a method of civic education developed in Brazil. It involves dialogue among oppressed people to help them discover the social injustices they are experiencing and to encourage the collaborative action necessary to transform their situations. Interest-group politics and adversarial legalism, characteristic of the U.S. system (Kagan, 1991; Kelman, 1992), have made critical consciousness a less attractive option in the past. However, its emphasis on civic education, dialogue, and learning makes it a process worthy of exploration in the future.

The dilemma of technology and expertise. The federal government acquired a central role in the development, application, and regulation of new technologies (DeSario and Langton, 1984). When sophisticated technologies outgrew Congress's ability to oversee them, new professional bureaucracies developed to serve in its stead. Private organizations experienced a simultaneous expansion of specialists and experts. Together, the two sectors eventually created a new "technostructure" of professionals who were expected to apply their specialized theories, models, and procedures to solving societal problems (DeSario and Langton, 1984). However, the limits of expert decision making began to surface. Scientific experts, good at achieving objectives, were not particularly good at defining them. Moreover, the science they espoused did not preclude them from making value choices in the name of objectivity and neutrality. As the public became more uneasy about technology and expert power, especially as the failures of technology became more apparent (*e.g.,* Love Canal, Three Mile Island, Agent Orange), citizens began to demand greater participation in complex technological issues such as air and water management, control of hazardous wastes, nuclear power and DNA research (DeSario and Langton, 1984). Yet the match between citizens and experts does not necessarily produce a level playing field. As Zimmerman notes, "nuclear power provides the prototypical example of technological authoritarianism" (Zimmerman, 1995:89). We lack the structures and procedures to integrate technocratic and democratic contributions. To the extent the deliberative processes described in Part 3 continue to unite experts and citizens in collaborative problem solving and decision making, then we can say with some confidence that progress is being made in addressing the dilemma of technology and expertise.

To the extent that these two groups fall back into their separate corners, then technocracy and democracy will continue to be the "chief protagonists in the technological struggle" (DeSario and Langton, 1984, p. 224).

The dilemma of time. A constant criticism of direct citizen participation is that it takes too much time. The business of government requires expeditious treatment, especially during crises when "split-second" decisions have to be made. The more people who are involved in some decisions process, the harder it is to act with dispatch. True, it is more difficult to make decisions as the number of people increases. However, this argument has less sway when we examine the cases that employed direct citizen participation to address budget problems (Roberts, 1997; Weeks, 2000). Not only were large-scale public deliberations effective in cutting budgets, they also were instrumental in maintaining civility throughout the process. As long as there was some latitude in terms of time—four months in one case at the local level—then direct citizen participation was found to be a viable option. When we factor in the argument that time is money, and that public deliberations are expensive with all the planning, facilitation, staff and resources needed to support them, we still have to consider what it costs *not* to have public deliberations. There is the potential for implementation disruptions and failures, costly litigation when citizens challenge administrative decisions, not to mention lost good will and opportunities for social learning. So unless these long-term costs are factored in, the counter-argument can easily be made that the dilemma of time is more of an issue for those who want to retain their administrative prerogatives rather than build a community of citizens who need to learn how to make hard choices in a resource-constrained world.

Related to the dilemma of time is the nature of the problem under consideration. "Hard" problems take more time for consideration. Siting a toxic waste facility, cutting a budget, and strategically planning for the future all are good examples of these types of problems. Often referred to as "wicked problems" (Rittel and Webber, 1973; Fischer, 1993; Roberts, 2001), their formulations are ambiguous and inconclusive, their resolutions are imperfect and temporary, and their criteria for judgment are difficult to assess independently of the social actors involved (Day, 1997). These intractable problem situations do not lend themselves to technical resolution and routine decision making. They require tradeoffs and value choices among competing options and solutions. Growing numbers of social scientists (*e.g.,* Gray, 1989; Chrislip and Larson, 1994; Huxham, 1996; Chisholm, 1998; Susskind, *et al.,* 1999; Mandell, 2001; Sullivan and Skelcher, 2002; Straus, 2002) have concluded that the only way to cope with wicked problems is through "increased doses of participation" (Day, 1997, p. 430). Collaborations among citizens, experts, and administrators over strategic plans, budgeting, and environmental concerns in Parts 3 and 4 of this volume certainly give evidence that this strategy can be effective. Citizens often expressed appreciation for the opportunity to be directly involved in policy matters that they considered to be relevant and important. Rather than criticize direct citizen participation for its inability to be efficient in crisis situations (and that criticism may not stand when all the long-term costs and consequences are factored into the equation), it may be just as important to assess its effectiveness in coping with wicked problems. Although direct citizen participation *takes* time, it also *affords* time for meaningful dialogue and deliberations. Indeed, proactive citizen involvement may be just what is needed to prevent wicked problems from becoming crises in the future.

The dilemma of the common good. The issue of the common good is not just about direct citizen participation. It is about *direct, deliberative citizen participation*—the ability of citizens to reason together and to come to public judgments with their peers in *face-to-face meetings* about issues of public concern. We know that a number of trends are threatening this ability. Although citizen access and personal involvement may be on the rise with the growing use of public initiatives, referenda, public opinion polls, and teledemocracy, these techniques aggregate individual interests, they do not enable direct contact and interaction. Traditional mechanisms for citizen participation—party involvement, voluntary associations, and membership in advisory and advocacy groups—have the potential to be deliberative, but they usually are not (Fishkin, 1991; 1997). In terms of civic engagement, there has been movement from direct toward indirect participation in civic organizations as professional staffs are hired and citizens become dues-paying members who substitute money for time. Some, in fact, have referred to the period of 1930 through 1995 as the "bureaucratization of civic engagement" (Skocpol and Farina, 1999). Additionally, as nonprofit agencies sign on to deliver social services through partnerships, alliances, joint ventures, and networks, these arrangements that professionalize and privatize civic life center on the efficiencies of production rather than the deliberation of public concerns. The question that prompts much discussion and debate is where is the *public space* where citizens can directly reason and learn with one another about issues of public interest?

The new participatory mechanisms such as large-group collaborations introduced in Parts 3 and 4 belie these trends and give evidence that it is possible to create a public space for social learning even in complex, modern societies.[1] The King et al. (1998) evaluation study in Part 5 also provides strong support for learning through deliberation and demonstrates how receptive people are to engaging in meaningful dialogue with one another. Deliberative polling, a new technique that has possibilities for the future, was mentioned in several articles. It brings together a cross sample of the electorate to deliberate over questions of public policy, aided by experts who provide the facts in language that can be understood by the layperson. The numbers of people involved in these experiments are small thus far, but measurements before and after these deliberations indicate learning among the participants does occur (Fishkin, 1991; 1997). The wonderful example of the World Trade Center deliberations, as noted above, has profound implications for large-scale deliberations. Not only did more than 4,000 citizens learn from one another, public officials also learned that when the public is deliberatively engaged, their policy recommendations can be thoughtful and substantive. And finally, the ideal of community as a living space, not just a marketplace, is very much alive in Box's (1998) work on citizen governance. He advocates rethinking the structure of local government by redefining the roles of citizens, elected officials, and administrators. The intent is to shift responsibility from the professionals and elected representatives to the citizen through new mechanisms such as the coordinating council, citizens' boards, and the "helper" role for public service practitioners. These and other recommendations for change, along with the evidence collected in this volume, indicate that the search for a "space" to deliberate about the common good still motivates a great deal of creative thinking and action. While not conclusive, these are hopeful signs and positive avenues for experimentation in the future.

NEXT STEPS

Direct citizen participation captivates our attention and imagination. There is something very seductive about the idea that people ought to be directly involved in the decisions that affect their lives. Despite the warnings of its dangers, limitations, impracticality, and expense, especially in large, complex, heterogeneous, technologically advanced twenty-first century societies, it still remains an ideal that animates many of our theories and beliefs. Its appeal continues to attract and fascinate us.

The practice of direct citizen participation is another matter. We struggle to ensure that our public deliberations are inclusive of all citizens, not just a subset. Our ability to organize, plan, and deliberate with thousands of people strains the limits of our social technology. We are in a continual search for new practices and techniques that enable us to be directly involved in a way that creates a public space for learning while at the same does not hinder the work of government. The disappointments and failures in direct citizen participation over the last fifty years have been well chronicled.

The gap between our ideal and its practice, rather than deter us, appears to have energized us. Over the last decade, there has been a surge in the number of books and articles written on the subject of direct citizen participation, dialogue, deliberation, collaboration, and the use of information technology to support the democratic process. Creative experiments with direct citizen participation are occurring in the field in increasing numbers. The deliberative democratic project, our "social experiment," is still very much alive. Although the tensions still plague us, the articles document that substantial progress has been made in coping with them.

The next steps in this journey will proceed on two interrelated paths. The first path compels us to track and evaluate what innovative practitioners in the field are doing. Social technology (designing and managing large groups of people for deliberative problem solving and decision making) is advancing at a rapid rate thanks to their inventiveness and creativity. Practitioners are energized, and as two innovators behind Listening to the City have commented: "The values are there, the strategies are there, the people are there. It is simply up to all of us to make it happen" (Lukensmeyer and Bringham 2002, p. 365).

Scholars have a role to play in these evaluations. A number of critical questions need to be addressed:

- Do the public deliberations involve substantive issues of concern to the public? Are the problems "wicked" enough to warrant the expenditures of public resources that will be required to plan, conduct, and follow up on the deliberations and integrate their results into government problems solving and decision making?
- How are participants selected? Are all individuals and groups invited, and do they attend and actively participate?
- Does the process enable participants to learn from one another, and what is it they learn? Do citizens' views of their fellow participants change as a result of these deliberations, and, if so, how do they change?
- Does the social technology used to organize the deliberations level the playing field among the participants and provide everyone with the resources, information, and expert support that they need to come to public judgments?
- What do the public officials learn from participants? To what extent does the deliberative process affect their roles as public officials? How do their views of citizens change as a result of the deliberative process?
- Do public deliberations achieve their stated intentions? Do the outcomes inform new policy and procedures?
- Do those *not in attendance* trust the outcomes of the deliberative process? The general citizenry will want to know that these efforts are credible and truly represent an attempt to learn and discover about the common good rather than be used as another platform for interest-group politics, behind the scenes manipulations, or a cover for decisions already made.
- Do the outcomes of these deliberations have the potential for unintended consequences, and, if so, is there an attempt to consider what they might be and how one might deal with them?
- Can new information and computer technology be *a substitute for* face-to-face deliberations,[2] or can they only be used as *a support for* face-to-face deliberations?

The second path, related to the first, requires better theory building about direct, deliberative citizen participation, especially as it pertains to administration. The least developed area of all the topics addressed in this volume, it needs careful attention from scholars. Theory building can proceed on many different levels as we saw in Part 6. At the micro level, it would be helpful to know what motivates citizens to participate. What keeps them invested in social learning and direct, deliberative participation? What discourages them from being engaged? Knowing when and how citizens learn also would be important. For example, is it possible for all citizens to listen, learn, and solve problems together, no matter what their backgrounds, personal characteristics, educations, and situations? What enhances their learning and what inhibits it?

At the group level, it would be useful to have better theory on how deliberative groups function. What type of leadership enables this learning, and what are the implications for public officials when they assume the role of steward of the learning process? Which design options and techniques of facilitation, organizing, and problem solving are supportive of the learning process? Does computer-assisted groupware facilitate the deliberative process, or does it distract participants' attention and impede face-to-face dialogue? Often referred to as collaborative technology, the question is whether groupware can support higher level learning activities as well as it supports administrative functions.

At the macro level, we need to understand how larger political, technological, economic, and historical forces may shape or inhibit direct, deliberative citizen participation. As other countries seek to emulate Western democratic traditions, it is important to question whether the model is applicable to those who have not had a democratic tradition or those who recently have emerged from totalitarian rule. Is the social learning process a necessary condition for democracy to take hold, or is social learning a consequence of a democratic system? If there is an evolutionary process that prepares people for the responsibilities and requirements of direct, deliberative citizen engagement, then the model might not be appropriate for all countries and situations. On the other hand, what better way to teach people how a democracy functions than to engage the citizens in problem solving and decision making about issues of importance to them?

No matter what the level of analysis, it must be remembered that central to any evaluation or theory building exercise concerning direct, deliberative citizen participation is the issue of power (Aleshire, 1972; MacNair, et al., 1983). Citizen deliberations intentionally seek to level the playing field among the participating social actors *during the deliberations*. Whatever power base individuals bring to the table, all share the right to be there, to be heard, and to be part of the learning process. Privileged status, whether it is based on expertise, money, or position, does not give some participants the right to control the agenda or the outcomes, especially when the issues are "wicked" and alternative solutions are based on values not science.

Moreover, it is important to recognize that it is not just how much power a social actor has, but it is the power distance among the social actors that is the critical variable (Kipnis, 1976; Kanter, 1977; Pfeffer, 1981). Evidence for the "power equalization" hypothesis indicates greater consensual, cooperative behavior between and among people when power is more equally distributed among them. Unequal power tends to produce exploitative actions in the more powerful, while more equal power results in more effective and collaborative outcomes (Bacharach and Lawler, 1981; Rubin and Brown, 1975). Research on conflict also supports this view. Although conflict can arise between people of equal power, the most pervasive conflict comes from dominant and subordinate groups—the "haves" and the "have-nots" (Deutsch, 1973, p. 93). Thus, power equalization, or conversely, power distance among participants, should be a central feature of future evaluations and theory-building exercises on citizen deliberations.

The two paths—evaluation and theory building—eventually converge as we attempt to understand the conditions under which direct, deliberative citizen participation is or is not appropriate. Wholesale application of direct citizen participation has not been advocated in this volume of articles, nor is it expected to be a viable option in all cases, in all situations. Rather, its use has been recommended in "wicked" situations (Rittel and Webber, 1973; Fischer, 1993; Roberts, 2001), when problem formulation is ambiguous, judgment criteria are difficult to establish, and solutions are valued-based and do not lend themselves just to technical reasoning and analysis. This is an important step, but more guidance than this is needed for public administrators who, as we saw in Part 2, are caught in a maelstrom of competing views on how to conduct the public's business. On the firing line between government and citizens, their role conflicts pull them in different directions—from being efficient, responsive professionals to being co-learners and stewards of the public trust. When should they rely on indirect citizen participation through top-down directives from legislative and executive authority, and when should they open up the problem solving process to invite more "grass-roots" citizen participation?

One possible answer comes from the "safety valve" principle (Roberts, 2003). It is suggested that direct, deliberative citizen engagement is utilized to the extent there is dissatisfaction with current government policy and procedures. The higher the level of dissatisfaction, the more likely that direct citizen engagement will be employed as a mechanism to reduce dissatisfaction levels. To be effective, however, its use must be predicated on power sharing and social learning among the participants of a deliberation. If direct involvement is used or seen to be used as a tool for the purposes of manipulation or co-optation, then the levels of dissatisfaction among participants, as well as observers, are likely to increase, setting up a cycle of instability and distrust between the government and its citizens.

No matter which theory one explores or which path one pursues in the study of direct, deliberative citizen participation, the undertaking will be complex and challenging. But for those who believe that our democracy is in trouble, that citizens' voices are muted by manipulation and moneyed interests, that adversarial democracy, by pitting citizen against citizen, threatens the commonweal and our collective future, the effort may be well worth making. For others who remain skeptical about the benefits direct citizen participation, especially its deliberative version, they owe it to themselves to observe at least one of these occasions in action. Many who witness them are awed by the fundamental wisdom of people, who, when given the chance, are able to rise to the occasion and publicly deliberate about the common good. One recent example is the New York Daily News columnist Pete Hamill, who listened to the deliberations over the World Trade Center. His words are a fitting way to end our volume of collected works and a good beginning to the next phase of the "social experiment" in direct, deliberative citizen participation.

> We came to the vast hangar at the Javits Center expecting the worst. Put 5,000 New Yorkers in a room, charge them with planning a hunk of the New York future, and the result would be a lunatic asylum. . . . None of that happened. . . . From 10 a.m. to 4 p.m. they were presented with basic issues about the rebuilding of those 16 gutted acres in lower Manhattan. At each table they debated in a sober, thoughtful civil way. They voted, offered comments, and moved on to the next item on the agenda. . . . And because the process was an exercise in democracy, not demagoguery, no bellowing idiots grabbed microphones to perform for the cameras. . . . In this room, "I" had given way to "we." Yes, the assembly was boring to look at, too serious, too grave, too well-mannered for standard TV presentation. And it was absolutely thrilling. . . . We have a word for what they were doing. The word is democracy.[3]

NOTES

1. See the research on collaboration to find other examples of participatory approaches (Gray, 1989; Chrislip and Larson, 1994; Huxham, 1996; Chisholm, 1998; Susskind, *et al.,* 1999; Mandell, 2001; Sullivan and Skelcher, 2002; Straus, 2002).

2. See the following links that are attempts to develop online dialogues without the face-to-face interaction: *Web Lab,* http://www.weblab.org/ (accessed June 8, 2007); *Information Renaissance,* http://www.info-ren. org/ (accessed June 8, 2007); and *e-thePeople,* http://www.e-thepeople.org/ (accessed June 8, 2007).

3. As quoted in Lukensmeyer and Brigham (2002, pp. 365–366).

REFERENCES

Aleshire, R.A. 1972. "Power to the People: An Assessment of the Community Action and Model Cities Experience." *Public Administration Review,* 32 (September): 428–42.

Aron, J.B. 1979. "Citizen Participation at Government Expense." *Public Administration Review,* 39(5): 477–85.

Bacharach, S.G., and E.J. Lawler. 1981. *Bargaining, Power, Tactics, and Outcomes.* San Francisco: Jossey-Bass.

Box, R.C. 1998. *Citizen Governance: Leading American Communities into the 21st Century.* Thousand Oaks, CA: Sage.

Chisholm, R.F. 1998. *Developing Network Organizations: Learning from Practice and Theory.* Reading, MA: Addison Wesley Longman.

Deutsch, M. 1973. *The Resolution of Conflict: Constructive and Destructive Processes.* New Haven: Yale University Press.

Fischer, F. 1993. "Citizen Participation and the Democratization of Policy Expertise: From Theoretical Inquiry to Practical Cases." *Policy Sciences,* 26(3): 165–88.

Freire, P. 1970. *Pedagogy of the Oppressed.* New York: Seabury Press.

Huxham, C., ed. 1996. *Creating Collaborative Advantage.* Thousand Oaks, CA: Sage.

Kagan, R.A. 1991. "Adversarial Legalism and American Government." *Journal of Policy Analysis & Management,* 10(3): 369–405.

Kanter, R.M. 1977. *Men and Women of the Corporation.* New York: Basic Books.

Kelman, S. 1992. "Adversary and Cooperationist Institutions for Conflict Resolution in Public Policymaking." *Journal of Policy Analysis & Management,* 11(2): 178–206.

Kipnis, D. 1976. *The Powerholders.* Chicago: University of Chicago Press.

Lukensmeyer, C.J., and S. Brigham. 2002. "Taking Democracy to Scale: Creating a Town Hall Meeting for the Twenty-First Century. *National Civic Review,* 91(4): 351–66.

MacNair, R.H., R. Caldwell, and L. Pollane. 1983. "Citizen Participants in Public Bureaucracies: Foul Weather Friends." *Administration & Society,* 14(4): 507–24.

Mandell, M.P., ed. 2001. *Getting Results Through Collaboration: Networks and Network Structures for Public Policy and Management.* Westport, CT: Quorum Books.

Paglin, M.D., and E. Shor. 1977. "Regulatory Agency Responses to the Development of Public Participation." *Public Administration Review,* 37(2): 140–48.

Pfeffer, J. 1981. *Power in Organizations.* New York: Pitman.

Rittel, H.W.J., and M. Webber. 1973. "Dilemmas in a General Theory of Planning." *Policy Sciences,* 4: 155–69.

Roberts, N.C. 1997. "Public Deliberation: An Alternative Approach to Crafting Policy and Setting Direction." *Public Administration Review,* 57(2): 124–32.

Roberts, N.C. 2001. "Coping with Wicked Problems: The Case of Afghanistan." In *Learning from International Public Management Reform,* ed. L. Jones, J. Guthrie, and P. Steane, Vol. II: 353–75. Amsterdam: JAI Press.

Roberts, N.C. 2003. Arenas and Forums of Citizen Participation: Building a Theory. Paper presented to the 7th National Public Management Research Conference, October 9–11, Georgetown University, Washington, DC.

Rubin, J.Z., and B.R. Brown. 1975. *The Social Psychology of Bargaining and Negotiation.* New York: Academic Free Press.

Skocpol T., and M.P. Fiorina. 1999. "Making Sense of the Civic Engagement Debate." In *Civic Engagement in American Democracy*, ed. T. Skocpol and M.P. Fiorina, 1–23. Washington, DC: Brookings Institution Press.

Straus, D. 2002. *How to Make Collaboration Work*. San Francisco: Barrett-Koehler.

Sullivan, H., and C. Skelcher. 2002. *Working Across Boundaries: Collaboration in Public Services*. New York: Palgrave/Macmillan.

Weeks, E.C. 2000. "The Practice of Deliberative Democracy: Results from Four Large-Scale Trials." *Public Administration Review*, 60(4): 360–72.

Zimmerman, A.D. 1995. "Toward a More Democratic Ethic of Technological Governance." *Science, Technology, & Human Values*, 20(1): 86–107.

INDEX

Boldface page references indicate boxed text, charts and tables.

Academia, 486–487
Active accountability, 386
Active citizenship involvement (ACI), 420–421, 424
Activists, 485
Adams-Morgan School experiment, 156–157
Adaptive approach, 212, 214–215, **214**
Administration. *See* City managers; Public administration
Administrative state model, 20, **20**
Administrators. *See* City managers; Public administration
Adonis, Andrew, 321
Advisory Commission on Intergovernmental Relations, 9, 266
Agencies, 328–329. *See also specific names*
Agnes Recovery Act (1972), 261
Agriculture and water quality Citizens Panel (1984), 270–274, 277
Allen, William H., 95–97
Almond, Gabriel A., 424
Alternative schools, 159
Altshuler, Alan A., 165–166, 172
American Assembly process, 240, 282–283
American Bar Association Project on Standards for Criminal Justice, 177–178
Anacostia School District (Washington, D.C.), 156–158
Andersen, David F., 286
Anderson, Eric, 52, 54, 56, 60
Angell, John, 170, 176
Anti-Semitism, 151
Area Wide Council (AWD), 357–363
Arendt, Hannah, 100
Aristotle, 10, 82, 317
Army Corps of Engineers, 366–367
Arnstein, Sherry R., 6–7, 86, 132–133, 270, 441, 446
Arzube, Juan, 196
ASPA Centennial Agendas Project, 38
Association for Improving the Condition of the Poor (AICP), 95
Atomic Energy Commission, 450
Auburn (Alabama) citizen survey
  background information, **246–247**, 248
  citizen and council priorities, 251–252
  conclusions, 252–253
  results, 248–251, **249, 250, 251**
Austin, David M., 338
Authentic citizen participation
  barriers to
    administrative processes, 339, 392–393
    current practices and techniques of participation, 339
    nature of life in contemporary society, 339, 390, 392
    overcoming, 394–395, **396–397**, 398–399

Authentic citizen participation *(continued)*
  current framework of participation and, 339, 387–388
  desirability of effective, 384, 386–387
  necessity of effective, 384, 386–387
  overview, 339, 383–384
  public administration and, 388–389, **389**
  reframing participation and, 388–390
  resources for information about, **384–385**
  unauthentic citizen participation versus, 390, **391**
Authority system model, 19, **20**
Aydelotte, James, 442

Bailey, Stephen K., 29–30, 33
Baker, Ernest, 6
Ball, Sir James, 116
Barber, Benjamin R., 44, 100, 207–208, 298, 421, 491
Barner, Carol, 416
Basic Car Plan (Los Angeles), 169
Battistoni, Richard, 101
Beesley, Michael, 105
Bell, Daniel, 268
Benefit-cost analysis, 206
Benhabib, Seyla, 298
Berman, Evan M., 417
Berry, Francis Stokes, 286
Biller, Robert, 43–44
Bland, R., 227
"Blueprint" approach, 121, 200–201
Bohm, D., 218
Bollen, Kenneth A., 426
Boston school reform (1970s), 157
Bottom-up approach, 240, 289, 292, **293**
Box, Richard C., 485, 495
Brady, Henry E., 422, 434, 486
Brewer, Gary, 42
Brudney, Jeffrey L., 244–245
Bruere, Henry, 95–97, 100
Bryson, John M., 294
Buchanan, William, 53, 58–59
Buckman, Fred, 290
Budget process and citizen participation. *See also* Citizen surveys in budgetary and policy-making process; International City/County Management Association (ICCMA) survey
  culture and, 122, 226–228
  institution structure and, 122, 226–228
  overview, 122, 226, 234
Bundy Plan, 147–149
Bureau of Indian Affairs, 8
Bureau of Land Management (BLM), 459–460
Bureau of Municipal Research (BMR) (New York), 93–96, 101–102

Bureaucratic Phenomenon, The (Crozier), 160
Burns, James MacGregor, 73

California Coastal Act (1972), 375, 377
California Coastal Commission hearings
    overview, 339, 374–375
    study
        citizen participation data, 378, **379**
        conclusions, 381–382
        discussion, 380–381
        findings, 377–378
        hypothesis, 376
        methodology, 376–377
        overview, 375–376
        staff recommendations, **377**, 378–380, **378**
California Department of Transportation (Caltrans),
        370–372
California Transportation Plan, 370
California's Proposition 13, 78
Caltrans, 370–372
Caravalho, George, 57
Carey, William, 82
Carnegie, Andrew, 95
Carnegie Foundation for the Advancement of Teaching,
        35
Carter, Jimmy, 27, 209
Cates, Camille, 34
Center for New Democratic Processes, 266–267, 270–274
Change, 27, 34, 44
Church, Charles, 53–54
Churchill, Winston, 315
Citizen Jury, 297
Citizen participation. *See also* Authentic citizen
        participation; Deliberative democracy; Direct
        citizen participation; Education; Indirect citizen
        participation; Police; Policy analysis; Prosecution
        and adjudication; U.S. cities survey of citizen
        participation
    active, 420–421, 424
    bridge between government and, 78, 89–90
    broad, representative, 309
    in Community Action and Model City Programs
        attitudes toward, 128
        conditions necessary, 132–133
        in future, 133–134
        implementation, 126–127
        meanings, 125–126
        objectives, 129–132
        overview, 120, 124–125
        restrictions, 127–128
        techniques, 133
    in corrections, 181–183
    definitions, 6–7, 401
    democracy and, 3
    education for, 35–36, 100–101, 395, **396–397**, 398
    effective, move toward, 331
    electronic, 240–241
    evaluating
        Caltrans and, 370–372
        overview, 339, 365
        participation questions, 365–367
        research, 367–370, **368**
    faith in, 420, 424–425
    framework
        current, 387–388, **387**
        new, 388–390

Citizen participation *(continued)*
    ideal, 308–309
    impacts, 402–403
    indirect, 3–4
    individual, 238–239
    informed, 309
    institutionalized, 243
    "ladder of participation" and, 7
    large group, 239–240
    levels of, 401–402
    mechanisms of, 237–238
    modern organizations and, 193
    Philadelphia Model Cities Program and, 356–357
    process issues, 238
    reasons for, 402, 461–465, **463**
    in regulatory decision making, 378, **379**
    small group, 239
Citizen Participation in Public Policy symposium, 9
Citizen surveys in budgetary and policy-making process.
        See also Auburn (Alabama) citizen survey; Budget
        process and citizen participation
    non-use of, 243, 245, 247–248
    overview, 238, 243, **246–247**, 252–253
    prominence of, 243
    use of, 243–245
Citizens. *See also* Citizen participation; Value-centered
        perspective
    bridge between government and, 78, 89–90
    change and, desire for, 27
    as clients, 20, **20**, 24, 474–476, 480–482
    as co-investors, 24
    as coproducers, 24
    as customers, 24, 93, 107, **109**, 480–482
    development of, 101, 395, **396–397**, 398
    empowering, 22, 395, **396–397**, 484
    government and public administration systems and,
        473
    as interest-group advocates, 20–21, **20**
    as owners, 24, 95–97, 108, **109**
    as partners, 476–478
    perspectives on, 6–7
    public administrators and, 5
    roles, 19–20, **20**, 485–486
    as social learners, **20**, 21–23
    as subjects, 19, **20**, 478–479
    types of, 7, 485
    as volunteers and coproducers, **20**, 21, 24
    as voters, 20, **20**, 479–480
Citizens Panels
    on agriculture and water quality (1984), 270–274,
        272, 277
    criteria for successful
        cost effectiveness, 269–270, 275
        effective decision making, 268, 274–275, **276**
        fair procedures, 269, 274–275, **276**
        flexibility, 270, 275
        meeting, 274–275, **276**, 277
        participant selection, 267–268, 274
        recommendations should be followed, 270,
            275, 277
    overview, 239, 266–267
    policy polling and, 208
City Beautiful Movement, 8
City hall services, 111–115
City Management Association's Future Horizons
        Committee, 59

City managers
  current
    community building, 50–53, 59
    facilitative leadership, 53–55, 59
    form of government, 55–56
    process-oriented management, 57–59
  Davis interviews, **51**
  overview, 23, 49
  in past, 49–50
  responsibilities, 60
  roles, 59–60
  values, 60–61
Citycard project, 321–322
Civic education, 35–36, 100–101, 395, **396–397**, 398
Civil society model, **20**, 21, 319
Civilian review boards, 173–174
Civism
  movement, 34–35
  origins, 27–29
  overview, 22, 26–27
  problems facing, 26–27
  recovery of
    democratic theory, 29–32
    organization theory, 32–34
  traditions, 27–29
Clark, Kenneth, 146
Cleveland, Frederick A., 95–96
Cleveland, Harlan, 27, 32
Clients, citizens as, 20, **20**, 24, 474–476, 480–482
Clinton, Bill, 63–64, 107
Coastal Zone Management Act (1972), 9
Coerciveness, 478–479
Collaboration, 217–218, **219–220**
Colleague Model, 170
Colorado River and State Water Project, 280–281
Common good, 11, 14, 494–495
Communication skills, 85–86
Community, 6, 31, 50, 67–68. *See also* Community
    control
Community Action Agencies (CAAs), 9, 124–125, 346–
    351. *See also* Study of Community Representation
    in Community Action Agencies
Community Action Programs (CAPs)
  citizen participation in
    attitudes toward, 128
    conditions necessary for, 132–133
    in future, 133–134
    implementation, 126–127
    meanings, 125–126
    objectives, 129–132
    overview, 120, 124–125
    restrictions, 127–128
    techniques, 133
  establishment of, 8–9, 120
Community-based crime prevention groups, 84–87, **87**
Community building, 50–53, 59
Community control
  Altshuler's definition of, 166
  connotation of, 88
  in education
    emergence of, 146–147
    evaluating, 151–152, **153**, 154–156, **154**
    increasing, 159–160
    institutional change and, 120, 160
    of schools, 159
  in policing, 174–175

Community Development Block Grant funds, 447
Community development programs
  learning process approach, 194, 200–201, **202**
  modernization and, 193–194, 198–200, 202–203
  overview, 120–121, 193–194
  The East Los Angeles Community Union, 194–196,
    200–203
  United Neighborhood Organization, 194–198, 200–203,
    202
Community dialogues. *See also* Deliberative democracy
  Eugene (Oregon), 300–303, **302**, 305–307
  Fort Collins (Colorado), 305–308
  overview, 240, 298–300, **299**
  Sacramento (California), 300–301, 303–305
Community Redevelopment Agency (CRA), 198
Community schools, 159
Comparative fit index (CFI), 427
Consensus-building for integrated resources planning
  consensus-building process and, 282–283
  issues, 279, 280–282
  lessons from, 284
  overview, 239–240, 279
  politics of water and, 279–280
Consolidation, 167
Constitutional theory, 316
Cooper, Terry, 41, 194, 198–199
Cooperation, 87, 167
Coordination, 87, 167
COPE, 223
Coproduction, 83, 87–90
CORE, 145
Corporations, 328–329
Corrections and citizen participation, 181–183
Cortner, Hanna J., 284
Creighton, James L., 461–462, 467
Crime displacement, 85
Crime prevention groups, 84–87, **87**. *See also* Policing
Criminal justice system, 164–166, 183–184. *See also*
    Corrections; Policing; Prosecution and adjudication
Critical consciousness, 493
Cronbach's alpha, 425, 429
Crosby, Ned, 239, 297, 311
Crozier, 160
Culture, 121–122, 228
Customer-centered model of citizenship, 24, 93, 107, **109**,
    480–482
Cutting, Fulton, 95

Dahl, Robert, 267
Daneke, Gregory A., 245
Davis, E.M., 169
Davis, Raymond G., **51**
De Sola Poole, Ithiel, 44
Decentralization
  administrative, 165, 172
  Altshuler's definition of, 165
  citizen participation in education and, 151–152, **153**,
    154–156, **154**
  corrections and, 182
  in federal government, 33
  policing and, 166–168
  political, 165
  prosecution and adjudication and, 177–180
  real, 33
Decision making
  creative, 34

Decision making *(continued)*
  group, support systems for, 223
  process, 446–447, **446**
  regulatory, study of
    citizen participation, 378, **379**
    conclusions, 381–382
    discussion, 380–381
    findings, 377–378
    hypothesis, 376
    methodology, 376–377
    overview, 339, 375–376
    staff recommendations, 378–380
  styles, 451, **451**
DeHaven-Smith, Lance, 239–240
Delegation, 479–480
DeLeon, Peter, 121, 394
Deliberative democracy. *See also* Public deliberation
  analysis
    broad, representative participation, 309
    deliberative participation, 309–310
    ideal participation, 308–309
    informative participation, 309
  community dialogues and
    Eugene (Oregon), 300–303, **302**, 305–307
    Fort Collins (Colorado), 305–308
    overview, 240, 298–300, **299**, 300
    Sacramento (California), 300–301, 303–305
  elements
    broad public participation, 297
    credible results, 298
    informed public judgment, 297
    opportunities for deliberation, 298, 310–311
    overview, 297
  overview, 240, 296
  results, 310–311
  terms for, alternative, 296
Deliberative Polling, 297
Democracy. *See also* Deliberative democracy;
        Direct citizen participation; Indirect citizen
        participation
  alternative models of, 316–319
  citizen participation and, 3
  constitutional, 315–316
  direct, 317
  individual rights and, 315–316
  participatory, 193, 314–315
  Schumpeter's view of, 6
  theories of, 29–32, 67
Democratic government, understanding, 30–31
Democratic team model, 170–172
Demonstrations Cities and Metropolitan Development
        Act (1966), 9
Denhardt, Janet Vinzant, 23
Denhardt, Robert B., 23
Denton, Eugene (Gene), 57–58
Deprofessionalizing public bureaucracies, 81–83, **84**
Detroit team policing, 168
Developmental theory, 223
Devolving service responsibility, 81, 83–84, **84**
Dewey, John, 6
Dienel, Peter C., 267, 270
DiIulio, John Jr., 93
Direct citizen participation
  ambivalence about, 3, 10
  assessments of, 337–342
  current context of, 19

Direct citizen participation *(continued)*
  debate about
    in opposition, 3, 5, 11–13
    in support, 3, 5, 10–11
    tensions over, 5
  definition, 5
  dilemmas of
    common good, 14, 494–495
    excluded/oppressed groups, 13, 492–493
    overview, 5
    risk, 13–14, 493
    size, 13, 238, 491–492
    technology/expertise, 14, 493–494
    time/crisis, 14, 494
  evaluation, 496–498
  in future, 496–499
  in government levels, 119
  at group level, 497
  historical perspective, 5, 7–10
  indirect citizen participation versus, 4
  at macro level, 497
  at micro level, 497
  pervasiveness of, 491
  in practice, 495–496
  "social experiment" of, 4–5, 496
  in theory, 495–496
  theory-building and, 497–498
Directive approach, 212–213, 214–215, **214**
Disasters, 254–256. *See also specific type*
Discourse theory, 68
Discursive democracy. *See* Deliberative democracy
Diversity, 54, 122
Domestic policy review (DPR), 209
Downs, Tom, 55–56
Drucker, Peter, 34
Dryzek, John S., 21, 206–207, 298
Duty, 6

Ebdon, Carol, 122
Ecclesia, 7–8
Econometric models, 206
Economic analysis and development, 45–46, 206
Economic Co-operation and Development (OECD), 318
Economic Opportunity Act (EOA) (1964), 8, 120, 124
Economy and aspirations, 292, **293**
Education and citizen participation
  alternative schools and, 159
  Bundy Plan and, 147–149
  community control and
    emergence, 146–147
    evaluating, 151–152, **153**, 154–156, **154**
    increasing, 159–160
    institutional change and, 120, 160
    schools, 159
  decentralization and, 151–152, **153**, 154–156, **154**
  integration and, failure of, 145–146
  Ocean Hill-Brownsville experiment and, 149–151
  overview, 120, 143–144
  professionalism and, expansion of, 144–145
  school board, 144
  urban school reform (1970s) and, 156–158
Education for citizenship participation, 35–36, 100–101,
        395, **396–397**, 398
Efficient Citizenship (BMR publication), 97
Eggers, William D., 114
Eisenhower, Dwight D., 239, 282

Eisinger, Robert M., 480
Elazar, D., 226, 228, 233
Electronic bureaucracy model, 318
Electronic democracy, 240–241, 317–319, 323–325. *See also* Information technology (IT) and democratic process
Electronic "town meeting," 319
"Elite syndrome," 121
Emergency management. *See* Emergent citizen groups
Emergent citizen groups
  characteristics, 256–260
  disasters and, 254–256
  at emergency times, 257–258
  implications, 262–264
  at non-emergency times, 258–260
  other types of emergence and, 260–261
  overview, 239, 254–255
Empowerment, 22, 395, **396–397**, 398, 484
England, Robert E., 244–245
Environmental Impact Statements (EIS), 209
Environmental Protection Agency (EPA), 99, 222, 450
Equal Opportunity Act (1964), 365
Equity and coproduction, 88–89
Eugene (Oregon) community dialogue, 300–303, **302**, 305–307
Evolutionary continuum of administration-citizen interaction
  coerciveness, 478–479
  delegation, 479–480
  overview, 442, 478, **479**
  responsiveness, 480–482
Excluded/oppressed groups, dilemma of, 13, 492–493
Executive action, 217, 220–221

Facilitative leadership, 53–55
Faith in citizenship involvement (FCI), 420, 424–425
Farnham, David, 481
Federal Advisory Committee Act (1972), 9
Federal and Land Policy and Management Act (FLPMA) (1976), 459
Federalist Papers, 10
Feldman, Ofer, 422
Feltey, Kathryn M., 339, 484
Field, Alexander J., 106
Fiscal stress and service delivery alternatives, 80–84
Fischer, F., 388
Fischer, Frank, 208
Fishkin, James S., 239, 297, 311
Flathman, Richard, 30
Flood Recovery Task Force, 261
Foner, Eric, 44
Ford Foundation, 288
Fore, Karmen N., 240
Forest Service, 99
Fort Collins (Colorado) community dialogue, 305–308
Fox, Charles J., 486–487
Fox, Daniel, 132–133
Frederich, Carl, 40
Frederickson, H. George, 22, 50, **51**, 55, 59–60, 61, 93, 480
Freedom, 11, 31
Freeman, Joe, 61
Freeriders, 485
Freire, Paolo, 493
Fried, Morton, 41
Frug, Gerald, 42

Gaebler, Ted, 63–66, 93–94, 480
Gardner, Howard, 52
Garvey, Gerald, 93
Gawthrop, Louis, 38
Gellhorn, Walter, 173–174
General managers. *See also* Public deliberation
  approaches of, 212–215, **214**
  challenges facing, 212
  examples
    Randall at Rosemount School District, 215–216
    Randall as State Commissioner of Minnesota Public Education, 216–217
  overview, 121, 212–213
Generalizability and coproduction, 89
Generative approach, 212–215, **214**
Generative learning, 217–218, 220
Gianakis, Jerry, 413
Giddens, A., 398
Gittell, Marilyn, 120
Glass, James J., 244
Glazer, Nathan, 83
Goel, Madan L., 420, 422, 424
Goldhammer, Keith, 144
Goldschmidt, Neil, 287
Golembiewski, Robert T., 476, 484
Goodness fit index (GFI), 427
Goodsell, Charles T., 79, 106
Gore, Al, 63–64
Gormley, W.T., 9
Government performance, improving. *See* Reinventing government
Government and public administration (G&PA) systems
  accuracy of endeavors of, testing, 475
  citizens and, 473
  role of, 484–485
Green Paper "Government Direct," 318
Greer, Colin, 143
Gross, E., 329
Gutmann, Amy, 298
Guyton, Edith M., 416

Habermas, Jürgen, 298, 441
Hamel, Gary, 286
Hamill, Peter, 498
Hart, David K., 34
Hatry, Harry P., 244, 247, 252
"Haves" and "have-nots," 7, 497
Hays, Dennis, 49
Hays, Steven W., 481
Head Start, 9
Health Decisions (Oregon), 297
Henry, Nicholas, 41
Hess, Karl, 176
Higher Learning in the Nation's Service (report), 35
Hildreth, W. Bartley, 286, 294
Hirschman, Albert O., 481–482
Hobbes, Thomas, 418
Holden, Reed K., 106
Homogeneity, 122
Hood, Christopher, 65
Horton, Sylvia, 481
Housing Act (1949 and 1954), 8
Housing Community Development Act (1974), 9
HUD, 357, 360
Huntington, Samuel P., 455
Huntsman, Carole A., 24

Ideal speech, 441
Incremental model, 29, 34
Indian Division of the Public Health Services, 8
Indirect citizen participation
  advantages of, 3
  critiques of current models of, 319–321
  direct citizen participation versus, 4
  emergence of, 315
  liberal, 320
  process of, 317
Individual rights, 315–316
Information management model, 318
Information overload, 329–330
Information technology (IT) and democratic process
  alternative models of democracy and, 316–319
  Citycard project, 321–322
  critiques of current representative democracy and,
    319–321
  downside, 323–325
  equitable access to IT and, 331
  in future, 329–331, 331–332
  impact
    agencies, 328–329
    citizens, 325–327
    corporations, 328–329
    media, 327–329
  individual rights and, 315–316
  information overload and, 329–330
  information's role, 331–332
  "knowledge gap" and, 331
  overview, 240–241, 314–315
  policy information and, 330–331
  potential, 321–323
  "remote-intimacy" dimensions and, 326
  "techno-affection" and, 326
Institute of Community Studies, 152
Institutional structure, 122
Integrated resources planning (IRP), 279, 284. *See also*
    Consensus building for integrated resources planning
Integration of schools, failure of, 145–146
Interdependencies, 22–23, 42–46
Interest-group politics, 12
Intergovernmentalizing service delivery, 81–82, **84**
International City/County Management Association
    (ICCMA) survey
  conclusions, 234
  conference (1997), 52
  findings, 229–234, **230**, **231**, **232**, **233**
  methodology, 228–229
  overview, 122, 226, 228
  reasons for citizen participation and, 461–462
  U.S. cities survey of citizen participation and, 403
International City Management Association, 245

Jackson, Andrew, 8
Jacobson, Willow S., 240
Jefferson, Thomas, 12
Johnson, Gerald W., 238
Joreskog, Karl, 427
Juster, Robert J., 238
Justice, 31
Juvenile Delinquency Demonstration Project, 8

Kaboolian, Linda, 65
Kakabadse, Andrew, 240–241
Kakabadse, Nada K., 240–241

Kamensky, John, 65
Kansas City (Kansas), 49
Kaplan, Abraham, 206
Kaufman, Herbert, 74, 89
Kawakami, Koichi, 422
Kearney, Richard C., 481
Kelly, Janet M., 239
Kelly, Rita Mae, 434
Kennedy administration, 9
Kennedy School of Government (Harvard), 288
Kenney, John P., 170, 176
Kessler, 284
Kettering Foundation, 386
Kettl, Donald, 93, 107
King, Cheryl Simrell, 63, 67–68, 73, 339, 420, 484, 495
King, David C., 423
King, Norm, 56, 58
Kissler, Gerald R., 240, 288
Kittredge, William P., 240
Kitzhaber, John, 288, 290, 292
Klobus-Edwards, Patricia, 245
Kloman, Erasmus, 338–339
Knoke, David, 41
"Knowledge gap," 331
"Knowledge society," 268
Korosec, Ronnie, 413
Korten, David, 121, 194, 200–201
Kouzmin, Alexander, 240–241
Kramer, Robert, 420
Kweit, Mary Grisez, 462
Kweit, Robert W., 462

"Ladder of participation," 7
Lakewood Plan, 167
Language, 22–23, 42–46
Lasswell, Harold, 206
Laumann, Edward, 41
Law Enforcement Assistance Administration, 164–165
Learning, 22–23, 42–46, 217–218, 220
Learning organization, 194, 200
Learning process approach, 194, 200–202, **202**
Leavitt, Mike, 460–461
Legal Aid, 9
Leonard, Jerry, 164
Levine, Charles, 24
Lewin, Kurt, 436
Liberalism, 315
Light, Paul, 99
Likert, Rensis, 32
Lindblom, Charles E., 29, 207
Lipset, Seymour Martin, 78–79
LISREL VIII, 340, 426, 429
Lobbying, 320
Local government managers. *See* City managers
Locke, John, 82, 418
Long, Norton, 81
Los Angeles
  community organizations, 194–198
  school reform (1970s), 157
  team policing, 169
Loyalty, 90, 100–101
Lynn, Lawrence E., 65

Madison, James, 10, 470
Magna Carta, 8
Majone, Giandomenico, 209

March, James G., 208
Marx, Karl, 314
Mathews, David, 35
"Maximum feasible participation" clause, 365
Mazmanian, Daniel, 366–367, 382
McGee, Richard A., 181–182
McSwain, C.J., 388
Media, 26, 327–328, 486–487
Mediated democracy. *See* Indirect citizen participation
Meising, Paul, 286
Member Agency/Metropolitan Agency Technical Group, 282–284
Menger, Carl, 105
Menke, Ben A., 82
Merton, Robert, 206
Meter, Elena C., 372
Metropolitan Water District (MWD) case study, 239, 279–280
    consensus-building process and, 282–284
    issues, 280–282
    lessons from, 279, 284
    overview, 239–240, 279
    politics of water and, 279–280
Milbraith, Lester W., 420, 422, 424
Mill, John Stuart, 10–11, 116, 314
Miller, Gerald J., 286, 294
Miller, Hugh T., 486–487
Miller, Jessica, 442
Miller, S.M., 38
Minnesota Public Education, 216–217
Mitchel, John Purroy, 95
Mitroff, Jan I., 465
Mobilization of bias, 10
Model Cities Programs. *See also* Philadelphia Model Cities Program
    citizen participation in
        attitudes toward, 128
        conditions necessary, 132–133
        in future, 133–134
        implementation, 126–127
        meanings, 125–126
        objectives, 129–132
        overview, 120, 124–125
        restrictions, 127–128
        techniques, 133
    establishment of, 9, 120
Modernization, 193–194, 198–200, 202–203
Moe, Ronald, 94
Moote, Margaret A., 284
Mora, David, 54–56, 58
Morrill Acts (1862 and 1890), 8
Mosher, Frederick, 94
Mosher, William E., 36
Mulgan, Geoff, 321
Murphy, M. Brian, 44
Murphy, Patrick V., 168
Murray, Michael A., 447
Myren, Richard A., 120

NAACP, 145
Nachmias, David, 106
Nagle, Thomas T., 106
Nalbandian, John, 23, 433
National Association of Community Schools, 159
National Association of Schools of Public Affairs and Administration (NASPAA), 398

National Council on Crime and Delinquency, 165
National Environmental Policy Act (1969), 9
National Governors Association, 287–288
National Grange, 8
National League of Cities, 462
National Performance Review (NPR), 64, 107
National Service Corps, 9
Neo-managerialism, 481
New Deal, 8, 42
New Public Management (NPM)
    alternative to, lack of, 64
    citizens as clients, 474–476
    citizens as partners, 476–478
    debate of citizens as clients versus partners, 477–478
    evolutionary continuum of administration-citizen interaction and
        coerciveness, 478–479
        delegation, 479–480
        overview, 442, 478, **479**
        responsiveness, 480–482
    in future, 487–488
    multidimensional perspective
        academia's role, 486
        citizens' role, 485–486
        collaboration between clients and partners, 482–484, **483**
        G&PA role, 484–485
        media's role, 486–487
    old public administration and, 64–67
    overview, 442, 473–474
    public administrators as entrepreneurs in, 73
New Public Managerialism, 474. *See also* New Public Management (NPM)
New Public Service (NPS) model
    background information, 63–64
    definition, 63
    dominance of, 419
    implications, 74–75
    lessons from
        accountability isn't simple, 72–73
        public interest is aim not by-product, 69, 71
        serve citizens, not customers, 71–72
        serve rather than steer, 69
        think strategically, act democratically, 71
        value citizenship and public service above entrepreneurship, 73–74
        value people, not just productivity, 73
    old public administration versus, 64–67, **70**
    overview, 23, 63
    roots, 67–68
    tenets of, 23
New York City
    schools
        decentralization of, 151–152, **153**, 154–156, **154**
        integration of, 146–151
        team policing, 168–169
Newton, 114
NIMBY (not-in-my-backyard) groups, 239, 386, 453, 493
Normative theory (Renn and Webler), 441
Normed fit index (NFI), 427
Nunnaly, Juan C., 429
Nye, Joseph S., 423

Ocean Hill-Brownsville experiment, 149–151
O'Connell, Brian, 485

Office of Economic Opportunity (OEO), 120, 124, 146–147
O'Leary, John, 114
O'Leary, Vincent, 182–183
Oligarchy, 12
Olsen, Johan, 208
Ombudsmen, 173–174
O'Neill, Robert Jr., 56
Operating productivity, improving, 81–82, **84**
Operation Neighborhood (New York City), 168–169
Oregon Benchmarks, 287–289
Oregon Shines (I and II), 288–294
Oregon State University, 288
Oregon's strategic plans
   development of, 287–290
   findings, 290–291
   lessons from, 291–294
   original, 287–288
   process, 290
   recommendations, 291
   updated, 288–290
   value of, 290–291, 294–295
Organization theory, 32–34
Organizational humanism theory, 68
Orum, Anthony M., 422
Osborne, David, 63–66, 93–94, 480
Owner-based model of citizenship, 24, 95–97, 108, **109**

Page, Benjamin I., 244
Paine, Thomas, 44
Palfrey, Colin, 419
Paris, David, 207
Parks and recreation services, 113–115
Parsons, David W., 419
Participation evaluation matrix, 368, **368**
Participation Mechanism Index, 404, **405**
Partnerships, 55
Pateman, Carole, 416
Pecorella, Robert, 120–121
Pell, Richard, 38
Pericles, 82
Perkins, Jan, 53, 55–56
Perot, Ross, 319, 328
Perpich, Rudy, 216
Peters, B. Guy, 480, 484
Philadelphia Model Cities Program
   Area Wide Council and, 357–363
   citizen participation and, 356–357
   city hall and, 359
   court case and, 360–361
   impact, 362–363
   judicial ruling and, 361
   lessons from, 363–364
   mayor and, 359
   overview, 338–339, 356
   racial divisions and, 358
   school demonstration (November 1967) and, 359–360
   Washington and, 357, 360
Philadelphia school reform (1970s), 157
Pico-Union Neighborhood Council (PUNC), 198
Plato, 314, 325
Plausibility criterion, 427
Pluralism, 10, 20
Pluralist system model, 20–21, **20**
Pocock, J.G.A., 44

Policing and citizen participation
   assessing, 176–177
   civilian review boards, 173–174
   community control, 174–175
   decentralization and, 166–168
   democratic team model, 170–172
   involvement, methods of, 172–173
   ombudsmen, 173–174
   overview, 120, 164–166
   team policing, 168–170
Policy analysis
   citizen participation in
      framework, 461–470
      nature of issue and, 464–468, **465**
      overview, 442, 458–459
      purpose-issue matrix and, 468–469
      purposes, 461–465, **463**
      Utah Growth Summit and, 460–461, 464, 467–468
      Utah Wilderness Debate and, 459–461, 464–465, 467–468
      views about, 458–459
   democratization of, 206–208, 210
   domestic policy review and, 209
   "elite syndrome" in, 121
   overview, 121, 205–206
   participatory, 330–331
   policy polling and, 208–210
Policy information, 330–331
Policy-making process. *See* Citizen surveys in budgetary and policy-making process
Policy polling, 208–210
Policy sciences. *See* Policy analysis
Policy sharing, 208
Political/market economy model, **20**, 21
Poor, role of, 97–98
Populist model, 318–319
POSDCORB (Planning, Organizing, Staffing, Directing, Coordinating, Reporting, and Budgeting), 29
Postmodern Public Administration (Fox and Miller), 487
"Power equalization" hypothesis, 497
Practitioner-client hierarchy, 388
Presidential election (2000), 10
President's Commission on Law Enforcement and Administration of Justice, 173, 178, 181–182
Privatizing service delivery, 80–81, **84**
Probation volunteer program, 180–181
Problem solving, 55–56
Procedural rights, 316
Process-oriented management, 57–59
Professionalism of school bureaucracies, 144–145
Progress Board, 288
Progressivism, 94
Prosecution and adjudication and citizen participation
   assessing, 181
   corrections, 181–183
   decentralization and, 177–180
   involvement, methods of, 180–181
   probation volunteer programs, 180–181
Public administration. *See also* Public administrators
   authentic citizen participation and, 388–389, **389**
   enabling structures and processes of, **395–396**, 398–399
   models, 19–22, **20**
   Mosher's view of, 36
   philosophy
      contemporary, 39–40
      implications of, 46

Public administration
  philosophy *(continued)*
    interdependencies and, 22–23, 42–46
    language and, 22–23, 42–46
    learning and, 22–23, 42–46
    overview, 22–23, 38–39
    Reagan and, 39
    state and, 40–42
  public confidence in, decline in, 78–79
  schools, 28–29, 33–34
  state model, 20, **20**
  taxpayer's revolt of 1978 and, 78
Public administrators. *See also* City managers; Public
    administration
  citizens and, 5
  re-educating, **395–396**, 398
  roles, 19–20, **20**, 34
Public Agenda Foundation (Yankelovich), 298
Public deliberation. *See also* Deliberative democracy
  cases
    Randall at Rosemount School District, 215–216
    Randall as State Commissioner of Minnesota Public
        Education, 216–217
  in general management's generative approach, 212–
      213, 223
  outcomes, 223
  overview, 121–122, 212–213
  structure
    executive action, 220–221
    generative learning, 217–218, 220
    overview, 217
    process, 221–223
    stakeholder collaboration, 217–218, **219–220**
    strategic question and issue identification, 217–218
  using, 223–224
Public judgment, 11
Public management and citizen participation. *See* Vroom
    and Yetton Model
Public-sector performance and citizen participation study
  alternative models and, 421–423, 427, **428–429**
  conclusions, 435–437
  contribution of, 437
  discussion, 433–435
  findings
    descriptive statistics and intercorrelations, 429–431,
        430, **431**
    evaluation of models, **428–429**, 431–433
  limitations, 436–437
  methodology
    measures, 424–427
    procedure, 423–424
    sample, 423–424
    tools, 423–424
  overview, 340, 416–417
  paradoxical relationship of, 434–435
  positive relationships and, 435–436
  public administration viewpoint and, 417–421
Purpose-issue matrix, 442, 468–469, **469**
Putnam, Robert D., 50, 68

Quarantelli, E. L., 239

Rabin, Jack, 286, 294
Racism, 145, 151
Radio watch programs, 85
Rainey, Hal, 480

Randall, Ruth, 215–217, 221–222
Rational actor paradigm, 206
Rational model, 33–34
Rawls, John, 31
Reactive approach to general management, 212–213,
    214–215, **214**
Reagan administration, 45
Reagan, Ronald, 27, 39
Redford, Emmett S., 107, 207
Reinventing government
  analysis, 94, 98–100
  Bureau of Municipal Research (New York) and, 93–96,
      101–102
  citizenship education and, 100–101
  customer-centered public administration, 24, 93
  information exchange and, 101
  overview, 24, 93–94
  owner-centered public administration, 24, 93, 95–97
  poor and, 97–98
Reiss, Albert J., Jr., 176–177
Relative fit index (RFI), 427
Renn, 441
Reporting skills, 85
Representative democracy. *See* Indirect citizen
    participation
Representative system model, 20, **20**
The Republic (Plato), 314
Resident participation. *See also* Study on Community
    Representation in Community Action Agencies
  active, 347–349
  adversary, 347–349
  limited, 347–349
  overview, 338, 341
Responsible Citizenship (Mosher), 36
Responsiveness, 480–482
Reynolds, James, 207
Rhodes, Rod A.W., 419
Rice, Tom W., 50
Rimmerman, Craig A., 433
Risk, dilemma of, 13–14, 493
Roberts, Nancy, 121
Robert's Rules of Order, 222
Rockefeller, John D., 95
Romzek, Barbara, 61
Rooke, Dennis, 105, 115–116
Roosevelt, Franklin, 42
Rosemount School District (Minnesota), 215–216
Rosenbloom, David H., 94, 106
Rosener, Judy B., 339, 462
Rosenwein, Robert E., 416
Ross, Bernard H., 106
Rousseau, Jean-Jacques, 3, 10–11, 82, 418
Rubin, I., 227, 233
Ruder, Karma, 52, 55–56

Sabatier, Paul, 382
Sacramento (California) community dialogue, 300–301,
    303–305
"Safety valve" principle, 498
Sagasti, Francisco, 465
Sandel, Michael, 67
Sardar, Ziauddin, 323
Scale, dilemma of, 13, 238, 491–492
Schachter, Hindy Lauer, 24, 104, 108
Schaefer, Paul, 239
Schlozman, Kay L., 486

Schneider, William, 78–79
Schon, Donald, 58
School board, 144
Schumpeter, J., 6, 10, 12
Scott, Jewel, 55
Scott, William G., 34
Selective Service Boards, 8
Self-help, 83
Senate Rules Committee, 375
Service delivery models
  community-based crime prevention groups and, 84–87
  coproduction concept and, 87–90
  deprofessionalizing bureaucracies and, 81–83, **84**
  devolving service responsibility, 81, 84, **84**
  fiscal stress and alternatives, 80–84, **84**
  gap between citizens and public employees and, 90
  intergovernmentalizing, 80, 82, **84**
  operating productivity improvements, 80–82, **84**
  overview, 24, 78–80
  privatizing, 80–81, **84**
Shapiro, Robert Y., 244
SHARE, 395, 398
Sharp, Elaine B., 88–89
Simon, Herbert, 29
Size, dilemma of, 13, 238, 491–492
Slocombe, D. Scott, 284
Smith, Adam, 106
Smith, Gerald E., 24
Social contract, 418
Social learning system model, **20**, 21–22
Socrates, 320
Sorbom, Dag, 427
Southern California fires (1970), 254–255
"Spillover effect," 10
Stakeholder collaboration, 217–218, **219–220**
Stallings, Robert A., 239
State model of strategic planning
  bottom-up approach and, 240, 289, 292, **293**
  Oregon
    development of, 287–290
    findings, 290–291
    lessons from, 291–294
    original plans, 287–288
    process, 290
    updated plan, 288–290
    value of, 290–291, 294–295
  overview, 240, 286–287
State and the public, 40–42
Stewart, Scott L., 240
Stipak, Brian, 419, 436
Stivers, Camilla, 4, 63, 67–68, 73, 386, 420
Strange, John H., 120
Strategic issue identification, 217–218
Strategic planning, 240, 286. *See also* State model of strategic planning
Strong democracy. *See* Deliberative democracy
Structural equation model (SEM), 427
Study on Community Representation in Community
  Action Agencies
  conclusions, 352–354
  federal policy and, 352
  findings
    impact of participation, 345–346
    target-area participation on CAA board, 343–344
    target-area participation through employment of
      nonprofessionals, 345

Study on Community Representation in Community
  Action Agencies
  findings *(continued)*
    target-area participation through target-area
      associations, 344
    variations among CAAs, 346–351
  local community and, 352
  overview, 338, 341–343
Substantive rights, 316
Successive-limited comparison model, 29
Sullivan, William, 43
Sumberg, Alexander F., 50
Sundeen, Richard A., 87
Susel, Bridget O'Neill, 339, 484
Sweat equity, 90
Syracuse (New York) team policing, 169
Szilagyi, Miklos N., 323

Task Force Report on Police (report), 166, 168
Taxpayer's revolt (1978), 78
Team policing, 168–170
Technology, dilemma of, 14, 493–494. *See also*
  Information technology (IT) and democratic
  process
Teledemocracy, 329. *See also* Information technology
  (IT) and democratic process
Tenement House Department (New York), 97
Terry, Larry D., 64, 480
The East Los Angeles Community Union (TELACU),
  194–196, 200–203
Theory building, 441–442, 497–498
Theory of Justice, A (Rawls), 31
Thomas, John Clayton, 54–55, 384, 441–442, 461
Thompson, Andres A., 476
Thompson, Dennis, 298, 434
Thompson, James D., 33, 368
Time, dilemma of, 14, 494
Tocqueville, Alexis de, 43, 314
Total quality management (TQM), 107
Tripp-Jones, Sandra, 57, 59
Tugwell, Rexford, 42
Tuler, Seth, 441

Unauthentic citizen participation, 390, **391**
Unitary democracy. *See* Deliberative democracy
United Federation of Teachers (UFT), 148
United Neighborhood Organization (UNO), 45, 194–198,
  200–203, **202**
"United We Stand" alliance, 328
Urban League, 145
Urban Renewal Act (1954), 8
Urban school reform (1970s), 156–158
U.S. cities survey of citizen participation
  conclusion, 412–413
  findings
    amount of participation, 406, **407–408**, 409
    impacts of participation, 411–412, **411**
    reasons for participation, 409–411, **410**
  framework, 401–403
  International City/County Management Association
    and, 403
  methodology, 403–406
  overview, 339–340, 401
U.S. Constitution, 6, 10
U.S. Department of Justice Standards and Goals,
  164–165

U.S. Supreme Court, 10
Utah Growth Summit, 460–461, 464, 467–468
Utah Wilderness Debate, 459–461, 464–465,
    467–468

Value-centered perspective
  analysis, 115
  citizens and
    as customers, 107, **109**
    overview, 106–107
    as owners, 108, **109**
    in value model, **109**, 110
  city hall services and, 111–113
  field research, 110–111
  findings, 111–115
  implications, 115–117
  merit of, 117
  overview, 24, 104–105
  parks and recreation services and, 113–115
  value and, meaning of, 105–106
Value model, 108, **109**, 110
Values, 60–61, 75, 105–106
Van Wart, Montgomery, 108, 110
Ventriss, Curtis, 22–23, 120–121
Verba, Sidney, 420, 422, 424, 486
Vigoda, Eran, 340, 419, 442, 474, 476
Villarroy, Pedro, 196–197
Voice and Equality (Verba), 420
Voluntarism, 83
Volunteer programs, 180–181, 484
Voting procedures, voluntary, 329
Vroom, Victor, 444–446
Vroom and Yetton Model
  assessing various paths, 450–452, **451**
  conclusion, 453–455
  contingency factors, 452–453
  findings, 448–453, **449**
  methodology, 447–448
  overview, 441–443
  public involvement in public management and
    decisions, 449, **449**
    matrix guide to, 454, **454**
    promise of, 453–455, **454**

Vroom and Yetton Model
  public involvement in public management and *(continued)*
    questions, 445–446, **446**
  theory, 443–447
Waldo, Dwight, 29, 67, 479
Walker, Olene S., 461
Walters, Lawrence C., 442
Walzer, Michael, 42
Wang, XiaoHu, 339–340
War on Poverty (1960s), 8
Watchdogs, 485
Water
  agriculture and quality of, Citizens Panel (1984),
    270–271, **272**, 277
  politics of, 279–280
Water Quality Act (1972), 271
Waterman Place (St. Louis), 114
Watkins, David, 53, 57
Watson, J., 238
Webb, Kenneth, 244, 247, 252
Weber, Max, 40, 199
Webler, Thomas, 441
Wechsler, Barton, 286
Weeks, Edward C., 240
Weikert, Lynne A., 480
Whitaker, Gordon P., 89
White, Mervin F., 82
White, O.F., 388
"Wicked problems," 386, 494
Wilderness Act (1964), 459
Wilkes-Barre (Pennsylvania) flood (1972), 260–261
Will, George, 41
Wilson, James Q., 176
Wilson, Woodrow, 28, 72, 479
Winner, Langdon, 332
Wodraska, John R., 239–240
Wolin, Sheldon, 45, 67, 83–84
Woller, Gary M., 418
World Trade Center site planning, 492, 495, 498

Yankelovich, Daniel, 239, 297–298, 311
Yetton, Philip, 444–446

Zelikow, Philip D., 423

ABOUT THE EDITOR

Nancy Roberts is a Professor of Defense Analysis in the Graduate School of Operational and Information Sciences at the Naval Postgraduate School in Monterey, California. She received a Ph.D. from Stanford University, an M.A. and B.A. from the University of Illinois, and a Diplome Annuel from the Cours de Civilization Francaise at the Sorbonne. She has published extensively in the areas of public entrepreneurship and innovation, stakeholder collaboration, dialogue and deliberation. Her recent work focuses on "wicked problems" such as the organizational challenges of peace operations and post-conflict reconstruction. She is the coauthor of *Transforming Public Policy: Dynamics of Public Entrepreneurship and Innovation* (1996) and editor of *The Transformative Power of Dialogue* (2002).

Roberts is also a coeditor of a book series on *Research on Public Management* for Information Age Publishing, an Associate Editor of PAR, and serves on the editorial boards of *Public Management, The American Review of Public Administration, International Public Management Journal,* and *International Public Management Review.* She has served as a consultant for numerous public and private sector organizations and is Codirector of the Institute for Whole Social Science in Carmel, California. She teaches courses on *Tracking and Disrupting Dark Networks, Planning and Organizing in Complex Networks,* and *Coping with Wicked Problems.*